AARON BURR

A Biography

By NATHAN SCHACHNER

AARON BURR, 1802

From a portrait by John Vanderlyn

AARON
BURR

A Biography

By

NATHAN SCHACHNER

A PERPETUA BOOK

A. S. Barnes & Company, Inc.

New York

PRINTED IN THE UNITED STATES OF AMERICA

To
MY WIFE,
HELEN

CONTENTS

viii CONTENTS

ACKNOWLEDGMENTS

In the writing of this book I have gone largely to the sources, both published and unpublished, for my factual material. This has necessitated the cooperation of many individuals, libraries, and historical societies, and, in every case, such assistance has been freely and gladly given.

I am indebted to the following for permission to quote from manuscript letters, journals, diaries and other documents in their possession: New York Historical Society, The Historical Society of Pennsylvania, The New Jersey Historical Society, American Antiquarian Society, Yale University, Princeton University, Columbia University, Thomas F. Madigan, Inc., Dr. Waldo F. Leland, of Washington, D. C., and Mr. Edward Coykendall, of Kingston, N. Y. A further word of thanks must be tendered to the staffs of these institutions, and of those vast depositories, the New York Public Library and the Library of Congress, for unwearied and always cheerful aid.

For permission to quote from printed material, acknowledgments are gratefully given to Dodd, Mead and Company and Walter McCaleb, whose *Aaron Burr Conspiracy* is already a classic; to Professor Isaac Joslin Cox, whose researches have led to a better understanding of early Spanish-American relations; to the Buffalo Historical Society and Dr. Paul D. Evans, whose thesis, *The Holland Land Company*, based primarily on Dutch archives, is an interesting commentary on one of the first of American land booms; to Mr. Meade Minnegerode, co-author with Mr. Samuel Wandell of *Aaron Burr*, based upon much patient research; to Houghton Mifflin Company and Professor Samuel E. Morison, author of the definitive *Life and Letters of Harrison Gray Otis*.

For permission to reproduce portraits and other illustrative material, I am indebted to the estate of Dr. John E. Stillwell, whose privately printed *The History of the Burr Portraits* is a veritable treasure-house of Burriana, to Gabriel Wells, of New York City, and to various art galleries and institutions.

In conclusion, I must publicly avow my private thanks to Professor Francis L. D. Goodrich and Mr. Thomas G. Schwartz, of the College of the City of New York, for the liberality with which they have permitted me unlimited access to the rich resources of their Library.

NATHAN SCHACHNER

New York City
January, 1937

ILLUSTRATIONS

CHAPTER I

ANCESTRAL VOICES

1. RESPECTABLE BURRS

I HAVE never known, in any country," declared John Adams, second President of the United States, " the prejudice in favor of birth, parentage and descent more conspicuous than in the instance of Colonel Burr." [1]

The phraseology of the testy old man, reminiscing publicly in the year 1815, was singularly inept, for neither his own context nor the facts themselves disclose that Aaron Burr's meteoric rise, nor, for that matter, his as precipitous fall, was in anywise influenced by a general public preoccupation with the incidence of " birth, parentage and descent."

Nevertheless the major premise remains intact. It would be difficult, in that early period of American history, to discover another whose lineage, on either branch of the convergent family tree, was as proudly intellectual, as earnestly God-fearing, as solid and substantial in the things of the world, as that of Aaron Burr.

The first paternal Burr of whom there is any authentic public record was a certain Jehue, who migrated with Winthrop's fleet in 1630 to the bleak and uninviting shores of Massachusetts for the greater glory of God and the possible enhancement of his own economic status.

There is no reason to doubt that he found satisfaction on both counts, for he very early occupied a solid niche in the affairs of that theocratic Colony. In Roxbury, where he first settled, he was appointed Overseer of Roads and Bridges; when, seized with restlessness and lured by the reports of broad, fertile acres, he pushed on to Agawam, in the newly established Colony of Connecticut, he was soon its Tax Collector, probably the first. When he finally removed to Fairfield, in the same Colony, he was chosen Town Commissioner and representative in the General Court. In short, by the time he died in 1672 he had placed the name of Burr on a very respectable basis indeed.

Nor did his descendants let him down. They increased and multiplied in accordance with the Biblical injunction, and they steadily and uninterruptedly added new laurels to the family escutcheon. Their roots went deep into the Town of Fairfield; their influence spread over the Colony. They became deputies and members of the Council, lawyers and magistrates. Their activities ranged from officiating at witch trials to service in the House of Deputies. They became wealthy landowners and they went to war. They were captains, and majors and colonels, and, from all accounts, acquitted themselves most creditably.

Jehu Burr, Junior, for instance, one of four sons sired by Jehue the Elder, followed in his father's footsteps, representing Fairfield in the Court of Deputies and then in the Standing Council. He was one of the first in the youthful Colonies to advocate actively the adoption of a public-school system supported by state funds. This notable heresy of his, however, met with defeat at the hands of his sterner associates. He died in 1692, leaving ten children.

Major John Burr, his brother, achieved his warlike title in the ever-enduring Indian Wars. He, too, was a deputy, a senator, and later a magistrate. It was his proud distinction to be one of the judges at the trial of Mercy Desborough in 1692 for practices that smacked strongly of witchcraft. He voted equally with his fellows for the death sentence.

Then there was Judge Peter Burr, son of Jehu, Jr., who was graduated from that early cradle of the arts and theology, Harvard, and went into the law. He held at one time or another most of the offices within the gift of Connecticut, and ended as Chief Judge of the Superior Court. He died in 1724, perhaps the most eminent of the early Burrs.

There were others, too. Colonel John Burr, grandson of Jehue, Sr., who found time from his political and judicial activities to behave very gallantly in the New England expedition against Port Royal. Nor did they prevent him from becoming one of the largest landowners in the Colony. His estate at the time of his death in 1750 was valued at 15,288 pounds, an immense sum in those days.

Colonel Andrew Burr, grandson of Major John, followed the regular pattern. Law, magistrate, Speaker of the House, and a distinguished soldier who participated in the capture of that formidable fortress, Louisburg. His death occurred in 1763.

Nor were these all. Others of the Burrs, not mentioned, had claim to a certain prominence and the seated respect of their fellows. There were ministers of the Word of God among them, as was natural in pious New England, and they married well, all of them, forming a close-knit web with the first families of the Colonies, so that the strain was deepened and enriched.

Aaron Burr's grandfather on the paternal side, Daniel Burr, strangely enough, had little to commend him as far as positive achievements were concerned. It was true that he was comfortably wealthy and the owner of broad, well-tended lands in Fairfield, but these were inherited matters. He was a good, honest gentleman who minded his own affairs and tended his acres without too much ado in the world at large. But in one particular he was notable. He begot Aaron, who in due time was to become the Reverend Aaron Burr, the second President of Princeton College, and who in turn fathered Aaron Burr, the subject of this biography.[2]

2. The Odor of Sanctity

The Reverend Aaron Burr was an important figure in the intellectual and religious movements of the pre-Revolutionary era. Unfortunately, even to those who are at all aware of his existence, he is completely overshadowed by the fierce torrents of light — and of heat — that have beaten interminably upon his brilliant and enigmatical son. Only at Princeton, of which institution he was almost the sole begetter, do they still do him honor. Which is a pity, for he deserves better of posterity.

He was born January 4, 1715, within the limits of the present town of Fairfield, in the Colony of Connecticut. He duly attended the College of Yale at New Haven as all well-born young men of the Colony were accustomed to do. There he proved to be a studious, brilliant youth, small, well-formed, and quick of wit, even as his son after him. A graduate at the age of nineteen with honors in Latin and Greek, he won a scholarship that permitted two further years of graduate study at the College.[3] But, he writes in 1736, suddenly "God saw fit to open my eyes and show me what a miserable creature I was." Fortunately, however, "it pleased God at length to reveal his Son to me in the gospel as an all-sufficient Saviour, and I hope inclined me to receive him on the terms of the gospel." [4] Whereupon he promptly offered himself as a candidate for orders.

This was not a novel course for the young students of the time. The formalism into which the Protestant churches of England and America alike had set as in a mold had aroused much protest from the earnestly religious. The revolt came almost simultaneously in the Old and New Worlds. Jonathan Edwards, Burr's future father-in-law, had started a hornet's nest in Boston; John Wesley had performed the same service in England, and was even now, in this year of young Aaron's conversion, proselytizing with great enthusiasm among the heathen Indians and the more heathen white folk of the Province of Georgia. George Whitefield was stirring the congregations of London in his master's absence to a frenzy and was soon to depart for his torrential tour of America.

The yeast of discontent fermented rapidly. The early Protestantism, the Calvinism of old, had jellied into something suspiciously like the authoritarian hierarchies of the Catholic and Episcopalian Churches. Salvation and the approaches to God were locked gates, the keys of which were closely held by the official ministry, and woe betide any man who sought grace and salvation outside the official folds.

Now, this had not been Calvin's doctrine, nor the doctrine of Luther and Hus. Narrow in their vision they might have been, cheerless and dour in their conceptions of a merciless and vindictive God who separated with harsh finality the elect from the damned, but never had they dreamed that their names would be used as a smoke-screen for the very things they detested and despised more than all else. What was their quarrel with the ancient Churches? That priest and deacon and bishop and pope had interposed themselves between man and his Maker. Protestantism was a *personal* religion, a meeting of man's naked soul with God. No minister might intervene except to exhort and advise and direct.

The revival of pure religious emotion that swept the Colonies was an attempt to restore that early nakedness. It caught the Colleges, whose very inception and maintenance were for the greater glory of God and the generous nurture of new ministers to preach the Gospel. No wonder young Aaron, reared of pious parents, surrounded by religious influences, was converted. It was quite the fashion.

" My first sermon," he wrote, " was preached at Greenfield, and immediately after I came into the Jerseys. I can hardly give any account why I came here. After I had preached for some time at Hanover, I had a call by the people of Newark; but there was scarce any probability that I should suit their circumstances, being young in standing and trials. I accepted of their invitation, with a reserve, that I did not come with any views of settling. My labours were universally acceptable among them, and they manifested such great regard and love for me, that I consented to accept of the charge of their souls." [5]

He had found his life-work. Regularly ordained in 1738, the Reverend Aaron Burr was to remain for almost a score of years as the pastor of the First Presbyterian Church of Newark.

His fame increased apace. The so-called Great Awakening was now in full swing — that remarkable religious revival of which we have just spoken. It swept the emotional depths that lay underneath the hard New England Puritan crust like fire through stubble grass. Jonathan Edwards was thundering in Massachusetts. Whitefield had finally come across the sea and was rousing vast concourses of people to frenzies of religious hysteria. Mr. Burr, intellectual and classicist though he was, was nevertheless sufficiently young and ardent to cast himself headlong into the stream.

Already he had been in communication with Jonathan Edwards. He made religious pilgrimages in 1739 and 1740 to drink at the spiritual fountainhead. And once again in the year 1740 to hear Whitefield preach. When the clamoring people crowded unyielding walls to suffocation, the great revivalist shifted the vast concourse of souls eager to be saved out into the reaches of Boston Common. As many as ten thousand hearkened to his fiery discourse in a single session. So great was the press that in one church there was panic, and some five were killed and many more seriously injured.

The Reverend Aaron Burr was deeply impressed. He laid the basis of a close friendship with the Englishman, and confided to his diary that he was becoming more and more pleased with the man.[6] In any event, he returned to his pastoral flock filled with a new zeal for the Lord's work. He preached to his rapt followers in his soft, mellifluous voice, his periods elegantly studied and composed, yet capable of arousing enthusiasm almost as extreme as the sterner quantities of Jonathan Edwards, or the vehement exaltations of George Whitefield.

Very early he became a leader in the Great Awakening. His sermons achieved publication and sold widely. He viewed with alarm the parlous and sinful state of the times, as all revivalists must; he glanced with awful trembling at the prospect of eventual popish domination; he saw Braddock's disaster as a visitation of God upon them for their sins; and he animadverted on politics, on French Bourbonism, and on the defenseless condition of the Colonies.[7]

Meanwhile he was gaining new laurels in a different field. Pious parents sent their sons to him to be taught English and the classical languages. His parsonage at the corner of Broad and William Streets in Newark was his schoolhouse. He proved to be the perfect pedagogue. The pupils loved him and imbibed from his lips a thirst for learning. The school grew and the circle of his teaching widened. He wrote a Latin Grammar that rapidly became standard and passed through numerous editions.

But there was something lacking. The Great Awakening had grown and burgeoned mightily under the zealous ministrations of Edwards, Burr and others. Yet there were still untapped wells of souls to be sought out and saved. Out in the hinterlands, on the frontiers, in Pennsylvania and the Southlands, were men and women and little children who perished because there were no preachers of the right persuasion to exhort and open their eyes.

So there were conferences. A training-school for the Presbyterian faith was urgently needed, a breeder of missionaries to the unenlightened. Nor — considering that the Reverend Aaron was himself a teacher of the humanities and a lover of fine books and finer thoughts — were the other adjuncts of learning to be disregarded.

Accordingly, in 1746, Aaron Burr, Jonathan Dickinson, John Pierson, Ebenezer Pemberton, and other gentlemen, both lay and of the cloth, petitioned Jonathan Belcher, Governor of the Province of New Jersey, for " the Establishment of a publick Seminary of Literature in New-Jersey." [8]

The good Governor was an enthusiastic devotee and friend of Mr. Burr, and sympathetic with the general aims of the petitioning gentlemen. The charter was granted, and Jonathan Dickinson became the first President of the infant College of New-Jersey.[9]

The College was first established in May, 1747, at Elizabethtown under very modest auspices. President Dickinson's tenure of office, however, was pathetically short, for he died in August of the same year. The *eight* students who comprised the institution were thereupon removed to Newark and installed under the ministering wing of the Reverend Aaron Burr. In September, 1748, a new charter was applied for and granted, and Aaron Burr was unanimously chosen the second President of the College of New-Jersey.

Whereupon the College prospered and waxed mightily. President Burr threw himself into his duties with gusto and alacrity. One suspects that they were more congenial to his sensitive soul than even the pursuit of the Great Awakening. " Under his immediate Tuition and Government," exulted the Trustees, " this Society has flourished far beyond the most raised and sanguine Expectations. The Number of Students has increased, in the short Space of five Years, from Eight or Ten, to about Sixty; besides near Forty in the Grammar-School." [10]

It was not all smooth sailing, however. The College, perforce, for want of accommodations, was conducted at the parsonage, along with President Burr's other multifarious duties. He still was Pastor of the First Presbyterian Church of Newark; he still was an active agent in the religious ferment of the times. And the management of the two-story, double stone building with its wing kitchens, barn, yard piled high with winter logs, garden and adjoining pasturage, as well as the temporal care of the attendant pupils, was soon to become a difficult task for a ripely mature bachelor. There was only one solution — marriage!

The Reverend Aaron Burr was thirty-seven. He was a famous preacher, the President of a College, his personality winning and his culture deep. It is a wonder that he had managed to evade matrimony thus long. He cast speculative eyes around, and decided rather suddenly on Esther Edwards, daughter of Jonathan Edwards, his old friend and co-worker in the tillings of the Lord. They were married on June 29, 1752, in Newark. She was only twenty-one and one of eleven children. The Reverend Jonathan Edwards had likewise heeded and obeyed the Biblical injunction.

The circumstances of this hasty courtship and marriage were rather curious. They excited a great deal of comment and some good-natured jesting at the time. The New York *Gazette* referred to it as a marriage " in the patriarchal mode " and wittily advised the pupils to follow the teacher in this as in all other matters.[11]

A young student of the College described the whole affair for the benefit of his parents in language that deserves quotation. " In the latter end of May," he wrote, " he [Burr] took a journey into N England, and during his absence he made a visit of but three days to the Rev. Mr. Edward's daughter, at Stockbridge, in which short time, tho' he had no acquaintance with nor, indeed, even seen the lady these six years, I suppose he accomplished his whole design; for it was not above a fortnight after his return here before he sent a young fellow . . . into N Engld. to conduct her and her mother down here.

" They came to town on Saturday evening, the 27th ulto., and on the Monday evening followg. the nuptial ceremonies were celebrated. . . . I think her a person of great beauty, tho' I must say that, in my opinion, she is rather too young (being 21 years of age) for the President." [12]

Yet this same observant young critic was obliged to confess shortly after that " I can't omit acquainting you that our President enjoys all the happiness the married state can afford. . . . From the little acquaintance I have with his lady, I think her a woman of very good sense, of a genteel and virtuous education, amiable in her person, of great affability and agreeableness in conversation, and a very excellent Oeconomist." [13]

He was not mistaken in his judgment. For the remainder of their lamentably short lives they were to be happy and utterly content with each other, despite the disparity of their years.

With the appearance of Esther Edwards the lines of greatness converged. To the sturdy heredity of the Burrs was added now the taint of genius that the Edwards possessed, not to mention the alleged ducal nobility of the Pierponts.

3. HIGH PRIEST OF CALVINISM

For Esther's father was that overwhelming Jonathan Edwards, theologian and Calvinist extraordinary, whose presence cast a huge shadow over colonial America immediately prior to the Revolution.

Born in 1703 of a line of respectable ministers and wealthy lawyer-merchants, he achieved the seemingly quite usual " soul awakening " while an undergraduate at Yale. He entered the ministry, preached a space in New York and was invited back to New Haven to teach. There he met Sarah Pierpont, daughter of a minister and Professor of Moral Philosophy at Yale, was smitten with the sweet sight of God's handiwork, and married.

He soon received a call to preach at Northampton, Massachusetts, and it was in that community that he reared the tremendous edifice of his theologic doctrine and wrote those voluminous volumes that are the despair of students of religious philosophy today. It was in that small community that he builded the largest Protestant congregation in the world, and preached unremittingly for twenty years to hysteria-ridden, emotionally unstrung auditors.

It is difficult to appraise Jonathan Edwards' work adequately. Many have tried it — the great divine has not suffered from a lack of biographers or interpreters. But too often they have fallen back on the more dramatic and sensational elements of his career. The Great Awakening, of which we have spoken in connection with the Reverend Aaron Burr, was, in America, largely his doing. But he was neither the originator nor the founder; the roots go back to England, to the Wesleys and to Whitefield whom Edwards met and admitted to closest friendship.

It is true that he was a Puritan of Puritans, that he remodeled the primitive Calvinism and fashioned it into a logical, coherent intellectual system. It is also true that he held forth in his pulpit with stern, unbending righteousness, flaying savagely the alleged

sins of his time, the dancing, the bundling — that he thundered
the everlasting wrath, and drew for the horrified, yet fascinated
gaze of his congregation the flames of Hell, the predestined dam-
nation that awaited all but the elect — that he detailed pitilessly
for their delectation the last refined agonies of the irremediably
lost.

But there was something more to the man, to the cause that he
sponsored. Religion had become formal, theocratic, a thing of
government and power rather than of personal inner light. He
made his dramatic decision to save the ancient Calvinism, to restore the old Congregational dominance, where the minister was
but the servant, the exhorter, rather than the fount of all salvation. But he was caught, wittingly or unwittingly, in forces far
removed. The Great Awakening, with its evangelical fervor and
revivalist frenzy, as has been pointed out, was not a local manifestation; it was a worldwide movement.

Edwards, as well as Wesley, perceived that the trouble with the
Church was that it had not reached the masses it pretended to
serve. The religion of Calvin and the Puritans had congealed into
a narrow aristocracy, essentially associated with wealth and birth.
The lowly, the vast incoherent people to whom Christ had
preached, were outside the fold, left to their own devices, barred
from the seats of the haughty, comfortable congregations of the
established towns. It was to bring these lowly into the fold, to
bring emotional, personal religion to the inchoate frontiers, that
the revivalists labored.

Theologically, Jonathan Edwards and John Wesley were poles
apart, but in their social objectives they were essentially the same.
The great divine's work was one of the earliest notes in American
life for a more democratic regime, religious as well as political. It
was a failure religiously. The Congregationalists were left ultimately divided and torn. Neither Edwards nor Aaron Burr, the
elder, sensed the full implications of what they were doing, of
the unloosing of democratic forces that necessarily ensued, of the
strange fruit of which they had helped plant the seed.

The Reverend Jonathan Edwards especially failed. He was deposed from his own parish after twenty years because he was too
unyielding, too harsh and narrow in his applications of theology
to everyday life. The emotional fervor had died out slowly among
his congregation — being but human people — while their pastor
grew more and more harsh in his personal judgments and in his
delineations of the requisites for salvation. The final and disastrous conflict between shepherd and flock arose out of the admis-

sion of sinners to the Sacrament. The congregation, uneasy and increasingly restive, insisted on a more liberal rule. But Edwards was adamant — only the saintly, the elect, were admissible. Being of the elect was no light matter. It required a blaze of inner illumination, a public confession that one had been touched with the divine, pure essence, a long, searching catechism and probation period from which many otherwise quite good and worthy people shrank. Not all of them were exhibitionists.

As a result Jonathan Edwards was cast out by a narrow majority and moved to Stockbridge, in western Massachusetts. This was a frontier settlement in the heart of the Indian country, subject to all the hardships of primitive life, to the ravages of wild beasts and of wilder Indians who seemingly did not appreciate to the full his missionary activities. His family, including little Esther, went with him, to share the fatigues and dangers and grinding poverty with uncomplaining fortitude. It was from Stockbridge that the Reverend Aaron Burr retrieved Esther and brought her back to Newark to preside over his bachelor establishment and the young students of the College.

4. THE DAUGHTER OF PURITANS

That the harshness and unfailing gloom of Puritan households have been greatly exaggerated and overdrawn is sufficiently proved in the person of Esther Burr herself. She had been reared in the very pith and center of the Calvinist domain, yet all contemporary accounts and the more concrete evidence of her own unpublished letters and private diary disclose an alert, lively young woman, sincerely and unaffectedly religious, it is true, but not untouched with normal feminine frailties, a proneness to laughter and gossip, and a certain light, skimming touch on sex and marriage that consort oddly with the supposedly sacred nature of those hoary institutions. And she adored her father, that thundering fount of wrath and brimstone and hellfire!

She slipped easily and graciously into the life at Newark. Her father saw to it that her spiritual welfare was not neglected. On September 17, 1753, the Reverend Jonathan Edwards of Stockbridge wrote to the Reverend Aaron Burr of Newark with all formality that the Church of Stockbridge at a meeting had unanimously recommended Mrs. Esther Burr, formerly Edwards, of their Communion, as worthy of entering " your stated Communion as a member in full standing." [14]

But there were other things that interested her. Their first child was born May 3, 1754, and was christened Sarah Burr — known ever after to her family and intimates as Sally. Yet, with Sally, an infant barely six months old, in her arms, she could still write her sister Lucy, at Stockbridge, all the gossip of the town. Curiously this news showed a fine preoccupation with the fundamentals of life — births, marriages and deaths. " Miss Elez-h Eaton is like to be married. . . ." she reports, " ant you glad? Now I think of another piec of News. Joseph Woodruffs Wife has got a fine Son. One thing brings another, I thought I had no news. Mrs. Serjent is like to have a Child, pray what do you think of this? I know you will laugh . . . Loyer Ogdens Wife lately lay in with Twains, two Daughters & lost em both." [15]

She loved her minister-teacher husband. When he had gone to Boston on College business, she confided to her diary and her friend, Miss Prince, of that Puritan and maritime stronghold, that " O my dear it seems as if Mr. Burr had been gon a little Age! & it is yet but *one Fortnight!* I dont know what I shall do with myself the rest of the time. I am out of patience already. I imagine now this Eve Mr. Burr is at your house, *Father* is there & some others, you all set in the Middleroom, *Father* has the talk, & Mr. Burr has the *laugh,* Mr. Prince gets room to stick in a word once in a while, the rest of you set & see, & hear, & make observations to your selves, Miss Janny amongst the rest, & when you get up stairs you tell what you think, & wish I was there too." [16] Dour, repressed Calvinist households!

There were consolations, however, for her husband's necessary absences. The Governor of New-Jersey, the estimable Jonathan Belcher, came to take her to the militia parade, and he and his lady stayed for tea.

Her life was a round of entertaining company, of dining from eight to ten ministers with dreadful regularity, of domestic affairs, of gossip, of attending sermons, of meetings of the Presbytery, of hearkening to the state of her soul and a little aghast at what she found, of tenderness for her husband, of antic fun withal and a quizzical attitude toward life.

Her diary is a remarkable document, filled to the brim with day to day matters, by turns sunny, sprightly, and religiously exalted.

" Pray what do you think every body marrye in, or about winter for," she inquires. " Tis quite merry, isn't it? I realy belive tis for fear of laying cold, & for the want of a bed fellow. Well, my advice to such ye same with ye Apostles, Let them marry — & you know the reason given by him, as well as I do — Tis better to Marry than

to — " But when it came down to cases, alas! " Cousin Billy Vance
is going to be Married — did you ever hear the like? Pray what
can he do with a Wife? He is more of a Woman than of a man." [17]

Of her husband she writes vehemently, passionately. " Do you
think I would change my *good Mr. Burr* for any person, or thing
or all things on the Erth? *No sure!* not for a Million such Worlds
as this [that] had *no Mr. B — r on it.*"

Life went on apace. The Lord's work had to be done; the training of the students, the needs of the infant College required the
unremitting efforts of the Reverend Mr. Burr. It was soon evident
that the cramped quarters of his parsonage were too limited, that
the multitudinous requirements on his time and energy were too
great to be united in a single individual. He had to decide between
the First Presbyterian Church and the College. He decided in
favor of the latter.

New quarters for the College had to be found. Meetings of the
Trustees were held. The matter was debated. Suitable sites were
discussed. The little village of Prince Town was finally decided
on. It was well situated, in the heart of good farming country
and great forests from which the winters' firewood could be readily
obtained; it was the halfway station on the stage lines between
New York and Philadelphia. The chief difficulty, however, was
the raising of sufficient funds.

A great campaign was instituted under the immediate personal
attention of President Burr. Governor Belcher, his close friend,
assisted in every way possible. Funds were solicited among the
elect and well-disposed in the Colonies; a vigorous drive was made
abroad. Contributions poured in from Scotland, Ireland and
" South Britain." Mr. Burr expressed his complete satisfaction
with the agreeable returns. Over 1000 pounds came in from Scotland alone. They would " be able before long," he hoped, " to
support a Professor of Divinity, that Office at present lies on the
President, with a considerable part of the Instruction in other
branches of Literature." [18]

Nor were the faithful the only sources of supply. The unregenerate disgorged too, via the worldly method of lotteries. Burr petitioned for, and received, permission from the Governor and
General Court of Connecticut to draw " a Lottery in their Colony
for the benefit of said College." [19] Similar permission was obtained elsewhere. In Philadelphia, in New York, in Boston, in the
South, the tickets were sold, the prizes distributed, and the resulting proceeds used to swell the College treasury.

President Burr did not withhold his own purse. He purchased

the lottery tickets on a generous scale — too generously, thought his somewhat resentful wife. " Mr. Burr has put Some Tickets into ye Philadelphia Lottery," she complains, " & I think we have lost enough by lotteries. We have lost about a hundred pounds York money by em, & I'm not willing to loose any more unless Duty evidently calls." [20]

Finally, in February, 1755, the contracts were let, and the building begun. He was busier than ever. To all his other duties was added the supervision of the slowly growing structures in far-off Prince Town. Yet he found time to exhort and preach with renewed vigor to his Newark flock. Mr. Burr, records his wife, " has been remarkably Stired up to be fervent in his preaching of late. O if the Lord would bless his labours! " [21]

Nor did he forget that learning, like charity, begins at home. Esther had received the normal girl's education. Her spelling was weird and wonderful, her command of foreign languages nil. Wherefore " we have a French Master in the House with us. He is lerning the Scholars french & Mr. Burr is lerning too, he knew Somthing of it before. Mr. Burr has had a mind [that] I should lern, but I have no time." Rebellion stirred in the wifely bosom, albeit somewhat apologetically. " The married women has Something else to care about besides lerning French tho if I had time I shoul be very fond of lerning." [22]

CHAPTER II

CHILDHOOD

1. A Son is Born

ON February 6, 1756, Esther Burr was "unexpectedly delivered of a Son," and "had a fine time altho it pleased God in infinite wisdome so to order it that Mr. Burr was from home." But, she rattled on, " I had a very quick & good time. A very good laying in till a but 3 weeks, then I had the Canker very bad, & before I had recovered of that my little Aaron (for so we call him) was taken very Sick so [that] for some days we did not expect his life. He has never been so well Since tho he is comfortable at present." ¹ His sister Sally was almost two now. There were to be no more children. Tragedy was lurking in the shadows.

But the protagonists did not know it at the time. They were still at Newark, in the parsonage at the juncture of Broad and William. The College buildings were growing slowly. Esther Burr was in raptures over them. " The College," she exclaims lyrically, " is a Famous building I assure you & the most commodious of any of the Colleges as well as much the largest of any upon the Continent. There is Somthing very Striking in it & a grandure & yet a Simplicity [that] cant well be expressed." ²

Her husband was noticeably more controlled in his enthusiasms. " We have begun a Building at Princeton," he wrote his Scotch correspondent, " which contains a Hall Library & Rooms to accommodate about an 100 Students, tho it will not any more of it be finished than is absolutely necessary at present, with an house for the President. We do everything in the plainest & cheapest manner, as far as is consistent with Decency & Convenience, having no superfluous ornaments." But he is satisfied. The students are behaving well. There are, in fact, some among them " that give good evidences of real Piety, & a prospect of special Usefullness in the Churches of Christ." ³ That, after all, was the all-important thing: The training of missionaries to spread the new unrest, the inner agitation, to all America.

Little Aaron was only six months old when a company of soldiers was quartered on the parsonage unexpectedly. Esther was not pleased. That night she scribbled in her diary: " 50 Soldiers to

Sup at this House & Lodge which Surprized me much, but they behaved better than I expected considering they came from Road Island. They are going for recrutes." [4] The Colonies, it seems, were not free from sectional prejudices.

The very next morning she set out with her infant son — Sally remained at home — " in a Waggon for Stockbridge." It was the long-anticipated, arduous journey to revisit her family. They welcomed her — mother, sisters, brothers, and the slightly bewildered, if still unbending Jonathan. To him she fled with the secret doubts that had troubled her soul — religious fears of which she did not wish her husband to know — and her father soothed, advised, and poured the sweet oil of his wisdom over their festerings. She came back via New York, feeling infinitely refreshed.

But alas! Poor little Aaron, who had stood the journey quite well, took immediately ill with a hoarse throat and violent fever. " The Doct Said he was affraid the Child would not live till morn." The frantic mother went through agonies, but in the morning the little one was still alive, to the vast astonishment of the learned doctor. He mended, did Aaron, but very slowly, and " O my dear," Esther cried to her confidante, Miss Prince, " help us to bless the Lord for his great mercies. I look on the Child as one given to me from the dead. What obligations are we laid under to bring up this Child in a peculiar manner for God? " [5] One wonders, had she lived, what sentiments she would have set down in her diary anent the strange course of her son's career.

In December, 1756, the College buildings having been put in a fair state of completion, they removed to Princeton. It was hard and wearing, this pulling up of stakes, this removal of an institution. Mr. Burr confessed to his friend, the great evangelist, Whitefield, that " the fatigue I have had in the care of the College this winter has been greater than ever, being obliged to do the duty of a Tutor as well as my own." But it did not matter. For, " blessed be God I never had so much comfort in my little Society. There has been a growing concern about the great things of religion among my pupils for some time past. Some of the most vain & careless greatly reformed and some enquiring the way to Zion." [6]

They were quite definitely in the throes of a great revival. Whether it was the sermons and exhortations of the President, or an intangible something that sweeps over even the most intelligent societies at times, the young students had received the inner illumination that comes from a state of grace and were acting accordingly.

But neither he nor his wife found any incongruities in the situation. It was the accepted mode of obtaining " Grace." Esther gave hallelujah. " Good news my dear," she penned joyfully. " I have to tell you this morning a Minnisters Son near Philadelphia hopefully received Comfort last Night in the Night. There was little Sleep amongst them. Some up all Night. Mr. Spencer Sat up till 1 o'clock then left there poor young cretures Seeking God. . . . Mr. Burr Says he thinks [it] evidently a Work of Grace." [7] And again, Mr. Burr told her that the " great part of the Schollars are gathered into one Room Crying in great distress & [that] another has received comfort. My Heart Exults at the thought [that] God is about to revive Religion in general." Esther Burr, in spite of certain worldly distractions, was a deeply religious woman.

The Princeton Revival made a great noise in the outside world. Inquiries poured in seeking first-hand knowledge of the late " remarkable occurrences." [8] President Burr was inordinately pleased, albeit exhausted. At no time had he been happier. But already the first clouds were gathering.

In May, Esther's sister became ill with the smallpox — there were always epidemics — and Esther had attended to her. In spite of her fears she escaped infection. The next alarm was for " Mr. Burr." He had played with a little dog they had taken home from her ill sister's home. A month of dreadful anxiety passed, and then the clouds lifted — temporarily. They were both still unscathed.

Meanwhile the children were growing apace. In September, 1757, the mother considered them with an impartial eye and jotted down the results on paper. " Sally has got pretty hearty again, is not much of a Baby, affects to be thought a Woman. Nothing She Scorns more than to be told She is a Baby or Child. We are about Sending her to School, but Mr. Burr is expecting [that] She will prove a numbhead." But as for her son, she sensed other things. " Aaron," she noted, " is a little dirty Noisy Boy very different from Sally almost in every thing. He begins to talk [a] little, is very Sly and mischievous. He has more sprightliness then Sally & most say he is handsomer, but not so good tempered. He is very resolute & requires a good Governor to bring him to terms." [9]

2. Swift Tragedy

And now, in swift and crashing crescendo, grim tragedy stalked the luckless family. President Burr was a slight, spare man, and the imperious demands of his situation had sapped his vigor. Still exhausted from the emotional orgy of the revival, he set off in

August, 1757, to Stockbridge to confer with his father-in-law. On his return from that tedious journey, he found it necessary to set off at once to Elizabethtown to meet Governor Belcher on business relating to the College. There he learned of the death of a friend's wife, and hastened to the house of mourning to preach the funeral sermon.

He took ill with a fever when he finally returned to Princeton, but, scorning mundane ailments, he took post to Philadelphia, once more on behalf of his beloved College. No sooner had he returned from there than the tidings were brought him of the death of Governor Belcher. It was a terrific shock. They had been close friends, and the College of New-Jersey was much beholden to the efforts of the Governor. He himself was by now quite ill, yet, disregarding all protestations, he went once more to Elizabethtown to preach a lofty and moving sermon at the bier of his friend. It was the last straw. He barely managed to get home and went immediately to bed, delirious. He never arose, dying quietly on September 24, 1757.

His death made a deep impression. His contemporaries knew that a great and good man had passed. His funeral took place in the College he had loved and labored mightily for; it was attended by a tremendous outpouring of people; the newly appointed Governor of New Jersey delivered a glowing eulogium, his praises were sung in press and pulpit alike, and finally his remains were deposited in the College churchyard.

The Reverend Ezra Stiles, preacher and tutor at Yale, heard of the sad event and sat down to his diary. " President Burr I was *Intimately* acquainted with," he said. " He was a little small Man as to body, but of great and well improved Mind . . . He was a hard Student. A good classical Scolar in the 3 learned Tongues: — was well studied in Logic, Rhet., Nat. & Mor Phil., the belles Lettres, History, Divinity, & Politics. He was an excellent Divine & Preacher, pious & agreeable, facetious & sociable, the eminent Xtian & every way the worthy Man. Like St. Paul his bodily presence was mean & contemptible, but his mental presence charmed all his Acquaintance. He was an Hon. to his College & an ornament to the Repub. of Letters." [10]

He left a not very large estate. His salary had been small and the demands on his purse heavy. But it was sufficient for the needs of his widow and their two small children.[11]

It was a terrible shock to poor Esther. Only by calling on the consolations of religion was she able to achieve a measure of peace. All the training of a lifetime was brought to bear. " O, dear madam," she wrote her mother, "I doubt not but I have your, and my honored father's prayers, daily, for me; but, give me leave to intreat you both, to request earnestly of the Lord that I may never despise his chastenings, nor faint under this his severe stroke; of which I am sensible there is great danger, if God should only deny me the supports that he has hitherto graciously granted." [12]

Her grief later gave way to exaltation, to a raptness that comes only to the zealot. Her rhapsodic outburst to her father, barely a month after the death of her husband, and with little Aaron, who had proved to be a delicate, ailing child, in the throes of another attack, smacks strongly of the glowing visions and the joyous renunciations of the Middle Ages. "God has carried me through new trials, and given me new supports," she cries. "My little son has been sick with a slow fever . . . and has been brought to the brink of the grave. But I hope, in mercy, God is bringing him up again. I was enabled to resign the child, after a severe struggle with nature, with the greatest freedom. God showed me that the child was not my own, but his, and that he had a right to recall what he had lent whenever he thought fit . . . A few days after this, one evening, in talking of the glorious state my dear departed must be in, my soul was carried out in such longing desires after this glorious state, that I was forced to retire from the family to conceal my joy. When alone, I was so transported, and my soul carried out in such eager desires after perfection, and the full enjoyment of God, and to serve him uninterruptedly, that I think my nature would not have borne much more. I think I had that night a foretaste of Heaven." [13]

Poor lady! She spoke wiser than she knew. For now calamity fell with renewed force upon them all. Young Aaron was better, but Jonathan Edwards was soon dead. He had been called by the Trustees to Princeton in January, 1758, to replace his deceased son-in-law as President of the College. The smallpox epidemic was still raging, and Edwards sought protection in inoculation. Unfortunately, the inoculation developed seriously, and on March 22, 1758, he died. A month before, his own father had preceded him.

His daughter Esther was not long to survive him. Already she had taken the smallpox taint, and on April 7, 1758, she, too, succumbed to the epidemic disease, aged twenty-seven.

Nor was the tale yet complete. The two orphaned children — Sally, aged four, and Aaron, aged two — had been hurriedly transported to Philadelphia and placed under the temporary care of

Dr. Shippen, a friend of the family. Their grandmother, Sarah Edwards, Jonathan's wife, journeyed there in September to take them to her own home. In less than two weeks she, too, was dead — of dysentery.

Father, mother, grandfather, grandmother, great-grandfather — all in the space of a year!

3. ORPHANS

The young orphans remained under the kindly care of Dr. Shippen until 1761, when Timothy Edwards, their uncle and eldest brother of Esther Burr, assumed their guardianship. They were taken to Stockbridge, and in 1762 were removed with Timothy and his family to Elizabethtown, New Jersey.

The Reverend Timothy Edwards — he, too, was of the elect — was not exactly the proper person to rear his high-spirited young charge. He inherited the sternness and straitlaced morality of his great father without those other and more winning qualities that had made him adored by his children. The reverend gentleman believed in strict obedience, in the gloomy repressions of an ultra-Puritanic household, in the free use of the rod and long, preceding moral exhortations and castigations. Small wonder that the boy rebelled. He ran away on several occasions; once, at the age of ten, getting as far as New York, where he shipped as a cabin boy on a boat making ready for sea. He was discovered by his guardian in time and incontinently hauled home.[14]

But Timothy Edwards was an honest, if somewhat narrow-visioned, gentleman. He accounted strictly to the Burr estate for the funds deposited in his hands for the support of the two children, and he dealt with them fairly according to his lights. Nor did Burr harbor any resentment against him in after years.

They were given private tutors, and Aaron, at least, made rapid progress. Sally, though not quite as keen-witted, did well by herself in the process of achieving an education. One of their tutors was Tapping Reeve, who fell in love with his young pupil, and eventually married her. They went to Litchfield, Connecticut, to live, and Reeve was to become a great lawyer, the founder of the first law school in the Colonies, and ultimately to be elevated to the Supreme Court of the newly formed State as its Chief Justice. All their lives there was to exist a warm friendship between Aaron Burr and his erstwhile teacher.

There were diversions, of course. Sailing and swimming, hunting, riding and fishing with young Matthias Ogden, a year his elder, and brother-in-law to Timothy on his wife's side. He, too, was a member of the Edwards' menage. This friendship persisted also in later years, surviving the mutual hardships of the campaign against Quebec, and outlasting the more perilous difficulties of maturity. Aaron Burr had a faculty even in these tender years of attaching warm loyalties to himself.

He did very well in his studies. An uncle, Pierpont Edwards, himself only thirteen, wrote of his small nephew and school-fellow, aged seven. " Aaron Burr is here, is hearty, goes to school, *and learns bravely.*" [15]

So well had he learned that at the age of eleven he was positive that he was sufficiently prepared for college. Naturally there was only one place to be considered — Princeton. His whole family fortunes had been bound up in a peculiar degree with the exist-ence of this institution for the breeding of Presbyterian ministers and incidental inculcation in the classical amenities.

He applied, and was refused — much to his disgust and mor-tification. Not because he was not qualified — the requirements for entrance were lamentably meager — but because of his ex-treme youth and tiny stature. " Little Burr " he was in youth and " little Burr " he was to remain throughout life. He was a handsome youngster, with small, delicate features inherited from his father, and glowing black eyes that were never to lose their luster even when old and buffeted by fate and the malice of his fellow men.

He went back to Elizabethtown, determined not to be thus unceremoniously cast aside. For two more years he studied at home, following the curriculum of the College faithfully. At the ripe age of thirteen he knocked at the doors of Princeton once again; this time, however, demanding not merely admission, but entrance into the Junior class. For had he not successfully accom-plished the required studies for the first two years?

His bold request was rejected, but, because of his special quali-fications and his Presidential background, he was graciously per-mitted to enter — as a Sophomore. This was in 1769. Dr. Wither-spoon was President, and the College was still officially known as the College of New-Jersey.

CHAPTER III

COLLEGE YEARS

1. THE INSATIABLE STUDENT

PRINCETON was a small village in those days. The College itself consisted of two buildings — Nassau Hall, the nobly proportioned eating, living and intellectual quarters of the students, and the President's home, with whose prospect in the course of construction Esther Burr had been so entirely enamored. Dense forests lay on every side, and other settlements were few and far between. But the New York-Philadelphia stage stopped overnight at the only tavern in the village, and brought regular news of the outside world, and provided a meeting-place where the young students could seek relief from the too chilly dogmas of moral philosophy.

The young boy of thirteen applied himself at once with the utmost diligence to his studies. He devoted from sixteen to eighteen hours of close application to his books. He ate and drank with Spartan abstemiousness, finding that a well-loaded stomach was conducive to mental and physical sluggishness. He was determined to keep up with the others of his class at whatever cost.

But this remarkable regime could not but undermine his constitution and lay the foundation for future disorders. His health gave way. When, however, he discovered at the end of the year that he had exceeded most of his companions in standing, he wisely decided to relax his furious pace. For the remainder of his college career he took his studies in their stride, easily and without the pale, sickly cast of the midnight lamp. Whereupon his health improved and he was able to devote himself to the other recreations that Princeton might afford.

For one thing he joined the literary societies. There were two of them, the American Whig and the Cliosophic, rivals in debate and a somewhat scurrilous paper warfare. He first became a member of the American Whig. With him in that organization were such future notables as James Madison, President of the United States, Philip Freneau, the Revolutionary poet and pamphleteer, Lighthorse Harry Lee, member of the Constitutional Convention, and Hugh Brackenridge, Judge of the Pennsylvania Supreme Court.[1]

In 1771, however, for some reason, he quit his associates and joined the rival society, the Cliosophic. According to legend he was one of its founders. But it had been in existence since 1765, when it was known as the Well-Meaning Society. William Patterson, Oliver Ellsworth, Luther Martin, Tapping Reeve and Robert Ogden — all names to conjure with — had been its organizers. It ran afoul of the Faculty and was suppressed in 1768 or 1769. In June of 1770 a group of future clergymen, all seniors, revived the corpse under the name of the Cliosophic Society. Burr joined some six months later.[2]

With this Society he remained until graduation, and after. His closest friendships — friendships that were to last far into manhood — were conceived and stimulated within the roster of the two societies. William Patterson, Governor of New Jersey, United States Senator and a Justice of the Supreme Court; Matthias Ogden, his boyhood chum, later Colonel and Brigadier General in the Revolutionary Army; Samuel Spring, chaplain of Arnold's expeditionary force and distinguished divine; Luther Martin, the renowned "bulldog of Federalism," who was to come to Burr's aid when Jefferson demanded his life, and who in turn was to be harbored and cherished in a lonely, sodden old age; Henry Brockholst Livingston, New York's Chief Justice and later of the United States Supreme Court; and Jonathan Dayton, Senator from New Jersey, whose fortunes and whose very life were to be intertwined with those of Aaron Burr.

There were others, too, equally distinguished, whose present friendship could not outlast the tides of political importunities and the slings and arrows of outrageous fortune. Of such were Morgan Lewis, long after to oppose his former comrade for the Governorship of New York, Jonathan Mason, Senator from Massachusetts, who failed him in his hour of bitterest need, and James Madison, who followed Jefferson's political banner into unrelenting enmity — and the Presidency of the United States.

A remarkably notable group — these young men of Princeton!

The Cliosophic Society never grew to be ashamed of its famous son. In the darkest of his years, when he was an outcast and all men's hands were turned against him, it delighted to show him honor. In 1812, just returned from his European exile, the Society promptly and somewhat defiantly elected Aaron Burr its President. In 1826 it repeated the gesture. When he died, public mourning was decreed for a period of thirty days and the Society turned out *en masse* to follow the last poor remains to their resting-place.[3]

2. Myths in the Making

It is from his college days on that the legends begin to cluster thick and furiously around the name of Aaron Burr. Probably of no one else in American history are there more unsupported, and unsupportable, tales in circulation. Some are innocuous; others, superimposed upon the known reserve of his life in those days when his name was already a hissing and a scorn in the mouths of the generalty, were tinctured with retrospective venom. The biographer must perforce tread warily among these fragile tales.

It is recorded that he played at billiards in the tavern and won thereby a certain small sum of money. This, it is said, so shocked the young man's conscience that he forthwith swore off all games of chance for stakes, and held strictly to his resolution through life.[4] But his Journal, that extraordinary account of his Continental journeyings, records on at least two occasions that he played cards — and for money. Once even, when literally starving, and without a sou in his pocket, he took the desperate chance and emerged " in possession of cash to the amount of 60 sous." [5]

Another legend is not so innocuous. It was the forerunner of a whole battalion of similar tales, all purporting to prove Aaron Burr a rake, a seducer, a scoundrel, a man without morals and without principles, wholly unfit to be invited into any decent man's home. Though, on analysis, not one of these infamous stories has emerged intact, yet a good deal of the spattering mire has managed to cling to his name down to this very day, with results that are obvious to the most casual observer.

This earliest *canard* was the touching story of the Lonely Grave. Catherine Bullock, so it went, a young lady of Princeton, was basely seduced by young Burr and as callously abandoned. In despair she committed suicide, and, as an eternal reproach to her betrayer, her outcast body was buried on the site of President Burr's house, where it still reposes in solitary judgment.

The facts, however, are quite at variance with this dark tale of passion and tragedy. She, it seems, was the niece of Colonel George Morgan, at whose home she was visiting from Philadelphia in a vain attempt to be cured of a tubercular condition. She died undramatically and quite correctly of that disease in the year, marked on her gravestone for all to see, 1792. Aaron Burr graduated from Princeton in 1772, just twenty years before. Actually, the " lonely grave " had been cut off from its respectable mates in the old Morgan burial-ground by the prosaic interposition of a new highway. Nor was the site ever the place of the house of President Burr.[6]

Of Aaron Burr's college compositions, several have been preserved for posterity, but they prove to be but the usual academic effusions on set topics that are always the delight of professors and the despair of students. Consider the subject matter. An Essay on Style, in which the youthful essayist condemns the "laboured ornaments of language, the round period, or the studied epithet," and justly, if platitudinously, proclaims that "there never was a ready speaker, whose language was not, generally, plain and simple."[7] He wrote also on Honor, on the Passions, on An Attempt to Search the Origin of Idolatry, and on Dancing. No sign anywhere of the literary art or the authentic fire. But then Burr was never to blossom into the literary life!

In his junior year he won first prize for "reading the English language with propriety, and answering questions on Orthography," and second prize for "reading the Latin and Greek languages with propriety."[8]

3. THE STUDENTS GET RELIGION

In Burr's last year at college there occurred one of those periodic frenzies known as "revivals" in which his father, the Reverend Mr. Burr, and his grandfather, the Reverend Mr. Edwards, had rejoiced so heartily. All regular business of the college was suspended, and students and professors alike wallowed in the emotional orgy. A large number hit the sawdust trail, and looked askance at young Burr when he held aloof. He was urged to remember his father, his mother, his grandfather, the entire ministerial line of Burrs and Edwards. Somewhat shaken in his intellectual skepticism by the continual exhortations — remember he was but a lad of fifteen at the time — he consulted in some perplexity the President of the College, Dr. Witherspoon. That canny Scotchman, whose practical good sense was opposed to revivals, though not daring openly to interfere, advised him against plunging into the emotional maelstrom. The raging excitement, he told the young applicant, was purely fanatical, without contacts in true religion. Whereupon Aaron felt relieved, and, thus fortified, was able to resist the call of the herd.[9]

Already, as a mere lad, Burr was conducting a goodly part of his correspondence in cipher; that practice which was to be maintained through life and was destined to contribute not a little to the tremendous popular clamor against him when the great " Conspiracy" unfolded. Always has this trait of secrecy and *sub rosa* concealments been held against Burr as pointing to certain dark and twisted convolutions in his being from which anything might be expected. But a little sane reflection should set the matter in its proper frame.

In the beginning, the practice of cipher writing may have been what has been normal to childhood in all ages. Though his friend, William Patterson, warned him almost immediately after graduation, that " the New-England people, I am told, are odd, inquisitive kind of beings, and, when pricked on by foolish curiosity, may perhaps open the letter, which I do not choose should be common to every eye." [10]

To a politician, however, or to any one who did not desire his mail to become public property, a cipher in that day and age was a practical necessity. The mails were not sacrosanct, the means of transportation crude, and, as Patterson pointed out, the people — elsewhere as well as in New England — curious. Ciphers were in common use among important men, just as code telegrams are universally used in business today. Time and again men like Washington and Jefferson interrupt their letters with the remark that they dare not entrust more to the insecurity of the mails, but must await a safer moment for further communication.

The students of Princeton were not exactly pampered. They were not permitted a free use of funds with which to indulge in worldly pleasures when their minds should be engrossed with the lovely symmetries of syntax and the noble proportions of ethical principles. Their spending money, given by doting parents or sterner guardians, was required to be deposited with the Treasurer of the College, and doled out by him to the necessitous student in such manner as not to cast undue temptation in his path.

When Aaron, for example, wished to visit in Philadelphia, he sent an humble chit to the purse-bearing Treasurer requesting a modest 4.10, which was happily granted.[11] But when, on the eve of graduation, he wrote, " As the Class are to be examined the Beginning of next week and I shall be obliged to spend a considerable sum I shall be much obliged to you if you will send me by the bearer George what you think fit," he committed a tactical error, for the Treasurer saw " fit " to send him the generous sum of four dollars! [12]

4. GRADUATION

He graduated from Princeton in September, 1772. His record was good but not outstanding. Another of those nameless legends has it that he graduated at the head of his class with a rating that has never been surpassed in the history of the university. There is not the slightest basis for this. As a matter of fact, while his exact standing is not known, he ranked neither first, second nor third in the class. He did not deliver the Latin Salutatory nor the Valedictory. Much is made of his honorary oration, entitled, ironically enough in view of certain phases of his later career, "Castle Building." But in those days of small graduating classes practically every graduate orated on Commencement Day.[13]

William Patterson, writing to their mutual friend, the Reverend Dr. Samuel Spring, already graduated and in orders, remarked that "the young gentlemen went through their exercises in a manner passable enough. The speakers were all tolerable — none of them very bad nor very good. Our young friend Burr made a gracefull appearance; he was excelled by none, except perhaps by Bradford." [14] Burr never was to blossom into the orotund type of oratory to which Commencement orations are peculiarly adapted. His talents lay in the direction of precision, cogency, and the swift marshaling of facts.

Patterson, as a matter of fact, had already advised young Burr on the subject. Said he: "Forbear with me while I say *that you cannot speak too slow.* Your good judgment generally leads you to lay emphasis on the most forcible word in the sentence; so far you act very right. But the misfortune is, that you lay too great stress upon the emphatical word. Every word should be distinctly pronounced; one should not be so highly sounded as to drown another." [15]

It was over; the tumult and the shouting and the fervent goodbyes. He was sixteen, precocious, young, small even for his age, a graceful, handsome lad, who already had attached male friends to himself and was beginning to flutter the feminine dovecotes. The world was before him.

But his guardian's good sense and his own desires declared in favor of delaying the plunge. Accordingly, Burr remained at Princeton after graduation for some months, reading extensively, laying the foundation for that love of books and searching inquiry that were to distinguish him throughout life, and withal amusing himself in a fashion not incongruous with his age, his looks and general disposition. He alternated between Princeton and Elizabethtown, where young Matthias Ogden, his best friend, joined him in boating, sailing the Kill van Kull, and in certain other adventures of which friend Patterson, more staid and accustomed to the cloistered air of Princeton, hinted in oblique phrases. "Our mutual friend, Stewart," he chides, "informed me you were still at Elizabethtown. You are much fonder of that place than I am, otherwise you would hardly be prevailed upon to make so long a stay. But, perhaps, the reason that I fear it, makes you like it. There is certainly something amorous in its very air." [16]

5. THE FOOTSTEPS OF HIS FATHERS

In such wise the summer of 1773 slipped by. With the coming of a sterner season, more serious thoughts intruded. It was time now to consider the future, the making of a career. As far as Timothy Edwards, his guardian, was concerned, the matter was settled. Nor did any other thought enter the heads of the whole tribe of Edwards, the more distantly related Burrs, the Faculty of Princeton, or of his numerous friends.

Aaron Burr was to become a minister of the gospel. His ancestry, his education, his uprearing, tradition, all imperiously demanded it. Already, back in May of 1772, while he was still a Senior in College, Samuel Spring, in the first flush of divinity studies, had hoped "to see the time when you will feel it to be your duty to go into the same study with a desire for the ministry. Remember, that was the prayer of your dear father and mother, and is the prayer of your friends to this time." [17]

It was hard for a lad of seventeen to oppose the expressed desires of those he respected and loved, and the even more crushing, if invisible, influences of form and tradition. There are no evidences that at any time he had been deeply religious, or possessed of the emotional, ecstatic nature of his immediate forbears. Such traits were foreign to his cool, analytical mind and reserved habits. His resistance to the pressure of the mob in the revival at Princeton had proved that.

Furthermore, he had read extensively, and seemingly a good part of that browsing had been done in books that were tinged with the spirit of skepticism and inquiry emanating thus early from the cosmopolites of France. A faint shudder of disgust must have passed over him at the thought of himself in decent black.

Nevertheless he trod for the moment the well-worn path of duty and conformity. He would at least give the matter a trial. So he repaired to the home of Dr. Joseph Bellamy, at Bethlehem, Connecticut, for instruction and guidance into the sacrosanct mysteries of the Presbyterian theology. The good Dr. Bellamy had been an apt pupil of Jonathan Edwards, and was himself by now a famous preacher and even more famous inductor into the ministry. His home had gradually assumed the proportions, if not the dignity, of a theological seminary.

He was pleased to receive Aaron into the bosom of his family in the autumn of 1773. Nor was Timothy Edwards, who had not long before closed his house in Elizabethtown and moved back to Stockbridge, less satisfied. His young ward must have sorely puzzled and perturbed the reverend gentleman; he had frankly given up all thoughts of restraint for a considerable period. But now, evidently, things were shaping up quite well.

It took Aaron Burr only a little while, however, to discover that the pursuit of chaste theology was not for him. The worthy doctor was an honorable, if somewhat indiscreet, instructor. He liked to employ the Socratic method for the purpose of testing the validities of the Calvinist dogma. This was a dangerous procedure with a lad of Burr's stamp. The theologian was evidently no match for his keen-witted pupil, whose weapons of debate had been tempered in the fires of the French philosophers, for soon Burr was writing with youthful exuberance to Matthias Ogden that he had Dr. Bellamy " completely under [his] thumb." [18]

Exuberance soon passed, however, and gave way to calmer and more considered reflections. The narrow path of Presbyterianism, the repressions preached by its great exemplars, the eradication of so much of life and humanity in the process, repelled him on this closer examination. " The road to heaven," he was convinced, " was open to all alike." [19] The keys were not irrevocably given to any one set of dogmas. Accordingly, and with mutual protestations of good will, he quit his mentor in the early summer of 1774.

Religion thereafter became for him a purely personal and private affair, not to be discussed in public or to be the subject of argument. He has been accused time and again of being an atheist. Perhaps he was — there is no manner of telling. Certainly his life was not put into the mold of any revealed gospel, nor was it at any time guided by the hope of rewards or fear of punishments in a hereafter. It is true that he attended a fashionable

REVEREND AARON BURR

AARON BURR, IN YOUTH

From a portrait by Gilbert Stuart

church in New York in afteryears, but that doubtless was a formal concession to the requirements of the time.[20]

It is probable, however, that he was a Deist, in the sense that Jefferson and Franklin were. It was a vague, comfortable phrase that could cover a great deal of inner skepticism. Surprisingly, the important figures of that period were not much given to prayer and religious observances. The old Gods had changed; new ones were taking their place,

6. IDYLLIC INTERLUDE

Burr's thoughts, now that the ministry had been definitely set aside, turned to law. This was the other great profession to which young men of good family and education inevitably tended. And it possessed certain characteristics that must have appealed quite strongly to his particular cast of mind.

The question arose, however, as to his tutelage in the intricacies of Blackstone and Coke. Pierpont Edwards or Tapping Reeve? Both good lawyers and both relatives. His guardian, Timothy, to whom he applied for advice, was grimly resigned. The decision of his obstreperous ward had been a blow to him. It was, he answered coldly, " a matter of indifference to me. I would have you act your pleasure therein." [21]

Left thus abruptly to his own devices, Burr chose Tapping Reeve. There were additional attractions at Litchfield besides the tutorial capacity of his brother-in-law. Sally Reeve, for instance, his well-beloved sister. The country, moreover, was pleasant; the young ladies numerous and quite pretty. Summer was just beginning, the sap was rising, and young spirits grew animated in anticipation. It was obviously no time to commence hard and serious work among the crabbed citations of the legists. Time enough for that in the sear of autumn.

But somehow when autumn came he still dallied. For he was feeling his oats, and the process seemed good. In short, he was eighteen! The winter passed, and the spring of 1775. All through the period he conducted a gay, lively correspondence from Litchfield with his friend Ogden in Elizabethtown. It was replete with much high-spirited nonsense and numerous allusions to casual love intrigues. There was an exchange of letters, conceived in anonymity, with a certain young lady, and couched in a phraseology at once sentimental and lofty. Ogden wrote of rumors in Princeton that Aaron had finally fixed his attentions on a single girl. To which Burr retorted that no two of the gossipers could agree on the same girl as the recipient of his favors. Then there was much laughter to be made out of Uncle Thaddeus Burr's transparent attempts to inveigle Aaron into matrimony with a young lady of fortune. Steady Matthias, himself engaged to be married, and fearing that the machinations of Uncle Thaddeus might finally involve his friend, breathed solemn warning against the proposed marriage with money unless " Love " and " Soul " were likewise involved.[22]

An idyllic interlude! The outer world seemed completely forgotten in this interchange of youthful exuberances and preoccupations with the lovely face of the youthful god, Eros. Yet that outer world was in a turmoil. The Colonies seethed with discontent and most articulate rage. There had been Navigation Acts and Stamp Acts, Committees of Correspondence and boycotts; Samuel Adams ranged up and down the land inculcating radical ideas and more radical actions; there had been a Boston Massacre and a Boston Tea Party. Events were marching with inexorable tread toward a definite, already visible goal.

It must not be assumed from the evidence of this correspondence alone that the vast issues which embroiled their fellow men left these dallying youngsters untouched. Aaron Burr never, at any period of his life, was to commit his profoundest thoughts or inner emotions to paper. His character, for all his outward fluency, was too essentially reserved, too chary of the power of the printed word, to place himself down thus irrevocably. This it is that makes the task of Aaron Burr's biographer such a blind groping in the dark. The *facts* of his life are there for all to read, but more often than not they are double-edged, susceptible of infinite doubt, because he left no clues to the inner motivations, the hidden springs which animated him; such clues as are ordinarily to be found in the unguarded or confidential letters of others.

One letter only of this period betrays an awareness of the parlous state of the times and a very definite insight into Burr's personal reactions. By August of 1774 passions had raised to such a pitch that a Barrington mob attacked and demolished the house of a man suspected of Toryism. The sheriff arrested eight of the ringleaders " *without resistance,*" and brought them on to Litchfield for safekeeping. The next day fifty horsemen, armed with clubs, rode into town to rescue the prisoners. Burr sallied forth to join in the prospective fray, but, to his vast disgust, the attempt was not made, and, crowning infamy, " the above mentioned *sneaks all gave bonds for their appearance,* to stand a trial at the next court for committing a riot." [23] The young amorist was rapidly becoming a fire-eater!

He was beginning also to apply himself to the study of the law. It was high time! But his progress was rudely interrupted by the sound of guns at Lexington. The War of the Revolution had commenced!

CHAPTER IV

SWORDS AND BULLETS

1. THE CALL TO ARMS

AARON BURR was then nineteen, some five feet six inches in height, slight of build, but wiry and capable of prolonged exertions. His year of so-called idleness, coupled with a healthy outdoor existence and the sports he loved, had rebuilt the reserves he had lost in that first year's arduous application at college.

The news of Lexington crashed like a thunderbolt into the placid existence and gallantries of Litchfield. Burr threw his books away forthwith. He was young, ardent, and enamored with the military life — he had been reading history of late, with especial attention to the accounts of battles and sieges and the stratagems of great soldiers. And the " rights of man," the " laws of nature," were phrases that spread their glamour for him equally with others of his age, and made righteous and just a revolt against the alleged tyranny of a far-off England.

He wrote immediately to his friend Ogden, urging him to come at once to Litchfield, so that they might volunteer for service together. Ogden was less impetuous; he wrote back that he must first make certain arrangements. Meanwhile events moved rapidly. The battle of Bunker Hill was fought, and the Americans had stood the test of a pitched battle with British regulars.

In an ecstasy of impatience Burr hurried to Elizabethtown to hasten his slothful friend; with such success, that in July, 1775, the two lads were riding into Cambridge where the hastily summoned American forces were encamped. They had with them a letter from John Hancock addressed to General Washington recommending " Mr. Ogden and Mr. Burr of the Jerseys." [1]

But here disillusionment awaited them. Washington had been only recently placed in command, and an almost impossible task presented itself to him. There were some 17,000 raw recruits in the scattered camps investing Boston; without the slightest semblance of discipline, unorganized, poorly armed, without uniforms or supplies. The officers were in little better state. Very few of them had either practical or theoretical knowledge of warfare.

A commissary had to be established, drills performed, powder and shot procured, companies organized — in short, an army had to be forged out of a mere conglomerate mass.

Naturally the harassed Washington had little time to hearken to letters of recommendation. If the eager volunteers ever got to the Commander with an offer of their services, they were evidently put off with vague phrases. In any event, they wandered about the camp, footloose, becoming increasingly disgusted with the wretchedness and disorder of the camp, wondering when the war was to begin. Nowhere in Burr's histories of military campaigns was there precedent for such squalor, ignorance, petty jealousies, inefficiency. Heroic exploits were far removed from the ragged men they met at Cambridge.

Young Aaron's spirits effervesced into a high fever at the disappointment. He betook himself to bed. The others, Matthias Ogden and their mutual friends, were no less disgusted. An expedition was being talked of; a secret whisper of a campaign against Canada. Volunteers were being called for. Ogden and the others were tired of inactivity, and here was adventure beckoning. They decided to join up.

But they tried to keep the news from their ailing friend. He heard their discussions inadvertently, however, and rose at once from his sick bed. He, too, was determined to go along. Ogden argued and expostulated; friends and relatives painted dark pictures of perils and fatigues and certain death; his sister Sally had already written that " if you are sick or wonded I will com and see you and I still assure you that the frightful nois of great guns nor the tho'ts of being in a Camp shall prevent my coming if ei :her of those should be the case." [2]

But nothing could shake him. Fever or no fever, he was joining the expedition forming under Benedict Arnold at Newburyport for the long dash through the Maine wilderness on Quebec. Ogden traveled comfortably by carriage the sixty miles to Newburyport. But Burr would have none of that. They were soldiers, not women. So he, and a few other volunteers whom he persuaded, started out September 14th, muskets and knapsacks on their backs, on foot to the appointed meeting-place.

Timothy Edwards, still legally his guardian, was alarmed for his hot-blooded young nephew. He sent a messenger post-haste to Newburyport with peremptory instructions to bring the fugitive back. Burr read the letter that was thrust into his hand, looked at the sturdy bearer, and inquired coolly: " How do you expect to take me back, if I should refuse to go? If you were to make any forcible attempt on me, I would have you hung up in ten minutes."

The messenger had been provided, however, against such a contingency. He produced a second letter from the uncle; this one no longer peremptory and harsh, but couched in affectionate and imploring terms. He dwelt exceedingly on the harrowing hardships to be endured on such an expedition, on Burr's present illness and a slightness of frame that would never endure to the end. In earnest accents he begged his ward to reflect and give up the idea.

Still the young volunteer was adamant. He answered the letter with many respectful protestations of regard, and a firm determination to carry on. Whereupon the messenger deposited with him silently a bag of gold that Edwards had sent along, and departed — alone.[3]

2. ON TO QUEBEC

The invasion of Canada was one of the earliest strategic moves of the Revolution. There were immeasurable advantages to be gained, both military and political, in winning over Canada to the cause. For one thing, there would be a solid and united front in America and a consequent increase in man-power and the resources of warfare; for another, it would eliminate a convenient base for British land operations against the rebellious Colonies.[4]

The idea was correct, the hopes based upon its success plausible, but unfortunately Washington and Congress had been furnished with distorted and misleading information. Certain negotiations had already been conducted with the Canadians, seeking their support. The old French settlers were not wholly unwilling to consider the matter; they were not exactly contented under the rule of England. But they were a prudent race and cautious against untoward commitments. If they could be assured of success, if the Americans could prove conclusively that they were well able to battle the might of England — well, then, Messieurs, we shall see . . . we shall see!

The American emissaries, unversed in these diplomatic murmurings, hastened back to report that all Canada was seething with revolt, that at the mere sight of an expeditionary force, the countryside would rise *en masse* and join in driving the English into the sea. These reports were promptly accepted at face value. Time was short, if the conquest of Canada was to be accomplished at all. General Guy Carleton, the British Governor, was an able soldier, and he was rushing fortifications with diligence and speed. Reinforcements were already on the way from England.

The capture of Ticonderoga and of Crown Point by the Americans opened a way along Lake Champlain into the heart of Canada. General Schuyler was placed in command of a force that would strike through at Montreal. On his sudden illness the command devolved on General Montgomery.

Simultaneously with this move, Arnold was to march with picked men through the untrodden wilderness of southwestern Maine and surprise and capture Quebec while Carleton was employed at Montreal. It was a desperate venture, but its very boldness and daring was in its favor. At that, the entire scheme missed complete success only by a hair's-breadth. The most important element of weakness, and one which was eventually to prove fatal, was the time equation. The maps of the Maine wilderness were not wholly accurate, and the passage took far longer than the calculated period. The surprise element was lost, Carleton was able to man Quebec adequately, and the wholly lukewarm Canadians, seeing that the fat was in the fire, lifted hardly a finger to aid their supposed allies.

Colonel Arnold's force (he had just received his commission) consisted of two battalions, of about 1100 men in total strength, chiefly mountaineers and frontiersmen from Pennsylvania and Virginia, accustomed to the wilderness. They left Cambridge in two detachments on September 11th and 13th, 1775, and reached Newburyport, the point of embarkation, on the 15th and 16th. Burr and his friends arrived at about the same time. On the 18th they embarked on board eleven transports and headed for Gardinierstown, at the mouth of the Kennebec River, where they put ashore on the 20th. Burr had been accepted as a gentleman volunteer by Arnold and was in high spirits. Along with him were young men whose names were to be linked with his in certain very important crises of his life. Besides Matthias Ogden, there were Samuel Spring and Jonathan Dayton, friends from college days, and — James Wilkinson. Of this worthy, much, much more anon.

From Gardinierstown, what with bateaux and marching, they traversed the six miles to Fort Western, up the river. From there, on September 25th and 26th, they pushed on in two battalions. Burr and his companions were assigned to Colonel Greene's division and started on the 26th.

They had for their perilous water journeying over 224 bateaux, "hastily built in the most slight manner of green pine," laden to the brim with men, provisions, cannon, equipment; two men in the bow, and two in the stern to handle each unwieldy craft. Thus equipped, they ventured without misgivings, sensing only high adventure ahead, into the unknown tangle of woods and swamps and rapids and mountains.

It was difficult, tedious work, far more so than any had anticipated. The current of the Kennebec, as they penetrated farther along its course, grew rapidly stronger and more shoal. Time and again the crews had to wade in the icy, rushing waters to haul the clumsy, overladen boats against its force. There were falls and rapids, too. The boats were unloaded, placed on the backs of straining men, together with the supplies and guns, and carried through hampering woods and swamps around the impasse. The weather was shifting too; every day it was perceptibly colder. On September 30th, only a few days along, it was already so cold that the soaked uniforms of the shivering men froze and refused to thaw out even near the fires.

The boats were leaking now, the crews were always in water, their clothes always drenched. Precious food supplies swept away in the torrents or grew moldy; ammunition became wet and was rendered useless. Portages increased in number and difficulty. The river became shallower and swifter, and the mountains were beginning. Snow was on their flanks, and continuous cold, penetrating rains set in. The water of the stream was icy. Rations were reduced to moldy pork and flour and a few barrels of unwholesome salt beef.

On October 8th they reached the headwaters of the Kennebec and there was a twelve-mile carry to the Dead River. This was the worst of all, through choked forests, swamps and miry lakes, across the looming flank of a mountain. The men were in a very bad state by now. Dysentery had weakened them, fevers and colds had sapped their strength; they were ill, exhausted, starved, their clothing in rags, drenched by the eternal rains, frozen by the sharp frosts of a Maine autumn. But they made it, and on October 16th set those boats that remained on the Dead River.

Arnold wrote letters to his correspondents in Canada, announcing his imminent arrival. Two Indians were the messengers. They and their letters fell into the hands of the British and gave the first warning of the approach of Arnold's expedition.

The Dead River was a deep, sluggish stream, black and ugly. It was too deep to pole and the bateaux had to be hauled with ropes by men on the banks. The rain fell torrentially. One bitter evening the river rose like a spring freshet and washed boats, provisions, guns and tents to irremediable destruction. The surrounding forest for hundreds of square miles became a vast, choked lake. The men died of hunger and exhaustion; pneumonia took its toll. Food was non-existent; everything was eaten by the desperate soldiers — dogs, moccasins, leather. And, to add to their miseries, it began to snow on October 25th. Winter and all its attendant terrors was at hand.

Finally, however, after indescribable hardships and superhuman efforts, they struggled with their few remaining boats over a terrible portage, surmounted the steep ridge of the Boundary Mountains, toiled down to Seven Mile Stream, and into Chaudière Pond. They were in Canada!

Burr and Ogden were participants in that dreadful march. They helped pole boats, waded in icy streams, struggled through swamps, ate dog meat when available, were ragged and hungry and footsore equally with the tough frontiersmen of Morgan and of Greene. Ogden kept a hurried journal, of which only a portion is preserved. On October 28th, he and Burr and two others, with " about $\frac{1}{2}$ of a pound of pork per man, and five pints, scant measure, of flour, which was to last us to the inhabitants," left the ridge of the Boundary Mountains and made their way by boat down to Chaudière Pond.[5] On the way they found one of Captain Smith's boats dashed on the rocks and all her lading lost. Because the stream was too swift they abandoned boat, and joining forces, seven all told, proceeded on foot, steering northeast, until they caught up with the rest of their Company. " At 3 o'clock we hailed Capt. Derborn and one more going down stream in a birch canoe. They informed us that Capt. Morgan had his boat split upon a rock, the most of his effects lost, and one man drowned." [6]

The next day they found the wreck of their informants' canoe. It was every man for himself. Discipline and ordered marching had long since vanished. They straggled through as best they might, singly and in couples and in little ragged, always hungry groups. Men died on the way and there was no one to bury them.

Meanwhile the rear division, under Colonel Enos, had held a council of war, and foreseeing only suffering and eventual death ahead in this frightful wilderness, had determined to abandon the expedition. Accordingly they turned back, taking with them the larger share of their scanty food and ammunition; for which Enos was afterward to be tried by court-martial and regrettably acquitted.

Arnold had pushed ahead of the toiling, still faithful detachment to Chaudière Pond. There he met a messenger from French sympathizers with the cheering information that there were " few or no regulars at Quebec, which may be easily taken." [7] He went on down the Chaudière River and on October 30th reached Sartigan, where there were, praise be, supplies to be purchased and sent back to his starving troops.

Ogden records their pathetic emotions at the vision of food. It was " the finest sight my eyes ever beheld . . . Scarce one of us but with tears of joy expressed the gratitude of his heart at seeing five horned cattle and two birch canoes loaded with mutton and flour brought forward by French men." It was November 2, 1775.

The wilderness march was over. From then on they traveled through settled country to their objective. But half the force had deserted, many had died in the terrible passage, and the rest were ill and exhausted.

After a rest at Sartigan, the little band, some 500 effectives, moved on to Point Levis on the St. Lawrence, directly opposite the frowning steeps of Quebec. The advance force camped on the ground November 7th; the last faint straggler came up by November 13th.

Meanwhile cheering news had been received from Montgomery. He had advanced into Canada, captured Chambly and St. John's in succession, and was pressing on to Montreal. General Carleton, hearing of the new threat caused by Arnold's sudden appearance, hastily abandoned Montreal to the foe and raced back to Quebec to put it in a state of defense.

Meanwhile there were no boats. The British had burned them all, and a frigate and a sloop patrolled the river. But somehow the Americans were able to purchase a supply from the natives, and secretly, the night of November 13th, 500 men crossed to Wolfe's Cove before the alarm was given. They met no opposition as they climbed in Wolfe's footsteps to the Heights of Abraham and encamped before the walls of Quebec.

A flag of truce to the English with a peremptory, threatening message to surrender was decided on. It was a gesture, nothing more.[8] Ogden, who carried the message, was, to his vast astonishment, promptly greeted with cannon balls. He tried it again on the following day, and the emphatic salute was repeated. Obviously the English were in no mood to listen to insulting demands.[9]

3. Siege and Assault

The besieging force was a mere handful; nor did it have any artillery with which to batter at the fortifications. The besiegers' position was far more hazardous than that of the ostensibly besieged. It was necessary, therefore, to wait for reinforcements and guns from Montgomery. Accordingly, the Americans retreated on November 19th to Pointe aux Trembles, on the St. Lawrence, some twenty miles west. Even as they quitted their positions before the city a sloop bearing General Carleton entered Quebec.

On November 20th Arnold heard from Montgomery about the victory at Montreal and the capture of 11 British vessels. He immediately dispatched young Ogden, now a Staff Captain, with a request for ammunition, clothing, and a proposal for a junction of their forces for a grand assault on Quebec. But nothing came. On November 30th Arnold sent another dispatch, expressing anxiety for the delay and for Montgomery's safe arrival. " I have not had the pleasure of hearing from you for ten days," it ran.[10]

This express was probably carried by Aaron Burr. For, on the very same day, November 30th, 1775, Arnold wrote another letter to Montgomery. " Dear Sir," it read, " this will be handed you by Mr. Burr, a volunteer in the army, and son to the former President of New Jersey College. He is a young gentleman of much life and activity, and has acted with great spirit and resolution on our fatiguing march. His conduct, I make no doubt, will be sufficient recommendation to your favor." [11]

Another legend concerning Burr must accordingly be placed in the discard. Notably, the flattering tale that young Burr had been sent by Arnold from Chaudière Pond to Montgomery, disguised as a Catholic priest, with news of Arnold's approach, and that Montgomery, pleased with the perilous task gallantly accomplished, forthwith appointed him to his Staff. Obviously, on November *30th,* Montgomery still did not know Burr.[12]

Burr never reached Montreal with these two letters. For Montgomery was already on his way up the river. On November 28th he had started forth and on December 1st he appeared in Arnold's camp. Burr evidently turned back on sighting the flotilla.

The reinforcements, however, consisted of only 300 men. The balance of Montgomery's army had been left with Wooster to hold Montreal. On December 2nd, the combined force, still under 1000, marched back to Quebec. Montgomery had brought artillery, and it was decided now to chance an assault.

Burr, armed with Arnold's strong recommendation, and because of his own personal qualities, had found favor with Montgomery. Immediately upon his arrival the commanding general attached the young volunteer to his own Staff as aide-de-camp. It was now *Captain* Burr, still aged 19!

Several schemes for the assault were proposed. Among them was a plan by Burr to scale the walls at the Cap Diamond bastion. This formidable fortress was supposedly impregnable, but the idea, though desperate, was not as forlorn a hope as it sounded. For the very reason that no attack would be reasonably expected there, the garrison should prove small, and, once at close quarters, the guns mounted in the bastion could not be depressed to inflict any damage on the attacking force.

Montgomery thought sufficiently of the plan to permit Burr to take 50 picked men and drill them in the use of scaling ladders. Which he proceeded diligently to do. But, to the ardent young Captain's great chagrin, the scheme was eventually dropped. It was decided instead to concentrate on a two-column attack on the Lower Town. It was believed that the wealthy citizens of Quebec would not view with equanimity the loss and possible destruction of their valuable warehouses along the riverfront, and would force Carleton to a speedy surrender. But Burr considered it then — and ever after — a fatal delusion.[13]

The attack finally took place on the night of December 31st. It was the last chance. The following morning the enlistment terms of some of the soldiers expired. Three New England companies — patriots all — had determined to quit, war or no war. Smallpox was prevalent, the officers wrangled, and food was giving out.

One detachment, headed by Arnold, was to approach the city from the General Hospital and storm the barrier at Sault au Matelot. The other, under Montgomery's personal leadership, was to make its way from Wolfe's Cove along the beach of the St. Lawrence and attempt to force the barrier and palisades on the opposite side of the Lower Town at Près de Ville. If both maneuvers proved successful, the two divisions were to combine at the foot of Mountain Street, within the Lower Town. A narrow picketed passage led to the Upper Town from there, and perhaps, if luck were with them. . . . These were the main assaults; there were to be three diversions. Arnold's column held 600 men, Montgomery's 300; the diversions 250. A pitiful force to assault a heavily fortified place, defended by every advantage of nature and 2,000 men!

They started in a blinding snowstorm, and the night was a shroud of ink and swirling white. But the English had been apprised of the impending assault, and fire opened almost immediately. Arnold's column withered under a storm of shot. Arnold himself fell, his leg shattered by a musket ball. Captain Daniel

Morgan took command and, with the few remaining men, swept around the precipice upon the first barrier. Here for the moment all seemed surprisingly well. The English guard was drunk with New Year's liquor, and the sound of battle had not penetrated their befuddled senses. Morgan raced over the barrier and on to the battery.

But the miraculous luck broke down. A solitary sailor, on sentry near the cannon — and liquorless — ran to the guns and discharged one of them. The guard tumbled out. Astounded, they beat a hasty retreat with Morgan and his men hot after them. But another battery intervened and the Americans paused for reinforcements. By his own account, Morgan ventured almost to the Upper Town " to see what was going on." He found everything in confusion, and no one in arms. Yet when he returned, they continued to wait and debate, he and his officers, while precious minutes fled. After all, they were only a handful, and they were clogged with prisoners. So the opportunity passed!

Aaron Burr was of course with General Montgomery's column. The way along the St. Lawrence was so encumbered with piled-up ice and deep snow-drifts that they did not reach the first palisade at Près de Ville until all chance for a surprise assault was over. The guard was alert at the barricade, waiting with lighted matches to the guns. Cautiously the little force crept closer to the great wooden pickets. Burr was at his General's side, so was John McPherson, the other aide-de-camp, and their Canadian guide.

Carpenters were called for. They succeeded in sawing out four of the pickets without giving the alarm to the garrison within. Encouraged by their success, the men crowded through, to repeat the same performance at the second barricade, well up on the precipice. When three of the posts were down, Montgomery and his two aides slipped through, then the Canadian guide, and some others. They were under the last sheltering point of the cliff. Around the bend waited the English at their cannons.

Suddenly the alarm was raised. Montgomery sprang forward unhesitatingly. " Push on, brave boys; Quebec is ours! " he shouted. Burr and McPherson were on his heels, the guide right behind, followed by a ragged column of assault.

A storm of cannister and grape swept the narrow pass. Montgomery went down, shot through the head; so did McPherson, the guide, and nine others. Burr stood almost alone, untouched.

The long column recoiled on itself, aghast at the disaster. Burr shouted to them to follow him, that he would lead them on. But Lieutenant-Colonel Campbell, second in command, and in the *rear* of the column, gave hasty orders to retreat. In vain did Burr stand exposed to the guns, exhorting the troops to press to the attack. The demoralized men were only too eager to obey the orders of the superior officer, and they fled, leaving their General dead in the snow.[14]

Meanwhile, the British, after that first fatal volley, had succumbed to panic and fled up toward the center of the town. On the field there was only Burr — and the dead! Finding themselves fleeing a phantom pursuit, the English returned sheepishly to their guns. Another opportunity had passed!

It is bootless to speak in " ifs." Yet, *if* Morgan's officers had not prevailed on him to wait for reinforcements; *if* the men had followed Aaron Burr instead of the more prudent Campbell, Quebec might have been captured that night, and the entire course of the War of the Revolution been profoundly changed. But to return to that snow-covered shambles!

According to Dr. Samuel Spring, an eye-witness, " as soon as the General fell, the American army fled in great consternation. . . . Burr returned back alone and attempted, amidst a shower of musquetry, to bring off on his shoulder, the body of Montgomery — but the General being a large man, and Burr small and the snow deep, prevented him." [15]

As a result, when, the next morning, the battle over, the British came down, they found the frozen corpse almost where it had fallen, and was carried by them up to the citadel for burial.

4. END OF THE VENTURE

The assault on Quebec had ended in failure. Montgomery was dead, Arnold wounded, and Morgan, who had finally returned with reinforcements — too late — had found his command cut to pieces and himself compelled to surrender. When morning came, the American forces counted their losses. They were staggering. More than half had been killed, wounded, or taken prisoner. Arnold, incapacitated, attempted to retire the command in favor of Colonel Campbell, but he was unacceptable to the other officers. It was he who had ordered the retreat at Près de Ville in the face of Burr's attempt to rally the column and press to the attack, and they felt that his prudence — or timidity — had lost them Quebec. Unanimously they elected Arnold.

The campaign was over, but the siege stubbornly carried on until May. Huddled behind breastworks, themselves fearing attack from the besieged, decimated by smallpox, hampered by heavy snowstorms and the severe cold, torn by internal dissensions and wrangling, they held on. Arnold quit to go to Montreal in April for treatment of his leg. Wooster took over, then Thomas. Finally, in May, 1776, by which time the British had been overwhelmingly reinforced, the fruitless siege was raised.

Captain Burr's gallantry in this ill-fated action elicited a sheaf of praise and commendation. Arnold declared he had "behaved extremely well" and appointed him Brigade Major.[16] General Wooster lauded him; his friend Bradford exulted that "your praise is now in every man's mouth . . . I make no doubt but your promotion will be taken care of. The gentlemen of the Congress speak highly of you."[17] Judge Reeve wrote with relieved anxiety. "Dear Burr, Amid the lamentations of a country for the loss of a brave, enterprising general, your escape from such imminent danger, to which you have been exposed, has afforded us the greatest satisfaction. The news of the unfortunate attack upon Quebec arrived among us on the 13th of this month. I concealed it from your sister [Sally] until the 18th, when she found it out; but, in less than half an hour, I received letters from Albany, acquainting me that you were in safety, and had gained great honour by your intrepid conduct."[18]

Meanwhile Matthias Ogden had left the army while it still huddled hopelessly before Quebec, and returned to New York. There he received an appointment as Lieutenant-Colonel in the 1st Jersey Battalion, and wrote forthwith to his friend that he had heard of a vacancy in General Washington's official family, and was pulling wires to obtain it for him.[19]

Burr felt the inactivity of the Canadian campaign keenly. It was dragging out to wretched failure, and he was, he told his sister, "dirty, ragged, moneyless and friendless." Nor had he conceived any particular esteem for his superior, General Arnold. He had thought him a bit more regardful of his own comforts than of the privations of his men during the Wilderness trek, and, while paying tribute to his undoubted bravery, considered him somewhat unprincipled on the moral side.

In April, 1776, Burr accompanied Arnold to Montreal, then on to Camp Sorrel, and by May he was at Fort Chambly, desperately eager to get home, to see his friends and family, to participate in a *war* once more.

So anxious indeed was he that Davis terms it desertion! But a letter from Burr to his sister, dated Fort Chambly, May 26, 1776, seems to put the quietus on this legend also.

"I have this Moment arrived from the Camp at Sorrel all well,"

he tells her. " I rec'd a Letter from you while at that Place — heard
of another taken Prisoner in Quebec and several more strolling
about the Country for the entertainment of the Army . . . Write
me no more till you hear from me again which I hope will be from
Albany. I shall if nothing extraordinary intervenes start for the
Southward the Beginning of next Week. *As I go on Public Business* I shall not probably have time to see you as I go down. I intend after that to make a week or two and enjoy it at Litchfield
with the best of sisters." [20]

En route through Albany, Burr heard that it would be agree-
able for General Washington to see him in New York. Ogden, now
a Colonel, had pulled his wires to good effect. Burr arrived in
New York about the second week in June. Davis sets the date as
May 20, 1776. But this is impossible. On May 26th, he was still at
Fort Chambly, and on June 5th he and Ogden, who had been
detailed to Fort George, missed each other on the road at Lake
George, the one coming down and the other going up.[21]

In any event he saw Washington and was invited to join his
staff, pending a satisfactory appointment. Burr accepted, and was
promptly installed at Headquarters, in the old Mortier Mansion
at Richmond Hill. Richmond Hill, whose history was already at
once venerable and glamorous, and that was to become so much
more famous and romantic from further association with the
name of the young aide-de-camp.

5. Major Burr of the Staff

Of young Burr's association with General Washington during
this period — he was only twenty — there has been considerable
ado. It is known that Burr wrote to John Hancock expressing a
desire to retire from the army, and that on June 22, 1776, Hancock obtained for him an appointment as aide-de-camp to General
Putnam instead. Accordingly the presumption has arisen — and
has been accepted as true down to the present — that the General
and his hot-headed young aide had quarreled, that Burr had become disgusted with Washington, that there had been constant
irritation between the two — not to speak of a certain dark and
nefarious amour which the General had uncovered.

The time element, hitherto overlooked, however, must effectually dispose of such suppositious imaginings. According to all previous accounts, Burr was with Washington for six weeks, during
which period a good many untoward events might have taken
place. Actually, with Burr at Lake George on June 5th, it was

impossible for him to have reached New York much before June 12th. Assuming a decent interval before he entered upon his duties, it must have been at least June 14th before he joined Washington's household. And on June 22nd he received his new appointment. Which brings his total service as Washington's aide-de-camp to not over eight days! Eight days — during which time he had already communicated his dissatisfaction to Hancock, who in turn was able to overcome the necessary red tape and furnish Burr with his commission.

On this calculation, Burr had barely been installed in Washington's household a day before he was evincing disgust and Washington was discovering illicit love affairs. Another explanation is much more satisfactory and credible, even though it does violence to hoary tradition. The appointment on Washington's staff had been a temporary one, a mere stopgap until a more satisfactory one could be found. Burr had left Canada because he desired *active* service. Staff Headquarters, with its routine of clerical work, was not to his taste. He came to the Colonies expressly, " by personal interview, to answer purposes which I scarce hoped the cold medium of ink and paper could effect." [22] This was undoubtedly an interview with Hancock, then President of the Continental Congress. The meeting must have taken place and the letter have been sent *immediately* on Burr's arrival, and *before* he had any personal acquaintance with Washington, to have achieved such quick results. Whatever ill-feeling or dislike there may have existed between the two necessarily arose at a later date.

Early in July, 1776, Aaron Burr entered upon his new duties with the rank and perquisites of a Major. He was eminently contented with his new post. Israel Putnam was Commander of the American forces in and about New York and, as such, was in a position to permit his warlike young aide to see real service very shortly. They got along very well together. Putnam had a real regard for Burr, and Burr was always to call the indomitable, if somewhat illiterate warrior, " my good old General."

Headquarters were established in the Warren House, at the corner of Broadway and the Battery, where Mrs. Putnam and her daughters presided in happy domesticity and mothered the handsome young aide.

For a while there were only clerical duties, the writing and revision of the General's orders with a due regard for the niceties and spelling of the English language, which Putnam was so often led wholly to disregard. Nor were the social amenities overlooked.

Besides the manifold attractions of New York for a handsome young officer, aged twenty, with a reputation already achieved for bravery in action, there was a new diversion. This was no less than the sudden appearance in General Putnam's household of a young beauty of the tender age of fourteen, cousin to the late General Montgomery and the daughter of a British officer stationed with the enemy forces on Staten Island. She was Margaret Moncrieffe, afterward to achieve a certain reputation in the courts of Europe as Mrs. Margaret Coghlan. Much, much later, she was also to publish her memoirs — an interminable catalogue of amours and escapades.

Friendless and alone at Elizabethtown, the young girl had thrown herself upon Putnam's mercy, and that kindly old man offered her at once shelter and succor in his own home where she " was received, with the greatest tenderness by Mrs. Putnam and her daughters." But, she goes on naively, " I seldom was allowed to be alone, although sometimes, indeed, I found an opportunity to escape to the gallery on the top of the house, where my chief delight was to view, with a telescope, our fleet and army on Staten Island." [23]

There was another delight, also. A certain young American officer about whom she rhapsodizes at length with the retrospective glow of later years. Aaron Burr. " Oh! " she cries rather self-consciously, and with due attention to the literary effect, " May these pages one day meet the eye of him who subdued my virgin heart, whom the immutable, unerring laws of nature had pointed out for my husband, but whose sacred decree the barbarous customs of society fatally violated. To him I plighted my virgin vow, and I shall never cease to lament, that obedience to a father left it incomplete. . . . I had communicated, by letter to General Putnam, the proposals of this gentleman, with my determination to accept them, and I was embarrassed by the answer which the general returned; he entreated me to remember that the person in question, from his political principles, was extremely obnoxious to my father, and concluded by observing ' that I surely would not unite myself with a man who, in his zeal for the cause of his country, would not hesitate to drench his sword in the blood of my nearest relation, should he be opposed to him in battle.' Saying this, he lamented the necessity of giving advice contrary to his own sentiments, since in every other respect he considered the match as unexceptionable." [24]

She does not name this " conqueror of my soul," except that he was an " American colonel." Yet Davis considers it a matter of common knowledge that Burr was the " gentleman " in question, even though he was only a major at the time. Perhaps he was! In any event Davis, by the deliberate omission of the above pertinent portions of the Memoirs, so garbled the text that it lent itself readily to his outright accusation that Burr had seduced the charming young ward of his General, and placed her errant feet on the path of later and more notorious years.[25]

There is also another story in connection with the youthful Margaret Moncrieffe. It appears that the young lady's frequent sessions on the roof with a telescope and her passion for painting flower pictures excited Burr's suspicion that the fair charmer might be nothing more or less than a British spy. These suspicions he communicated to his superior, and one day she was quietly removed to closer confinement at Kingsbridge, there to remain until she was sent back to her father within the British lines with a most ingenuous note, composed by the General himself.

" Ginrale Putnam's compliments to Major Moncrieffe," it read, " has made him a present of a fine daughter, if he don't *lick* her he send her back again, and he will previde her with a good *twig* husband." [26]

6. BURR RESCUES A BRIGADE

It was not all to be a nice balancing of the amenities, however. There was a war in progress. General Howe had landed in August, 1776, an army of 34,000 men on Staten Island, backed by a mighty fleet, all for the purpose of taking the City of New York. With New York as a military base, and with the fleet of His Majesty dominating the sea and the wide stretch of the Hudson River, it would be comparatively simple to cut the rebel Colonies neatly in twain.

To meet this peril Washington determined to hold the city at all costs. Yet he must have known that his position, with the men and armament at his disposal, was militarily indefensible. He was compelled to divide his already scanty forces. Long Island was open to the guns of the fleet and the attack of an overwhelming enemy. Let but Brooklyn Heights be seized, and low-lying Manhattan could be raked at will. With the frigates in possession of all the waterways, a defeat might speedily be converted into overwhelming disaster.

Others, better tacticians than he, saw this clearly. Young Aaron Burr, aide-de-camp to General Putnam, was one of these. Nay, he was the first to suggest that it would be sound and farseeing tactics to abandon the city to the British; first, however, setting fire to it, so that there would be no shelter or accommodations for their unwieldy host. A drastic measure, it is true, but militarily correct. *After* the retreat, General Nathanael Greene, and even John Jay, proposed like measures.[27] It may be that the enterprising aide pressed his suggestion with more vehemence than discretion, and that the commanding General resented it.

However, the event was to prove the wisdom of Burr's proposal. For Washington persisted in his attempts to hold the city. There were political repercussions and the matter of morale to be considered as well as abstract tactics. He fortified Brooklyn Heights, correctly seeing the strategic value of that rise of land, and there stationed the greater part of his too small forces. General Greene, chosen to command the Heights, took ill, and Generals Putnam and Sullivan were hurried over just as the British were about to attack.

By a clever flanking movement Howe turned the American left, under cover of a feigned frontal attack and the thunder of the ships' guns, and, on August 27th, the Americans were utterly defeated. Stirling and Sullivan were captured together with a thousand men; the rest driven back to an intrenched camp. But Howe, instead of attacking the demoralized troops at once, preferred to commence slow siege tactics, and Washington availed himself of the respite, the darkness, the rain, and a strong northeast gale that kept the British ships out of the East River, to ferry his bedraggled and disheartened army across to Manhattan.

Major Burr had proceeded with General Putnam to Brooklyn, where he had been charged with the inspection of troops and outposts. His reports were caustic and biting; he found the raw levies lacking in morale and wholly innocent of military efficiency — reports that the events of the next few days were thoroughly to justify. He even advised that the Heights be abandoned without a battle. On that dreadful night of terror and confusion he watched with somber eyes the battalions load into the wind-blown boats, so eager to get away that " those in the rear were mounting on the shoulders and clambering over the heads of those before them." [28] He had predicted just such a debacle!

With Brooklyn Heights lost, and the fleet commanding all the surrounding waters of Manhattan Island, only Howe's extreme and inexplicable dilatoriness prevented him from easily encompassing the capture of Washington's entire force and the probable conclusion, then and there, of the American Revolution. Nor was

Washington himself without fault here, as in the remainder of this most unmilitary campaign. It is true that he shifted half of his force to Kingsbridge, where the Westchester Hills were open to him for escape, but with the balance of his force he clung stubbornly to Manhattan, until Howe, girding himself at length and after two weeks' delay, landed in Kip's Bay, and drove the American troops before him in disgraceful rout, cutting off whole brigades, and harrying the remainder until they stopped, exhausted and breathless, on Harlem Heights.

It was during this disorderly retreat that Burr, singlehanded, and with the utmost coolness and daring, saved an entire brigade from destruction or capture by the pursuing British. Through some misapprehension, General Silliman's Brigade had been left stranded in the vast and disastrous confusion of that 15th day of September, 1776. General Knox, temporarily in command, without orders and wholly cut off from the fleeing army, moved his troops to Bunker's Hill, a small, crudely constructed fort at the juncture of what is now Grand and Mulberry Streets. There he determined to await the course of events.

While they huddled in increasing bewilderment, hearing the thunder of guns and the crash of musketry, Aaron Burr rode up and asked to know who commanded there. General Knox presented himself, whereupon Burr — a Major, it must be remembered, and twenty years old — demanded of the veteran General what he did there, and why he had not retreated with the rest of the army?

The General replied that retreat was impossible, that the enemy had already thrown a cordon across the upper island, and that he meant to defend himself in the fort. Burr laughed out loud. How can you defend this place, he inquired scornfully? You have no provisions, no water, no bombproof shelters. Why, he went on, with one mortar or a howitzer the British could take you within four hours. It is suicide to stay, General; you *must* retreat, and at once, to Harlem Heights.

Knox, however, was stubborn, and a bit addled by the rush of events. Besides, what did this little snip of an aide-de-camp mean by offering him advice in such assured, scornful tones! He would not attempt it, in spite of Burr's excited urgings.

Whereupon the young aide, seeing all too clearly the consequences of the superior officer's decision, determined on an act of the grossest insubordination. Turning from the obstinate General, he addressed himself directly to the frightened men and officers, who had crowded around, intent on the debate. Why, he exclaimed, if you remain here, men, before nightfall you will all be prisoners, crammed into a dungeon, or hung like dogs. Put yourselves under my command, he cried in ringing tones, and I'll engage to lead you off. Better that half of you die fighting, than all be sacrificed in this cowardly manner. And, while Knox puffed and stormed, the men cheered and agreed to follow this young Major who had appeared out of nowhere.

Burr knew the terrain intimately. He led them along devious back roads, galloping up and down their flank, scouting for sight of the enemy. At about four miles from town they ran into some British and were fired upon. Burr pushed his horse recklessly toward the concealment from which the musket shots had come, hallooing to his men to follow him. Fortunately it proved to be only a company on guard, who broke and fled at once before the onslaught. Burr and his two mounted attendants pursued the fleeing men and killed several of them.

Meanwhile the head of his column had taken the wrong road. He galloped back, hurried them to the left, away from the main force of the British, into a wood, and rode continually up and down the straggling column, encouraging the men with cheerful words, until he had led them into the camp of the American forces on Harlem Heights. Only a few men had been lost in the entire exploit.[29]

It was a gallant deed from inception to conclusion, rendered notable by a coolness and deliberation and envisioning of consequences unusual in a mere lad of twenty. Yet this rescue of an entire brigade was never mentioned in official dispatches. Perhaps the fuming General Knox had something to do with that. Perhaps General Washington still smarted under certain outspoken criticisms from the brash young aide that the event had proved only too overwhelmingly correct. And Burr would have been more than human not to have felt a certain resentment at the seeming slight.

The following day, on September 16, 1776, the panic-stricken troops rallied, defeated the combined British and Hessians in the battle of Harlem Heights, and with the respite thus achieved, were enabled to retire in good order.

7. MILITARY INTELLIGENCE

The campaign now stagnated. Howe again delayed and temporized, when bold moves might have meant the rout of the opposing army. Washington sent 13,000 men to White Plains, where Howe inflicted another defeat on October 28th, yet failed to follow up his victory. Burr was at White Plains, writing to Sally on the eve of battle. " I was near you tho unwittingly . . . Pray remind Seymour again of my Hat — I want it much. If I have any plain Metal Buttons on any of my old Cloathes I should be glad of them all. I have Cloath but cannot make it up for Want of some. If I have a Pr. of Leather Drawers send them & two Pr of the coarsest of my Winter Stockings." [30]

Then came disaster. Fort Washington and Fort Lee, the guardian sentinels of the Hudson, were taken; and Washington, who had joined the main body of his army at Hackensack, began his retreat through the Jerseys. Howe pursued with his accustomed leisureliness. Philadelphia seemed in danger of capture and Congress fled in alarm to Baltimore. General Putnam was ordered south to supervise the construction of lines of defense. Burr, still his aide-de-camp, and solidly entrenched in the bluff old man's affections, assisted. Then came the startling news of Trenton and the victory at Princeton. From the latter place Major Burr wrote in some bitterness to an inquiry of his old friend, Ogden, now a Colonel: " As to ' expectations of promotion,' I have not the least, either in the line or the staff. You need not express any surprise at it, as I have never made any application, and, as you know me, you know I never shall. I should have been fond of a berth in a regiment, as we proposed when I last saw you. But, as I am at present happy in the esteem and entire confidence of my good old general, I shall be piqued at no neglect, unless particularly pointed, or where silence would be want of spirit. 'Tis true, indeed, my former equals, and even inferiors in rank, have left me. Assurances from those in power I have had unasked, and in abundance; but of these I shall never remind them. We are not to judge of our own merit, and I am content to contribute my mite in any station." [31]

Burr never, through life, possessed that capacity to push himself and plead his own cause that is characteristic of your typically successful man. His spirit was too proud, too reserved, even at the height of his own political career. But it rankled nevertheless. Rightly or wrongly, he attributed the oversight of his promotion to the Commanding General, George Washington. There was a crying lack of good officers in the Revolutionary Army. And the twenty-one-year-old Major had sufficiently proved himself possessed of military genius and capacity for leadership.

Yet he continued to perform his staff duties with diligence and dispatch. Already he was showing a decided aptitude for the

Military Intelligence Service. He was quickwitted and observant as well as brave. He interviewed deserters from the British camp at Brunswick and prepared a careful account of " the Situation, Strength and Intentions of the Enemy . . . taken at Princeton, Mar. 10, 1777," for Staff use. At that time Putnam's entire division for the defense of Princeton and its environs consisted of some 350 effectives.[32]

Shortly after, Putnam was ordered to Peekskill to take command of the American lines across Westchester County. Once again, Burr was set to Intelligence work, a task at which he had proved himself most adept. On July 14, 1777, Putnam ordered him to proceed to the Sound and " transmit . . . without delay the intelligence you shall from time to time receive of the movements of the enemy, or any of their fleets." [33]

Chapter V

THE WAR GOES ON

1. Promotion

I T costs money to raise and equip troops, and money — that is, good hard cash as opposed to the product of the printing-press — was very much lacking in the coffers of the Continental Congress. Yet the war had to be fought, and farmers and mechanics induced to enlist by the dangling of bonuses and the prospect of a regular wage. So a vicious system arose. There were plenty of wealthy men in the Colonies — patriots, it must be understood — who, while unwilling to be taxed for the sinews of warfare, succumbed readily to the lure of self-glory and the luster of a military title.

Whereupon the privilege was accorded those with ample money-bags to raise regiments at their own expense, and in return, the illustrious name of the donor was forthwith attached to the troop, while the donor himself — merchant, trader, land speculator, whatnot — was commissioned a Colonel by a grateful Congress, and placed immediately in command. No wonder a good many of these regiments were slightly less than useful to the harassed commander-in-chief!

William Malcolm — a worthy, and wealthy merchant of the City of New York — was one of these. He raised his regiment, was duly commissioned, and behold, Colonel Malcolm's Regiment, completely accoutered and consisting of some 260 men, was ordered to a station on the Ramapo, in New Jersey. But war, even in an encampment, was not all beer and skittles, as the worthy and rotund Colonel soon discovered. In the first place he had taken as his officers the young sons of wealth and influence, and they were not only without any experience in military matters, but resented any interruptions in their former easy-going civilian life. The men in the ranks were the usual bonus hunters, and similarly averse to discipline and the harshness of the army. So that the regiment rapidly grew unmanageable, much to the alarm and inward quakings of its most unwarlike Colonel.

So it was that Major Aaron Burr was suddenly given an opportunity. He had been almost a year with General Putnam as Staff

Officer, without promotion. Now, dated June 29, 1777, he received official announcement from General Washington of his appointment as Lieutenant-Colonel in the Continental Army and his immediate attachment to the regiment commanded by Colonel Malcolm, then in camp on the Ramapo.

But the ambitious young soldier, who had been gnawing his inwards in silence, was not appeased by the belated recognition. The flood gates of his wrath opened in one of the most remarkable responses from a junior officer to a Commander-in-Chief on record.

" I am . . . constrained to observe," he penned sarcastically, " that the late date of my appointment subjects me to the command of many who were younger in the service, and junior officers the last campaign . . . I would beg to know whether it was any misconduct in me, or any extraordinary merit or services in them, which entitled the gentlemen lately put over me to that preference? Or, if a uniform diligence and attention to duty has marked my conduct since the formation of the army, whether I may not expect to be restored to that rank of which I have been deprived, rather, I flatter myself, by accident than design? " [1]

There is no record of General Washington's reply, but doubtless he silently laid this thinly veiled accusation alongside of certain other matters as cause for resentment against this very daring young man. Yet, in spite of his complaint, Aaron Burr was almost the youngest Lieutenant-Colonel in the Army. He was twenty-one!

The portly Colonel Malcolm was only too happy to welcome his newly appointed assistant. In spite of his youth and small size Aaron Burr had achieved for himself an enviable reputation, and he was a veteran of numerous campaigns. In fact, Colonel Malcolm was so grateful that he hastily offered to retire from the regimental scene altogether and leave the young officer completely in control as Acting Colonel. " You shall have all the honour of disciplining and fighting the regiment," he told him with a magnanimous gesture, " while I will be its father." [2]

Whereupon he retired with his family to a comfortable spot some twenty miles from the scene, breathing, no doubt, a huge sigh of relief. What, after all, had a peaceful merchant to do with war's alarms? Sufficient that he had his military title, that " Malcolm's Regiment " it was in all dispatches. A very nice young fellow, brisk and competent, was this new Lieutenant-Colonel Burr. He was very welcome to the job.

2. MARTINET BURR

Burr took charge at once. His hand was firm, yet even. He tightened the lax discipline, instituted a regular series of strict drills and rigorous inspections. The lounging, sullen men were made to toe the mark, and toe it with the alert smartness of well-trained soldiers. Those of his officers who resisted the new order of things, or could not accommodate themselves, were dismissed summarily from the regiment. For two months he labored incessantly. By the end of that period he had a disciplined group, increased by his efforts to 300 effectives, and, surprisingly, he had made himself the idol of the men in the ranks and of officers alike. He never employed whippings or other forms of corporal punishment, then quite the usual thing in the patriot army. The men knew him to be strict, yet fair and just, and ready to listen to their reasonable complaints. He tended the sick himself, and opened his private purse freely to the necessitous. " His attention and care of the men," averred a subaltern, " were such as I never saw, nor anything approaching it, in any other officer, though I served under many." [3]

Yet he found time from his arduous duties to meet, and visit socially, a certain Mrs. Theodosia Prevost, wife of an English officer, who lived in Paramus with her mother, her sister, and her five children.

In September, 1777, while the regiment still lay at " Suffren's, in the Clove," news was received that the enemy had gathered at Hackensack in great force and was advancing into the country. Colonel Burr immediately put his force into motion to oppose their passage. While on the march an express came from General Putnam ordering him to retire with the public stores into the mountains rather than risk battle with a greatly superior enemy. The young Colonel replied firmly to the messenger — he was forever disobeying orders he conceived ill-judged — that " he could not run away from an enemy he had not seen, and that he would be answerable for the public stores and for his men."

They arrived at Paramus, some sixteen miles away, by sunset. There they found considerable bodies of the militia, hastily assembled, in great alarm and disorder, and doing more damage to the neighboring farms than to the still-distant enemy.

Burr set them to work at once repairing the fences they had trampled down, and moved forward with thirty of his own men and some militiamen to act as guides to reconnoiter the enemy. He found the advance picket posts some three miles from Hackensack. He at once ordered his little troop into a nearby wood to get some sleep — they had marched under forced draft over thirty miles since noon — and went on alone to spy out the size of the opposing force. Within a half-hour he was back, had aroused his sleeping men, and led them stealthily between the outflung sentinels until only a few yards separated them from the main body of the pickets, without an alarm having been given.

The surprise was complete. Most of the enemy force was killed, and the rest taken prisoner without the loss of a single American. Still unresting, Burr sent an express back to Paramus to bring up the regiment and rally the country. But the British had had enough of this most unorthodox war. They retreated the very next day, leaving behind them the greater part of the cattle and plunder they had garnered. Burr wished to pursue and attack, but General Putnam had sent another, and this time peremptory order, commanding him to join without delay the main Continental Army, then in Pennsylvania.[4]

Burr bowed to the inevitable. By November, 1777, Malcolm's Regiment was at Whitemarsh, about twenty miles from Philadelphia. A few weeks later they went into winter quarters at Valley Forge. That long, dark winter of cold and starvation and suffering, while the British dined and wined in the warmth and luxury of Philadelphia; that winter when the fortunes of the embattled Colonies seemed at their lowest ebb!

It was still Malcolm's Regiment, but Lieutenant-Colonel Burr was to all intents and purposes its Colonel. Malcolm himself observed the gallant actions of his command with a " father's " pride, and from a safe distance. The Regiment was attached to General Conway's Brigade. Burr's Orderly Books for this period are full of the minutiæ of daily routine, enlivened with reports of courts-martial over which he presided, or the results of which were sent to him for approval.

For instance, Private Thomas McCalvy, who was accused of setting fire to gunpowder and thereby burning a fellow soldier's arm, was given two days' extra fatigue; while Thomas Barry, whose offense consisted in plundering the inhabitants, riotous and disorderly behavior, and " insolent and abusive language to officers," was adjudged worthy of 100 lashes " on the bare back." To which Colonel Burr appended in his firm, incisive hand, " the Above Sentences are Approvd." [5]

Or that other trial, partaking somewhat of the nature of the ridiculous. " Michl Brannon Accused with taking a Shirt out of

Coll. Burr's Room from among the Clothing without Liberty &
wearing the Same, & for Concealing the Shirt in another part of
the Room & not putting it among the Clothing." For which the
aghast court-martial sentenced him " to Receive 50 Lashes but on
account of his Youth beg Leave to Recommend him to the Comdg
Officers Clemency." Which recommendation his commanding
officer, one Captain Tom, duly noted and graciously remitted
half of the required number of lashes.[6]

It was this same Captain Tom, incidentally, for whom Colonel
Burr himself had interceded only a month before for having been
absent without leave.[7]

3. MUTINY

During that winter of 1777–8, Burr's active mind teemed with
plans. He hated the enforced idleness, the dreary round of routine, the loss of morale and the widespread suffering. He submitted to Washington a carefully thought-out plan for a sudden
attack against the British forces encamped on Staten Island, and
offered to lead it himself. Washington turned the plan down.
But there was another job which it was felt suited the young
Colonel's particular talents. What he had done with the erstwhile
rebellious, slack-living regiment he commanded had not escaped
notice.

A body of militia occupied an important strategic pass known
as the Gulf, some eight or ten miles away from the main camp.
Their discipline was of the loosest, and time hung heavy on their
hands. Some wit conceived the brilliant idea of raising false
alarms at regular intervals, so that the bored militia might enjoy
the spectacle of the hurried commotion and frenzied arming of
the troops at Valley Forge. Surely a nice, innocent pastime, especially in wartime! But the ragged, starving Continentals surprisingly resented being dragged out of their poor enough beds
to shiver in the cold. General McDougall, who had formed a vast
respect for young Burr's abilities ever since Brooklyn Heights,
suggested to Washington that he was the one man in camp to put
a stop to such nonsense.

Burr did. He took command of the regiment of practical jokers,
kept them under constant, unremitting drill all day, shifted them
by quick, forced marches from position to position, instituted a
system of rigid policing, made it his business to pay sudden surprise visits to the sentinel lines at all hours of the night and every
night, and kept them on the jump generally until the militiamen,

astounded at the taste of real army discipline, determined to murder this martinet youngster who was riding them ragged.

Burr heard of the conspiracy. Without saying a word, he secretly caused the bullets to be drawn from the muskets, and, that night, ordered the rebellious troops to be formed for retreat. Alone he marched along the sullen ranks, saber in hand, eying the men closely. Suddenly, as he came opposite one of the ringleaders, the man stepped forward, leveled his musket, shouted in a loud voice, "Now is your time, my boys," and snapped his empty gun. The young Colonel, quick as light, slashed down with his saber. The blade sliced through the mutineer's right arm, wounding it so badly that it had to be amputated the next day. That ended the mutiny, then and forever. There was some talk of a court-martial for this rough-and-ready method of enforcing discipline, but nothing came of it. Colonel Burr was evidently not a man to be trifled with.

In March, 1778, Malcolm's Regiment, commanded by Burr, was removed from Conway's Brigade and placed in the left wing of Lord Stirling's division. With the coming of summer the war emerged from its frozen quiescence into renewed activity.

The French had finally decided to join openly in the affray, and thereby made the purely local war one of worldwide proportions. Sir Henry Clinton had superseded the amiable, slow-moving Howe in command of the British forces at Philadelphia. With the advent of the French, and believing that the troops at his disposal did not justify a farflung front, he determined to evacuate the Quaker town and concentrate on New York as a base of operations.

Accordingly, he moved out, bag and baggage, and marched across the Jerseys to his proposed destination. Washington broke up camp at Valley Forge and started in pursuit. He caught up with the enemy at Monmouth, and engaged in battle on June 28, 1778.

Colonel Burr and his regiment were in the left wing of the American army, under Lord Stirling's command. Charles Lee, just returned from captivity with the British, and now Major-General, led the attack. At first the Americans were victorious; then Lee made those incomprehensible and disastrous moves which effectually threw away all chance for success and put the enemy in a position to threaten their left flank. Washington galloped up in a passion, swore roundly at the man who had snatched almost certain victory from his grasp, and ordered the lowering General off the field. Then he took personal command,

and re-established the lines; but it was too late. Clinton was able to withdraw his forces intact and pursue his interrupted march.

Colonel Burr commanded a brigade during the battle, consisting of his own regiment and some Pennsylvania troops. Shortly after the general action commenced, he discovered a detachment of the enemy breaking out of a patch of woods. Instantly he put his brigade into motion to stop the threat to Stirling's flank. To make contact it was necessary to cross a muddy lake over which a bridge had been thrown. Half of the brigade had passed over successfully under a galling enemy fire; the other half was advancing on the double-quick. Colonel Barber, aide to Washington, rode up with orders from his Chief commanding a halt. Burr protested that in their present position they were exposed to the concentrated fire of the enemy without adequate support, and that the balance of the brigade must cross before a halt could safely be called. Barber repeated that his orders were peremptory, and Burr was forced to obey. As a result, the divided brigade, sundered by the intervening bridge, suffered severely under the fire of an overwhelming enemy. Lieutenant-Colonel Dummer, second in command, was killed, and Burr's horse was shot under him. Sullenly and slowly, the advanced troops retreated back over the bridge. Another count in the reciprocal score between Colonel Burr and General Washington!

4. SECRET SERVICE

It was during this battle that Burr laid the seeds of that ill health which was to dog him for a considerable period, and force him eventually to resign from the army. The fatigue, the exertions, and the blazing sun, combined to give a case of sunstroke and a chronic diarrhea that only the severest regimen was able to overcome.

He was ordered immediately, however, to Elizabethtown, to gather intelligence of the enemy's possible future movements. He was instructed to ascertain " what are the preparations of shipping for embarcation of foot or horse? — what expeditions on hand? — whether up the North river, Connecticut, or West Indies? " [8]

Burr was already noted as a gallant officer, a disciplinarian and organizer, and a master of Intelligence. His activities in the latter branch of the service furnish the clue to the facility — which appeared almost miraculous to his political opponents in later life

— with which he was able to gain complete foreknowledge of their most secret plans and documents, and use that foreknowledge with crushing effect against them.

On the satisfactory completion of this mission he rejoined his regiment in time to receive orders to march at once to the fort at West Point. Almost immediately after, he was detached from regimental service for another very confidential mission. Sir Henry Clinton was in New York City and the patriots of the State were in an uproar over the numerous Tories in their midst, their activities and conspiracies. An oath of allegiance was prescribed by the Legislature under the egis of Governor George Clinton in order to separate the sheep from the goats. Those who refused the oath were to be transferred immediately within the enemy's lines and their property confiscated. It was no time, thought the patriots, for delicate handling of Tories or those who pretended a neutrality in the struggle.

There was a group of these gathered at Fishkill. It was Burr's task to convoy them, by sloop, and under a flag of truce, down the Hudson into the City of New York.[9] Considering that Burr already had " one, two or three trusty persons over to the city, to get the reports, the newspapers, and the truth, if they can," [10] is it not conceivable that these convoys were but a blind for more serious work; that thus he might safely get in touch with his agents and obtain the results of their spyings?

On his first voyage on the sloop *Liberty* to New York City, Burr added in his own handwriting to Governor Clinton's safe conduct: " Mrs. Prevost and Miss De Visme with one Man Servant in consequence of Lord Stirling's Leave to pass to N.York and return are admitted on board this Flagg." [11]

September, 1778, found Colonel Burr still detached from his regiment and engaged in regular trips out of Fishkill convoying prisoners down to the enemy lines, and, incidentally, establishing contact with his spies in New York.[12]

Meanwhile Major-General Charles Lee had been court-martialed and suspended for one year from the service for his conduct at Monmouth and for other good and sufficient reasons. Colonel Burr was indignant over the result; he felt that Washington had pursued the General with ill-judged hatred; that Lee was a far better tactician than his superior; and he did not hesitate to express his sympathy to Lee. The letter has been lost, but Lee's grateful reply is extant. He intends, he declares sarcastically, " whether the sentence is reversed or not reversed [by Congress], to resign my commission, retire to Virginia, and learn to hoe tobacco, which I find is the best school to form a consummate *general*. This is a discovery I have lately made." [13]

Burr's open advocacy of the deposed General certainly did nothing to better the somewhat strained relations between himself and Washington. The young Colonel was quite sincere in his belief that the Commander-in-Chief was a military leader of limited capacity; honest, it was true, and well-intentioned, but lacking the spark of genius and stubbornly set in his ways. He thought the entire plan of campaign around New York to have been a blunder of the first magnitude, the indecisiveness of the battle of Monmouth to have been due at least equally to Washington's tactical blunders as to Lee's disobedience of orders; the slow quiescence of the winter at Valley Forge had roused him to fury. Strangely enough, Burr's own predictions and suggestions had a remarkable way of becoming justified by the course of later events. He was without question an able officer and leader in his own right, and his actions were always direct, energetic, and carried out with unhesitating decision. Washington himself, in spite of his resentment at the implied and expressed criticism of this forward young officer, appreciated Burr's capacities as a soldier.

Burr was not alone, either then or now, in his animadversions. Conway, Lee, Gates, among the generals, and a substantial minority of the Continental Congress felt the same way. Nor have modern historians and students of military tactics been disposed to place Washington among the first flight of great military commanders. But what young Burr, too close to the imperfections of the picture, failed to see was that his commanding general possessed other qualities, equally as valuable, which were absolutely requisite to the binding together of the Colonies, and the patient, steady continuance of a disheartening and seemingly lost struggle.

5. NO MAN'S LAND

By October Burr's physical disabilities had increased to such an extent that a short retirement was essential. Accordingly he wrote to Washington requesting a leave of absence. " Sir, the excessive heat and occasional fatigues of the preceding campaign, have so impaired my health and constitution as to render me incapable of immediate service. I have, for three months past, taken every advisable step for my recovery, but have the mortification to find, upon my return to duty, a return of sickness, and that every relapse is more dangerous than the former. I have consulted several physicians; they all assure me that a few months retirement and attention to my health are the only probable means to restore it." He therefore asked for permission to retire — without pay, however, because " too great a regard to malicious surmises, and a delicacy perhaps censurable, might otherwise hurry me unnecessarily into service, to the prejudice of my health, and without any advantage to the public." [14]

Washington answered promptly and in very kindly and gracious accents. " You, in my opinion," he chided, " carry your ideas of delicacy too far when you propose to drop your pay while the recovery of your health necessarily requires your absence from the service. It is not customary, and it would be unjust. You therefore have leave to retire until your health is so far re-established as to enable you to do your duty." [15]

Washington was right. The illness had been incurred in the line of duty. Pay in such cases always continued. Nevertheless Burr rejoined his regiment at West Point, cutting short his leave, rather than accept an extended leave of absence with pay. It was too great a delicacy and matter of pride on his part, or perhaps he wished for no seeming favors from the hand of his commander.

In spite of debilitating illness, he continued to perform his duties with his usual competence. In December he was ordered to Haverstraw to command a brigade, consisting of Malcolm's Regiment, and parts of Spencer's and Patten's Regiments. From there, in January, 1779, he was transferred to the lines in Westchester County and placed in active charge of the entire area.

This was a most important assignment, and required an officer who combined tact, disciplinarianism, military intelligence and ability to an almost incredible degree. It was a remarkable tribute to a mere Lieutenant-Colonel to place him in command of this area. General McDougall was unquestionably responsible for Burr's transfer. The district was part of his military bailiwick, and he had never failed to push the young officer's fortunes whenever possible. With his kindly offices and the paternal friendship of General Putnam, as well as the talents that he had displayed on every possible occasion, it was a matter for wonder that young Burr had not been promoted long before this to higher rank. Ogden, only one year his senior, and greatly his inferior in ability, had been for over a year a full colonel, and was soon to be made a brigadier-general. The army was full of such instances. Yet Burr was being consistently overlooked when the promotion lists were published. Was he correct in his surmise that Washington was responsible for the patent neglect?

In any event, promotion or no, the proper care of the West-chester lines was most important to the well-being and safety of the American forces. They stretched from Fishkill and Croton on the Hudson through White Plains across to the Sound. Above was sound American territory, but to the east, northward along the Connecticut shore, the British were in the habit of landing raiding expeditions from their fleet and harrying and burning with much gusto and thoroughness. To the south, between Croton and Kingsbridge, the northernmost point of Clinton's army of occupation, there was confusion worse confounded. It was typical No Man's Land, held by neither army, and subject to marauding bands from both armies, or, rather, the riffraff of their camp-followers, who plundered the civilians indiscriminately, and who tortured and burned and robbed with a fine disregard pretended friend and foe alike. The supposed Loyalists were known as "Cowboys," and the equally hypothetical Patriots went under the euphonious appellation of "Skinners."

A great wail arose from the outraged district; and McDougall, finding that the former commanders were unable to cope with the situation, assigned to Burr the job of cleaning up the festering district, putting an end to the daily outrages, robberies and down-right murders, and of restoring discipline to the demoralized American forces themselves, who, it was more than suspected, participated in the avails, if not in the actual outrages themselves.

On January 9th, McDougall notified General Parsons that "Lieut Col Burr is gone down to Command the Troops sent from hence for the winter. He will have under his orders four Parties of choice Continental Troops of sixty rank and file. And orders have been given to enlist till the first of April four Serjeants Parties of eight Brave Young Men of the Militia well acquainted with each Post, to serve as Guides and light Troops for the Regulars. . . . Their present Possition is at Tarry Town, Young's, David Davis's, and Quaker Meeting House at the head of Purchase Street, in a few days I shall order Col Burr to advance the left in a south east line from Tarry Town, which I imagine by the Map will strike near Rye . . . You know Lieut Col Burr he will chearfully Harmonize with you; or any Officer from General Putnams Corps, which may be posted on our Left." [16]

Colonel Burr found matters in his district even worse than he had anticipated. Almost at once there was trouble — a serious affair that involved American troops and Lieutenant-Colonel Littlefield — the officer whom Burr had superseded — himself. Burr wrote in hot wrath to McDougall: "Colonel Littlefield, with the party [a scouting troop], returned this morning. . . . Notwithstanding the cautions I gave, and notwithstanding Colonel Littlefield's good intentions, I blush to tell you that the party returned loaded with plunder. Sir, till now, I never wished for arbitrary power. I could gibbet half a dozen *good whigs,* with all the venom of an inveterate tory. The party had not been returned an hour, before I had six or seven persons from New-Rochelle and Frog's Neck, with piteous applications for stolen goods and horses . . . I am mortified that not an officer on the ground has shown any activity to detect the plunderers or their spoil. I have got three horses, and a number of other articles, and have confined two soldiers who had them in possession. But these are petty rascals. I feel more pity than indignation towards them. They were honest men till debauched by this expedition. I believe some officers are concerned. If I can be assured of that (and I shall spare no labour) , you may depend on seeing them with a file of men. The militia volunteers excelled in this business. If I detect them I shall treat them with the same rigour, unless you advise to the contrary." [17]

But McDougall did nothing of the sort. He had sent Burr down to the Lines just for that purpose. " In all doubtful questions," he wrote back instantly, " which may arise on my orders as to the limits or legality of plunder in your front, *I authorize you to be the sole* judge." [18]

Burr, backed thus to the limit by the commanding general, proceeded to act with vigor and dispatch. Already, on January 12th, three days after his arrival, he had remanded one of the officers, Captain Brown, to Headquarters under arrest for " unbecoming behaviour." [19] And on this particular bit of business he did not rest until it had been thoroughly cleaned up. On February 15th he sent to McDougall " Mr. Veal a valuable good Man of this Neighborhood " with a complaint " he made some time ago to me about some Irregularities committed by the Scout under Col. Littlefield. Capt Williams and some others were in the House. John Paulding one of the Volunteers on that Party will swear that Cap. William's Servant had the Things and that they were given by Cap. William's Direction." And on February 19th he reported with obvious satisfaction, " I have already adopted the Mode of Treatment you prescribed for Tories. Captain Williams has the hard Money as my Letter of this Morning will inform you." [20]

To prevent any repetition of such disgraceful occurrences, and to tighten the discipline of the camp, Colonel Burr promulgated orders that were terse, direct and very much to the point. " No officer is to presume to purchase Forage on Public Acct or to Impress Horses or any thing whatever for Public or private Use unless by Order of the Commdg Officer on Pain of his severest Displeasure." Prisoners were to be sent immediately to him for examination, civilian movements through the lines were to be very carefully scrutinized; scouting patrols, which had been used as a blind for plundering expeditions, were restricted to two-mile limits except on express order; and especially " no pretence will be admitted as an excuse for the seizing of Horses or Goods without proper Instructions. Practices contrary to this order will be deemed Marauding and treated as a Capital Crime." Arms and ammunition to be cleaned and inspected regularly, sentinels to be alert and watchful for spies and thieves, officers to acquaint themselves thoroughly with the duties and instructions, and "all disaffected Persons who come to the Guards on frivolous pretences and without proper Papers are to be severely whipd on the Spot and sent back." Officers absent from their guard " before regularly relieved or without proper Authority will be immediately Arrested. The Commanding Officer is ashamed of the necessity he is under of Enforcing such Common points of duty which every Corporal is supposed to be acquainted with — much more Gentlemen of some Years Military Experience." The young Colonel's sarcasm could sting like a lash! And, in accordance with McDougall's explicit commands, 100 lashes were to be meted out to any sentinel who quit his post while on duty or who parted " with his Arms unless they are wrested from him." [21] Burr was determined to clean house at whatever cost! And he did.

It was not long before the results were plainly evident. He did not spare himself in the process. He seemed to sleep neither day nor night; his lightning descents upon remote outposts in the dead of night smote terror into the hearts of the slack and the indifferent; he weeded out the inefficient and the criminal among the officers, he made a complete register of all the inhabitants in the entire area, as well as an accurate map of the country. He was good at map-making; it was a practice that was to prove valuable in later years. He raised a corps of horsemen from the proved patriots of the neighborhood who served as an intelligence corps, and he had his most secret spies scattered over the countryside and penetrating even into the enemy lines. He effectually put an end to all plundering, so that even the known Tories were able to go to bed nights without fear. So remarkable was his espionage system, and his methods for the detection and punishment of unknown thieves, that, according to an eye-witness, " it was universally believed that Colonel Burr could tell a robber by looking in his face, or that he had supernatural means of discovering crime." [22] According to the same witness he gained " the love and veneration of all devoted to the common cause, and conciliated even its bitterest foes. His habits were a subject of admiration. His diet was simple in the extreme." He attended personally to the minutest details of his soldiers' comfort, to their lodgings, their diet, and even their sports when off duty. No wonder the men grew to idolize him, even as the men of Malcolm's Regiment had done before. He transformed them from negligent, discontented, plundering slackers to a disciplined, smart, and gallant command. Not a man deserted during his regime; there was not a single death from sickness. A most enviable record, indeed!

Nor were the enemy forgotten. Whereas their bands had been accustomed almost at will to break through the American defenses and harry and burn, the country back of the lines was now as safe as the streets of a peaceful city. All attempts to surprise Burr's clever guard system failed signally. Twice attacks were driven back with loss. He chased Governor Tryon, with 2,000 British, all the way back into Connecticut when that worthy attempted an attack. He led personally an assault upon a strongly fortified blockhouse held by Colonel Delancey at Delancey's Bridge, and took it without firing a shot or the loss of a single man.

6. Resignation

But his health, already heavily undermined, gave way completely under these incessant fatigues and arduous duties. His physician insisted on his retirement, otherwise he would not answer for the consequences. Very reluctantly, therefore, on March 10, 1779, he tendered his resignation.

It was accepted with real regret by General Washington. The Commander appreciated the value of his services, even though he had his private prejudices against the young officer. " Perfectly satisfied," he said, " that no consideration save a desire to reestablish your health could induce you to leave the service, I cannot therefore withhold my consent. But, in giving permission to your retiring from the army, I am not only to regret the loss of a good officer, but the cause which makes his resignation necessary." [23]

But Burr's old friend, Patterson, from a distance, put another construction upon the business. " I congratulate you on your return to civil life," he wrote, " for which (I cannot forbear the thought) we must thank a certain lady not far from Paramus. May I have occasion soon to thank her on another account; and may I congratulate you both in the course of the next moon for being in my line: I mean the married." [24] But of this lady and of Patterson's confident prediction more anon. For the present suffice it to say that Burr was definitely ill — he was to be a martyr to his ailment for a considerable time to come.

The effects of Burr's withdrawal soon manifested themselves. A good officer, Colonel Thompson, took over the command, but the British, apprised that the dreaded Burr was no longer on the ground, attacked and wiped out Thompson's Headquarters and took him prisoner. Colonel Green, who replaced him, was surprised and killed together with most of his men. The American lines were hurriedly shortened, leaving some twenty miles of country unprotected and subject to the old ravages. William Hull, an officer of the old command, wrote to his former Colonel sadly, " The ground you so long defended is now left to the depredation of the Enimy, and our friends in distressing circumstances." [25]

Burr, however, was not to be permitted immediately to recuperate. Even though now a civilian, at McDougall's request he consented to undertake another mission. The General, at Newburgh, had been unable, in spite of repeated attempts, to get word through to Washington of enemy movements. Burr consented to make the passage. " To whom it may concern: — Colonel Burr, being on very pressing public business, every magistrate will assist him in changing horses, and all friends of the country will also assist him. June 2nd, 1779. Alexander M'Dougall, Major-General." [26]

He got through successfully, and Washington, on hearing of McDougall's critical position, marched forthwith toward the Highlands with his forces.

7. THE WAR HORSE SNUFFS BATTLE

Colonel Burr may have thought he was through with battles and alarms after this, but the gods of war ordered differently. He sought peace and the restoration of a shattered constitution with friends at New Haven. The war pursued him. For, on July 5, 1779, a fleet of some forty sail under Sir George Collyer anchored off the Connecticut shore, preparatory to an attack on New Haven. Governor Tryon, that vindictive ex-Governor of the former province of New York, landed with 3,000 troops. The patriot inhabitants flew to arms; the Tories rejoiced, armed themselves and went forth to join the invaders. East Haven was plundered and set on fire, and the scattered militia driven back on the main town. " Near 2 M. Stone," reports the Rev. Ezra Stiles, of Yale, " Dr. Dagget Professor of Divinity was captivated. He discharged his piece and then submitted as Prisoner — they after this pierced and beat him with Bayonets & otherwise abused him, so that his Life was in danger for a month after." [27]

Burr heard the uproar and the sound of guns. Though he was confined to bed, he arose at once and volunteered to take command of the militia. But they were fleeing in a disordered rout. Then he heard that the students of Yale were hurriedly organizing in the College yard. He threw himself on a horse and galloped to the meeting-place, followed by some few of the militia who had rallied after him. The students enthusiastically placed themselves under the command of this veteran, scarcely older than themselves. More of the militia, shamefaced, joined.

The British were trying to force Darby Bridge, in order to gain lodgment in the town itself. Burr threw his force upon their left flank, and harried their march.[28] The enemy was compelled to retreat, but returned with artillery and reinforcements. Burr's little band was greatly outnumbered, and retired gradually, in good order. New Haven was captured, plundered, and burnt.

This, however, was the final act of the Revolutionary drama as far as Burr was concerned. The war went on, with varying fortunes, until the ultimate triumph and independence. The youthful veteran — he was twenty-three now — gradually regained his health by a careful regimen and a rigorous diet. On his retirement from the service, he was universally respected and acknowledged to be a brave, gallant, intelligent officer. The men in the ranks worshiped him and his brother officers testified to his worth. There was no dissenting voice, not even from those who had secretly withheld too rapid advancement. His thoughts now turned to civilian affairs — to his future career, and to a certain lady of Paramus.

Chapter VI

PRELUDE TO LIFE

1. Courtship and Law Books

A S a civilian, it became Burr's first duty to recruit his shattered health. This, however, was not to prove an easy task. It was to be over a year before he was sufficiently recovered to pick up the threads of his interrupted career. To the anguish of body there had been added another torment, no less keen because of its purely psychological character. He had fallen in love.

In 1777, while stationed at Ramapo, he had made the acquaintance of Mrs. Theodosia Prevost, who, with her younger children, her sister and her mother, resided at Paramus, but a short distance away. Her husband, Lieutenant-Colonel Jacques Marc Prevost, of the British Army, was then in the West Indies on duty with his regiment. Technically, therefore, she was an enemy; and to be treated as such.

But the American officers of the immediate vicinity did not consider her in that light. In spite of her marriage, she was herself of American birth and lineage. Her father, Theodosius Bartow, had been a lawyer in Shrewsbury, New Jersey. Her mother, Anne Stillwell, could trace her descent from Nicholas Stillwell, one of the earliest settlers and tobacco planters in the Colony of Virginia.

Theodosius Bartow died in 1746, immediately before the birth of a daughter, Theodosia. The widow, Anne Stillwell Bartow, shortly thereafter married Captain Philip de Visme of the British Army, by whom, at the date of his death in 1762, she had given little Theodosia five half-brothers and sisters.

Theodosia Bartow herself, at the tender age of seventeen, was married to Colonel Prevost, also of His Majesty's Forces. The young wife bore, in fairly rapid succession, five children to him — three daughters, Sally, Anne Louisa and Mary Louisa; and two sons, John Bartow and Augustine James Frederick, who, though but mere lads at the time of the Revolution, followed in their father's footsteps and were serving as ensigns with the British forces.

So that, during the entire course of the war, her position continued to be one of great delicacy and apprehension. In spite of her own impeccable ancestry, her husband and two sons were even then in arms against the rebellious Colonies; she was related in various ways to a whole swarm of active participants on the British side. Accordingly, there was much grumbling and covetous casting of eyes among the patriotic Whigs of Paramus and the vicinity.

New Jersey had followed the general trend and passed severe laws against Tories and British sympathizers. Many super-patriots demanded that they be executed forthwith against Mrs. Prevost; that her absent husband's estate be forfeited in accordance with law, and that she and her three little girls be forced to withdraw inside the British lines, where she belonged.

She had, however, numerous and powerful friends, who continued to exert themselves unweariedly on her behalf. Her home, the Hermitage, a great red sandstone house, was the popular resort of the American officers. There was an air of spaciousness, of culture and hospitality about the place that was exceedingly grateful to polished gentlemen whose nerves had become a bit exacerbated from the crudities and hardships of camp life. James Monroe, later to become a President of the United States, interceded vigorously in her behalf to stay the harsh execution of the laws. So did General Lee.[1]

She was also personally acquainted with General Washington. When her half-brother, Peter de Visme, was captured at sea by the Americans, she pleaded with the General for him to exercise his influence to promote an exchange. Washington declined, in the politest of terms, on the ground that he never interfered in the disposal of marine prisoners.[2]

Burr had become a frequent and welcome visitor at her home during the year 1777, and even when his regiment removed to other spheres of activity, he kept up a cordial communication and correspondence. In 1778 he managed to obtain permission for her and her sister, Miss de Visme, to pass to British-occupied New York and return to the American lines.[3]

It was a rather strange friendship that ripened gradually into something more intimate and substantial. She was ten years his senior, married to a British officer, and the mother of five children. She was not beautiful — contemporary opinion did not consider her so, nor do her portraits belie the rumor. She had indeed a disfiguring scar on her forehead, the result of a burn. She was pious, too, and viewed with a certain abhorrence her youthful admirer's skeptical attitude toward revealed religion. Furthermore, her health was precarious — no doubt the cancer that was ultimately to prove fatal was already gnawing at her vitals. She was not rich, and she was the wife of another.

Burr, on the other hand, though slight of form, was a striking figure in any company. He impressed men with his lofty demeanor and military erectness, with his proved bravery and wide knowledge. He fascinated all women with his polished and courtly air, his charming manners, his graceful demeanor and flattering attentions. He was young and handsome, of excellent family, and his jet-black eyes pierced all beholders with their almost unbearable brilliance.

Yet Mrs. Prevost held certain qualities that were rare and unusual. Besides a consummate grace and charm, she was exceptionally well read and cultured in an age when women were not considered the proper recipients of an education. She and Burr had many interests in common — they loved books and paintings, they both welcomed the impact of general ideas, and they found exciting possibilities in discussions on the respective merits of Voltaire, Rousseau, Lord Chesterfield, and the French precursors of the enlightenment. The Hermitage was well stocked with the latest volumes from France and England, and Burr delved eagerly into their fascinating contents.

But — she was married to another! It is quite probable that the turmoil aroused in Burr by the anomalous condition of their relations had something to do with the gradual breakdown of his health. He was also justly disturbed over the unremitting efforts of the patriots to dislodge her from their midst and to seize control of her rather slender fortune.

In September, 1779, Burr was in New Haven sighing dolefully for New Jersey — and Mrs. Prevost — yet refusing to return. He wrote his friend Billy Patterson that he saw no company, partook of no amusements, and that he was always grave. His delicacy did him credit. By this time, evidently, he had fathomed the state of his feelings for Mrs. Prevost, and had realized that the matter could be allowed to proceed no further. Yet his interest in her affairs did not flag. Patterson wrote in response to his anxious inquiry that " I cannot tell you what has become of Mrs. Prevost's affairs. About two months ago I received a very polite letter from her. She was apprehensive that the commissioners would proceed. It seems they threatened to go on. I wrote them on the subject, but I have not heard the event." [4]

Then came the news that Colonel Prevost had died in the West Indies. The repercussions of this startling shift in their relations are fairly obvious. Instead of sighing for the unattainable, the be-

loved woman was now within reach. He hurried to Paramus to
condole — and console. Up to this time, since his resignation from
the army, he had drifted aimlessly. But now he became imbued
with new energy. Law, at which he had only begun to nibble at
the outbreak of the Revolution, engaged his attention once more.
He actually commenced to read under the direction of a Mr.
Osmer in Connecticut. He wrote to his friend, Colonel Robert
Troup, who was most eager that they study together. But Troup
preferred Mr. Stockton of Princeton as a tutor, and urged Burr to
join him at Princeton.[5]

But something happened to delay Burr's plans. The ferment,
the excitement, had been too much for him. On February 16, 1780,
he was writing Patterson from Middletown in melancholy accents.
" My health, which was till of late very promising, seems to decline
a little. This circumstance will oblige me to alter my course of
life . . . My health will bear no imposition. I am obliged to eat,
drink, sleep and study, as it directs." [6] To Robert Troup he
avowed strong objections both to Mr. Stockton and to Princeton,
and suggested Patterson, now Attorney General of New Jersey, as
a better friend and more efficient tutor.[7]

For a considerable period Burr continued to shift restlessly from
one place to another, still unable to come to grips with his chosen
profession. There was considerable talk, also, concerning his very
manifest interest in Paramus and in the dwellers at the Hermitage.
Few, however, were aware of the real situation. As late as June,
1780, Robert Troup was still in the dark. He even wrote his friend,
" The Miss Livingstons have inquired in a very friendly manner
about you, and expect you will wait upon them when you pass
this way. Since I have been here, I have had an opportunity of removing entirely the suspicion they had of your courting Miss De
Visme [Mrs. Prevost's young half-sister]. They believe nothing of
it now, and attribute your visits at Paramus to motives of friendship for Mrs. Prevost and the family. Wherever I am, and can with
propriety, you may be assured I shall represent this matter in its
true light." [8]

Indeed, Burr seems to have been present that night in the
Hermitage when Peggy Arnold, the wife of the traitorous Benedict
Arnold, heavily veiled and under close guard, halted there on her
way from West Point to New York. She was that Peggy Shippen
who had been a playmate of Burr's for some years during his
childhood, and she was likewise intimate with Mrs. Prevost. To
the latter, so the story goes, she confessed her complete implication
in the conspiracy; though at the time, and for a considerable

period thereafter, she was universally believed to be the innocent victim of her husband's machinations.

Other matters were also worrying young Burr at this time. The state of his finances, for instance. His patrimony had, contrary to report, been rather modest. He had spent it with a careless, albeit warm-hearted, generosity, and a reckless disregard for the future. The pay of an officer in the Continental Army was miserably small, when measured in terms of gold currency, and even that pittance was not always available. Burr dipped into his own pocket for his own expenses, for the general welfare of his soldiers and brother officers. No call upon him for funds was ever refused. His friends, too, were forever borrowing. He tided Troup over some embarrassing financial stringencies with substantial loans, with the proffer of horses and an adequate equipage. He paid for a tutor to Mrs. Prevost's two boys, now out of the King's Service, to the tune of 60 pounds a year, New York currency. This rendered a double service — to the woman he loved, and to the tutor, one Major Alden, an impecunious Revolutionary friend.[9]

And, at about this time, he received unwelcome news. He had, to recoup his fortunes, taken a considerable share in the outfitting of the *Hawk*, an American privateer. Instead of bringing back fat prizes, however, she had been grounded off Long Island by a British warship, and the sea did the rest. It represented a substantial loss to Burr.[10]

He continued ill and distraught right through the autumn of 1780, taking the mineral waters in the " Clove," staying as much as possible at Paramus. Then he buckled down to the study of the law and serious work. Together with Troup, who had managed finally to escape from the clutches of Mr. Stockton, he placed himself in the charge of William Patterson, his old friend and college chum.

But he soon became dissatisfied. Patterson was a methodical, plodding man, whose ideas on the study of the law were along conventional and settled lines. He demanded a thorough grounding in theory, and a careful combing of ancient texts, before any attempt was to be made to learn the practical applications in office and court. An admirable, conscientious procedure, indeed, but — it would take two to three years before the young aspirant could branch out on his own!

This, Burr was not prepared to do. He was impatient, in a hurry now. For one thing, his funds had run out; for another, he had come to a fairly definite understanding with the widowed Theodosia Prevost, and marriage would have to be held off until he could earn a living. Even more important, it seems, was another consideration. In the high tide of resentment against Tories and lukewarm pettifoggers, the patriots of the still warring State of New York were agitating for a law disqualifying from legal practice all those who refused to take the new oath of loyalty. The law actually was passed in November, 1781. Inasmuch as the legal profession in New York was heavily Tory in its sympathies, the passage and enforcement of the proposed law meant a notable opportunity to young lawyers of the proper patriotic persuasion to step in and reap the harvest in a field from which their established elders had been ruthlessly removed. And it would be a case of first come, first served.

So, without any diminution in their continued friendship, Burr removed from Patterson's office in the spring of 1781 to that of Thomas Smith, a prominent New York attorney, who, because of the British occupation, was compelled to practise in Haverstraw. Smith had no such scruples as the steady-going Patterson, and agreed, for a specified consideration, to permit the impatient young man to study according to his own plan. Burr was to read law and propose questions based upon his readings in writing. These Smith was to answer, also in writing, with appropriate legal points and citations; and his answers in turn laid the basis for further questions.[11] It was a novel arrangement, but one evidently suited to Burr's peculiar genius.

He studied hard and diligently, spending from sixteen to twenty hours a day on his law. Yet he found time to keep up a steady correspondence with Theodosia Prevost. He had already proposed marriage, but she, being older and more experienced in the marital state, preferred to wait before yielding her final assent.

" Our being the subject of much inquiry, conjecture, and calumny," she wrote, " is no more than we ought to expect. My attention to you was ever pointed enough to attract the observation of those who visited the house. Your esteem more than compensated for the worst they could say. When I am sensible I can make you and myself happy, I will readily join you to suppress their malice. But, till I am confident of *this*, I cannot think of our union." [12]

They held long, learned conversations, through the mails, on authors and doctrines and systems of education. She was pleased with his enthusiastic admiration for Voltaire, but she delivered severe strictures on his manifest tendency to exalt Chesterfield above Rousseau as an educator. " The indulgence you applaud in Chesterfield," she told him, " is the only part of his writings I

think reprehensible. Such lessons from so able a pen are dangerous to a young mind, and ought never to be read till the judgment
and heart are established in virtue. If Rousseau's ghost can reach
this quarter of the globe, he will certainly haunt you for this
scheme — 'tis striking at the root of his design, and destroying the
main purport of his admirable production. *Les foiblesses de
l'humanité,* is an easy apology; or rather, a license to practice in-
temperance; and is particularly agreeable and flattering to such
practitioners, as it brings the most virtuous on a level with the
vicious." These were strong words to address to a young man
whose code of ethics and mode of life were to be influenced largely
by the easy-going morality, the polished urbanity and intellectual
emancipation of the English nobleman, but she hastened to soften
the blow by assuring him that " you have, undoubtedly, a mind
superior to the contagion." [13]

At the same time she was writing to Burr's sister, Sally Reeve,
and her husband, in the most lively and affectionate fashion. She
had already visited them at Litchfield. " I lament with you," she
wrote Reeve, " the indisposition of our dear Sally. If a tender
feeling for her sufferings, a most ardent wish for her recovery, &
your mutual happiness, are a recommendation to your esteem, I
have an undoubted claim." [14] It is evident that, though she still
held her young suitor at arm's-length, she had made up her mind
concerning the ultimate outcome.

2. SPECIAL DISPENSATION

By October, 1781, the bill for the disbarment of Tory lawyers
was already up for consideration in the New York Legislature, and
its passage practically assured. Burr had studied with Smith a
scant six months; his entire previous training in the law was, at
the most, another six months. Yet, for reasons heretofore suggested, he was desperately anxious to qualify at once for the practice of law. It was an opportunity that, once missed, could never
be retrieved.

But the code of rules governing admission to the Bar was clear
and unmistakable in its requirements. The candidate, before he
could appear for the preliminary examinations, must have studied
under competent tutelage for a period of at least three years.

It seemed an insuperable obstacle; yet Burr did not despair.
With characteristic energy and adroitness he set about obtaining
a suspension of the rules in his particular case. Already he had
laid the basis. Theodosia Prevost had seen Judge Hobart, of the

Supreme Court, in his behalf, and had received a favorable response.[15] Burr himself had communicated with Judge Robert Yates, who extended himself warmly for his youthful friend. It was a service that Aaron Burr, who never forgot favors received, was to repay many times over in their later political careers.

Armed with the approbation of these two justices of a Bench of three, he turned next to the sole remaining justice, Chief Justice Richard Morris. He hurried to Albany with additional letters of introduction, including one from his old General, Alexander McDougall, to General Philip Schuyler.

Arrived in Albany, he wrote Morris a letter in which he stated his case with a flattering mixture of logic and respectful admiration. " Sir, I do myself the honour to enclose you several letters, which were intended, I believe, to introduce me to your acquaintance, perhaps to your friendship." He had unfortunately found, he pursued, " a rule of unexpected rigour, which, if strictly adhered to, must effectually exclude me from this bar. Mr. Judge Yates gives me reason to hope this rule may be enlarged. If it should be deemed unadvisable to make one of such latitude as may include me within a general description, perhaps my particular situation may be thought to claim particular indulgence.

" Before the revolution, and long before the existence of the present rule, I had served some time with an attorney of another state. At that period I could have availed myself of this service; and, surely, no rule could be intended to have such retrospect as to injure one *whose only misfortune is having sacrificed his time, his constitution, and his fortune, to his country.*

" It would give me sensible regret were my admission to establish a precedent which might give umbrage to the bar; but, should your opinion accord with my wishes, with respect to the indulgence due to my particular case, the expression of it, to any gentleman of the profession, would doubtless remove the possibility of discontent." [16]

But, though Burr had armed himself at every point, the matter of breaking through the fixed inertia of rules of law was not to prove easy. He spent some anxious weeks in Albany, seeking interviews with the judges who were to pass on his fate, using every influence and special argument at his command. Yet still his petition dragged.

While waiting for the final decision, his stay complicated by sick headaches and the difficulty of finding rooms, he found himself suddenly catapulted into the midst of Albany society, where,

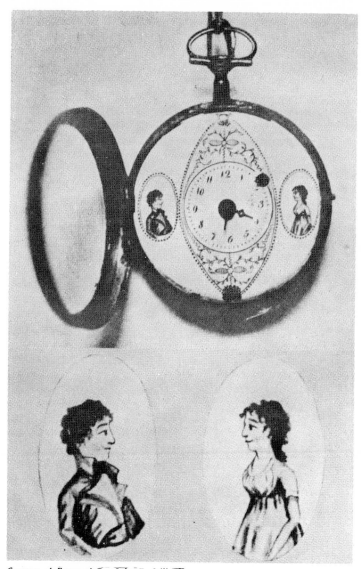

COLONEL BURR'S WATCH

Theodosia Prevost Burr   *Theodosia Burr*

THEODOSIA BURR

From a portrait by Gilbert Stuart

he wrote Mrs. Prevost, " there is scarce any age or sex that does not, either from information or acquaintance, know something of him "; that information, notably, " the whole history of Burr, and much of Theo, but nothing unfavorable," having been industriously broadcast by " an old, weather-beaten lady, Miss Depeyster." [17]

In fact, society opened wide its doors to the engaging, handsome young soldier. Philip van Rensselaer, one of the wealthiest and most respectable young men of the town, tendered his services, and insisted that Burr transfer his lodgings to the quarters of two maiden aunts of his. Miss Depeyster proved " a warm friend and advocate."

Meanwhile he was reading Rousseau in a vain effort to possess his soul in patience, and writing to Mrs. Prevost. His letters to the woman he loved, ten years his senior, are remarkable compositions. There is but little of love or of tender endearments in them, but much of books and ethics and philosophy; veritable didactic essays with more than a hint of the dictatorial. Already Burr's passion for the improvement and disciplinary education of all and sundry was beginning to show.

Behold the schoolmaster in this surprising address to the beloved!

" I am not certain I shall be regularly punctual in writing you in this manner every day when I get at business," he informs her, " but I shall, if possible, devote one quarter of an hour a day to you. In return, I demand one half of an hour every day from you; more I forbid, unless on special occasions. This half hour is to be *mine,* to be invariably at the same time, and, for that purpose, fixed at an hour least liable to interruption, and as you shall find most convenient. . . . The children will each have their sheet, and, at the given hour, write, if but a single word. Burr, at this half hour, is to be a kind of watchword." [18]

Or consider this abrupt and strange epistle. " You wrote me too much by Dom.," he declared. " I hope it was not from a fear that I should be dissatisfied with less. It is, I confess, rather singular to find fault with the quantity, when matter and manner are so delightful. You must, however, deal less in sentiments and more in ideas. Indeed, in the letter in answer to my last, you will need to be particularly attentive to this injunction. I think constantly of the approaching change in our affairs, and what it demands. Do not let us, like children, be so taken with the prospect as to lose sight of the means. Remember to write me facts and ideas, and don't torture me with compliments, or yourself with sentiments to which I am already no stranger. Write but little, and very little at once." [19]

One wonders with what mingled emotions this experienced woman of the world read these lines, and many similar ones exhibiting the same meticulous ordering of the lives of others — all for their own benefit and improvement, of course. But in spite of this, in spite of exhortations to make short memoranda (in cipher) of things later to be written, she loved him, and tenderly; and he loved her. They were to be quite happy during the all-too-short period of their marriage.

Meanwhile the Court was unaccountably backward in hearing Burr's plea for an exemption. The Bar of the State unanimously and enthusiastically opposed any deviation from the rule. This, indeed, was but natural, for they had vested interests that would be disturbed by the opening of the door to a possible flood of competitors. Not one lawyer in Albany could be found to appear for Burr on the motion. He argued it therefore himself, and ably. The Court listened attentively, and decided that, in view of his services to his country, they would dispense with the requirement as to length of time employed in studies, but that there would be no indulgence granted as to the legal qualifications themselves. This was fair and reasonable. Considerably greater indulgence was to be shown applicants for admission to the Bar of New York long after, at the termination of the World War.

The leading members of the Albany Bar chuckled grimly at that. *They* were the examiners. It would be hard if they could not find the means to reject this young upstart. But, to their vast surprise, Burr answered their most severe and critical questions with ease and assurance, and they were compelled, albeit reluctantly, to certify his qualifications to the Court. On January 19, 1782, he was licensed as an attorney, and on April 17th he was duly admitted to practice.

3. Theodosia Prevost Burr

A few months before, on November 20, 1781, the New York Legislature had finally passed the law disqualifying from practice all " attorneys, solicitors, and counsellors at law " who could not produce satisfactory certificates, showing their attachment to the Whig cause during the War. At one swoop the leading gentlemen of the Bar were dislodged from their lucrative profession. Only a handful of qualifying patriots remained — the *truly* patriot were still busily engaged in the Revolutionary service — and the whole tempting field was theirs.

Burr looked the situation over and decided to open his office in Albany. The town was small, but comparatively wealthy. It was the resort of the great upstate patroons and landowners; it was the mart of a flourishing fur trade with the Indians, and — during the War — the channel for illicit, but lucrative, bartering with the enemy via Canada.

He decided also that it was time to marry. Though he was practically penniless by now, he had no doubts as to the future — success in the profession of law seemed assured.

Accordingly he hastened back to Paramus, where, on July 2, 1782, "Aaron Burr of the State of N. York Esqr and Theodosia Prevost of Bergen County, State of N. Jersey," were "joined in lawful wedlock." [20]

The wedding, Theodosia declared in lively fashion to her new sister-in-law, Sally Reeve, was "attended with two singular circumstances, the first is that it cost us nothing. Brown and Caty [the latter a half-sister of Theodosia, and the former, Dr. Brown, Caty's husband] provided abundantly and we improved the opportunity. The fates led Burr on in his old coat; it was proper my gown should be of suitable gauze; ribbons, gloves, etc., were favors from Caty. The second circumstance was that the parson's fees took the only half Joe Burr was master of; we partook of the good things as long as they lasted and then set out for Albany, where the want of money is our only grievance." But "the attention of my dear Burr is not to be equalled" and "the air of Albany is healthy, beer in perfection." [21]

The newly married couple — and the bride's two young boys — did not suffer long from want of money. (The three girls seem never to have become a part of the Burr household — evidently they were taken over and reared by the Prevosts.) There was, as has been stated, a sudden paucity of lawyers, and Burr, of good family, attractive, intellectual, and assiduous in his devotion to his profession, had no difficulty in obtaining soon a veritable swarm of clients.

In spite of his immediate success, however, he rightly felt that New York, the metropolis, held greater prospects for a lawyer. As soon, therefore, as the preliminary treaty of peace was signed in 1783, Burr made preparations for the transfer of his family and office down the Hudson. After several abortive negotiations, he finally decided on the Verplanck house as his new home and law office, "in Wall Street, next Door but one to the City Hall." [22]

By November, 1783, just as the English marched out of New York, and the triumphant Americans moved in to take their place, he was safely installed in his new quarters, a bit dubious, it may be, over the adventure and the additional expense, but resolved, nevertheless, to make a go of it.

The Burrs brought with them from Albany an addition to the family. On June 21, 1783, a girl baby, Theodosia Burr, named after the mother, was born. " Providence smiled upon our wishes . . . and blessed us with a lovely daughter," the former Mrs. Prevost wrote joyfully to her brother-in-law, Tapping Reeve. " My suffering was shorter than my most sanguine hopes had dared to flatter, & have ended in my perfect recovery . . . will you believe me Reeve, when I tell you the dear little girl has the eyes of your Sally, and promises to be as handsome. I would also have given her her name; but Burr insisted on calling her Theo — assure my sister from me that I submitted with the greatest regret." [23]

Later, on June 20, 1785, there was to be a second child to their marriage — also a girl baby.[24] This time Theodosia Burr's wishes were to control, and the child was named Sally. But Sally did not survive long. She died sometime in October, 1788. There were no others. Little Theodosia, however, was to grow into brilliant womanhood, the sensation of her day, the living epitome of her father's rules and regulations, his philosophy and system of education, at once the worshiper and the worshiped, and ultimately a fruitful source of legend and myth because of her tragic, untimely end — Theodosia, in whom the blood of Aaron Burr and of his forbears flowed with undiminished vigor.

Burr was not mistaken in his assumptions when he removed to New York. The Tory lawyers hastily evacuated the town with the British, fearing the wrath of the approaching Americans. With them went wealth and respectability and prestige. But a new crop appeared; young, vigorous attorneys fired with enthusiasm and the proper patriotic spirit, and soon to prove themselves more keen, more brilliant, greater in every respect than the stolid, if substantial, men they displaced. Besides Aaron Burr, there were Alexander Hamilton, John Jay, Robert Troup, Rufus King, James Kent, and others; names that soon became inextricably interwoven with the history of the new nation.

Business prospered, his office was filled with clients, and his name moved rapidly to the foreground in the legal profession. He was happy in his marriage; Theodosia Burr proved a tender, understanding and wise wife, a fit mate intellectually and spiritually for him. Their letters, on those occasions when the law called him to Albany or Westchester or New Jersey, were no longer prim, repressed dissertations that foreswore sentiment and dealt only in " general ideas "; they were ardent, personal, loving, filled with domestic incidents, laments over continued absences, accounts of little Theo's illnesses.

She writes him: " My Aaron had scarce quitted the door when I regretted my passiveness. Why did I consent to his departure? Can interest repay the sacrifice? can aught on earth compensate for his presence? . . . My Aaron, dark is the hour that separates my soul from itself . . . Heaven protect my Aaron; preserve him, restore him to his adoring mistress." [25] One would scarcely recognize the rather frigid bluestocking who once had written a set composition on the respective merits of Rousseau, Voltaire and Chesterfield.

But then again, it would be difficult in the following letter to detect that ardent young lover who had exhorted his mistress to eschew sentiment and confine herself to " general ideas." Writes Burr: " I run from court to waft you a memorandum of affection. . . . I cannot leave this till Sunday or Monday. Then to Westchester Court. The return to joy and Theo. cannot be till Thursday or Friday . . . I read your memorandum ten times a day, and observed it as religiously as ever monk did his devotion. Yesterday I burnt it. To me it seemed like sacrilege." [26]

Marriage had mellowed the didactic young man. There was little Theo, also, whom he adored, and the two Prevost youngsters, whom he loved as devotedly as though they were his own.

There were flaws, however, in the unalloyed bliss. In spite of the rapid growth of his law practice, Burr was already suffering from that state of financial destitution that was destined to become chronic with him. His inheritance had been dissipated with careless, generous fingers during the War. Now that he was married and responsible for the needs and welfare of a family, the money that he made so readily, slipped even more readily and easily through his fingers. Never was he to learn the value of those shining bits of tinsel. He loved good food, good wine, stately houses, splendid furnishings, books and paintings and lavish entertainment. He could never resist an appeal to his pocket, whether based on need, alleged acquaintance, or a common service during the Revolution. He was liberal and generous to a fault. As a result, no matter what he earned, he spent much more, and constantly the specter of innumerable borrowings and the dates of approaching payments loomed to torment and engross his energies with frantic scurryings and borrowings from Peter to pay Paul.

More important, at this immediate time, was the constant ill-health of Theodosia Burr. It runs like a dark thread throughout their married life, thickening and overwhelming everything else with its shadow as the cancer spread within her vitals.

" My [constitution]," she told Tapping Reeve despairingly, " is quite worn out, & my spirits entirely exhausted, my mind and memory much impaired. I believe I have been as near a state insanity as possible, indeed there are hours in which I am confidant it still threatens me; how often do I wish the conversation of my friends to releive those horrors that can never be described — how often I feel the want of that tenderness, that kind pity that you have so freely granted me . . . Thus abandoned to nature & my own efforts, I pass many succeeding lingering hours — there are cares, & circumstances that demand my attention, & rouse my feelings, when these pass off my mind relapses to its former melancholy companions who are ever in waiting . . . In the morning I wake with regret — at night I lye down with the hope of never waking to the disappointments of another day." [27]

Poor lady! The shadow of death was already upon her, and it evoked an expression as eloquent in its deep-seated melancholy, as somber and tragic in its rooted despair, as anything in all literature. But this was later, when her invalidism had become confirmed and no longer subject to a facile optimism.

In the meantime she was happy, keeping house for her " adored Aaron," watching her two sons grow to sturdy manhood, the baby Theo an endless source of joy and loving nonsense, maintaining constant communication with Sally and Tapping Reeve, for whom she displayed a surprising affection. " Is it possible," she exclaimed to Sally, " you can suspect your Theo of ingratitude, of a fickle heart. Do you believe I can ever forget your friendship & your tender attention, the consolations you gave me when none but you could console. Your brother was the first friend I ever made, you the second. That place you still hold in my heart & ever will." [28]

4. ENTERING WEDGE

There was a good deal of law business to be handled. Litigation over the confiscation of Tory estates proved immensely fruitful, with young Burr and young Hamilton already on opposite sides of the fence. There was also politics to be considered. Already, in

June, 1783, he had been considered for an appointment under the new government. Judge Hobart, of the New York Supreme Court, had urged his merits in the proper quarters. But Burr, hearing of this, declined to be considered as entering into a scrambling competition for any office. It was a trait — this pride of self — which had already shown itself in the army and which was to be responsible for so much in his future career. Hobart, thus rebuffed, answered a bit sarcastically. "However pure your views may be [in seeking an office], I fear you must be contented with the character of a private gentleman so long as you determine to avoid a competition; for I am told there are long lists of applicants for all the offices in the city and county of New-York." [29]

Nevertheless the rising young lawyer could not avoid the political lists — and competition. The politics of the infant State, and of the Nation too, for that matter, were still inchoate and shifting. The Revolutionary War had only recently ended, and idealism and martial enthusiasm still held their glamour, albeit they were fading a bit at the edges. The terrific struggle over the adoption of the Federal Constitution was still to begin — that struggle in which definite cleavages, ineradicable differences, were to emerge between class and class, between sections, between economic strata of society, between fundamental political philosophies, and harden into definite and violently opposed parties.

At the present, during the years 1783 and 1784, such cleavages, though they necessarily existed, had not shown themselves sharply and distinctly. Those who had favored the Revolution and participated actively therein were Whigs and patriots; those whose sympathies had been with the Empire or who had disclosed a certain lukewarmness were Tories and properly to be anathematized. Politics still were based on these broad and simple divisions, and the personalities of the candidates for office the chief consideration.

Burr early attracted notice. His obvious abilities as a lawyer, his breeding, his talents, his notable family, forced his name on the attention of the electors. He did not wish for office — at this time he had no hankering for the political fleshpots. But in spite of his manifest inertia, he was nominated for the State Assembly from the City of New York, and elected in April, 1784. George Clinton was then Governor, as he was to remain for a good many years, and the State was functioning politically under a Constitution adopted in 1777, in the very first years of the War.

Chapter VII

CHIEFLY LEGAL

1. Political Interlude

THUS, almost unwillingly, Burr embarked on his political career. The Assembly then met in New York, so that his legislative labors did not interfere very much with the continuance of his law practice. It was as a lawyer that Burr was determined to make his mark, not as a politician. He was in constant need of money, and the pay of a legislator was pitifully small. Furthermore, he still held aloof with that formidable reserve of his from the heat and squabblings of office holding. It is small wonder, then, that he did not take his new duties at first with the proper seriousness.

The first session of the Legislature opened October 12, 1784. The Assembly Journal discloses that he did not appear in his seat until November 5th, over three weeks later, and that his attendance for the balance of the session was exceedingly perfunctory. The record is blank of any measure proposed by him, or of any participation in debate.[1]

Certainly not an enviable record. But the leaven was stirring. For, when the Assembly convened for its second session on January 27, 1785, Burr was promptly on hand, and this time took a considerably more active part in the public discussions and voting.

On February 14th, he was placed on a joint committee to revise the laws of the State — an important assignment. The following day, a bill entitled " An Act incorporating the several tradesmen and mechanics of the city and county of New-York " came up for a vote. On the face of it an innocuous, routine bill. But Burr's motion to reject it met with an instant storm of abuse. In spite of the tumult, however, and in spite of the fact that he was the only member of the Assembly from the city who dared fight the proposal, he persisted in his opposition. His motion was nevertheless defeated, and the bill passed.

The Council of Revision — a peculiar constitutional body, composed of the governor, the chancellor, and the judges of the Supreme Court, before whom all bills must be laid for approval — vetoed the measure in the very terms and with almost the very phrases that Burr had used. It was, they stated, a scheme whereby the price of labor might be artificially increased; its charter made its bylaws dependent largely on the will of the Mayor and Aldermen of the City of New York, which must necessarily lead to political power and control; it set up a privileged aristocracy in trade, inasmuch as its limited numbers would prove a hindrance to immigrant mechanics and non-members; and, most cogent argument of all, the charter set up forty-three designated persons as the governing body, possessing almost absolute powers, including the right of self-perpetuation in the continuance of their regime and the exercise of full discretion in the choice of the commonalty of mechanics.[2]

It is obvious that many of these provisions were inherently dangerous, and that Burr was right in vigorously opposing such an incorporation. It was not a labor union, nor even a guild on Old World lines. It was an instrument to be used by certain politicians lurking in the background. But Burr had displayed an immense courage in breasting the popular clamor. The disgruntled partisans tried to instigate riots and threatened an assault on his house. He refused, however, all offers of aid from his friends, going about his business alone and unprotected as coolly as ever he had led his troops in action. He had brought himself forward at one bound from the general anonymity of the Legislature.

More important, however, was his determined fight to force the Legislature into the prompt and unequivocal abolition of slavery in the State of New York. A bill had been introduced in the Assembly purporting to free all those thereafter born from bondage. Burr moved to amend it to the effect that freedom should apply universally and at once. His motion met with defeat, and the unamended bill was finally passed, Burr voting stubbornly in the negative. It was, he felt, a weak compromise.

The Senate did not concur in certain provisions, and the bill came back for further consideration. Steadily and consistently, on every point, Burr's vote was for the greater enlargement of the negro's freedom and the immediacy of his release, even on such controversial questions as the right to vote, to hold positions of trust, to be admitted as witness or juror, and to intermarry without penalties. The bill was finally defeated, not to emerge again until 1799, when Burr was again in the Legislature.[3]

When the Legislature adjourned on April 27, 1785, Burr had the consciousness of having performed his duties actively and well. His name had been brought into the public view, he had achieved a reputation for courage, he had made many friends — and some enemies.

But he refused to continue in politics. His ambitions still moved in a narrower, more personal circle. The law fascinated him; its sense of achievement and financial rewards were glittering. And his expenses were steadily growing heavier. So that, for a period of years, he devoted himself exclusively to his practice and his family, touching politics merely at its periphery and but lightly.

He took no part in the heat and uproar that attended the making of the Constitution, or in the greater uproar that attended its ratification in New York and elsewhere. One does not even know how he stood on these burning and all-important questions. Alexander Hamilton was afterward to refer to his attitude as " equivocal," but Hamilton's comments on Burr must always be taken with caution.[4] There was nothing equivocal about his attitude. He simply took no public stand on the matter, equally with thousands of other private citizens.

New York ratified the Constitution, but only after battle had raged, more intense even than the physical conflicts of the Revolution. Perhaps the issue involved was more fundamental than the earlier struggle. It was a fight between the *haves* and the *have-nots;* between the proponents of a strong central government and those who believed in the essential sovereignty of the states; between those who favored resumption of specie payment and those who thought inflation a better course. There were innumerable cross-currents and strange bedfellows. Returned Tories found themselves fighting for the Constitution, and Revolutionary radicals for local control. Two parties emerged, Federalist and anti-Federalist — those who favored ratification and those who did not.

In New York Governor George Clinton, John Lansing, New York's delegate to the Constitutional Convention, and Melancton Smith violently opposed ratification. Alexander Hamilton, his father-in-law, General Philip Schuyler, the Livingstons, William Duer, the war profiteer, and John Jay were as violently in favor.

So inflamed were the discussions, so fundamental the dissensions, that even after adoption and the final victory of the Federalist forces, the parties continued, and steadily widened the breach. But Burr continued to hold himself aloof, his politics generally unclassifiable. He was generally considered an old Whig, in that he had favored a policy of proscription against the Tories, but he had taken no part in the fray when Hamilton had actively campaigned against such a policy. He leaned, no doubt, toward the anti-Federalists, but he was an independent then as later. He cared nothing for tags or party labels, and voted with equal indifference for measures proposed by either party. Such independence from party lines and tags is the clue to much that puzzled and enraged his contemporaries in later political affrays. Then, as today, the man who transcended his party's edicts was a traitor, a double-dealer, a trimmer, a Mugwump, a son of the wild jackass!

2. PRACTICING ATTORNEY

Burr went happily back to his law. His reputation steadily grew. He was rapidly forging to the forefront of the legal profession in the State and probably in the United States. It did not take long for him to become, together with Hamilton, an acknowledged leader of the Bar. Clients poured in, fees waxed large, other lawyers employed him as counsel or requested his opinions on moot points in writing.

The Docket of his cases in the Mayor's Court of New York City for the years 1784 to 1788 discloses him as an extremely busy trial attorney, handling matters as various as the conversion of horses that had strayed from their owners, trespass on land, protested notes, assault and battery, and contracts for the sale of merchandise. In short, the usual grist that goes through the legal mill.[5]

The amounts ranged from a few pounds, New York money, to much more substantial sums, and the fees charged were in proportion. This should dispose, once and for all, of that much repeated legend that Burr refused to handle any matter under a minimum fee of £40. This legend is based on a false reading of a statement of his, which has been used time and again to charge him with mercenary qualities, usually in unfavorable contrast to the admitted modesty of Hamilton's fees.

The statement is contained in a letter he wrote to Peter van Schaack. He says: " I have never undertaken the management of a Cause of any moment in error under £40." [6] There are two distinct limitations to be noted in this assertion. First, that it relates only to matters on appeal (Causes in error) ; second, that the cause be one of *moment* — in other words, substantial in character and in the amount involved. When it is further considered that appeals were argued before the Supreme Court in Albany, involving a long, tedious journey of days, Burr's avowal becomes considerably more modest, and would be applicable to any practicing attorney of the time.

His clientele was large and varied. It included his old Colonel, William Malcolm, now once more a prosperous New York merchant; he managed large landed properties in Maine for remote

English clients; [7] he represented the famous De Peyster family,[8] and was for years general counsel for the even more famous tribe of Livingstons, the most powerful family in the State. His bill, rendered the Estate of Robert G. Livingston in 1789, on a running account of six or seven years, discloses a total of over £10,-000, New York money! [9]

It has been estimated that his annual earnings exceeded $10,000 a year, a huge sum in those days, and it is claimed that he received as much as that for a single fee.[10] No one in his day exceeded him in legal income. His first partner was William T. Broome, the son of the Treasurer of the New York Chamber of Commerce. He had several thereafter, notably William Coleman, who later was to edit the New York *Chronicle* and defend his former partner vigorously, though opposed to him in politics.

The restrictions against Tory lawyers were lifted in 1786, but the raising of the ban did not affect Burr's prestige or success at the Bar. It was said at the time that in all his life Burr never lost a case that he personally conducted. The obvious retort to such an assertion is, as all lawyers are aware, that the successful one's practice was either severely limited or that he chose his cases with care. Burr chose his cases with care. He refused to appear in court on a matter of whose eventual success he was not fairly confident.

More important, he prepared his cases thoroughly. He was indefatigable in research, he marshaled his facts and precedents with telling precision and irresistible force. He obtained every scrap of available evidence; he " pursued [says a legal friend] the opposite party with notices, and motions, and applications, and appeals, and rearguments, never despairing himself, nor allowing to his adversary confidence, nor comfort, nor repose. Always vigilant and always urgent, until a proposition for compromise or a negotiation between the parties ensued. ' Now move slow ' (he would say) ; ' never negotiate in a hurry.' " [11]

Another lawyer avowed that Burr had defined law as " whatever is boldly asserted and plausibly maintained " and that he acted accordingly. This anonymous informant went on further to say " that Colonel Burr was not a deep-read lawyer; that he showed himself abundantly conversant with the general knowledge of the profession, and that he was skilful in suggesting doubts and questions; but that he exhibited no indications of a fondness for the science, nor of researches into its abstruse doctrines; that he seemed, indeed, to hold it and its administration in slight estimation." [12]

It is difficult to appraise adequately the legal talents of the great lawyers of the past. The learning and ability of judges may be determined from their reported opinions, but there is no such test for the intangible things that go into the making of a great and successful lawyer. His work is essentially ephemeral, transmitted only through the colored and prejudiced impressions of others. Nevertheless, a careful analysis of the few briefs and opinions that have been preserved leads to conclusions somewhat similar to those just quoted.

Burr's mind was agile and active; he seized the essential points of an argument with unerring insight, and possessed the faculty of reducing an elaborate, difficult discussion to a single luminous point. He was always a strict practitioner, addicted to every legal technicality, never soliciting his opponent's favor nor indulgent in overlooking the errors of others, but courteous to his adversary and eminently polite. Yet it is true, from the available evidence, that he did not penetrate into the inner philosophy of the law, the broad consideration of its abstract principles, of fundamental justice. Nor did he object, when the occasion offered, to the use of technical arguments to gloss over matters in which equity and justice seemed to rule otherwise. This, however, cannot be considered as an indictment. Such has been the uniform custom of lawyers and judges of whatever time or clime. It is inherent in the very structure of the law.

In court as well as in the office, Burr was irresistible. He valued oratory but little. He pleaded his cause in a conversational tone, never declaiming, never diffuse, compacting his argument in small compass, covering the essential points thoroughly and concisely. " I have not the talent of making long harangues," he told the court.[13] His argument was prepared to the last detail before he entered the courtroom. He was quietly sarcastic, yet immensely impressive. His manner was courtly, despite his small stature, and his air one of dignity and perfect breeding.

A contemporary described the contrast between Burr and Hamilton, the two acknowledged leaders of the Bar, in action. Hamilton would exhaust a case, and his hearers, with a wealth of elaborate detail on every point, on every possible objection. He would speak for two or three hours, fluent, loftily eloquent, orotund. Burr would then arise in rebuttal, select with uncanny care two or three vulnerable, yet vital points in Hamilton's argument, and quietly demolish them in a few cogent words. Then he would sit down, leaving all the rest of his adversary's elaboration untouched. But in twenty minutes he had completely destroyed the effect of Hamilton's hours of effort.[14]

General Erastus Root, himself one of the best lawyers of the day, remarked that the two rivals were equal in reasoning powers and scholarship, but that Burr would say as much in half an hour as Hamilton in two. " They were," he continued, " much the greatest men in this State, and perhaps the greatest men in the United States." [15]

An Englishman, traveling in America, averred that " his [Burr's] distinguished abilities attracted so decided a leaning of the Judges in his favour, a deference for his opinions so strongly marked, as to excite in no small degree the jealousy of the bar. So strong was the impression made by the general respect for his opinions, that exclamations of despair were frequently heard to escape the lips of the Counsel whose fortune it was to be opposed by the eloquence of Mr. *Burr*. I am aware that this language wears the colour of panegyric; but the recollections which the facts must excite in the breasts of his candid rivals, will corroborate its accuracy." [16]

3. DOMESTICITY

By 1786 the Burrs had moved to 10 Little Queen Street, or what is now known as Maiden Lane. In 1789 they removed once more to quarters on the corner of Nassau and Maiden Lane, more spacious, with garden and wonderful grapes. In 1791 they were at No. 4 Broadway, to remain there until the final hegira to Richmond Hill.

Mrs. Burr's two boys, John and Augustin Prevost, joined their stepfather's legal staff and applied themselves diligently, faithfully and loyally to their work. Between Burr and his stepsons there was always to be mutual affection and devotion.

Between Burr and his wife ardent love had deepened to an abiding trust. His law practice took him on numerous, extended trips, but always they were in each other's thoughts. He writes from Philadelphia that " I have been to twenty places to find something to please you, but can see nothing that answers my wishes." [17] She replies that " all, in silent expectation, await the return of their much-loved lord, but all faintly when compared to thy Theo." [18] And little Theo, by now a plump, beautiful little baby of almost two, equally adored her father. Says her mother: " Your dear little daughter seeks you twenty times a day; calls you to your meals, and will not suffer your chair to be filled by any of the family . . . O, my Aaron! how many tender, grateful things rush to my mind in this moment; how much fortitude do I summon to suppress them! You will do justice to their silence; to the inexpressible affection of your *plus tendre amie*." [19]

Sally, the second child, was born, and died. Mrs. Burr herself, as her letters testify, was in perpetual ill health. She finds herself unable to climb stairs; she is prey to frequent fits of melancholia. But little Theo is a constant source of joy. " Your dear little Theo grows the most engaging child you ever saw. She frequently talks of, and calls on, her dear papa. It is impossible to see her with indifference." And again, " I really believe, my dear, few parents can boast of children whose minds are so prone to virtue. I see the rewards of our assiduity with inexpressible delight, with a gratitude few experience." [20] And still again, " Your dear Theodosia cannot hear you spoken of without an apparent melancholy; insomuch that her nurse is obliged to exert her invention to divert her, and myself avoid to mention you in her presence. She was one whole day indifferent to everything but your name. Her attachment is not of a common nature." [21]

There was much of prescience in these observations. The singular and overwhelming attachment between Theodosia Burr and her father is still one of the great devotions in all history. Nor was her mother far behind. Her letters are instinct with the breath of a lofty and noble nature; all her life was laid at the feet of Aaron Burr. He reciprocated in kind, though not to the extent and sacrificial depths of his wife. How could he? He was a man of affairs, immersed in the world of men, of law, of politics, of a hundred and one distractions. Whereas she, held to a round of domesticity, afflicted with an incurable disease, brooded on her love and fed it with small, still hands. " Tell me, Aaron, why do I grow every day more tenacious of thy regard? Is it possible my affection can increase? Is it because each revolving day proves thee more deserving? " [22]

Burr's letters are tender, thoughtful, considerate, breathing a manifest sincerity. Every remedy of which he hears is promptly reported home in the steadily lessening hope that here is finally the cure; he buttonholes every doctor, in Philadelphia, in Albany, in New York, seeking the causes of that obscure disease which is wasting his beloved Theo. He truly and devotedly loved her — even though he had become involved in certain disputes with her relatives.

General Maunsell, her uncle, residing in London, had originally approved of the marriage. He had written his sister-in-law, Mrs. Watkins, a widow in New York, and in search of legal advice, that " Mr. Burr will counsel you in all this. I hear a great character of him, and I think Theo was lucky in meeting so good a man." [23]

But when he came to America the following year (1784) to attend to certain real estate interests in New York and to act with Burr as co-Trustee under the will of Mrs. de Visme, Theodosia's mother, the tune changed. Burr took exception to the General's inquisitorial inquiries into his management of the estate. Furthermore, the military man seems to have bogged down completely in a mass of figures. They quarreled. What happened thereafter is vague. The General was arrested in 1787. It has been assumed that his incarceration was at Burr's instance, but there is no basis for such an assumption in Maunsell's simple statement that Burr paid him " the sum of £87: 10: 11, *as on that day I was arrested,* and he paid for me £125 out of all the money he had of mine in his hands." [24] If anything, it would seem that he was being assisted in his extremity.

In any event there was a definite break with the English branch of Theodosia's family. Maunsell was later to splutter to another relative: " Liddy tells me that Mr. Burr expects a seat in congress, and that he had taken *Big* Symmon's house in Wall Street. As I shall never more have any intercourse with him, or his family, his changes in life give me no concern, or pleasure; he is no friend to your house." [25] And Burr was to remark sarcastically to his wife: " You have really a Distressing family. I hope it has by this time diminished." [26]

But this latter remark was contained in a letter remarkable for its general bitterness of tone and fault-finding. Burr was ill at the time — as he constantly was during the middle years of his life — Mrs. Burr was ailing and a bit querulous, and she had crossed him in several ways. A single letter cannot be made the basis for a general trend of affairs, as has been attempted. As a matter of fact, within a few days thereafter, their correspondence is again replete with the tenderest and most warm-hearted expressions. The cloud had vanished.

Chapter VIII

THE POLITICIAN EMBARKED

1. Preview

MEANWHILE politics had been steadily growing more exacerbated and party lines more sharply delimited in New York State. The Federal Constitution had been fought over and adopted in 1787. Governor George Clinton had been its bitterest opponent, preferring the prestige and power of a semi-independent State. Names were being called, in spite of the unanimity with which George Washington had been elected President. Already the lines were being drawn for the agrarian revolt under Jefferson and others.

The situation in New York was rather peculiar. Under the State Constitution of 1777 it was comparatively easy for the few with power, influence and wealth to rule the many. It could not in any modern sense of the term be considered a democracy. Nor, for that matter, could the political set-up of any other State in the newly formed United States.

The government consisted of a Governor, a bicameral Legislature — the Assembly, 70 members elected annually, and the Senate, 24 members chosen for terms of four years. These were the nominal government; actually there were two other bodies specified in the Constitution that held as much, if not more, of real power. The Council of Revision, composed of the Governor, the Chancellor and Judges of the Supreme Court, was vested with veto power over all legislation, subject to be overridden by a two-thirds vote of *each* branch of the Legislature. The Council of Appointment was even more curious. It consisted of four Senators nominated and appointed by the Assembly, who, together with the Governor, appointed all state officials with the exception of the Governor, Lieutenant-Governor, and State Treasurer. The patronage was enormous, ranging from Supreme Court Judges down to justices of the peace and auctioneers. It can readily be seen what a powerful and flexible weapon this Council could be in the hands of unscrupulous politicians.

Suffrage was heavily restricted. To be permitted to vote for members of the Assembly there were property qualifications — to wit, one must be a freeholder with a freehold of the value of £20, or the renter of a tenement of the annual value of 40 shillings, and a taxpayer to boot. For the Senate and for Governor the qualifications were much more stringent. The prospective voter must be a freeholder possessed of a freehold worth £100, over and above all debts and incumbrances. In 1790 there were only 1303 out of a total of 13,330 adult male residents of New York City with the requisite property qualifications to vote for Senators and for Governor.[1] Ten percent of the citizenry, in other words, ran the government; ninety percent to all intents and purposes were largely or completely disfranchised.

It is small wonder then that the State found itself in the grip of a few powerful families. The Clintons generally; in Westchester the Morrises and Van Cortlandts; along the Hudson the Livingstons and the Coldens; in Albany the Van Rensselaers and Schuylers; and to the west Sir William Johnson. All of them were owners of princely domains and exceedingly wealthy. Together they could have dominated the State with irresistible influence. Actually they were usually at cross-purposes, and the Clintons, in the person of the veteran and perennial Governor, George Clinton, rode the conflict of interests and of families with an agility that commands the admiration of the beholder.

The situation has been stated rather succinctly, if with undue simplification. " The Clintons had the *power,* the Livingstons had *numbers,* the Schuylers had *Hamilton.*" [2]

Alexander Hamilton had married the daughter of General Philip Schuyler, of Revolutionary fame, and a land speculator and canal builder extraordinary. Already had the young West Indian made his mark in state and national politics. He was decidedly a Federalist with all that the name implies; he had fought valiantly and hard for the Constitution; he was soon to be the first Secretary of the Treasury and the power that motivated the President of the United States. Yet he cannily realized that political influence must have a local habitation and a name, and set to work to entrench himself strongly in New York.

Accordingly there ensued a jockeying for position. The Clintons were in control. An alliance between the Livingstons and the Schuylers (Hamilton) might oust the ruling family. It simplified matters, too, that the Livingstons were equally with the Schuylers of the Federalist persuasion. Governor Clinton was well aware of the situation. He needed counterbalances. The other families were too feudal — and feudist — in their characteristics to promise much help. He was in trouble.

Meanwhile, in April 1788, Burr had been nominated once again as candidate for the Assembly from New York City by the anti-Federalists. The ticket was advertised in the newspapers and hand-bills as follows:

" The sons of liberty, who are again called upon to contend with the sheltered aliens [Tories], who have, by the courtesy of our country, been permitted to remain among us, will give their support to the following ticket: —

" *William Denning, Melancton Smith, Marinus Willet, and Aaron Burr.*" [3]

The ticket went down to ignominious defeat. The Federalists won overwhelmingly, and it looked gloomy for the gubernatorial election the following year. Burr does not seem to have canvassed for votes very actively. No doubt he had permitted his name to be entered at the urging of friends who were active. It was known in advance that defeat was certain. He still was not very politically minded.

The Federalists now had a majority in the State Senate and had gained heavily in the Assembly. They were jubilant and assured of success in the coming gubernatorial contest. Clinton seemed doomed to be ousted from the seat he had held so long. It was routine, of course, for him to be renominated on the anti-Federalist ticket.

On February 11, 1789, a meeting of citizens was called in New York City, mostly Federalist in complexion, to nominate an opposition candidate to Clinton. It is noteworthy of remark that they were not all Federalists. Personalities still entered into the consideration of office-holders, though with ever-decreasing force. Judge Robert Yates was nominated to contest the seat with Clinton. Aaron Burr attended this meeting, and was appointed, with Hamilton, Troup, and William Duer, to a committee of correspondence to promote Yates' election.[4]

Yates was now a moderate Federalist. Burr was certainly not. He had run on the opposition ticket only the year before. Yet he appeared now to vote for and advance actively the candidacy of a Federalist. Several considerations entered into this seeming abandonment of his own party.

In the strict sense of the term he never was a party man. Aside from the fact that his interest in politics had been comparatively slight, he was essentially a moderate in disposition. He was too coolly intellectual and keenly logical to yield to fanatical extremes on either side. Furthermore, he did not consider this particular contest as one involving national principles. It was a contest of

men, of personalities. And Robert Yates was his close, his personal
friend. He remembered gratefully the time when Yates had eased
the way for his admission to the bar and the ties had deepened
and strengthened ever since. He owed no allegiance to George
Clinton.

Clinton defeated Yates, but by an uncomfortably close vote.
And the Federalists won majorities in both branches of the
Legislature. Clinton more than ever was determined to strengthen
his lines. His eye fell on Aaron Burr. Burr was a comparatively
young man, only thirty-three years of age, of excellent family and
background, and had risen by his own unaided efforts to the top
of his profession. Though he had supported Clinton's antagonist
in the recent election, he was still in fact an anti-Federalist. And,
most important of all, he had no entangling alliances in the welter of interfamily quarrels that made of New York politics such
an intricate web.

Clinton acted swiftly and decisively. He appointed his late opponent, Robert Yates, to the Chief Justiceship of the Supreme
Court, and thereby eliminated him from future political consideration. Then he attempted to attach Burr to himself by offering
him the office of State Attorney General. On September 25, 1789,
Burr accepted, after some hesitation. He was reluctant to give
up his law practice.

2. STEPPING-STONE

The Attorney-Generalship was just then a particularly important position, involving immense labors and the determination
of a host of knotty legal questions. The respective obligations and
status of the State and Federal governments had not been thoroughly worked out as yet, and it was necessary to discriminate between claims that were legitimately the obligation of the State
and those which might be thrust upon the Federal nation. There
were an enormous number of claims arising out of the chaos of
the Revolution; creditors clamoring for immediate payment, soldiers for back pay and because of disabilities incurred, damages
alleged to have been sustained by expropriation and confiscation,
losses arising out of the depreciated currency.

Burr found himself at once submerged under a welter of pe-
titions that a harassed Legislature promptly shifted to his desk for
legal consideration. There were no precedents, no well-established
principles by which he could test the validity of individual claims.
Accordingly, commissioners were appointed by the Legislature to

report a basis for orderly settlements. The commission consisted of Gerard Bancker, State Treasurer, Peter T. Curtenius, State Auditor, and Aaron Burr, as Attorney General.

The report, when submitted, was Burr's creation. It was a masterful and exhaustive study, codifying the groups of claims, establishing uniform rules of procedure for their orderly examination, and treating all classes of claimants with rigorous fairness and impartiality. The Legislature entered the report on April 5, 1792, unanimously, and it was made the basis for all future settlements.

As Attorney General, Burr was also ex-officio a Land Commissioner. The other members of the commission were J. A. Scott, Secretary of State, Gerard Bancker, State Treasurer, Peter T. Curtenius, State Auditor, and Governor George Clinton.

The State of New York was possessed of 7,000,000 acres of unappropriated land. This immense domain literally cried for settlement, and the State Treasury as vehemently required funds. Yet sales along normal lines were proceeding slowly. In order to quicken the tempo the Legislature in 1791 authorized the commissioners of the Land Office to dispose of any waste and unappropriated lands, in such parcels and on such terms and in such manner as they deemed in the public interest. It was a broad designation of powers that opened the door wide to what actually followed.

Under this unlimited authority the Commission sold forthwith, during the year, 5,542,173 acres for a total purchase price of $1,034,483. Less than 20 cents an acre average. But included in this total was one regal donation — it could hardly be called a sale — to Alexander McComb of 3,635,200 acres at 8 pence an acre, payable in five annual instalments without interest, with a discount of six per cent for immediate payment. The other parcels, even those of considerable extent, were disposed of at much higher rates, ranging from a shilling to 3 shillings an acre.

Instantly an outcry arose. Ugly charges were bandied back and forth. The Federalists pounced upon the matter and elevated it to a distinct major scandal. Talbot, from Montgomery County, rose in the Assembly and offered some severely condemnatory resolutions. He intimated very plainly that Clinton and his friends had personally feathered their nests in the matter of the sale to McComb. An investigation was instituted. But, though on the face of it favoritism, if not corruption, seemed rampant, no factual evidence was forthcoming. Talbot's resolutions were finally rejected by the Assembly, and the report of the Land Commission (and, inferentially, their conduct) was approved by a vote of 35 to 20.

Burr's complicity in this transaction is the subject of dispute. Davis claims that " these resolutions [Talbot's] exempted Col. Burr from any participation in the malconduct complained of, inasmuch as the minutes of the board proved that he was not present at the meetings (*being absent on official duty as Attorney General*) , when these contracts, so ruinous as they alleged, to the interest of the state, were made." [5]

Hammond, however, maintains that the resolutions made no such express exemption, though they *did* refer only to " such of the commissioners as had an agency in the sales." He is skeptical, moreover, of Burr's alleged absence, alleging that Davis cited no supporting evidence. He feels that inasmuch as the transactions complained of extended over a period of months, Burr must have known and, knowing, approved of what was being done. [6]

An examination of the facts must dispose of the controversy summarily, in Burr's favor. The Legislative grant of powers to the Commission was made on March 22, 1791. The letters that passed between Burr and Theodosia prove that he was away from New York — at Kingston, Claverack and Albany — from at least the beginning of June, 1791, engaged on a " very laborious task," and that he did not return until sometime in August. [7] And in October he was in Philadelphia, ready to embark on his Senatorial duties, already resigned from his office as Attorney General. The entire scandal over the land sales occurred during his absences, and after he was no longer a member of the Commission. He must therefore be absolved of all possible complicity.

As for the routine duties of his office, it was said that " in State prosecutions, a disposition to aggravate the enormities of the accused was never attributed to him." [8]

3. INTO THE ARENA

The next step in Burr's political career was one of those wholly unexpected twists of fortune, of a sudden concatenation of events, that appear with strange regularity in the lives of all famous men. It was responsible for the translation of Burr from a purely local celebrity to the national stage, where the eyes of the entire country could be focused upon him, and the basis laid for his subsequent meteoric and sensational rise to prominence.

Philip Schuyler and Rufus King had been appointed the first

United States Senators from the State of New York by joint resolution of the Legislature. Schuyler had drawn the short term and
his office expired March 4, 1791. Naturally he was a candidate
again, and the Legislature being safely Federalist, his reappoint-
ment was expected to be a routine affair. There were seemingly
no candidates in opposition. He was a man of power and influence,
with the prestige of a brilliant Revolutionary record and a great
family to back him up. There was Alexander Hamilton, his son-
in-law, too. But subtle influences were at work.

To understand these, one must rehearse the story a bit. The
Federalists had won the Legislature and barely missed unseating
George Clinton in 1789 by a coalition of Schuylers and Livingstons. The Livingstons were Federalist — had they not worked
valiantly for the Constitution? — but they were likewise ambitious. They viewed with increasing discontent and a jaundiced
eye the manifest tendency of the Schuylers (meaning Hamilton)
to arrogate to themselves the spoils of office, both in local and in
national affairs, and to dominate almost exclusively the Administration of President Washington.

It had been expected that a Livingston, as well as a Schuyler,
would have been chosen to represent the State in the United States
Senate. Instead, Hamilton set up Rufus King, only recently arrived from Massachusetts. It had also been expected that the venerable head of the family, the Chancellor, Robert Livingston, was
to have been granted the Chief Justiceship of the Supreme Court
of the United States. John Jay was given the honored position.
Everywhere they turned they saw the fine Machiavellian hand of
Hamilton, exalting the Schuylers and their allies, quietly shoving
the too-powerful Livingstons aside. It was an alliance in which
there was no comfort.

George Clinton, too, was surveying the scene with political
forevision. Alone, the anti-Federalists could not do anything in
the Legislature. But if the Livingstons, ostensibly Federalist, were
to join. . . .

A vote was taken. Schuyler's name was the only one proposed.
He was rejected. Had the heavens fallen the supporters of Hamilton could not have been more profoundly startled or surprised.
But the fact remained — Schuyler had been considered, and emphatically disposed of.

Whereupon Burr's name was promptly put in nomination. In
the Assembly he received a majority of 5; in the Senate, with only
16 voting out of a possible 24, he was chosen by an overwhelming

vote of 12 to 4. On January 19, 1791, Aaron Burr, aged not quite thirty-five, thus found himself the next United States Senator from the State of New York!

A good deal of controversy has raged over his particular part in the surprising debacle. It has been held, chiefly by his inveterate enemies, that he had anticipated just such an event, that he had intrigued and insinuated himself into the graces of the individual members of the Legislature. The facts warrant no such interpretation.

The movement had been essentially one against Philip Schuyler on the part of the disgruntled Livingstons, with the efficient co-operation of the Governor. It was a case of *beat Hamilton!* When it came to the question of a successor, however, there were certain delicate considerations involved. Clinton could not bring forth his own candidate, or an out-and-out anti-Federalist. The Livingstons were in no mood to tear down one group in order to exalt another. Besides, they were still Federalist in politics.

The answer was of course an independent, a moderate, a man of undoubted talents and popularity, a man who had not completely identified himself with any faction and yet whose character and ability would win the approval of the generalty of the voters. Another gubernatorial election, it must be remembered, was impending.

Aaron Burr seemed to be such an available choice. He was anti-Federalist, yet he had supported Yates against Clinton. His term as Attorney General had proved eminently satisfactory. His eminence as a lawyer was unquestioned. He was on good terms with the tribe of Livingstons; he was friendly from college days with Brockholst Livingston and had acted as counsel for Robert G. Livingston, recently deceased, for a good many years. He was acceptable also to Clinton. The old Governor had already appraised the rising young independent, and desired to attach him to his chariot-wheels. In the coming close election he did not wish a recurrence of 1789.

So, out of a complex of forces, Burr emerged into the arena of state and national politics, possibly much to his own surprise. But in the doing he had gained fierce and unrelenting enmities.

General Schuyler and Hamilton were furious. There was no question in their minds that Burr, and Burr alone, had by his arts prepared and fired the mine. Schuyler nursed his wrath in secret and wrote to his son-in-law: " As no good could possibly result from evincing any resentment to Mr. Burr for the part he took last winter, I have on every occasion behaved toward him as if he had not been the principal in the business." [9] He did not realize that it was the Livingstons who had betrayed him.

But a secret wrath, nursed under a smiling countenance, bottles to dangerous compressions. Hamilton likewise accepted it as a personal and family affront, as well as a considerable setback to his own political fortunes. He required every vote he could get in the Senate, and he was intimate enough with Burr to know that in the new Senator he had acquired a formidable antagonist. Most of Hamilton's measures, sponsored by him in pursuit of a definite plan, had squeezed through Congress by the closest of margins and only after extended fighting. Besides, all his well-laid plans for the total assumption of power in New York, the pivotal state of the Union, were wholly upset by this unexpected defeat. No wonder he began to hate Burr from that day on as the author of his misfortunes, and was to pursue him throughout his career and down to the last tragic dénouement with a bitter and personal venom unsurpassed in the history of American politics.

Of all this Burr at the time had no inkling. The grudge was covered with a smiling face, with an outward friendliness, as before. Burr and Hamilton had been necessarily thrown much in each other's company; they had visited each other and appeared in court as associated counsel or as opponents with an equal courtesy and friendship. But Hamilton's secret malice was to dog Burr's footsteps relentlessly, to cross his path time and again, to warp all of Burr's life in the crucible of a distilled venom, and to terminate abruptly in the death of the maligner. Even that death was to pursue Burr still further like the Erinyes of old.

CHAPTER IX

THE GENTLEMAN FROM NEW YORK

1. STRICTLY PROFESSIONAL

IN the meantime the prospects were fair and the skies unclouded. Burr wound up his duties as Attorney General and put his personal affairs in order. Theodosia admonished him anxiously that " it is . . . of serious consequence to you, to establish your health before you commence politician; when once you get engaged, your industry will exceed your strength; your pride cause you to forget yourself." [1]

Congress then met in Philadelphia, and Burr established himself in that city of Quakers, politicians and financiers sometime in October, 1791. He found lodgings in a house " inhabited by two widows. The mother about seventy, and the daughter about fifty. . . . The old lady is deaf, and upon my [Burr's] first coming to take possession of my lodgings, she with great civility requested that I would never attempt to speak to her, for fear of injuring my lungs without being able to make her hear. I shall faithfully obey this injunction." [2]

The Second Congress of the United States opened on October 24, 1791. The First Congress had been the scene of much tumultuous debate, of the forging of a new nation. Hamilton had pushed his schemes for assumption of State debts, for payment of all governmental securities at par, for a National Bank, through Houses that were divided almost equally into enthusiastic supporters and bitter opponents. The great measures of government had been passed. President Washington heaved a sigh of relief and Hamilton permitted himself to relax. The Second Congress was a period of comparative quiet, of marking time. Within its halls parties had not yet fully crystallized. The loose appellations of Federalist and anti-Federalist still held their original meaning, based as they were on the Constitutional fight of 1787. Actually Congress voted on the basis of approval or disapproval of Hamilton's operations. Within a few years, however, as the depression that commenced in 1792 deepened, the issues were more baldly stated, and party lines became fixed and unalterable.

Already the fight between Jefferson and Hamilton in the Cabinet had assumed the stage of a dangerous, if smoldering, fire. Hamilton's principles had been definitely and logically formulated. Jefferson's, if still a trifle inchoate, were steadily crystallizing. The great planting interests of the South had nothing in common with the mercantile, bond-holding classes of the North. Virginia led the Southern States, Massachusetts those of the North. The South could not hope to make successful headway on its own; it was therefore necessary to seek alliances.

Accordingly, in the summer of 1791, Jefferson and Madison made a leisurely trip through New York, ostensibly on a botanizing excursion. But apparently, as S. E. Morison has felicitously put it, they were in search of a certain rare plant, the *Clintonia borealis*. They saw George Clinton — quite casually, of course — they met the Livingstons, who had just given Philip Schuyler his *coup de grâce;* and they spoke to Aaron Burr. An understanding was arranged — the beginning of the political alliance of New York and Virginia — that was to ripen slowly and bear considerable fruit.

Burr threw himself into his new duties with unremitting energy. He now saw clearly the path ahead. Law was to be discarded in favor of politics as the ultimate career. He was too keenly analytical and appraising to hold any particular illusions about the matter. He was not swayed by violent hatreds or dogmas; he did not believe that political opponents were necessarily rascals. In an era when invective and diatribe were almost the sole political arguments, he was amazingly urbane and courteous. He ran neither with the hares nor with the hounds, nor suffered himself to be overwhelmed and blinded by party passions and prejudices. He considered the exercise of public office in the nature of a career, even as the " careerists " in the British civil offices consider it to this day. It was a life-work, not as lucrative as the law perhaps, but offering its own peculiar rewards in the feeling of power, of satisfied ambition, of the efficient smoothness of geared wheels to be set in operation, of public service even. In short, politics was a profession, and Burr determined to treat it as such.

It was this attitude which set Burr apart from the others of his time, and made him an enigma to them and to the following generations as well. It was too cool-headed, too analytical an attitude. They could not understand his complete objectivity, his utter contempt for the innumerable dogmas that aroused the emotions and clouded sheer reasonableness, his steady, unswerving, unhurried movement toward a clearly developed objective. They were amateurs in politics — even Jefferson, Hamilton, John Adams,

Madison and the rest. Amateurs, that is, in the sense that politics was not their life-work, a science to be studied calmly and mapped in accordance with certain intellectual rules. To them it was an avocation, something inextricably involved with their passions and instinctive economic reactions. They theorized, and philosophized, and rationalized what they did with subtle generalizations. Burr never generalized. Each political problem stood on its own feet. He studied it unemotionally, determined on the appropriate means to secure the desired end, and unhesitatingly put them into motion.

Not that Jefferson or Hamilton or the others were not *practical* politicians. They were, and immensely skilful at the job indeed. The distinction is one between *practical* and *professional.* Burr was the latter. The term has now, and had then, certain vaguely distasteful connotations. There is no reason for this, any more than its use in any other field. The political field requires skill, training and the development of orderly technique, even as the law or engineering or medicine. Other nations have recognized this simple principle; America perhaps has not even yet.

But Burr was a new phenomenon on the American scene. His contemporaries did not understand him; there is no clear understanding of him today. He fought political battles as he fought law suits, as he had disposed of his forces in war — as though they were problems in chess, intellectual exercises. In a day when party passions reached an unbelievable pitch, when pamphlets and the press frothed at the mouth, when physical warfare threatened, Burr rode serenely above the storm, appraising, marshaling his forces, hewing to a predetermined line. It accounts in great part for his brilliant upswing; it accounts in still greater part for his abrupt downfall. His own associates were uneasy, distrustful of him, instinctively hostile to his methods, though employed on their behalf. They preferred the bludgeon to the rapier; they preferred the ecstasy of aroused emotion to the smooth working of a geared and irresistible machine. Burr was a portent of a new force in American politics and they did not like it. They feared what they could not fathom; they sensed a danger to their own positions in his Old World urbanity and polish.

Yet though Burr was admittedly ambitious — which is no crime — and though he treated politics as an intellectual exercise, he was an immensely valuable force in the growing nation. The whole Jeffersonian campaign pivoted on his tactics; admittedly the agrarian revolt would not have triumphed when it did had it not been for him. Now that he had entered politics as a definite field of endeavor, he was on the side of the masses, of the popular discontent. Yet it must not be conceived that this was a matter of demagoguery.

He was as far removed from the demagogic as it was possible to be; he disdained exhortations, tub-thumpings, appeals to the emotions; he disdained even to defend himself when attacked in personal terms. Essentially his was an aristocratic nature, whose ideal was the Chesterfieldian gentleman, reserved, impenetrable, proud. Nor was the popular side necessarily the vote-getting side. The masses were disfranchised, inarticulate at the ballot-box. The property qualifications saw to that. New York State, his own bailiwick, in 1789 had a population of 324,270, yet the voters numbered only 12,353. The rest of the country followed the same general proportions. And this handful of the electorate comprised the men of means, of property, of respectability, the men who inevitably were conservative and chary on behalf of their vested interests. They would naturally — in most sections — gravitate to the party of Federalism.

Burr's choice of Republicanism must then be laid to an intellectual conviction, not to motives of personal interest. He could have gone as far, perhaps even farther, as an avowed Federalist. Most of his friends were of that persuasion — Robert Troup, Judge Yates, William Patterson, Jonathan Dayton. The ever-present fear that Burr might some day turn suddenly and wrest the scepter of supremacy from his hands may have had considerable to do with Hamilton's persistent sniping.

Burr was the true aristocratic liberal. He followed the fortunes of the French Revolution with enthusiastic admiration and careful analysis, a combination that only he could compass. " From an attentive perusal of the French Constitution, and a careful examination of their proceedings," he wrote, " I am a warm admirer of the Essential parts of the plan of government which they have instituted, and of the talents and disinterestedness of the members of the National Assembly." [3] To this admiration he steadily adhered. In later life he became a student and ardent disciple of Jeremy Bentham, the great English economist and liberal. He helped disseminate Bentham's ideas in America, and sought his close friendship when in exile. His was the Continental spirit. In Europe he had his fellows; in America at this time he was alone. Therein was his strength and his tragedy.

2. SENATORIAL DUTIES

The Senate met behind closed doors. Debates were secret, and only skeletal outlines were permitted to reach the light of day. It is therefore extremely difficult to appraise properly this portion of Burr's career. Yet he was evidently active in the debates and very well thought of by his confrères. A contemporary remarks that " deference [was] shewn his opinions by his senatorial colleagues," and that " it was . . . universally acknowledged, that no other State was so respectably represented as the State of *New-York,* in the combined talents of Mr. *Burr* and Mr. King." [4]

However, the Annals of Congress give verification to contemporary opinion and furnish a fairly accurate guide to his standing and to his position on men and measures.

The Senate opened with due solemnity on October 24, 1791. On October 25th, the fledgling Senator from New York was made chairman of a committee to draft the Senate's address to the President of the United States.[5] And almost immediately thereafter he was given a host of committee assignments. Included in these were some of considerable importance.[6]

In the Second Session, starting on November 5, 1792, he commenced a persistent campaign to abolish the shroud of secrecy in which the Senate proceedings were enveloped, and to throw open the doors to the public during all debates. At this particular time the motion was defeated by a large majority.[7]

The message of President Washington on the Indian troubles and the necessity for a larger military establishment came in for a great deal of warm debate and maneuvering. Burr was the chairman of the committee that considered the message, and there were rumors abroad concerning his stand, and the probability that he had been offered a military command as a reward for the position he took. He denied it peremptorily — to his wife, it must be understood, not to the general public. He made it a fixed rule of life never to deny rumors or accusations. " You may expect a host of such falsehoods as that about the Indian war," he declared. " I have not been offered any command. When the part I take in the bill on that subject shall be fully known, I am sure it will give entire satisfaction to my friends." [8]

Burr, regardless of self-interest, was always to be a warm supporter of a strong military establishment. His Revolutionary service had left a deep impression on his mind; he was always to appreciate complimentary references to his soldiering far more than those concerning any other phase of his career.

He devoted himself arduously to his duties. He was not content with the ordinary routine of the average Congressman. He wished to perfect himself in his profession, to become able to act intelligently and with understanding on measures of government. Especially was he interested in foreign relations. But, pursuant to a highly monarchical policy, the archives of the Department of State were not available to Congress. Only those matters and such particular correspondence which the President was graciously willing to present to its attention, could be inquired into by the legislative branch of the Government.

Burr resented this, and applied to Thomas Jefferson, Secretary of State, for permission to examine the archives of the Department mornings before the regular opening time. Permission was granted. Burr threw himself into his researches with characteristic energy. He was there every morning promptly at five, copied or made extracts until ten, when the doors were formally opened. Then he attended sessions of the Senate, and spent his evenings studying and digesting his notes. Then, one fine day, Washington heard of the practices of the Senator from New York, and put a stop to it by peremptory order.

" Thomas Jefferson presents his respectful compliments to Colonel Burr, and is sorry to inform him it has been concluded to be improper to communicate the correspondence of existing ministers." [9]

3. Eyes on New York

But national politics were not all that occupied the attention of Senator Burr during that pregnant year of 1792. His home State was seething with ferment and recriminations, and wisely he paused in his labors in the Senate to keep sharp eyes on the local situation. Already he saw with exceeding clarity that New York in great measure held the balance of power between conflicting sections of the country, and that he, as a moderate and comparative independent, might, by the employment of a cohesive and durable organization, swing the balance with delicate precision in the pivotal State.

Governor Clinton's term was due to expire in March, 1792, and by the first month of the year the political campaign was in full swing. There was talk that the aging Governor would decline to run again, but Burr knew better. George Clinton was not the man to resign easily the reins of office.

On the Federalist side, however, matters were in a state of confusion. Judge Yates was first offered the nomination. He was the logical candidate, inasmuch as he had missed election in 1790 by a mere handful of votes. But to their vast surprise and no little alarm, he declined, alleging as a sufficient reason that " he apprehended his pecuniary affairs would be injured if he was placed in the chair of Government." But the suspicious Federalists smelled a rat. Schuyler, in great perturbation of spirit, hastened to call on him, and wrote Hamilton that after considerable argument, " I am led to believe that he will not yield to Mr. Burr's views. I shall, however, in a day or two bring him to an explicit declaration on the subject." [10]

The cat was out of the bag. It was the small, erect, imperturbable figure of Burr, newly elected Senator, a comparative newcomer on the political stage, that was from now on to cause sleepless nights and political nightmares to the older and ostensibly more experienced statesmen of New York.

There were forces at work pushing Burr for the gubernatorial nomination with might and main. Nor were these forces restricted to one party. Both Federalists and anti-Federalists felt the subterranean upheavals, and suffered queasy sensations in the pit of the stomach in consequence. It is easy to comprehend Hamilton's indignation and astonishment at receiving the following analysis of the situation from a loyal henchman, one Isaac Ledyard. " On my arrival here [in New York], finding that a tide was likely to work strongly for Mr. Burr, I grew more anxious." Judge Yates, it is to be calculated, by " supporting Mr. Burr will best please most of his ancient friends [Yates had originally been an anti-Federalist] and tend to restore him to their confidence, and also that the candidate in question has a personal dominion over him." Schuyler himself, it seems, feared " that if Mr. Clinton and Mr. Burr were to be the only competitors, and his friends thrown out of the scale, it would be doubtful which succeeded." Ledyard proceeded to argue that the candidacy of a strict Federalist in a three-cornered fight would mean Burr's election; that the only hope of opposing him was to support Clinton, but that, he felt, would be " a dereliction of sentiment," and not to be thought of.

Furthermore, he pointed out to Hamilton, " if B. finally succeeds, and you have not the merit of it, it will be an event extremely disagreeable to me," and, though he left it to implication, to all Federalists who were hungering for office. With that in mind, the hungry Ledyard sought repeated interviews with Burr to

" procure from him an *artless* declaration of his sentiments, both with respect to the Union, on present grounds, and also with respect to you."

Burr must have smiled secretively at the advent of the alarmed politician, and evaded with glittering phrases that satisfied the none too subtle Ledyard, who went on to report that " he [Burr] has expressed a sincere regard for the safety and well-being of the former. With respect to yourself, he expresses an entire confidence in the wisdom and integrity of your designs, and a real personal friendship, and which he does not seem to suppose you doubt of, or that you ever will, unless it may arise from meddling interveners." And Ledyard closed with a sentence that must have thrown Hamilton into a veritable fury. " Unless you have grounds of objection which I do not know of, I ardently wish that the result of your interview with General Schuyler may be an adoption of the candidate." [11] In other words, Aaron Burr!

Hamilton had many " grounds of objection," not all of which were for public consumption. He marshaled his forces against the open threat to his hitherto unquestioned supremacy in New York Federalist politics. Pressure was brought to bear on Yates. Van Rensselaer was offered the nomination to cement the loyalty of his powerful clan. He declined. In desperation Hamilton turned to John Jay, and obtained his reluctant consent to quit the Supreme Court Bench and make the campaign. At a great meeting in New York City, held on February 13, 1792, John Jay was nominated by acclamation. Judge Yates appeared and announced his support, thereby quieting all rumors; the other supposed recalcitrants pledged their aid. It was a love feast, and Hamilton breathed easier.

Meanwhile the anti-Federalists, or Republicans, as they now preferred to be called, had their own difficulties. The campaign to ignore Clinton and to give the nomination to Burr went on with unabated vigor. A great many good Republicans, notably in New York City, considered Burr the stronger candidate. The regular forces girded their loins and Clinton used the great power of his patronage. On February 15, 1792, the Republicans met, the hall was packed with Clinton supporters, and the Governor was nominated.

In spite of these regular nominations, however, the politicians of both parties were disturbed. The sentiment for Burr had not subsided. On February 27, 1792, an open letter appeared in the Albany *Gazette,* under the pseudonym of " Plain Farmer," urging

Burr's name on the moderates of both parties because of his superior qualifications and because " he did not belong to either party." [12]

Burr, from Philadelphia, took stock. His friends in New York, the little band of devoted followers, whom already he was building up into a smooth, efficient machine, had engineered the excitement under his able, if secret, leadership. He had good cause to be satisfied with the results. He had thrown a considerable scare into the old-line politicians. It is not to be believed that he actually desired the nomination at this particular time. It would have been premature. There was much spade-work still to be done. But he had, without showing his hand, proved his power. With Hamilton there would be no compromise; nothing but bitter feud. But Clinton sought him out, as the event showed, and offered satisfactory terms for his withdrawal. A third party candidacy would have been fatal to Clinton's chances.

Accordingly, on March 15, 1792, Burr announced through the newspapers that he was not a candidate for the office, and the campaign was on between Clinton and Jay.

4. BURR DECIDES AN ELECTION

The election was warmly contested and exceedingly close. When the ballots were all in, the result was still in doubt. By law the votes had to be canvassed by a joint committee of the two branches of the Legislature — six Senators and six Assemblymen. The ballots were required to be delivered to the Sheriffs of the respective counties, who were to place them in boxes, seal and deliver them to the Secretary of State. He in turn delivered them on the second Tuesday in May to the Board of Canvassers, who thereupon broke the seals, counted the votes and announced the results. Their decision, declared the law, was to be binding and conclusive.

Excitement grew more and more tense as the canvassing date approached. There were rumors of irregularities, of a determination to seat George Clinton in the gubernatorial chair by fair means or foul. The majority of the committee were Republican in politics and Clinton's personal friends and henchmen.

Nor were the rumors entirely false. When the ballots were duly opened, it was discovered that John Jay, if all the ballots were declared valid, had been elected by a majority of almost 400 votes. But at once the Republicans on the Board of Canvassers discovered irregularities in the votes that had been delivered to them from the counties of Otsego, Clinton, and Tioga, all from the upper portions of the State.

The irregularities were of a highly technical nature, not impugning in any way the honesty or probity of the balloting in the three suspect counties, nor the integrity of the officials who had handled the votes. But, claimed the majority of the Board, the exact letter of the law had not been complied with, and therefore the entire votes of the counties must be rejected. Tioga had given a substantial majority to Jay; the votes of the other two counties were approximately even. If all three were rejected, Clinton was elected by a vote of 8,440 to 8,332. If accepted, Jay was the next Governor.

The minority of Federalists, however, raised such a clamor that the dominant faction hesitated to dispose of the matter thus summarily, and it was finally agreed to obtain the opinion of eminent lawyers for their guidance. The lawyers chosen were Aaron Burr and Rufus King, both United States Senators.

The two Senators conferred, and found that they, too, disagreed, each following the bent of his political convictions. Burr thereupon proposed that they should decline to announce any public decision, but King refused and forthwith sent this opinion in writing to the Board. It was to the effect that the ballots of the disputed counties be declared valid. Whereupon Burr promptly forwarded *his* opinion that the ballots of Tioga and Otsego were void, and concurring with King only insofar as Clinton County was concerned.

Which left the Canvassers pretty much where they had been before. Yet, with a fine disregard of the proprieties, they proceeded to reject the votes of *all* of the counties, including Clinton, by a strictly partisan vote of 7 to 4, and George Clinton was declared elected.

At once the State was swept by a flame of excitement. The Federalists shouted to the heavens that Jay had been deliberately cheated out of the election, that the Canvassers had been corrupt and partisan; they held public meetings, and denounced Clinton as a usurper. Civil war even threatened. But Jay remained calm and opposed all violent measures, much to the disgruntlement of the hotheads in his party. Instead, an appeal was taken to the Legislature as a whole from the acts of its Committee.

On November 6th, the Legislature met, and on November 21st, it took up the matter of the disputed canvass. The majority of the Board presented their case in a document drawn for them by Burr, actively enlisted in Clinton's behalf. He now, as a special pleader, even defended the action of the Board in rejecting the vote from Clinton County, though he had before, as an allegedly impartial arbitrator, declared it to be valid.

The Legislature, by a vote of 35 to 22, dividing along familiar lines, found that the majority of the Canvassers had not been " guilty of mal or corrupt conduct in the execution of the trust reposed in them by law," and that, according to the statute, the judgment of the committee " shall in all cases be binding and conclusive," and hence not to be set aside by the Legislature.[13] The controversy was ended, and George Clinton was Governor.

The Legislature had evaded the fundamental issues, but the historian is not permitted to do so, or to overlook Burr's part in the transaction. These issues must accordingly be examined.

In Otsego County, the commission of Richard R. Smith, the Sheriff, had expired on February 18, 1792. His successor, Benjamin Gilbert, though appointed on March 30th, did not actually qualify into office until May 11th. On May 3rd, however, the ballots of the county had already been delivered to the old Sheriff, Smith, and by him turned over to the Secretary of State. The point at issue was whether such a delivery was within the meaning of the statute, which provided that the " Sheriff of the County " deliver the ballot-boxes. In other words, was Smith still Sheriff, or had he been superseded by Gilbert?

Rufus King maintained that Smith was the Sheriff *de facto* until the new incumbent qualified; that it was ridiculous to assume that the non-action or delay of the Council of Appointment in filling the vacant office could void the duly deposited ballots of an entire county. Burr took the opposite view in a long and closely woven argument that is a masterpiece of casuistry and technical legal learning. He declared that the law was specific and allowed for no leeway; that in England a statute was required to permit sheriffs to hold over pending the appointment of a successor, and he cited this as proof positive that at common law such a right did not exist. Inasmuch as the common law obtained in New York, and as no such statute was on the books, it followed that Smith was no longer Sheriff at the time he delivered the ballot-boxes. Burr also made much of the fact that the old Sheriff, Smith, had already another public office, and hence would be in the awkward position of holding two incompatible public offices at once.[14]

His argument limps in several respects. In the first place, he erred in his assumption that the existence of an English statute presupposed that the original common law had been necessarily to the contrary. There were then, and are now, many statutes on the books, both in England and the United States, that are merely reaffirmations of the old common law. Furthermore, the doctrine of hold-overs in office, pending the election or qualification of a successor, was even then thoroughly established by precedents for ministerial duties. The delivery of ballot-boxes is purely ministerial in function. Rufus King's argument, however, while sound and correct in its assumptions, was inferior to that of Burr in the marshaling of data and precedents, in the skill and plausibility with which they were advanced.

In the case of Tioga, the pivotal county, it appeared that the Sheriff " delivered the box containing the ballots to B. Hovey, his special deputy, who set out, was taken sick on his journey, and delivered the box to H. Thompson, his clerk, who delivered it into the Secretary's office." [15]

King was doubtful about this as a legal delivery, but, taking into consideration that " the election law is intended to render effectual the constitutional right of suffrage . . . it may be reasonably doubtful whether the canvassers are obliged to reject the votes of Tioga." A weak, ineffectual opinion that was bludgeoned down by Burr's ringing assertion that " the ballots of this county cannot, by any fiction or construction, be said to have been delivered *by the sheriff.*" [16]

But there *were* precedents for such a redelegation of power by a sheriff's deputy, which, unfortunately, King had failed to discover. The English case of Parker *vs* Kett, 1 Salkeld 95, had so ruled, and later, in New York, the State Supreme Court was to follow the English decision.[17]

In Clinton County, the Sheriff entrusted the box to his servant for delivery, making him a deputy by *parole* for the occasion. Both King and Burr concurred in their original opinions that such a designation was proper.

The outcry continued, and both parties busied themselves in obtaining the opinions of other eminent lawyers to back up the legal arguments of their respective champions. It is hardly necessary to say that both were eminently successful in finding the necessary concurrences. To King's opinion were added those of Robert Troup, Cornelius J. Bogart, Thomas Cooper and others, chiefly from New York.

Burr bestirred himself actively in his own behalf. His reputation as a lawyer and to some extent his political fortunes were at stake. He spread his net wide over the legal luminaries of the nation.

" This business has become of considerable personal Importance to me," he wrote his brother-in-law, Tapping Reeve, " & must therefore command a little of your attention." He had also enlisted the services of another relative, Pierpont Edwards, who had agreed to obtain signatures of approval from a half-dozen leading members of the Connecticut Bar. Reeve was to urge the matter on Trumbull, Bradley and Sedgwick, all likewise of Connecticut.[18]

He also solicited and obtained the support of Edmund Randolph of Virginia, of Jonathan Sergeant of Philadelphia, who had been Treasurer of Princeton in Burr's college days. He went as far afield as Paris, where James Monroe, Minister Plenipotentiary, was called upon for assistance. He enclosed the necessary papers and opinions, declaring that "those decisions, and of course my opinion, have been the subject of much animadversion and declamation; they were in short attacked with every thing but reason and law. The discontent of the friends of Mr. Jay or rather of the enemies of Mr. Clinton became clamorous and was expressed by resolutions and addresses of tumultuous meetings." In order to achieve public approbation of his course, Burr proceeded, "the persuasion must principally be wrought by the authority of great Names (for it cannot be expected that the public will reason on law points)." And if possible, Monroe was, besides rendering his own opinion, to request those of Patrick Henry and others in the South, charging all expenses to Burr.[19]

In short, Aaron Burr threw himself into the matter with every weapon and every resource that his powerful and agile mind could discover. Though, as he wrote Jacob De Lamater, "it would, indeed, be the extreme of weakness in me to expect friendship from Mr. Clinton. I have too many reasons to believe that he regards me with jealousy and malevolence."[20]

This was, in a measure, true. For Clinton could not but view with considerable uneasiness the rising star of Burr. Accordingly, he determined to repeat the tactics that he had employed with Judge Yates. In an access of seeming gratitude for the timely aid of the youthful Senator, he nominated him to the Council of Appointment on October 2, 1792, as a Judge of the State Supreme Court. Burr saw through the scheme and promptly declined the honor. He had no intention of being shelved.

Chapter X

INTERMEDIATE YEARS

1. Hamilton Calls Names

ARON BURR had, by the latter part of 1792, definitely committed himself to the Republican ranks. He had, earlier in the year, been seriously considered as a candidate by the Federalists in New York; he had held aloof from active assistance or persuasion during the campaign; his voting in the Senate had been fairly non-partisan in character; but, with the advent of the disputed election, there was no longer any question as to where he stood. The Federalists were infuriated at his decisive part in the transaction, Hamilton considered him now as his most dangerous antagonist in state and national affairs, and the repercussions spread far and wide. He was a national figure, and the Republicans of other States observed the youthful Senator with a new and more thoughtful interest. They consulted with him, and listened with respect to his opinions in the councils of the still somewhat inchoate party.

An influential Pennsylvania Republican urged that " your friends everywhere look to you to take an active part in removing the monarchical rubbish of our government. It is time to speak out, or we are undone. The association in Boston augurs well. Do feed it by a letter to Mr. Samuel Adams. My letter will serve to introduce you to him, if enclosed in one from yourself." [1]

The second national election for the Presidency of the United States was then in full swing. The first had been attended with practical unanimity. George Washington had been made President by acclamation; John Adams Vice-President by an overwhelming majority.

But now, in 1792, parties had definitely emerged. There was still no opposition to the reelection of Washington, though the magic of his name had faded considerably. There were a good many underground rumblings at his seeming monarchical tendencies, and especially at the strangle-grip that Hamilton held upon his Administration.

Nevertheless the Republicans determined to move cautiously. They attacked a more vulnerable figure — John Adams, the Vice-

President. A serious effort was put forth to unseat him. The strategy was good. Washington must necessarily resign his office at the end of the term — he had already expressed his disinclination for further public honors — and the Vice-President would be the logical heir to the vacant throne.

Three men were mentioned by the Republicans as candidates: Governor George Clinton of New York, Thomas Jefferson, and Aaron Burr.

Burr went quietly to work to build his political fences — chiefly in Massachusetts, Connecticut, Pennsylvania and South Carolina. In New York he was already a power. It was not that he expected to achieve the Vice-Presidency in this particular election, but he took the professional, long view. There would be other campaigns and other years, and an organization was not built in a day. Already, the year before, he had been secretly busy in Massachusetts.[2]

But quietly and discreetly as he moved, the Federalists got wind of his doings and became alarmed. Their consternation was greater, it seems, than over the avowed candidacy of George Clinton. Rufus King sounded the tocsin. " If the enemies of the government are secret and united," he warned Hamilton, " we shall lose Mr. Adams. Burr is industrious in his canvass, and his object is well understood by our Antis. Mr. Edwards is to make interest for him in Connecticut, and Mr. Dallas, who is here and quite in the circle of the Governor and the party, informs us that Mr. Burr will be supported as Vice-President in Pennsylvania. Should Jefferson and his friends unite in the project, the votes of Mr. A. may be so reduced, that though more numerous than those of any other person, he may decline the office." [3]

Hamilton literally frothed at the mouth on the receipt of this startling information. He lost his head completely. Wherever he turned, the smiling, secretive figure of Burr was looming more and more in his path to thwart his plans, personal, private and political. They had begun as rivals at the New York Bar, and Burr was his only competitor to preeminence in that field. Then Burr had committed the unforgivable crime — he had wrested the senatorship from Hamilton's father-in-law. The next step had been to sow discord in the ranks of Hamilton's own party, and to create the first serious threat to his leadership in the State. It had been only by herculean efforts that the thrust had been averted. Burr had countered then by doing more than anyone else to wrench the governorship from Hamilton's candidate when Jay's election had seemed assured. In the Senate he had fought Hamilton's measures

ALEXANDER HAMILTON

From a portrait by John Trumbull (?)

RICHMOND HILL MANSION

From a wash drawing

in season and out. And now he was attacking the basis of government itself.

There is no doubt that Hamilton's obsession concerning Burr was definitely pathologic in nature. He differed profoundly with others — notably Jefferson — and the roots of disagreement were far more fundamental than his differences with Burr; yet always the fight was waged along strictly political, if vigorous lines. With Burr, however, it partook of a completely personal and vindictive nature. There was no attempt to attack Burr's political creed or acts, but he did attack, with a veritable frenzy of vituperation and venomous malice, his private honor, his integrity, his scrupulousness, his ambition.

There has been a tendency to seek the hidden reason for Hamilton's secret hate in some rivalry in love between the two men, a rivalry in which Hamilton had been supplanted or defeated. Both men were notably gallant in love, and, at first blush, the theory might seem a colorable one. But it must be remembered that at this period Theodosia Prevost Burr was still alive, and there is absolutely no evidence that, during her lifetime, Burr was anything but a tender, devoted and faithful husband. This aside from the consideration that the hypothesis is based on but the merest wisps of rumors, such as have always gravitated irresistibly around the enigmatic personality of Burr. It *is* possible that somehow, somewhere, Burr had offended Hamilton in his tenderest spot — his vanity.

Hamilton sent a copy of King's letter forthwith to President Washington, with a gloss that was a model of moderation. " Mr. Burr was here [in Philadelphia] about ten days since and every body wondered what was meant by it," he commented. " It seems to be explained. Yet I am not certain that this is any thing more than a diversion in favour of Mr. Clinton." 4

When he wrote to others, however, he cast all moderation to the winds. He poured out a torrent of letters, scattering them broadcast with reckless profusion, endlessly repeating his charges, hammering them home, seeking everywhere to undermine confidence in the hated enemy. It is important to note that these communications were all addressed to fellow Federalists, who ordinarily should not have required such extensive propaganda. Is it possible that the real underlying motive for Hamilton's hatred was the uneasy fear that Burr, who had numerous personal friends in the Federalist ranks, might eventually supplant him in the councils of his own party?

Hamilton used King's letter as the text for his sermon. To an unnamed Federalist he wrote: "Mr. Clinton's success I should think very unfortunate; I am not for trusting the government too much in the hands of its enemies. But still, Mr. C. is a man of property, and in private life, as far as I know, of probity. I fear the other gentleman [Burr] is unprincipled, both as a public and a private man . . . He is determined, as I conceive, to make his way to be the head of the popular party, and to climbe *per fas aut nefas* to the highest honors of the State, and as much higher as circumstances may permit. Embarrassed, as I understand, in his circumstances, with an extravagant family, bold, enterprising, and intriguing, I am mistaken if it be not his object to play a game of confusion, and I feel it a religious duty to oppose his career." *Religious duty,* indeed!

" I have hitherto scrupulously refrained from interference in elections," he went on with a wild disregard for the truth, " but the occasion is, in my opinion, of sufficient importance to warrant, in this instance, a departure from that rule. I, therefore, commit my opinion to you without scruple; but in perfect confidence. I pledge my character for discernment, that it is incumbent upon every good man to resist the present design." [5]

Strange language, even for those times, certain to make a deep-seated impression on men who perhaps did not know Burr personally, who looked upon Hamilton as their leader, and who knew that he was intimately acquainted with the object of his opprobrium. Loose language, too, for there is nothing definite, nothing tangible about the repeated accusations; and an examination of Burr's career, both public and private, during this period, discloses nothing on which these charges could possibly be hung.

As the letters flowed from Hamilton's facile pen he grew more and more unrestrained. To another Federal politician he repeated almost verbatim the old charges, and proceeded further: " Mr. Burr's integrity as an individual is not unimpeached. As a public man, he is one of the worst sort — a friend to nothing but as it suits his interest and ambition . . . 'Tis evident that he aims at putting himself at the head of what he calls the ' popular party,' as affording the best tools for an ambitious man to work with. Secretly turning liberty into ridicule, he knows as well as most men how to make use of that name. In a word, if we have an embryo Caesar in the United States, 'tis Burr." [6]

To Steele, however, who, as a member of Congress, was well acquainted with the victim, he writes far more cautiously, and with an inconsistency that is deliberate. " My opinion of Mr. Burr is yet to form — " he says surprisingly, " but, according to the present state of it, he is a man whose only political principle is to *mount at all events,* to the highest legal honors." Moreover, he insinuates, " imputations, not favorable to his integrity as a man, rest upon him, but I do not vouch for their authenticity." [7] This, almost a month after he had pledged his character and reputation for discernment to the authenticity of identical statements!

To King, his friend and lieutenant, he lets the cat out of the bag. He thanks him for his warning anent Burr's activities, and promises complacently that " a good use will be made of it in this State," and in all the States to the south of New York.[8]

Yet outwardly, Hamilton was seemingly on the friendliest of personal terms with Burr. And if Burr knew of the pernicious sniping against his character, he, too, made no sign. But slowly, with the inevitability of a Greek tragedy, the mills of the gods were grinding toward a predestined end.

2. Withdrawal and a Bargain

An unpublished letter from John Beckley, a Pennsylvania politician, addressed to James Madison, dispels somewhat the fog that has hitherto seemed to shroud the inner mechanism of the Republican strategy in the election of 1792 and Burr's part therein. He tells of " a meeting which was had last evening between Melancton Smith, on the part of the republican interest of N. Y. (specially deputed) and the principal movers of the same interest here [Pennsylvania], to conclude *finally* & *definitively* as to the choice of a V. P. — the result of which was, unanimously, to exert every endeavor for Mr. Clinton, & to drop all thought of Mr. Burr." And, he proceeds, Colonel Burr had assured him " that he would cheerfully support the measure of removing Mr. A[dams] & lend every aid in his power to C[linton]'s election." [9]

Burr was as good as his word. Washington received a unanimous vote. Against him there was no open opposition. But John Adams met with difficulties. He received 77 out of a possible 132 ballots. George Clinton, with the Republican caucus behind him, obtained 50 — the second votes of New York, Virginia, North Carolina and Georgia. Kentucky cast 10 for Jefferson, and Aaron Burr received a solitary salute from South Carolina. New York, chiefly because of Clinton and Burr, had marched with the agrarian South.

It is important to remember the outcome of that caucus in Philadelphia at which Burr was dropped in favor of Clinton. It is quite plausible to assume that certain assurances had been made

to him in return for his withdrawal. At any rate, Burr was to claim
after the Presidential election of 1796 that there had been such a
bargain, and that the South had violated its share in the agreement.

3. RICHMOND HILL AND THE ARTS

Hamilton had been correct in at least one of his many accusations against Burr. He *was* extravagant. He loved to live well, to
entertain lavishly and with abounding hospitality; he sought out
young, struggling talent, and helped it with unobtrusive generosity along the road to recognition and fortune.

Abraham Mortier, Commissary to the King, had leased in 1768
from Trinity Church for a period of 99 years a little hill that overlooked the Hudson in what was then the outskirts of New York
City. Today it is approximately the area enclosed by Clinton
Place, Varick and Van Dam Streets. On this plot of farm land he
built himself a stately mansion with wide porticoes, noble rooms,
and an unequaled vista of rolling country, lordly river, and pleasant meadows. The house and its little eminence became known as
Richmond Hill, and its fame spread far and wide.

During the Revolutionary War General Washington had used
it as his Headquarters, and Burr had then obtained his first
glimpse of it. John Adams next occupied the house while Vice-
President. His remarkable wife, Abigail, grew lyric over its
charms. "The house in which we reside," she exclaimed to her
sister, "is situated upon a hill, the avenue to which is interspersed with forest trees. . . . In front of the house, the noble
Hudson rolls his majestic waves, bearing upon his bosom innumerable small vessels." And, beyond, "rises to our view the
fertile country of the Jerseys, covered with a golden harvest, and
pouring forth plenty like the cornucopia of Ceres. On the right
hand, an extensive plain presents us with a view of fields covered
with verdure, and pastures full of cattle. On the left, the city
opens upon us, intercepted only by clumps of trees, and some
rising ground, which serves to heighten the beauty of the scene,
by appearing to conceal a part. In the back ground, is a large
flower-garden, enclosed with a hedge and some very handsome
trees. On one side of it, a grove of pines and oaks fit for contemplation." [10]

And to a friend she rhapsodized: "I have a situation here,
which, for natural beauty may vie with the most delicious spot I
ever saw." [11] When the Adamses were forced to move to Philadelphia in 1790, on the transfer of the Capital to that city, she

mourned sadly, thinking of departed glories, that " Bush Hill is a very beautiful place. But the grand and sublime I left at Richmond Hill." [12]

This was Burr's opportunity to gain possession of the coveted Paradise. He took over the lease in 1791, furnished the great mansion with splendid furnishings, landscaped the grounds, widened and dammed Minetta Brook into a pond, and proceeded to entertain visiting celebrities in princely style. No distinguished Frenchman, exile or traveler from his native land, but spent hospitable weeks as his guest. Tallyrand, Volney, Louis Philippe, Jerome Napoleon, and others remembered with pleasure Richmond Hill and its cultured host. His library was always stocked with the very latest imported volumes. He gave instructions to a London bookseller to forward him at once the very best of the newer publications. He received Gibbon's monumental work, the writings of William Godwin, of Mary Wollstonecraft, of Jeremy Bentham, volumes on history, economics, and military tactics.

As a patron of literature and the arts he was famous in his day. John Davis was gratefully to record that Burr, " cultivating literature himself, loved to encourage it in others; and . . . with a condescension little known to patrons, sought out my obscure lodgings in a populous city, and invited me to his house." [13]

The famous painter, John Vanderlyn, owed far more to Burr's far-seeing and generous patronage. Vanderlyn, born in Kingston, New York, had come to Philadelphia to study art under the tutelage of the master, Gilbert Stuart. Lacking funds to continue, he returned to Kingston, where he made some striking copies of certain portraits that Stuart had lent him. One of these was a portrait of Burr. This was sold to Peter Van Gaasbeck, of Kingston, a member of Congress and a friend of Burr. Burr learned of the young painter and expressed a desire to assist him.

He wrote Van Gaasbeck: " I understand that a young Mr. Van De Lyne, who lived a short time with Stewart the Painter, left him for want of the means of suitable support.

" You must persuade him to allow me to remove that objection. If he was personally acquainted with me, he would, I am confident, accept this proposal without hesitation. I commit to you then to overcome any delicacy which he may feel on this head. I shall never imagine that I have conferred on him the slightest obligation, but shall be infinitely flattered by an opportunity of rescuing Genius from obscurity.

" He may draw on J. B. Prevost, New York for any sum which may be necessary for his outfit. And on his arrival in this City, where Mr. Stewart now lives, he will find a letter from me, addressed to him (Mr. Van De Lyne) pointing out the channel of his future supplies, the source of which will never be known except to himself . . . This arrangement is intended to continue as long as it may be necessary for Mr. V. D. L. to cultivate his genius to highest point of Perfection." [14]

Burr made this generous gesture at a time when he was head over heels in debt, when he owed substantial sums of money to the very Peter Van Gaasbeck whose aid he was enlisting on behalf of Vanderlyn. In an accompanying letter to Van Gaasbeck he replies to an evident request for funds that " something might perhaps be devised to fulfil in part your wishes. I am still however equally distressed, as when I last wrote you, in my finances . . . I have experienced . . . disappointments to a very distressing degree, and it will be six months before I shall be relieved, unless some unknown good fortune intervenes." But Burr's was an essentially buoyant and optimistic nature. He continues: " It will however give you pleasure to learn (& therefore only I mention it) that if I weather the storm, of which there can be no doubt I shall be as rich as a reasonable man need wish. I mention my distresses by way of apology for myself, in not having answered your letters in a more *effectual* and *satisfactory* way. And I mention my prospects to console you for the disappointment & to keep up your hopes & spirits." [15]

Nevertheless he fulfilled his assumed obligations to the young painter with a princely munificence. He had Vanderlyn study under Stuart for a year. When the master acknowledged that " you are wasting your time with me; now you are ready for Europe . . . I have taken you as far as I can," Burr brought him to Richmond Hill for the spring and summer of 1796, and diligently proceeded to advertise him as a splendid portraitist. He gained him many commissions; among them the portraits of Albert Gallatin, M. Adet, the French minister, and others. Not to speak of Burr himself and little Theodosia.

In September he sent Vanderlyn to France to continue his studies, with a liberal supply of money and letters of introduction. In two years he was back, again under Burr's tutelage. As long as Burr lived, the painter was to find in him a friend, a patron, an ardent admirer. Later, much later, when Vanderlyn had become famous, and achieved worldwide recognition, he was to remember gratefully the unselfish aid of Aaron Burr.[16]

4. FINANCIAL LEGERDEMAIN

It is obvious that Aaron Burr's expenses were enormous. Besides Richmond Hill, which he treated as a country estate, he retained his town house at No. 30 Partition Street. The upkeep of both establishments, the lavish entertainment, the largesse and patronage, the education of his daughter, Theodosia, imposed a drain on his resources with which not even his tremendous earning capacity could keep pace.

He was always in debt, always borrowing, always having notes falling due without the wherewithal to make payment. Throughout his life finances were to be a monotonous refrain, coloring his thoughts, engrossing his energies, weaving a pattern that was eventually to enmesh him in an impenetrable web. Yet never for a moment did he consider the possibility of reducing his expenses, of living on a less lavish scale. In the darkest days of his exile, he was to spend the last poor *sou* he possessed for some trinket that had engaged his fancy, and which, he thought, might brighten the face of far-off daughter or grandson. Then he would tighten his belt cheerfully against hunger and cold. It was something inherent, ineradicable.

As far back as 1791 there are constant references in his letters to notes of hand. He borrowed money from his friends, from usurers at exorbitant rates of interest. He paid as high as 15 percent per annum. His friends endorsed for him. And they were to rue their kindness; not because Burr was dishonest, but because his affairs had become so involved that, struggle as he might, he could never escape the nightmare multiplication of overdue notes. He had reared for himself a veritable inverted pyramid of paper, and the structure was toppling.

He borrowed from his clients too, because he could not help it. He and Hamilton had acted as joint counsel for Le Guen in a very complicated mercantile litigation against Gouverneur and Kemble. After several years' tortuous progress through the courts, the matter ended in victory for their client. On June 2, 1795, Burr received a fee of $2500 for his services, of which $1750 had already been assigned to two of his creditors. Both Hamilton and Burr borrowed heavily from Le Guen. Burr obtained several loans, one of which, for some $6000, was to end in a dispute over alleged repayments, and was to drag acrimoniously for almost thirty years. Marinus Willett, General John Lamb, Le Guen, Pierpont Edwards, Colonel John Nicholson, Peter Van Gaasbeck — all friends

— appear again and again in his correspondence as endorsers who are involved in his whirlwind of extensions and renewals.

" When I took your last endorsement payable at *twenty* Days," Burr mournfully confessed to the disgusted Marinus Willett, " I expected that the Sale of my property would have been completed before the expiration of that time. It has happened otherwise and the Note becomes payable to day which obliges me to ask for a further endorsement." [17]

By 1796 the clouds were gathering ominously. " As to pecuniary matters," he informed a friend, involved with him by the usual endorsements, " I am very sorry both for your sake and my own that I can say nothing agreeable. I have met with the most vexatious and ruinous disappointments, and it is I assure you with extreme difficulty that I keep along." [18]

And in 1797 the storm was crashing about his ears. Robert Troup, his old-time personal friend and present bitter political enemy, was writing to Rufus King, now Minister to England, that Burr has " during the present session paid little or no attention to his duties in the Senate. It is whispered that his money engagements are embarrassing to him." [19] The matter had become common knowledge.

It was General Lamb who bore the brunt of Burr's financial legerdemain. The correspondence between them is staggering in its proportions. Their transactions commenced back in 1795. They began modestly with a direct loan of $3500 and by the end of 1796 had reached a total of over $22,000, of which approximately $5000 was still unpaid. Besides which, Lamb was endorsed on a considerable amount in outstanding notes.[20]

By 1797 his affairs with General Lamb had reached the desperate stage. On December 9, 1796, Burr asked for " the other 2000 before three oclock "; on December 10th, " it is with reluctance that I ask your endorsement to the enclosed "; on December 17th, he had reduced certain notes by $2400 and was sending the renewal notes along for endorsement — this time without reluctance. Day by day the notes passed back and forth in bewildering succession.

Finally, in desperation, Burr offered to sell all his possessions at Richmond Hill to Lamb in settlement of their mutual accounts, and Lamb agreed. But another creditor pressed, and Lamb, on March 29, 1797, wrote magnanimously, " However desireable it might be to me to have your house on the terms you proposed, Yet if it will as you say enable you to settle with the holder of one of your Notes, I consent to release you from your offer. At the same time I must intreat you to provide in some other Way for the balance due me." [21]

And, on June 17, 1797, Burr did sell to Sir John Temple, English Consul General, " all and singular the household goods furniture and things mentioned and expressed in the Inventory or Schedule hereto annexed, and now remaining in the Mansion house and on the Farm and piece of Land belonging to the said Aaron Burr." [22]

The glories of Richmond Hill had departed. The place in which Theodosia Prevost Burr had spent the last years of her life, the graceful mansion over whose festal board young Theodosia had presided with dignity and astonishing aplomb, the walls that had echoed to laughter and brilliant conversation and the tread of a distinguished company, were now vacant and bare — stripped ruthlessly of mahogany armchairs, Turkey carpets, mirrors, satin haircloth sofas, Venetian blinds, fluted-post bedsteads, Dutch liquor cases — all the luxurious furnishings in which Burr had taken such pride — sold now for a pittance of $3,500 to pay a single debt!

Nor did the empty walls of Richmond Hill last much longer. They were pawns in the desperate game he was playing with creditors. Later Burr was compelled to mortgage his leasehold, and much later, after his trial for treason, John Jacob Astor, with his hawklike eye for valuable land, took advantage of Burr's necessitous condition, and purchased the leasehold, subject to the mortgage, for the sum of $32,000. It was this parcel that Astor was to cut up into lots, to be leased out at heavy rentals, and which contributed mightily to the foundation of his millions. [23]

All these were but drops in the endless ocean of Burr's tangled finances. He would sit at home whole days in anxious expectation of promised funds, heartsick and weary. When he could write Lamb that " you perceive by the enclosed, that I am nearly through with your endorsements . . . In truth I could not see you with pleasure while these matters were unsettled," [24] his volatile spirits rebounded.

But these canceled endorsements were evidently of only a single series of notes, because in 1798 Lamb was calling on him frantically for immediate aid. The creditors had tired of pressing Burr and were now concentrating on Lamb. Judgments had been obtained and executions were impending. Burr's property — whatever could be found — had also been seized.

Burr, then in Albany, felt the matter keenly. " I will return to N York," he advised by post, " and superintend the Sales of my own property untill you shall be exonerated. That your peace of mind should be disturbed or personal safety endangered by an act of friendship and generosity to me is the most humiliating event of my life — and I shall be most wretched untill I hear the Course the business has taken. Though a writ of error can at any time be procured in an hour, yet the possibility of any inattention by which you might be for a moment exposed to indignity from people who would delight in torturing me through you, leave me no rest or peace." [25]

And finally, on May 6, 1799, General Lamb was actually arrested by Richard Harison, as counsel for impatient creditors, on executions primarily against Burr. Burr went frantically to work to help the innocent victim of his own difficulties. He proffered himself and David Gelston as bail; Harison insisted on additional security — certainly Burr's signature was no inducement — and suggested either Colonel Rutgers or Alexander Robertson.[26] Burr managed to satisfy Harison, and Lamb was released, to disappear out of the records of Burr's finances.

Eventually the whole precarious structure of notes and mortgages was to come toppling about Burr's ears, and was to be primarily responsible for that last desperate venture on the Washita and at Blennerhassett's Island which led to ruin and disgrace.

5. EXPERIMENT IN EDUCATION

Despite his financial difficulties, however, and despite his preoccupation with law and politics, Burr found time to supervise with meticulous exactitude the rearing and education of his little daughter, Theodosia.

He had very definite ideas on the subject of education, especially of female education. He resented the bland assumption of the day that women were inferior to men in mental capacity, and he was determined that *his* daughter should prove to the world that, given equal opportunities, the female brain was equally competent with the male. It became an obsession with him, almost the guiding passion of his life. He had married Theodosia Prevost because of her intellectual endowment.

" It was a knowledge of your mind," he told her in later years, " which first inspired me with a respect for that of your sex, and with some regret, I confess, that the ideas which you have often heard me express in favour of female intellectual powers are founded on what I have imagined, more than what I have seen, except in you. I have endeavoured to trace the causes of this *rare* display of genius in women, and find them in the errors of education, of prejudice, and of habit . . . Boys and girls are generally educated much in the same way till they are eight or nine years of age, and it is admitted that girls make at least equal progress with the boys; generally, indeed, they make better. Why, then, has it never been thought worth the attempt to discover, by fair experiment, the particular age at which the male superiority becomes so evident? " [27]

Burr determined to make the experiment. Little Theo was to be his laboratory guinea-pig, his shining example. The blood of many educators flowed in his veins. And he had just finished reading, with a mounting excitement, a certain volume he had recently received from England.

" You have heard me speak of a Miss Woolstonecraft [*sic*]," he hastened to inform his wife, " who has written something on the French revolution; she has also written a book entitled ' Vindication of the rights of Woman.' I had heard it spoken of with a coldness little calculated to excite attention; but as I read with avidity and prepossession every thing written by a lady, I made haste to procure it, and spent the last night, almost the whole of it, in reading it. Be assured that your sex has in *her* an able advocate. It is, in my opinion, a work of genius. She has successfully adopted the style of Rousseau's Emilius; and her comment on that work, especially what relates to female education, contains more good sense than all the other criticisms upon him which I have seen put together." Astonished, he inquires, " is it owing to ignorance or prejudice that I have not yet met a single person who had discovered or would allow the merit of this work? " [28]

But then, Aaron Burr possessed a singularly flexible and open mind, and new ideas were eagerly welcomed. Besides Mary Wollstonecraft, there had been Jeremy Bentham, and others, including Gibbon, whose monumental work had just been published, of whom he was perhaps the first in America to appreciate the importance.

So, with the theoretic background of the author of the " Vindication," of Rousseau, of Chesterfield, of Godwin and Voltaire, he set about molding in earnest the genius of little Theo.

The course of training that he imposed was rigorous and exacting. It was Spartan in its insistence on regularity and self-discipline, yet it was compounded with ideas and methods that were far ahead of his time.

At the age of eight, he was insisting, " I hope Theo. will learn to ride on horseback. Two or three hours a day at French and arithmetic will not injure her. Be careful of green apples, etc." [29] And Mrs. Burr was complaining in return that Theo had too many avocations to make much progress. Nevertheless " she begins to cipher " and " I take care she never omits learning her French lesson." But, she continues, " I don't think the dancing lessons do much good while the weather is so warm," and " as to music, upon the footing it now is she can never make progress, though she sacrifices two thirds of her time to it. Tis a serious check to her other requirements." [30]

However, a little later she is able to report with some pride that " Theo is much better; she writes and ciphers from five in the morning until eight, and also the same hours in the evening," and that " she makes amazing progress with figures." [31]

Nor was the elder Theodosia herself exempt from her husband's educational drive. " To render any reading really amusing or in any degree instructive, you should never pass a word you do not understand, or the name of a person or place of which you have not some knowledge. . . . Lempriere's Dictionary is that of which I spoke to you. Purchase also Macbeau's; this last is appropriate to ancient theocracy, fiction and geography, both of them will be useful in reading Gibbon, and still more so in reading ancient authors, or of any period of ancient history." Gibbon, Plutarch's Lives, Herodotus, Paley's Philosophy of Natural History — all these he recommends. " The reading of one book will invite you to another," he continues. " I cannot, I fear, at this distance, advise you successfully; much less can I hope to assist you in your reading. . . . I am inclined to dilate on these topics, and upon the effects of reading and study on the mind; but this would require an essay, and I have not time to write a letter." [32]

As for the little girl, her education proceeded apace, in accordance with a preconceived plan. " You may recollect," Burr reminded his wife from his Senatorial duties in Philadelphia, " that I left a memorandum of what Theo was to learn. I hope it has been strictly attended to. Desire Gurney [her tutor] not to attempt to teach her anything about the ' concords.' I will show him how I choose that should be done when I return." Then suddenly he bursts out into a passion of words that give the clue to the driving purpose which not for a moment would he allow to waver. " If I could foresee that Theo would become a mere fashionable woman," he exclaims, " with all the attendant frivolity and vacuity of mind, adorned with whatever grace and allurement, I would earnestly pray God to take her forthwith hence. But I yet hope, by her, to convince the world what neither sex appear to believe — that women have souls! " [33]

This was the man who too often has been portrayed as the heartless gallant, the unthinking seducer of innumerable women, the mere luster after their flesh!

He exhorted the younger Theo as well as the elder. " I received your french english Letter by Major Prevost," he told her. " It is a very good one, but not half long enough . . . How many tunes can you play? and can you play them so that any one except your Master will know one from the other?

" Major Prevost indeed gives me a fine report of you, but in two or three weeks I shall come & see for myself, and I now tell you that I shall expect to see the most accomplished Girl for her years in the whole world. Take Care that I be not disappointed." [34]

By 1793, Theo was ten, and corresponding regularly with her father in Philadelphia. She sent him a fable and a riddle, which, " if the whole performance was your own, which I am inclined to hope and believe, it indicates an improvement in style, in knowledge of French, and in your handwriting. I have therefore not only read it several times, but shown it to several persons with pride and pleasure." [35] The martinet educator was after all a very human father.

He insisted that she keep a journal, in which " you are to note the occurrences of the day as concisely as you can; and, at your pleasure, to add any short reflections or remarks that may arise." For her guidance he enclosed a sample. The sample is well worth quoting entire.

" Learned 230 lines, which finished Horace. Heigh-ho for Terence and the Greek grammar to-morrow.

" Practiced two hours less thirty-five minutes, which I have begged off.

" Hewlett (dancing master) did not come.

" Began Gibbon last evening. I find he requires as much study and attention as Horace; so I shall not rank the reading of *him* among amusements.

" Skated an hour; fell twenty times, and find the advantage of a hard head and

" Ma better — dined with us at table, and is still sitting up and free from pain." [36]

All their lives, father and daughter were to maintain a felicitous bantering in their correspondence. But the sample is memorable for another reason. It outlined a pretty heavy regimen for a child of ten.

His letters continued to be preoccupied with her lessons, her journal, her spelling, the style of her writing, her progress. Even to the very slightest detail. But a new note was creeping into his letters. The cancer was taking its last toll of his tortured wife. She was taking laudanum now, steadily, and soon even that was failing to give relief. Burr was in Philadelphia, attending the session of Congress. He consulted with the famous Dr. Benjamin Rush, with other doctors. He suggested numerous remedies, some with medical sanction, some without, hoping against hope. Mrs. Burr became bedridden; it was an event when she appeared at dinner with the family. Her nights and days were painful beyond bearing. Burr wished to leave his Senatorial duties and rush to her bedside. She forbade it. On May 18, 1794, Theodosia Prevost Burr died, suddenly, with only little Theo at her side.

They had been very happy together, though in the last years the shadow of her invalidism had fallen across their marriage. They had loved, they had admired and respected each other. He had been faithful and tender, and she had adored him. Only after her death, and it was to be long after, did Burr begin those innumerable little affairs of gallantry and mere sexual assuagement which were to become notoriously associated with his name.

6. ASPASIA

Theodosia Burr, the younger, at the age of eleven, had become the sole mistress of the great establishment at Richmond Hill. She had as companion and playmate a French girl of about her own age: Natalie de Lage, the daughter of Admiral de Lage of the French Navy. She had been separated from her mother by the exigencies of the Revolution, and brought to New York by her nurse. Burr gave the child an asylum, and adopted and educated her as his own. He had a veritable passion for adopting and rearing children. Throughout his long life they inhabited his households, and he never distinguished, in the abundance of love and generous dealing that he lavished upon them, between the children of his own blood and those of a strictly legal relation. Natalie de Lage was eventually to marry the son of General Sumter of South Carolina.

Theo made an excellent head to her father's house. She entertained his guests, even during his frequent absences, with a gentle gravity and bearing beyond her years that excited the admiration of the most distinguished. She grew swiftly to remarkable womanhood, the most brilliant of her day. She was learned in the classics, in modern languages, in history, philosophy and the sciences. She danced and sang and played the piano with taste and feeling. She had ranged widely and well in literature, and she could quote for hours from the masterpieces of poetry. Yet she was no bluestocking, no mere pedant; even though Burr was writing in 1797, "and do you regret that you are not also a woman? That you are not numbered in that galaxy of beauty which adorns an assembly-room? Coquetting for admiration and attracting flattery? No. I answer with confidence. You feel you are maturing for solid friendship. The friends you gain you will never lose; and no one, I think, will dare to insult your understanding by such compliments as are most graciously received by too many of your sex." [37]

The testimony of contemporaries and of her extant portraits is overwhelmingly to the contrary. She was beautiful with a proud lift of head and an aristocratic mold of features; wherever she went half the eligible young males of the town sighed fruitlessly after her — and a good many of the older, more substantial men, too. She was beloved equally by women as by men. She was " elegant without ostentation, and learned without pedantry." She danced " with more grace than any young lady of New York." [38] Her wit sparkled and warmed; she possessed her father's airy sense of humor. She was the living proof of the success of Aaron Burr's seemingly repellent system of education. Had he not thrown his great talents and energy into politics he could have become a great educator.

She adored her father, and he worshiped her. Which in itself was a tribute to his methods. It was a love as pure and noble and unselfish as anything in the realm of history, yet it was based on a frank and full understanding between the two. Her faith in him never wavered, even during the darkest days of his career, and in return he bared his soul to her candid gaze. He hid nothing, not even those things that most men wish to hide even from themselves. The Journal of his wanderings in exile, that astounding portrayal of a stripped human being, was written in the plainest language for her eyes alone. It was a bond that the passing years strengthened, and when it was sundered by her tragic death, something snapped in his soul too, never to mend.

" The happiness of my life," he had written, " depends on your exertions; for what else, for whom else do I live? " [39]

Chapter XI

PARTY GROWTH

1. Republican Cockades

IN spite of domestic affliction, of bewildering finances, of educational dogmas, Burr hewed vigorously to the line of his chosen profession — politics.

The Third Congress opened in Philadelphia on December 2, 1793, amidst scenes of domestic passion and foreign muddlements. The French Revolution had been hailed by those of the budding Republican persuasion with ardent sympathy and unexampled enthusiasm. Burr from the very first thought it the beginning of a new era in the history of the world's enlightenment. The Federalists viewed the hysteria, however, with jaundiced eyes. They had triumphed over certain tendencies to radicalism in the United States, and the unfettered forces that rode the Revolution were seemingly oblivious to all settled property rights. The Federalists much preferred the British system, and turned naturally to England as the haven of all sound conservatism. It was to be pro-French against pro-English as much as South against North, agrarian against industrialist.

The shipping interests of New England had built up a flourishing trade with England, and the war which broke out between France and Great Britain in 1793 brought the United States headlong into the welter of European politics. For one thing, American commerce was bound to suffer as a result of the war. For another, the United States was still formally the ally of France, and had guaranteed the independence of the French West Indies, now subject to imminent attack by the English Navy.

Washington desired no war and proclaimed neutrality in the European struggle on April 22, 1793. Meanwhile Citizen Genêt had landed in America as the representative of the Revolutionary French Government. He was without doubt the worst possible diplomat that the French could have accredited to the United States. It was his duty, he thought, to dragoon the laggard country into war immediately on the side of his beloved France, and he proceeded to effect it by the most violent and open propaganda, by vicious attacks on the American government, by incendiary speeches and open appeals to popular passions.

At first he seemed eminently successful. The Republicans received him with open arms and continuous ovations. It turned his head completely. He insulted Washington openly for his stand on neutrality, organized Jacobin clubs, and boasted of his ability to overthrow the existing American government.

Burr had at first welcomed Genêt along with the others. Then disturbing rumors reached him, and he wrote John Nicholson to inquire whether they had any foundation in fact. "We have a rumor here, (very grateful to the Tories)," he said, "that Genet has come to an open rupture with the President — That he has publicly threatened to appeal to the people, that as preparatory to this Step he goes about visiting the Mechanics and the lower orders of people, leaving cards at their houses when they are not at home! And the rumors add that it is in Contemplation of the President and his Ministers to dismiss the French Plenipo." [1]

His information was correct. In August, 1793, Genêt's recall was demanded, and early in 1794 he was removed and his arrest ordered by Robespierre and the Directory. But Genêt had no taste for the guillotine. Instead, he married the daughter of Governor Clinton of New York and settled into the peaceful pursuits of a country gentleman.

Burr took his seat promptly in the opening days of the session. Matters of considerable importance were in the offing. The Senate was pretty closely divided between the adherents of the Administration and the Opposition. Burr was a member of the Opposition. The first matter that engaged their attention was an assault on the Bank of the United States, Hamilton's pet creation, and an anathema to the agrarians. On January 16, 1794, bills were introduced to bar the personnel of the Bank from membership in Congress, and to divorce the United States from stockholding in the Bank and all political connection therewith. Both bills were defeated by a narrow majority of one, Burr voting yea.[2]

On February 20th, Burr won in his long struggle to force open sessions of the Senate, except where secrecy was specifically required.[3]

On February 28th, the question of Albert Gallatin's seat in the Senate came up for consideration. The future Secretary of the Treasury was of Swiss birth, and, arriving in the United States in 1780, had promptly risen to prominence in the radical ranks. It was maintained by those who wished to bar him from the seat to which he had been elected that he had not been sufficiently long in the country. Burr made a very able speech in his behalf that attracted much favorable comment, but the motion to seat him was defeated 12 to 14.[4]

Meanwhile, foreign affairs had been moving steadily to the foreground. England, as mistress of the seas, had been ruthless in her disregard of American interests. France seized the opportunity to attach the new nation to herself. She opened her colonies in the French West Indies, hitherto tight shut within the walls of a rigid mercantilist system, to the ships of neutrals. That meant largely the United States. England countered by declaring all neutral vessels engaged in such trade liable to seizure. Hundreds of American ships were seized under this ruling, and under an additional order declaring contraband all vessels carrying the goods of French citizens. It was a deadly blow to the American shipping interests. Hitherto Federalist, they began to listen with attention to Republican doctrines. The Southern planters were also deeply interested in the controversy. They still owed large sums to English merchants on pre-Revolutionary debts, and war with England might involve the abrogation of the Treaty of 1783 whereby the government warranted that there would be " no lawful impediment to the recovery of the full value in sterling money of all bona fide debts heretofore contracted."

President Washington laid down a temporary embargo, but it was ineffective. On March 28, 1794, he sent a message to Congress calling for measures to put teeth in the embargo. The message was referred to a committee of which Burr was chairman. He was heartily in favor of an airtight embargo directed against England alone, but the bill he reported out, though it passed the Senate, was defeated in the House, and a less stringent measure was adopted in its stead.[5]

The Republicans persisted. On April 28th a new bill was introduced, which recited the injuries sustained by the United States by reason of British violation of their rights as neutrals, and resolving to forbid all importations from that country. On this measure the two factions in the Senate split in clearcut fashion. The Federalists, in spite of the losses sustained by their mercantile adherents, determined that such a course would bring about considerably greater losses and must eventually lead to war with England. Accordingly they voted solidly against the bill. The Republicans, Burr included, voted as solidly for it. The division was close, 13 to 13, and was decided only by the casting vote of Vice-President Adams.[6]

Meanwhile Lord Grenville, of the British Ministry, had made

a conciliatory gesture, and Washington hastened to take advantage of it. On April 16th, Washington nominated to the Senate Chief Justice John Jay as envoy extraordinary to Great Britain to negotiate for a redress of the existing grievances.

Burr was up in arms. John Jay, though personally his friend, represented everything against which he was fighting. He was a Federalist, a conservative of the deepest dye, an Anglophile. American interests could not safely be entrusted to such hands. It was almost a one-man battle to prevent confirmation. He argued that the present minister, Pinckney, could handle the negotiations sufficiently well, and that it was inadvisable for a judge of the Supreme Court to hold an additional office at the pleasure of the executive. Nevertheless the nomination was confirmed by a vote of 18 to 8.

Jay wrote his wife with some bitterness that " yesterday the Senate approved of the nomination by a great majority. Mr. Burr was among the few who opposed it." [7]

Meanwhile, more local measures were also engaging his attention. Hamilton's program of internal taxation met his steady resistance, usually futile. He opposed taxes on snuff and sugar, and labored mightily against the obnoxious carriage tax, comparable in its scope to the present Federal taxation of automobiles.[8]

The Ohio Company, a huge land grab and settlement venture, petitioned Congress to be relieved of the terms of its contract with the government and for an outright donation of the lands north of the Ohio River. The bill was turned over to a committee of which Burr was chairman. Senator George Cabot told Manasseh Cutler, the Company's active lobbyist, that Burr was very bitter against the Company, and warm in favor of the French, whose interests were involved.[9] But, as a result of extensive bribery, and a shady deal with William Duer of New York, land speculator extraordinary and a man of weight in Federalist councils, the petition was granted in its essential terms over Burr's opposition.

The Session terminated in June. Burr emerged with a national reputation. He had been the active, able leader of the forces of the Opposition. He was generally recognized as such by Federalists and Republicans alike, though not without some inward qualms on the part of the Southern Republicans, who placed their sectional interests above everything else.

Oliver Wolcott, Secretary of the Treasury, cited the opinion of an unnamed Virginia politician, obviously well acquainted with the Senate, on Burr.

" The two most efficient actors on the political theatre of our country," he quotes, " are Mr. Hamilton and Mr. Burr . . . I have watched the movements of Mr. Burr with attention, and have discovered traits of character which sooner or later will give us much trouble. He has an unequalled talent of attaching men to his views, and forming combinations of which he is always the centre. He is determined to play a first part; he acts strenuously with us in public, but it is remarkable that in all private conversations he more frequently agrees with us in principle than in the mode of giving them effect. . . . I shall not be surprised if Mr. Burr is found, in a few years, the leader of a popular party in the northern states; and if this event ever happens, this party will subvert the influence of the southern states." [10]

In this private communication lies the key to the political situation that developed later. The Virginia group viewed with alarm the rapid rise of Aaron Burr to leadership and power. They represented a closed corporation, seeking chiefly the special interests of their own territory, which to them meant the interests of the planter aristocracy. Already the Virginia dynasty was in the process of formation. Burr represented a real threat to its continued leadership. They had not bargained for this when the compact with New York had been made. The Clintons could be handled — they were rather provincial in their ambitions — but not Burr. He had talents and energies that could not readily be overlooked. It is possible that already, in 1794, the Virginians had determined to sidetrack this formidable Northerner.

2. Almost Minister to France

Meanwhile Gouverneur Morris was arousing the ire equally of the French Republic to which he was accredited and of the Republicans at home. France considered him a monarchist and opposed to the Revolution, and demanded that he be recalled. Inasmuch as Washington had just made a similar demand for the return of Citizen Genêt, he could do no other than acquiesce. The Republican faction in Congress insisted on, and received, Washington's informal consent to the appointment of a member of their party as Minister to France.

The Republicans of the Senate and many of those in the House met in caucus, and decided to propose Burr's name. Madison, Monroe and a House Representative waited on the President to communicate their party's wishes. Washington hesitated (aside from his recollection of Burr as a supremely self-confident, impertinent youngster during the Revolution, his mind had been thoroughly poisoned by the secret whisperings of Hamilton), then remarked " that he had made it a rule of life never to recommend or nominate any person for a high and responsible situation in whose integrity he had not confidence; that, wanting confidence in Colonel Burr, he could not nominate him; but that it would give him great pleasure to meet their wishes if they would designate an individual in whom he could confide." [11]

One detects in his very phrasing the characteristic syllables of Alexander Hamilton. The committee reported to the caucus, and found the Republicans unanimous in their insistence on Burr. They so reported back to Washington, who grew warm and declared angrily that his decision was unalterable. He would accept Madison or Monroe, but never Burr. Both of these gentlemen declined the office, the Senatorial caucus waxed equally warm, and would make no other recommendation. On the committee's third visit, Washington refused to receive them, and Randolph, the Secretary of State, shunted them off with soft words. Later, on May 27, 1794, James Monroe was nominated by Washington and confirmed by the disgruntled opposition. Later, much later, in the famous X Y Z dispatches of 1798, the then American envoys to France narrated that they had been told by Talleyrand's agents that " intelligence had been received from the United States, that if Col. Burr and Mr. Madison had constituted the mission, the differences between the two countries would have been accommodated before that time." [12]

3. The Jay Treaty

The second Session of the Third Congress opened on November 3, 1794, but the Senate had no quorum until Burr appeared on November 18th. He found Washington's message on the Whiskey Insurrection in Pennsylvania waiting for consideration. Senator King, his colleague, in a committee report that heartily endorsed Washington's stand, could not resist the opportunity to include certain political animadversions. Burr rose to demand the expungement of these remarks, but the Federalists forced their retention.[13]

Burr was particularly active this session. He sponsored numerous motions and amendments, usually meeting with defeat at the hands of the Federalist majority, and he was given many important committee assignments. He fought vigorously, though in vain, against proposed modifications of the redemption provisions of the public debt, calculated to raise the price of existing government securities and make bond issues demand instruments at the option of the subscriber.[14]

Then John Jay returned to the United States with the treaty he had negotiated, and Washington called a Special Session of the Senate on June 8, 1795, to consider its adoption. The Senate met behind closed doors in executive session, though Burr had insisted, in accordance with his lifelong principles, on full publicity to the debate.

At once the fireworks started, with Burr leading the opposition. The treaty was thoroughly abhorrent to the Republicans, and especially to the Virginians. It was essentially a partisan document, with certain concessions to Northern interests and not even a sop for the South. Even Washington himself was dissatisfied, but he was afraid that its rejection would plunge the nation into an immediate war. In all charity to Jay, it must be confessed that the treaty he had negotiated did prevent an outbreak of hostilities, though it must also be confessed that another envoy, abler perhaps, and less afflicted with a certain myopism in favor of Great Britain, might have gained much more substantial concessions.

In any event, the Opposition, led and skilfully marshaled by Burr, fell upon the proposed treaty hammer and tongs. Burr bore the brunt of the fray. On June 22nd he moved to postpone further consideration of the treaty and to recommend to the President that he negotiate further for certain alterations therein, notably, that the articles relating to refuge or shelter given armed vessels of States at war with either party (a direct slap at France) be expunged; that the concessions to British fur-traders and settlers over the border from Canada be eliminated; that the citizens of the United States have the same rights in British North American ports and rivers that British citizens had in those of the United States; that the British settle satisfactorily for the value of negro slaves carried away by them contrary to the terms of the Treaty of 1783 (this was a long-standing grievance in the South) ; that damages for the illegal retention of frontier posts be also assessed; that the provisions concerning trade with the British West Indies be expunged or made much more favorable to the United States (in this instance Burr was assisting the Northern interests) ; and that no sections be permitted which restrained the United States from " most favored nations " clauses in their commercial arrangements with other foreign powers (this was a remarkable abnegation of American sovereignty on Jay's part, and a further direct slap at France) .[15]

On the whole, the amendments and proposals he offered were

fair and gave only substantial justice to all sections of the United States. But doubtless it was too late to obtain any better treaty — the damage had been done — and under the existing circumstances it was perhaps wiser to accept it as it stood, halting and lame though it was.

In spite of the fact that Burr's speeches against the treaty promptly became famous — Gallatin wrote his wife " I am told that Burr made a most excellent speech " [16] — the Federalists, by adroit negotiations with certain viable opponents, and the suspension of Article XII, relating to the West Indies trade, which, incidentally, was done for the benefit of their *own* constituent merchant and shipping interests, finally jammed through the treaty on June 24, 1795, by a vote of 20 to 10.[17]

When the news leaked out to a stunned and incredulous country, a howl of execration went up. Popular fury with the betrayers rose to fever pitch. Giant mass meetings were held to oppose the " nefarious plot against the liberties of the people," Hamilton was stoned, Jay burned in effigy, and the Republicans, as well as a goodly number of Federalists, frothed at the mouth. Burr became the hero of the hour. Nor did he lose hope to the very end. It was possible, he thought, to persuade the President not to sign the pernicious document. As late as July 5th he wrote Monroe, then in Paris, that " the Country is considerably agitated with [the treaty]. Many of the merchants who were most devoted to Mr. Jay and to the administration, express themselves decidedly and warmly against it . . . A memorial against the ratification is circulating in this Town." [18] But Washington signed the treaty, and the fight was over.

4. REPUBLICAN DEFEAT

Meanwhile Burr had been keeping a wary eye on New York State politics. Slowly, but steadily, with infinite skill and resource, he was building his machine, binding to himself a little group of enthusiastic young men who expressed for him a fanatical loyalty — William P. Van Ness, Colonel John Swartwout, Matthew L. Davis, and others — utilizing certain organizations originally of vague and grandiose aspirations, and welding them into compact, irresistible political bodies.

The Republicans had had rather hard sledding in the State, in spite of Clinton's precarious triumph over Jay in the election of 1792. The Federalist Legislature had promptly taken its revenge. The real power in the State was the Council of Appointment, whose members were appointed by and from the Legislature, with the Governor as Chairman. It was the Council that distributed the patronage, and it is an axiom of politics that the wielder of the patronage holds all power.

Hitherto the Governor had contended, and it had not been questioned, that under the Constitution it was the Governor's privilege to nominate for office, and the Council's duty to confirm or reject. But now, with a packed Federalist Council, under the leadership of Philip Schuyler, still nursing his thirst for revenge under a smiling face, the Council boldly proclaimed that nominations might be offered by any member of the Council, and that the Governor as Chairman merely held the casting vote in case of a tie. This interpretation, with a cohesive Federalist majority, meant that the Republican Governor had been shorn of all power. Clinton protested vigorously, but the Legislature backed the child of its own creation. All State offices were promptly filled with those of the Federalist persuasion, and the power of patronage cracked whiplike in preparation for the next gubernatorial election in 1795.

Angry, discomfited, and seeing the handwriting on the wall, Clinton refused to run again. Once more Burr's name was mentioned for the candidacy, but he, equally with Clinton, read aright the signs of forthcoming Federalist victory. Judge Robert Yates, who, chiefly because of his friend Burr's persuasion, had returned to the anti-Federalist fold, was thereupon nominated. John Jay, from whom the previous election had been stolen, was the obvious candidate of the Federalists. He was elected by a heavy vote, with a concomitant party majority in both Houses of the Legislature. The sun of Republicanism seemed to have set in its solitary Northern stronghold. But Burr, in the intervals of his Senatorial duties at Philadelphia, proceeded quietly with the slow solidifying of his forces in New York City, content to wait, biding his time. As a professional politician, he always took the long view, and temporary defeats could not disturb his imperturbable poise. Nor was he unduly distressed when the spring elections of 1796 continued the large majorities of the Federalists in the Legislature.

The Fourth Congress met on December 7, 1795. The stirring debates and turbulent sessions of the preceding Congress anent the Jay Treaty were but memories, but the exacerbated passions were not easily allayed. France, deeply offended at the outcome, was beginning to strike back at American commerce in retaliation. But her raids were still tentative and comparatively unimportant. Local issues absorbed the attention of embattled politicians. The next year, 1796, was a Presidential year, and it was already known that Washington was to refuse reelection — which left the field wide open to all comers. So it was that Congress marked time to a large extent.

Tennessee was clamoring at the gates of the Union for admission as a State. Burr, whose eyes were already turning westward, and who, in spite of his aristocratic rearing and personal elegance, was fascinated by the rude and turbulent democracy of the frontier, worked for and spoke in favor of the bill. It was defeated. Yet his efforts were remembered with gratitude by the great Western Territory, and when, in June, 1796, Tennessee finally achieved Statehood, its first Representative in Congress, Andrew Jackson, sought out Aaron Burr at once for advice and guidance, and thereupon conceived a profound admiration and a vast respect for the Northerner that was to last throughout life.[19]

Burr also advocated and voted for a bill seeking relief for those imprisoned for debt under Federal process, so that they might claim the benefit of the bankruptcy laws of their respective States.[20] In both state and nation he was unwearied in his advocacy of more liberal laws on bankruptcy, and for the alleviation of the harshness of the various statutes covering imprisonment for civil debts. In view of the tangled state of his own finances at the time, his enemies whispered that his interest in the matter was purely personal. That, however, may be doubted; his own precarious affairs simply brought the barbarous provisions of the existing law more forcibly to his attention.

5. VIRGINIA BREAKS A PROMISE

By the time of the national election of 1796 the two political parties had grown to definite maturity. The confusion, the shifting of forces, the vague inchoateness of 1792 was gone from the American scene forever. Two great opposing principles locked horns in a battle to the death. Federalism and all that it implied had dominated the national government since its inception; now for the first time its control was being seriously threatened.

The two parties grew out of different conceptions of the fundamentals of government, of the opposition of conservative and radical on the political side; on the economic side it was a sectionalism based on divergent industrial conditions, a contest between the capitalist and the agrarian, the creditor and the debtor. Essentially it was South against North, with New York and Pennsylvania borderline States possessing an economy at once industrial and agrarian. Jefferson had early realized that his beloved Virginia was doomed to eternal defeat without the aid of these two States. That was why he had started a newspaper in Pennsylvania under the minor poet, Philip Freneau; that was why he had gone botanizing into New York; that was why George Clinton had received Southern votes in the election of 1792, and Burr had been promised certain things for 1796.

Jefferson had finally resigned from his uneasy office in Washington's Cabinet and was prepared to make a definite bid for power in this election. The country was strongly discontented. The farmers had not obtained what Hamilton had foreshadowed under his dispensation. There had been a depression which had hit the artisan and mechanic classes of the North rather hard, and they were willing to consider the Republican gospel. Though Jefferson and his Virginia planter-aristocrats sniffed rather disdainfully at the thought of an alliance with these greasy, clamorous individuals, so discordant to the ideal agrarian civilization of which they dreamed, Aaron Burr, equally aristocratic, had no such qualms. In fact, he was the first to perceive the political value of these sweaty, turbulent artisans, and utilized them as the very basis of his organization. Thus it was that, unwillingly, the Virginians made their alliance with Burr — with secret reservations. With Clinton, and the chameleon Livingstons, they were more at home — they, too, were essentially agrarian in their viewpoint, and would always be content to act the tail to the Virginia kite.

Arrayed against them were the Federalists, entrenched in power, the followers of Hamilton, the merchant and commercial classes, the security holders, the speculators, the professions and the intellectuals, the budding industrialists. But there was secret dissension. Vice-President John Adams was necessarily their candidate for the Presidency. He could not be dislodged openly. But Adams had resented Hamilton's overwhelming influence in the councils of Washington and his own comparative impotence. He was stubborn and crabbed, and honest. Hamilton realized that with the election of Adams his own power would wane, and accordingly, with clandestine craft, he intrigued in favor of Thomas Pinckney of South Carolina, who was ostensibly the candidate for the Vice-Presidency. He urged Northern and Eastern Federalist friends of his to give an equal number of votes to both Adams and Pinckney, hoping that by some means Adams would be omitted from the Southern electoral tickets. This actually did happen in South Carolina, Pinckney's own State — and the means were obvious. Its electors divided 8 for Pinckney and 8 for Jefferson. But the Northern Federalists, as always, while acknowledging Hamilton's intellectual leadership, paid little or no attention to his numerous exhortations and intrigues. Rhode Island, New Hampshire, Massachusetts and Connecticut voted overwhelmingly for Adams and split their second votes between Pinckney and favorite sons, with the result that Hamilton's attempt to elevate Pinckney to the Presidency collapsed utterly.

On the Republican side there was no open dissension. Jefferson was chosen by informal correspondence and various caucuses to be the standard-bearer for the Presidency, and Aaron Burr, in accordance with the understanding arrived at in 1792, was to be the candidate for the second office. But underneath the surface, even as among the Federalists, there appeared certain small signs of a rift. John Beckley was writing to Madison from Philadelphia on June 20, 1796, that " it is . . . an idea strongly urged by Swan to play off Chancellor Livingston for V. P. upon New York & Jersey, as the most likely means of a successful diversion there." But Beckley hastens to add, rather unconvincingly, that " he is however strongly in favor of Burr's election," and that " upon the whole however, if no great schism happens in Virginia, I think it morally certain that Mr. Jefferson and Col. Burr will be elected." [21]

Burr was fairly confident too. " The approaching election for President," he wrote Monroe, " will be, on both sides, urged with much activity. Jefferson & Adams will I believe be the only candidates. The prospect of success is in favor of the former." [22] And, while on a flying trip to Boston, prominent men had informed him that the two candidates would be nearly equal in their votes.[23]

The election was held amid scenes of great excitement and much subterranean intriguing. In those days of slow communication and travel, the results of the meeting of the various electoral bodies could not be determined for a considerable period. On November 22nd Burr was writing his uncle, Pierpont Edwards, at New Haven, for information. " Pray favor me with one line respecting your hopes from the Electors of Connect. & R. I. The Jefferson Ticket will have a large Majority in Penna. unless the votes of the three Western Counties should have been *stolen or fraudulently suppressed,* which there is some reason to apprehend." [24]

But by December 16, 1796, Hamilton was able to write with considerable relief to Rufus King that " it is now decided that *neither Jefferson nor Burr* can be President . . . The event will not a little mortify Burr. Virginia has given him only one vote." [25] Hamilton evidently believed that his great opponent had been intriguing to oust Jefferson from the Presidency, even as he himself had been feverishly engaged against Adams. But it happened that the shoe was on the other foot.

When the final results were announced, it was found that John Adams had been elected President with 71 electoral votes, Jefferson Vice-President with 68. The rest trailed — Pinckney had 59, Burr had 30, with a scattering for various favorite sons. The election had been perilously close — a slight shift would have placed Jefferson in the President's chair. But Burr had excellent reasons, aside from non-election, for being extremely disturbed at the result. His votes were scattered as follows: Tennessee, 3; Kentucky, 4; North Carolina, 6; Pennsylvania, 13; Maryland, 3; and Virginia, 1.

It was the Virginia vote that could not be explained away to his satisfaction, or to the satisfaction of any one else. Virginia was closely held by Jefferson and his friends; its electoral vote had gone solidly for Jefferson, yet but a lone vote had been cast for Burr, his running mate. Hamilton had commented gleefully on the situation, Beckley early in the campaign had expressed fears about the issue. There were other States to the South also where, strangely, Burr had been overlooked by Republican electors under the domination of Jefferson.

But he was too good a politician to show outward resentment at what he considered treachery. He had lived up to his part of the bargain with meticulous faith, and had campaigned mightily for the success of the party ticket. He realized now that the leaders of the Southern Republicans were determined that their Northern ally should not wax too powerful. Yet he said nothing, except privately and among friends. He had it in his power to wreck the party irrevocably between 1796 and the next election, but he never permitted emotion or resentment or passion to sway his decisions. He had staked his political fortunes on the eventual success of Republicanism; he must continue on the chosen path.

CHAPTER XII

BURR STOOPS TO CONQUER

1. THE LOWLY ASSEMBLYMAN

BURR'S term as Senator was approaching its end. The close of the Congressional session in 1797 marked the finish of his Senatorial career. The New York Legislature, now strongly Federalist in its complexion, with John Jay in the gubernatorial chair, returned Philip Schuyler in his stead. The proud General and patroon of an ancient family had nursed his spleen long enough. Now he had his revenge, and both he and his son-in-law, Hamilton, were content. They had crushed their enemy.

But Burr had not been taken by surprise. He had expected nothing else and had laid his plans accordingly. From national politics he returned to the local scene. He had neglected it too long, and a herculean task awaited him. It was nothing more nor less than to oust the triumphant and seemingly impregnably intrenched Federalists from their control of the State, and to assume definite and unquestioned leadership for himself. Burr, however, never desponded, never despaired. His was an unbounded energy, controlled and channelized by a first-rate brain.

The first step in his carefully prepared campaign was to inject himself into a strategic position in State politics. The spring election of 1797 for the Assembly gave him his opportunity. He ran on the ticket from New York City and was promptly elected. So also was young De Witt Clinton, nephew to the old ex-Governor — as yet an unknown quantity in State politics. All over the State there were Republican gains, but not enough to damage substantially the Federalist majority.

It was seemingly a considerable comedown from United States Senator, national figure, aspirant for the Vice-Presidency, to the lowly condition of a local Assemblyman. Burr did not mind. He had but stooped to conquer. Nor were his opponents entirely deceived. Schuyler, recently exultant at his own triumph, wrote with considerable apprehension to Hamilton: " Mr. Burr, we are informed, will be a candidate for a seat in the Assembly; his views it is not difficult to appreciate. They alarm me, and if he prevails I apprehend a total change of politics in the next Assembly — attended with other disagreeable consequences." [1] Neither of these gentlemen made the mistake of underestimating Aaron Burr.

Meanwhile Hamilton was running into substantial difficulties of his own. The odorous Mrs. Reynolds affair had burst upon him like a bombshell. Callender, a Republican hack writer of the particularly vicious breed that seemed to spawn with remarkable fecundity in those days, had just published documents that seemed to involve Hamilton in the grossest of fraudulent financial transactions, dating back to 1792 and his incumbency in the office of the Treasury. An investigation then by Senator Monroe and two Republican members of Congress had elicited from Hamilton the astonishing confession that the entire affair was an attempt at blackmail on the part of one James Reynolds because of certain illicit relations that he, Hamilton, had maintained with Mrs. Reynolds, his wife. Monroe and the others had professed themselves satisfied at the time and the matter had seemingly been dropped. Now that the scandal had broken into public print, however, Hamilton was compelled, in order to maintain his political honor, to reveal in a pamphlet the stain upon his private honor. The whole unsavory amour with all its sordid details was exposed to the eyes of a gloating world. It was a very courageous act; only Grover Cleveland in all the annals of American politics was to possess a similar courage.

But there were repercussions. An acrimonious correspondence took place between Hamilton and Monroe, whom, rightly or wrongly, Hamilton considered responsible for the exposure of his shame. On July 18, 1797, he wrote Monroe a demand for an explanation of certain inferences, which was couched in such language that Monroe could only consider it as a challenge. Monroe retorted that if " you meant your last letter as a challenge to me I have then to request that you say so, and in which case have to inform you, that my friend Col. Burr — who will present you this . . . is authorized to give you my answer to it, and to make such other arrangements as may be suitable in such an event."

Monroe then forwarded the correspondence to Burr and requested him to act as his second in the event Hamilton had challenged. Hamilton, on the other hand, had assumed that Monroe had challenged *him*. The affair was ultimately settled by mutual disavowals, and Burr, as intermediary, drafted a memorandum of agreement satisfactory to both parties. [2] By an ironic twist of fate Burr was thus early interposing his good offices between Hamilton and a possible death on the dueling field.

2. ALMOST A BRIGADIER

While waiting for the Assembly to meet, Burr kept in touch with national affairs. Jefferson was writing him from Philadelphia, where he was filling acceptably the none too arduous duties of a Vice-President under the American Constitution, that "some general view of our situation and prospects, since you left us, may not be unacceptable. At any rate, it will give me an opportunity of recalling myself to your memory, and of evidencing my esteem for you." After a résumé of the situation in Congress he proceeds to inquire as to the trend of affairs in New York, from which, he presumes, "little is to be hoped." If, however, Burr could give him "a comfortable solution" of "certain painful and doubtful questions" it would "relieve a mind devoted to the preservation of our republican government in the true form and spirit in which it was established." [3]

To which Burr replied in similar vein that "the moment requires free communication among those who adhere to the principles of our revolution. The conduct of some individuals of the [Jay] Treaty Majority has disappointed me a good deal. That of the executive something also, but much less." He had been "led to hope that a more temperate system would have been adopted. All such expectations are now abandoned. The gauntlet I see is thrown and the fruit of our War with Britain is again in jeopardy . . . It would not be easy neither would it be discreet, to answer your inquiries or to communicate to you my ideas with satisfaction to either of us, in the compass of a Letter. I will endeavor to do it in person." [4]

Burr's maneuvers in New York were known to Jefferson, and in accordance with a prearranged plan. And Burr was watching like a hawk the national situation. The Federalists, as he had noted, were interpreting the Jay Treaty in a way to antagonize France. France responded by raids on American shipping. For two years John Adams negotiated, trying desperately to stave off a threatened war. The Federalists were gleeful. The country was forgetting England as the arch-enemy and turning all its resentment and wrath upon their old ally, France. The Federalists artfully fanned the flames, and tried to force the stubborn old President into a situation from which he could not possibly extricate himself without a declaration of war. Adams resisted the pressure, Federalist though he was. But even the Republicans were becoming disgusted with French arrogance and utter disregard for

American rights, though they insisted that the situation had been brought about by Federalist tactics.

The famous X Y Z affair intervened. The stupid and incomprehensible reception of the American envoys by the French government, the outrageous cynicism with which Talleyrand, through his agents, Mr. X, Mr. Y and Mr. Z, demanded open bribes, raised a veritable frenzy of excitement. A state of undeclared war existed between the two countries, with pitched naval battles, and privateers raiding each other's commerce with relish and impunity.

The American army and navy were rapidly strengthened. Washington was called out of retirement to head the forces as commander-in-chief. Subordinate generals were promptly appointed. At Washington's suggestion, and much to Hamilton's delight, the latter was appointed second in command. President Adams, hampered by his Cabinet, which he had inherited from his predecessor in office and which assumed to dictate policies to him as it had to Washington, nevertheless considered Colonel Burr for a post in the newly formed army. He had always had a high opinion of Burr's abilities. As he narrates the story, " I proposed to General Washington, in a conference between him and me, and through him to the triumvirate [Hamilton, Pickering and Pinckney], to nominate Colonel Burr for a brigadier-general. Washington's answer to me was, ' By all that I have known and heard, Colonel Burr is a brave and able officer; but the question is, whether he has not equal talents at intrigue.' How shall I describe my sensations and reflections at that moment? " continues Adams. " He had compelled me to promote, over the heads of Lincoln, Gates, Clinton, Knox, and others, and even over Pinckney, one of his own triumvirate, the most restless, impatient, artful, indefatigable and unprincipled intriguer in the United States, if not in the world [Hamilton], to be second in command under himself, and now dreaded an intriguer in a poor brigadier! He did, however, propose it to the triumvirate, at least to Hamilton. But I was not permitted to nominate Burr. If I had been, what would have been the consequence? Shall I say, that Hamilton would have been now alive, and Hamilton and Burr now at the head of our affairs? What then? If I had nominated Burr without the consent of the triumvirate, a negative in Senate was certain. Burr to this day knows nothing of this." [5]

Poor John Adams! He was not even master in his own house! The record speaks for itself. He was also to declare in retrospect that it was Hamilton's intention in 1799 to make an offensive and

WATER OFFICE.

THE Directors of the Manhattan Company, desirous to render the object of their institution as generally useful to the inhabitants of the city as it was capable of, determined to attempt to furnish families with a plentiful supply of water for every domestic purpose at all times, and not, as is the case in most cities of Europe, to give it at intervals of from 24 to 48 hours; but it is feared the abuse that is made of their good intentions will probably oblige them to alter the mode of distribution; previous to any alteration, however, they have resolved first to try to correct the evil. I am therefore directed to inform those who take the water from the Company, that where a wilful or negligent waste of it is permitted, the lateral pipe leading to such house will be cut off as soon as detected; and also to notify, that in case it can be discovered and proved that the water is given or sold to any person or persons, who do not pay the Company for it, that the pipe from whence such be taken shall not only be cut off, but the persons so defrauding the Company shall be prosecuted in a court of law for the damages resulting, and for which purpose I will give a reward of ten dollars to any person who will give the requisite information. It is hoped that those who are well wishers to the institution will use their influence to prevent the malpractices alluded to.

     JOSEPH BROWNE, *Superintendant of Water Works*
New-York, May 22d, 1802.

A CIRCULAR ISSUED BY THE MANHATTAN COMPANY, 1802

COLLECT POND, 1802, NOW CROSSED BY CENTER STREET, NEW YORK CITY

From an old print

defensive alliance with Great Britain and provoke war with France. In which case it was Adams's opinion then, " and has been ever since, that the two parties in the United States would have broken out into a civil war; a majority of all the States to the southward of Hudson River, united with nearly half New England, would have raised an army under Aaron Burr; a majority of New England might have raised another under Hamilton. Burr would have beaten Hamilton to pieces, and what would have followed next, let the prophets foretell." [6]

While John Adams's retrospective prophesying need not necessarily be swallowed whole, it is an interesting indication of the profound respect which he, and others, entertained for Aaron Burr's talents, and his recognition of the fact that the two great antagonists in the country were Burr and Hamilton; two giants, one of whom must eventually give way.

3. STRANGE BEDFELLOWS

Burr busied himself during the first session in quietly consolidating his position. He was still advocating more liberal bankruptcy laws and the speedy and immediate abolition of slavery, as well as a tax on woodland and unproductive property in the hands of speculators for the rise that seems a remarkable forerunner of the modern theories of Henry George. The Republicans nationally had been compelled, because of the storm over France, to lie low and say nothing. Burr was conspicuous for his strong advocacy of fortifications for New York Harbor. In this matter he worked amicably with the Federalists. His stand puzzled Robert Troup, now bitterly his opponent. Troup was not very bright politically. He wrote Rufus King, marooned in London, that " Burr has been re-elected a member of the State Legislature for this City. He was a member the last year — and his conduct very different from what you would imagine. Some conjecture that he is changing his ground. He concurs with us decidedly in measures for defence of our port." [7]

In fact, Burr went farther. At the 1798 elections, as Troup had remarked, he had been returned to the Assembly in spite of another Federalist sweep in the State. John Jay had been reelected over Livingston, now safely and completely a Republican. But in New York City Burr and his friends held the reins. John Swartwout, his most loyal lieutenant, entered the Assembly with him, while De Witt Clinton, still outwardly meek and subservient, went to the State Senate.

All through the summer of 1798, while the fever of preparations against France was at its height, Burr was the most ardent advocate of State preparedness. He even cooperated with Hamilton, much to that worthy's astonishment. It must be remembered that Colonel Burr had always been enamored of the military life, and, while he still preferred French republican doctrine to the British monarchical system, French provocations had been extreme. In the event of a war forced on the United States by French aggression there would be no question as to his stand.

All through the summer of 1798, he was in active correspondence with Colonel Ebenezer Stevens, in command of the New York City area. He requested detailed information of his fortifications, arms, and special needs, together with an estimate " of the probable cost of an *impregnable castle* to contain from 75 to 200 Cannon, Howitzers & Mortars." He had assumed practically the entire responsibility of obtaining the necessary funds for the work from the Legislature. " The business of the appropriations goes on slowly," he wrote Stevens, " but it in fact advances. It has been infinitely fatiguing & laborious to me, yet I do not despair of accomplishing something which shall gratify my fellow citizens." [8]

And on another occasion he wrote the Colonel that the legislators from the northern counties of the State, whose constituents, though Federalist, would not be exposed to the attacks of a foreign sea power, " seem to be in very *ungiving* humor. We apprehend much *secret* opposition from Mr. Jones. A letter from Genl Hamilton to him might be useful." [9]

The threatening war had made strange bedfellows. Aside from Burr's undoubted patriotism at this time, he was stealing his opponents' thunder. In New York, at least, the Federalists could not accuse the Republicans of truckling to a foreign foe, of a lack of patriotic fervor.

In fact, when the Assembly met on August 9th, it was Burr who was made chairman of the committee to study and act on Governor Jay's message relating to the defense of New York City. On August 10th he reported promptly that the harbor defenses were wholly inadequate, based on the confidential information he had received from Stevens, and brought in a bill calling for an appropriation of $1,200,000. On his motion the bill passed the Assembly, but soberer thought prevailed, and on a recommission, the decision was reversed. Thereafter Burr fought valiantly for bills calling for progressively less amounts, until the northern members were placated, and the sum of $300,000 was appropriated.[10]

Troup was more and more puzzled at these tactics of the friend of his youth. He wrote at considerable length to King.

"Our Legislature met on the 9th of August last and . . . granted 300,000 dollars for fortifications & *unanimously* agreed upon an address to the President on the conduct of France. The address upon the whole considering that Burr was in the Assembly & much superior in talents to any of the opposite party is better than I expected." Nor does he understand why Burr continues in the Assembly, an office so obviously beneath his talents. "His object cannot be precisely developed. Some suppose it to be a state bankrupt law in which he is said to be deeply interested. Others conceive that he has the government in view. It is certain that he has not discovered a desire to resume his stand in the *Senate*. No doubt is entertained that after the publication of the despatches from our envoys to France his conduct showed strong symptoms of a wish to change his ground. He was active & apparently zealous in our measures for defending our harbour. He was particularly courteous to Hamilton, and some of the most intelligent of his party have gone so far as to say he certainly expected an appointment in the army." [11]

Certainly Burr kept his own counsels and pursued his own path. Neither party associates nor political opponents realized that he was adopting the only course possible to keep the Republicans afloat during a period of angry passions and Federalist reaction. Yet when Republican principles were directly attacked, he acted with decision and despatch. For Troup continues, in a still greater fog of misapprehension: "Yet before the appointment of General officers took place and in the midst of conciliating appearances he became bail for the appearance of one Bourk who was apprehended upon a warrant . . . for a most infamous libel upon the President." [12]

Here, indeed, the Republicans were on sure ground. In the midst of the agitation against France, the Federalists had jammed through Congress the infamous Alien and Sedition Acts. They were as vicious in their tendencies as — at least those relating to sedition — they were unconstitutional. Here was a direct assault on the freedom of speech and of the press guaranteed in the Bill of Rights. Under the provisions of the Acts, all criticism of public officials by the opposition might be construed as criminal libel, as sedition itself. Here, indeed, as Burr was quick to see, was an issue on which the Republicans could regain all the ground they had lost by the arrogant aggressions of their ally, France. The issue was to become notably alive and burning throughout the nation the following year, and in New York Burr did his utmost to fan the flames of popular indignation.

In the Session of January 2, 1799, Burr continued his steady drive for a bankruptcy law, and his efforts were finally rewarded in the Assembly on January 16th. And also that other measure which he had advocated in season and out — the abolition of slavery in New York — met now with success, though it did not go quite as far as he would have wished. The act provided that every child of slave parents thereafter born was to be free, on condition however that until the age of 28 it was to remain the servant of the mother's owner. Furthermore, Burr was chairman of the Committee on Taxation and worked diligently to provide a scientific, equitable and efficient system that would reorganize the State's finances.[13]

On February 7, 1799, John Swartwout, Burr's lieutenant, under his direction introduced an important measure for the consideration of the Assembly. He proposed that the State be divided into districts, and that Presidential electors be voted for directly by the people of the several districts. Hitherto Presidential electors were elected by the Legislature in joint session, and hence they were not responsive to the popular will, except by indirection — that is, such popular will as could be determined within the narrow limits of the property qualifications for voters. Burr, through Swartwout, now proposed to make the elections more immediately direct.

The scheme was the opening gun in his grand strategy for the oncoming Presidential election of 1800. If, as seemed probable from the then complexion of New York politics, it would prove impossible to elect a majority of the Legislature, at least a part of the electoral College might be secured through the votes of New York City and other Republican strongholds. Otherwise, a bare Federalist majority in the Legislature could insure a unanimous Federalist delegation.

The bill was argued on a strictly partisan basis, each faction realizing to the full its implications. With a Federalist majority in control of the Assembly, Burr's talents for negotiation were extended to the utmost. There was a group of some eight to ten Federalists whose party affiliations were not of the strongest. In addition, most of them were personally well disposed to Burr. He proceeded to work on them with unequaled arts. Especially did he labor with Judge Peck and General German of the western counties. He flattered them, selected the former to bring in the electoral resolutions, and did everything in his power to identify them with the Republicans. The Federalists aided him unwittingly by their ill-judged resentment against the two men. By the time he was through, the bill had passed the Assembly. In the Senate, however, where his influence was not so great, it went down to defeat.[14]

This disposition, though seemingly a blow at the time, in the final outcome proved to be the salvation of the Republican hopes. But then Burr, for all his political acumen, could not have foreseen exactly what was to happen. The campaign, however, bore its own peculiarly fruitful results. He had definitely succeeded in alienating Peck and German from the Federalist ranks, and their support in 1800 was to prove particularly valuable in the western portions of the State.

Meanwhile the agitation against the Alien and Sedition Acts was sweeping the country. Editors, publicists, political opponents of the Administration, were being daily clapped into jail on charges of libel and sedition. Matthew Lyon, Republican Congressman from Vermont, had been arrested and fined; Judge Peck, in New York, was involved in the circulation of a petition against the laws by Burr's clever maneuvers, and was promptly arrested by the indignant Federalists. All this was grist for the Republican mills.

Virginia and Kentucky rose in arms against the suppression of their local liberties and proclaimed in a series of Resolutions that Congress had transcended its constitutional powers, and that they, as sovereign States, took it upon themselves to declare the offending Acts nul and void. There was even talk of secession. The Federalists frothed at the mouth. Resolutions were offered in the New York Legislature in sharp rebuke of the two recalcitrant States, declaring in no uncertain terms " that the right of deciding on the constitutionality of all laws passed by the Congress of the United States appertains to the judiciary department; and . . . an assumption of that right by the legislatures of individual states is unwarrantable, and has a direct tendency to destroy the independence of the general government." [15]

This was quite true. Burr and Swartwout, however, staged an intricate and lengthy parliamentary fight to avoid the record of a hostile vote. They almost succeeded, going down to defeat only by the cracking of the Federalist party whip.

4. The Holland Land Company

Scandal meanwhile was gathering in a cloud of whispers around Burr. It related to his activities during the preceding session in connection with the Holland Land Company. A duel was to be the outcome, though it did nothing to clear the atmosphere. Even to this day the cloud has persisted. Accordingly the affair is well worth careful and impartial examination.[16]

Burr's finances through these years had been in a desperate way. His combined income from the practice of law and the salaries accruing from public office had been wofully insufficient to meet the mounting pyramid of notes, endorsements, mortgages, and unsecured debts. To recoup his fortunes Burr embarked on a series of land speculations. Fabulous sums were in the air; men of the highest rank, from George Washington to William Duer and Robert Morris, engaged eagerly in the boom. Robert Morris, Duer, John Nicholson and a host of others, had dealt in millions of acres, and had made millions.

Nor was the speculation in virgin American lands confined to the natives. Europe became infected with the frenzy, and invested huge sums for the rise. Of alien investors the Dutch were perhaps the most active. They started as early as 1791, when one Theophile Cazenove, a Dutchman himself, became the American agent for a group of Dutch firms interested in the speculation.

In 1792 six of these firms united as the Holland Land Company for the purpose of making extensive purchases of land, and for the purpose of resale to the Dutch public at a profit.

Cazenove purchased on behalf of the Company huge tracts in western New York, comprising 1,500,000 acres, from Robert Morris; and another great area in Pennsylvania. In 1796 the Company incorporated solely as a stock-selling proposition, and induced their gullible compatriots, bitten by the delirium of fabulous profits in far-off America, to subscribe heavily.

Meanwhile a native venture, the Pennsylvania Population Company, sponsored by John Nicholson, had already entered the field, and controlled 450,000 acres north and west of the Allegheny. Burr held 100 shares out of a total of 2500 of the stock of this company, which he had purchased in 1793.[17] But the continued pressure for cash compelled him to offer it for sale in 1795.[18] He could find no purchaser, however.

Cazenove was buying heavily for his principals into this Company, at about the time that Burr was trying to step out. Encouraged by this manifestation of renewed interest, Burr decided to plunge again, this time with Cazenove. In 1796 he borrowed heavily from all available sources and contracted to purchase from the Holland Company 100,000 acres of land in the Presque Isle area, at 12 shillings an acre, payable in instalments. The covenant held a penalty of $20,000 in case of a default in performance on his part. As security for this penalty, Burr assigned to Cazenove the bond of Thomas L. Witbeck, payable to Burr, in the penal sum of $20,000, and, as additional security, a mortgage on his holdings in the Pennsylvania Population Company.[19]

Manifestly this immense purchase of land was purely speculative in its origin. Burr hoped to dispose of the same at a handsome profit before he would be compelled to make good on the terms of his contract. But the market for lands had become completely glutted, and the bottom dropped out of the boom by the end of 1796. Burr was left holding the bag, with a contract which came due in 1797. He was unable to pay on his commitment, and was threatened with the heavy penalties contained in the agreement.

Meanwhile trouble was also brewing for the Holland Company. Pennsylvania, in which they held vast tracts, was the only State in the country that permitted aliens to hold land without limitation. In New York, where their holdings were even larger, this was not the case. Accordingly, when the tentative purchase was made in 1792 of the Genesee tract from Robert Morris, Cazenove instigated the introduction of a bill into the New York Legislature to grant his principals full rights in the land. The bill was defeated heavily, due, it was thought, to the opposition of the Clintons, who seized this opportunity to strike indirectly at their enemy, Morris.

At the next session the bill was introduced again, this time to pass the Senate, but to meet with defeat in the House, where the Clintons were strong. In a desperate attempt to force the measure through, Cazenove retained Hamilton, who worked with Samuel Jones to obtain the passage of a general alien holding act. His influence achieved a measure of success. A bill was passed permitting the holding of lands by aliens for a period of seven years.[20]

This, however, was not sufficient for the purposes of the Holland Company and they tried again, still employing Hamilton. This time Philip Schuyler, Hamilton's father-in-law, became interested. He was now the President of the Western Inland Lock Navigation Company, which required additional capital for its enterprises. He negotiated with the Holland Company. In return for the use of their funds in *his* Company, he succeeded in push-

ing a measure through a subservient Legislature which raised the
period of alien tenure to twenty years, and incorporated the astounding condition that the Holland Company pay over to Schuyler's Canal Company the sum of $250,000 as a loan, or in purchase
of shares of stock.[21] It was a particularly unblushing example of
political and financial logrolling.

But the boom was already collapsing, and Cazenove refused to
go through with the bargain unless unrestricted tenure in land
was granted his Company. A respectable lobby was thereupon
built up. There were many other foreigners in the same boat —
Colonel Charles Williamson, later to become deeply involved in
the Burr " Conspiracy," was then agent for a group of English investors in American lands — and the large native landowners were
also in favor. The best customers for their holdings were the gullible Europeans.

To Cazenove it seemed that now was the time for the supreme
effort. He enlisted Burr's services, as he had done before with
Hamilton. Burr, too, was personally interested in the successful
termination of the matter. With unrestricted alien tenure, it
might be possible for him to market his contract lands abroad.

Burr went to work at once. He was a much better negotiator
and persuasive agent than Hamilton. The Act of April 2, 1798,
crowned his efforts with complete success. There had been little
opposition in the Senate, where Thomas Morris was in charge of
operations. But the Assembly was a different proposition. Besides
the usual opponents to all forms of alien privilege, there was the
Schuyler and Hamiltonian faction, now definitely in the opposition. With the passage of a new and unrestricted bill, their hopes
for the subsidy of $250,000 for their canal projects went glimmer-
ing. So they rallied righteously to the defense of the American
citizen against the foreign capitalist.

Burr looked the situation over and realized it was a case of
meeting fire with fire. Besides deft political management, unscrupulous bribery of venal legislators was indicated. This Cazenove unblushingly proceeded to do, and the bill was passed.

Cazenove justified the use of bribe money to his Directors in
Holland as small in amount compared with the sums that the
Canal Company had been attempting to extract.[22] This money
was charged on the books as counsel fees. The total paid was
$10,500 — $3,000 went to Josiah Ogden Hoffman, the State Attorney General, $1,000 to Thomas Morris, State Senator, $1,000 to
Mr. L—— (even in the private records the name was kept religiously secret), and $5,500 to Aaron Burr! [23]

But as against Burr this evidence is not as damning as it might seem on the face. There is still in the Company archives an engagement on the part of Burr to repay this sum of $5,500 within two years, and a penal bond for double that amount.[24] Evidently, as far as Burr was concerned, the transaction was a loan, a favor no doubt resulting from his services to the Company, but nevertheless not in the category of a direct bribe. Of this sum, $2,050 was paid on his order direct to Buckley and Dayton for his account — another strong bit of evidence that in the eyes of all parties concerned, the loan was not considered in any wise reprehensible. The loan was never repaid, and the bond was eventually canceled in the general settlement of accounts between Burr and the Holland Company.

Judge Benson, of the Council of Revision, wrote to Cazenove in naive surprise over the final passage of the bill that " there has been such a combination of views, objects & interests not only wholly dissimilar but even directly opposed to each other in promoting or at least in acquiescing in this law as infinitely surpasses anything I have hitherto seen in the notable business of Legislation, as conducted with us. I believe that I may venture to assure you there is reason to suppose that the prevailing motive of some in agreeing to it was merely to disappoint others by depriving the Canal Company of a loan." [25]

Meanwhile Burr was still bound on his unfortunate contract. He joined with Cazenove and other speculators in the same predicament to give James Wadsworth a power of attorney to seek possible purchasers in England or on the Continent for the undigested lands. Communications were poor, and the reports that filtered through seemed to indicate in 1798 that Wadsworth was on the verge of successfully negotiating the deal. But the Holland Company, in the person of Cazenove, was not disposed to wait. He pressed Burr for payment in accordance with the terms of his contract. This in spite of the fact that Burr had been chiefly instrumental in the passage of the Alien Tenure Bill.

Witbeck, who had given his bond for $20,000 on Burr's behalf, became uneasy. His own credit was being affected by the outstanding obligation. He therefore insisted that Burr take up his bond, and on Burr's refusal, or inability to do so, applied directly to Cazenove. He finally became so importunate that Burr, with Cazenove's consent, took it up and offered Frederick Prevost's bond in its stead. Prevost, it must be remembered, was Burr's step-son, and by now had achieved a substantial position in the community. His bond was as good as, or better than, Witbeck's. Cazenove accepted — there was also the mortgage on Burr's 20,000 acres in the Pennsylvania Population Company — and the switch was arranged; all other terms and conditions, it being agreed, to remain the same. Yet Cazenove was to claim to his Holland principals, and to others, that the change of bonds was a big favor to Burr and " large compensation for his efforts in behalf of the alien bill." [26] At least the claim was another indication that the loan of $5,500 was not in the nature of a bribe.

Evidently by this time Cazenove and Burr were not on the friendliest of terms. Cazenove began to press for performance of the contract. Burr was unable to raise the necessary cash, and the supposed deal in Europe had fallen through. In December, 1798, Burr offered to return the lands and cancel the contract. Cazenove insisted on the penalty in addition. They parted without decision, to renew negotiations in May, 1799. It was finally agreed that the Holland Company would accept the return of the contract land; but that, in addition, Burr was to convey to it absolutely as and for damages the 20,000 acres of Presque Isle property. In exchange, the covenants of the contract were to be canceled, Prevost's bond given up, and certain advances made by Cazenove to Burr, described by the latter as " several thousand dollars," were to be included in the general settlement. These advances were without doubt the loan that had borne the suspicious earmarks of a bribe. The transaction was now closed.

But not from the political point of view. Cazenove talked — possibly to Hamilton, the legal counsel for the Company. Hamilton talked to others — including John B. Church, his brother-in-law. An election was in the offing. Church whispered and made derogatory remarks concerning Burr's probity, including something about bribes. Burr heard of the whispering campaign and promptly called Church out.

Troup wrote to King about it. " Mr. Church fought a duel yesterday with Col. Burr. A day or two ago Mr. Church in some company intimated that Burr had been bribed for his influence, whilst in the Legislature, to procure the passing of an act, permittg the Holland company to hold their lands. One of the company mentioned it to Burr. A challenge ensued. A duel was fought. Burr had a ball through his coat. Church escaped. After the first fire, and whilst the seconds were preparg to load a second time, Church declared he had been indiscreet and was sorry for it, and thus the affair ended. Church wanted proof of the charge — but it has long been believed." [27]

And continued to be believed. Burr never explained in public.

It was not his custom. But later he wrote an unnamed friend a private account of the transaction, ending proudly: " This, sir, is the first time in my life that I have condescended . . . to refute a calumny. I leave it to my actions to speak for themselves, and to my character to confound the fictions of slander." [28] A very dangerous position indeed, for a professional politician!

A careful consideration of the facts discloses unquestionably that Burr had received no bribes or favors of any kind from the Holland Company. The final settlement of his affairs with Cazenove, in spite of Cazenove's own animadversions on the matter, contain all the essentials of a strict business deal. The Holland Company could have done no better in a court of law. Even had they foreclosed on their lien and called for a forfeiture of the bond, they would only have been entitled to the actual damage sustained. It is doubtful whether the return of their lands intact, in addition to absolute title to 20,000 acres belonging to Burr, was not a settlement entirely to their advantage. Burr's own account, when compared to the records of the Holland Company recently unearthed, seems fundamentally honest. Only in one particular does it err, and that is on a matter of dates. He claimed that the offer to switch bonds was made long after the passage of the Alien Act, when actually it occurred within a month.

But on another count Burr cannot escape unscathed. It was not exactly the best ethics for a member of the Legislature who was involved financially with an interested group seeking favors from that Legislature, to undertake the management of their cause on the floor of the House. Nor was the fact that he advised, or was only aware of, the consequent bribery and corruption, conducive to the highest political standards.

It must be confessed that others were tarred with the same brush, and in a far worse predicament. It was a remarkably venal Legislature. What of Thomas Morris, the manager of the bill on the floor of the Senate, of the State Attorney General, of other legislators who received direct and incontrovertible bribes? What of Alexander Hamilton himself, and Philip Schuyler, United States Senator, who openly bartered legislative enactments for the benefit of a monstrous bribe to their Canal Company? Burr was perhaps the least blameworthy of all in the whole shady transaction.

5. WATERING A BANK

New York City had long been suffering from a lack of water. It depended chiefly for its supply on a single pump in Chatham

Street, fed from a pond known as the "Collect," on the site where the Tombs, that gray, grim prison, now stands. In 1789 Edmund Randolph described the situation to his wife. "Good water is difficult to be found in this place, and the inhabitants are obliged to receive water for tea, and other purposes which do not admit brackish water, from hogshead brought about every day in drays." [29]

This deficiency of water, coupled with the wretched sanitary arrangements then in vogue, lent itself readily to the rapid spread of epidemics. In 1795 yellow fever invaded New York City and caused 525 deaths; in 1798 it raged again with frightful virulence. Before the epidemic burnt itself out, 1,524 had died. Something quite evidently had to be done about the situation.

In the Legislative Session of 1799 Burr introduced a bill quietly into the Assembly entitled "An Act for Supplying the City of New-York with Pure and Wholesome Water." The Board of Directors of the prospective Corporation were Daniel Ludlow, John Watts, John B. Church, Brockholst Livingston, William Edgar, William Laight, Paschal N. Smith, Samuel Osgood, John Stevens, John Broome, John B. Coles, and — modestly last — Aaron Burr.

The purposes of this new incorporation, entitled the Manhattan Company, and capitalized at $2,000,000, were obviously to fill a pressing need. It was to supply the City of New York with an adequate supply of water, and, in pursuance of this laudable endeavor, it was empowered to condemn land, erect dams, turn streams and rivers, dig canals and trenches, dykes and reservoirs, and lay pipes and conduits, "*provided,* That the said company shall, within ten years from the passing of this act, furnish and continue a supply of pure and wholesome water, sufficient for the use of all such citizens dwelling in the said city, as shall agree to take it on the terms to be demanded by the said company; in default whereof, the said corporation shall be dissolved." [30]

Fair enough, highly laudable, and seemingly innocuous. But there was another innocent-seeming provision. And it was in connection with this appendage that Burr rose to the heights of political agility and finesse. It read: "*And be it further enacted,* That it shall and may be lawful for the said company to employ all such surplus capital as may belong or accrue to the said company in the purchase of public or other stock, or in any other monied transactions or operations not inconsistent with the constitution and laws of this state or of the United States, for the sole benefit of the said company." [31]

To understand the dynamite concealed in this rider, it is necessary to view the financial situation of New York at the time. There were two banks in the entire State — the Bank of New York, and a branch of the Bank of the United States. Both were wholly under Hamilton's domination, and exclusively Federalist in politics. They were powerful weapons in the Hamiltonian arsenal of tactics. Through them Federalist merchants were favored with loans and substantial accommodations in the necessary pursuits of their business, while merchants of Republican tendencies were politely informed that the banks were unable to extend them any credit. It may readily be seen that such a weapon, used with ruthlessness, might convert certain wavering merchants to the Federalist cause. And it *was* used with the necessary ruthlessness.

The Republicans tried in vain to break this strangling grip of the banks. The Legislature, under the control of a Federalist majority, refused point-blank to issue any new bank charters, especially to Republican incorporators. It was necessary, therefore, to employ guile. Burr was the master mind at this sort of thing. The idea of the Water Company was born. It was a public-spirited enterprise, and non-political. There would be no difficulty in ensuring its passage. The rider seemed mere surplusage. The fact that most of the incorporators and directors were Republicans did not penetrate the legislative mind. Was not John B. Church — he who was soon to meet Burr on the dueling field — Hamilton's own brother-in-law?

On March 28, 1799, the bill passed the Assembly quietly, without even the record of a vote.[32] In the Senate Burr maneuvered the bill with such skill that, with the aid and assistance of unsuspecting Federalist Senators, it was referred to a select committee for consideration, instead of, as was usual, being placed before the entire Senate functioning as a committee of the whole. Davis contends that to this select committee of three Burr disclosed his intention to run a bank in connection with the chief business of the proposed corporation, or even possibly to form an East India Company for foreign trade.[33] This may or may not be so; there is no corroborating evidence.

But it is quite obvious that the generalty of the legislators, either in the Assembly or in the Senate, knew nothing of these intentions. The committee reported the bill favorably, and it passed the Senate. But in the Council of Revision, to which all bills must be sent for approval, the Chief Justice smelled a rat. He objected to the charter on the ground of that added novel and unusual clause, justly foreseeing the uses to which it might be put.

Nevertheless he was overruled in the Council, and the bill became a law on April 2, 1799.

The Chief Justice was right. There was a rush to subscribe to the stock of the Manhattan Company, mainly by Republicans, and almost immediately the Bank of the Manhattan Company blossomed into existence. Burr's tactics had been eminently successful, and now, equally with the Federalists, the Republicans had their bank where accommodations might be obtained by Republican merchants and well-wishers. No longer could Federalist control of credit act as a political force in New York elections. The bank flourished and waxed mightily, like the proverbial green bay tree, and to this day it is a great and respected institution in the City of New York.

The Federalists rubbed their eyes and shouted treachery from the housetops. The members of the Legislature, that is, those of the Federalist persuasion, proclaimed that they had been tricked and deceived by the slippery Colonel Burr. An inflammatory pamphlet circulated, crying the deception, and maintaining with considerable vehemence that the bank was to be a party machine, ministering solely to the personal ambition of Mr. Burr. Nothing of course was said about the similar management of the existing Bank of New York and of the branch of the Bank of the United States, a supposedly governmental institution.

The Federalists lashed themselves into a veritable frenzy. Their best weapon had been taken away from them. Troup, that irrepressible purveyor of news to the distant envoy to England, hastened to inform him that " the most respectable mercantile & monied interests in the City are decidedly opposed to the measure . . . I have no doubt that if the company carry their schemes into effect they will contribute powerfully to increase that bloated state of credit which has of late essentially injured us by repeated & heavy bankruptcies." [34] He, too, forgot to mention that the " bloated state of credit " he decried was the sole doing of the Federalist banks, or that the Republican merchants were lean enough in all conscience.

But an election to the Assembly was impending, and the incorporation of the Manhattan Company was a splendid political weapon in the hands of the Federalists. As a result, many Republican artisans, uneasy in the presence of any bank, which they had been taught by Jefferson to consider as the invention of the devil himself, and standing to gain nothing from the new reservoir of credit, hearkened to the stream of propaganda, and voted the Federalist ticket. Darker tactics also were employed. Burr, a candidate for reelection to the Assembly, and the whole Republican slate in New York City, went down to defeat by an overwhelming majority of 900 votes. The Bank had proved a boomerang. Burr had miscalculated. There was political dynamite implicit in the charter, and he should have waited until *after* the election for the incorporation.

Like most of the acts of Burr's life, this episode has remained clouded in suspicion and misunderstanding. The Federalist thesis of double-dealing, chicanery and slippery morality on the part of Burr has been accepted in the main by his biographers. Especially do they feel that it was a shabby trick to promise the pest-ridden City of New York a pure water supply, and then cynically to foist a bank on the community instead.[35]

The first part of the thesis must fall of its own weight. The trick in the establishment of the bank — and trick no doubt it was — was well within the realm of the permissable in practical politics. The Federalists had their banks; they had used them as political weapons to favor their own followers; they had refused to permit the granting of any further charters. The Republican bank *per se* was not tainted with wrongdoing — it was and continued to be a legitimate business enterprise — and Burr was well within his rights to achieve it by the means he did. There had been no bribery, no corruption, such as had tainted the Holland Company affair. The Chief Justice had recognized the implications of the offending clause, yet the bill had passed. Burr had simply outmaneuvered and outsmarted his duller opponents.

The second part of the thesis — that the health of the people of New York had been used as a political football — is of graver import and must be examined. Evidently no one has done so before. It has always been considered that the Manhattan Company either did nothing at all about the expressed purposes of the charter, or did only sufficient to keep within the mandatory provisions — and no more. The records, however, are emphatically to the contrary.

When the Bank of the Manhattan Company commenced operations, the main business of the company was not thereupon sidetracked. It was attended to in earnest and serious fashion, and with all possible speed. As soon as the Charter went into effect, a Committee was appointed by the Board of Directors to study the situation. The Committee consisted of John B. Coles, Samuel Osgood and John Stevens. They reported to the Company before the end of the year (though the charter permitted a ten-year grace period) that " we must depend altogether on the supply which a well, or wells, sunk in the vicinity of the city, are capable of furnishing. On this head there is, however, every reason to believe the Springs which supply Water to the Tea-Water Pump and to the Collect are very copious, and may probably be adequate to the supply of Water for culinary purposes, at *least*. But in order to distribute the Water, thus procured, into the several quarters of the city, it will be necessary to raise it by some sort of Machinery." A " Steam Engine," in fact, was essential, and inquiries as to terms had already been made of a " Mr. Nicholas Roosevelt, of Second River." His terms, it seemed, were satisfactory, and the Committee advised their acceptance. They felt able, by the next winter, to supply 2,000 houses with an abundant supply of water at the rate of $8 per house. The Committee then proceeded to delve thoroughly into the question of piping, and after much deliberation and consideration of technical data, decided in favor of wooden pipes over those made of iron. There would be a considerable delay in the manufacture of iron piping (though the charter permitted them ten years), and the additional expense would have to be charged against the householders in the water rates. Furthermore, iron, in the existing state of its metallurgy, was generally an unsatisfactory metal for the purpose. The mains were to be laid " Down the Broad-way to the Government House, down Beekman-street, and down Wall Street," a distance of 2,970 yards. A reservoir was to be dug from wells near the " Collect," and estimates for all of these jobs were appended to the report.[36]

The work went on, with all the resources available at the time. Burr took an active part; so active that much later, while in exile, he was able to give advice to Swedish engineers on the feasibility of draining a lake, and to remark that " they bore logs (for conduit pipes) by hand with an auger, having no such machine as we used at New York for the Manhattan works." [37]

On March 25, 1808, long after Burr had been dissociated from the Company, a supplementary Act passed the New York Legislature giving the Manhattan Company the right to sell to the City of New York " all their . . . water works, pipes, conduits, canals, and all matters and things appertaining to the same, and the real estate appurtenant to the said works, and also all their right to supply the said City with water," and permitting the Company to continue in existence as a purely banking corporation.[38]

It was not until 1835 that the supply of water through the facilities of the old Manhattan Company was finally deemed inadequate. The Commissioners then reported that their water was still being furnished at an average rate of $9.63 per household. It must be remembered that the City had far outgrown its original limits, and that by 1835, the science of engineering hydraulics had made appreciable advances. It is a tribute to the founders of the Manhattan Company that their system had taken so long to become antiquated.

6. THE POT AND THE KETTLE

In 1799, however, the uproar continued unabated, cleverly fed by the Federalist politicians. Robert Troup's letters are illuminating as to the tactics employed. " Burr has for two years past been a member of the assembly & by his arts & intrigues he has done a great deal towards revolutionizing the state. It became an object of primary & essential importance to put him & his party to flight. The Manhattan company bill . . . gave not a little strength to our opposition against him. The election was the most animated I have ever experienced. All men of property & respectability stood forth, and appeared to act as if they were persuaded that every thing valuable in society depended on the success of their efforts. The merchants in particular were zealous & active. The consequence was that we have obtained a glorious triumph." [39]

On June 5, 1799, he was forwarding additional information to the effect that the news of the new bank " has seriously alarmed the two existg banks — and induced them to curtail their discounts very considerably." It was a political method of bringing pressure to bear upon the New York merchants, as the sequel seems to show. For, Troup continues, " the opposition given to this company by the great body of our monied & mercantile interests is astonishg . . . The odium it has caused against Burr had a powerful tendency durg the election to oust him & his partisans . . . We have at last prevailed upon the merchants to exert themselves. In the last election they were essentially useful. *They told the cartmen that such of them as supported the democratic ticket would be dismissed from their employ. The consequence was we had a strong support from the cartmen . . . Mr. John Murray spent one whole day at the poll of the Sevth Ward somtimes called the cartmen's ward or the Livingston's stronghold — and his presence operated like a charm . . .*

" We have received congratulations upon [the election] from various parts of the state and of the continent. It is considered as formg a new era in the annals of federal politics. If Burr had continued two or three sessions more in our Legislature it is a pretty prevalent opinion that he would have disorganized the whole state." [40]

These astounding revelations of the inner workings of the Federalist campaign are made by Troup with the most obvious approval of the tactics employed. No angry howl went up from the respectable and the great in the party councils. They were eminently right and proper. Yet these were the men who called Aaron Burr unprincipled, without virtue, ambitious, immoral, unscrupulous — indeed, every epithet within the resources of political and personal invective! Which proves merely that politics is an ancient institution, and has changed but little in the course of centuries.

Aaron Burr was defeated, and his Republican cohorts with him. It was a clean sweep, and Federalist hopes rose throughout the country. The most dangerous exponent of Republicanism in the nation had been crushed, seemingly for all time. New York was solidly in the Federalist column; only an earthquake could alter the political situation within the short course of a year. In 1800 there would be a Presidential election. John Adams — or Pinckney — was already as good as elected. No wonder they showered congratulations upon victorious Hamilton, Schuyler, Troup *et al.*

Nevertheless Aaron Burr was to furnish just that earthquake. For the last time they had underestimated his resources, his essential resilience of mind and body, his subtle brain and imperturbable aplomb, his inability to confess defeat. They were never to make that mistake again.

CHAPTER XIII

THE SECOND AMERICAN REVOLUTION

1. BURR DRAFTS A TICKET

T HE Republicans — in the person of Jefferson — had fallen just short of ousting Adams from the Presidency in the election of 1796. During the four year interim they had been busy strengthening their organization by constant correspondence, agitation, and pamphleteering. The economic discontent had deepened and widened among those classes to whom the Republican appeal was especially directed — the farmer and the " proletariat " of the towns. Some of the shippers and merchants, even, had become amenable to their gospel — notably those whose ships and cargoes had been seized by the British on the high seas.

But these advantages were to a large extent offset by the unacknowledged war with France, to which Revolutionary country the Republicans had somewhat too enthusiastically hitched their wagon. From the offensive they were compelled to pass to the defensive; only Burr had been clever enough to avoid the issue by his stand on armaments.

The Federalists, however, had lost this tactical advantage by their advocacy and passage of the unpopular Alien and Sedition Acts. The Republicans quickly seized upon the issue that had been thus thrust into their hands. They raised lusty cries about the freedom of the press, the rights of personal liberty. They inveighed against the aristocrats and the moneyed classes who held the poor farmer in subjection. For the moment, the issue of France versus England was considerably soft-pedaled.

The Federalists, on the other hand, rallied *their* stalwarts — the holders of public securities, the investors in bank and industrial stocks, the large shipowners and manufacturers, the New England clergy. A campaign of unprecedented bitterness and hate was in the making. A war between alien nations could not have been attended with more vicious propaganda, with greater outbursts of passion. Federalist and Republican avoided each other in the street or at private gatherings; to the Republican, the Federalist was a monarchist, a swollen creature of money-bags not unlike the caricatured Wall Street banker of later years; to the Federalist, his Republican opponent was a wild-eyed anarchist with blazing torch and the horns and hooves of a medieval devil. The first Revolution had been taken away from the Revolutionists. Another Revolution was now impending.

To understand the election of 1800 and its outcome, it is necessary to understand the election machinery of that period. There was no direct voting by the people of the nation for the officers of Government. There was not even a general election day. The electors in eleven of the States were chosen by the Legislatures of those States, meeting in joint session. In five only was there even the semblance of a popular, direct vote. Under the provisions of the Constitution then in force, the electors cast their votes for two men, without any distinction between them as to office. The candidate receiving the highest number of all the ballots cast became President, the candidate with the second highest number, Vice-President.

It is obvious, therefore, that the National campaign was actually determined in the local elections for members of the respective State Legislatures. Given a Federalist or Republican majority in the combined Houses of any Legislature, no matter how small, the vote of that majority would insure a unanimous delegation of electors from that State of the same political complexion. Hence the campaign had to be conducted on state, not national lines, and all energies were accordingly directed to the election of Legislatures of the proper political persuasion. But even this could not involve an appeal to the general population. The great mass of the people was notably disfranchised. The rigid property qualifications took care of that. A mere one-fifteenth of the adult male white population of the country were voters. Of these, still fewer exercised their franchise because of the difficulties in reaching the polls on the prescribed day, and because of the fact that the voting was non-secret. In those days of inflamed passions it required courage to vote in the public eye against the desires of the powerful and influential. It is well to keep in mind the picture of that stalwart merchant, Mr. John Murray, sacrificing an entire day in order to keep under his watchful eye the cartmen, his employees, when they came to the polls to vote.[1]

The Southern States were on the whole safely Republican; the New England section as safely Federalist. It was early realized that the election would turn in large measure on the electoral votes of New York, Pennsylvania and South Carolina. Of these the most important was New York. Unless that State could be carried, it would be almost impossible for either side to win.

The first States to vote for members of Legislature were New York, Massachusetts and New Hampshire. Their elections took place early in the spring. By common consent New York was recognized as the all-important, the pivotal State. All eyes turned in breathless fascination to its internecine struggle for supremacy as the few, all too few, voters were marshaled and counted and marched to the polls.

The State was seemingly Federalist. Hamilton's forces had won overwhelmingly in the election of 1799; the old Legislature was Federalist and John Jay was Governor. All the power of patronage, of the massed hordes of office-holders, was on their side.

But the Republicans did not despair. Aaron Burr examined the situation and found reason for optimism. He had detached certain valuable men in the western counties from the Federalist ranks — Judge Peck and General German especially. He had friends in Orange County, Peter Van Gaasbeck and others, to whom his name was an inspiring slogan. The State outside New York City would be close in its division. Hence New York City would prove the decisive factor. It was true that he had been beaten in the last election, but that had been the result of certain local factors. He had learned his lesson from former errors.

The Republican leaders unanimously left complete charge of the New York campaign to Burr. They recognized in him a brilliant tactician, the one hope they had of carrying the State, and thereby carrying the nation. The Clintons and the Livingstons remained on the sidelines. Jefferson, sitting anxiously in Philadelphia, relied on him implicitly. In January, 1800, in the very earliest stages of the campaign, he wrote to Monroe expressing his confidence in the result " on the strength of advices." In March, he was informing Madison that the election was safe if New York City could be carried. This on the representations of Aaron Burr.[2]

The supreme struggle centered on New York City. Both parties put forth their utmost efforts. Hamilton, facing the most desperate fight of his career, was campaigning like a madman. The Federalists backed him solidly. But the whole brunt of the Republican attack rested on Burr. In the beginning he had very little support. The Clintons and the Livingstons were strangely lackadaisical. They appeared to be sulking in their tents. The situation called for every ounce of energy, every dram of Burr's much vaunted diplomacy and finesse.

His first move in the campaign was a tactical one. He did not put forth his list of candidates for the Assembly and the State Senate until the Federalists had published theirs. Much of his strategy depended on the makeup of the Federalist ticket. Matthew L. Davis, Burr's lieutenant and future biographer, wrote to Gallatin on March 29, 1800, that " the Federalists have had a meeting and determined on their Senators; they have also appointed a committee to nominate suitable characters for the Assembly . . . Mr. Hamilton is very busy, more so than usual, and no exertions will be wanting on his part." But, continued Davis with justifiable pride, " fortunately, Mr. Hamilton will have at this election a most powerful opponent in Colonel Burr. This gentleman is exceedingly active; it is his opinion that the Republicans had better not publish a ticket or call a meeting until the Federalists have completed theirs. Mr. Burr is arranging matters in such a way as to bring into operation all the Republican interests." [3]

The event was to justify the brilliance of this strategy. For Hamilton committed a blunder. His blunder was conditioned chiefly on his secret malice towards John Adams, the titular head of the party. All *his* strategy was bottomed on the driving aim to unseat Adams for the Presidency and push his own ally, Charles Cotesworth Pinckney, of South Carolina, into the chair. To accomplish this, it was necessary, naturally, to elect a Federalist Legislature in New York, but it was equally necessary to place in office men who would be amenable to his plans when it came to the choice of Presidential electors. Accordingly, he called a secret caucus of his most pliant followers and nominated a slate of mediocrities, of mere tools to his ambition; men who would vote as he cracked the whip. It followed that there could be no outstanding Federalists on such a ticket; *they* would not have lent themselves readily to such work.

The caucus and the ensuing nominations were clothed with the utmost secrecy. But Burr had been waiting patiently for just this moment. Not for nothing had he been chosen time and again for Intelligence Service during the Revolution. As part of his political strategy he had built up an efficient espionage system, the details of which are still veiled in obscurity, but whose results savored of black magic to his befuddled opponents.

John Adams was to relate with considerable complacency — though it eventually cost him the election — how Hamilton had " fixed upon a list of his own friends, people of little weight or consideration in the city or the country. Burr, who had friends in all circles, had a copy of this list brought to him immediately. He read it over, with great gravity folded it up, put it in his pocket, and, without uttering another word said, ' Now I have him all hollow.' " This story, Adams averred, he had received from personal witnesses.[4]

Burr proceeded at once to stage the next step in his planned strategy. This was to oppose to the Federalist mediocrities a Republican ticket of men of such outstanding reputation that, on the basis of personalities alone, the voters must perforce exercise their franchise in behalf of the Republicans. But this was easier said than done.

The New York Republican party was not a welded unit, an organization united in a common cause. It was split into factions, each ambitious in its own right and jealously suspicious of all the others. The Clintons had dominated the scene for many years; they feared now Burr's rise to a commanding position. Between them and the Livingstons, recent converts to the Republican gospel, there existed a feud of long standing and a clash of political ambitions. There was also a host of other factions, swayed by local issues and mutual animosities. Yet to win the election, it was necessary to obliterate these personal and political feuds, and weld all contending factions into a solid and powerful fighting unit. Worse still, it was necessary to persuade, cajole or threaten the leaders, the great heads, the sulkers in their tents, to come forth and stand as candidates for seats in the lowly Legislature. Burr had stooped to conquer in 1797, but he was a *professional* politician. These others were not. It was a seemingly impossible task that he had undertaken.

Burr nevertheless had determined on his course. In the management of men and factions he had never risen to greater heights; perhaps in American history there has been no comparable accomplishment. He called into play all the resources of his remarkably attractive personality, of his powers of persuasion, of his political acumen and resourcefulness. His ticket was already drawn. It consisted of the ablest men of the party, men whose names were clarion calls to victory. George Clinton, many times Governor of New York, General Horatio Gates, with the glamour of the Revolution still upon him, Brockholst Livingston, eminent lawyer and member of a mighty clan, Samuel Osgood, Postmaster-General during Washington's Administration and ex-member of Congress, John Swartwout, Burr's own lieutenant, Henry Rutgers, Elias Nexen, Thomas Storm, George Warner, Philip I. Arcularius, James Hunt and Ezekiel Robins, each man representing some interest or faction and of more than local prominence. Every branch of the Republican party was represented in this New York City ticket.

The problem now was to make them run. Many — the Clintons among them — considered the prospect, aside from other and more personal considerations, as hopeless. The Federalists were in the saddle in New York City, and could not be unseated. To the ignominy of running for petty office, would be added the greater ignominy of defeat. Burr was not to be denied, however. He saw each proposed candidate personally, exercised on him all the arts of which he alone was capable, argued of the greater patriotism, the eventual success of the cause to which they were all committed, made each man feel the subtle force of his flattery — that on him, and him alone, depended the success of the movement. They were obdurate, eying each other with dour suspicion, refusing to yield. Burr redoubled his blandishments, his arguments; organized committees that waited upon the stubborn gentlemen with additional pleas.

Finally, after superhuman efforts, Brockholst Livingston reluctantly agreed that, if George Clinton and Horatio Gates both ran with him on the ticket, he would not withhold his consent. With this opening breach in impregnable walls, Burr rushed to Gates. Gates was his personal friend and warm admirer.[5] After much argument, Gates finally yielded, conditioned, however, on Clinton's similar acceptance.

Everything now depended on the ex-Governor's attitude. Burr brought all his forces into play. He himself, and committees which he formed, literally camped on the obstinate old man's doorstep. He had here to contend with, among other motivations, an ineradicable jealousy of himself. Clinton had held the power in New York for a long time. Should the Republicans win this campaign, through the efforts of Aaron Burr, a new star would be in the ascendant. Finally, however, party pressure became too great to be borne. He yielded, grudgingly, to this extent, that his name might be used without his express disavowal, but that he would not campaign in his own behalf. He even went so far, according to Davis, who was a member of the committee, as to express certain very unflattering sentiments respecting Thomas Jefferson, the leader of the national ticket.[6]

Once the leaders had capitulated, the lesser fry hastened to follow suit. The ticket was complete. It was unfolded to Republican gaze at the house of J. Adams, Jr., on William Street. The surprised rank and file, who had known nothing of what was taking place behind the scenes, arose and cheered deliriously. The nominations were endorsed unanimously.

When the news broke on the startled Federalists, they were

dumfounded. Burr had kept his secrets well, for Hamilton had nothing like the organized espionage of his opponent. Here was a ticket composed of great names, of national figures, to which they had to oppose a group of men without reputation, without standing, known to all and sundry as Hamilton's personal henchmen. Hamilton himself was paralyzed. Then he swung into action. The Federalist press hysterically attacked Jefferson, Madison and Clinton as plotters of destruction, subverters of the Government. Unfortunately, Clinton was almost the only one of the *local* ticket amenable to such attacks. Livingston and Osgood had supported the Constitution, Gates had hardly dabbled in politics.[7]

2. TAMMANY MARCHES TO THE POLLS

But Burr was not depending solely on the merits of the ticket he had evolved. For years he had been slowly but steadily employed in the forging of an irresistible political machine. Fundamentally, it was based upon a group of young men of ability and enthusiasm whom he had gathered around him after careful deliberation. The Swartwout family, John and Robert, and later, young Samuel; Matthew L. Davis, William P. Van Ness, talented and the wielder of a trenchant polemical pen, with his brothers, Peter and John, Theodorus Bailey, John Prevost, his stepson, David Gelston, and others. A group fired with fanatical loyalty and devotion for their Chief, captivated by his fascination, brilliance and unfeigned interest in their welfare, a group that acted and fought with formidable unanimity. These were the young men at whom the Federalists, and later the Republicans themselves, directed their sneers as the " little band," the " Myrmidons," and who were to be called proudly by Theodosia " the Tenth Legion."

There was also another group, much larger in numbers, and sprawling at first with considerable looseness over the city, whose political potentialities Aaron Burr was the first to discover. This was the Society of St. Tammany, or Columbian Order, founded in 1789 by William Mooney, an ex-soldier, who kept a small upholstery-shop at 23 Nassau Street. It was the normal successor to certain organizations of the Revolutionary era — the Sons of Liberty and the Sons of St. Tammany — groups of mechanics, laborers, and the dispossessed generally, who espoused independence and a vigorous war, and decried and ridiculed opposing Tory societies possessing the grandiose appellations of St. George, St. Andrew and St. David. These predecessors of Tammany dissolved at the end of the war, only to re-form during the struggle over the Constitution. They had followed George Clinton in his first battles, but had disbanded again under the dissolving acid of Hamilton's victories.

William Mooney, however, a private during the Revolution, resented the emergence of a new order of aristocrats, the Society of the Cincinnati. This was composed of officers only, who proposed for themselves and their families hereditary membership and resplendent insignia, leaving the common soldiers who had fought the Revolution out in the cold, politically as well as socially. Hamilton became the President of the New York Chapter. Burr was also a member.

In protest, Mooney organized the Society of St. Tammany, with a mumbo-jumboism of Indian titles — Sachems, Grand Sachems, Sagamores, Scribes and Wiskinskies — utilizing all the secret ritual and outlandish forms dear to the American heart. The years were floral seasons, the months " moons "; there were tribes of the Eagle, Otter, Rattlesnake, Bear, Fox and Tiger (which last was to become synonymous with the Society) ; their meeting-place was called the Wigwam, and Barden's Tavern was their first place of assignation.[8]

Originally the Society was non-partisan in politics, but gradually it shifted to anti-Federalist sympathies. Its members endorsed the French Revolution, toasted " Liberty " and " Freedom," and evinced an unconcealed hatred for the aristocrats and those of monarchical tendencies, as well as a vaguer and more unformulated resentment of the possessing classes in general. The backbone of the Society's membership consisted of mechanics, artisans, laborers and cartmen.

But the Society was not a political force. Its membership considered the Wigwam in the main a social rendezvous, where nightly, after the day's arduous labors, the men gathered to smoke, drink ale, and swap stories and anecdotes of a kind. Fitz-Greene Halleck was to sing of them,

> " There's a barrel of porter at Tammany Hall,
> And the Bucktails are swigging it all night long."

Burr had long had his eye on this loose-bound Society of Tammany. He saw the enormous possibilities it held. As far back as 1796 he had set to work to make it his own. He never joined the Order; it is doubtful if he ever set foot within its smoky, odorous precincts. But he gradually achieved control, becoming in fact though not in name, its real leader, and thereby started Tammany on the long road of political domination in the City of New York, a domination which has continued with but few interruptions to the present day. Mooney remained for a while the titular leader, but he was no more than a mere tool. Many of Burr's "little band," at his command, joined the Society of St. Tammany, in due time to become its Sachems and Grand Sachems, its prime movers: Davis, John and Robert Swartwout, John and William P. Van Ness, Isaac Pierson, John P. Haff, Jacob Barker, and others. "Burr was our chief," Davis acknowledged later.[9] Through his lieutenants Burr regulated the policies of Tammany, whipped its members into a fighting organization, marshaled them on election day to the polls in obedience to his orders. He was Tammany's first "Boss," the first of a long line. Yet he was not "one of the boys," in any sense of the phrase.

By 1798 the Society, under his powerful, if invisible domination, had entered upon its purely political phase. Its meeting-place was shifted to the "Long Room," kept as a tavern by Abraham Martling, an Ex-Sachem. The adherents of Burr, in the days of his disgrace, were to be called the "Martling Men." The Federalists, holding their noses, contemptuously termed the rendezvous "the Pig Pen." It was, in fact, a small, dark room in a shabby, one-story frame building.

Unfortunately, most of the Tammanyites were disfranchised by the existing property qualifications. Burr addressed himself to this problem and solved it by means of a clever scheme. Poor Republicans, propertyless and landless, clubbed together and purchased as joint tenants sufficient land to come within the law. The salient feature of a joint tenancy is that each participant therein, no matter how large the group, in law is the owner of the entire parcel. The substantial men of property who had originally placed their limitations in the Constitution against the rabble did not envisage the loophole through which Burr was to drive his massed cohorts to victory. Nor is it to be doubted that the wealthier Republicans, or the new Bank of the Manhattan Company, surreptitiously supplied the requisite funds for the purchases.

Burr's tactics in this respect were extended widely the following year. In November, 1801, 39 landless Republicans purchased jointly a house and plot of ground in the Fifth Ward, with the result that these additional votes turned the tide in the next Ward election. And in the Fourth Ward, a similar real-estate transaction at 50 Dey Street carried the day in the City Common Council. The Federalists howled "fraud" and their aldermen moved to cast out the ballots as illegal. They had a majority of one. But Edward Livingston, Mayor of the City, was Republican, and his vote created a tie, an impasse, and complete nullification of Federalist efforts.[10]

Nor was this all. Burr still had not reached the end of his resources in this momentous election. He realized that finances, the backbone of a successful campaign, had never been placed upon a systematic basis. He organized committees to collect funds in a house-to-house canvass. He sent solicitors to the wealthier Republicans, bearing with them slips on which the proposed contributions were already listed — as determined by himself. He scanned his lists with care and attention. No one escaped. A certain rich man, noted for his parsimony, was down for $100. " Strike out his name," observed Burr. " You will not get the money, his exertions on our behalf will cease, and you will not even see him at the polls." He came across another name. This man was liberal, but notably lazy. " Double the amount of his contribution," Burr remarked, " and tell him no labor will be expected of him." [11] Mark Hanna was but to put Burr's methods into practice on a larger scale.

Burr did more. He card-indexed every voter in the city, his political history, his present disposition, his temperament, habits, state of health, and the efforts necessary to get him to the polls. He organized precinct and ward meetings, saw to it that speakers were in constant supply, spoke himself. Modern politics — the politics of localism whereby national majorities are compounded — was being born.

Meanwhile Burr himself was standing for the Assembly from Orange County, not from New York City. He had many friends in that county who could be relied on to put him through safely. It is claimed that the reason for this shift in his own candidacy was to permit him to devote his entire efforts to electioneering in New York. It is also possible that he thereby avoided the embarrassing issue of the Manhattan Bank which had helped defeat him the year before.

The polls in New York City opened on April 29th and closed May 1st. Political leaders of the entire country watched with fascination the drama of that election. Hamilton, seeing the handwriting on the wall, rode frenziedly on a white horse from poll to poll, haranguing the voters, declaiming in a twelfth-hour effort to turn the tide. Handbills flooded the city. The Republicans worked ceaselessly. Davis penned a hasty note to Gallatin at the height of the excitement. " This day he [Burr] has remained at the polls of the Seventh ward ten hours without intermission. Pardon this hasty scrawl. I have not ate for fifteen hours." [12]

The polls closed at sunset. By late evening the result was known. The Republicans had swept their ticket into office by an average majority of 490. Burr's masterly generalship had been almost exclusively responsible for the result. Every one knew it, every one acknowledged the fact. The Republican Assemblymen and Senators from New York City were sufficient to create a Republican majority in the joint Houses. Burr had also been successful in Orange County. A unanimous Republican delegation of Presidential electors from New York State was assured.

An analysis of the vote in New York City discloses certain interesting sidelights on the fundamental makeup of the two parties. In order to vote for State Senators, it must be remembered, possession of freeholds of at least £100 in value was required. Necessarily, such voters were representative of the substantial, propertied classes, especially within city limits. Haight, the ranking Federalist candidate, received 1126 votes in New York City, as against 877 for Denning, the leader on the Republican list. But the outlying rural districts, where the farmers were, overcame this majority and elected the Republican.

For the Assembly, the property qualifications were substantially less, and Burr's methods of joint tenancy and ownership had made practically every Republican dweller in the city into a voter. Here George Clinton, the leading Republican candidate, received 3092 votes as against 2665 for Furma, the highest among the Federalists.[13] Wealth and commerce gravitated substantially to the Federalists, farmers and landless workers to the Republicans.

The news of the smashing New York victory was carried by swift expresses to Philadelphia, the seat of the Government. Wild exultation overcame the Republicans, while the Federalists sank into gloomy depression. Hamilton had let them down. The Senate was in session, but such was the confusion and hasty assemblage of party conclaves that the further transaction of business became impossible, and the Senate was compelled to adjourn.

In New York, Hamilton was stunned. He knew only too well what the result portended. The success of the Republicans nationally, the ousting of the Federalists from the seats of the mighty, his own eventual downfall as the leader of the party. The prospect appalled him. Ordinarily an intellectual machine of the first order, he gave way to one of his not infrequent emotional outbursts. He called a secret meeting of his followers and determined upon trickery to snatch back victory from defeat.

In his own handwriting, he sent Governor John Jay a most remarkable document. He proposed nothing more or less than the immediate convening of an extra session of the existing Legislature, which was Federalist in complexion. At this session a bill was to be jammed through, depriving the Legislature of the right to choose the Presidential electors, and placing such power in the hands of the people of the State by districts. Thereby, he stated, the impending debacle could be averted, and a respectable minority of electors chosen to vote for the Federalist candidates for President and Vice-President. " It is easy," he wrote, " to sacrifice the substantial interests of society by a strict adherence to ordinary rules . . . the scruples of delicacy and propriety, as relative to a common course of things, ought to yield to the extraordinary nature of the crisis." [14] An astounding proposition, especially from a man who never tired of accusing Burr of political chicanery and loose ethics. Hamilton once again had lost his head. An election had just been held, in accordance with law. The people had registered their convictions, knowing full well what issues were at stake. Hamilton was proposing now to defeat their will — *after* he and his party had formulated the rules. For his scheme was nothing more or less than that which Burr and Swartwout had legitimately advocated *prior* to the election, and which the Federalists themselves had defeated.[15] But then they had been certain of victory. It all depended on whose ox was gored.

To Jay's eternal credit, however, he made a notation on Hamilton's letter, " proposing a measure for party purposes, which I think it would not become me to adopt " and buried it among his private papers, where it was discovered after his death.[16]

Burr's spy system was still functioning with uncanny efficiency. The very next day after Hamilton's proposal was despatched, a copy of it appeared in a Republican newspaper. The public read it with incredulity. A Federalist editor, who had not been in on the secret caucus, denounced it in unmeasured language as a base slander, an infamous lie.

The new Legislature duly met, with a Republican majority of 22 on joint ballot, and elected 12 Republican Presidential electors from New York.

3. CLINTON OR BURR?

Burr's victory in New York turned all eyes upon him as a strong and powerful leader whose wishes must be consulted and heeded. The Republican party chiefs — the Senators, Congressmen, and officials assembled in Philadelphia — were now compelled to consider him in any plans that might be adopted for the forthcoming election. Nominations for national office, as they are known today, were nonexistent. Candidates were agreed upon at informal discussions or caucuses of influential leaders, who proceeded to write to all their friends, urging the caucus choice upon them.

Immediately after the results of the New York election were known, the Republican members of Congress foregathered in Philadelphia to choose such informal candidates. It was obvious that Thomas Jefferson would be the choice for the Presidency. It was just as obvious that the Vice-Presidency must go to New York as the Northern stronghold of Republicanism.

But here the obvious ended, and disputes arose. Three possible candidates were suggested — George Clinton, Chancellor Livingston, and Aaron Burr — representatives of the three political factions in the State. Each had his ardent supporters. Davis wrote to Gallatin, a caucus member, pushing Burr's claims to the nomination. Clinton, he said, was old, infirm, and seemingly averse to further public life. As to Livingston, " there are objections more weighty." There was a definite prejudice against his name and family, and doubts as to his firmness and decision. " Colonel Burr," he concluded, " is therefore the most eligible character. Whether he would consent to stand I am totally ignorant," but " if he is not nominated, many of us will experience much chagrin and disappointment." [17]

Meanwhile Gallatin, in puzzlement, was writing his wife, that " the New York election has engrossed the whole attention of all of us, meaning by us Congress and the whole city. Exultation on our side is high; the other party are in low spirits." But the burning question now was, " Who is to be our Vice-President, Clinton or Burr? This is a serious question which I am delegated to make, and to which I must have an answer by Friday next. Remember this is important, and I have engaged to procure correct information of the wishes of the New York Republicans." [18]

This was the decision, then, at which the caucus had arrived — to permit the New Yorkers to decide for themselves. Gallatin was given the delicate task, and he promptly assigned it to James Nicholson, his father-in-law, and an influential politician in New York.

What happened in the course of this mission is shrouded in an after-envelopment of inky mystery. Several years later, when

Cheetham's charges flew thick and fast, and Van Ness as vigorously retorted, diametrically opposed stories were laid before the public, and the truth is still not fully understood.

But in May, 1800, all this was in the limbo of the future. Nicholson first met with various Republicans and then, in accordance with his instructions, sounded out both Clinton and Burr on the question of their candidacies. On May 7, 1800, he reported to Gallatin that " I have conversed with the two gentlemen mentioned in your letter. George Clinton, with whom I first spoke, declined." Clinton, in fact, " thinks Colonel Burr is the most suitable person and perhaps the only man. Such is also the opinion of all the Republicans in this quarter that I have conversed with; their confidence in A. B. is universal and unbounded. Mr. Burr, however, appeared averse to be the candidate. He seemed to think that no arrangment could be made which would be observed to the southward; alluding, as I understood, to the last election, in which he was certainly ill used by Virginia and North Carolina.

" I believe he may be induced to stand if assurances can be given that the Southern States will act fairly. . . . But his name must not be played the fool with." [19]

Burr had forgiven, but not forgotten. Virginia and the Southern States had knifed him in 1796; he wished for no repetition of that treachery now that the chances of election were particularly bright. This private communication of Nicholson to Gallatin requires careful consideration. Gallatin was his son-in-law, its contents confidential. He had no reason for stating anything but the truth. For one thing, he acknowledged that Burr's resentment against the South was justified. It must be remembered, moreover, that Gallatin was definitely attached to Jefferson, though at this time friendly with Burr.

More important, however, is Nicholson's account of what took place in his conferences with Clinton and Burr. Several years later, when the storm clouds swirled, and the political axes were sharpening for Burr, Nicholson was to change his story. But definite pressure had been brought to bear. It was political suicide for a politician to stand out against Jefferson and the Clintons, and immediately before his new version was carefully written down — never to be published during his lifetime, however — he had been appointed to Federal office by Jefferson, on the recommendation of De Witt Clinton.

This account purported to substantiate Cheetham's, and Clinton's narrative of the conferences, and to dispute the counter-charges of Aristides (William P. Van Ness) . As far as Nicholson is concerned, the record must stand on the relative merits to be given these two documents.

As to Clinton, *his* statement also never saw the light of day. But he had furnished the material to Cheetham for his assertion that Burr had deliberately jockeyed him out of the nomination. In this communication, addressed to his nephew, De Witt Clinton, dated December 13, 1803, he declared, " I believe it can be ascertained beyond a doubt that our republican Friends in Congress were . . . in my favour in case I would consent to be held up as the Candidate for that Office and that it was only on my declension that Chancellor Livingston and Mr. Burr were to be proposed. To this effect Mr. Gallatin . . . wrote to his Father in law Commodore Nicholson, who shewed me his Letter and importuned me very earnestly to authorize him to express to Mr. Gallatin my consent." [20] But no such inference can be drawn from Gallatin's letter to his wife, dated May 6, 1800, previously quoted. Unfortunately Gallatin's own letter to Nicholson has been lost.

Clinton went on to say that at first he declined the nomination, but on further solicitation, " I finally agreed that in answering Mr. Gallatin's Letter he might mention that I was averse to engage in public life yet rather than that any danger should occur in the Election of President . . . I would so far consent as that my name might be used without any Contradiction on my part. It being understood however that if elected I would be at liberty to resign without giving umbrage to our Friends and he agreed to draught a Letter to Mr. Gallatin & shew it to me." On the face of it, this was a very strange decision to which Nicholson had assented. A Vice-Presidential candidate who refused to campaign for office, and who, if elected, would resign and leave the new Republican Government in a state of almost irremediable confusion! Nevertheless, according to Clinton's story, Nicholson returned the next day with the letter he had drafted to Gallatin, which Clinton thereupon read and approved. But, " when he left my House he went to Mr. Burr's where Mr. Swarthoudt [*sic*] and some others of Burr's Friends were, he disclosed to them the Business he had been on and shewed the Letter. On reading of it Mr. Burr was much agitated, declared he would have nothing more to do with the Business, That he could be Governor of the State whenever he pleased to be. This conduct alarmed Mr. Nicholson and to appeaze Mr. Burr and his Party he consented to alter the Letter to Mr. Gallatin to an unqualified declension on my part and by this means Mr. Burr's nomination was effected."

To which Nicholson, on December 26, 1803, two weeks later,

and over three years after the event, concurs in almost identical language. He adds, however, certain curious details as to the methods employed by Burr and his friends to persuade him to an alteration of the all-important letter to Gallatin, which, if true, speak volumes for Nicholson's incredible gullibility and Burr's even more incredibly clumsy tactics. For example — Burr is alleged to have rushed out of the room after he read Clinton's qualified consent to stand as a candidate, crying out " that he would not give up the certainty of being elected Govr to the uncertainty of being chosen V.P.," when, in fact, no proffer of the latter position had as yet been made to him. That he sent back two friends to Nicholson, pacing the room alone, to whom the bewildered politician again divulged the contents of the fatal letters. They read them, and " one of them declared with a determined Voice that Colo. Burr should accept and that he was obliged so to do upon principles." Whereupon they also left the room, only to return immediately with Burr, who " with apparent reluctance consented." [21]

An astonishing story, indeed, which Cheetham was to employ with telling effect when it was decided to read Burr out of the party. A story full of patent absurdities and contradictions, and not at all in accordance with earlier documentary material.

However, on the receipt of Nicholson's letter of May 7th, there was held, on May 11, 1800, " a very large meeting of Republicans, in which it was unanimously agreed to support Burr for Vice-President." [22] The ticket was complete. Thomas Jefferson of Virginia for President, and Aaron Burr of New York for Vice-President.

4. HAMILTON WRITES A PAMPHLET

The campaign proceeded with new vigor. That same month New Hampshire and Massachusetts held their elections for Legislature, and the Republicans polled astonishing votes, though failing of absolute majorities. The Federalists were thoroughly disgruntled, and torn by internal dissensions. Hamilton and his closer friends were determined that this time, come what may, they would displace John Adams and exalt Pinckney in his stead. Not that this was an open or public avowal of intentions: Hamilton was burrowing secretly and in the dark. He wrote with feverish intensity to all his friends and those whom he felt he could influence, urging them to cast aside Adams and throw their weight to Pinckney. On May 8, 1800, when New York's vote was still in doubt, he wrote Sedgwick that New York, if Federalist, would not go for John Adams unless a firm pledge was given that Pinckney would be equally supported in the Northern States, and ended significantly that "our welfare depends absolutely on a faithful adherence to the plan which has been adopted." [23]

On May 10th, in another communication to Sedgwick, he was even more open in his avowals. "For my individual part," he affirmed, "my mind is made up. I will never more be responsible for him [Adams] by my direct support, even though the consequences should be the election of *Jefferson*." [24] This, within three days after his letter to Governor Jay, in which he advocates the most unscrupulous measures on the ground that Jefferson's election meant the "overthrow of government," "revolution," "Bonaparte," "atheist in religion," and "fanatic in politics"!

John Adams became aware of Hamilton's machinations and exploded with wrath. There was no way he could get at Hamilton himself. But he proceeded to rid his Cabinet of Pickering, Secretary of State, McHenry, Secretary of War, and Wolcott, Secretary of Treasury; all friends and satellites of Hamilton. He had erred in not having taken this step long before. The damage was done.

Furious, Hamilton threw what little discretion he had left to the winds. The belated action of Adams was a declaration of war against himself. He promptly set himself to write a pamphlet — against the advice of his cooler-headed friends — in which he assailed the Administration and John Adams personally in the most intemperate language. Only on the repeated pleadings of his friends did he consent, albeit reluctantly, not to publish it anonymously to the world. Instead, it was agreed that Hamilton was to sign the pamphlet and that it was to be circulated privately among the leading Federalists for their consideration.

He forgot Burr, however, who had eyes and ears in the most secret councils of the enemy. The pamphlet had been sent to the editor of the New York *Gazette* to be printed, with due cautions as to secrecy. Somehow — the means employed has been the subject of several unsubstantiated versions — a copy of the printed pamphlet came into Burr's hands even before Hamilton received his own. And Burr promptly saw to it that it was printed, with appropriate fanfares, in the Republican *Aurora* and the New London *Bee*. It made a sensation. The Republicans pounced upon the damning pamphlet with infinite glee. The Federalists — those not of the immediate Hamilton persuasion — were shocked. Adams fumed. The party split wide open.

Now that New York was safely Republican, Burr turned his organizing talents to those New England States where elections were still to be held, notably in Connecticut and Rhode Island, where he had a host of friends. Troup was still keeping Rufus King informed of his movements and getting no satisfaction out of them. " Burr," he wrote in August, " whom Mr. Church calls our chief consul, is in very high glee. He entertains much company & with elegance. I understand he is in a day or two going to the Eastward & I presume on business of the coming election." [25]

The following month Troup was telling King that " Burr has just returned from the Eastward where he has been for the purpose of effecting a division of the New England vote . . . I recollect no period of Burr's life in which he has been more complacent than since our last election in this city." [26]

Hamilton was growing more and more worried. He had resigned himself to the defeat of his party; in fact, he even preferred the election of Jefferson " the atheist in religion " and " fanatic in politics " to that of John Adams. Adams and Burr — these were his two overwhelming hatreds, the red rags to his flaming passion. By August, however, he was thoroughly alarmed. Perhaps, through some sleight-of-hand, Burr might squeeze out even Jefferson for the premier position. This was not to be endured. Already, in August, he was telling James A. Bayard, the Federalist Congressman from Delaware, that " there seems to be too much probability that Jefferson or Burr will be President. The latter is intriguing with all his might in New Jersey, Rhode Island, and Vermont; and there is a possibility of some success in his intrigues . . . if it is so, Burr will certainly attempt to reform the government *à la Buonaparte*. He is as unprincipled and dangerous a man as any country can boast — as true a Cataline as ever met in midnight conclave." [27] Hamilton was very fond of such loose words as " intrigue," " unprincipled " and " dangerous."

To his horror, however, he discovered that other prominent Federalists were not imbued with his shuddering hatred of Burr; in fact, reading the signs aright, they were even this early considering certain possibilities involving Burr. Worse yet, the first suggestion of them came from no less a person than George Cabot of Massachusetts, high priest of Federalism, member of the all-powerful Essex Junto, hitherto devoted to Hamilton's interest.

" The question has been asked," he told Hamilton, " whether if the federalists cannot carry their first points, they would not do as well to turn the election from Jefferson to Burr? They conceive Burr to be less likely to look to France for support than Jefferson, provided he would be supported at home. They consider Burr as actuated by ordinary ambition, Jefferson by that and the pride of the Jacobinic philosophy. The former may be satisfied by power and property, the latter must see the roots of our society pulled up and a new course of cultivation substituted." [28]

In the light of subsequent events, Cabot's estimation of Jefferson's uncompromising nature was to prove wofully inadequate. One wonders therefore how much of truth there is in his unflattering characterization of Burr. All of the Federalists were to hammer the matter of his ambition. The accusation was true enough. It was also true that he was actuated by no particular philosophy of government or vision of a theoretic Utopia. But, judging from his record, there seems no doubt that had the Federalist plans been successful, they would have been sadly mistaken about their ability to sway Burr.

5. DOWNFALL OF FEDERALISM

Slowly the returns from the several States filtered in through the summer and autumn of 1800. The tension was becoming unbearable. New Jersey went Federalist, in spite of Burr's exertions. Connecticut, too, was safely in the Federalist column. As the autumn waned, and the snows set in, it became more and more apparent that the final result would depend on three States — Pennsylvania, where the fight was waged with violence and bitterness, little Rhode Island, and South Carolina, Pinckney's home State.

On November 26th, Rhode Island appeared to have gone Republican, but the outlook was dark in Pennsylvania and South Carolina. The Republicans everywhere became gloomy, but Burr was still optimistic. He wrote his uncle, Pierpont Edwards, an active Republican of Connecticut, that "you despond without reason. If we have R. I. Jefferson will have a majority even without Pena or S. C. But in S. C. there is every reason to believe that *he* will have the whole Eight." [29] Observe the significant underscoring. Burr evidently feared that the second votes would go to Pinckney, the favorite son, and not to himself. In which case, as the election was shaping up, Burr would be defeated. This situation explains largely his special activities in the politics of that State, which were exhibited later as evidence of dark and nefarious plottings. Of course he had to campaign for himself in South Carolina. Jefferson was reasonably certain of *his* votes. Burr's were doubtful.

Three days later he received further reports, which he hastened to pass on to his uncle. "S.C. will probably give an unanimous vote for Pinckney & Jefferson. Maryland 5 & 5 — N.C. 8 & 4 — Penna probably no vote. If your people (New England) have

cut P[inckney] from two or three Votes — J[efferson] will be Prest
— otherwise doubtful." [30] Burr was well aware of Hamilton's underground activities against Adams. And also, by this time, he
seems to have resigned himself to his own non-election.

On November 20th he had already received an express from
Georgia advising that Pinckney " appeared to entertain no other
hope than that of compromizing so as to run his own Name with
Jefferson." [31] The Federalists had broken party lines. Remembering certain sad experiences in 1796, Burr had good reason to fear
that such a compromise might find favor in the South and leave
him out of the picture completely.

No wonder, then, that complaints reached Madison, who bestirred himself promptly. He wrote to Monroe that Gelston, Burr's
lieutenant, " is uneasy lest the Southern States should not be true
to their duty. I hope he will be sensible that there was no occasion for it. It seems important that all proper measures should
emanate from Richmond for guarding against a division of the
Republican votes, by which one of the Republican Candidates
may be lost. It would be superfluous to suggest to you the mischief resulting from the least ground of reproach, and particularly
to Virginia, on this head." [32]

To Jefferson, Madison wrote with equal vigor. Gelston " expresses much anxiety and betrays some jealousy with respect to
the *integrity* of the Southern States in keeping [Burr] in view for
the secondary station. I hope the event will skreen all the parties,
particularly Virginia, from any imputation on this subject;
though I am not without fears that the requisite concert may not
sufficiently pervade the several States." [33] This last, coming from
a member of the Virginia group, is clear evidence that Burr's
fears were not mere fancies, and casts a retrospective glance at 1796.

These communications show a sufficient justification for Burr's
insistence that he be deprived of no Republican vote anywhere.
The election was still very much in doubt — Pennsylvania had not
voted as yet, South Carolina seemed likely to favor Pinckney over
Burr, and the final vote of the Presidential electors would in any
event be exceedingly close. A single ballot might mean the difference between election and non-election.

South Carolina, however, was to be the last State to choose its
electors — not, in fact, until December 2nd, two days before the
final date for the delivery of the electoral votes. Pennsylvania now
held the center of the stage. If Pennsylvania elected a full college
of Republican electors, a Republican would be the next President
without any assistance from South Carolina. But Pennsylvania

was in the throes of a violent political upheaval. It ended in a compromise. Both Republican and Federalist electors were chosen, with a majority of one in favor of the Republicans.

South Carolina proceeded to do the unexpected. It cast its electoral votes unanimously for Jefferson and Burr, and the Republican ticket swept to triumphant victory. The Revolution of 1800 was an accomplished fact; the Federalists, holders of the reins of government since its inception, were out of office. Yet, in spite of their defeat, in spite of the demoralization that had attended their campaign, honeycombed as it was by the bitter feud between Adams and Hamilton, the result had been perilously close. The final results were: Jefferson — 73, Burr — 73, Adams — 65, Pinckney — 64, Jay — 1. A switch of 250 votes in the city of New York had decided the national election, and this small shift was to be credited solely to the agency of Aaron Burr. The Republican party had triumphed because of him.

CHAPTER XIV

JEFFERSON OR BURR

1. PREMONITORY MURMURS

THE Republicans had won. But an unprecedented situation had arisen. Jefferson and Burr were tied in the number of votes received. Owing to the peculiarities of the Constitution, the electors of the various States had cast their ballots for two men, without differentiating between them as to which was to be designated President and which Vice-President.

As early as November, Madison had perceived the possibilities, but refused to believe that any danger could arise out of the anomalous situation.[1] Jefferson had correctly gauged the situation also, and seemed to have taken certain precautions, which, however, did not prove effective. On December 2nd, Peter Freneau was writing him that one South Carolinian elector had been expected to vote for George Clinton instead of Burr, to insure the Presidency to Jefferson, but that he had failed to do so.[2]

Jefferson himself was still confident on December 12th that his plans had not wholly gone astray, notwithstanding South Carolina's defection. He had other strings to his bow. On that date he was informing Thomas Mann Randolph that " it was intended that one vote should be thrown away [in South Carolina] from Colo. Burr. It is believed Georgia will withhold from him one or two. The votes will stand probably T. J. 73, Burr about 70, Mr. Adams 65." [3]

Nevertheless, to dispel certain small doubts, he wrote a very canny and carefully worded congratulatory letter to his running-mate on December 15th. " It was badly managed," he told Burr, " not to have arranged with certainty what seems to have been left to hazard. It was the more material, because I understand several of the high-flying federalists have expressed their hope that the two republican tickets may be equal, and their determination in that case to prevent a choice by the House of Representatives (which they are strong enough to do) , and let the government devolve on a president of the Senate." Under the Constitution, in case of a tie, the choice of a President was to be decided by a majority of the House of Representatives, voting as States, from the two highest candidates.

MATTHEW L. DAVIS

From a miniature

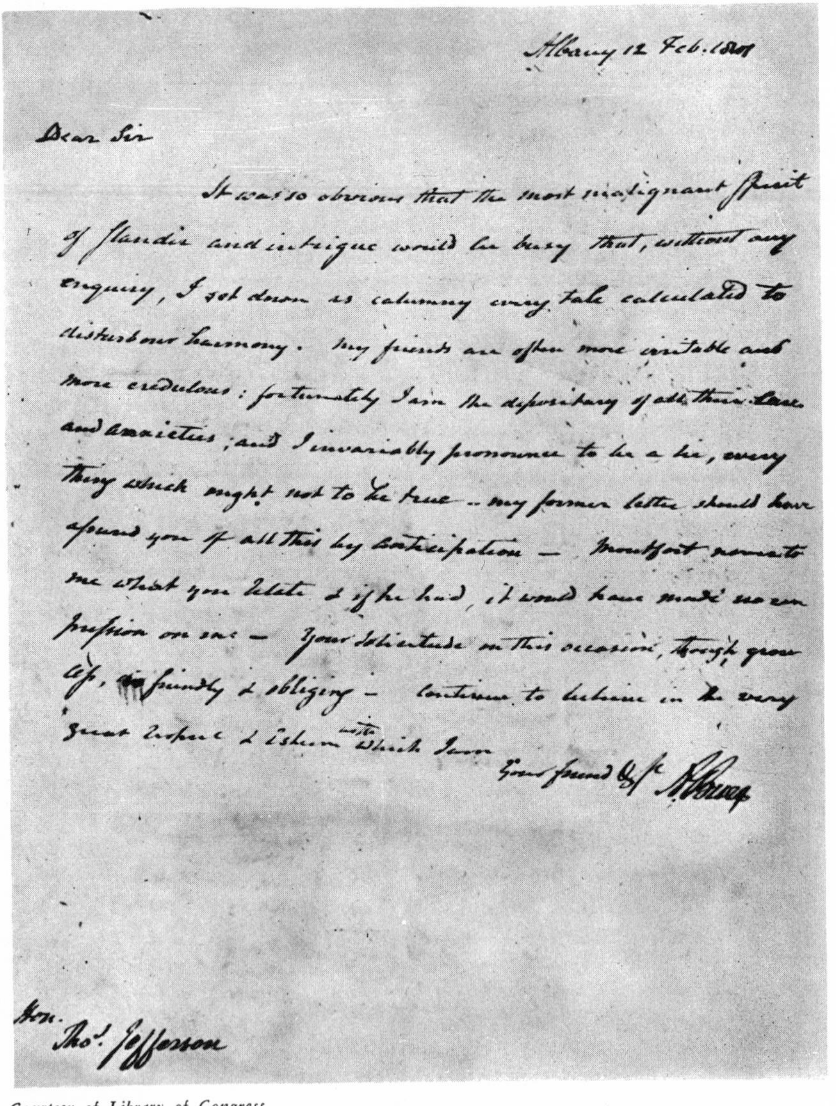
Albany 12 Feb. 1801

Dear Sir

It was so obvious that the most malignant spirit of slander and intrigue would be busy that, without any enquiry, I set down as calumny every tale calculated to disturb our harmony. My friends are often more irritable and more credulous: fortunately I am the depository of all their cares and anxieties; and I invariably pronounce to be a lie, every thing which ought not to be true — My former letter should have assured you of all this by anticipation — Mountfort never wrote to me what you relate & if he had, it would have made no impression on me — Your solicitude on this occasion, though groundless, is friendly & obliging — Continue to believe in the very great respect & esteem with which I am

Your friend & st A. Burr

Hon. Thos. Jefferson

Courtesy of Library of Congress

HITHERTO UNPUBLISHED LETTER FROM BURR TO JEFFERSON

"Decency required," he continued, "that I should be so entirely passive during the late contest, that I never once asked whether arrangements had been made to prevent so many from dropping votes intentionally as might frustrate half the republican wish; nor did I doubt, till lately, that such had been made." This is confusing, and refers evidently to a former statement of his in the same letter that South Carolina, Georgia and Tennessee might withdraw certain votes from Burr. He was blowing hot and cold. In one breath he disavows all complicity in any set-up which might deprive Burr of the Vice-Presidency; in another he fears the possibility of a tie between them.

However, "while I must congratulate you, my dear sir, on the issue of this contest; because it is more honorable, and, doubtless, more grateful to you than any station within the competence of the chief magistrate, yet, for myself, and for the substantial service of the public, I feel most sensibly the loss we sustain of your aid in our new administration. It leaves a chasm in my arrangements which cannot be adequately filled up. I had endeavoured to compose an administration whose talents, integrity, names, and dispositions should at once inspire unbounded confidence in the public mind, and ensure a perfect harmony in the conduct of the public business. I lose you from the list, and am not sure of all the others." [4]

This section of Jefferson's letter is fairly clear in its tenor, though there has been a tendency to wrap it in confusion. The confusion, if any, lies in the preceding paragraph, in which he was attempting to safeguard himself against all eventualities. Jefferson had marked Burr for a place in his Cabinet, in the event that he would gain the Presidency and Burr be defeated for the second office by a Federalist. Burr, however, was to be Vice-President, and hence unavailable for a Cabinet position. Jefferson was already aware of the comparative futility of being a Vice-President.

But Burr had also anticipated the possibility of a tie, and on December 16th had written to General Samuel Smith of Baltimore, a Republican Congressman and close friend to Jefferson: "It is highly improbable that I shall have an equal number of votes with Mr. Jefferson; but, if such should be the result, every man who knows me ought to know that I would utterly disclaim all competition. Be assured that the federal party can entertain no wish for such an exchange. As to my friends, they would dishonour my views and insult my feelings by a suspicion that I would submit to be instrumental in counteracting the wishes and expectations of the United States. And I now constitute you my

proxy to declare these sentiments if the occasion should require." [5]
Forthright, explicit, unmistakable in meaning. In those days of
limited newspapers and poor dissemination of news, such letters
were the accepted medium for the public avowal of views. This
letter was to become famous.

He replied to Jefferson's communication on December 23rd.
His response seems to have been overlooked by historians and
biographers generally. Yet it throws a flood of light on his stand
and on the hidden mechanism of the election.

" Yesterday," he begins, " Mr. Van Benthuysen handed me your
obliging letter [of December 15th]. Gov. Fenner is principally responsible for the unfortunate result of the election in R. I. So late
as September, he told me personally that you would have every
vote in that State and that A[dams] would certainly have one &
probably two: this he confirmed by a Verbal Message to me
through a confidential friend in October. He has lately given some
plausible reasons for withdrawing his name from the republican
ticket. I do not however apprehend any embarrassment even in
case the Votes should come out alike for us. My personal friends
are perfectly informed of my wishes on the subject and can never
think of diverting a single Vote from you. On the contrary they
will be found among your most zealous adherents. I see no reason
to doubt of you having at least nine States if the business shall
come before the H. of Rep."

In other words, Burr, while insisting that he be not knifed in
the South, where he could not oversee the result, had expected
that Rhode Island would drop a vote or two from him and ensure
Jefferson's election to the primary office. He had been assured of
this by the Republican Governor himself. But Fenner, for private reasons, had at the last moment decided not to run as elector,
and his substitute had voted equally for Jefferson and Burr. Here
Burr named names. Jefferson was in possession of this information. When the lid blew off and Cheetham proclaimed to a believing world Burr's faithlessness and treachery during the entire
course of the election, Jefferson had the means of inquiring from
Fenner as to the truth of Burr's allegations. He chose not to do so.
In fact, in spite of Jefferson's asseverations that he had kept his
hands off the Southern electors, the evidence points at least to the
activities of his lieutenants in withdrawing votes from Burr in
South Carolina, Georgia and Tennessee. Had *that* been done, and
Rhode Island had followed suit, Burr might have been nosed out
by Adams. Yet, as Madison's correspondence and the letter of
Nicholson to Gallatin indicate, the arrangement had originally
been for *none* of the Southern States to do this very thing.

In answer to the second part of Jefferson's communication, anent his Cabinet arrangements, Burr proceeded to remark that " as far forth as my knowledge extends, it is the unanimous determination of the Republicans of every grade to support your administration with unremitted zeal: indeed I should distrust the loyalty of any one professing to be a Republican who should refuse his services. There is in fact no such dearth of Talents or of patriotism as ought to inspire a doubt of your being able to fill every office in a manner that will command public confidence and public approbation. As to myself, I will chearfully abandon the office of V. P. if it shall be thought that I can be more useful in any active station. In fact, my whole time and attention shall be unceasingly employed to render your administration grateful and honorable to our Country and to yourself. To this I am impelled by the highest sense of duty as by the most devoted personal attachment." [6] Which proffer of services was also carefully to be lost sight of by Jefferson. When he had safely gained the Presidency, he preferred to have the dangerous Burr in the innocuous position of Vice-President. He could more easily be handled there.

2. THE FEDERALISTS TAKE STOCK

The world seemed to have come to an end for the Federalists. Nurtured as they were in the welter of party passions, and accustomed to the use of epithets and slogans for so long that they had conditioned themselves into a blind belief in the actuality of their own phrases, they felt that the triumph of the Democrats — one of the many names they applied to the Republican party — spelled unlimited disaster. Jacobins, French-lovers, infidels, Constitution-destroyers! — what would happen to the nation when this pernicious breed, under the egis of Jefferson, seized the reins of government?

The Federalist leaders, in Congress and out, scurried into caucus to decide their course. The more hotheaded, especially those from New England, openly advocated secession of their States from the Union, rather than submit to the domination of Virginia and its Southern allies. Others, almost as impulsive, seized upon the tie between Jefferson and Burr, and the consequent throwing of the election into the House of Representatives, where the Federalists were in the majority, as a manifest working of Providence. Let us, they cried, refuse to vote either candidate into office, and by what, they maintained, " would only be a *stretch* of the Constitution, name a President of the Senate *pro tem*," and permit him to exercise indefinitely all the functions of government. This course of action had a very respectable number of Federalists in its favor.

But the majority agreed finally on another plan — to vote Aaron Burr into the Presidency of the United States, as the lesser of two evils. On December 2nd, Gouverneur Morris, prominent Federalist, recorded in his Diary the reasons for this choice. " It seems to be the general opinion," he wrote, " that Colonel Burr will be chosen President by the House of Representatives. Many of them think it highly dangerous that Mr. Jefferson should, in the present crisis, be placed in that office. They consider him as a theoretic man, who would bring the National Government back to something like the old Confederation. Mr. Nicholay comes to-day, and to him I state it as the opinion, not of light and fanciful but of serious and considerable men, that Burr must be preferred to Jefferson." [7]

The plot brewed and bubbled over. All considerations of the known and expressed will of the people in favor of Jefferson, of public honor and decency, fell upon heedless ears. The Federalists were desperately determined that the hated Jefferson be not exalted over them. As for Burr, he was personally on good terms with many of them, they felt he was more moderate and less given to chimerical adventures, and that his course in office would not be as conducive to violent upheavals.

Federalist Robert G. Harper, hitherto a satellite of Hamilton, wrote Burr from Baltimore that " I advise you to take no step whatever by which the choice of the House . . . can be impeded or embarrassed. Keep the game perfectly in your own hands, but do not answer this letter, or any other that may be written to you by a Federal man, nor write to any of that party." [8] A wholly unsolicited communication, and there is no record of an answer. It asked for none, nor did it require any. Burr had already written an open letter to General Samuel Smith, also of Baltimore, in which he had stated his position in clear and unmistakable terms.

Hamilton, when he heard of this strong and concerted movement among the Federalists, was stunned. In the first place, he was supposedly the overlord of the party, yet these men, his henchmen, had not even taken the trouble to consult him. In the second place, the mere thought of Aaron Burr, whom he hated with a blasting hate, as President of the United States, was conducive to nausea. At first these rumors of what was going on behind his back were difficult to believe. He wrote Oliver Wolcott, old line Federalist, that there had been some talk of preferring Burr to Jefferson, but he hoped it was not so. Much as he was opposed to Jefferson, he would rather have him in office than Burr, whose " private character is not defended by his most partial friends. He is bankrupt beyond redemption, except by the plunder of his country . . . If he can, he will certainly disturb our institutions, to secure to himself *permanent power,* and with it *wealth.* He is truly the Cataline of America." Hamilton was becoming more and more reckless in unsubstantiated, and unsubstantiable, charges, as well as in phrase-making. Then, surprisingly, this guardian of the morals of a nation continued in quite another vein. " Yet it may be well enough to throw out a lure for him, in order to tempt him to start for the plate, and then lay the foundation of dissension between the two chiefs." [9] One wonders, in the face of this, whether Hamilton had instigated the craftily worded letter that Harper had sent to Burr.

But Hamilton was not long to continue in this vein. He soon discovered that the Federalist leaders had taken the bit in their mouths, and were running wholly away from his leadership and counsels. They were in earnest. It was no mere *lure* they were dangling before Burr; they grimly intended to go through with their scheme. They had come to the conclusion that the only hope of salvaging something from the wreck lay in Burr. Harper visited Morris and told him that it would be " advisable for the House of Representatives to give him their voice, without asking or expecting any assurances or explanation respecting his future administration. He thinks Burr's temper and disposition give an ample security for a conduct hostile to the democratic spirit which Mr. Harper considers as dangerous to our country, while Mr. Jefferson, he thinks, is so deeply imbued with false principles of government, and has so far committed himself in support of them, that nothing good can be expected from them." [10]

And Sedgwick was telling Hamilton that Burr " holds to no pernicious theories, but is a mere matter-of-fact man. His very selfishness prevents his entertaining any mischievous predilections for foreign nations. The situation in which he lives has enabled him to discern and justly appreciate the benefits resulting from our commercial and national systems; and the same selfishness will afford some security that he will not only patronize their support but their invigoration." [11] This in answer to Hamilton's condemnation of Burr as selfish, profligate, unscrupulous.

Hamilton was not to be convinced by these arguments. As he saw the tide running strongly for Burr among his own followers, he grew desperate, hysterical even. He threw himself into the breach with every epithet, every mouth-filling phrase at his command. He wrote feverishly, angrily, to every Federalist leader, in vain attempt to stem the tide. He argued and threatened and cajoled and painted black, horrendous pictures. The letters went out in an endless stream, wordy, repetitious, almost facsimiles of each other. He told Robert Troup, almost his sole loyal supporter, that " if the federal party play so dangerous a game as to support Burr, and he should succeed in consequence of it, he will withdraw from the party and from all public concerns." [12] He wrote to Sedgwick, Bayard, Wolcott, Rutledge, Morris, Otis, Cabot, practically every Federalist in Congress. He was right in this — that Burr in office would be less amenable to Federal compromise and threats than Jefferson. The event showed that Jefferson was willing to compromise, to placate. But the Federalist leaders did not know this at the time. They feared with an unholy fear Virginia domination and the theories of the physiocrats. They considered other things as well. Burr " has no political theories repugnant to the form of the constitution or the former administration," wrote Theophilus Parsons to Otis. " His ambition & interest will direct his conduct — and his own state is commercial & largely interested in the funded debt. If he will honorably support the government for which he has undoubted talents, he will have the support of the federalists and some of the Jacobins whom he may detach — and his election will disorganize and embarrass the party who have given him their votes." But, on the other hand, others of the Federalists " are fearful of his activity of his talents & his personal courage. They consider Jefferson as a man cautious thro' timidity — that he will fear to go the lengths of his party, & will thereby disgust many of them; and proceeding slowly the chapter of accidents may furnish opportunities of self defence which the vigour of Burr will not admit of." [13]

Hamilton, aside from his personal obsession over Burr, was clearer-minded in foreseeing the future than the others. He had been in intimate contact with Jefferson in Washington's Cabinet, and he realized that the Federalists had less to fear from his activities as President than from Burr. He said as much to Wolcott. If the movement to elect Burr should succeed, he warned, " it will have done nothing more or less, than place in that station a man who will possess the boldness and daring necessary to give success to the Jacobin system, instead of one, who for want of that quality, will be less fitted to promote it." And, significantly, considering that Hamilton was forever harping on the single string of Burr's cynical amenability to anything that would promote his inordinate ambition, " let it not be imagined that Mr. Burr can be won to the federal views. It is a vain hope." [14]

" If there be a man in the world I ought to hate, it is Jefferson," he wrote Morris. " With Burr I have always been personally well. But the public good must be paramount to every private consideration." [15]

To each, Hamilton directed those arguments which seemed to him the most effective in the particular case. To Bayard of Delaware he termed Burr a man " without probity," " a voluptuary by system," that, being in debt, " with all the habits of excessive expense, he cannot be satisfied with the regular emoluments of any office of our government. Corrupt expedients will be to him a *necessary* resource. Will any prudent man offer such a President to the temptations of foreign gold? " [16]

When Bayard responded in terms that did not show any undue alarm over these terrific qualities, he repeated his charges, with embellishments. Rather Jefferson, he cried, even though " his politics are tinctured with fanaticism," and " he is crafty and persevering in his objects; that he is not scrupulous about the means of success, nor very mindful of truth, and that he is a contemptible hypocrite." In spite of all this, he repeats, rather Jefferson than Burr, who " is a man of *extreme* and *irregular* ambition; that he is *selfish* to a degree which excludes all social affections; and that he is decidedly *profligate*." Hamilton had come a long way in the use of billingsgate. Why, he continued, " if Burr's conversation is to be credited, he is not far from being a visionary." This in answer to the Federalist argument that he was a " matter-of-fact man." " He has quoted to me *Connecticut* as an example of the success of the democratic theory, and as authority, serious doubts whether it was not a good one. It is ascertained, in some instances, that he has talked perfect *Godwinism*." This of course should strike horror into the hearts of all good Federalists, as should also the following: " I have myself heard him speak with applause of the French system, as unshackling the mind, and leaving it to its natural energies; and I have been present when he had contended against banking systems with earnestness, and with the same arguments that Jefferson would use." Furthermore, Hamilton maintained, Burr had gone so far as to quote approvingly Napoleon's phrase, " *Les grand âmes se soucient peu des petits moraux.*" (Great souls care little for small morals.) [17]

But Hamilton's long harangues made little impression on his former followers. He seemed pitifully alone in his opposition. Few listened, fewer still were swayed by his declamations. The expiring Congress was soon to meet in session to count the ballots, and, with a tie in prospect, the House of Representatives was to choose a President.

3. REPUBLICAN FEARS

The Republicans were literally beside themselves with rage and fear at the Federalist machinations. They had won a glorious victory, and now, through the interposition of a peculiar set of circumstances, the fruits were about to be snatched out of their eager hands. It was not that they feared, at that time, any wavering in Burr's loyalty to Jefferson, or the cause of Republicanism. It was, as Jefferson had indicated, the open and avowed boast of the Federalists that they would prevent an election altogether, and continue to hold the reins of power, through the medium of a Federalist President of the Senate.[18]

In this view he was not far mistaken. To a good many of the scheming Federalists, Burr's name was a mere pretense. Read what Samuel Sewell, member of Congress and later Chief Justice of the Massachusetts Supreme Court, has to say to Otis: " Another purpose may be effected by a steady and decided vote of the federal party for Mr. Burr: it is possible that an election at this time and with the materials you will be confined to, may be wholly prevented. This is most desirable." [19]

General Samuel Smith rushed to publish Burr's letter of disclaimer to him, as he had been authorized to do. It made no difference in the Federalist plans. They went right ahead with their determination to vote for Burr, and stalemate Congress into an impasse. Some even surmised that perhaps Burr would not be very angry at being aided by them in this fashion.[20]

The Republicans did not know whom to blame for having permitted themselves to be maneuvered into this unprecedented situation. The air was filled with mutual recriminations. McHenry gleefully reported " that the democrats in Congress are in a rage for having acted in good faith, that they swear they will never do it again and mutually criminate each other for having done so now, each declaring if they had not had full confidence in the Treachery of the others they would have been Treacherous themselves, and not acted as they promised to act at Philadelphia last winter viz: to give equal votes for Jefferson and Burr." [21]

Yet still no word of blame for Burr, or of his actions in the present crisis. In fact, nothing but a chorus of approval on the part of the Republicans. Jefferson himself was writing his daughter on

January 14, 1801, that " the Federalists were confident at first they could debauch Col. B. . . . His conduct has been honorable and decisive, and greatly embarrasses them." [22]

George Clinton, too, who later was to aid his nephew, De Witt Clinton, in the instigation of vicious attacks upon Burr's course of action, now declared that " I have Reason to believe from Burr's explicit declaration to me that he will not countenance a Competition for the Presidency with Mr. Jefferson." [23]

And Caesar Rodney was writing Joseph H. Nicholson, Republican Congressman, that " I think Col. Burr deserves immortal honor for the noble part he has acted on this occasion." [24]

Jefferson appointed Albert Gallatin the leader of his strategy in the ensuing session of Congress. Gallatin hurried to Washington and started work, quietly checking on every member of the House, preparing for every possible contingency. Jefferson himself, also on the ground, hovered watchfully in the rear, saying nothing for publication, sawing wood. He, too, was preparing, feeling the pulse of the nation over the proposed usurpation, asking for opinions from his friends. Madison was a bit doubtful. " Will it be best to acquiesce in a suspension or usurpation of the Executive authority till the meeting of Congress [the newly elected one] in December next, or for Congress to be summoned by a joint proclamation or recommendation of the two characters having a majority of votes for President? My present judgment favors the latter expedient." [25]

Joseph H. Nicholson was far more forthright. " In the Event of a non-election in consequence of federal Machinations," he asserted, " Virginia would instantly proclaim herself out of the Union." [26] There were hotheads in both parties.

Jefferson inclined to Madison's view, but only in case of eventualities. He personally was willing to have the House of Representatives elect. Failing that, other measures must be taken. " The federalists . . . propose to prevent an election in Congress," he wrote Tench Coxe. " The republicans propose to press forward to an election. If they fail in this, a concert between the two higher candidates may prevent the dissolution of the government and danger of anarchy, by an operation, bungling indeed and imperfect, but better than letting the legislature take the nomination of the Executive entirely from the people." [27]

Meanwhile, during all this preliminary turmoil and uproar, where was Burr? He was attending quietly to his duties in the New York Legislature to which he had been elected. The Session had commenced on November 4, 1800, and adjourned on November

8th until January 27, 1801. Burr attended its debates until February 17th, right through the balloting in Washington. There was something else engrossing his attention at this particular time. His adored Theodosia, the child he had reared in accordance with a rigorous system of education, was now a young woman of eighteen, beautiful, brilliant beyond all expectations — and about to be married. The bridegroom was Joseph Alston, a South Carolina young gentleman of fortune, a plantation owner, twenty-two years old, amiable, with some talent, and in due time to rise, with certain shoves from Aaron Burr and Theodosia herself, into the Governor's chair of his native State. He was, however, not quite up to his remarkable wife.

They were married on February 2, 1801, amid scenes of festivity. Almost immediately the bridal couple commenced their journey southward, on their way to the Alston ancestral home in Charleston, South Carolina. They were first to stop at Baltimore, however, where Burr promised to join them by the 28th at the latest.[28] These duties and preoccupations kept him in Albany, and busy. Yet he expressed his position on the matter of the proceedings in Washington time and again, and with great force. It has been stated repeatedly that he kept a discreet silence, wholly diplomatic in origin, and that secretly he was not averse to accepting the mantle of the Presidency which the Federalists were offering to throw over his shoulders. The record, however, tends to disprove this contention.

On January 16, 1801, Burr wrote in congratulatory vein to Albert Gallatin, whom he knew to be the leader of the Jeffersonian forces in Congress. " I am heartily glad of your arrival at your post. You were never more wanted, for it was absolutely vacant." As for the question that was agitating the nation at the time, " Livingston will tell you my sentiments on the proposed usurpation, and indeed of all the other occurrences and projects of the day." [29]

Edward Livingston, young Congressman from New York, was a member of the great clan, and Burr's close friend. Indeed, it was to be asserted by the ineffable Cheetham that Livingston was the intermediary between Burr and the Federalists in the great conspiracy to place Burr in the Presidency; a charge which Livingston was emphatically to deny. More important, however, than his denials, more important even than the close communication evidenced above between Livingston and Gallatin, is the testimony of a private and confidential letter he wrote to Matthew L. Davis — that Davis who was Burr's lieutenant in the Society of St. Tammany, and to whom certainly he would have unbosomed himself if treachery had been afoot. This is what he said, however, immediately before the House began its fateful sessions:

"I can now speak with some degree of confidence and have great pleasure in assuring you that all the little intrigues of falling ambition, all the execrable plans of violence and usurpation will in a few hours after you read this be defeated by the election of Mr. Jefferson." A prophecy which was, to be sure, a bit premature. He continued, "You may I think rely as fully on this information as on any that the nature of the case will admit . . . but if any unforeseen event should disappoint our hopes and wishes, you may rest assured that our City shall never be disgraced by any temporizing plan or acquescence in usurpation on the part of its representatives and I think I may without danger give this pledge for all those with whom he acts." [30]

Gallatin himself was well satisfied with Burr's attitude. He had already written his wife that "A more considerable number [of Federalists] will try actually to make Burr President. He has *sincerely* opposed the design, and will go *any lengths* to prevent its execution." [31]

The Federalists were resorting to trickery. Robert G. Harper had written Burr a seemingly incriminating letter, Gouverneur Morris, the same Federalist who had determined to support Burr in spite of Hamilton, was nevertheless telling General Armstrong (according to Jefferson): "How comes it that Burr who is four hundred miles off, has agents here at work with great activity, while Mr. Jefferson, who is on the spot, does nothing?" Matthew Lyon, vociferous Republican Congressman, was also to tell Jefferson that he had been approached by a Federalist from Rhode Island with the following words: "What is it you want, Colonel Lyon? Is it office, is it money? Only say what you want, and you shall have it." [32]

If these conversations actually took place as reported, they show the measures employed by the Federalists to embroil Burr with Jefferson to the prejudice of Burr. Jefferson meticulously noted them down in his *Anas,* as well as certain other second-hand conversations, long after the event. But evidently other attempts were made, and these were intended to prejudice Burr against Jefferson. Burr, however, did not keep *Anas,* or any similar repository for all the gossip he heard. Nevertheless Jefferson was alarmed at the possible reaction of his running-mate to these insidious rumors. His letter to spike these is well worth quoting.

"It was to be expected," he says, "that the enemy would endeavor to sow tares between us, that they might divide us and our friends. Every consideration satisfies me you will be on your guard against this, as I assure you I am strongly. I hear of one stratagem so imposing and so base that it is proper I should notice it to you. Mr. Munford, who is here, says he saw at New York before he left it, an original letter of mine to Judge Breckenridge, in which are sentiments highly injurious to you. He knows my handwriting, and did not doubt that to be genuine. I enclose you a copy taken from the press copy of the only letter I ever wrote to Judge Breckenridge in my life. . . . Of consequence, the letter seen by Mr. Munford must be a forgery, and if it contains a sentiment unfriendly or disrespectful to you, I affirm it solemnly to be a forgery . . . A mutual knowledge of each other furnishes us with the best test of the contrivances which will be practiced by the enemies of both." [33] Yet, while he was penning these sentiments and defense of himself against a forgery, so well done that it fooled a friend who was familiar with his handwriting, he was hoarding in his *Anas* for future use every rumor, every bit of second-hand gossip against Burr.

This alleged forgery, indeed, gave Burr a splendid chance, if he desired, to justify an open alliance with the Federalists to capture the Presidency. Professional politician and tactician that he was, if he had in truth been conspiring secretly to supplant Jefferson, he would not have failed to jump at the heaven-sent forgery. Instead, he wrote back to the anxious candidate in terms calculated to dispose for all time of this ready-made opportunity. His letter has missed the eyes of historians. Jefferson never saw fit to publish it.

" It was so obvious," he wrote, " that the most malignant spirit of slander and intrigue would be busy that, without any inquiry, I set down as calumny every tale calculated to disturb our harmony. My friends are often more irritable and credulous; fortunately I am the depositary of all their cares and anxieties; and I invariably pronounce to be a lie, every thing which ought not to be true. . . . Montfort never told me what you relate & if he had, it would have made no impression on me." [34] It must be confessed that Burr, the slippery intriguer, as he has so often been painted, emerges from this particular situation with all the honors.

4. THE HOUSE VOTES

February, 1801. Washington, the new capital of the United States, raw, unfinished, its streets by turn mud-holes and knee-deep in snow, was jammed to bursting. Space in the boarding-houses was at a premium; prominent men slept on rude cots, on draughty floors, and were glad enough to obtain such accommodations. Intrigue was in the air, conspiracy stalked the passageways. Excitement, anxiety, showed on every face. Congress was in session. The counting of the ballots was the province of the Senate and House jointly, Thomas Jefferson presiding over the unsealment of his own fate. But every one knew the result, even before the day. There was a tie between the two leaders of Republicanism.

It was in the House of Representatives that the true drama would unfold. Congressmen from 16 States, voting by States, held in their hands not only the individual fates of Jefferson and Burr, but perhaps of the nation as well. It was an open secret that the Federalists were determined on one of two courses, either to supplant Jefferson with Burr, or to drag matters into an impasse, from which, by some feat of legerdemain, the Federalists would emerge triumphant and in control of the Government.

The nation watched, and rumbled with excitement and alarm. The Republicans cried to the skies their execration of Federalist tactics. There was talk of secession, of the forcible seizure of government, even. It was said that armed men were congregating in Pennsylvania and in Virginia to resist such a subversion of the election returns. The Governors of these States were reported to be ready to call out their troops for a sudden descent on Washington. There was dark talk of assassination of any one who assumed to don the purple in place of the beloved Jefferson. It had been suggested by the Federalists that a law be passed placing John Marshall, Chief Justice of the United States, in the seat of the mighty. To which the Republicans retorted that blood would flow before they would permit such a usurpation.

The Federalist newspapers were almost unanimously for Burr, especially in New England, where his ancestry stood him in good stead. " He is," quoth one, " the grandson of the dignified Edwards, the great American luminary of Divinity, and a son of President Burr who was also a burning and shining light in the churches." [35] And the same paper boasted, in answer to Republican threats, not deigning even to consult the object of its exordium, that " our General [Burr] if called upon can assure them that he has seen southern regiments in former times and knows what they are composed of." [36]

There were dissenting notes, notably in those newspapers under Hamilton's control.[37] Hamilton, who wandered vainly on the periphery of his party, still seeking to argue its leaders into voting for Jefferson. At the Tontine Coffee House in New York, presiding at a dinner tendered to Oliver Wolcott, he gave the bitter toast: " May our government never fall a prey to the dreams of a Condorcet nor the vices of a Cataline." [38]

On February 11, 1801, Congress opened in an atmosphere of unexampled tenseness. It was bitter cold and Washington was blanketed with snow. The electoral votes were counted in joint session, Jefferson reading the results. A tie. Then the House retired to its own chambers, and settled down to the real business.

On February 8th, Bayard of Delaware had already offered a resolution that in the event of a tie, the House would continue to ballot until a President was chosen. The Federalists held an absolute majority in numbers. But the voting was to be done by States, not by individuals. Each State was to be counted as a unit, by a majority of votes within its delegation. Not only that, but the Constitution required for an election an absolute majority of all the States; in this instance nine.

The first vote was taken in breathless silence. The members leaned forward eagerly in their seats when the result was announced. It was indecisive. Eight states had cast their votes for Jefferson — New York, New Jersey, Pennsylvania, Virginia, North Carolina, Kentucky, Georgia and Tennessee. Six States had voted for Burr — New Hampshire, Massachusetts, Rhode Island, Connecticut, Delaware, and South Carolina. Two States, their delegations tied, cast blanks — Vermont and Maryland. Eight for Jefferson, six for Burr; nine States required for an election.

The divisions within the States are interesting. They may be summarized as follows.[39]

	Jefferson	Burr
New Hampshire	0	6
Vermont	1	1
Massachusetts	3	11
Rhode Island	0	2
Connecticut	0	7
New York	6	4
New Jersey	3	2
Pennsylvania	9	4
Delaware	0	1
Maryland	4	4
Virginia	14	5
North Carolina	6	4
South Carolina	1	4
Georgia	1	0
Kentucky	2	0
Tennessee	1	0
	51	55

Burr had an actual majority of votes cast.

The details are important. The Republican members of the State delegations voted, from all available reports, solidly for Jefferson. Included were the six Republicans from New York, headed by Livingston, Burr's personal friend. Also those from New Jersey, where Burr's influence was supposed to be strong. The Federalists, on the other hand, though in possession of a majority in numbers and in States, did not vote as solidly for Burr. There were a few recalcitrants, who did not follow the caucus. They were sufficient to keep Burr from an immediate election. It is impossible from the evidence to determine how many of these few voted for Jefferson from sincere motives, how many followed Hamilton in his violent exertions to avert the menace of Burr, or whether, behind the scenes, this method had been taken to create a stalemate, and prepare the ground for a later usurpation of power by the Federalists. Had the Federalist caucus been binding on all its members, Burr would have been elected President on the very first vote.

Outside, a snowstorm raged, the House was cold and draughty, but the members settled down to a long and weary balloting. Joseph Nicholson, Representative from Maryland, had left his sick bed in a high fever, toiled through the snow, and had bedded again in the House, in order to cast his vote for Jefferson in his State delegation, and thus create a tie. Thereby he prevented Maryland's vote from going to Burr.[40] Harrison Gray Otis viewed him as he lay on his rude cot, voting through interminable days, with a certain admiration. " It is a chance that this kills him," he wrote his wife. " I would not thus expose myself for any President on Earth." As to the first day's work, he went on to say, " we have agreed not to adjourn, but we have suspended balloting for *one* hour to eat a mouthful. Perhaps we shall continue here a week. No conjecture can be formed how it will terminate, but if we are true to ourselves *we* [the Federalists] shall prevail." [41]

The voting started at one in the afternoon on February 11th, and continued, with interruptions only for hasty snatches of food, until eight the following morning. Twenty-seven ballots were taken without the slightest change in the result. Both forces were steadfast in their determination to see it through.[42]

At 8 A.M. of February 12th, the wearied Representatives adjourned until noon in order to get a little sleep. " They looked banged badly," observed Uriah Tracy, one of their number, " as the night was cold, & they had the most of them not slept a wink: and those who had, were none the better for it: as it was caught in a chair or on the floor in a Cloak." [43] Then they resumed for more ballots. Still no change. Whereupon they adjourned until the following day.

Meanwhile Gallatin, fighting to hold his lines intact, received a letter from Burr, expressing astonishment at the advices that had come to him from the field of battle. " My letters for ten days past had assured me that all was settled and that no doubt remained but that J. would have 10 or 11 votes on the first trial. I am, therefore, utterly surprised by the contents of yours of the 3rd. In case of usurpation, by law, by President of the Senate pro tem., or in any other way, my opinion is definitely made up, and it is known to S. S. and E. L. On that opinion I shall act in defiance of all timid, temporizing spirits." [44]

Burr understood quite clearly the motives that actuated at least some of the Federalists, in their advocacy of himself. He was prepared for such an emergency. So were Jefferson and Madison. They had already discussed the situation together and laid their plans.

February 14th passed, with three more ballots; thirty-three in all. Not a single vote had shifted. On February 15th, Jefferson wrote to Monroe that " if they [the Federalists] could have been permitted to pass a law for putting the government into the hands of an officer, they would certainly have prevented an election. But we thought it best to declare openly and firmly, one and all, that the day such an act was passed, the Middle States would arm, and that no such usurpation, even for a single day, should be submitted to." In fact, the Republicans were already declaring for a Convention, at which the government would be completely reorganized and the Constitution amended, from a " democratical " point of view.[45]

Doubtless Burr was advised of these plans. It is also inconceivable that Gallatin, floor leader for Jefferson, should not have exhibited openly to the recalcitrant Federalists the threat of action contained in Burr's letter to himself.

Yet the voting went on, sluggishly, day by day, while the whole country seethed with wild rumors and alarms.

On February 16th came the first break. It had all along been obvious that it required very little shifting to decide the Presidency either way. To put Jefferson into the office was a mere matter of a single vote. James A. Bayard, solitary Representative from Delaware, cast the ballot of his State. Should he change his vote from Burr, Jefferson would have the necessary nine States. Should a single member of either the Vermont or Maryland delegation, presently voting for Burr, decide to shift, such State, now voting blank because of a tie within its ranks, would be sufficient to break the deadlock. In other words, any *one* of six men, from the designated States, had it in his power to make Jefferson President.

To elect Burr required a little more effort. To gain the requisite nine States, it was essential to divert a Jeffersonian voter in Maryland and Vermont, the tied States, and also one in New Jersey, whose ballot Jefferson was receiving by a precarious majority of *one*. In other words, *three* men would have to shift to his camp.

This, however, was not very difficult to accomplish. For this statement there is the authority of Bayard himself. Not long after the event, he wrote Hamilton in disgusted mood that though he was willing at first to take Burr, " I was enabled soon to discover that he was determined not to shackle himself with federal principles." An attempt had been made by the Federalists to treat with Burr in exchange for the election. David A. Ogden, Hamilton's law partner, was chosen as the emissary. But Burr explicitly refused to entertain any terms whatever, and Ogden wrote to the conspirators advising them to " acquiesce in the election of Mr. Jefferson, as the less dangerous man of the two." [46]

With the testimony of Ogden in mind, what happened becomes all the more clear from Bayard's narration to Hamilton. " When the experiment was fully made," he said, " and acknowledged upon all hands to have completely ascertained that Burr was resolved not to commit himself . . . I came out with the . . . declaration of voting for Jefferson."

" The means existed of electing Burr," he went on to declare, " but this required his co-operation. By deceiving one man (a great blockhead) , and tempting two (not incorruptible) , he might have secured a majority of the States. He will never have another chance of being President of the United States; and the little use he has made of the one which has occurred, gives me but an humble opinion of the talents of an unprincipled man." [47]

A remarkable document indeed, written by one Federalist, strategically the leader of their forces in the House, to another — and that one, Hamilton. Burr *could* have been elected, had he not turned down decisively all overtures from the Federalists. Bayard declared so now; David A. Ogden, Hamilton's own law partner, was to declare so later in a public forum. Certainly, had Hamilton any evidence of Burr's alleged intrigues, he would not have scrupled to use it then and in the Gubernatorial election of 1804, to his opponent's disadvantage. The record is clear, even without considering those declarations of Bayard, made years after the event, when extraneous considerations might have entered into the picture. One phrase in Bayard's letter is illuminating, as evidence how Hamilton's characterizations of Burr, by constant reiteration, had been so impressed on the minds of even intelligent men, that they became almost automatic in response. Burr, it seems, was " an unprincipled man " for not having yielded to the Federalist blandishments and usurped the Presidency! Posterity was to adopt a similar uncritical choice of adjectives.

Before leaving finally the violently disputed matter of Burr's alleged conspiratorial involvement in the Federalist campaign for his election, several additional bits of evidence remain to be adduced. One is a letter from William Cooper, Federalist Congressman, addressed to Thomas Morris during the very peak of the weary session. " We have postponed, until to-morrow 11 o'clock, the voting for president. All stand firm. Jefferson eight — Burr six — divided two. *Had Burr done any thing for himself, he would long ere this have been president.* If a majority would answer, he would have it on every vote." [48]

The other is the memorandum of a conversation, jotted down by Martin Van Buren many years after the event, with Judge John Woodworth, who had been one of the New York electors, and close to the Clintons. De Witt Clinton, it seemed, had expressed a fear that Burr might induce one of the electors to throw away a vote from Jefferson and thereby elect Burr. Woodworth, however, found " Burr's conduct in that affair entirely unexceptionable," and discovered no evidence of any attempt to oust Jefferson. Furthermore, though politically allied with the Clintons, he had been in close contact with Burr during the entire period of the Congressional balloting. According to the old Judge's recollection, Burr repeatedly reprobated the Federalist stand as an attempt to defeat the will of the people, and said strongly that " extreme measure should be resorted to to render their efforts unavailing," and on one occasion went so far as to say that in his opinion the success of their undertaking would " justify a resort to the sword." [49]

5. THE HOUSE ELECTS

On February 16, 1801, James A. Bayard of Delaware determined to break the interminable deadlock. Burr had been approached and found adamant against Federalist blandishments. The temper of the country was too alarmingly ominous to attempt the *coup d'état* that had been contemplated. There was only one thing to do — to try to obtain from Jefferson certain concessions in return for voting him into office. Here again controversy has raged.

Bayard gave his side of the story in a sworn statement which became a matter of court record. According to him, he, Baer and Craik of Maryland, and Morris of Vermont, the holders of the balance of power, had determined to vote together. When it was seen that a break must come, the four Federalists met and decided to make terms with Jefferson. They applied to Nicholas of Virginia as the intermediary. If Jefferson would assure them on certain points, they would arrange to switch these three States to him and make certain his election. They wished assurances that he would not, once in office, take any measures that might disturb the public credit, that he would maintain an adequate naval establishment, and that he would not remove subordinate administrative public officers from their posts because of their political faith. Nicholas refused to approach Jefferson, whereupon the four Congressmen turned to General Samuel Smith of Maryland.

" I told him," swore Bayard in 1806, " I should not be satisfied or agree to yield till I had the assurance of Mr. Jefferson himself [on the moot points] . . . The general . . . proposed giving me his [Jefferson's] answer the next morning. The next day, upon our meeting, General Smith informed me that he had seen Mr. Jefferson, and stated to him the points mentioned, and was authorized by him to say that they corresponded with his views and intentions, and that we might confide in him accordingly." [50]

That same day, February 17th, on the thirty-sixth ballot, the members from Vermont and Maryland who had voted for Burr cast blank ballots, and the votes of their States were registered for Jefferson; Bayard of Delaware and the South Carolina delegation refrained from voting altogether. The result was — ten States for Jefferson, four for Burr, and two not voting. Jefferson was elected President, Burr Vice-President, and the most bitterly contested election in all American history was closed.

But there were scars left. For one thing, the charges that Jefferson had compromised his principles in achieving the office. He resented them intensely, and wrote interminable defenses of himself in his *Anas*. For had he not, in a letter to Monroe, already stated emphatically that "many attempts have been made to obtain terms and promises from me. I have declared to them unequivocally, that I would not receive the government on capitulation, that I would not go into it with my hands tied." [51]

When Bayard's deposition was published in 1806, Jefferson told in his Diary that " this is absolutely false. No proposition of any kind was ever made to me on that occasion by General Smith, nor any answer authorized by me. And this fact General Smith affirms at the moment." However, as he wrote on and on, he qualified this statement somewhat. " I do not recall," he now recorded, " that I ever had had any particular conversation with General Samuel Smith on this subject. Very possibly I had, however, as the general subject and all its parts were the constant theme of conversation in the private tête-à-têtes with our friends. But certain I am, that neither he nor any other republican ever uttered the most distant hint to me about submitting to any conditions, or giving any assurances to anybody, and still more certainly, was neither he nor any other person ever authorized by me to say what I would or would not do." [52]

But Smith, in a deposition similar to that of Bayard, unwillingly admitted that he had spoken to Jefferson about the inquiries put to him by Bayard, and that Jefferson had told him that he would not dismiss officers of the government on political grounds only, especially with reference to Mr. M'Lane of Delaware, Bayard's friend, and that " Mr. Bayard might rest assured . . . that Mr. Jefferson would conduct, as to those points, agreeably to the opinions I had stated as his." [53] The whole dispute, then, seems to boil down to a question as to whether or not Jefferson *knew* for what purpose Smith was asking these questions, and whether or not he had directly *authorized* the answers given to Bayard. Which, on the face of it, seems rather an academic distinction. Certainly Jefferson was too good a politician not to have realized why Smith had sought him out in special conference to discuss certain matters which could only have emanated from Federalist sources.

Bayard must be considered honest in his reporting, as far as he was aware of the facts. By the very intemperateness of his language he absolved Burr from all complicity. On February 16, 1801, after he had determined to negotiate with Jefferson, he wrote Bassett that " tomorrow we shall give up the contest. Burr has acted a miserable paultry part. The election was in his power, but he was determined to come in as a Democrat, and in that event would have been the most dangerous man in the community. We have been counteracted in the whole business by letters he has written to this place." [54] One wonders what letters he refers to.

Bayard was to make other assertions against Jefferson, this time in a speech addressed to the Judiciary Bill on the floor of the House, February 4, 1802. Among other matters, he charged directly that Jefferson in a frenzy of fear that he might not gain the Presidency, had assured himself of certain votes by the bribery of promised appointments. Claiborne, who held the sole vote of Tennessee in his hands, received the Governorship of the Mississippi Territory, Linn of New Jersey, whose vote would have shifted that State from Jefferson to Burr, was given the profitable office of supervisor of his district, Edward Livingston was since made District Attorney for New York, and his brother, the Chancellor, Minister to France. And above everything else, M'Lane, for whom Bayard had directly spoken, was continued in office, in spite of the efforts of disgruntled Republican politicians to oust him. Not to speak of Theodorus Bailey of New York, friend to Burr, who had voted for Jefferson and was soon thereafter made postmaster of New York.[55]

6. CAUSE AND EFFECTS

The election was over, but irremediable damage had been done. Jefferson had never been too comfortable with Aaron Burr, and now, because of his narrow escape, Burr was doubly to be feared and distrusted. In spite of all Jefferson's protestations of friendship, it may be that he actually believed Burr had intrigued for the office. In fact, Hamilton had been at the greatest pains to inform Jefferson and the Livingstons alike of Burr's alleged plots and maneuvers, and thereby sown with skilful hand the seeds of distrust within the camp of his enemies.[56] In any event, from this day on it was Jefferson's deliberate purpose to remove Burr from his path, and crush him so thoroughly that never again would he be able to rise and trouble the dreams of the Virginia dynasty. The chapter of Burr's enemies was now complete. Alexander Hamilton, Thomas Jefferson, George and De Witt Clinton, the entire Livingston clan. Deadly, powerful enemies, still working in secret, nibbling stealthily at the sources of Burr's power, all still opposing smiling faces to his sight, and all the more dangerous because of that. They ringed him round in an ever-tightening circle, patient, inexorable, waiting for the right moment to crush him. From this moment on, Burr was a marked man. No stratagem was too low, no maneuver too foul, to encompass his destruction. Once more he stood alone, dependent solely on his own resources, on the little group of devoted followers in New York City, on the personal friends he had made. All the machinery of politics, the machinery he had done so much to create, was now to be used against him with irresistible pressure. Aaron Burr, Vice-President of the United States.

CHAPTER XV

VICE–PRESIDENT BURR

1. PRIDE GOETH

ON March 4, 1801, three men stood facing each other in the chamber of the Senate of the United States — Thomas Jefferson, President-elect, Aaron Burr, Vice-President-elect, and John Marshall, Chief Justice. Three men mutually distrustful, mutually inimical, whose duty it was to carry on the government and interpret the laws of the nation, who were to meet again in implacable conflict and under even more dramatic circumstances within a few short years. The oaths of office were administered; the new President read his Inaugural Address — a placating document in which, remarked Henry Adams, Jefferson seemed anxious to prove to his opponents that actually there had been no revolution at all.[1] The new Republican government was formally launched.

The new incumbents found themselves confronted, not merely with a complex of problems, both foreign and domestic, inherited from the old Federalist regime, but with another inheritance even more burdensome, and, to their minds, considerably more vicious. This was the famous midnight appointments of John Adams, who, seeing the twilight of the Federalist gods almost upon him, sat in his study until the very last stroke of his expiring term, signing appointments to office as fast as he could write. Chiefly they were made to the Judiciary, whose limits the Federalist Congress had thoughtfully extended for just such an emergency, and whose incumbents held tenure for life on good behavior.

Jefferson was confronted with a *fait accompli,* as well as with a horde of hungry Republican partisans seeking office under the new administration. Yet he had promised Bayard — so at least Bayard claimed — that no Federalist administrative office-holders would be disturbed for political reasons. It was a promise which, if made, he was compelled to ignore, except in isolated cases. The pressure placed upon him was tremendous. He tried to compromise, proclaiming a doctrine in his famous reply to the New Haven remonstrants that to the victors belong at least one-half the spoils.

" If a due participation of office," he wrote the merchants of

New Haven, "is a matter of right, how are vacancies to be obtained? Those by death are few; by resignation, none. Can any other mode than that of removal be proposed? This is a painful office, but it is made my duty, and I meet it as such."[2]

It was a difficult task with which he was confronted, and one that meets every change of party administration. Grover Cleveland was much later to use almost identical phrases when the same knotty question arose.

Aaron Burr watched the scene with somber eyes and inscrutable thoughts. He was an outsider, the skeleton at the feast. As Vice-President, technically his duties were confined to presiding in the Senate. The government hummed and buzzed with activity, the new Cabinet met and discussed questions of policy and administration, but the man who had done more than any other to achieve the revolution, to place them all in office, wandered disconsolately alone. Jefferson who had only a few months before lamented that Burr's absence from his councils would leave an irremediable gap, now politely passed him by, with cold, formal words of courtesy, seeking no way in which to avail himself and the government of the undoubted talents of the Vice-President of the United States.

Yet Burr said nothing. It is inconceivable that he did not perceive the frostiness in the atmosphere, that he was not at least partially aware of the massed forces of his enemies, and who they were. He even returned to New York to assist George Clinton in his ever-renewed race for the Governorship, once more to oppose Hamilton at the polls. Clinton was elected by a large majority.

As far as the outer world knew, Burr was still a party man in good standing, at the height of his power and popularity. The hollowness of the structure, due to the boring of innumerable termites, was not yet visible. Possibly he felt that by such a show of party activity, by the maintenance of a discreet silence, he could placate his enemies. Thereby he made the mistake that no professional politician dare make without courting disaster. He underestimated the venom with which he was regarded.

He had already made another blunder during the course of the campaign. He could have cast honor aside and seized the Presidency, as Clinton had done with the Governorship in the contest with Jay, as Rutherford B. Hayes was to do in the campaign against Tilden. Failing that, the matter called for the most vigorous measures. He had done all he could, at least so he thought, with letters and announcements and avowals, to dissociate himself from the Presidency. A professional politician should have done more. Burr should have quit Albany, Theodosia's wedding, the

Assembly, forgotten his wonted reserve, and hastened to Washington to declare in ringing public accents his denunciation of the unspeakable tactics of the Federalists. Thereby he might have avoided the creeping, insidious rumors that were finally to overwhelm him. Yet, with a due regard for human nature, it is doubtful whether such a course would have avoided the secret enmity of Jefferson. An office which is palpably the gift of another excites certain inner resentments. And the matter was too deeply rooted in more fundamental oppositions.

By aiding George Clinton to regain the Governor's chair, Burr unwittingly sealed his doom. New York was not big enough for the Clintons and Aaron Burr both. Sooner or later the struggle would have to be fought to the death. And the Clintons now had the power and the backing of the Federal Government, a situation which they were quick to capitalize. It was not so much the aged Governor who led the pack. A new leader had emerged to take his place. De Witt Clinton, his nephew, young, vigorous, thoroughly unscrupulous and talented. He knew what he wanted and spared no means to achieve his ends. New York State must once more be the inviolable bailiwick of the Clintons, and the shadow of the Vice-President of the United States darkened the Clinton sun. It must be removed forthwith.

The old Legislature, being Republican, had appointed a majority of Republicans to the all-powerful Council of Appointment. De Witt Clinton was one of these, and promptly assumed the leadership of his group in a struggle for power with the then Governor, John Jay, Federalist. Both factions turned a complete somersault in their respective stands. Whereas, under Governor Clinton, a Federalist majority had proclaimed over his protests the right of initiation of nominations, now it was the Republicans who asserted that right over a Federalist Governor. A long struggle ensued, until the Legislature, to cut the Gordian knot, declared for a Constitutional Convention to settle that and certain other problems. The Convention met October 13, 1801, in Albany. Burr was nominated as a delegate from Orange County, and in deference to his high position, the Convention promptly elected him President. Under his able leadership the Assembly was reorganized, with district apportionments according to the new census, and the powers of the Council of Appointment, under Article XXIII of the Constitution, were construed. As against the invariable claim of each succeeding Governor, Federalist or Republican, that he alone possessed the power of nomination, the Convention decided that such power was vested concurrently in the Governor and each of

DeWITT CLINTON

From a portrait by John Wesley Jarvis

"A GENUINE VIEW OF THE PARTIES IN AN AFFAIR OF HONOR AFTER THE FIFTH
SHOT, AT HOBUKEN, 31st JULY, 1802"

From a contemporary cartoon of the duel between DeWitt Clinton and Swartwout

the members of the Council. Which in effect gave all power to the Council — the Governor having but one vote out of five.[3]

This, it seems, may be considered the greatest blunder of Burr's entire career. As President of the Convention, as Vice-President of the United States, as a Republican whose popularity was still ostensibly unrivaled, and considering his talents for persuasion, it is quite probable that he could have swayed the Convention to adopt the position taken by Jay, and by George Clinton himself. By aiding and abetting in a triumph for De Witt Clinton and his personal henchmen in the Council, Burr had delivered himself into the hands of his enemies. More than anything else was this act to bring him crashing. Politicians do not operate in a void, beating their luminous wings in vain. They require substantial nourishment, with feet solidly planted on a firm foundation — notably, offices and the perquisites thereof. Now all appointments were placed in the hands of De Witt Clinton, who knew exactly the nature of the weapon which had been given to him by his rival, and did not hesitate for an instant to use it. " The meekness of Quakerism," he is alleged to have remarked, " will do in religion, but not in politics." George Clinton, secretly averse to Burr though he was, would never have used his power of nomination with the ruthlessness, the simple brutality, which his nephew employed. But of that more anon.

2. THE SPOILS OF OFFICE

Aaron Burr realized that his continued political strength depended entirely upon the organization he had built up in New York State, and especially in New York City. But, as has been stated, such an organization could not exist *in vacuo,* and certainly not when the party to which it was pledged had achieved all power, both State and national. There were offices to be filled, and the workers and tillers in the political fields required to be fed. Burr was as well aware of this tremendous principle as any one of his time.

The Clintons opposed him — of that he was definitely certain. But he relied, in State politics, as heretofore, on the balance-wheel of the Livingstons. He thought they were still his allies, and so was not unduly alarmed. Edward Livingston in the House, and General Armstrong in the Senate, both of the Livingston faction, were his friends. Others of the clan were personally his clients and even associated with him in certain vague speculations.[4] As long as the alliance existed, the Clintons would be impotent, New York would be safe, and even Jefferson, President of the United States, would not dare tread unduly on his feet.

For the moment his strategy seemed correct. In conjunction with these two members of the Livingstons, and with Albert Gallatin, Jefferson's new Secretary of the Treasury and erstwhile leader of his cohorts in the House, he arranged a careful list for the disposal of the Federal patronage in New York. It was a surprisingly moderate and reasonable list. Every faction in New York politics was given its due representation. The appointments in which Burr was particularly interested were those of John Swartwout as Federal Marshal and Matthew L. Davis as Naval Officer or Supervisor. In addition he would have been glad to see David Gelston appointed Collector of the Port, and Theodorus Bailey Supervisor.[5]

This list, it must be remembered, had been arrived at by a conference of the New York Republicans in Congress, Burr and Gallatin. It was submitted to Jefferson. He read it and saw his opportunity. Without the power of patronage, Burr would be cut off from his base of supplies and rendered impotent. Yet he did not wish to show his hand too openly. Whereupon he sat down and wrote a letter to Governor Clinton.

" The following arrangement was agreed on by Colonel Burr and some of your senators and representatives, — David Gelston, collector; Theodorus Bailey, naval officer; and M. L. Davis, supervisor." But objections have been made to this list — by whom, Jefferson does not state. What does the Governor think about it? [6]

The Governor, or rather De Witt Clinton, evidently thought plenty. Jefferson had tipped them off that Burr was *persona non grata* with the Administration, and that he would view with a tolerant and benevolent eye the downfall of their, and his, rival. It was not that he was particularly fond of the Clintons. He simply disliked and feared Burr more.

The appointments unaccountably lagged. John Swartwout, it is true, received the office of Marshal. Jefferson did not wish to declare open war immediately, and there were no good reasons that could be adduced against this particular appointment. Bailey withdrew his application, on the promise, it was understood, of a postmastership. The fight thereupon concentrated on Davis, Burr's particular lieutenant. There was the question, Jefferson said vaguely, of the present incumbent, a Federalist named Rogers. He was not prepared for *wholesale* dismissals of honest and efficient administrators. Perhaps he was sincere in the general theory; he certainly was not in the particular instance. New York, under the Clintons, and Pennsylvania, under Governor McKean, were even then witnessing a veritable slaughter of Federalist office-holders. *They* held no illusions about an equitable division of the spoils.

Burr heard something of what was going on behind the scenes. He wrote in angry tones to Gallatin. " Strange reports are here in circulation respecting secret machinations against Davis," he declared. " He has already waived a very lucrative employment in expectation of this appointment . . . The opposition to him, if any, must proceed from improper motives, as no man dare openly avow an opinion hostile to the measure." [7]

But Gallatin, though personally inclined to Burr's position, and a power with Jefferson, could do nothing in this particular matter. The months dragged. Burr communicated with Jefferson direct, to receive only the shifty response that Gallatin had not mentioned the subject to him. Which was obviously a lie, for Burr had insisted that Gallatin show Jefferson what he had written. Whereupon Davis determined to beard the lion in his den — the President was then at Monticello. But first he passed through Washington to see Gallatin, who received him with embarrassment, and attempted to dissuade him from the proposed journey. Failing that, Gallatin gave him a letter addressed to Jefferson which is remarkable for its frankness. He inveighed against what he termed " the general spirit of persecution which, in that State particularly, disgraces our cause and sinks us on a level with our predecessors." He viewed with disgust the way in which the Council of Appointment, under De Witt Clinton's domination, had extended its removal of Federalists, no matter how competent, " to almost every auctioneer " — surely not a political office. However, he concluded, if Rogers, the then Naval Officer, must be removed, he would strongly recommend Davis for the vacancy.[8]

To this letter, which he gave to Davis, he added another, by private post, even more remarkable in its language. For the whole strategy of the Virginians with respect to Burr was herein mercilessly exposed. The Administration had been in office a bare six months, yet already certain points were under secret consideration.

" There are . . . two points . . . on which I wish the Republicans throughout the Union would make up their mind," he wrote. " Do they eventually mean not to support Burr as your successor when you shall think fit to retire? Do they mean not to support him at next election for Vice-President? " In the next election, he thought, though Madison would have been preferable, " it seems to me that there are but two ways, either to support Burr once more, or to give only one vote for President, scattering our votes for the other person to be voted for. If we do the first, we run, on the one hand, the risk of the Federal party making Burr President, and we seem, on the other, to give him an additional pledge of being eventually supported hereafter by the Republicans for that office." And the second course would mean a Federalist Vice-President. The Administration was determined not to follow either alternative, and the only remedy for this particular dilemma was to distinguish constitutionally between the two offices. This was actually done soon after. The Twelfth Amendment put an end forever to the possibility of a repetition of 1800–1.

As for Burr personally, Gallatin continued, " I dislike much the idea of supporting a section of Republicans in New York, and mistrusting the great majority, because that section is supposed to be hostile to Burr, and *he* is considered as the leader of that majority. A great reason against such policy is that the reputed leaders of that section, I mean the Livingstons generally, and some broken remnants of the Clintonian party who hate Burr (for Governor Clinton is out of the question and will not act), are so selfish and so uninfluential that they can never obtain their great object, the State government, without the assistance of what is called Burr's party, and will not hesitate a moment to bargain for that object with him and his friends, granting in exchange their support for anything he or they may want out of the State." Shifting to the matter of Davis's application, he warned Jefferson that " it is not to be doubted that . . . his refusal will, by Burr, be considered as a declaration of war . . . I do know that there is hardly a man who meddles with politics in New York who does not believe that Davis's rejection is owing to Burr's recommendation. On that as well as on many other accounts I was anxious to prevent Davis's journey." [9]

The warning fell on deaf ears. Jefferson plumbed the future better than did Gallatin, though even he could not have foreseen the extent of Burr's blunder in the Constitutional Convention in giving all power to his deadliest enemy, De Witt Clinton. A combination of Federal and State patronage would be sufficient, he knew, to remove all supports from Burr's political prestige. Furthermore, he knew what Burr himself was still not wholly aware of. The Livingstons had deserted to the enemy. This was in great part Jefferson's own doing. He had flattered the clan with important offices and more important promises. The Chancellor became Minister to France, Edward Livingston was given by the Clintonians the lucrative office of Mayor of New York, worth $10,000 a year, besides the office of District Attorney. The new Secretary of State was of their family; they held New York judgeships and had a representative in the United States Senate.

Jefferson read Gallatin's long letter in Monticello and smiled. Davis was already there. " Mr. Davis is now with me," he wrote back. " He has not opened himself. When he does, I shall inform him that nothing is decided nor can be till we get together at Washington." [10] Jefferson had a positive talent for effective evasion.

Davis was never appointed. As late as March 25, 1802, Burr was still writing with a note of pathos to Gallatin, " As to Davis, it is a small, a very small favor to ask a *determination*. That ' nothing is determined ' is so commonplace that I should prefer any other answer to this only *request* which I have ever made." [11] Jefferson had not even taken the trouble to answer Burr's previous letters on the subject, except for one formal reply that, addressed as it was to the Vice-President of the United States, was by its very terms a direct slap in his face. Especially when Burr had good reason to believe that Jefferson had not been so meticulously upright in other cases. He made it a general rule, Jefferson said coldly, not to answer letters " relating to office . . . but leaving the answer to be found in what is done or not done on them." [12]

He forgot to mention his turning Burr's list of proposed appointments over to Governor Clinton for his opinion. He forgot also to mention that the objections to this list had come directly from Samuel Osgood, a Clinton henchman, and had been acted on with unseemly haste by himself. On April 24, 1801, Osgood had written to Madison to protest against the appointment of the three candidates from New York City on the ground that they were " entirely devoted to the Vice-President." He insisted, in fact, that no appointments be made of any Burrites, whose " Republicanism has been and still is questioned by many." Only Clintonites, he declared, should receive the Presidential approval.[13]

The war had been joined. Burr was out in the cold. In the State, De Witt Clinton had made a clean sweep of all Federalist officeholders, over his own uncle's futile protests, and forthwith filled the vacancies, down to the smallest auctioneer, with relatives and friends. But the lion's share was reserved to his new allies, the Livingstons, who must be held content at all costs. Of the six or seven thousand appointive offices, not a single one went to known Burrites. When, in desperation, Burr turned to Jefferson, he met with a more evasive, but just as effective, lack of support. A few scattered crumbs of Federal patronage, it is true, were grudgingly granted him, but not enough to satisfy his clamorous adherents. They could not know the inner workings of the conspiracy against their chieftain; they saw only that he was unable or unwilling to satisfy what they conceived to be their just demands. How long could they continue loyal under these circumstances? What fruitful ground would they yield later to the carefully sown seeds of suspicion against their former idol?

The story of Mr. Furman, a Republican with a natural desire to become Federal Marshal in New Jersey, conveys its own moral. On January 5, 1801, he wrote William Edgar, Burr's business associate in certain speculations, that he had, the week before, " the honour and pleasure of being introduced to the great little Burr." On March 2nd he was writing that " Mr. Burr is gone to his Post in which I hope he will be a terror to evil doers and a praise to them that do well."

On May 25th, he was abjectly grateful to Edgar and Burr both. " Thanks thanks for your prompt application to the vice [Burr] for his Interest in my behalf, nor can I make any other returns to that good man who has undertaken so arduous a task for the good of our country, in which he can have no other views, as I doubt not his professional business is more productive." The dulcet notes of an expectant office-seeker.

On August 6th, the note is still there, but a bit restrained. " When I applied through you to offer my Service as Marshall of this State, it was *as much* to gratify some of my friends as myself." He has heard, however, of others making application for office through their *Congressmen,* and seemingly with greater success than himself. But, he proceeds, " I concluded to let my application rest upon what was said by you to the Vice . . . I am bound to thank you for the application to Mr. Burr, and him for his willingness to grant it." Perhaps this is sarcasm.

In any event, by October 18, 1802, the floodgates of bitterness are opened. Another had been made Marshal, and it was all Burr's fault. " I am waiting, I cant say with patience," he writes, " to be able to form some Judgment respecting the conduct of Mr. B. Pray inform me what is the Opinion of those who have a knowledge of the business." This is a reference to Cheetham's attacks. In fact, the once dulcet politician is willing to add the strains of retrospective suspicion to the savage harmonies that are filling the air. " Believe I mentioned to you," he contributes, " that Col. Hunt and my self was invited to a Dinner last year when Mr. B. was there, the party consisted of Gentlemen that were so different in sentiments that Col. H. and myself could not account for the cause that induced Mr. R. to make such a Collection; but the matter seems to be opening now so as to account for it; if what is publishing is true, and it seems to carry the marks of fact." [14]

The evolution of a disappointed office-seeker, and an intimate picture of how Burr's fall was accomplished by his enemies.

3. GRIM PROSPECTS AND IDLE DALLIANCE

" Never in the history of the United States," wrote Henry Adams in his classic volumes on Jefferson's Administration, " did so powerful a combination of rival politicians unite to break down a single man as that which arrayed itself against Burr; for as the hostile circle gathered about him, he could plainly see not only Jefferson, Madison, and the whole Virginia legion, with Duane and his ' Aurora ' at their heels; not only De Witt Clinton and his whole family interest, with Cheetham and his ' Watch-tower ' by their side; but — strangest of companions — Alexander Hamilton himself joining hands with his own bitterest enemies to complete the ring." [15]

By the beginning of 1802 Burr stood not alone in this realization of his political solitude. Astute observers in both parties were fast becoming aware of the hue and cry that snarled at his heels. Thomas Truxton, on his way to Tripoli and glory, wrote sympathetically. " My friends in politiks are aware of your situation and how cautious you ought to be just now. And there are those here who you dont know — that have lately been at Washington and have heard enough to drop from certain characters, to convince them and this society [Norfolk, Va.] that you are not in the confidence of — [Jefferson?]." [16] And one Federalist was writing to inform another that " I have the best evidence that Burr is completely an insulated man at Washington; wholly without personal influence." [17]

De Witt Clinton, smug with the good work he had accomplished in New York, journeyed to Washington to take his seat in the Senate, and establish more intimate contact with the Administration. From Washington he wrote back exultantly to General Horatio Gates, erstwhile friend to Burr, and now alienated by Clinton's tortuous plottings, that " I find on my arrival here that our opinion of a certain character as formed at N. York is confirmed by that of our friends who have had better opportunities of looking into the business. Little or no consequence is attached to him in the general estimation here, and he will soon appear to every eye in his true colors." [18] Already, at this early date, February

25, 1802, Clinton was planning the vicious Cheetham attacks on his rival.

The Senate had begun its sessions on December 7, 1801. Burr was then still in New York negotiating for the sale of a sizable part of Richmond Hill, only to see the negotiations blow up almost at the last moment. William Edgar was the agent in the transaction, and there had been such rumors circulated about the true worth of the property by those " either utterly ignorant of the value or . . . from improper Motives," that Burr in anger withdrew it from the market.[19] The sale was necessarily a forced one, due to an ever-recurring financial crisis. Already he had been compelled to sell out his stock in the Manhattan Company, or a goodly part of it, thereby paving the way for his eventual dispossession from the Directorate by the Clinton forces. The powerful tool he had forged for Republican interests was wrested from his grasp as the opening blow in a well-planned campaign. John Swartwout and other Burrites were cast out in the same relentless purge. Even his financial speculations suffered from the secret machinations of his enemies. Brockholst Livingston, almost the last of his personal friends among the tribe of Livingstons, withdrew suddenly from a speculation of Burr to which he had promised financial support, and sailed hastily to the Madeira Islands to avoid his former friend's accusing eye.[20]

Yet none of these defections, these alternate pinpricks and bludgeonings of fortune, could depress the eternally rebounding spirits of Burr. The resiliency of his nature is probably his outstanding characteristic. He was forty-six, already on the heights, and to the unthinking, with even more brilliant prospects ahead. But Burr knew that he was slipping — that whichever way he turned, the path led down — unless a miracle occurred. Yet never once did he give up his abounding faith in the ultimate miracle, never once did his keen brain stop its scheming and restless planning. He was alone now. His wife was long dead, and Theodosia, in whom his whole soul was wrapped, had gone to Charleston to live with her husband, twenty days' journey away.

No longer does he act the schoolmaster with this child of his loins and of his brain. His letters are more human, lighter in vein; gay, witty, utterly charming. The moralizing has disappeared; so have the stern preachments. They breathe of a wholly delightful relationship, brimming over with tenderness, with the frankness of complete understanding. Hints of gallantries and a succession of dim-seen fair ladies parade across the pages, clothed in oblique language, but evidently holding no secrets from the understanding Theodosia. The Vice-President is still the gallant, the irresistible. The ladies succumb readily and willingly, nor did any of them appear to complain. Neither did his daughter, who in fact jested with him. A light-hearted acceptance of sex was a characteristic of both. Why then should the moralists of a later generation see fit to hold Burr up to opprobrium?

4. THE JUDICIARY BILL

But Burr was not forgetting public duties in private dalliances. He appeared in the Senate on January 15, 1802, and assumed his seat in the Vice-President's chair with consummate dignity and repose. The slipshod Senators, accustomed to slouching in their seats and loud talk and the noisy munching of apples and cakes, felt the subtle change in the atmosphere. They straightened up, they conducted their debates with an added decorum under the watchful, yet always courteous eye of the Vice-President. Burr was the perfect presiding officer.

On February 9th, General Armstrong, Senator from New York, suddenly resigned, and De Witt Clinton as suddenly was appointed in his place. Burr saw his enemy thus at close quarters, yet did not permit his easy calm to waver for a moment. But his friends charged that the shift in offices had been the result of a deal with the Livingstons.

Burr found the Senate in the middle of a violent and exacerbated debate on the Judiciary Bill. The Federalists, faced with the certainty of Republican victory, had rushed a bill through the previous session which reduced the number of Supreme Court Justices, after the next vacancy, to five. This was done, charged the Republicans angrily, to prevent the appointment of a Republican to that august Bench.[21]

In a further attempt to rescue the Judiciary from the oncoming Republican flood, John Marshall, bulwark of Federalism, was hastily appointed Chief Justice, and a horde of new circuit and district judgeships created, and as quickly filled, in the famous " midnight appointments " of John Adams.

The Republicans, and Jefferson in particular, very properly resented these tactics, especially as the judges, all Federalists, held office for life, and would oppose a formidable barrier to Republican measures. On January 6, 1802, Senator John Breckenridge of Kentucky moved the repeal of the National Judiciary Act. The new courts and the new judges, he argued, were not only mere surplusage and a heavy charge upon the straining finances of the Government, but they had been created for political purposes. The Federalists avoided the real issue and took their stand on the Constitution, which guaranteed to incumbent judges their offices during good behavior. Many even of the Republicans, though disapproving heartily of the additional offices, felt the force of the Constitutional argument, and paused in indecision.

Burr moved into this atmosphere of charged passions and political exacerbations. Every action, every change of his expression, was eagerly noted and commented upon by the opposing factions. The two parties were almost evenly divided in the Senate, and there was a frantic marshaling of forces. Every one knew by this time that war had been joined between Burr and the Administration, and the Repeal was a pet Jeffersonian measure which involved the very prestige of the Administration.

By January 25th, the excitement had grown to fever heat. The two parties were jockeying for position, and it became hourly more and more noticeable that the balance of power was being shifted into the hands of the inscrutable Vice-President. Bayard was writing, " Mr. Ross [Federalist Senator from Pennsylvania] has arrived and Mr. Ogden [Federalist Senator from New Jersey] hourly expected. These gentlemen will balance the Parties and place the scales in the hands of the Vice President. It is a situation he will endeavour to avoid and it is not certain how he would act. He openly disapproves some of Mr. Jefferson's projects and particularly the abolition of the internal taxes. There are *none* of them for which he has manifested much respect." [22]

But Burr could not avoid the issue. On January 26, 1802, the usual motion was made to pass the Judiciary Bill to a third reading. A vote was taken. It was a tie — 15 to 15. All eyes turned to the presiding officer. In calm, even tones he announced his casting vote. *Yea!* The bill forthwith proceeded to its third reading.[23]

The significance of this vote has been lost on historians. Only Gouverneur Morris seemed to have understood, and later recorded with some heat that " there was a moment when the Vice-President might have arrested the measure by his vote, and that vote would, I believe, have made him President at the next election; but there is a tide in the affairs of men which he suffered to go by." [24]

This may well be believed. Had Burr stopped the bill in its tracks, not Hamilton nor any one else could have prevented the Federalists from acclaiming him with joyous shouts as their champion. It might not have led to the Presidency; certainly it would have made him Governor of New York in 1804.

Yet Burr voted to break the tie and advance the bill, when he had the opportunity to bury it. His action on the following day has been analyzed and pulled to pieces by commentators, and his enemies were prompt to seize upon the incident and belabor it to good effect. But no one except Morris mentions his far more determinative vote of January 26th. Even his friends, outside the scene of battle, passed it by, and believed, as did his decriers, that Burr wished to defeat the Judiciary Bill. With this in mind, his own explanation of the reasons for his decision on January 27th must be accepted as credible.

On that day, Jonathan Dayton of New Jersey moved that the " Bill be referred to a select committee, with instructions to consider and report the alterations which may be proper in the Judiciary system of the United States." He argued in support of his motion that he considered it a " conciliatory motion," that " both parties should unite their labors with a view to revise and amend the whole Judiciary system." Colhoun, another Federalist, added that there was time enough in the present session to iron out all differences, that " if the report made by the committee should prove agreeable, there would be time enough to bring in another bill. This attempt to harmonize all parties can do no injury, while on the other hand, a system might be framed that gentlemen may be better pleased with than even a repeal of the act." 25

The Republicans were adamant, however, and when the motion came on for a vote, once more the Senate divided on strict party lines. Again Burr had the casting vote. This time he voted *Yea,* and the bill was recommitted. In announcing his decision, he essayed an explanation of his stand. " He felt disposed," he said, " to accommodate the gentlemen in the expression of their wishes, the sincerity of which he had no reason to question, to ameliorate the provisions of the bill, that it might be rendered more acceptable to the Senate. He did this under the impression that their object was sincere. He should, however, discountenance, by his vote, any attempt, if any such should be made, that might, in an indirect way, go to defeat the bill." 26

It is difficult to see how Burr's position can be quarreled with. It aimed at that very reconciliation of which Jefferson had spoken so grandiloquently in his Inaugural Address. It was a mere recommittal, not a burial of the bill. Its passage within the next few days proves this convincingly. Had he wished, as he was charged by those seeking his downfall, for a betrayal of Republican interests to the Federalists, he could have accomplished it the previous day by killing the bill altogether.

On February 2nd, under the lash of Jefferson, Breckenridge moved to discharge the committee, and bring the bill once more before the Senate. The political complexion had changed in the interim. Howard, a Federalist, was now absent, and Bradley, a Republican, had been hurried into the Chamber. The motion passed 16 to 14. Thereafter, by straight party votes, all amendments to the bill were relentlessly defeated, until, on February 3rd, the bitterly contested Repeal went through by the narrow margin of a single vote.[27] On March 3rd, the House concurred.

Burr's actions, carefully considered, must be held as rigorously fair and impartial. So keen a student as the late Senator Beveridge, himself a parliamentarian of no mean note, has so designated Burr's conduct.[28] Prominent Republicans wrote him in warm commendation of his stand. Yet the occasion was too good for his enemies to pass by. They concentrated on the second vote, and overlooked the first. The chorus yapped at his heels with a growing lust for his blood. It was to be added to the list of his crimes.

The Washington correspondent to the *Gazette of the United States* wrote with mixed feelings of the ensuing situation. " Col. Burr's vote to refer the bill, for destroying the judiciary, to a select committee has greatly puzzled the Virginia party . . . indeed his whole conduct is incomprehensible to them. Instead of lodging and boarding (as Mr. Jefferson did when Vice-President) at an Inn, he has taken a handsome suite of rooms and lives in the style of a perfect gentleman. All invitations to drink Toddy, and play cards, at Tunnicliff's Hotel, with the Virginians, have been declined, and he is not upon terms of familiarity with any one of them. It is said he has no great personal respect for the Virginia members, and indeed from what I've seen of them they are not calculated to excite the veneration of such a gentleman as Mr. Burr." [29]

5. Sundry Errors in Tactics

Burr was fumbling now, untrue to his own conception of the professional politician. He seems to have lost his grip. There were two courses conceivably open to him. One was to adopt a waiting policy within the ranks of his own party, efface himself as much as possible, do nothing that might provide his enemies with material against him, and await the inevitable breaks of fortune. The other was to ally himself openly with the defeated and disgruntled Federalists, who were milling about in the utmost confusion, without competent leadership. Hamilton had proved wanting; in fact, his activities had been directly responsible for the election of

Jefferson. Burr had many friends in that party, and his essentially moderate convictions on most questions were not too far removed from Federalist dogmas.

He did neither one nor the other. By his very impartiality in the matter of the Judiciary Bill he had exasperated both factions. This was creditable to him. But his appearance at a banquet of prominent Federalists met to celebrate the birthday of their departed and already mythic leader, George Washington, was the clumsiest kind of strategy. It was obviously a bid for Federalist support, but he had determined that it must be accorded him on his own ground. Burr, in spite of universal opinion to the contrary, showed no signs of compromising his underlying Republican principles. As a matter of fact, his chief political quarrel with Jefferson arose from Jefferson's manifest disposition to compromise, to yield on those very principles which had been proclaimed so strongly before the election. Burr was ready to unite with the Federalists, it is true, but he insisted on writing the platform. Time and again he was to hold stubbornly to this point: now; in the preceding campaign; in the election of 1804. A strange position indeed for the " pliant and slippery intriguer " of tradition to take.

A year or so previous, Burr would have handled the Federalist negotiators with consummate ease. Now he blundered badly into the trap that was set for him. The leaders, without taking the rank and file into their confidence, had invited him to the birthday feast. Bayard baited the trap.

" We knew," he wrote Hamilton in explanation, " the impression which the coincidence of circumstances would make on a certain great personage; how readily that impression would be communicated to the proud and aspiring lords of the Ancient Dominion; and we have not been mistaken as to the jealousy we expected it would excite through the party." [30]

The feasting and wining was almost over when Burr appeared dramatically, and took his seat as the guest of honor. When toasts were called for, he arose, fingered his glass, looked around the flushed and expectant faces, and proposed, " *The union of all honest men!* "

The rank and file were startled. The toast meant to them only one thing. A direct bid for union of Federalists and dissident Republicans under Burr's leadership against the regnant Virginia faction. And that, without question, was exactly Burr's intention.

The leaders — those who had engineered the invitation — smiled secretly. They hastened to spread the news of the fatal toast. It reached the ears of the Virginians, who reacted just as

Bayard thought they would. It was a direct insult to them, a flaunting in their faces of all their actions since they had broken their first promise in 1796. It roused them to a new pitch of fury. Burr's own adherents were somewhat taken aback. The Federalists, approached thus crudely, proceeded to make political capital of the situation.

The ethical Hamilton wrote gleefully, " We are told here [in New York] that at the close of your birthday feast, a strange *apparition,* which was taken for the Vice-President, appeared among you, and toasted ' the union of all honest men.' . . . If the story be true, 'tis a good thing, if we use it well. As an *instrument,* the person will be an auxiliary of some value; as a chief, he will disgrace and destroy the party." [31] Certainly Burr had blundered.

He had already been guilty of another capital error, the reason for which is difficult to understand. It was an innocent enough bit of business, yet he should have realized that every move and every act of his was being subjected to the minutest scrutiny; that this act in particular might readily be distorted and twisted against him, no matter how honorable his motives might have been.

Toward the end of 1801, John Wood, a hack writer of the chameleon breed with which the political woods were then swarming, sent to press a voluminous pamphlet entitled " A History of the Administration of John Adams." A good deal of the material had been furnished by William Duane, editor of the Republican *Aurora,* and Jefferson's first line of offense in the party press. Ward and Barlas, New York printers, set up some 1250 copies, and advertised them for sale. Burr heard of the forthcoming volume, and managed to obtain a prepublication copy.

The book was in the best party traditions of the day — a fierce, acrimonious attack on John Adams and all his works; slanderous, vicious, full of the most outrageous lies. As against this, there were fulsome and labored eulogies of Jefferson and Burr himself, the godlike leaders of Republicanism. Burr grimaced with distaste over libelous matter and eulogies alike. It was stupid, unentertaining, and a direct invitation to libel suits by the outraged John Adams. In fact, Brockholst Livingston, to whom the publishers had submitted the proof-sheets for a legal opinion, had advised that the " History " contained much material that was actionable. So too thought Burr.[32]

Inasmuch as the offending volume was being published in the ostensible interests of the Republican cause, it might do the cause it pretended to serve considerably more harm than good. Accordingly, Burr took it upon himself to surpass the offensive " History " by offering to purchase the entire issue. Duane himself, who was later to join the attacks on Burr because of this suppression, wrote him privately on April 15, 1802, that " I think it fortunate that the pamphlet of Mr. Wood has not yet been published, and that it would be much more so if it were not ever to see the light . . . I consider it, upon the whole, as a hasty, crude and inconsistent production, calculated to produce evil than the least good — as it would be attributed to the republicans." [33] There might also have been in the back of Burr's mind the thought that such a vicious assault on John Adams, with whom he had always been on personal good terms, coupled as it was with thick-laid eulogy of himself, might alienate New England from the " union of all honest men " which he was then contemplating.

Before the bargain was consummated, however, Cheetham and Duane received private information of the negotiations, and one of the printed volumes was surreptitiously spirited away. Burr actually paid $1000 for the edition; unavailingly, it seemed. A new edition was hastily printed from the text of the purloined copy and offered for sale on June 2, 1802. He had been overreached. Nevertheless he was willing to drop the entire matter.

But it was not permitted to rest thus quietly. De Witt Clinton, skulking in the rear, saw in this minor incident the chance for which he had been waiting so long. Hitherto he had sniped persistently at Burr in secret; now, he felt, was the time to come out into the open. The strange toast at the Federalist banquet, the distorted rumors of Burr's part in the Repeal of the Judiciary Act, the long-pursued campaign of whispered calumny, had had their cumulative effect. Burr's popularity was now sufficiently undermined for a concerted attack to bring him toppling. He therefore unleashed his jackal, Cheetham, with orders not to rest until the quarry had been brought down.

James Cheetham, an English radical, had been compelled to quit his own country rather hastily. He came to New York in 1798, and offered his peculiar journalistic talents to the highest bidder. In partnership with a cousin of De Witt Clinton, and secretly backed by the great man himself, he started a daily Republican newspaper in the city, called the *American Citizen*. Tradition has it that Burr had aided in the establishment of the party newspaper. Whether he did or not, Cheetham came to the parting of the ways at the initiation of the quarrel between the two

Republican leaders. With canny foresight, he elected to go along with Clinton, his financial backer.

Cheetham chose his time well for the initiation of his attacks. Burr had left Washington on April 26, 1802, to visit his beloved Theo in South Carolina. She was expecting shortly the birth of a child. On May 26th, while Burr was twenty days' journey away, and unable to hit back, Cheetham opened his campaign in the columns of the *American Citizen*. He began with the charge that the suppression of Wood's book was a deliberate attempt on the part of Burr to ingratiate himself with the Federalists; he issued a scurrilous pamphlet entitled " The Narrative of the Suppression by Col. Burr of the History of the Administration of John Adams," in which he belabored the point with artful insinuations and wholly unsupported assertions. Duane, of the *Aurora,* took up the cry. He was Jefferson's acknowledged mouthpiece, thereby lending the whole affair an official tinge. This was the same Duane who only a month before had himself suggested a suppression of Wood's volume as wholly advisable.

Two wholly unexpected allies rushed to the absent victim's defense. One was John Wood himself, who, hack though he was, felt that Burr had been unjustly treated. He brought out a counter pamphlet in which he set forth the true facts and the justifiable motives which had induced Burr to suppress his work.[34]

Cheetham replied with a new blast, grandiloquently called " An Antidote to John Wood's Poison," which was but a mere reiteration of former charges. Cheetham knew then what modern propagandists and advertisers have only recently learned. There is no statement, no assertion, no matter how fantastic or absurd, which may not be given the color of truth by constant and assiduous hammering.

His second champion was, strangely enough, the rival newspaper, the New York *Evening Post.* This was the organ of the Federalist party, and supposedly run in the interests of the Hamiltonian faction. But its editor, William Coleman, had not long before been law partner to Aaron Burr, and he proceeded to take up cudgels in his behalf. On May 26th, " Fair Play " — a pseudonym for Coleman himself — announced that for several weeks there had been menaces and threats in the *Citizen* promising certain dark unfoldments on Burr, which, on appearance, " only amounts to this, that the Vice-President has purchased the copyright of a certain book." [35]

Cheetham, however, was not through. This had been merely

his opening gun. On July 16, 1802, he unleashed his second battery — an advertisement of a pamphlet entitled " A View of the Political Conduct of Aaron Burr." This was the heavy assault, to be followed by daily columns of abuse in the *Citizen*. In this outrageous document Burr's career was examined in venomous detail from the days of the Revolution. Burr, charged Cheetham, had not even been a good soldier. He had veered later from party to party; every act of his in the Legislature had been motivated by an intention to wreck the budding Republican interest, even when he advocated and voted for Republican measures. His attitude had been " listless," his part in the Republican success of 1800 trivial; in short, Burr had never committed an honest act in his life. And now, for the first time, appeared the most serious allegation of all. Burr had conspired to defeat Jefferson in the recent election and elevate himself to the Presidency. A loose, reckless charge, unsupported by the slightest shred of documentary evidence, of anything that could be considered at all probative by disinterested, analytic observers. But Cheetham named names in profusion, and narrated alleged incidents with such a wealth of circumstantial detail that the uncritical reader could not but be impressed. It was a veritable orgy of downright lies and innocent occurrences dressed by innuendo and blatant assertion in outward clothing of the most damning texture.

Coleman struggled vainly against the unleashed torrent. He was, however, handicapped by a moderate regard for the truth and by the fact that he, a Federalist, was defending a political enemy. This later was adroitly played up by Cheetham.

Aaron Burr returned to New York on June 23rd, to find his native city a seething cauldron, and himself the target of a furious onslaught. He had brought back with him to Richmond Hill Theodosia and her infant son, born May 29, 1802, and named in his honor Aaron Burr Alston. A slashing defense was manifestly indicated. But Burr, for all his long years of political experience, was still possessed of that strange trait of reserve and contempt for mere personal attacks which had stood him in ill stead on numberless occasions. It was this aversion to any defense of his actions that, without doubt, contributed largely to his eventual discrediting. He was never to realize the power of public opinion, and its capacity for absorbing slanders. A public character must be prepared to nail lies promptly and decisively, before they have a chance to soak in, to take root. After that, no amount of denial, no evidence whatever, can undo the harm already done, or shake convictions already formed.

His attitude was best expressed in a letter to his son-in-law. " As to the publications of Cheetham and Wood," he wrote scornfully, " it is not worth while to write any thing by way of comment or explanation. It will, in due time, be known what they are, and what is Dewitt Clinton, their colleague and instigator. These things will do me no harm personally." [36]

Therein he was terribly wrong. These charges, unanswered at the psychologic moment, were to complete the task of his ruin and bury him so deep he could never rise again. His friends, his still devoted " Tenth Legion," pleaded with him to defend himself. He refused.

The persecution grew more and more vindictive. It extended to every line of action: political, financial, social even. All communications were cut off between the Clintonites and the Burrites. The Manhattan Bank joined in the fray. Burr had been compelled to sell most of his stock, while Clinton had been steadily consolidating his position. At a hotly waged election, Burr and John Swartwout were swept out of the Directorate. The institution Burr had founded was now a merciless weapon against him in the hands of the enemy.

In the process, De Witt Clinton permitted himself certain unguarded phrases against Swartwout. Swartwout promptly challenged. The duel took place on July 31, 1802. They fired three times at each other ineffectually. The fourth exchange left Clinton unwounded and placed a ball in Swartwout's leg. Swartwout insisted on continuing, unless Clinton signed a written apology. Clinton refused. On the fifth interchange Swartwout was again wounded. He swayed, yet stood his ground with stubborn bravery. Clinton refused to continue, or to apologize, saying, however, that he had no personal enmity against Swartwout. Whereupon the duel ended. But here, as in every matter involving Burr, controversy has raged. Clinton, it is said, terminated the duel by declaring that " I don't want to hurt him [Swartwout], but I wish I had the *principal* here — I will meet him when he pleases." [37] And every one knew that it was Burr he meant. Whereupon a new war started in the newspapers.

But this alleged challenge was obviously an afterthought. For the account of the duel first published on August 4th by Richard Riker, his own second, made no mention of this remark.[38] It was only after a rather intemperate discussion between the two seconds, conducted publicly in the newspapers, as to *how* the duel terminated, that Riker alleged the making of the offensive remark. To which *Truth* promptly rose to inquire " *why* if he is anxious to *fight* this *Principal* does he not call on him for the purpose. I dare say the Principal, whoever he may be, will not shrink from an interview with *De Witt Clinton*." [39] Whatever else may be said of Burr, no one then or since has ever accused him of lacking in physical courage.

When it was too late, Burr awoke to the irremediable damage which Cheetham's unanswered attacks were causing his reputation and political fortunes. On November 25, 1802, after enduring in silence six months of untrammeled abuse, he founded the New York *Chronicle-Express* to defend himself and further his own faction in the scurrilous war of newspapers and pamphlets. Not only had the harm been done, however, but he erred in installing as editor a very cultured, kindly gentleman, Dr. Peter Irving, brother to Washington Irving. The newspaper achieved quite a genteel and literary flavor, but Dr. Irving was manifestly unfit for the knockdown and drag-out methods that were indicated. He opposed reason to violent and opprobrious tactics, he opposed gentle ridicule to brute reiterations. To the historian his defense of Burr is crushing and unanswerable. He obtained public refutations from David A. Ogden and Edward Livingston, both alleged by Cheetham to have been emissaries of Burr. He printed Burr's own positive and unequivocal denial of any attempt to displace Jefferson — the first time Burr had condescended personally to notice the vicious assaults upon his honor.[40] The public read, and turned eagerly to the more sensational columns of the *Citizen*. On November 16, 1802, the Albany *Register*, hitherto aloof, joined the fray against Burr. So did most of the other Republican newspapers. The orders had gone out to crush Burr.

These emanated probably from Jefferson himself, who managed, nevertheless, to remain skilfully in the background. As early as December 10, 1801, Cheetham had sent for his inspection a long draft of the proposed campaign against Burr, and, in response to a request from the President, he followed it up on January 30, 1802, by a draft of his future article on the suppression of Wood's History. This, it must be remembered, was months before the matter broke into public print.[41] On April 23, 1802, Jefferson wrote Cheetham — and this was just before the campaign was to begin — that " I shall be glad hereafter to receive your daily paper by post, as usual . . . I shall not frank this to avoid post office curiosity, but pray you to add the postage to your bill." [42]

Late in 1802, or early in 1803, Cheetham forged another link in his unremitting attack by the publication of a pamphlet entitled " Nine Letters on the Subject of Aaron Burr's Political

Defection." They contained no new matter, merely reiterations of stale charges, but Cheetham was now compelled to take notice of the steady flow of denials from all the parties he had named in the earlier pamphlet. To these he could only oppose what he himself admitted to be " presumptive testimony," evidence several times removed, anonymous people vouching to conversations had with other similarly anonymous individuals.[43] Against Ogden's denial he took refuge in the ridiculous assumption that Hamilton, Ogden's law partner, was himself involved in the plot.[44] Of such gossamer were his charges spun.

A whole year too late, another and far more redoubtable champion arose. Burr had finally roused himself to the utter danger of his spineless course and determined to strike back, and strike back hard, at all his enemies. In December, 1803, a pamphlet appeared, signed modestly, " Aristides," and called simply, " An Examination of the Various Charges Exhibited Against Aaron Burr."

The title does not give any real inkling of the dynamite contained in those few black-letter pages. It was far more than a defense of Burr; it was a bitter, relentless, excoriating attack on all of his enemies within the Republican party — which necessarily included pretty nearly every politician of prominence in New York, and extended with irreverent gestures to the President of the United States himself and the entire Virginia dynasty. Nowhere in all polemic literature, with the exception of the famous " Junius " letters, is there anything comparable to this performance. Burr's back was now to the wall and his anonymous defender lashed out with barbed language and accusations that sank deep into the most insensitive hide. No one was spared, all were flayed alike; the mighty as well as the lowly. The Clintons had long hated Burr, it was declared, and sought his downfall. George Clinton, old and doddering, had " sighed for " the Vice-Presidential nomination, and had spoken in very unflattering terms of Jefferson. As for De Witt Clinton and his colleague, Ambrose Spencer, they were " destitute of all honor, probity, or talents, of all attachment to the general welfare." Clinton himself was " the acknowledged leader of a band of hired calumniators," his mind, " matured by the practice of iniquity, and unalloyed with any virtuous principle, pointed him out as fit for every vice." He had filled every office with relatives, hirelings and the pliant. On him Aristides turned the heaviest artillery of his excoriation.

Then he turned his unflattering attention to the Livingstons.

The old Chancellor himself was "destitute of solid and useful knowledge . . . a capricious, visionary theorist"; Tillotson, Secretary of State, "had travelled the country round, like a hungry spaniel, begging an office as he went"; Richard Riker, District Attorney, was "a vain and contemptible little pest"; while as for the ineffable James Cheetham, he was "an open blasphemer of his God, a reviler of his Saviour and a conspirator against the religious establishments of his country." Brockholst Livingston was "a man who has been extricated from debts, to an incalculable amount, by means which have never been explained, but is now rioting in luxury and wealth." Jefferson himself had rewarded those who voted for him with lucrative appointments, had in fact bid for the Presidency.[45]

Overnight the pamphlet was a sensation. The indicted men writhed under the allegations, the blasting characterizations. At last Cheetham was being answered in his own language, and with a pen dipped in gall and wormwood. De Witt Clinton roared with rage, and threatened the publishers, Ward and Gould, that "you have it in your power to protect yourselves from the consequences of a private prosecution by giving up in writing the name of the author and making satisfactory apology for your very improper conduct in permitting yourselves to be the instruments of the most virulent and execrable attacks on private characters ever known in this country." [46]

Ward and Gould refused, feeling confident in the backing of the Burrites. But this proved a thin reed. Clinton and others whose full-length portraits had been boiled in oils, started suits for damages, two of which went to judgment. The remainder dragged until 1805, to be terminated finally by abject apologies on the part of the publishers.[47]

Cheetham essayed a rather weak reply to the barbed arrows of Aristides, called "A Reply to Aristides," which was a defense of the personages attacked and a stale reiteration of stale and already smashed charges against Burr. This was in 1804, when events were moving with breath-taking rapidity.

Not until the furore had subsided was it discovered that "Aristides" was no other than William P. Van Ness, Burr's most talented lieutenant. Meanwhile, as a result of the heated controversies, Robert Swartwout fought a duel with Richard Riker and wounded him slightly. John Swartwout was ousted from office by the aggrieved Jefferson for distributing "so atrocious a libel" and, what was worse, daring to affirm it to be true.[48] Burr reluctantly commenced a libel suit against James Cheetham for the sole purpose of placing on record the sworn statements of James A. Bayard and Samuel Smith of Maryland, relative to Jefferson's bargaining for the Presidency. Interrogatories were issued and testimony taken. Then he dropped the whole matter. By this time he was deeply involved in his Western expedition, and he considered the subject as entirely profitless. But his friends, those loyal " Martling men," " the Tenth Legion," " the little band," by whatever name you wish to call them, were fighting for political existence against overwhelming odds. For the sake of their own political fortunes as well as to clear the memory of their leader, they refused to let the matter die. They commenced another suit, a " wager suit " between two dummies, and once more obtained the depositions of the participants in that long-rumored deal. Even these, however, remained unpublished until 1830, and then only were made public by the sons of James A. Bayard, to clear *his* memory from the pert insinuations of Jefferson's recently released *Anas*.

In the eyes of the outside world, Burr had sealed his fate with the publication of the pamphlet by Aristides. But his fate had actually been determined long before. It was even better, perhaps, to force all the secret elements of opposition out into the open and into acknowledged, public warfare. In 1802 W. C. Nicholas was writing De Witt Clinton rather warily about the political effect of the attacks on Burr, and acknowledging that " our situation was like that of a man who submits to the loss of a limb to save his life." [49]

And Gallatin was warning Jefferson, also in 1802, " that transaction — I mean the attack on Mr. B. by Cheetham — has deeply injured the Republican cause in this State." [50] But Jefferson was politically wiser than his Secretary. He knew that Burr had to be cut down this early to avert a reassemblage of his scattered forces by 1804, when another election would be pending. To grapple with him then would be suicidal, and might mean Federalist victory. Within a year or two most people forget, and time heals factional wounds quite readily.

How well Jefferson knew his politics and politicians may be exemplified by the course of Martin Van Buren, then young and fresh from the tutelage of Aaron Burr. He had been too well taught, perhaps, for he absorbed the *machine* efficiency of his master without those other tangible qualities which softened the bare political bones. In 1804, Van Ness was engaged in a desperate effort to rally Burr's cohorts. He wrote Van Buren, " You know that Mr. Burr is the intended victim of villainy and persecution against which it is the duty of every friend to freedom to sustain him . . . I wish you to reflect maturely before you take a side — and when you do never change." [51]

But Van Buren, later to become President of the United States, was all that Burr was ever claimed to be. The simon-pure politician, anxious only for the integrity of his own skin, peeps out of his reply. " Feeling Possessed of Strong personal prejudices for Mr. Burr and feeling a pure and disinterested affection for some of his most intimate friends amongst whom it is with pleasure that I name you as first in my esteem," he commenced unctuously, and then proceeded to the meat of the matter, " Upon the most mature [and] passionate reflection however I am truly Impressed . . . that the support of Col. Burr would not under existing Circumstances be proper, . . . and in giving this opinion I wish to be understood, as not at all embracing the truth or falsity of the Charges." [52]

CHAPTER XVI

THE LAST STRUGGLE FOR POWER

1. ESCAPE FANTASIES

THOUGH the storm had actually broken, Burr's resilient and essentially imaginative nature seemed to throw off with ease all despondency and sense of defeat. His letters were never as gay and sprightly as they were now. The world was a cosmic jest and he studied its variegated face with ironic humor. Only when it came to Theo and his little grandson, dubbed almost immediately with a hundred endearing pet names, did he show the slightest concern. Theo had emerged an invalid from the ordeal of childbirth. It was thought that the semi-tropic Carolinian climate was too enervating for her. Burr took her back to New York with him, and she tried the waters of Saratoga and Ballston Spa for relief, but without much success. She was to remain a semi-invalid for the balance of her life. Finally she returned to Charleston and her husband, taking the little boy with her. Burr was disconsolate. New York, Washington even, became suddenly lonely and empty. Not even his deceased wife had plumbed the full depths of his devotion. This was to be achieved in all the world by but two persons — his daughter Theodosia, and his grandson, Aaron Burr Alston.

These were the deeps. The surface texture of his being imperiously demanded other consolations — the remedial pattern of sex and the society of woman. He had been a widower for over a decade, he was forty-seven, still handsome, irresistible, the Vice-President of the United States. Glimpses of little *contretemps,* of small gallantries and affairs of the heart, begin to peep through the airy persiflage of his letters. He was a splendid catch, and many a lady set herself to achieve the conquest. One at least almost succeeded, hidden forever in his detailed accounts to an amused Theodosia under the name of Celeste. But her feminine wiles, her *no* when she meant *yes,* gave the half-hearted lover his chance to escape before it was too late. " They made me laugh," wrote Theo of his letters, " yet I pity you, and have really a fellow feeling for you. Poor little Rippy, so you are mortgaged! But you bear it charmingly . . . Spasmodic love. It is really quite new

. . . Poor Starling! " [1] And when the father announced the termination of the love affair, for all his experience a little bewildered at feminine twists and turns, the daughter knew exactly what had happened. " As to Celeste," she scolded, " she meant, from the beginning, to say that awful word — yes . . . you took it as a plump refusal, and walked off. She called you back. What more could she do? I would have seen you to Japan before I would have done so much." [2]

There were others too, a long line of vanished ladies, all wearing the decent anonymity of initials, of pseudonyms, yet obviously all well known to Theo, the solitary recipient of his confidences. They were a definite need, an escape fantasy, possibly, from the harassments of the outer world.

Burr continued to preside in the Senate, with a distinction which no other Vice-President has ever lent to the office. Friend and political foe alike were unanimous in their testimony as to that. Said the Federalist Senator Plumer, " Burr presides in the Senate with great ease and dignity. He always understands the subject before the Senate, states the question clearly, and confines the speakers to the point. He despises the littleness and meanness of the administration, but does not distinctly oppose them or aid us." [3]

As Vice-President, he could do no more than direct the course of debate, preserve order and confine speakers to the issue. On the great and pressing problems of the day — the Louisiana Purchase, foreign relations, the delicate negotiations with France, Spain and England — in all of which he was profoundly interested, he could neither act nor express an opinion even. He was an outlaw in his own Administration, a lonely figure against whom all hands were turned.

Such small solace as he could obtain was received from the always loyal College of his youth. Princeton, in the person of Governor Bloomfield of New Jersey, conferred on him the degree of Doctor of Laws, and accepted gratefully his proposal to present the College with a portrait of his father, second President of that already venerable institution.[4] A little later, his help was required in a more tangible way. The College had been swept by fire, and Burr subscribed a substantial sum to the rebuilding fund.[5]

2. JEFFERSON IN THE SADDLE

At the beginning of 1804, political thoughts were already pointing toward the Presidential election of the following year. As to the Republican candidate for President, there was no doubt whatever. Jefferson was the unanimous choice, and would be re-elected by an overwhelming vote. The Federalists were badly disorganized, and less than half-hearted in their efforts. Jefferson had used his office so skilfully that he had driven a huge wedge into the ranks of his opponents. He had placated and soothed wherever possible, he had wielded the patronage with telling effect; more, he had shown the jittery Federalists that Jacobinism was not the anarchical, revolutionary *bête noire* they had expected. It was hard sometimes to distinguish the policies of his Administration from those of an orthodox Federalist. The Executive powers had not been weakened by one jot; in the purchase of Louisiana " the strict constructionist " had stretched the Constitution until it literally cracked. He had gone to war with Tripoli in the best military tradition; and the Hamiltonian system — funded debt and bank, the anathemas of old — had not been disturbed in the slightest detail. Moreover, the country was prosperous. No wonder the Federalists deserted in droves to the fleshpots of Republicanism.

In the ranks of his own party, however, Jefferson was implacable. He had nothing more to fear from the Federalists, but Burr was an ever-present threat to the continued existence in power of the Virginia group. Madison, Monroe, these were the heir-apparents.

So successful had been the campaign of vituperation and accusation against Burr that, when the Congressional leaders of the party met in informal caucus to discuss nominations, his name was barely mentioned for the Vice-Presidency. George Clinton, aged now and feeble, achieved his ultimate dream without opposition. It was part of the bargain with Jefferson for having dragged Burr down. Jefferson knew that Clinton presented no serious threat in the future against Madison, whom he was already grooming for the event of his own retirement. But Clinton's nomination opened the field in New York, where he had been Governor.

Burr cast his eyes in the direction of his own home State. There, if at all, would be the place to recoup his political fortunes. He would have to start from the beginning, and rebuild anew the careful edifice which had been shattered by the patronage and the paper warfare of his enemies. Let New York once more come into his grasp, and he would be in a position to dictate terms to those who now scorned, yet secretly feared him. Nor was the task as hopeless as it seemed. His " little band " was still active and devoted; Tammany had stuck to him loyally and remained recalcitrant to the blandishments of the Clintons and the Livingstons. And Burr still possessed many personal friends among the New York Federalists. Their party had been smashed almost beyond repair in the recent elections, and, under the Jeffersonian dispensation nationally and the Clinton regime locally, there seemed but little difference in principles between the two parties.

Before he turned to New York, however, Burr made a last desperate attempt to settle matters with Jefferson by a personal interview. The President set down the facts of that strange conference with malicious glee. We have only his word as to what took place, and Jefferson's word, as noted before, was sometimes not quite trustworthy.

Burr, said Jefferson, called on him privately, recapitulated his history since coming to New York " a stranger " and finding " the country in the possession of two rich families," and assured him that he had accepted the Vice-Presidential nomination only " with a view to promoting my [Jefferson's] fame and advancement, and from a desire to be with me, whose company and conversation had always been fascinating to him." The Clintons and Livingstons, Burr said, had soon turned hostile and excited calumnies against him, but his attachment to Jefferson was as strong and sincere as ever. He believed, however, that " it would be for the interest of the republican cause for him to retire; that a disadvantageous schism would otherwise take place," but that he did not wish to retire under fire, as that would be construed as an avowal of defeat. Wherefore, to prove to the world that he still possessed the favor of Jefferson, he asked him to bestow some outward mark of such favor upon him for all to see.

Jefferson thought he was hinting for some appointment, and turned the conversation " to indifferent subjects." As for the published attacks, he assured Burr, forsooth, he " had noticed it but as the passing wind." In short, Jefferson bowed him out with evasions, and hastened back to his library to record how " I had never seen Colonel Burr till he came as a member of Senate. His conduct very soon inspired me with distrust. I habitually cautioned Mr. Madison against trusting him too much . . . When I destined him for a high appointment, it was out of respect for the favor he had obtained with the republican party, by his extraordinary exertions and successes in the New York election in 1800." [6]

It was in any event a most extraordinary interview, and, at the best, betrayed the desperation with which Burr surveyed the future. In earlier years his proud spirit would never have humbled itself to beg any favor, no matter how slight, from one whom he knew to be his inveterate enemy. And he had humiliated himself in vain.

Burr now turned definitely to New York as his sole hope for salvation. The gubernatorial election was to take place in the spring, and his friends proceeded at once to whip up waning enthusiasms in his behalf. His enemies hailed his approach with furious activity of their own. Already had they prepared their lines. De Witt Clinton had resigned, after a short period, as United States Senator, and General Armstrong was returned again to the Senate. The Clintons and the Livingstons were shifting their pawns about with remarkable agility. Whereupon De Witt Clinton was promptly appointed Mayor of the City of New York, and as promptly filled all city posts with political hirelings in an effort to break the power of Tammany. The Manhattan Bank was mobilized and all its resources poured into the impending battle. Should Burr win, not all the aid of the national administration could save the Clintons from ruin.

When Burr had presented himself for the fatal interview with Jefferson, the latter had already been warned of his plans by De Witt Clinton. "A certain gentleman [Burr] was to leave this place yesterday morning," he wrote. "He has been very active in procuring information as to his probable success for governor at the next election. This, I believe is his intention at present, although it is certain that if the present Governor will consent to be a candidate, he will prevail by an immense majority." This was before George Clinton had been offered the Vice-Presidential nomination. "Perhaps a letter from you may be of singular service." [7]

But Jefferson refused to commit himself in writing. He still preferred to work through subterranean channels. "I should think it indeed a serious misfortune," he replied, "should a change in the administration of your government be hazarded before its present principles be well established through all its parts; yet on reflection you will be sensible that the delicacy of my situation, considering who may be competitors, forbids my intermeddling even so far as to write the letter you suggest. I can therefore only brood in silence over my secret wishes." [8]

Jefferson had assured Burr in their interview that as in the past he had "never interfered directly or indirectly" to influence any election, so, he said, "in the election now coming on, I was observing the same conduct, held no councils with anybody re-

specting it, nor suffered any one to speak to me on the subject." [9]
In spite of this assurance, he found no qualms, however, as he
himself admitted later, in sending a warning posthaste to the
Clintons advising them of Burr's proposed plans and putting
them on their guard.[10] His vaunted neutrality was a sham.

3. Burr for Governor

The Clintons and Livingstons were in command of the Republican machinery of the State. They nominated Chancellor Lansing, an able, trustworthy man. At first he accepted; then, on
February 18, 1804, he threw consternation into the hearts of his
supporters by publicly announcing his declination on the ground
that he had accepted solely in the interests of establishing a union
of factions, but that " subsequent events have induced me to believe that my hopes on this subject were too sanguine."

These " subsequent events " were the upsurge of considerable
Burr sentiment. In New York City, the Burrites, in spite of Clinton's exertions, were very powerful. In almost every county of
the State distinguished Republicans declared openly for his
candidacy. In Dutchess and Orange Counties sentiment was particularly strong in his favor. On February 18th, the very date of
Lansing's declination, the Burr forces met at the Tontine Coffee
House in Albany, and, amid scenes of enthusiasm, formally nominated Burr for Governor. New York City held its meeting two
days later to the same effect. A ticket was drawn up, and Oliver
Phelps of Ontario County chosen as his running-mate for Lieutenant-Governor.[11]

The Clinton faction grew alarmed. Burr was stronger than
they had suspected, and they were still without a nominee. On
February 20th they called another caucus and hastily proposed
Morgan Lewis, Chief Justice of the State Supreme Court, and a
member of the Livingston clan — and he as hastily accepted.

Burr knew, running as an independent Republican alone, that
he could not hope to defeat the regular Republican machine, intrenched as it was in patronage and the organization of government. His only hope lay in attracting the Federalists to his standard. They were disorganized, hopelessly routed. They had not
even a candidate to offer. No one could be found to accept the
burden of sure defeat.

But the moribund figure of Alexander Hamilton rose once
again to block his path, to put the last link in the chain with which
his Republican enemies had almost surrounded him. Hamilton

had been sulking in his tent, a discredited leader. Now he roused himself to do battle for a last time with the man he hated above all others. It was more than a matter of mere personal emotions, however. It was a bid to regain the commanding leadership in his own party, that overwhelming prestige he had once enjoyed. Revolt, long muttered, had blazed forth. He had driven Federalism into the ground with his tactics, grumbled certain New England members, erstwhile meek and subservient. New issues had arisen, involving New England closely, and Hamilton was paying them no heed. It was time, they declared openly, to shift the mantle of leadership to one more capable of command. But of that more anon.

The Federalists met secretly in Albany to determine whether they, as a party, should support Burr, or run their own candidate. Hamilton attended with a written statement of his views. He descanted at length on the general untrustworthiness of Aaron Burr, repeated all the old accusations, and begged the assembled Federalists rather to vote for Lansing, whose declination was still not known, to vote for the Devil himself, if need be, than for the independent candidate.[12]

The Federalists were unimpressed. They were growing weary of Hamilton's obsession. Only through the support of Burr could they hope to regain even the crumbs of office once more. Gaylord Griswold, Federalist Congressman from Herkimer County, even went so far as to write a letter for publication, in which he urged all his friends to vote for Burr, charging Hamilton's opposition to a " personal resentment towards Burr." [13] There were other forces at work, too, of which Hamilton was as yet unaware — notably the New Englanders, with secret aims of their own.

The issue was joined. Morgan Lewis, regular Republican, against Aaron Burr, independent Republican, with the avowed support of most of the Federalist party. Senator Plumer, who had noted on February 10th that Burr had no chance for success, on February 28th sang another tune. " Burr yesterday again took his seat in the Senate. His journey to New York was, I presume, necessary to make arrangements for the approaching gubanatorial election. His prospect of success encreases; many of the federalists in that State will exert themselves in his favor." [14]

Meanwhile, outside events concurred. Louisiana had been annexed — a dangerous addition, thought the Federalists, to Republican territory — and Jefferson was proceeding inexorably to the impeachment of Federalist judges. In only this had he shown himself at all revolutionary: in his constant aversion to the entire Judiciary system. Impeachment was his remedy.

To his plans the Federalist Congressmen from New England could at first only interpose despair. Their ranks had crumbled, the Virginians were in the saddle, and in the attack on the Judiciary they saw only the ultimate destruction of all sacrosanct property rights, of freedom itself.

Despair gave way to secret conclaves, in the course of which four New England Senators — Pickering of Massachusetts, Plumer of New Hampshire, Tracy and Hillhouse of Connecticut — together with Roger Griswold, Congressman from Connecticut, and others from the House, agreed that desperate times demanded desperate measures. In short, New England, now at a disadvantage within the Union, must declare the compact of the States at an end, and forthwith secede. At once the conspirators stirred into a bustle of frenetic activity. They wrote to those in their respective States whom they felt most likely to heed, sounding them out, apprising them of their plans. Pickering, the head and front of the movement, wrote George Cabot that the separation "must begin in Massachusetts. The proposition would be welcomed in Connecticut; and could we doubt of New Hampshire? But New York must be associated; and how is her concurrence to be obtained? She must be made the centre of the confederacy. Vermont and New Jersey would follow of course, and Rhode Island of necessity." [15]

This, then, was the very heart of the problem. Without New York, the conspiracy must be doomed to defeat. *With* New York, it would flourish as the green bay tree. So the plotters turned to Aaron Burr. He was the key to the situation. He was an outlaw in his own party; his resentment would make him amenable. With him as an ally, New York might be captured and made an integral part of a Federalist nation.

They sounded him out in Washington early in 1804. Timothy Pickering, James Hillhouse, William Plumer and others dined with him. Hillhouse, watchful of the effect, declared that the United States " would soon form two distinct & separate governments." Others expressed themselves in similar fashion. Burr participated in the conversation with his usual easy grace. Plumer, well pleased, took home with him the impression that Burr " not only thought *such an event would take place — but that it was necessary it should.*" Unfortunately, in the silence of his own study, when Plumer tried to analyze Burr's remarks, he found " nothing that he said that necessarily implied his approbation

of Mr. Hillhouse's observations." Whereupon he became attentive
to Burr's after talk and discovered " perhaps no man's language
was ever more apparently explicit, & at the same time so covert &
indefinite." [16] Which may be ascribed to Plumer's disgruntlement
at not having been able to pin Burr down to an acceptance of
their plans.

The conspirators did not give up, however. Burr was most essential to them. The old Essex Junto — George Cabot, Fisher
Ames, Stephen Higginson, Theophilus Parsons — as well as Hamilton, were all opposed to the idea. They admitted the premises,
but denied that secession was the proper remedy.

Pickering wrote rather optimistically to Rufus King that " the
Federalists here in general anxiously desire the election of Mr.
Burr to the chair of New York; for they despair of a present
ascendancy of the Federal party. Mr. Burr alone, we think, can
break your Democratic phalanx; and we anticipate much good
from his success." [17]

Roger Griswold was more practical. He tried to ascertain Burr's
views, but obtained little information. " He speaks in the most
bitter terms of the Virginia faction," Griswold told Oliver Wolcott, " and of the necessity of a union at the northward to resist it;
but what the ultimate objects are which he would propose, I do
not know." But Griswold was determined to find out. " I have
engaged to call on the Vice-President as I pass through New York,"
he continued. " He said he wished very much to see me, and to
converse, but his situation in this place did not admit of it, and
he begged me to call on him at New York . . . Indeed, I do not
see how he can avoid a full explanation with Federal men. His
prospects must depend on the union of the Federalists with his
friends, and it is certain that his views must extend much beyond
the office of Governor of New York. He has the spirit of ambition
and revenge to gratify, and can do but little with his ' little band '
alone." [18]

The interview took place on April 4th in the house of Burr in
New York. But all Griswold's insistence could elicit nothing further from Burr than that " he must go on democratically to obtain
the government; that, if he succeeded, he should administer it
in a manner that would be satisfactory to the Federalists. In respect to the affairs of the nation, Burr said that the Northern
States must be governed by Virginia or govern Virginia, and that
there was no middle course; that the Democratic members of Congress from the East were in this sentiment, some of those from

A warning to Libellers.

AARON BURR is closeted with his satellites in dark divan. He is using every wicked art to promote his own election. He is surrounded by a little party of discontended men, who are attempting to destroy our republican administration, with a view that they may procure offices. He has employed detestable hirelings to vilify and abuse our most faithful public characters. Can we pardon the abuse which the villainous wretch, Aristides, has heaped upon our worthy President, THOMAS JEFFERSON, by representing him as a weak and fickle visionary; in fine as an ideot, incompetent to preside over the affairs of a great nation? a more formidable charge could not have been advanced against this illustrious character, for it is as fatal to desert a cause from weakness as to betray it by treachery. Aaron Burr and his disgraceful associates have exceeded all bounds—they have carried calumny, slander, and detraction to a greater heigth than was ever done before. They have established a News-Paper for no other purpose than to abuse private characters. No men are so vulnerable as themselves. If decency would permit, I could tell such tales of all of them as would put them down for ever. I shall forbear. But let the disgraceful debauchee who permitted an infamous prostitute to insult and embitter the dying moments of his injured wife ; let him look home. Degraded as he is, beyond contempt in the opinion of all good men. Vain Dotard! Does he aspire to public honor? Let this hint suffice—Let it shew what I could relate—I know their rottenness of characters, and could torture the very marrow of their bones.

" I could" some tales " unfold, whose lightest word would harrow up thy soul ;
" freeze thy young blood; make thy two eyes like stars, start from their spheres ; thy
" knotty and combined locks to part, and each particular hair to stand an end like quills
" upon the fretful Porcupine."

Basilisk beware! an eye keen as the lightning—A voice powerful as the thunder of the heavens is near thee—Revoke not the power which can crush thee in an instant. At present it beholds thee with sovereign disdain and with contempt ineffable—Child of the dust—Little Puppet of the day—It can sport with thee—It has a merciful spirit ; but there is a point of endurance, beyond which, it is not to be controuled.

SYLPHID.

BURR-LEWIS CAMPAIGN POSTER, 1804

THE following hand-bill was circulated in the year 1801, by the Federal party. It is now re-published for the *gratification* of those Federal gentlemen who are now supporting "this Cataline." The original may be seen at the office of the Citizen.

Aaron Burr !

At length this Cataline stands CONFESSED in all his VILLAINY—His INVETERATE HATRED of the Constitution of the United States has long been displayed in one steady, undeviating course of HOSTILITY to every measure which the solid interests of the Union demand—His POLITICAL PERFIDIOUSNESS AND INTRIGUES are also now pretty generally known, and even his own party have avowed their jealousy and fear of a character, which, to great talents adds the deepest dissimulation and an entire devotion to self-interest, and self-aggrandizement—But there is a NEW TRAIT in this man's character, to be unfolded to the view of an INDIGNANT PUBLIC!—His ABANDONED PROFLIGACY, and the NUMEROUS UNHAPPY WRETCHES who have fallen VICTIMS to this accomplished and but too successful DEBAUCHEE, have indeed been long known to those whom similar habits of vice, or the amiable offices of humanity have led to the wretched haunts of female prostitution—But it is time to draw aside the curtain in which he has thus far been permitted to conceal himself by the forbearance of his enemies, by the anxious interference of his friends, and much more by his own crafty contrivances and unbounded prodigality.

It is time to tear away the veil that hides this monster, and lay open a scene of misery, at which every heart must shudder. Fellow Citizens, read a tale of truth, which must harrow up your sensibility, and excite your keenest resentment. It is, indeed, a tale of truth! and, but for wounding, too deeply, the already lacerated feelings of a parental heart, it could be authenticated by all the formalities of an oath.

I do not mean to tell you of the late celebrated courtezan N———, nor U———, nor S———, nor of half a dozen more whom first his INTRIGUES have RUINED, and his SATIATED BRUTALITY has afterwards thrown on the town, the prey of disease, of infamy, and wretchedness—It is to a more recent act, that I call your attention, and I hope it will create in every heart, the same abhorrence with which mine is filled.

When Mr. Burr last went to the city of Washington about 2 months ago, to take the oath of office, and his seat in the August senate of the U. States, he SEDUCED the daughter of a respectable tradesman there, & had the cruelty to persuade her to forsake her native town, her friends and family, and to follow him to New-York. She did so—and she is now IN KEEPING in Partition-st. Vice, however, sooner or later, meets its merited punishment. Justice, though sometimes SLOW, is SURE. The villain has not long enjoyed this triumph over female weakness. The father of the girl has at length after a laborious and painful search, found out the author of his child's RUIN, and VENGEANCE will soon light on the guilty head———Fellow-citizens, I leave you to make your own comments on this complicated scene of misery and vice,—I will conclude with a single observation.—Is that party at whose head is this monster, who directs all their motions and originates all their nefarious schemes worthy of your support?

A CONTEMPORARY ELECTION BROADSIDE, 1804

New York, some of the leaders in Jersey, and likewise in Pennsylvania." [19] And with that Griswold had to be content.

Burr's interview with Griswold cannot be tortured into an expression of approval of secessionist sentiments. He welcomed Federalist support, it is true, but he must go on *democratically* to obtain the government. He wished the North to govern Virginia, not *vice versa*, but " there was no middle course." A clear warning, it seems, against all thoughts of disunion. Yet it is persistently alleged that Burr had joined the New England Conspiracy, and would, if elected, have piloted the Northern States to secession.

The campaign was both active and acrimonious. Handbills fluttered in profusion, the newspapers roared, Cheetham accused Burr of keeping a seraglio, of being " a disgraceful debauchee who permitted an infamous prostitute to insult and embitter the dying moments of his injured wife." [20] With these assertions ringing in their ears, the electors of the State of New York marched to the polls.

When the votes were counted, it was seen that Morgan Lewis had been elected over Burr by a vote of 30,829 to 22,139. New York City gave Burr a small majority of 100 votes, but the tide upstate swept strongly for Lewis. The Republican party had been thoroughly poisoned against him — only his immediate adherents supported him within its ranks — while the unceasing opposition of Hamilton had alienated a sufficient number of Federalists to insure his defeat. The debacle in New York had shattered all Burr's dreams of rehabilitation. Though Vice-President of the United States, the future held only a political blank. His enemies had finally triumphed.

Chapter XVII

TRAGIC DUEL

1. Provocation

NO man in public life had exhibited such utter forbearance and outward good-humor under years of public calumny, lies, insinuations, innuendoes and accusations directed not only to his political life but to his private character and morals, as Aaron Burr. But now, with the ruins of his career thick about him, the myriad poisoned barbs he had hitherto brushed carelessly aside began to stick and fester. His enemies stood in a tight ring about him, watchful for the least sign of recovery in the victim they had downed.

The bright armor of pride and indifference with which this professional politician, this Chesterfieldian aristocrat, had encased himself, was now pierced beyond repair. He turned on his enemies, determined to strike back — hard. At the beginning of the nineteenth century there was but one method open to a man of honor to negate imputations against his private, as opposed to his public, character. That was the duel. Burr had fought not many years before with John B. Church; John Swartwout had been twice wounded by De Witt Clinton; Coleman, the editor of the *Post*, had killed Captain Thompson; Hamilton's own son had fallen on the dueling field a short time before. Gates had fought, so had Randolph, and later Andrew Jackson was to become a famous duelist and kill his man. Monroe and Hamilton had been on the verge of pistols; Hamilton had acted as second to Colonel Laurens in his duel with General Lee, and had himself proposed to be the first to meet the alleged traducer of Washington. Robert Swartwout had severely wounded Richard Riker — but the catalogue is endless. There was hardly a man of any prominence in those days who had not been on at least one occasion an early riser, with pistols for two, and coffee for one. It was the accepted mode, the sole recourse to gentlemen for slights, real or fancied, upon their characters. It is true that voices were beginning to rise in protest against the barbarous code of the duello, but they were still muted and weak against the strong course of tradition. It is with this in mind that the ensuing affair must be considered, and not with the overlaid prejudices of a modern age.

Even before the gubernatorial battle, Burr had told Charles Biddle, en route from Washington to New York, " that he was determined to call out the first man of any respectability concerned in the infamous publications concerning him." [1]

Which left James Cheetham out of the picture, and brought De Witt Clinton very much into the foreground. Burr knew as well as the rest of the world that Clinton was the instigator and only begetter of the Cheetham libels. It was quite probable that Burr had him in mind when he spoke. But the fates decided otherwise. While Burr was brooding over his wrongs and determined to take the necessary steps to avenge them, there appeared in the Albany *Register* certain letters which diverted Burr's wrath to Alexander Hamilton as the arch-enemy and author of all his misfortunes.

Hamilton had spoken of Burr with his accustomed immoderateness of language at a dinner party given by Judge Tayler of Albany. This was during the campaign. Dr. Charles D. Cooper, Tayler's son-in-law, listened attentively and wrote forthwith an electioneering letter to Andrew Brown, of Berne, in which he said " Gen. Hamilton . . . has come out decidedly against Burr; indeed when he was here he spoke of him as a dangerous man and ought not to be trusted." [2] The letter was dated April 12, 1804.

On April 23, 1804, Cooper wrote another letter, addressed to Philip Schuyler. This letter contained dynamite. " General Hamilton and Judge Kent have declared, in substance, that they looked upon Mr. Burr as a dangerous man," it asserted, " and one who ought not to be trusted with the reins of government. If, sir, you attended a meeting of Federalists at the City Tavern where General Hamilton made a speech on the pending election I might appeal to you for the truth of so much of this assertion as related to him . . . I could detail to you a still more despicable opinion which General Hamilton has expressed of Mr. Burr." [3]

Whom the gods wish to destroy, they first make mad. With the probable connivance of Schuyler, Hamilton's father-in-law, these letters were published in the Albany *Register,* to be copied and quoted by other journals, and to make their endless rounds in the campaign literature of the day.

" *I could detail to you a still more despicable opinion which General Hamilton has expressed of Mr. Burr.*" This was the fatal sentence, the one which Burr could not afford to overlook. De Witt Clinton was wiped out of his mind for the moment; all his attention was concentrated on Hamilton. This, of course, was not the first time Hamilton had spoken disparagingly of Burr's moral and personal character. In fact, the vague phrases of Cooper were mild compared to the sentiments Hamilton had expressed time and again both in private speech and private letter. But never before had any of his damning communications achieved the pitiless glare of publicity. The recipients had read his accusations, and filed the incriminating documents away in their own portfolios. It is too much to believe that Burr had not been fully aware this long time past of Hamilton's secret thrusts, and that they had not rankled. But as long as they were confidential, and not susceptible of open avowal, he deemed it wiser to ignore them and meet Hamilton with accustomed courtesy and outward friendliness. Now, however, Hamilton's private opinions had become public and open for all to see. They could no longer be ignored. By the code there could be only one answer.

No human motive is entirely simple. Mingled with these considerations were quite probably others, obscurely working in the recesses of Burr's mind. Hamilton had been his fatal genius — had blocked him at every turn. There had been the legitimate occasions of political controversy; there were other occasions, not quite as legitimate. Such, for example, as the thwarting of his appointment as Minister to France, as Brigadier-General in John Adams's Army. He had opposed him by fair means and foul, had split the Federalist ranks when they would have supported him, had stopped his election to the Governorship, had sniped persistently with hints and dark innuendoes that had spread like a rank contagion, and invoked among men a vague distrust of Burr, his private morals, his public ethics, his whole personality.

On June 18, 1804, Burr set the wheels of an inexorable destiny in motion, wheels which were to destroy Hamilton's body and, more fiendishly even, to blast Burr with contemporaries and posterity alike. On that day, William P. Van Ness appeared at Hamilton's home and silently handed him a formal communication. Hamilton read it through slowly, feeling already the first touch of the grinding wheels. It said, " Sir, I send for your perusal a letter signed Charles D. Cooper, which, though apparently published some time ago, has but very recently come to my knowledge. Mr. Van Ness, who does me the favour to deliver this, will point out to you that clause of the letter to which I particularly request your attention. You must perceive, sir, the necessity of a prompt and unqualified acknowledgment or denial of the use of any expressions which would warrant the assertions of Mr. Cooper. I have the honour to be Your obedient servant, A. Burr " [4]

Icily direct and to the point, correct in every detail. Hamilton stared at the enclosed clippings, turned to the silently formal Van Ness and said that the matter required consideration, and a reply would be shortly forthcoming. It was not, however, until June 20th, that Van Ness received the awaited response. It was lengthy and argumentative, quite unlike Burr's stripped phrases. " I have maturely reflected on the subject of your letter of the 18th inst.," it began, " and the more I have reflected the more I have become convinced that I could not, without manifest impropriety, make the avowal or disavowal which you seem to think necessary." Then he proceeded to analyze the offending phrases, to twist and turn them, to argue their exact meaning with the subtlety of a lawyer for the defense. He spoke of the justifiable " animadversions of political opponents upon each other," and called Burr's attention to the fact that he had not been interrogated as to the precise opinion which was ascribed to him. " I stand ready," he concluded, " to avow or disavow promptly and explicitly any precise or definite opinion which I may be charged with having declared of any gentleman . . . I trust, on more reflection, you will see the matter in the same light with me. If not, I can only regret the circumstance, and must abide the consequence."

He must, he declared, " abide the consequence." The immemorial phrase, attesting to a willingness to accept a challenge, if and when given!

Burr retorted promptly that " political opposition can never absolve gentlemen from the necessity of a rigid adherence to the laws of honour and the rules of decorum. I neither claim such privilege nor indulge it in others." Which was true. Charles Biddle wrote much later that he " never knew Colonel Burr speak ill of any man." [5] Burr went on to point out that " the common sense of mankind affixed to the epithet adopted by Doctor Cooper [*despicable*] the idea of dishonour. The question is not whether he has understood the meaning of the word, or has used it according to syntax and with grammatical accuracy, but whether you have authorized this application, either directly or by uttering expressions or opinions derogatory to my honour. Your letter has furnished me with new reasons for requiring a definite reply."

It has, I believe, slipped the attention of most commentators that at this point in the correspondence Hamilton could have avoided a duel by a prompt disavowal of having used any language at the Tontine Coffee House which involved a *despicable* opinion of Burr. Hamilton, however, let the opportunity pass by; probably because there were too many Federalists who remembered his remarks. It was ridiculous, of course, for him to have demanded from Burr, for avowal or disavowal, a list of the exact statements alleged to have been made. Burr had only Cooper's letter to go on.

Hamilton read this short, sharp note, and told Van Ness " that it contained several offensive expressions, and seemed to close the door to all further reply." Accordingly, on June 25th, Van Ness waited on him again, this time with what was no doubt a formal challenge. But Hamilton had reconsidered what was tantamount to a defiance, and handed him a letter, dated three days earlier. " If by a ' definite reply ' you mean the direct avowal or disavowal required in your first letter, I have no other answer to give than that which had already been given. If you mean any thing different, admitting of greater latitude, it is requisite that you should explain."

Hamilton was obviously unwilling to enter upon a duel with Burr, yet he was in a tight situation. The memory of all the things he had said about Burr now rose to plague him. He could not disavow them all. It was for this reason that he resorted to what might seem the veriest quibbling tactics.

Burr read this note attentively, and remarked coldly to Van Ness that it was not sufficient. Whereupon Van Ness conferred with Mr. Pendleton, to whom Hamilton had confided the task of representing him. Now the ground was broadened. Burr was no longer content with the disavowal of a single incident. He now demanded, reported Van Ness, " a general disavowal of any intention, on the part of General Hamilton, in his various conversations, to convey expressions derogatory to the honour of Mr. Burr." In his struggles to escape from the ignominy of a single denial or apology, Hamilton had but enmeshed himself more closely in the web of circumstance. From this point on, events march with the inevitableness of a Greek tragedy. In spite of Pendleton's assurance to Van Ness that he believed Hamilton would have no objections to making such a declaration, Hamilton could not possibly make such a disavowal without digging his own grave, politically, socially and personally. There were literally hundreds who possessed much too damning evidence of Hamilton's opinions on Burr for him to withdraw. He must needs proceed to his fate. He declined to make the requisite generalization, but he was willing now to avail himself of the loophole which Burr had first offered.

Pendleton read a prepared statement that " in answer to a letter properly adapted . . . he would be able to answer consistently with his honour and the truth, in substance, that the conversation to which Doctor Cooper alluded turned wholly on political topics, and did not attribute to Colonel Burr any instance of dishonourable conduct, nor relate to his private character; and in relation to any other language or conversation of General Hamilton, which Colonel Burr will specify, a prompt and frank avowal or denial will be given."

Had Hamilton agreed to this statement earlier in the controversy the duel could have been averted. He had delayed too long, however. The basis for discussion had broadened. Now, by his hedging, he gave Burr public reason to believe that Hamilton *had* used contumelious language concerning him. A man who demands specific instances for him to avow or disavow, and who refuses to say generally that he had never impugned his opponent's honor, thereby makes a practical admission that he had. Which was precisely what Burr retorted in his next communication, and continued to insist upon a general denial or declaration.

To which Pendleton answered that the matter had gone far beyond its original scope — which it had — and that it aimed at nothing less than an inquisition into Hamilton's most confidential conversations. "Presuming, therefore," he added significantly, "that it will be adhered to, he [Hamilton] has instructed me to receive the message which you have it in charge to deliver."

To this there was only one answer. On June 27, 1804, Van Ness delivered Burr's formal challenge.

2. APOLOGIA

On Hamilton's representations that he was engaged in certain court matters which required completion, the date of the duel was ultimately set for the morning of July 11th; the place Weehawken, just across the river, in New Jersey. This was a favorite meeting-place for the duelers of the time, as outside the jurisdiction of New York, readily accessible, and as readily left.

For two weeks the principals and their seconds went about their normal business, meeting in public, disclosing nothing by their manner or conversation to an unknowing world. They even met to celebrate the Fourth of July, at a banquet of the Society of the Cincinnati, of which both were members and Hamilton the President. Hamilton was wildly hilarious, even to the extent of leaping on a table and singing a song. Burr was quiet and reserved as usual, leaning on his elbow, and gazing earnestly into the face of the man he was soon to meet with pistols. He left the festivities early. On June 23rd, knowing quite well that he was shortly to meet Hamilton, there was Theo's birthday to be celebrated, even though Theo was hundreds of miles away. They "laughed an hour, and danced an hour, and drank her health at Richmond Hill." [6]

On July 10th, the day before the duel, Burr wrote Theo, " having lately written my will, and given my private letters and papers in charge to you, I have no other direction to give you on the subject but to request you to burn all such as, if by accident made public, would injure any person. This is more particularly applicable to the letters of my female correspondents." There was very little he could leave any one, " I mean, if I should die this year," he told her. " If I live a few years, it is probable things may be better." He directed the disposal of certain objects of sentimental value to friends and relations, and wound up with a heartfelt, " I am indebted to you, my dearest Theodosia, for a very great portion of the happiness which I have enjoyed in this life. You have completely satisfied all that my heart and affections had hoped or even wished. With a little more perseverance, determination, and industry, you will obtain all that my ambition or vanity had fondly imagined. Let your son have occasion to be proud that he had a mother. Adieu." [7]

Then he wrote other letters. One to Joseph Alston, Theo's husband, arranging for the disposition of his estate and the payment of his debts. " I have called out General Hamilton, and we meet to-morrow," he advised. " If it should be my lot to fall . . . yet I shall live in you and your son. I commit to you all that is most dear to me — my reputation and my daughter." Even on the point of imminent death, however, the educator could not resist one final exhortation. " Let me entreat you," he concluded, " to stimulate and aid Theodosia in the cultivation of her mind. It is indispensable to her happiness and essential to yours. It is also of the utmost importance to your son. She would presently acquire a critical knowledge of Latin, English, and all branches of natural philosophy. All this would be poured into your son. If you should differ with me as to the importance of this measure, suffer me to ask it of you as a last favour. She will richly compensate your trouble." [8]

Hamilton spent his days in winding up his legal business, and preparing his *apologia* for the benefit of posterity. This is a remarkable document. In it he avowed that he was opposed to dueling on religious and moral principles, that his wife, children and creditors required his continued life, that he was conscious of no ill will to Burr distinct from political opposition. He conceived, however, that it was impossible to avoid the issue, because " it is not to be denied that my animadversions on the political principles, character, and views of Colonel Burr have been extremely severe; and, on different occasions, I, in common with many others, have made very unfavorable criticisms on particular instances of the private conduct of this gentleman." He hoped to be believed that he had not censured Burr on light grounds, " though it is possible that in some particulars I have been influenced· by misconstruction or misinformation . . . As well, because it is possible that I may have injured Colonel Burr, however convinced myself that my opinions and declarations have been well founded, as from my general principles and temper in relation to similar affairs, I have resolved . . . to reserve and throw away my first fire, and I have thoughts even of reserving my second fire, and thus giving a double opportunity to Colonel Burr to pause and reflect." As for those who might inquire why he did not refuse the duel altogether, there was " a peculiar necessity not to decline the call. The ability to be in future useful, whether in resisting mischief or effecting good, in those crises of our public affairs which seem likely to happen, would probably be inseparable from a conformity with prejudice in this particular." [9]

This, then, was the answer. Hamilton felt his leadership involved; he was fighting not alone Burr, but the recalcitrant New Englanders headed by Pickering, and he would have fallen irreparably in the estimation of his own party, had he declined the encounter.

3. PISTOLS FOR TWO; COFFEE FOR ONE

The morning of the 11th dawned misty and red. Burr was the first upon the ground, attended by Van Ness. John Swartwout, come to waken him, had found him in deep and tranquil slumber. Then appeared Hamilton with Pendleton. The parties saluted each other with formal courtesy, and the seconds proceeded with the necessary arrangements. Pistols loaded, the two antagonists took their allotted positions. The word was given. Both parties presented and fired. Burr remained erect, but Hamilton raised himself convulsively, staggered, and pitched headlong to the ground. Burr advanced towards Hamilton with a manner and gesture that appeared to Hamilton's second to be expressive of regret, but Van Ness urged him to withdraw immediately from the field, so as not to be recognized by the boatmen or the surgeon in the barge which was already approaching.[10]

Afterwards, there was to be considerable disagreement between the seconds as to whether Hamilton fired first, or whether in fact he fired in the air, in accordance with the intention expressed in his pre-mortem statement. The matter aroused violent controversy at the time, but is now of purely academic importance. He had agreed to a duel, and must abide the necessary results. Burr could not have known of his secret determination to reserve the first fire. Van Ness always maintained, and with considerable vehemence, that Hamilton had fired first, and *at* his friend.

The doctor found Hamilton dangerously wounded and had him hurriedly transported to New York, where he lingered in great agony for thirty-one hours before he died.

At one bound Alexander Hamilton had achieved martyrdom and a posthumous exaltation of devotion that had never been granted him during his lifetime. The City of New York draped itself in mourning. Bells were muffled, flags were furled; everywhere the most extravagant sorrow manifested itself. Hamilton's remains were buried with military honors under the auspices of the Cincinnati, attended by a vast concourse of people. Gouverneur Morris pronounced the funeral oration to weeping thousands, though, in the privacy of his Diary, he recorded that he would find the proposed address rather difficult, considering Hamilton's birth, vain, opinionated character, monarchical opinions, and wrong ideas generally. To Colonel Smith, who urged him to the task, he said flatly that " Colonel Burr ought to be considered in the same light with any other man who has killed another in a duel; that I certainly should not excite to any outrage on him." [11]

There were others, however, who would and did. The Clintons were especially active in expressions of horror at the *murder* of their dear friend, Alexander Hamilton, and did not hesitate to incite the population to wreak vengeance on the author of such a foul deed. Wild rumors were industriously set in circulation, wilder accounts of the duel. Burr, it seemed, had spent the days before the duel in alternate revelry and target-shooting to increase the deadliness of his aim, while Hamilton had settled his affairs, remained in the bosom of his family, and otherwise conducted himself as a most irreproachable citizen. Burr had worn silk the day of the duel, since silk was known to deflect bullets; Hamilton had refused to shrink from the speeding missile. Burr had laughed and rubbed his hands in glee when Hamilton fell, and regretted only that the missile had not lodged directly in his heart. In short, it was cold-blooded, deliberate murder. Cheetham took up the cry; even Coleman went along. All over the nation processions were held, mass meetings convoked in honor of the departed hero; while Burr's name was made the target of intense execration.

Those very Federalists who had been secretly working against Hamilton's domination were now the loudest in their wails. Hamilton was safely dead, and his apotheosis might be used to rally the fainting cohorts. The populace, roused to frenzy, threatened to burn Burr's house about his ears. They shouted opprobrious doggerels, vile alike in meter and sentiment, paraded and demonstrated.

> " Oh Burr, oh Burr, what hast thou done,
> Thou hast shooted dead great Hamilton!
> You hid behind a bunch of thistle,
> And shooted him dead with a great hoss pistol! "

In short, the duel was made the occasion for the release of a great many hidden wishes. The Federalists thought to ride back to popularity and control on the wave of national emotion; the Clintons saw in it their final chance to destroy Burr forever.

In the South and the West, however, the affair was viewed in simpler, calmer fashion. It was but a duel, similar to hundreds of others; it was, moreover, from all the available evidence, thoroughly justified, if ever a duel could be justified. Burr actually increased in stature among the hot-blooded planters of the South and the hair-trigger frontiersmen of the West. He had killed his man.[12]

John Randolph thought Burr's " whole conduct in that affair does him honor " and that the published correspondence reminded him " of a sinking fox, pressed by a vigorous old hound, where no shift is permitted to avail him." [13]

4. INDICTED FOR MURDER

Burr was aghast at the tumult and the shouting and the storm of execration which promptly descended upon his head. He had killed Hamilton in fair duel; he had had, he conceived, more than ample provocation for the encounter; why, then, should this particular affair of honor be viewed differently from all others? He had not realized to the full the extent of the insidious campaign that had been directed for years against his reputation. Men's minds had been prepared to believe the worst of him. Certain adjectives had been attached to his name for so long that they were matters of automatic response. He did not know how to fight back. When it came to calling names the talents of Van Ness had to be impressed. In politics the best defense is a violent offensive. His intellectual equipment was marvelously adapted to moving measures, and men in the mass, with abstract precision and in the

form of a mathematical problem. But he did not possess the demagogic art of impressing himself upon the *emotions* of men. Even
when sincere, his bland imperturbability and air of reserve
aroused an uneasy belief that he was inwardly mocking the beholder. There was an air of subtlety about the man which was resented by those of simpler mold. This was a mistake. Your true
politician veils his cleverness with an outward mask of transparent
simplicity and pretends to a wholly common denominator with
his constituents. So that the nation was only too eager to believe
the worst of this polished, courtly gentleman, whose courtliness
they could not penetrate.

For eleven days after the duel Burr remained in New York, waiting for the noise to subside. Under Cheetham's incitement, however, it mounted to furious heights. A coroner's jury was summoned by the City Administration — composed of Clintonites — to
inquire into the duel. It was proposed to indict Burr for murder, though the alleged act had been committed in another
state.

On July 18th, Burr wrote with bitterness to Alston that "the
event . . . has driven me into a sort of exile, and may terminate
in an actual and permanent ostracism . . . Every sort of persecution is to be exercised against me. A coroner's jury will sit this evening, being the *fourth* time. The object of this unexampled measure is to obtain an inquest of murder . . . I am waiting the report
of this jury; when that is known, you shall be advised of my
movements." [14]

Yet, in spite of manifest anxiety and the uncertainty even of
life itself, this amazing man could find time to pay suit to a certain
lady, known to Theo as *La G.*, with whom, on July 20th, an interview was expected, " which if it take place, will terminate in something definitive." [15]

The interview probably did not take place. For, on the following day, it was decided by Burr's friends that New York was
entirely too dangerous a place for him. The populace was threatening, plans were afoot to attack and destroy Burr's house, the coroner's jury was certain to bring in a presentment of murder.

Accordingly, at 10 A.M. on July 21st, Burr left Richmond Hill
unostentatiously in company with the ever-faithful John Swartwout, to embark on a waiting barge in the Hudson. He first went
to Thomas Truxton, at Perth Amboy, who welcomed him and put
him up for the night. Swartwout returned to New York and Burr
proceeded in Truxton's carriage to Cranberry, twenty miles farther, where he changed carriages and went on to Philadelphia.

He was now out of the jurisdiction of the two States concerned in the duel — New York and New Jersey. The Vice-President of the United States had been compelled to flee like any common criminal.

In Philadelphia, Burr stopped at the house of A. J. Dallas, Republican politician and an old friend. He showed himself in the streets, went about his daily affairs with outward calm and composure.

Meanwhile New York was seething. The coroner's jury issued warrants to apprehend all his friends for questioning. Davis refused to answer, and was committed to jail. Swartwout, Van Ness, and others evaded service by going into hiding, but managed to keep Burr informed of the turn of events by fast messengers.[16]

Early one morning, Burr found himself staring at a hasty message from Swartwout, dated August 2nd. " The jury agreed to their verdict," it read. " Wilful murder by the hand of A. B., William P. Van Ness and Nathaniel Pendleton accessories before the fact." However, three jurors dissented, and the public was beginning to react. Morgan Lewis, the Governor of the State, " speaks of the proceedings openly as disgraceful, illiberal and ungentlemanly." [17] In fact, they were more than that: they were wholly illegal. New York had no jurisdiction of the crime, if crime it was. The duel had taken place on the Jersey shore. For the first and last time in the history of the United States, a Vice-President had been made the subject of a murder presentment; even, as it proved, of an indictment for the same offense. For New Jersey rose to the public clamor, and pushed through such an indictment, as it had a *legal* right to do. New York's Grand Jury, having received competent counsel, dropped the murder charge, and substituted for it an indictment for having uttered and sent a challenge — a misdemeanor.

5. SOUTHERN JOURNEY

With two indictments hanging over his head — one of them capital in effect — Philadelphia also became dangerous territory. Pressure was being brought to bear on Governor Lewis of New York to demand Burr's extradition from Pennsylvania and he was fearful of the consequences. He made plans, therefore, to flee to the South. Yet, even now, he could not resist the irresistible dictates of his nature. He had taken up with Celeste again, still toying with the thought of matrimony, and, he lightly advised Theo, " If any male friend of yours should be dying of ennui recommend to him to engage in a duel and a courtship at the same time

. . . I do believe that eight days would have produced some grave event; but alas! those eight days, and perhaps eight days more, are to be passed on the ocean." [18]

In the middle of August, Burr secretly embarked, with the youngest of the Swartwout brothers, Samuel, and a slave named Peter, for Georgia. He had decided to seek refuge with a friend, Senator Pierce Butler, at his feudal plantation on St. Simon's, an island near Darien. He traveled under the name of R. King (was he thus mocking the Federalist ex-Senator and Minister to England?) and he preserved his incognito even in that remote establishment. There he waited for the hue and cry to die down; in fact, he was a fugitive from justice.

But even in exile, Burr's restless mind was not still. The Southern journey held more in it than a mere escape into hiding. Burr was never to submit tamely to the bludgeonings of fortune. He could not be crushed. He had lost all chance for the Presidency, he had lost even New York, he was under indictment for murder. His enemies triumphed in the belief that Aaron Burr was in the discard, that he could never survive the combined weight of his misfortunes. An ordinary man could not. But Burr was not an ordinary man. He was forever scheming, forever revolving new plans in his fertile brain, living always in the present and the future, sloughing off the past with contemptuous gesture. For some time now he had been thinking in terms of the South and the West. As early as 1802, he had shown himself intensely interested in the vast territories held under foreign control to the South and Southwest — the Floridas and Louisiana.

On February 2, 1802, he had written Alston, " it has for months past been asserted that Spain has ceded Louisiana and the Floridas to France; and it may, I believe, be assumed as a fact. How do you account for the apathy of the public on this subject? To me the arrangement appears to be pregnant with evil to the United States. I wish you to think of it, and endeavour to excite attention to it through the newspapers." [19]

Spain was a weak power, and could eventually be dispossessed by an aggressive United States. France, however, was strong, and would in turn prove a dangerous neighbor with aggressions of her own. And perhaps, already the germs of the " Conspiracy" were incubating. Now, by 1804, they had matured into a ripe, considered plan of action. The necessity of flight had given Burr the chance to make certain investigations without exciting too much comment. Posing as a London merchant, he took various journeys through the southernmost State of the Union, scouting the land, making inquiries as to local sentiment. A great storm swept the low coast, in which Burr was caught on his travels. It spread devastation and ruin over wide areas. His host's plantation suffered severely, the rice crops were destroyed, buildings were carried out to sea, and nineteen negro slaves were drowned.

In September, Burr traveled south into Florida, then a Spanish province. This journey was the true reason for his Georgian residence. He was investigating the situation, spying out the land, making those maps at which he was particularly skilful, to be stored away for future use.

By the time of his return from Florida, the agitation to the North had subsided. The South had never been fully involved. Congress was soon to meet, and Burr was still Vice-President of the United States and the Presiding Officer of the Senate. Late in the month of September he took boat to Savannah, where he was actually serenaded by a band of music and greeted by a concourse of citizens. He could have remained there indefinitely, basking in the unwonted hospitality, but he was anxious to see Theo, her husband, and their little son, his namesake.

He stopped over with them for a while, then traveled by slow stages to Washington, meeting with a surprising warmth of welcome along the route; everywhere being feted and dined by the Republicans. To them he was something of a hero. On October 31st he wrote Theo wryly that " Virginia is the last state, and Petersburgh the last town in the state of Virginia, in which I should have expected any open marks of hospitality and respect." [20] The State of Jefferson, Madison and Monroe.

He arrived in Washington on November 4th, having heard on the way that Bergen County, New Jersey, the locus of the duel, had finally indicted him for murder, and that his house and furniture had been sold for about $25,000 to satisfy clamorous creditors, leaving almost $8,000 worth of debts still unsatisfied. He was penniless, in debt, ostracized and under indictment.[21]

Yet Burr could always extract airy humor from any situation. On December 4th, he informed Theo about " a contention of a very singular nature between the states of New-York and New-Jersey . . . The subject in dispute is which shall have the honour of hanging the vice-president. I have not now the leisure to state the various pretensions of the parties . . . nor is it yet known that the vice-president has made his election, though a paper received this morning asserts, but without authority, that he had determined in favour of the New-York tribunals . . . Whenever it may be, you may rely on a great concourse of company, much gayety, and many rare sights; such as the lion, the elephant, etc." [22]

But powerful influences were already being employed in his behalf. He still had many personal friends in the United States Senate, and a situation had arisen which changed the open and covert hostility of the Jeffersonian forces to an almost fawning cordiality. That situation will be discussed in the next chapter. As a result, however, a round-robin letter had been drawn by Senator Giles of Virginia, Jefferson's whip in the Senate, and signed by the leading Republican members, petitioning Governor Bloomfield of New Jersey to quash the proceedings against Burr.[23] To which Bloomfield, though an old friend of Burr, was compelled to reply that the State Constitution gave him no such power.[24]

It was beginning to be perceived that, because of the situation aforesaid, the indictments in either State would be allowed to die quietly, and that Burr would not be molested. There was evidently some talk among his friends that he should present himself boldly for trial in New Jersey and remove the menace of an unquashed indictment forever, but Burr decided against such a course. While he was writing Theo that the New-Jersey affair, which had alarmed her, " should be considered as a farce " [25] he was writing also to Charles Biddle, in a hitherto unpublished letter, that " the best informed persons in this City . . . do aver that an impartial jury cannot be had in Bergen. The pious Judge B[oudinot] preached their [sic] that if they did not pursue vengeance to effect, their harvests would be blasted and that famine and pestilence would desolate the Land — Now surely the Judge ought to be exempt from these curses, for his Zeal is still unabated — but seriously speaking, it is asserted by high authority that if you had the right of selecting, you could not get 12 men to whose impartiality and discernment the cause could be trusted." [26]

AARON BURR, 1802-1804

From a portrait by John Vanderlyn

THEODOSIA BURR ALSTON, 1802

From a portrait by John Vanderlyn

Chapter XVIII

THE IMPEACHMENT OF JUSTICE CHASE

1. Jefferson Suddenly Courts Burr

ON November 5, 1804, Aaron Burr quietly appeared in the Senate Chamber and took his seat in the chair of the Presiding Officer. Senator Plumer of New Hampshire, staunch Federalist, and but recently a party to the Secession Conspiracy, stared at him aghast. In the bitterness of his soul he wrote a friend that " Mr. Burr, the man whom the Grand jury in the County of Bergen, New Jersey, have recently indicted for the murder of the incomparable Hamilton, appeared yesterday & to day at the head of the Senate! This is, I believe, the first time that ever a Vice President appeared in the Senate the first day of a session. It certainly is the first time, & God grant it may be the last, that ever a man, so justly charged with such an infamous crime, presided in the American Senate. We are, indeed, fallen on evil times! " [1]

The Federalists in the Senate, excluding certain close friends, followed Plumer in treating Burr with great coldness, and avoiding speech with him as far as possible. But the Republicans (or Democrats, as they were beginning to term themselves) showed an attentiveness, a cordiality that the astonished Plumer could only attribute to joy at Hamilton's demise. " Burr is still with us," he exclaims. " He is avoided by federalists, but caressed & flattered by democrats from the President to the door keeper. General rules will not apply to Mr. Burr; he is an exception to them. No man is better calculated to brow beat & cajole public opinion." [2]

Plumer was mistaken. Though a few rejoiced at the killing of Hamilton, far more important issues accounted for the seemingly impossible change of front on the part of the Administration. Jefferson had girded his loins for a death-struggle with the Judiciary, last stronghold of Federalism, and under John Marshall's powerful guidance, an insuperable obstacle to the untrammeled expression of the people's will. As long as the Judiciary held even the threat of annulment of Congressional enactments and Executive decisions alike over their respective heads, as enunciated by Marshall in the case of Marbury vs Madison, so long was the United States not truly a democratic nation. Jefferson's plan of campaign was simple. He had caused the Judiciary Bill to be repealed, but the judges in office held life tenure, subject to good behavior. This was the Constitutional loophole. On charges of misbehavior, they could be impeached and removed from office by Congress.

Justice Pickering had been the first to feel the weight of Jefferson's disapproval, even though it was alleged he was insane. Burr had presided at what was truly a tragic farce, and only his incomparable dignity in the Chair held the judicial trial on a high level of solemnity and decorum.[3]

The case of Justice Samuel Chase, however, was of far greater importance, and destined by Jefferson to establish a precedent whereby he could unseat even the mighty Marshall himself. Chase was accused of browbeating and bullying tactics on the Bench, of using his high office as a springboard for violent political denunciations of the Democrats, of temperamental unfitness. On March 10, 1804, Samuel Chase was indicted by the House on a strictly partisan vote, and the articles of impeachment handed up to the Senate.

The importance of the impending trial before the Senate was realized by Federalists and Republicans alike. On its outcome depended the course of government for decades to come. But Aaron Burr was still Vice-President, and the Presiding Officer of the Senate. On the studied conduct of the Presiding Officer much depended. His rulings, his admission or non-admission of evidence, his entire method of procedure, could very easily sway a closely divided and excited Senate one way or another. And Burr was a famous lawyer, familiar with every legal technicality, to whose iron discipline the Senate had submitted on numberless occasions. Twenty-three votes were necessary to convict; the Republicans had twenty-five, and the Federalists nine. A defection of three Republicans to the solid Federalist ranks would bring Jefferson's carefully prepared structure crashing to ruin. There were at least five who were doubtful or hesitating. One of these was Senator John Smith of Ohio, an intimate friend of Burr. Others could be swayed by him, should he feel urged to extend his arts. At all times he was a dangerous antagonist, and especially now. Jefferson decided he must be placated at all costs, and his natural resentment turned away with oil and flattery.

By December 23rd a great light burst on Plumer. He was writing now that Burr is " flattered and feared by Administration." [4] Nothing was too good for the man whom they had thought crushed, ostracized, a pariah. Plumer observed that " Mr. Jefferson had shewn more attention & invited Mr. Burr oftener to his house within this three weeks than ever he did in the course of the same time before. Mr. Gallatin . . . has waited upon him often at his lodging — & on one day was closetted with him more than two hours. The Secretary of State, Mr. Madison . . . accompanied him on a visit to M. Terreau [sic] the French Minister." Giles was busy circulating his petition to the Governor of New Jersey, and " the Democrats of both Houses are remarkably attentive to Burr . . . Duane, in his Aurora, has declared in his favour." [5]

Nor was this all. More tangible proofs were to be offered Burr of the Administration's sudden access of warmth and good will. J. B. Prevost, Burr's stepson, was appointed Judge of the Superior Court at New Orleans; James Brown, his brother-in-law, was made Secretary of the Louisiana Territory; and *James Wilkinson,* whom Burr had considered his closest of friends since they had participated in the siege of Quebec, and now Commanding General of the American Army, was given in addition the Governorship of the Louisiana Territory: a combination of civil and military authority that Jefferson ordinarily would never have stomached.

There can be no doubt that these appointments were made at Burr's suggestion, and in a studious effort to avoid his enmity during the forthcoming trial.[6] Burr must have smiled his slow, courteous smile at the hullaballoo, the flattery, the sudden cordial attentions of all the members of the Administration; and it is equally certain that he avoided any direct commitments in exchange. He knew quite well why the tempting bait was being offered, that underneath, there had been no change in the hostility of the Virginians, and he went his way, keeping his own counsel. He was not, however, averse to using these gifts of offices for his own purposes. It is significant that all appointments were made in the newly purchased Louisiana Territory and the separate, though adjacent, Territory of Orleans. His plans were soon to be translated into action; those plans of which he had dreamed back in 1802, because of which he had only recently journeyed into Florida. The placing of three good friends in positions of responsibility and influence on the borders of Spanish Territory would prove of invaluable assistance in the future. Claiborne of Tennessee, however, to his great disgust and annoyance, had received the important post of Orleans' Governor. Claiborne was an honest nincompoop and was destined to arouse the alien citizenry of New Orleans to turbulence. Plumer records on

December 12th that "after the Senate was adjourned the Vice-President observed at the fire that the Senate had agreed to advise to the appointment of Claiborne when not a single Senator beleived he was qualified for the office." To which Senator Bradley retorted " that the President's dinners had silenced them — & that Senators were becoming more servile." [7] Jefferson was well acquainted with the methods of ingratiation.

2. Trial and Acquittal

The trial of Justice Samuel Chase opened on January 2, 1805, to crowded galleries in the Senate. It was well known that the Supreme Court itself was on trial in the person of Chase, and that, should he be convicted, other impeachments were pending, even of the great John Marshall himself, who had only two months before dared to enunciate the doctrine that the Supreme Court had the right and the power to declare Acts of Congress invalid as contrary to the Constitution.

Chase had been impeached on eight articles, the most important of which alleged that in charging the Grand Jury at Baltimore he had denounced in unmeasured terms Republican principles and violently assailed Republican acts and purposes. The House had chosen seven managers to conduct the prosecution, and John Randolph of Roanoke was put forward to lead the fight. For the defense there was a far more imposing array of legal talent, headed by Luther Martin, the Federalist bulldog, anathema now and to become even more so in the future to Jefferson. Associated with him were Robert G. Harper, Charles Lee, Philip B. Key, and Joseph Hopkinson, all brilliant lawyers and skilful politicians as well.

Burr arranged the setting for the trial with careful detail and a flair for the dramatic. The nation was seething with partisan propaganda, great issues were at stake, Jefferson hovered in the background, moving invisible strings, and the trial might, if not properly ensconced, descend to the level of political hustings. To Burr had been given the sole power of making the arrangements.[8]

The Senate Chamber glowed with the trappings of a great theater. To the right and left of the President's chair, in which the slight, carefully attired Burr was seated in state, were two rows of benches, fronted by desks covered with crimson cloths. These were for the Senators, constituting the Court. A specially built semicircular gallery, of three rows of benches, was elevated above the well of the amphitheater on pillars and draped in dark green hangings. Two boxes flanked them. These were crowded with the ladies of officialdom, gaily dressed, perfumed, enjoying the spectacle as a splendid show. On the floor beneath this temporary gallery were three more rows of benches, arranged in tiers, covered also with green cloth, where sat the Representatives, watching their champions and the impassive Senators. On the right was a box for diplomats, foreign representatives, members of the Cabinet. High overhead was the permanent gallery, to which the general public was admitted. A cleared passage led from the President's chair to the door of the Chamber, and on either side of this aisle were blue-draped stalls, occupied on the right by the managers of the House, and on the left by the lawyers for the defense. A very impressive show indeed, and one which, coupled with the pale dignity and flashing eye of the President of the Court, stilled all whisperings and shufflings and commotions.[9]

From the very first rap of his gavel, Burr swayed and dominated the proceedings. He gave his rulings on moot points promptly, unhesitatingly, with clear precision and legal exactitude. Federalists and Republicans alike watched him with hawk-like eyes, seeking for signs of partisanship. They were to be disappointed. When the trial was over, universal approbation for his conduct was in everyone's mouth, friend and foe alike. He had lent new luster to his office, he had made the trial, begun in sordid political passions, a memorable example of judicial dignity and orderly proceeding.

Manasseh Cutler told Dr. Torrey that " the trial has been conducted with a propriety and solemnity throughout which reflects honor upon the Senate. It must be acknowledged that Burr has displayed much ability, and since the first day I have seen nothing of partiality." [10]

The Washington *Federalist*, bitterly hostile to him, declared that " he conducted with the dignity and impartiality of an angel, but with the rigor of a devil." Senator Plumer, who, though one of the Judges, from the first took a wholly partisan view of the proceedings, and who was especially unfriendly to Burr for the " murder " of Hamilton, filled the early days of his Diary with splenetic references to Burr's conduct. He had not been quick enough to give Chase a chair — according to Parliamentary practice, the accused was not entitled to a seat — he had interrupted Chase several times while he was reading a lengthy application to the Court, he demanded that the Court hold longer sessions so as to bring the trial to a fairly early conclusion. Worse still, he informed Senators — Judges of the Court — that it was their duty to remain in their seats during the course of the trial, and not to leave whenever they wished — which angered the haughty Senators, who already knew, without the benefit of testimony, which way they were going to cast their votes. Plumer, one of those so rebuked, wrote angrily in his Diary, " Mr. Burr has for this few weeks assumed the airs of a *pedagogue* — & rather considered the senators as his scholars than otherwise."

But the worst offense Burr committed was to insist that the Senators refrain during the examinations from wandering casually all over the Chamber, and from munching apples and cakes. " Mr. Wright said he eat cake — he had a just right so to do — he was faint — but he disturbed nobody — He never would submit to be schooled & catechised in this manner . . . Burr told Wright he was not in order — sit down — The Senate adjourned — & I left Wright and Burr scolding. Really, *Master Burr*," exploded Plumer when he got home, " you need a ferule, or birch, to enforce your lectures on polite behavior! " [11] One wonders what manner of trial the Senate would have conducted if any other but Burr had presided.

But as the trial moved forward, with speed and precision, and Randolph fulminated and thundered, and Luther Martin roared back in his great voice, and Burr held an even balance between the contending factions, even Plumer came at length to unwilling respect and admiration. When Chase was acquitted on all counts, though a majority had voted " guilty " on three of the eight articles, Plumer, relieved of his anxiety, could then view Burr's conduct with more candor and impartiality. On March 1st he wrote, " Mr. Burr has certainly, on the whole, done himself, the Senate & the nation honor by the dignified manner in which he has presided over this high & numerous Court." [12]

Jefferson had been defeated in his assault on the Judiciary. Burr, in spite of bribes and flattery, had done nothing to assist or rebuff the prosecution. He had been a fair Presiding Officer when impartial conduct was not exactly a virtue in the eyes of the Administration.

3. A LONG FAREWELL

The great trial ended on March 1, 1805. Burr's term of office as Vice-President expired on March 4th. Already it had been his dubious privilege to announce the election results to the Senate. Thomas Jefferson, President; George Clinton, Vice-President. His own public career was ending.

On March 2nd, he rose quietly from the Chair where he had sat for four years. The Senators, lounging in weariness after the tenseness of the preceding months, straightened up. There was that in the Vice-President's manner which demanded attention. He spoke to them, extemporaneously, and as his voice rose and fell in the hushed Senate Chamber, a wave of emotion quivered over his auditors. They were listening, they knew, to a great speech, the greatest they had ever heard. It was Burr's farewell address.

The speech itself is but a lifeless thing as it is summarized in the various accounts of the time. The magic of the occasion, the impressiveness of that short, erect figure, the grandeur of his bearing, the simplicity of his voice, too deep for tears, the knowledge that a glamorous, talented man was about to pass from the stage he had occupied so long — these were the things that blurred Senatorial eyes, and confused them into speechless emotion.

Plumer reported it; so did John Quincy Adams, newly elected Senator; so did the Washington *Federalist*. None of them could recapture the strain. But the *Federalist* remarked, " It is . . . said to be the most dignified, sublime and impressive [speech] that ever was uttered. . . . The whole Senate were in tears, and so unmanned that it was half an hour before they could recover themselves sufficiently to come to order, and choose a vice-president pro tem . . . At the president's . . . two of the senators were relating these circumstances to a circle which had collected round them. One said that he wished that the tradition might be preserved as one of the most extraordinary events he had ever witnessed. Another senator being asked, how long he (Burr) was speaking, after a moment's pause, said he could form no idea; it might have been an hour, and it might have been but a moment; when he came to his senses, he seemed to have awakened as from a kind of trance." [13]

The varying accounts of the text of the speech agree in the main on its essentials. The official account prepared by the Senate reporter is perhaps the most accurate. First Burr touched lightly on the necessity of changing certain rules of the Senate, then he spoke of his personal relations with the members. He had not knowingly done or attempted any injuries to any of the Senate, nor had he any to complain of. " In his official conduct, he had known no party, no cause, no friend, that if, in the opinion of any, the discipline which had been established approached to rigor, they would at least admit that it was uniform and indiscriminate." He paused a moment, and then spoke his peroration. " He challenged their attention," wrote the reporter, " to the considerations more momentous than any which regarded merely their personal honor and character — the preservation of law, of liberty, and the Constitution. This House, said he, is a sanctuary; a citadel of law, of order, and of liberty; and it is here — it is here, in this exalted refuge; here, if anywhere, will resistance be made to the storms of political phrenzy and the silent arts of corruption; and if the Constitution be destined ever to perish by the sacrilegious hands of the demagogue or the usurper, which God avert, its expiring agonies will be witnessed on this floor."

After which, he took leave of his colleagues in touching accents, "perhaps forever," with expressions of personal respect and prayers, and consoling himself, and them, with the reflection that, though they separated, they would still be engaged in the common cause of disseminating principles of freedom and social order.[14]

Whereupon, noted John Quincy Adams, he left the Chair and the room, quietly and without ostentation. He had spoken his swan song, and for the moment the hearts of all were softened to the effulgence of his passing.

Mr. White moved a resolution of thanks to Burr " for the impartiality, integrity, and ability with which he had presided in Senate, and their unqualified approbation of his conduct in that capacity. It passed unanimously." [15]

Several weeks before, in anticipation, Senator Smith of New York had moved a bill to grant Burr the franking privilege for life. It had never been given previously to any retiring Vice-President. After some debate, the measure passed by a vote of 18 to 13, every Republican voting *yea* and some of the Federalists, including the critical John Quincy Adams. But the House did not approve of their colleagues' action. On March 1, 1805, it buried the bill in the Committee of the Whole from which it was never to emerge.[16]

4. L'Envoi

The door of the Senate had closed on Aaron Burr with abrupt finality. He was an outsider, a stranger now in the scenes of public life. Plumer, personally resentful because of Hamilton, was moved to reflection and analysis. " This man, but for his vices, might have held the first office in the gift of the Nation," he wrote his son. " He certainly is an able man — he is ambitious — But he is fallen & I much doubt if he can ever rise again . . . I saw him after he was no longer in office. And my pity involuntarily was excited in his favor. He appeared dejected, gloomy, forsaken by all parties. Mr. Jefferson owes the presidency to the conduct of Mr. Burr. Mr.

Jefferson is in power, but he will not give Mr. Burr any office. Governor of the Territory of Orleans, or Attorney Genl of the United States, either of them, would have been acceptable. But these are given to men of far less talents than Burr. Mr. Jefferson appears to afford no countenance to the man who served him so effectually. The reasons for this, 1st it would be unpopular; 2nd jealousy of his talents, & 3rd fear that if Burr had the means he would injure him." [17]

Bankrupt in fortune, with two indictments suspended over his head, his creditors waiting with writs of execution and body attachments, unable to return to New York to resume his law practice, homeless and adrift in Washington, execrated by most Federalists, feared and suspected by all Republicans, small wonder that the great frontiers of the nation beckoned now with irresistible force. Fortune, fame, power — all shimmered over the farther reaches of the continent like a mirage. Aaron Burr, aged forty-nine, was ready to slough off the old life and pioneer the new.

Chapter XIX

BACKGROUNDS FOR THE CONSPIRACY

1. Westward the Course of Empire

THE thirteen original Colonies had been but a thin, longitudinal strip stretching precariously along the eastern seaboard of the American continent. Beyond the Alleghanies lay vast uncharted regions of forest and plains, and the remote escarpment of the Rockies; to the south and southwest the tangled swamps and barrens of the Floridas, the bayous of the Gulf coast, the farther plains of Texas and the great deserts of what are now New Mexico and Arizona.

Two other great European powers competed with England for domination of the New World. France held Canada and claimed all of the Continent from the Alleghanies to the Rockies. Spain, gorged with South America, swollen with the fabulous riches of Mexico, had pushed upward into California and the fertile plains of Texas. The Floridas, too, were Spanish by right of discovery and settlement.

England and its Colonies, however, never yielded certain vague pretensions to the land west of the Alleghanies, and bold pioneers, traders and fur-trappers pushed in ever-increasing numbers over the mountain barrier, in defiance of alleged French sovereignty. As yet the Spanish settlements were too remote for infiltration. Clashes inevitably arose between the French and the pushing colonists, which led, through a succession of stages, to the drawing of the American colonies into the vortex of the greater European war between the parent nations.

By the Treaty of Paris, England, victorious against the European coalition, took Canada and the Ohio Territory from the French, and Florida from Spain. France, to reconcile the Spanish Government to its losses in a war fought primarily for French interests, ceded to Spain the Louisiana Territory.

Once the menace of France had been removed, the colonists flocked in even greater numbers into the almost virgin Ohio Territory, only to meet with unexpected restrictions imposed on that great area by the mother country. Forced back once more to the line of the Alleghanies, resentment festered and grew, and contributed to some extent to the eventual American Revolution.

By the Treaty of 1783, after a war in which the original antagonists had all participated, the annexed territories were reshuffled.
England was compelled to disgorge Florida to Spain, the Ohio
Territory was turned over to the new nation, the United States,
while France found herself holding the bag, at least as far as any
territorial gains on the American continent were concerned. Hitherto the French had been the great antagonists of the American
colonists; now, for the first time, the latter found themselves opposed along a thousand miles of vague and unsurveyed border by
a new people, the Spanish.

At first there was but little friction. Only on the southeastern
frontier, between sparsely populated Georgia and even more
sparsely populated East Florida, were there any points of contact.
But the opening of the Ohio Territory by various Ordinances
of Congress soon put a different complexion on the situation. The
Americans moved forward in successive waves into the land beyond the Alleghanies. First the trappers, then the Indian traders,
then the pioneer settlers, seeking ever to the west new land, new
resources, new freedom.

In an incredibly short period they had overrun great areas, and
had formed thriving communities along the Ohio River and its
tributaries. But, though there were still huge stretches in which
wild animals and Indians roamed almost unmolested, already the
frontiersmen were clamoring for new worlds to conquer, new
territories to open to their ineradicable greed for westward expansion. It was this restless urge, to move always westward, to find
new sources of fur and trade, to appease a boundless land-hunger
made necessary by wasteful methods of farming, that dominated
the American scene right down to the extinction of the last frontier in the latter part of the nineteenth century.

But now these hardy spirits found themselves thrusting against
the enclosing wall of Spanish possessions. The trans-Mississippi
country was barred to American traders as well as settlers; East
and West Florida blocked access to the warm waters of the Gulf
of Mexico and to the West Indian islands. The Mississippi River,
in the last miles of its course, ran wholly through Spanish territory, as did every other river to which the settlers west of the Alleghanies had access. There was no way of marketing the crops and
products of Ohio, Tennessee and Kentucky, except by arduous
transport over the formidable barrier of the mountains to the
Eastern States, or by submitting to the whims and political
caprices of the Spaniards.

The Easterners, occupied with their own particular problems, were comparatively indifferent to the plaints of the Western territories. To the Westerners, the future lay still farther west and south, along the rivers, the natural highways of the period. But Spain blocked these natural outlets. There followed then a period of complex intrigues and rival ambitions, of mutual raids and economic barriers, of illicit trade and bribery and corruption. It is difficult to unravel the tangled skein of events, to apportion with impartial hand an abstract justice between the contending factions. The Americans of the West saw their economic life, both present and future, slowly throttled by the iron grip of Spain on the mouths of the rivers which tapped their territory; they resented the peculiar alienness of the Spaniard, his ways that were not their ways — and therefore wrong; they resented fiercely the closure of the Spanish provinces to settlement and trade.

The Spaniards, on the other hand, viewed with alarm the aggressive, pushing qualities of the American frontiersmen; they noted with indignation the manifest contempt of the Westerners for Spanish regulations and laws, and they justly feared the insatiable appetite of this new nation for land, and more land. Once it would be permitted to pierce the Spanish domain at any point whatever, eventual absorption or forcible conquest would prove but a matter of time.

In the light of these obvious facts, Spain decided upon a vigorous counter-attack. The Ohio Territory was, geographically, a natural unit with Spanish possessions. There was no such barrier between them as separated the Eastern States from their Western possessions. The rivers which traversed one, emptied through the other into the Gulf. Eventually one must swallow the other. The Spaniards determined to swallow the Ohio.

But not by force. Intrigue was their natural element, as rude violence was that of the Western frontier. They sent agents up the Ohio to propagandize and foment dissension. They employed and paid well certain key Americans in Ohio, Kentucky and Tennessee to agitate for a separation from the Eastern United States, which, they insinuated, was manifestly indifferent to their special needs, and for a submission to the gracious and benevolent rule of His Majesty, the King of Spain. Gold was poured in profusion into the coveted area to bribe and corrupt the Territorial Legislatures. Of the American agents, the most prominent was James Wilkinson. Like a dark, funereal thread he appears again and again in the strands that went to make up the life of Aaron Burr. Soon it will become incorporated into the very warp and woof.

When these secret measures seemed lacking in success, the Spaniards decided on a bolder policy of coercion. They shut their frontiers completely, instigated the Indians within their borders to raid adjacent settlements, confiscated American boats and American shipments down the Mississippi, and imposed crushing imposts on American commerce through New Orleans, the chief port of exit for the West.

The frontier clamored to Congress for aid and protection against the treacherous Don; but Congress, representing the East, considered the West as merely a pawn in the diplomatic game. The West demanded war on Spain, and the conquest of Louisiana and the Floridas, so as to satisfy its two great hungers — land and access to the sea. There was talk even of secession, and a war on its own.

Finally, in 1795, after a decade of resentment, muddled politics and economic confusion, the Federal Government roused itself and negotiated a treaty whereby the Mississippi River was opened to navigation, and Americans given the right of free deposit for their goods in the port of New Orleans, pending sale or transshipment to the West Indies and Europe. Temporarily, the West and South were placated by these concessions on the part of Spain. There was a boom in the West, immigrants thronged in from the East to take advantage of the richer economic possibilities, land rose in value, commerce expanded, and the bolder and more restless spirits looked with longing eyes still farther to the west.

But new grievances soon arose. The crowded frontier was knocking already at the gates of inviolate Spanish territory, the Indian raids across the border increased in number and in violence, traders who slipped into Louisiana and West Florida in defiance of Spanish edicts were arrested and their stocks confiscated, and, to cap the climax, on October 16, 1802, Juan Ventura Morales, Spanish Intendant, or Governor, of Louisiana, without authority from his home government, took it upon himself to proclaim the right of deposit of American goods in New Orleans forfeited.

The news threw the West into a veritable frenzy of excitement. The border flamed; passion rose to fever-pitch. Economic strangulation stared the country in the face. Legislatures met to consider the prospects, men picked up their long rifles, cleaned and oiled them carefully, inspected primings and weighed their supply of bullets.

Henry Clay, a rising young Kentucky lawyer and politician, declared that " the whole country was in commotion and, at a nod of the Government, would have fallen on Baton Rouge and New

Orleans, and punished the treachery of the perfidious Government." [1]

In the end, the unauthorized action of Morales was disavowed by his home government, but the storm had been raised and passions unleashed that could not so readily be allayed. In the midst of these alarms and turmoils another report was brought to the Western country that added new clamors and new alarms. This was the news that Spain was preparing to cede, or rather to retrocede, the Louisiana Territory to France.

Napoleon was now the Man on Horseback in the European scene, and Talleyrand, subtle and tortuous in diplomacy, using speech to conceal his thought, was his Minister. Charles IV was King of Spain, and Don Manuel Godoy, nicknamed " the Prince of Peace " for his assumed leanings toward policy as a weapon of government rather than war, was his Prime Minister. Godoy was a bit tired of the constant agitation and diplomatic confusion resulting from Spanish possession of New Orleans and Louisiana. He was engaged, as the tail to the French kite, in an almost interminable war with England, and this comparatively undefended stretch was more of a liability than an asset. But he was moved by other considerations as well. He was farseeing enough to realize that Spain could not long continue to hold this precarious possession in the face of the vigorous, constantly advancing nation on which it bordered; a nation which, rightly or wrongly, considered Louisiana in foreign hands an unjust restriction of its expansive powers. Godoy had other fish to fry nearer home. Besides, should England or the United States — especially the latter — decide on a war of conquest, patriotic fervor might lead them ever closer to the alluring vision of Mexico. And Godoy very decidedly wished to retain Mexico and South America. The sinews of Spain's power, the supply of gold and metals she required, came from those enormously rich provinces.

Napoleon, on the other hand, was revolving in his head grandiose schemes of world domination. France still had not given up the dream of a vast empire on the American continent, though her possessions had been wrested from her grasp. Louisiana would be the entering wedge once more. It was a *quid pro quo.*

Godoy did *not* want Louisiana any more; furthermore, the interposition of the French between Mexico and the restless Americans to the east would enable him to sleep easier of nights. But Godoy *did* want additional territory in Italy. Accordingly, on October 1, 1800, after lengthy negotiations, a secret treaty was entered into between France and Spain at San Ildefonso, whereby Spain agreed to retrocede to France the Territory of Louisiana and — this with considerable reluctance — the Floridas. In return, France agreed to aggrandize to the Spanish Duchy of Parma a considerable territory in Italy. So secret was this treaty, fraught as it was with enormous possibilities to the United States, that Jefferson, six months later, was still unaware of its existence.

"With respect to Spain," he wrote Claiborne, Governor of the Mississippi Territory — that area which Godoy had ceded to the United States in 1795 against the wrath of the French — " our disposition is sincerely amicable, and even affectionate. We consider her possession of the adjacent country as most favorable to our interests, and should see with an extreme pain any other nation substituted for them." [2]

Within a short time, however, " extreme pain " must have assailed him. For the news of the secret treaty gradually leaked out, first in the form of rumors, then in more tangible and definite shape. Godoy, who found Talleyrand unable or unwilling to live up to his part of the bargain, evaded as long as he could the cession of the American territories. But pressure which could not be ignored was finally brought to bear, and he promised to deliver, if, among other things, France bound herself never to alienate Louisiana to the United States. One of the chief reasons for Godoy's willingness to cede that territory in the beginning had been to set up a buffer state between Mexico and the United States. Talleyrand and Napoleon gave the necessary assurances, with tongue in cheek. A date was set for the official transfer.

If Jefferson had suffered " extreme pain," the West was almost beside itself at the news. Instead of Spain, weak and corruptible, whose officials could be brought to wink at infractions of the prohibitory laws, a strong, ruthless nation was now to encamp on its doorstep. Instead of eventual easy conquest of Louisiana, Napoleon as a neighbor would be afflicted with a fatally similar vision of expanding empire.

Jefferson was compelled to listen to the clamorous demands. The West and the South, the vitally interested sections, were strongholds of Republicanism. Burr had written vigorously of the retrocession to his son-in-law. He was keenly alive to its necessary consequences.[3] Jefferson, the pacifist, now spoke sharply — in public — of the possibility of war with Spain. For, in the meantime, to complicate the situation, Morales had closed the port of New Orleans. In private, he threatened Napoleon with a similar catastrophe. He even spoke of " marrying " the English Navy to effectuate his threats. Napoleon was not unduly alarmed, and continued to demand from Spain immediate occupation, while a bedeviled Spain was yielding on the closure of the port to the Americans.

Before the negotiations with Spain were satisfactorily ended, however, John Randolph of Roanoke, already tilting at Jefferson, moved in the House for the examination of all the documents relating to the violated right of deposit. Pichon, the French Minister, wrote to Talleyrand that " however timid Mr. Jefferson may be, and whatever price he may put on his pacific policy, one cannot foresee precisely what his answer will be. . . . If he acts feebly, he is lost among his partisans; it will be then the time for Mr. Burr to show himself with advantage." [4]

For the matter had widened. It was realized by Randolph and Burr alike that the closure of New Orleans had been instigated by the French in order that it might be considered a *fait accompli* when they came to take possession. It was a skilful attempt to place the onus of a deliberate French policy upon a scapegoat Spain. Even if Spain disavowed Morales, there was no doubt in the minds of Randolph and Burr, or in the minds of Westerners generally, that France, once in possession, would re-enact the ordinance, and close the Mississippi entirely to American shipping.

Jefferson tried to stifle the growing clamor, and succeeded in holding the House down to a conditional resolution. But the West was not so easily stilled. State Legislature after Legislature met and adopted resolutions worded in the strongest language. Demands poured in unending flood upon Washington for the seizure of New Orleans before the French troops, veterans of the campaign against Toussaint L'Ouverture, could be landed, and fortify themselves into impregnable positions.

There was but one way out for the harassed President. He emphatically did not want war with Spain and France both, and the specter of Aaron Burr, waiting grimly for an opportunity to recoup his political fortunes, goaded him on and sharpened his wits. He would purchase the port of New Orleans and the contiguous territory in order to obtain an outlet on the Mississippi, and, in addition, the Floridas, valuable both as outlets and for expansion to his beloved South.

It is not necessary here to examine the extended and weary negotiations, the sudden and surprising offer of the entire Louisiana Territory by a newly beleaguered Napoleon who had seen his dream of New World Empire fade in the smoke and ruins engendered by Toussaint L'Ouverture — that has been done many times before.

AARON BURR, 1805

From an Original Drawing by Favret de Saint Mémin

GENERAL JAMES WILKINSON

From an engraving by Favret de St. Mémin

Suffice it to say that Jefferson seized the opportunity — though there were serious doubts as to constitutionality, and New England was decidedly opposed — and the deal was consummated for $15,000,000. Napoleon, however, could not include the Floridas, which had been eliminated from his bargain with Spain. The treaty of purchase was signed on May 2, 1803.

Immediately, serious difficulties arose. Spain, when she heard of the astounding sale, was furious. She pointed out that Napoleon's title was wholly defective. He had not lived up to the Treaty of San Ildefonso, which required that he obtain for Spain the expansion of the Duchy of Parma, and, worse yet, from the point of view of the buyer, he was selling that which he had expressly agreed never to alienate without the consent of Spain. And Spain certainly did not consent.

As a matter of fact, she used strong language to Napoleon. " This alienation," d'Azara insisted to Talleyrand, " not only deranges from top to bottom the whole colonial system of Spain, and even of Europe, but is directly opposed to the compacts and formal stipulations agreed upon between France and Spain." [5]

Cevallos, Spanish Minister for Foreign Affairs, in his protest, frankly avowed the real purposes of Spain. " The intention which led the King to give his consent to the exchange of Louisiana was completely deceived. This intention had been to interpose a strong dyke between the Spanish colonies and the American possessions; now, on the contrary, the doors of Mexico are to stay open to them." [6]

Nevertheless, Napoleon drove ahead with his bargain, and Spain, being the weaker power, was compelled to acquiesce. On November 30, 1803, New Orleans was formally handed over to the French, and twenty days later, on December 20, 1803, it was formally transferred to the American commissioners in symbolic token of the entire Louisiana Territory. The commissioners were W. C. C. Claiborne, Governor of the Mississippi Territory, and General James Wilkinson, of the American Army. The United States of America had more than doubled in size.

The West went wild with joy. It had achieved the way-station to its ultimate goal. For the present, there was plenty of land, and the Mississippi was an American river from source to mouth. The South was decidedly more moderate in its rejoicing. The Floridas still belonged to Spain. Nor was Spain, resentful over what it considered sharp practice, willing to sell, even for the munificent price of $2,000,000. There were other difficulties, too. What, in fact, had the United States bought? Napoleon had no clear title, and he had frankly given what the lawyers call a quitclaim deed. In other words, just what had been ceded to him without warranties of any kind on his part. The boundaries of the new accession even were not known, especially on the eastern frontier. Just where did Louisiana leave off and West Florida, still Spanish, begin? Talleyrand shrugged his expressive shoulders when the American envoys politely inquired on this point, and returned as politely that no doubt the Americans would be able to settle that little detail themselves.

This the resourceful Americans proceeded to do. They had been sent abroad to purchase the Floridas, not merely New Orleans. It is true that Louisiana was thrown into the bargain, but the Floridas, so vital to the South, still belonged, it seemed, to Spain. Whereupon they evolved an ingenious theory, viz., that actually the Louisiana Territory *included* the Floridas, even though Napoleon himself had not known it. The theory, in truth, was so ingenious that it made Talleyrand, veteran diplomatist that he was, stare in amazement, and wonder if, after all, he had not underestimated the cleverness of these Americans.

Livingston was so enthusiastic that he convinced himself of the justice of this stand, and wrote to Madison that " the moment is so favorable for taking possession of that country that I hope it has not been neglected, even though a little force should be necessary to effect it. Your minister must find the means to justify it." [7] The bland European chancelleries had nothing to teach Americans in the way of rationalizations and cynical diplomacy.

Jefferson seized upon this interpretation with eagerness; so did a Republican Congress in which the Southern expansionists were in the saddle. Congress, under the impassioned lash of John Randolph, fire-eater extraordinary, even legislated as though West Florida were actually a part of the United States, and tried to prod Jefferson along the road of forcible possession. But there Jefferson balked, even though his words were warlike, and though he had rushed troops to Natchez.

Outwardly, however, war with Spain seemed inevitable. Spain stubbornly refused to accept Livingston's interpretation of her own treaties, and she was prepared to meet force with force if West Florida should be invaded. In retaliation for her wrongs, she closed all her borders tight against further American penetration of any kind. She resented also what she deemed the exorbitant demands of the United States in connection with the Spoliation Claims. Don Carlos Martinez de Yrujo, Marquis of Casa Yrujo, her Minister to the United States, who originally had been most friendly to the Jeffersonian faction, even to the extent of marrying the daughter of Governor McKean, now turned vigorously hostile in behalf of his native land. So, too, did Turreau, the French Minister, and especially so did Anthony Merry, Minister from England, whose bitterness against Jefferson and Madison was all the more intense because it was bottomed primarily on social and personal reasons. All of these diplomats engaged in violent intrigues against the Government. Yrujo protested vigorously and publicly, obtained and paid for opinions of American lawyers concerning the injustice of the American claims, and engaged in downright bribery of the Press to advocate the cause of Spain. Merry went further. His home was the headquarters of all the intriguers in Washington. Pickering and the Federal disunionists received his official aid and support. In fact, the conspirators kept Merry advised of the secret aims of the American Government in the pending boundary dispute, and, reported Merry, when the day of disunion came, " they naturally look forward to Great Britain for support and assistance whenever the occasion shall arise." [8] What difference between Pickering, Griswold, Hillhouse and Company, and Aaron Burr — granting the premise that Burr actually plotted disunion?

2. HAMILTON AND MIRANDA

This, then, was the situation when Aaron Burr ended his term as Vice-President on March 4, 1805, and found all former doors irrevocably closed to him. All Europe was at war, either on the side of Napoleon or of William Pitt, his great English antagonist. The United States was on unfriendly terms with both France and England, and breathing fire and snorting thunderous words at Spain over West Florida. The Mexican Colonies had themselves become infected with the prevalent unrest. The French Revolution had unleashed noble catchwords which reverberated around the world and brought new hope and strength to the oppressed everywhere. *Liberty, Equality, Fraternity!*

In spite of the Spanish authorities, in spite of the dread chambers of the Inquisition, the unrest spread in Mexico, in South America. Insurrections were suppressed in blood and the screams of the tortured, but the movement continued underground. The United States watched the progress of plotting and insurrection alike with a keen interest, encouraged the movement with moral support. The West, however, was willing to proceed more openly. Spain was hated with a consuming hatred. It was democracy against autocracy, liberty against oppression. And Mexico beckoned afar, fabulous, incredibly wealthy. The South wanted the Floridas. Both sections had a fierce contempt for the " treacherous Don," would welcome with eagerness filibustering expeditions, and would enlist by the thousands in an outright war.

Burr was not the first American in public life to look longingly at Mexico, and South America even. In 1798 Hamilton had listened avidly to Francesco de Miranda, a native of Venezuela and soldier of fortune *par excellence*, whose dream it was to free all South America from the rule of the Spaniard and set himself up as the Washington of his native province. He sought aid in England, but received no satisfactory assurances. He turned to Hamilton and the United States, where his welcome was warmer. Hamilton envisioned himself as the all-conquering General and entered enthusiastically upon his schemes. A plan of campaign was drawn. " Every thing is smooth," wrote Miranda, " and we wait only for the fiat of your illustrious president to depart like lightning." 9 But the " illustrious president," who happened to be John Adams, was in no hurry to encourage a wild adventure simply because Hamilton saw himself as the Man on Horseback. The scheme died under the withering blight of his disapproval, and thereby added fuel to Hamilton's hatred. For had the latter not already written to Rufus King that " with regard to the enterprise in question . . . the command in this case would very naturally fall upon me; and I hope I should disappoint no favorable anticipations." 10 He was still indignant over wasted opportunities the following year. He complained to McHenry, " It is a pity, my dear sir, and a reproach, that our administration have no general plan." At least, he thought, " we ought certainly to look to the possession of the Floridas and Louisiana, and we ought to squint at South America." 11

Miranda, however, was not discouraged. After years more of proselytizing among the European nations without substantial success, he determined in 1805 that the United States was his final opportunity. All the signs pointed to an immediate war between the United States and Spain, and his own private plans concerning South America would fit neatly into the picture. He landed in New York in November, 1805, and became an overnight sensation. A host of adventurers flocked to his standard; even Jonathan Dayton, ex-Senator of the United States, and close friend to Burr, was involved. So, too, were John Swartwout, still United States Marshal, and William S. Smith, Surveyor of the Port of New York.

Miranda, a self-styled General, hired a ship, the *Leander*, and proceeded to purchase arms and supplies, and enlist men openly for a filibustering expedition against his native country. He did more. He went to Washington and was cordially received by Madison and dined by Jefferson. Afterwards, when Spain angrily protested against this encouragement of a warlike expedition from American soil against her territories, both Madison and Jefferson were to deny any complicity in Miranda's schemes. But Miranda loudly insisted that Madison was fully aware of his purposes, and the Secretary of State, by his own account, cannot be completely exonerated.

In any event, Miranda returned to New York, boasting of Governmental assistance, and completed his preparations. Over a month later, the ship sailed publicly from New York Harbor, armed to the teeth, making no secret of its destination. In fact, ten days before sailing time, Miranda had written to Madison bidding him a formal goodbye, adding that the matters he had communicated to him " will remain, I doubt not, in the deepest secret until the final result of this delicate affair. I have acted here on that supposition, conforming myself in everything to the intentions of the Government, which I hope I have seized and observed with exactitude and discretion." [12] This shifty transaction, and the Government's subsequent disavowal, should be remembered in connection with the almost exactly similar instance of Burr's own relations with Jefferson and Madison later on.

Miranda's expedition came to an inglorious end. The ship was captured by the Spaniards before it ever reached the mainland, and at once the inevitable repercussions commenced in Washington. Yrujo laid the damning evidence before Madison — it was bad enough without Miranda's written leave-taking of Madison, of which Spain fortunately was not aware — and under the lash of his charges, the Government was compelled to move. Swartwout was removed as Marshal, Smith as Surveyor, and Smith and Ogden, owner of the *Leander*, were formally indicted for violation of the laws. Smith's case eventually came on for trial. He was acquitted by a jury handpicked by Swartwout, and the entire incident was considered closed.

Burr had held aloof from Miranda's plans, inasmuch as they conflicted to a large extent with his own, and because, as he told Charles Biddle, " Miranda was a fool, totally unqualified for such an expedition." [13]

He had, in fact, been approached by Miranda with a view to enlisting his services. But Burr exercised his unequaled talent for evading a forthright encounter and Miranda retired, disgruntled and nursing a resentment which was to flare up at a much later date during Burr's period of exile.[14]

Filibuster was in the air, war with Spain was imminent, while Mexico and the Spanish possessions in the Americas ever held an ineradicable attraction for American adventurers. Burr was neither the first nor the last of a long line of expansionists; though it was his fate to become the most tragical.

3. FOREIGN AID

Burr had long been revolving certain plans in his mind, ante-dating even his duel with Hamilton. The date of their inception may perhaps be fixed with an air of certainty. On May 23, 1804, James Wilkinson, on his way back from New Orleans, where, as one of the American commissioners, he had formally taken possession of Louisiana Territory, wrote Burr that " to save time of which I need much and have but little, I propose to take a Bed with you this night, if it may be done without observation or intrusion." [15] Burr was then Vice-President. He had been recently defeated in the gubernatorial election in New York; all his former hopes of political rehabilitation had come crashing to earth. It was time to look about him. Wilkinson was in command of the American forces on the Spanish frontier. He was much more than that, but it is extremely doubtful that Burr had any inkling of his Spanish connections at the time.

What more natural than to assume that it was Wilkinson who first impregnated Burr's fertile brain with the dazzling possibilities of a career of arms and glory, of personal aggrandizement at the expense of Spain. He had first-hand knowledge of the situation, his friends and subordinates were spying out routes and Spanish defenses, he was in command of the Army, Mexico was in the throes of insurrection, and — relations between the United States and Spain pointed to the imminence of war. Note the secrecy, the insistence on freedom from " observation " in the proposed visit.

At this hasty meeting, Spain, Mexico, the Southwest, were discussed. Wilkinson — this, of course, is all pure surmise, based merely upon the logic of later events — dangled glittering bait before Burr's dazzled vision. He knew whereof he spoke, and the means seemed at hand. It is quite likely that at this stage of the affair Wilkinson was sincere — with his usual mental reservations in case matters turned out badly. They talked far into the night, and, when Wilkinson left, a definite scheme of action had been determined on, and a cipher arranged for future communications. Wilkinson went back to his command on the border, to prepare the way. Burr went on to the tragedy of his duel with Hamilton, his flight, and return to Washington. In any event, the scheme had to wait on the end of his term in office — a Vice-President could not engage in filibusters or private wars.

In the meantime, he had seized the chance to explore Southern sentiment and to survey the East Florida terrain. When Jefferson, engrossed with the impeachment of Justice Chase, sought his favor, Burr recommended Wilkinson's appointment as Governor of Louisiana, Brown, as Secretary, and Prevost as Judge in New Orleans. Edward Livingston, his friend of former days, had left New York under a cloud, and settled in New Orleans, where he had already achieved a considerable measure of influence. The very heavens, it seemed, were smiling on the meditated enterprise. He enlisted the services of certain other chosen spirits, men of influence and then at loose ends. They eagerly associated themselves with him. Jonathan Dayton, whose term as United States Senator from New Jersey was about to expire, was one of these. He had married Matthias Ogden's sister, was himself a close friend to Burr from boyhood days. Furthermore, he was interested in a projected canal around the Ohio Falls, and held on speculation some 25,000 acres of land between Big and Little Miami Rivers. The city of Dayton, Ohio, was later to be named after him. While Burr involved him in the Spanish adventure, he in turn interested Burr in the canal project. There was a considerable fluidity about the entire business. Burr was chiefly anxious to redeem his fortunes; and land speculations, canal projects, settlement in the West, even the practice of law in that area, and subsequent re-entry into politics, revolved in his mind together with Wilkinson's scheme of warlike endeavor.

He approached others, members of Congress, men chiefly from the West, and already predisposed to engage in a venture which was certain to be extremely popular among their constituents. All of them were personal friends and imbued with a great admiration for Burr's talents and military abilities. They were Senator John Smith of Ohio, General John Adair, Senator from Kentucky, and Senator John Brown from the same state. Matthew Lyon, erstwhile Congressman from Vermont, and now Kentucky's representative in the House, seemingly had a finger in the pie. So had Andrew Jackson, Major-General of the Tennessee militia, who had admired Burr enthusiastically ever since he had been in

Congress. There were others, of lesser note: personal adherents, like young Samuel Swartwout, young Peter Ogden and Comfort Tyler of New York, who had been in the New York Legislature with Burr.

In short, it must not be considered that the scheme proposed by Wilkinson and engineered by Burr, was the ordinary filibuster, insufficiently prepared and poorly planned. Men of substance and influence were involved, featuring the East as well as the West, while the remote Territories, contiguous to Spain's dominion, were almost wholly controlled by the conspirators. Furthermore, Wilkinson had evidently assured Burr of hearty support in New Orleans, where there existed a Mexican Association with a membership of 300, dedicated, it seems, to the cause of revolution in Mexico. Daniel Clark, the most substantial merchant of the City and Territory, was interested. There was still another in the secret: a British army officer, Colonel Charles Williamson. Burr had been associated with him in the old days of the New York land boom, when Williamson had represented a group of British investors, and he had remained on terms of complete intimacy with him ever since.[16] To him would be entrusted the delicate matter of obtaining British cooperation for their schemes. Great Britain, as the Mistress of the Seas, had the power to advance or nullify any adventure relating to Spain's domain in the Americas.

But an adequate attempt on Spain's possessions required a considerable amount of money. Burr had none himself — financially he was bankrupt. The others had some, but not very much. He appealed to his son-in-law, Joseph Alston, for assistance. Alston was wealthy, probably the largest plantation owner in his State. His imagination took fire at the scheme, what with Theodosia's deft kindling, and he subscribed certain sums and went surety later for the borrowing of still greater amounts. Theo threw herself heart and soul into her father's plans. No doubt she envisioned for him a glorious future that even his own optimistic faculty could not encompass. When all was collected, and accounted for, there still was considerably less than the barest minimum required. This situation, however, had been thoroughly anticipated by Burr and Wilkinson in their original discussions. A sum beyond the resources of private individuals was indicated, and even the use of regular troops and naval forces. The United States Government could not be considered, in spite of prospective war. At this moment — June, 1804 — Burr was *persona non grata* with the Administration. There was only Great Britain. She was the logical nation to approach for funds and military assistance. She was at war with

Spain; she had nibbled at Miranda's first proposals, and she had both money and naval power.

But, the conspirators evidently argued, a bald approach based on these simple facts would lead to curt dismissal. A scheme was accordingly concocted, whether at Burr's instigation, or Williamson's, familiar as he was with the processes of the British administrative mind,[17] or Wilkinson's, there is no present possibility of assurance. But the probabilities point to Wilkinson's fine Machiavellian hand in these transactions. They indicate, by their sleight-of-hand agility, methods, and total lack of sustaining morals of any kind, his own previous career of chicanery and slipperiness as a Spanish agent and spy.

For this scheme was undoubtedly an unpardonable bit of trickery and false dealing, and represented a very definite moral obtuseness on the part of the proponents. Though it is likely that Wilkinson, with a long career of successful endeavor in similar matters behind him, had suggested the plan, Burr cannot be acquitted of complicity. He not only adopted the proposals, but conducted the negotiations. This episode, says Beveridge, "was the first thoroughly dishonorable act of Burr's career." [18] He has been accused of much, but aside from the doubtful ethics of his advocacy of the Alien Holding Bill, his record, in public as well as in private life, was considerably cleaner than that of most rival politicians. It is the ironic touch of fate that these secret dealings with the British, and later with the Spanish themselves, were not known until they were unearthed by Henry Adams in the archives of the foreign Chancellories. Here, if anywhere, was there seeming proof of Burr's traitorous intent, of his general moral obliquity. Yet he was actually hounded and persecuted and scorned for transactions in which his only fault had been perhaps a too great resistance to the temptations of accidental opportunity.

Burr had just fought his duel with Hamilton — this was in July, 1804 — and had fled to Philadelphia in consequence. There he found Anthony Merry, British Minister, summering and nursing his personal resentments against the Administration in particular and Americans in general. He had, forsooth, been slighted in the important matter of social precedence, and his petty mind was filled with spleen. A vain, irascible, weak man, as poor a diplomat and ambassador as Great Britain had ever sent from her shores. A good deal of a fool too, and easily hoodwinked. The conspirators counted on that.

At the beginning of August, Burr sent Charles Williamson to Merry with an astounding proposition. Merry listened to Williamson — who, after all, was notably connected in England — with gullible eagerness. In fact, he snatched the bait before it was well presented. Visions of himself as the dominant arbiter of American destiny, dreams of a spiteful revenge against Jefferson and Madison, dazzled his poor wits and addled his already scrambled mental processes. Without further ado he sat down and wrote a long letter to his home Government.

" I have just received an offer from Mr. Burr, the actual Vice-President of the United States (which situation he is about to resign) ," he reported, " to lend his assistance to his Majesty's government in any manner in which they may think fit to employ him, particularly in endeavoring to effect a separation of the western part of the United States from that which lies between the Atlantic and the mountains, in its whole extent. His proposition on this and other subjects will be fully detailed to your Lordship by Colonel Williamson, who has been the bearer of them to me, and who will embark for England in a few days." [19]

Here, if anywhere, is treasonable intent, definite and avowed, similar to that of the New England Disunionists, even to the appeal to England for support. Jefferson would have given much to have been able to lay his hands on this communication, and the others that followed voluminously. But the situation is not as simple as all that. To obtain Merry's cooperation at all, it was necessary to bait him with the prospect of that which he most desired — the wrecking of the American Union and the downfall of Jefferson. Without him, it would be almost impossible to obtain British funds and support. He was the channel through which these must flow.

But it was on Williamson's mission that Burr relied to unfold the true state of affairs. Only recently have the details of that mission been disclosed. The discovery of Williamson's letters among the Melville Papers in the Newberry Library of Chicago by Professor I. J. Cox has placed a new interpretation on what has hitherto been shrouded in considerable mystery.[20]

Burr in the meantime had let matters rest. He had proceeded south on his exploration of Florida, and had returned to resume his Vice-Presidential duties in Washington, waiting to hear some word from his envoy to England. But no word came. Neither to himself, nor to Merry from his superiors. It was most disturbing.

Williamson, however, had been delayed by a long and perilous trip across the Atlantic, which threatened, as he wrote, to disappoint the expectations of many in America. Immediately on landing he reported to his patron, Lord Melville, First Lord of the

Admiralty, and possessed of Pitt's private ear.[21] Melville was favorably disposed to Miranda's enterprise, and Williamson urged assiduously both Burr's and Miranda's plans upon him, as mutually complementary and offering certain success. He emphasized again and again that these two schemes would effectually prevent the French from taking over the Spanish colonies, a probability that was most disturbing to English diplomacy.[22] These reports and communications extended over a period of a year, and, according to Professor Cox, nowhere in the confidential and frank exchanges between the two Englishmen, protégé and patron, is there the slightest mention of Burr in connection with Western separatism. Always it is Mexico and the Spanish possessions which Burr is represented as being ready to attack, with British help, and always it is joined with Miranda's plan to free South America, as a single grand, embracing policy for the consideration of the British Government.

Even much later, after Burr's efforts had collapsed ignominiously, and he had been tried for treason, Williamson refused to relax his efforts on behalf of his friend. For Burr, as will be seen, persisted in his schemes, in spite of exile, in spite of disgrace. In Williamson's letters of 1807–8, he mentions his further communications with the British Cabinet, in which Burr's name is invariably associated with a proposal for the reduction of Mexico. Now, it is true, Williamson mentions Western separatism, but for the first time, and as something apart from Burr's own schemes.[23] This, it must be remembered, was the period of the Chesapeake incident, Jefferson's embargo, and definitely embittered relations between Great Britain and the United States. Williamson had become definitely anti-American, in the interim. Burr, Williamson now thought, might lead a political revolt of the Northern merchant classes against the ruinous policy of the Virginia Dynasty, and thereby justify British approval, yet still not a single word linking Burr and the West. Certainly these unbuttoned communications, coupled with the classic researches of Professor Walter McCaleb, must dispel forever the rooted belief that Burr's plot, conspiracy, or whatever it may be called, was an attempt to disrupt the Union.

Williamson found himself unable to do anything. For this there were several reasons. Napoleon, at this time (1804–5), was threatening to invade England with a vast Armada, and the Government could not afford to engage in distant expeditions. Lord Melville, Williamson's patron, had come under a cloud due to alleged irregularities in his accounts, and a Commission was even then engaged in an examination of his affairs. In 1806, he was actually impeached and removed from office, though there seems to have been no probative evidence of any guilt. His impeachment was chiefly a matter of subterranean politics. But thereby the strongest prop for the Burr scheme was removed from the Cabinet.

Early in 1805, Williamson saw the handwriting on the wall, and requested permission from Melville to return to America, and there keep alive the readiness of his friends to join any expedition which Great Britain might wish to undertake against *South America*.[24] Evidently Melville requested that he stay. For, on January 3, 1806, and again on January 6th, he was writing, this time to Lord Justice Clerk, with a new view of Burr's plan, requesting that he show it to Melville, who " will take, I dare say, Measures to give his Opinions to the only Man in the Nation [Pitt] that can, after all, act on them." England, he urged, must act without delay. With a small fleet in the Gulf of Mexico and an outlay of less than £200,000, he " would expect before next August to see 50,000 North Americans with Colonel Burr at their head, far on their March to the City of Mexico." [25]

Here, in small compass, is the entire " Conspiracy." To seize Mexico, to obtain sufficient money from England to pay all expenses and leave the bankrupt participants a tidy sum over and above for themselves. This latter was reprehensible, perhaps, but, at the risk of belaboring the point, nothing that could possibly be construed as treason to the United States.

Within a few days thereafter William Pitt, Prime Minister of England, was dead, and Lord Melville driven from office. Thereby all hopes of English participation collapsed. Williamson returned to America in disgust, landing in April, 1806, only to find that matters had gone even more badly with his friends, and the country decidedly hostile to England and Englishmen. By August of the same year he went back to his native country, to resume, a year later, his pressure on behalf of his friend Burr, and the plans dearest to his heart. But, as will be seen, the episode was ended, and not to be revived.

With the English situation in mind, it is easier to understand what was happening in the United States. Burr was seriously disturbed over the complete absence of information from his English emissary. To him he had confided far more than to the inept gullibility of Anthony Merry. But the weeks became months, and the months a year. Great Britain was far distant — and an inscrutable blank. His term of office was expiring, and all his plans were marking time.

4. CREOLE GRIEVANCES

Meanwhile, another situation had arisen in New Orleans, focal point for any expedition against Mexico by land or sea. The United States, under the Treaty of Session, had promised the inhabitants that they would be admitted as soon as possible to citizenship in the United States, and vested with all the rights, privileges and immunities accruing thereto. This promise had been broken, on the high ground that the mixed population, Creole, French, Spanish and American, was not fit for self-government. The sensitive habitants, Creole chiefly, resented the imputation, resented their helpless dependency, and hated their new Governor, W. C. C. Claiborne, worse than they had ever hated Spain.

Accordingly, they sent three representatives to Washington armed with a list of their grievances, and a demand that the Government live up to its pledge. On March 2, 1805, Congress yielded to the extent of granting a General Assembly and a promise of admission to the Union when and if the population reached a total of 60,000. This, however, did not content the angry Deputies, and they growled to Merry — the willing ear to all malcontents, conspirators, and plotters — that they did not think much of the Union and regretted extremely that they had ever been forced into any connection with it.[26]

Burr sympathized with the disgruntled Deputies. He was sincere in believing that they were entitled to citizenship, and he possessed a peculiar interest of his own in their mission. The Mountain had come to Mahomet. He became intimate with them, encouraged their plans, and spoke of his own. They could be of mutual assistance. New Orleans had been cut off from a lucrative trade with Mexico and Texas on its annexation to the United States. The Mexican Association, seeking Mexican independence, and composed of prominent citizens of New Orleans, was already agitating secretly in furtherance of that object. With Burr in control of Mexico, either as an independent nation or as a part of the United States, New Orleans' commerce would revive, and a new and unprecedented era of prosperity commence. The Deputies listened and were impressed.

No sooner was Burr out of office than he hastened again to Merry. Williamson, it seemed, had failed him, and Merry must once more be the vehicle of his proposals to England. He tempered his story to suit Merry's peculiar frame of mind. Merry took fire and sent forthwith another despatch to his Government — in triplicate — and marked " Most secret."

" Mr. Burr, (with whom I know that the deputies became very intimate during their residence here) has mentioned to me that the inhabitants of Louisiana seem determined to render themselves independent of the United States, and that the execution of their design is only delayed by the difficulty of obtaining previously an assurance of protection and assistance from some foreign Power, and of concerting and connecting their independence with that of the inhabitants of the western parts of the United States, who must always have a command over them by the rivers which communicate with the Mississippi. It is clear that Mr. Burr (although he has not as yet confided to me the exact nature and extent of his plan) means to endeavor to be the instrument of effecting such a connection." Again Burr was dangling Merry's pet scheme before his own eyes, yet evading — as Merry was fumblingly aware — any definite complicity of his own. Plumer, long before, had discovered somewhat ruefully that Burr could manage to give a general impression which was not at all justified by what he actually said. In return for these nebulosities, Burr merely asked the use of a British squadron at the mouth of the Mississippi and a loan of half a million dollars. Should England refuse, he insinuated artfully, he would apply to France, who, he knew, would " be eager to attend to it in the most effectual manner." This, too, Merry swallowed, in spite of the fact that France had only recently delivered the property, and been glad to get rid of it. He also duly forwarded Burr's scheme for remitting the money — a very clever method whereby it would have come at once into Burr's own hands, and no questions asked.[27]

Burr, however, did not intend to wait supinely at Washington for a reply. In those days of tedious communication, at least four months must intervene. The West, the Mississippi, New Orleans beckoned — and beyond. The West, because it was there that he expected to recruit the major part of his filibustering expedition. The Mississippi, because that was Wilkinson's stronghold, and further plans must be discussed. New Orleans, because that was the springboard for all ventures, and he wished to establish contact with the Mexican Association, Judge Prevost, Edward Livingston, and the Deputies themselves on their home ground. Beyond — meant — Mexico. Burr had an unequaled talent for topography, mapping, and the plotting of strategic routes.

With a fine audacity he applied to Yrujo, the Spanish Minister, for a passport to Mexico. Yrujo, who had once before granted him leave to enter Florida, was thoroughly suspicious this time. Perhaps Wilkinson had already commenced his remarkable campaign of duplicity, playing both ends against the middle, and relying on his own extraordinary agility to come out on top, no matter which way the game went. Yrujo refused the passport, and wrote at once to Casa Calvo, one of the Spanish boundary commissioners who was still lingering in New Orleans, advising him to warn all Mexico to watch out for Burr, and to arrest him if he should set foot in Spanish territory.[28] Yrujo, at this stage of the game, was obviously under no illusions as to Burr's real purposes.

Each of the Foreign Ministers, not one of whom was friendly to the United States, had a different and bewildering version of Burr's activities. Merry had heard only of the promised Western Secession and the appendage of Louisiana to that kite; Turreau, the French Minister, was certain it involved only Louisiana, and perceived Wilkinson's connection with the affair; [29] Yrujo alone was in command of the proper information. Which leads, as has been stated, directly to the aforesaid Wilkinson. Of this gentleman, perhaps too little has been said. To follow the intricate web of plot and counterplot, the march of events and Burr's eventual entrapment, it is essential to understand the talents, character, and previous career of General James Wilkinson.

5. "THE FINISHED SCOUNDREL"

James Wilkinson was born in Maryland in 1757, studied medicine as a boy, and threw it over to volunteer at the beginning of the Revolution. Rapidly achieving a Captaincy, he was in the column led by General Sullivan to reinforce Arnold at Quebec after the assault on that fortress had failed. There, at the age of 17, he met Burr, not much older than himself, and they became friends. After that their paths separated, but correspondence continued. Wilkinson became Brigade-Major on Gates' Staff, and rose to Brigadier-General after Burgoyne's campaign. His indiscreet talk, so it is claimed, resulted in the discovery by Washington of the Gates-Conway cabal. He resigned under a cloud; to return, however, eighteen months later, as Clothier-General to the army, a position at once filled with fascinating possibilities of profit and a reasonable assurance of safety. At the end of the war he went to Kentucky to seek his further fortune, as so many discharged soldiers and officers were doing.

With the money he had saved from his salary and possible perquisites as Clothier-General, he soon became a trader and person of consequence. In 1787 he journeyed by flatboat to New Orleans to extend the theater of his operations and establish a profitable trade connection with the Spaniards. He not only disposed of his cargo of flour, tobacco, butter and bacon, but he perceived a new field for his talents. American citizens were subject to heavy restrictions and onerous duties in the trade with the Spanish provinces, and Wilkinson, who had become friendly with Governor Miro, decided to become a Spanish subject — in secret. This, however, was not enough. To obtain special privileges and a pension from the credulous officials, he boldly proposed to them that he, and he alone, could wrest the western part of the United States away from the East and place it " under the protection or vassalage of his Catholic Majesty." [30]

On August 20, 1787, he took a secret oath of allegiance to Spain, and presented a memorial to the Governor in which he described in florid language the grievances which Kentucky held against the Union, and a procedure whereby Spain could take advantage of the situation and attach Kentucky to its own dominion. This latter would require Wilkinson's return to his former home, where he would proceed to work for disunion. Naturally, it was essential that certain sums of money be placed in his hands as the sinews of warfare.[31] This document was called No. 13 in the list of official documents, which number was later transferred to Wilkinson himself in all cipher communications between the various officials of the Spanish Government. This was done at Wilkinson's own request, for reasons that are obvious.

On September 17, 1789, the new Spanish subject and secret agent presented another memorial in which he hedged a bit — he now suggested that Spain permit free and unlimited immigration of Kentuckians into Louisiana, and thereby sap the West of its boldest and hardiest citizens. A day later he acknowledged receipt of $7,000 from Miro, euphemistically called a " loan," " but must ask you," he begged that official, " that no one outside of the confidential servants of the crown shall know of this loan." [32]

Thus armed, he returned to Kentucky to initiate subterranean intrigues for the secession of the Western lands and for a submission to Spain. He managed to gather around him a certain group, but, in spite of wild rumors and alarums, and a promiscuous distribution of bribes, the conspiracy failed to gain momentum.

Whereupon Wilkinson, though still drawing funds from Spain, hastened to insinuate himself into the American armed forces once again. His secret change of citizenship was unknown. By 1799 he had labored to such good effect that he was appointed General of the newly opened Mississippi Territory. Hamilton, Washington and McHenry, Secretary of War, in a remarkable interchange of letters, agreed that his talents were great, his character more than doubtful, his connections with Spain so open to suspicion as to cause McHenry to warn against " saying any thing to him which would induce him to imagine government had in view any hostile project, however remote, or dependent on events, against any of the possessions of Spain." [33] But, on Hamilton's recommendation, all concurred in promoting him to command of the forces on the Spanish border as Major-General, on the high ground, as Hamilton neatly put it, that " he will be apt to become disgusted, if neglected; and through disgust may be rendered really what he is now only suspected to be." [34]

Wilkinson was now in a position to be really valuable to his Spanish employers. Already, in 1796, he had cashed in on a more modest Generalship. " In the Galley the Victoria, . . . there have been sent to Don Vincente Folch nine thousand six hundred and forty dollars, which sum," ordered Baron de Carondelet of Don Tomas Portel, " you will hold at my disposal, to deliver it the moment an order may be presented to you by the American General Don James Wilkinson." [35]

The skein of his intrigues grew more and more entangled. In 1797 an American named Power was sent by Spain northward with what was said to be a mule load of gold for the American General, then stationed at Detroit. His grand opportunity came in 1804, however, immediately before he came north to spin ambitious visions for the delectation of the Vice-President of the United States. Jefferson was then considering approvingly Livingston's interpretation of what constituted the boundaries of Louisiana. Spain was apprehensive and a trifle jumpy. Don Vicente Folch, Governor of West Florida, and Casa Calvo, Spanish Boundary Commissioner, met Wilkinson, American Boundary Commissioner, secretly at New Orleans. Wilkinson upbraided them for having failed to deliver his promised pension of $2000 a year for the past ten years. He was going, he said, to Washington, and if Folch paid him what was due, he would report to him all the plans and purposes of Jefferson and his Cabinet, for, he declared, he knew " what was concealed in the heart of the President."

After some dickering, it was agreed for the present to pay Wilkinson immediately $12,000 of the $20,000 he demanded, and to forward his famous " Reflections " to Spain for consideration, together with his further demands, to wit, that he receive the balance of $8,000, and for the future, a pension of $4,000 a year.[36]

In return for these concessions, Wilkinson advised strongly against any yielding by the Spaniards in the West Florida dispute.

West Florida, he said, must act as a barrier to further western expansion by the United States, and thus help save Mexico from future conquest. Then he hastened north, to discover what was " in the heart of the President," and to use his old friend, Aaron Burr, as a tool for the furtherance of his own secret ambitions. For this is a consideration which requires some thought. To Burr he unfolded a dazzling scheme of Mexican conquest, with West Florida as a subsidiary lure. But this occurred just after he had received $12,000 from Spain, with prospects of more in the near future, and to whom he had hinted darkly of aggression against West Florida and Mexico.

Is it possible, therefore, that Burr's Conspiracy was merely a potent threat to be employed by Wilkinson in proving the enormous value of his services to Spain, and as a means of extracting much larger sums of money from his frightened employer? It may be that thus early, at the very inception, Wilkinson already envisaged his course of action. Later events seem to justify this view. Of course, in the event that the United States declared war, and Burr *had* managed to achieve British help and the use of a modest half million of dollars, it would then have been more profitable to jettison his former connections, and reap gold, glory and a possible empire for himself. There is this also to be said. Burr was Vice-President; as such, he could be useful as a medium for the passage of secrets of State, the direct channel into " the heart of the President." Certainly it was through Burr that Wilkinson received his additional promotion to the Governorship of Louisiana, thereby making him the most powerful personage in all America in the eyes of Spain. Burr, it seems, for all his perspicuity and remarkable talents, was not a good judge of human character. He was easily taken in. Wilkinson was but one of the many in whom he was deceived.

Later on, when the lid blew off, and Daniel Clark of New Orleans, furious at certain imputations directed against himself, openly accused Wilkinson of being in the Spanish pay, Folch came to his spy's rescue with a solemn affidavit that Wilkinson's relations with Spain had been of a highly honorable nature and in no way detrimental to the United States; and that, in the archives under his control, there existed no document showing Wilkinson ever to have received a pension or gratuity of any sort from Spain. Largely on the strength of this affidavit, Wilkinson was whitewashed by a Congressional Committee.[37]

But, a few months later, on January 26, 1809, the honorable Spaniard wrote Wilkinson privately, " My dear friend: I believe that you are already well convinced that I have acted as is befitting a faithful servant of the noble Spanish Monarchy, and that I have sincerely fulfilled the obligations which friendship imposes upon me. I have done even more, for I have sent to the archives of Havana all that pertains to the ancient History, persuaded that before the United States are in a situation to conquer that capital you and I, Jefferson, Madison, with all the Secretaries of the different departments, and even the prophet Daniel [Clark] himself will have made many days journey into the other world." [38] James Wilkinson, whom John Randolph was truly to call " the finished scoundrel "!

Chapter XX

WESTERN JOURNEY

1. Houseboat on the Ohio

ON March 29, 1805, Burr was writing Theo from Phila-delphia, " In ten or twelve days I shall be on my way west-ward. . . . the objects of his journey, not mere curiosity, or pour passer le temps, may lead me to Orleans, and perhaps far-ther." [1] Mexico, in other words.

To Alston he wrote, " In New-York I am to be disfranchised, and in New-Jersey hanged. Having substantial objections to both, I shall not for the present, hazard either, but shall seek another country. You will not, from this, conclude that I have become pas-sive, or disposed to submit tamely to the machinations of a ban-ditti. If you should you would greatly err." [2]

On April 10, 1805, Burr started out from Philadelphia on his long-anticipated Western " tour." His first objective was Pitts-burgh, to which he journeyed on horseback in the company of Mr. and Mrs. Gabriel Shaw. There he found a " floating house," which he had ordered in advance, " sixty feet by fourteen, con-taining dining-room, kitchen with fireplace, and two bedrooms: roofed from stem to stern; steps go up, and a walk on the top the whole length; glass windows, etc. This edifice costs one hundred and thirty-three dollars." [3] With this vehicle he intended floating down the Ohio and Mississippi to New Orleans, making certain stops on the way.

He arrived on April 29th and departed the next day. Wilkinson was to have joined him there, on his way to St. Louis to assume his new duties as Governor of the Louisiana Territory, but he was delayed, and Burr went on alone. Thirty-six hours later, he caught up with Matthew Lyon, ex-Vermont Congressman, and settled now in Kentucky, who had left Pittsburgh by barge the day be-fore him. They lashed their boats together and proceeded down the river. Lyon was to depose later that Wilkinson had inquired of him early in 1804 what could be done for Burr. Lyon had sug-gested that he go to Nashville to practice law, and from there achieve a seat in Congress. Wilkinson thought it was a good scheme, but Burr was not at all enthusiastic over the prospect. Instead, according to Lyon, Burr wished him to broach the subject of an embassy to Jefferson. Lyon refused to intervene.[4]

On the way, they stopped at an island in the middle of the Ohio River, some two miles from Parkersburg, and no great distance from Marietta, Ohio. This island and its occupants were destined to play a very considerable part in the events of the next year or two. Harman Blennerhassett, its owner, was of Irish birth. Falling heir to an estate of some $100,000, he abandoned his native land and his legal profession, married an Englishwoman, and took ship to America in 1796. Traveling at a leisurely sightseeing pace, he discovered the Ohio and the island. He fell in love with their natural beauties, purchased the island, and proceeded to make it the show place of the Western country. His home was in the palatial English style, on a slope fronting the river. Around it he made wide, smooth lawns, planted gardens in profusion, with long rows of shrubs and hedges in the English fashion, and settled down to play the role of an English country gentleman in the heart of the wilderness.

The man himself was six feet tall, slender, slightly stooped, nearsighted, with a prominent nose, timid, and somewhat scholarly. He loved to play at chemistry, astronomy, and the sciences in general, and he performed acceptably on the violin. While the grandeur with which he had surrounded himself had taken some $50,000 from his inheritance, he still had enough left to run his manor and live in style — at least for a while.[5]

Burr evidently had met him before, and quite likely, in his desperate need for funds, had already turned his attention to the eccentric Irishman. But Blennerhassett was away in the East when Burr arrived, and it devolved on his wife to do the honors. In the short space of an afternoon, Mrs. Blennerhassett became completely fascinated by the very fascinating ex-Vice-President, and, under deft and diplomatic questioning, disclosed much of their private affairs and financial entanglements. Burr pigeonholed the information and left, after dinner, with many courteous protestations of regard.

He arrived in Cincinnati on May 11, 1805, where he found Jonathan Dayton and Senator John Smith — both by appointment — and several old army acquaintances. The West was full of ex-army officers. It is not to be doubted that he expatiated to them of his plans for leading a special expedition against Spain and her colonial possessions. Perhaps he hinted even of Mexico. This proselytizing was indeed one of the chief purposes of this lengthy journey. It is also quite likely that his old army friends responded with considerable enthusiasm. The West hated Spain, and Burr's military talents were well known to them. But the proposals, it seems, were conditioned wholly upon the understanding that the United States would soon declare war upon Spain. Burr had made that quite plain. Such, at least, was later to be the unanimous contention of all those who had joined the proceedings. Dayton, naturally, continued to stir up favorable sentiment after Burr's departure; he was one of the prime movers.

There were other matters discussed at these conferences besides a warlike descent on Spanish territory. That would take place in the future, and depended on certain contingencies. Other schemes were in the air, more peaceful in character, in which the participants were equally interested. Burr, Wilkinson, Dayton, Smith, John Brown.

The Ohio River broke at Louisville into a swirl of rapids that proved a serious obstacle to navigation. At low water it was necessary to unload the cargoes of vessels from either end of the river, transport them painfully around the rough passage, and reload where smooth water began again. A canal had been discussed for some time as a remedy for this situation. Louisville objected — that village profited immensely from the break in navigation. But various land speculators, whose holdings along the river would benefit from a canal, joined forces to press the issue. General Benjamin Hovey, of New York, petitioned Congress on January 17, 1805, for a grant of 25,000 acres in Indiana for himself and his associates, on receipt of which they would engage to build the canal. The Senate referred the petition to a committee — Dayton of New Jersey, Brown of Kentucky, and Smith of Ohio. They reported favorably on the proposition, but Congress defeated the bill. Whereupon the associates turned to the Indiana Legislature for the requisite charter. The triumvirate on the Senate Committee, however, had themselves become interested in the idea. They joined forces with the original proponents. Burr, in the Vice-Presidential chair, had noted the proceedings in the Senate, and he, too, was interested. It was without doubt one of the matters that took him West at this particular time. For the new Indiana Legislature was meeting for the first time in June, 1805.

The Indiana Canal Company was actually incorporated in August, with a capitalization of a million dollars, and the usual clauses for the construction and operation of a canal. But there were certain other curious clauses in the charter relating to monied ventures which were strangely reminiscent of another charter, viz., that one which had been granted to the Manhattan Company in New York some years before. The suspicion deepens to certainty on a perusal of the names of the Board of Directors for the initial year. Jonathan Dayton, John Brown, Davis Floyd, Benjamin Hovey and Aaron Burr.[6]

The canal was never built by this company — it was finally to be constructed on the Kentucky side by a different corporation — but this failure should not be charged to Burr. He was soon enough to become involved in a glut of situations that drove all thoughts of the corporation he had sponsored from his mind. But the Company *did* set up a bank possessing the power of emitting paper currency — which was certainly Burr's idea; and it was later claimed by opponents of the Company that this had been its real purpose from the very beginning.[7]

The groundwork for this scheme having been laid, Burr's next stop was Louisville, where he took to land to avoid the rapids, and traveled by horseback to Frankfort, in Kentucky, which he reached May 20th. Here he sojourned with Senator John Brown — also by appointment. Both the canal and Spanish projects were discussed. Then he met John Adair, United States Senator, probably at Lexington, to whom Wilkinson, following on Burr's trail, and only a few days behind, had sent a note ahead by messenger. " I was to have introduced my friend Burr to you," he wrote, " but in this I failed by accident. He understands your merits, and *reckons* on you. Prepare to visit me, and I will tell you all. We must have a peep at the unknown world beyond." [8] Very definitely this points to far lands — Mexico. Long afterward, Adair declared that " the intentions of Colonel Burr . . . were to prepare and lead an expedition into Mexico, predicated on a war between the two governments; without a war he knew he could do nothing. On this war taking place he calculated with certainty, as well from the policy of the measure at this time as from the positive assurances of Wilkinson, who seemed to have the power to force it in his own hands." [9]

This was close to the truth. Wilkinson was on his way to become Governor as well as General. His forces were soon to oppose the Spanish across the Sabine River, a very contentious boundary. If Jefferson were reluctant to proceed to extremities, it required only a " border incident " to force the issue. Already Wilkinson and Burr must have discussed the matter, and Burr was now taking it up with Adair.

From Lexington, Burr went on to Nashville, Tennessee. The fiery Andrew Jackson, General of Militia, admirer of Aaron Burr, and boundless in his contempt for the " Spanish Don," was the next port of call. Everywhere Burr had been received with profuse cordiality, hospitality, and expressions of respect. The West remembered his activities in its behalf, he had been Vice-President of the United States, and his duel with Hamilton, which had damned him in the effete East, was here only an evidence of his personal courage. Hamilton, moreover, had been somewhat of a Devil in the rude Western mythology, just as Jefferson, with his democratic principles, was something of a God. It is difficult to believe that Burr, after this Western journey, could possibly have been possessed of any illusions as to the willingness of the West to secede from the Union. He was too shrewd a man not to have observed the almost unanimous sentiment for Jefferson and Democracy. Wilkinson himself, in the earlier turbulent days, when Spain held the Mississippi and New Orleans, and the Federalist East neglected its Western possessions shamefully, had not been able to whip up much enthusiasm for that particular project.

But if Burr's reception heretofore had been cordial, in Nashville it was overwhelming. He arrived there on May 29th, and was promptly taken in tow by Andrew Jackson. From miles around, the populace thronged to see the man of whom it was already rumored that he was prepared to scourge the contemptible Spaniard out of America. A great parade was organized in his honor, music blared and cannon roared; there was feasting and dancing, and he was compelled to deliver a speech to the cheering crowds. They clamored that he lead them at once against Spain, and he was forced to moderate their transports. He was in truth the man of the hour. Jackson, bursting with pride over this " lion " in his Hermitage, offered his services, then, in the future, at any time. Burr accepted them gracefully, but said the time was not yet.

To Theo, Burr merely wrote (he was keeping a journal of the trip for her private delectation) that " I have been received with much hospitality and kindness, and could stay a month with pleasure; but General Andrew Jackson having provided us a boat, we shall set off on Sunday, the 2nd of June." [10]

In fact, he left on June 3rd, floated down the Cumberland River to the place where it emptied into the Ohio, a distance of about 220 miles, and there found his " ark " waiting. On the 6th he reached Fort Massac, sixteen miles below, where Wilkinson and his entourage, come straight down the Ohio, were expecting his arrival. They spent four days at the fort together; then they parted. Burr was furnished by Wilkinson with " an elegant barge, sails, colours, and ten oars, with a sergeant, and ten able, faithful hands " for the balance of his journey down the rivers to New

Orleans, while the General, after some delay, proceeded alone to St. Louis to assume his gubernatorial duties.[11]

For seven days they rowed swiftly and uneventfully down the Ohio, and along the broad and muddy waters of the Mississippi, until they reached Natchez on June 17th, a distance of nearly eight hundred miles. Here Burr was surprised to find a substantial community, whose planters, many of them men of education and refinement, entertained him with lavish hospitality. A short stay, and he pushed on, until, on June 25th, his men rested on their oars. They had reached New Orleans, the first goal of this particular journey.

That turbulent, cosmopolitan town welcomed him with an enthusiasm which surpassed anything he had before experienced. Not even Nashville's reception could be compared with this. The Deputies had already returned from their unsatisfactory mission in Washington, and the one note of praise they had brought back with them had been for the sympathetic Vice-President of the United States, the only man in all the East who had understood their special problems. All classes of society joined to do him honor. He had with him also certain letters of introduction, furnished by Wilkinson. One was addressed to Daniel Clark, wealthiest merchant of the town, whose eyes were steadily fixed on the almost fabulous trade of Mexico. " This will be delivered to you by Colonel Burr," it read, " whose worth you know well how to estimate. If the persecutions of a great and honorable man, can give title to generous attentions, he has claims to all your civilities, and all your services. You cannot oblige me more than by such conduct; and I pledge my life to you, it will not be misapplied. To him I refer you for many things improper to letter, and which he will not say to any other." [12]

There was another letter, addressed to Casa Calvo, Spanish Commissioner, still lingering unaccountably in New Orleans. Wilkinson requested him to " serve this gentleman, he is my friend . . . Your great family interests will promote the view of Colonel Burr and the great interest of your country will be served by following his advice . . . Do as I advise you and you will soon send to the devil that boastful idiot W. C. C. Claiborne." [13]

With this letter, the stew of many diverse and marvelous ingredients begins to thicken. Wilkinson, in New Orleans, could no longer withhold his identification with Burr's projects, as he had in the East. It was necessary therefore to sugarcoat the pill for Spanish consumption, inasmuch as he did not intend to lose that lucrative source of supplies unless it were to his advantage. Accordingly, Burr was being presented to the Spaniards as his confederate, ready to do Spain's bidding. In short, he intended to arouse the old cupidity for a Western empire which would include Kentucky, Tennessee, and the return of Louisiana. Thereby Spanish suspicions would be lulled as to the real objects of Burr's descent upon New Orleans. With this in mind, the later approach to Yrujo in Washington and Philadelphia becomes more explicable.

To Clark, however, and the members of the Mexican Association, another facet was displayed. This was the true picture. The conquest and liberation of Mexico, with consequent free and unlimited trade for the merchants of New Orleans; the subjugation of West Florida and its attachment, politically as well as commercially, to themselves. It is at this point that the only doubt as to Burr's, and Wilkinson's, somewhat divergent courses may be entertained.

The newly sliced Territory of Orleans, comprising the city and the contiguous country, was not happy over its transfer to the United States. The dominant Creoles had not liked Spanish government, it is true, but the American officialdom which had descended on them, in the person of Claiborne of Tennessee, was not to be borne. He was well-meaning, perhaps, but stupid, and possessed of that peculiar American talent for regarding American institutions, system of education, manners, customs, etc., as God's own peculiar largesse, and all others as foreign and therefore inferior. The Creoles were a proud, cultured race, who found their sensibilities, their methods, their religion even, exquisitely exacerbated by the stupid, unmeaning grossness of the American Governor. There is no doubt that in 1805 they would have preferred independence under the protecting egis of England or France to their present humiliating state of subjection to a remote commonwealth. And perhaps Burr was considering this, too, — it is hard to say from the available evidence. If he were, however, it was a secondary consideration — to be ticketed for the future. First there was Mexico — and possibly West Florida. To subjugate these required not only the aid of New Orleans, but of the West also. Independence for the Orleans Territory, though it was to be dangled as a bait for British, French and Spanish gold, was a remote contingency; certainly not by forcible means. Negotiation, perhaps, when Burr ruled in Mexico; not otherwise.

In any event, Burr was feted and dined and given the keys to the city. He met the Mayor, John Watkins, and James Workman, Judge of the New Orleans County Court, both members of the

Mexican Association; he met and conferred with Daniel Clark; he renewed old acquaintance with Edward Livingston and talked to Judge Prevost, his step-son; he met Americans and Creoles alike, society of high and low degree; and delightfully, he was invited to visit the Ursuline nuns, where " all was gayety, wit, and sprightliness " and man of the world and those withdrawn felt the reciprocal tug of each other's charm.[14] For the Catholic authorities of New Orleans were ready to support any scheme pointing to the independence of Mexico, and they promptly appointed three priests as Burr's agents to the secret leaders of the revolutionists. And Burr saw Casa Calvo, handed him Wilkinson's letter, and exercised all his talents to soothe the Spaniard's natural fears.[15]

2. YRUJO STARTS A BACKFIRE

On July 10th, having accomplished the chief purposes of this preliminary tour and survey of the situation, Burr turned eastward to carry his plans into effect. He had good reason to be satisfied with the results already obtained, even though he had been unable to penetrate into Mexico. Everywhere he had been hailed with acclaim, everywhere he had found the populace eager to be led against the Spaniard. The commencement of hostilities would be the signal of a great outpouring, and Burr intended to lead the irregulars. The Regular Army was under Wilkinson's command. It required, therefore, only a forward move by the Administration, or, failing that, the establishment of a *fait accompli* by Wilkinson.

Reluctantly Burr tore himself away from New Orleans. He had thoughts even of settling permanently in that coming metropolis of the South. Daniel Clark furnished him with horses, and he rode overland to Natchez, where he tarried nearly a week. Then on through an untracked wilderness, most of the way on foot, following the line of division between West Florida and the United States, along the Yazoo, through " a vile country, destitute of springs and running water — think of drinking the nasty puddle-water, covered with green scum, and full of animalculae." Then across the Tennessee, "a clear, beautiful, magnificent river," about " forty miles below the muscle shoals," and on to Nashville and General Jackson once more, arriving safe, if much fatigued, on August 6th.[16] It was a Homeric journey.

Nashville outdid its former tremendous welcome. A great public dinner was held, at which Burr and Jackson appeared arm in arm, to the accolade of cheers and the fluttering of feminine hearts.

On August 13th he was still "lounging at the house of General Jackson, once a lawyer, after a judge, now a planter; a man of intelligence, and one of those prompt, frank, ardent souls whom I love to meet." [17]

Finally he summoned fortitude to his aid and went on to Lexington, retracing his earlier steps; then, on August 31st, he was once more the guest of John Brown at Frankfort. The following day he doubled back again, this time to proceed to St. Louis, and General James Wilkinson. There was much to be discussed, notes to be compared, and the future to be plotted.

But at St. Louis he found that certain clouds had appeared on a hitherto spotless horizon. Wilkinson had been hinting vaguely to certain of his officers of schemes in hand whereby they could recoup their fortunes, and volunteering wholly unnecessary information to the effect that " a military government was best " for Louisiana, that the French inhabitants could not understand a republican form, and that the Americans in the Territory were " a turbulent set, the mere emptyings of jails, or fugitives from justice." Major Bruff, one of those thus approached, made it plain that he would have no part in any such transaction.[18] Wilkinson was not always seeing eye to eye with Burr; many times the crosscurrents of their thoughts and separate actions were clashing — more and more, as time wore on. In any event, this episode made Wilkinson pause and reflect.

There was another, more serious, and doubtless the one that finally determined the valiant General to jettison his confederate and seek his advantage elsewhere. Yrujo had not been idle during Burr's absence. It was not enough that he had warned all Spanish officials to be on their guard. He was alarmed, in the existing delicate state of affairs between the United States and Spain, over the prospect that Burr's proposed filibuster against Mexico might start a conflagration which would sweep Spain out of the Americas. To avoid this, he skilfully started a backfire which would discredit Burr and his aims completely. Stephen Minor, an American in the pay of Spain — even as Wilkinson — was given instructions. Minor was well worth his salary. He industriously circulated rumors in New Orleans, in Natchez, in all the Territory, that Burr's real purpose was to separate the Western country from the Union — by force if necessary — and to unite them all in one great Empire with the Spanish possessions.[19] It was this rumor, traveling east and north, gathering strength and fabulous accretions on the way, that brought about Burr's eventual downfall. The report arrived at St. Louis almost simultaneously with Burr, and was sufficiently ominous in its texture to cause Wilkinson not only to reflect, but to change the entire purport of his own private plans with the agility of a molting snake.

Daniel Clark sent him the news, in a letter dated September 7th, bearing under its veneer of airy lightness an unmistakable note of warning. "Many absurd and wild reports, are circulated here [New Orleans]," he wrote, "and have reached the ears of the officers of the late Spanish government, respecting our ex-vice president. You are spoken of as his right hand man; and even I am now supposed to be of consequence enough to combine with generals and vice-presidents . . . Entre nous, I believe that Minor, of Natchez, has a great part in this business . . . he is in the pay of Spain, and wishes to convince them he is much their friend . . . Were I sufficiently intimate with Mr. Burr, and knew where to direct a line to him, I should take the liberty of writing him . . . The tale is a horrid one, if well told. Kentucky, Tennessee, the state of Ohio, the four territories on the Mississippi and Ohio, with part of Georgia and Carolina, are to be bribed with the plunder of the Spanish countries west of us, to separate from the union." [20]

Wilkinson became alarmed. If the United States, as well as Spain, was aroused against Burr, and his own name involved, he was a ruined man. From this time on, he definitely determined to dissociate himself completely from Burr. Already a new plan was germinating in his fertile brain — treacherous, a base betrayal of friendship, it is true — but calculated at once to save his own skin, and to achieve a measure of profit from the wreckage. This, however, was to be a last resort.

In the meantime, he seems to have said nothing to Burr of Clark's disturbing letter, though it must have arrived while Burr was still in St. Louis. For Burr did not leave until September 19th; the letter was dated September 7th, and was sufficiently important to be sent by fast messenger. The average time of passage was ten days. It was better, he thought, to keep his confederate temporarily in ignorance, while he decided on his own course. It was not until November, some two months later, that he wrote to Burr about it, now safely in the East. Burr replied on January 6, 1806, that "your friend [Clark] suspects without reason the person [Minor] named in his letter to you. I love the society of that person; but surely I could never be guilty of the folly of confiding to one of his levity anything which I wished not to be repeated. Pray do not disturb yourself with such nonsense." [21]

And it was not until March 8, 1806, that Wilkinson answered

Clark with a scornful reference to " the tale of a tub of Burr," and dropped the subject forthwith.[22]

Meanwhile Wilkinson had conceived an expedient to get rid of Burr. Evidently he pulled a long face — not disclosing the source of his distrust — and advised Burr in friendly fashion that perhaps it would be wiser to drop their plans temporarily, that the time was not ripe, etc. etc. In the meantime he would be glad to help Burr get back into political life. In fact, he would furnish him with a letter that would do the trick. Which he did.

Burr, unknowing of the background of alarm and meditated dissociation, accepted the letter in good faith, though, from the sequel, he had no intention of presenting it. There was no reason that he could see for Wilkinson's sudden weak-kneedness.

The letter was addressed to Governor William Henry Harrison, of the Indiana Territory, at Vincennes. " I will demand from your friendship a boon in its influence co-extensive with the Union; a boon, perhaps, on which the Union may much depend," Wilkinson wrote darkly, " a boon which may serve me, may serve you, and disserve neither . . . If you ask, What is this important boon which I so earnestly crave? I will say to you, return the bearer to the councils of our country, where his talents and abilities are all-important at the present moment." [23] A boon, indeed, to Wilkinson. With Burr peacefully settled in Indiana, and returned to Washington as a Congressman, he could boast to Spain that it was his influence alone which had turned the dreadful energies of that infamous conspirator, Aaron Burr, from all thoughts of Spanish conquest. Naturally, such notable services would be requited with a special honorarium. In the event that the storm broke from the American side, he could then claim — as in fact he did — that it was this meeting in St. Louis which made him, for the first time, suspicious of Burr's intentions, and point to this letter as proof that he was trying to render Burr and his schemes innocuous. A very subtle, wriggling man indeed!

On September 23rd Burr was speaking cordially to Governor Harrison of a number of things, but not of the contents of this letter. From Vincennes he turned eastward, his preliminary mission accomplished. He passed Blennerhassett's Island in October, to find its master still away, and his impressionable wife also. Then back to Washington late in November, still ignorant of the blaze of rumor that had been dogging his footsteps all the way, only a few days behind, yet never quite catching up. The West was kindling to the fire as it rolled along, credulously, casting the faint remembrance of fainter hints, expressions and gestures of the unknowing victim as further fuel upon the conflagration, indignant all the more because, in its open-hearted hospitality, it had been taken in by the suave, courtly Easterner.

In the East, Yrujo — at least it seems to have been Yrujo — was busy building a second backfire so as to surround the proposed filibusterer against his beloved country, and destroy him. A series of *Queries* appeared anonymously in the *Gazette of the United States* — Yrujo had long before shown his talent for achieving anonymous publication in American newspapers — asking certain questions which by their very vagueness were calculated to excite the deepest alarm. " How long will it be," demanded the Querist, " before we shall hear of Colonel Burr being at the head of a revolutionary party on the Western waters? Is it a fact that Colonel Burr has formed a plan to engage the adventurous and enterprising young men from the Atlantic States to Louisiana? Is it one of the inducements that an immediate convention will be called from the States bordering on the Ohio and Mississippi to form a separate government? " Is it a fact that he intends to seize New Orleans, and how soon will he, aided by British gold and British ships, reduce Mexico and seize all its store of treasure? Is it a fact, etc., etc.? [24]

Never once a positive affirmation; just a series of hypothetical leading questions such as every skilful lawyer employs in cross-examination to bring matters before the jury without the dull necessity of adducing proof. The method, in fact, was remarkably successful. The newspapers of the country — forerunners of the headline hunters of today — played up the veiled charges with gusto, copied and recopied them until they had spread like a rash from Maine to Texas, meeting midway the onrushing smoke of Stephen Minor's rumors, and uniting to amplify and confirm each other.

Anthony Merry read the *Queries,* hearkened to the seething murmurs which had already invaded the capital, and became panic-stricken. The conspiracy had been discovered; all was lost! For these queries tallied neatly with the scheme which Burr had poured into his willing ears — so neatly, that again one wonders whether Wilkinson from the very beginning had not kept Yrujo apprised of the course of events.

Merry wrote to his Government in considerable agitation. " He [Burr] or some of his agents have either been indiscreet in their communications, or have been betrayed by some person in whom they considered that they had reason to confide." But the British Minister had committed himself too far with his superiors to retreat now, so, perforce, he closed on a lamely optimistic note. " It is, however, possible that the business may be so far advanced as, from the nature of it, to render any further secrecy impossible." [25]

3. FINANCES

Burr came back to Washington to find the press of the nation barking loudly at his heels, his journey the subject of speculation, his supposedly traitorous designs whispered from mouth to mouth. He hurried at once to Merry, seemingly unperturbed at the clamor, anxious only to find out whether or not the promised response from England had given him what he wanted — money chiefly, and a British naval demonstration in the Gulf secondarily. Jonathan Dayton, his lieutenant and most loyal confidant, who had been ill for a considerable period in the West, had preceded him by several days to report to Merry as to the progress of their plans.

But Merry had no news. The English Government was strangely silent to his feverish requests. Merry put it down to the loss of a packet boat — he was a master in the art of self-delusion. So, for that matter, was Burr. He could not see that his schemes were already doomed; he failed to read aright the growing sentiment of the country, or to realize the fatal power of the press. He had been guilty of a similar blind spot in connection with Cheetham's campaign. Worst of all, he was evidently a poor judge of character. There were too many men whom he accepted at face value, and confided in trustingly to his great hurt. Trust in General James Wilkinson was to prove his most outstanding and most tragic error.

Burr saw the bubble bursting when Merry told him he had not heard from England. His plans called for the commencement of his movement in the early spring of 1806. Without money, however — and his requirements were considerable — he could do nothing. He told Merry as much, and took pains to express his deepest disappointment. He even told him Williamson had written " that his Majesty's government were disposed to afford him their assistance." This statement was made out of whole cloth. Williamson, even if he *had* written to Burr, of which there is no evidence, had been engaged in a losing fight with the authorities in England, and knew it. It was necessary, Burr pursued, for an English fleet to " cruise off the mouth of the Mississippi at the latest by the 10th of April next, and to continue there until the commanding officer should receive information from him or from

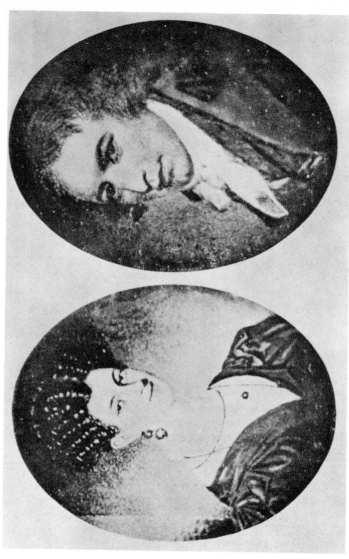

MR. AND MRS. HARMAN BLENNERHASSETT

From Daguerreotypes

ANDREW JACKSON

From a portrait by Asher B. Durand

Mr. Daniel Clark of the country having declared itself independent." Again that queer insistence on New Orleans. Actually, of course, the fleet was to act as a convoy for his expedition, which was scheduled to sail from New Orleans to Vera Cruz, and from there march overland to Mexico City. But the idea of New Orleans' independence seemed to have taken root. As for his Western journey — Western secession and the break-up of a nation that had humiliated him was Merry's abiding passion — Burr resorted to purposeful vagueness. It was necessary to keep Merry's interest alive, but Burr had nothing definite to report. In fact he had not even been considering the matter. At no time, even when witnesses came forward by the score, secure in the knowledge that thereby they gained governmental favor, was there the slightest whisper that he had mentioned secession on this journey. The best he could do was to hint that, once Louisiana was independent, and Mexico conquered, the West would find it profitable to secede and join in a vast new Empire. The one thing he did harp on was the matter of funds — £110,000 to be placed to the credit of John Barclay of Philadelphia and Daniel Clark of New Orleans. All of which Merry duly reported to Lord Mulgrave.[26]

Meanwhile Yrujo had been reporting to *his* Government that "the supposed expedition against Mexico is ridiculous and chimerical in the present state of things; but I am not unaware that Burr, in order to get moneys from the English Minister or from England, has made to him some such proposition, in which he is to play the leading role." [27] Evidently Yrujo had exact knowledge of Burr's most secret interviews with Merry, yet dismissed contemptuously without a word the " Western secession conspiracy." A letter dated June 25, 1807, addressed by Governor Folch to the Governor-General of Cuba, illuminates startlingly the curious foreknowledge of Yrujo and other Spanish officials concerning every move that Burr made during all this period. " It is necessary . . ." wrote Folch, " to inform your Excellency that during the disturbances of Burr the aforesaid general [Wilkinson] has, by means of a person in his confidence, constantly maintained a correspondence with me, in which he has laid before me not only the information which he acquired, but also his intentions for the various exigencies in which he might find himself." [28]

Rebuffed in his attempts to extract money from Merry, Burr was compelled to turn elsewhere for the funds he so vitally needed. He remembered Harman Blennerhassett, the Irish gentleman who had planted an English manor in the heart of the Western wilderness. He wrote him a letter regretting that he had missed him on his last journey. He alluded to Blennerhassett's talents, and spoke of them as deserving a less inactive sphere; he hinted that with his growing family his diminishing revenues might be recouped by certain plans Burr had in mind.[29] Blennerhassett in truth was finding the Island a drain on his resources, and even then was offering it for sale, with no bidders. Gentleman farming might do in England, but the wilderness was a hard taskmaster.

Blennerhassett took the bait at once. He wrote back on December 21, 1805 — though the letter was not to arrive until the middle of February — that " I should be honoured in being associated with you, in any contemplated enterprise you would permit me to participate in. The amount of means I could at first come forward with would be small. You might command my services as a lawyer [this to Burr!] or in any other way you should suggest as being most useful." [30] Poor, erratic soul! Not Burr himself was to suffer more in the dénouement!

This, for the moment, was a minor string to Burr's bow. The paltry few thousands that Blennerhassett might presently raise would be but a drop in the insatiable ocean of expense. Merry had failed him; France, in the person of Turreau, would certainly not listen to a scheme of Mexican conquest. France and Spain were allies. Then, in his desperation, he conceived a plan that was breathtaking in its audacity. So audacious, in fact, that almost one's sense of its moral obliquity is destroyed in the contemplation.

On December 5, 1805, Jonathan Dayton, the Man Friday, visited Yrujo, the Spanish Minister, in Philadelphia. He was there, he informed the sophisticated Spaniard, to disclose certain horrendous secrets, upon which he placed a modest price of thirty to forty thousand dollars. Yrujo encouraged him to proceed, thinking he knew what it was about; but to his surprise, Dayton unfolded himself in the role of a traitor — a traitor to Burr, his fellow conspirator. With a great show of frankness, Dayton disclosed in detail Burr's dealings with Merry, of the plans he had proposed to the British Minister for taking the Floridas and Mexico, and joining thereto the West; he told of Williamson's mission to England; he even talked of the exact measures to be employed, including the British fleet off New Orleans. In only one small particular did he stretch the matter. He said that the British Cabinet had received the scheme favorably, and that even then Mr. Pitt was considering it seriously.[31]

Was Dayton then actually double-crossing Burr? Not at all. It was Burr's own scheme. He had been in close conference with

Jefferson only five days before and had been informed, much to his astonishment, that there was to be no war with Spain. In fact, he was later to describe the situation to Wilkinson. "About the last of October our cabinet was seriously disposed for war with the Spaniards; but more recent accounts of the increasing and alarming aggressions and annoyance of the British, and some courteous words from the French, have banished every such intention." This necessitated a change in their plans. Fundamentally, the proposed invasion of Mexico was conditioned on a declaration of war. In such event the West would have rallied to Burr, and the expedition would have been earmarked for success. England, before its "increasing and alarming aggressions," would have been an ally both of Burr and of the United States. "On the subject of a certain speculation," he continued, "it is not deemed material to write till the whole can be communicated. The circumstance referred to in a letter from Ohio remains in suspense; the auspices, however, are favorable, and it is believed that Wilkinson will give audience to a delegation composed of Adair and Dayton in February. Can 25 — [boats?] be had in your vicinity to move at some few hours notification?" [32] This obviously is not the language of a conspirator plotting secession. He is disappointed in the prospect of a war — a war which would inflame the West with patriotism, and hurl them upon the Spaniard even as they longed. Again, and again, at the risk of belaboring the point, must this be made clear. The other scheme, referred to in a letter from Ohio which Wilkinson never produced, must have been the alternative plan — if the pending war failed — which Burr was in fact to attempt to put into execution. That is, the peaceful settlement of lands on the Washita in a vast colonization scheme, and the abandonment for the moment of dreams of Mexico.

So that, with the Mexican scheme dropped, no harm could be done by disclosing it, after the event, to Yrujo. Even in failure and collapse, some profit might be extracted from an alarmed Spain. Unfortunately, Burr did not know that Yrujo and the Spanish officials were already aware of everything that Dayton disclosed with such frightened whisperings. More, they knew even that England had failed Burr, that Jefferson had turned from trumpetings of war to meek, pacific smiles, and that the danger to their domains was temporarily past. Whereupon Yrujo dismissed Dayton with vague promises, to insure further revelations, and wrote home about this new and perplexing turn of events. For Wilkinson had not apprised the Spaniards of this new scheme. Burr had worked it alone, and evidently on the spur of the moment.

Failing to extract cash from the elusive Spaniard on this first visit, Dayton returned to the attack with a quick shift in his tactics. This time he admitted that Burr's plans had gone astray in London, but that a brand-new plan had been evolved. It was nothing less than to introduce into the City of Washington armed men, who, at a signal from Burr, would seize Jefferson, the aged George Clinton, and the President of the Senate. With the chiefs of the government in their control, the conspirators would then descend on the banks and the public arsenal, and declare Burr the head of the government. If the East roused itself in behalf of Jefferson, Burr would then burn the navy, except for sufficient shipping to take him and his followers to New Orleans, there to proclaim the independence of Louisiana and the Western States.[33]

There is no question that this astonishing scheme was merely a bogey to extract money from Yrujo. Nothing could have been further from Burr's real plans — had he even toyed with the idea, he certainly would not have disclosed it to Yrujo, who could do nothing to further, and much to block such a plot. Nevertheless, it was a thoroughly discreditable idea to broach, even as the mock plan of Western disunion to Merry, and betrays a growing moral obtuseness on Burr's part, not to speak of Dayton — which had been conspicuously lacking in former years. In the desperation of their need, plots and weird conspiracies were being hatched in infinite variety for the delectation of the foreign diplomats.

Strangely enough, this " almost insane plan," as Yrujo called it, attracted a certain degree of interest and respectful attention from the Minister, just as the conspirators had hoped. Forewarned, he had been wily enough; now that no one had tipped him off in advance, he was as gullible as Merry himself. For, he told Cevallos in his report, " I confess, for my part, that in view of all the circumstances it seems to me easy to execute, although it will irritate the Atlantic States, especially those called central — that is, Virginia, Maryland, Delaware, Pennsylvania, New Jersey and New York." Perhaps Burr and Dayton were cleverer in their methods than the bald documents would seem to indicate.

Yrujo gave Dayton $1500 outright for his pretended treachery to Burr, and solicited from his home government an additional $1000 for him as well as a pension of $1500 a year.[34] This was first blood for the pair. They actually obtained the extra $1000, but the pension was peremptorily refused. Cevallos, in Madrid, was in a better position to know the exact state of affairs, through Mexico and the spy listed in his secret Code Book as No. 13. On February

3rd he was telling Yrujo that England had troubles of her own at home, and that Dayton's "secret" had not been exactly a secret to him.[35]

4. RECRUITING

By the end of February, Burr was exceedingly dejected. Even the small pension Yrujo had promised could not restore his spirits. The larger sum that Dayton had demanded had been turned aside with polite Spanish evasions; Merry had obviously no standing with his own government; Williamson had evidently written and told him to expect little or nothing from England. The United States was farther away from war than ever before. Wilkinson had betrayed a strange inclination to discuss political campaigns rather than expeditions. The whole game no longer seemed worth the candle. Whereupon Burr took a deep breath and went to see his arch-enemy, Thomas Jefferson. This was on February 22, 1806, exactly two years after that famous toast about the "union of all honest men!" [36]

Jefferson was to record this last strange interview with a good deal of malicious satisfaction. According to Jefferson, Burr reminded him of his former services "in bringing on the present order of things . . . that he could do me much harm; he wished, however, to be on different ground," and hinted that he would be "in town some days, if I should have anything to propose to him." To which Jefferson replied that he was sorry, the public had withdrawn its confidence from Burr, and that as to his threats, he "feared no injury which any man could do me; that I had never done a single act, or been concerned in any transaction, which I feared to have fully laid open." [37] Of their conversation there is no other record.

In any event, Burr had humiliated himself once more. In a moment of bleak despair he had been willing to cast aside the plans of years, and assume the safety and orderliness of a governmental position. Jefferson very cheerfully and firmly closed that door to security. There was nothing left but to go ahead.

He reread Blennerhassett's letter, and sat down to answer it. "Your talents and acquirements seem to have destined you for something more than vegetable life," he wrote flatteringly, "and since the first hour of our acquaintance, I have considered your seclusion as a fraud on society." Burr had, it seemed, just such a project in mind, a speculation, as Blennerhassett himself had described. However, there was little expectation of its commencement until December, and "as the matter, in its present state, can not be satisfactorily explained by letter, the communication will be deferred until a personal interview can be had." [38]

He threw himself once more with all his old restless energies into the affair. Mexico — or colonization! Either way meant a new and possibly more abundant life. Alston was called upon again for funds; he spoke to Smith and Ogden, of Miranda fame. He started the enlistment of adventurous young men. He sounded out " General " William Eaton, a fantastic character who had the year before seated a pretender on the throne of Tripoli by an epic march with a motley array across burning desert sands. He was now in Washington, trying vainly to obtain Congressional reimbursement of moneys claimed to have been expended for the benefit of the American government, and exceedingly loud in denunciation of an Administration that had not backed up his Tripolitan adventure. He was a familiar sight in the Washington taverns, accoutered with an outlandish hat and Turkish sash, tossing off huge potations and hiccuping into his cups anent the base neglect of heroes by a republican government. Certainly the last person in the world to be inducted into the inner circle of a treasonable conspiracy.

Yet Eaton was to testify to that very thing at Richmond. According to him, Burr had spoken to him during the winter of 1805–6 of a military expedition he was organizing against the Spanish provinces, hinting that it was being done with the secret authority of the American government, and based upon the inevitableness of war with Spain. Eaton agreed to join, and the feasibility of penetrating to Mexico was discussed. Thus far, the story is quite plausible and proper. But then, Eaton maintained, Burr gave vent to " certain indistinct expressions and innuendoes," from which he deduced that " colonel Burr had other projects." Burr railed to him against the administration, and encouraged him in his resentment against Congress. Whereupon Eaton, the loose-mouthed, became suddenly subtle with Burr, pretended acquiescence, and thus brought that reserved and secretive individual to a full disclosure of his horrid plans. It was nothing less than a " project of revolutionizing the territory west of the Allegany; establishing an independent empire there; New-Orleans to be the capital, and he himself to be the chief; organizing a military force on the waters of the Mississippi, and carrying conquest to Mexico." In fact, he was offering Eaton a command in his all-conquering forces, second only to Wilkinson.[39]

But these treasonable plans for forcible disunion were not the only ones to be disclosed to this gentleman of deep potations and loud complaints, whom Burr had never seen before. There was more, much more. Burr, it seemed, now spoke even more wildly. He intended "overthrowing the present Government," and "would turn Congress neck and heels out of doors, assassinate the President, seize the treasury and Navy; and declare himself the protector of an energetic government." This, be it remembered, in the face of Eaton's constant objections and expressions of horror.[40]

Eaton, shocked at these revelations, did not know what to do. "I durst not place my lonely testimony in the balance against the weight of colonel Burr's character," he was to testify disingenuously. Of course, not a person in all Washington, with the exception of this lonely hero of Tripoli, but knew that Burr's character, in the eyes of officialdom, represented the very nadir of respectability. "I resolved therefore with myself," continued the self-made General naively, "to obtain the removal of Mr. Burr from this country, in a way honorable to him; and on this I did consult him, without his knowing my motive." Whereupon, in February or March, 1806, Eaton hied himself to Jefferson and suggested an ambassadorship for Burr, at Paris, London or Madrid, on the high ground that "colonel Burr ought to be removed from the country, because I considered him dangerous in it." But, strangely enough, he "perceived the subject was disagreeable to the president," and thereupon dropped it, keeping a discreet silence as to the details of the horrendous conspiracy he had just discovered. It is true he hinted vaguely about a possible Western insurrection in the distant future, but the interview was closed rather peremptorily by Jefferson. Whereupon Eaton, after a *full* disclosure to two unnamed representatives and a senator, who "did not seem much alarmed," returned to Massachusetts and thought no more of Burr and his revolutions until long after, when the whole nation was in a state of alarm, and Jefferson was ordering the country scoured for witnesses against the traitor Burr.[41]

The whole story is a tissue of inherent improbabilities. Burr had opened himself to this stranger as he had to no one else; then, after placing his very life in Eaton's hands, he had consented that the drinking warrior go to Jefferson and obtain for him an embassy. Eaton kept silence with the President, said nothing all the time that rumors were flying thick and fast, and only came forward when the whole weight of the government was being employed to crush Burr.[42]

On January 21, 1807, Senator Plumer found himself opposite

Eaton at a dinner table. That worthy expatiated at length on his exposure of Burr's treason. Only within the week, he said, had he disclosed the truth to Jefferson, and never before to any one else. After listening to the tirade, the caustic Senator felt impelled to confide to his Diary, " The more distant the time, the more distant from Burr, & the louder public opinion is expressed agt Burr — the fuller & stronger are the declarations of Eaton against the accused." [43]

Most remarkable of all, however, is the fact that almost immediately after Eaton placed his deposition in Jefferson's hands, Congress suddenly authorized the payment to him of $10,000 on a doubtful claim which had been before it for years, and which it had shown no previous disposition to honor. In March, 1807, the payment was promptly made by a government known for its dilatoriness in such matters. No court or jury could possibly accept Eaton's testimony at its face value.

At about the same time Burr spoke also to Commodore Thomas Truxton, an intimate friend of long standing, who had sheltered Burr in his flight after the duel. Truxton had commanded the American fleet in the brief struggle with Tripoli, had acquitted himself with the utmost gallantry, yet found himself now cooling his heels in Washington, under the manifest displeasure of the Administration. To Truxton, however, equally discontented with his condition, a friend, a man who knew how to keep silence, Burr disclosed no such treasonable design as that which Eaton claimed had been opened to him. Truxton was to testify that during the winter of 1805–6, Burr had frequently mentioned to him the subject of speculations in western lands, the proposed canal around Ohio Falls, the possibility of a bridge over that river, and had advised him to forget about the Navy, where, from Jefferson's known policy of attrition, nothing could be expected in the way of a career. Instead, said Truxton, " he wished to see or make me . . . an admiral; that he contemplated an expedition to Mexico, in the event of a war with Spain, which he thought inevitable." In fact, he asked Truxton to assume command of the naval end of the expedition. Truxton inquired if Jefferson were a party to the scheme, and on Burr's emphatic disavowal, declined to participate. The scheme, according to Truxton's testimony, involved the establishment of an independent government in Mexico, and he was told that Wilkinson " had projected the expedition." Many officers of the United States Army and Navy, Burr assured him, would join, as would thousands of Westerners.[44] Nothing about secession, nothing of assassination and seizure of government.

Burr turned also to Charles Biddle, another old friend, in the summer of 1806. To him he spoke of " a settlement on the Mississippi of military men; that the Spaniards he knew were ripe for a revolt, and it would make the fortunes of all those concerned in revolutionizing that country." When Biddle objected that it would lead to war with Spain, Burr replied that war must come in any event.[45]

By that time Burr had come definitely to the conclusion that his original plan for an immediate descent upon Mexico was premature. He had now switched to the colonization scheme. He had his eye on a huge tract of land that would suit his schemes admirably.

In 1797 the Spanish Government entered into a contract with Baron Bastrop whereby the latter bound himself to settle five hundred families on a tract of land, thirty miles square, abutting the Washita River in the Territory of Louisiana. In return, Spain agreed to convey title to the promoter, and obligated itself further to furnish the settlers with sufficient food for a period of six months. Governor Carondelet found himself unable to live up to this part of the agreement — the supplying of food — and in exchange, released Bastrop from the requirements of the contract relating to settlement. Bastrop claimed that his title to the land was not thereby impaired, and sold his rights to various persons who in turn conveyed to one Charles Lynch. Burr had already commenced negotiations with Lynch for the purchase of 350,000 acres of this grant. His intentions were obvious, and sufficiently specified in his conversations with Biddle. He would settle a large community of young, militarily disposed adventurers on the tract, which was now in the newly carved Territory of Orleans, and close to the Spanish border. There he would establish himself as a landed gentleman, surrounded by friends and congenial associates, and bide his time. Sooner or later, he felt certain, the United States must clash with Spain — sooner, if Wilkinson would do his part. At the first sign of hostilities, his settlers would march on the Spanish possessions and, in conjunction with Wilkinson and those of the American army and navy whom he could induce to join, sweep all before them. The country would rise and hail him as a deliverer, and the original dream of Mexico and a government of his own would be fulfilled.

5. Plot and Counterplot

On April 16, 1806, Burr wrote to Wilkinson: "The execution of our project is postponed till December; want of water in Ohio, rendered movement impracticable; other reasons rendered delay expedient. The association is enlarged, and comprises all that Wilkinson could wish. Confidence limited to a few. . . . *Burr* wrote you a long letter last December, replying to a short one deemed very silly. Nothing has been heard from Brigadier since October. Is Cusion et Portes right? Address Burr at Washington." [46]

The *Brigadier*, it seems, was a code word for Wilkinson, *Cusion* and *Portes* for the frontier officers whom Wilkinson was trying to interest in the Mexican venture, and *want of water in Ohio* meant funds were lacking, and that Merry had failed them. The letters mentioned were evidently Wilkinson's belated forwarding of Daniel Clark's warning, and Burr's reply thereto, though there is a discrepancy in the dates. Wilkinson, prepared to drop Burr completely and turn the whole affair to his own advantage, had since then been very careful about incriminating himself in writing. Burr was to receive no further communications from him.

While waiting impatiently to hear from Wilkinson, Burr turned again to Yrujo, who now seemed his last resort for adequate funds. This time he went to him direct, and dropped the pretense of Dayton's betrayal. He spoke of Western secession, of New Orleans, of subversion of the government — all the old treacheries which were peculiarly grateful to Spain, not to speak of England and France. He now asked point-blank for the sinews with which to carry out these schemes. Yrujo was impressed with the possibilities of success, and so advised his home government.[47] But he refused to disburse any further moneys to Burr until he had received instructions from Spain.

Whereupon Burr tried to alarm him. He suddenly stopped his visits, and Dayton once more appeared on the scene, explaining to the credulous Envoy that Burr, disgusted with his dilatoriness, had turned to England again, and had revived his original idea of a cooperative attack on the Spanish possessions. Dayton expressed himself as eager to protect Spain from Burr's scheme of conquest. In fact, he advocated the immediate reinforcement of the garrisons at Pensacola and Mobile, and, incidentally, felt that he should receive further honorariums for his good services.[48]

Unfortunately, Yrujo, though alarmed, was stubborn in his refusal to pay out any more sums from his private purse.

In which the event justified him. For Don Pedro Cevallos, who at first had been interested in the despatches from the United States, was soon to warn him against any further outlays of money to the adventurers, and finally, as both the American and the European scene cleared up favorably for Spain, declared flatly that the King would not in any way encourage Burr's designs.[49]

Pitt had died in England, and Merry's letter of November 25, 1805, had fallen into the hands of Charles James Fox, England's new Prime Minister, foe to Pitt's American policy, and well disposed to the United States. About June 1, 1806, Merry was astounded to receive a polite notification that His Majesty had graciously consented to accept his request for recall, and that his successor would soon be on his way to take over the British Ministry. Merry, never very bright, wrote vainly that he had never even entertained such an idea, much less suggested it, but Fox paid no heed to his plaintive protestations.

Almost immediately after the receipt of this dismissal, Burr called again on Merry. He would, he said, " though very reluctantly," have to address himself now to the French and Spanish Governments, inasmuch as Great Britain had proved herself shamefully lacking in consideration. He was playing Yrujo against Merry, and *vice versa,* with an agility worthy of a better cause. And both sources of a magical stream of funds failed him. As he told Merry, " with or without such support [his venture] certainly would be made shortly." [50]

CHAPTER XXI

NEVER TO RETURN

1. THE FATAL CIPHER

ON March 24, 1806, Burr was convinced that the earlier war temper of the Administration had passed away. He wrote Andrew Jackson that " you have doubtless before this time been convinced that we are to have no war if it can be avoided with honor, or even without." But Miranda's expedition had aroused his hopes again, and if it caused an embroilment of the United States " a military force on our part would be requisite, and that force might come from your side of the mountains." Wherefore, he advised Jackson to recruit both men and officers, because " I have often said a brigade could be raised in West Tennessee which would drive double the number of Frenchmen off the earth." [1]

Soon even this faint hope died. Miranda was ingloriously defeated, and Jefferson and Madison managed to evade responsibility, though not without some uncomfortable squirmings. Burr was reduced to his impotent manipulations of Merry and Yrujo. But with the coming of summer the situation suddenly changed. Spanish troops were reported on American soil. At least, that was the American contention. Spain claimed the territory involved belonged to Texas. Jefferson insisted that the Sabine River was the boundary-line between Louisiana and Texas — as indeed it is today — and that any attempt by the Spaniards to garrison themselves on the Louisiana side would be met with force. The Spaniards argued — and remained where they were — east of the Sabine.

A new flame of warlike anger swept the nation. General Jackson drilled his State militia and thought of Burr. General John Adair in the neighboring State did likewise. Smith and Brown roused themselves. Here at last was the chance for which they had been waiting so long. Jefferson felt the public pulse and acted for once with decision. He sent peremptory orders to Wilkinson, commander-in-chief of the American forces on the frontier, to drive the Spaniards beyond the Sabine at any cost. Wilkinson, initiator of the scheme of aggrandizement — Burr's confederate!

Everywhere the conspirators perked up. Their enthusiasm was unbounded. In Wilkinson's hands rested the decision of peace or war with Spain. He had been given what practically amounted to *carte blanche* by the President. By a single operation he could embroil the two countries in such wise that war would prove inescapable. And, with a declaration of war, with the West heated to patriotic frenzy, with Jackson forming his militia, all dreams of the conspirators *must* be realized. Texas, Mexico, West Florida, South America even! Visions of grandeur, dreams of empire!

And, in fact, Burr was not deluding himself. Francisco Viana, Inspector General of the Spanish troops in Texas, already was writing in considerable alarm that " the rumor grows that the American forces are gathering in Kentucky, and that our unpeopled lands, neophytes, and vassal Indians are to fall into their hands. And I have neither munitions, arms, provisions, nor soldiers wherewith to uphold our authority." [2]

Only Burr and Dayton, however, did not wax enthusiastic. Something had happened to Wilkinson — just what it was, they were not quite certain. After a blank silence of months, Burr's urgent note of April 16th had galvanized him into a reply. We know nothing of its contents except that it was dated May 13th. Concerning this letter much ado was to be made at the trial, until Wilkinson was goaded into challenging Burr to produce it. But Burr, it seemed, had voluntarily, and in the presence of a witness, put the letter out of his hand, " so it would not be used improperly against any one." [3] Wilkinson was too canny to have committed himself in writing, but evidently, from what happened next, his letter was wholly evasive and unsatisfactory to the conspirators.

Burr and Dayton conferred. Troops were being sent to the Sabine; a clash — if Wilkinson wished — was inevitable. It was necessary therefore to heighten his faltering spirits, to alarm him into swift action. Two letters were sent him by different messengers. One was from Dayton, carried by Peter V. Ogden, his nephew, and dated July 24, 1806. It read, " It is now well ascertained that you are to be displaced in next session. Jefferson will affect to yield reluctantly to the public sentiment, but yield he will. Prepare yourself, therefore, for it. You know the rest. You are not a man to despair, or even despond, especially when such prospects offer in another quarter. Are you ready? Are your numerous associates ready? Wealth and glory! Louisiana and Mexico! I shall have time to receive a letter from you before I set out for Ohio — OHIO." [4]

By such means did they expect to force Wilkinson's hand. On

receipt of such alarming information — entirely false, of course —
he would be compelled to precipitate a war in order to save his
own skin. The rest would follow. Louisiana meant the Bastrop
grant — perhaps even the independence of New Orleans; and
Mexico — *that* was the real goal!

Traveling with Ogden was another messenger — young Samuel
Swartwout, handsome, frank of bearing, youngest brother of the
Swartwout clan. He carried Burr's message to Wilkinson, dated
July 29, 1806, written in cipher. This was the famous message
which, when published, roused the whole country to a final, irrevocable conviction of Burr's guilt. Its exact wording will never
be known. Wilkinson took months, so he claimed, to decipher it;
he erased and made alterations in the original document to suit
his convenience and to save himself from implication — as he
brazenly admitted on the witness stand — and his published versions varied with the necessities of the occasion. In fact, the first
translation which he sent to Jefferson had been framed to justify
the arrest of one of Burr's messengers, and, deposed the copyist, he
had intentionally omitted " every thing which was calculated to
inculpate the General, or which might by exciting suspicion, have
a tendency to weaken his testimony." During the course of a relentless cross-examination, Wilkinson changed his testimony repeatedly concerning the decipherment of this famous document.
The translation was, he said at one time, hasty and inaccurate and
done piece-meal; at another, that it was a careful, tedious and
lengthy bit of work. The original translation had been lost, he
averred, and only substantially could he point out the differences
between the several translations and the original.[5] In short, a
pitiful, untrustworthy performance.

Burr and Wilkinson had agreed on three ciphers to be used
between them. A hieroglyphic cipher invented by Wilkinson and
one Captain Smith; an arbitrary alphabet cipher formed by Burr
and Wilkinson in 1799 or 1800; and a dictionary cipher which depended on the use of a certain edition of Entick's pocket dictionary as the key. The cipher letter of July 29th was written in all
three ciphers, as well as in English.[6]

In its generally accepted version the letter read as follows:
" Your letter, postmarked 13th May, is received. At length I have
obtained funds, and have actually commenced. The Eastern detachments, from different points and under different pretences,
will rendezvous on the Ohio 1st of November. Everything internal
and external favors our views. Naval protection of England is
secured. Truxton is going to Jamaica to arrange with the admiral

on that station. It will meet us at the Mississippi. England, a navy of the United States, are ready to join, and final orders are given to my friends and followers. It will be a host of choice spirits. Wilkinson shall be second to Burr only; Wilkinson shall dictate the rank and promotion of his officers. Burr will proceed westward 1st August, never to return. With him goes his daughter; the husband will follow in October, with a corps of worthies. Send forthwith an intelligent and confidential friend with whom Burr may confer; he shall return immediately with further interesting details; this is essential to concert and harmony of movement. Send a list of all persons known to Wilkinson west of the mountains who could be useful, with a note delineating their characters. By your messenger send me four or five commissions of your officers, which you can borrow under any pretence you please; they shall be returned faithfully. Already are orders given to the contractor to forward six months' provisions to points Wilkinson may name; this shall not be used until the last moment, and then under proper injunctions. Our object, my dear friend, is brought to a point so long desired. Burr guarantees the result with his life and honor, with the lives and honor and the fortunes of hundreds, the best blood of our country. Burr's plan of operation is to move down rapidly from the Falls, on the 15th of November, with the first five hundred or a thousand men, in light boats now constructing for that purpose; to be at Natchez between the 5th and 15th of December, there to meet you; there to determine whether it will be expedient to seize on or pass by Baton Rouge. On receipt of this, send Burr an answer. Draw on Burr for all expenses, etc. The people of the country to which we are going are prepared to receive us; their agents, now with Burr, say that if we will protect their religion, and will not subject them to a foreign Power, that in three weeks all will be settled. The gods invite us to glory and fortune; it remains to be seen whether we deserve the boon. The bearer of this goes express to you. He is a man of inviolable honor and perfect discretion, formed to execute rather than project, capable of relating facts with fidelity, and incapable of relating them otherwise; he is thoroughly informed of the plans and intentions of Burr, and will disclose to you as far as you require, and no further. He had imbibed a reverence for your character, and may be embarrassed in your presence; put him at ease, and he will satisfy you." [7]

It was on this letter that Jefferson was to act finally and belatedly, and, as if to atone for his long delay, pursue Burr with a venomous persecution unparalleled in the Presidential annals of the United States. It was on this letter that the country was roused to execration and rage against the traitor, and left it for posterity to follow suit with uncritical zeal. Yet John Marshall, Chief Justice of the United States, was to declare flatly that there was no taint of treason to the United States in this allegedly incriminating document, nor in any of the evidence adduced to support the charge. And an examination of the epistle substantiates his decision in every particular.

What does it contain? A statement of an expedition, formed of Eastern and Western detachments, to be supported by an English navy and a group of American naval officers, as well as army officers associated with Wilkinson, directed against a country whose people wish to be protected in their religion and not be subjected to a foreign power, a people whose agents were then with Burr. Obviously Mexico, and nowhere else. The people were Catholic, and naturally reluctant to be placed under a Protestant rule of suppression; they did not intend to cast off Spain and receive France, England or the United States in its stead. Secret agents from Mexico were active in Washington and Philadelphia, and Burr had been in close touch with them ever since the Catholic Bishop of New Orleans had sent missionary priests into Mexico to make contacts for him. It was neither New Orleans nor Louisiana, where the majority of Burr's supporters were American Protestants and uninterested in religious protection. In fact, Burr queries whether it would not be advisable to capture Baton Rouge, the important city of Spanish West Florida. Wilkinson himself realized at the treason trial that this communication, as it stood, even with his alterations and erasures, was poor evidence of a scheme to revolutionize any part of the United States. Accordingly, he availed himself of the latter part of the letter which recommended young Swartwout to him, and claimed, without corroboration of any kind, that Swartwout had buzzed the real dark project of secession into his horrified ear.

The letter itself is turgid and bombastic in the highest degree, quite at variance with Burr's usual style and reserve of language. It was written so for a purpose, even as Dayton's accompanying letter had been. Both were in the same vein as Wilkinson's own mannered affectation, and were intended to tickle his vanity and move him to the long-contemplated action. There were falsehoods in it — many of them, though Swartwout was to deny vigorously that the original cipher had made any mention of Truxton and Alston. These, he claimed — and he had helped put the letter into code — were interpolations by the doughty General.

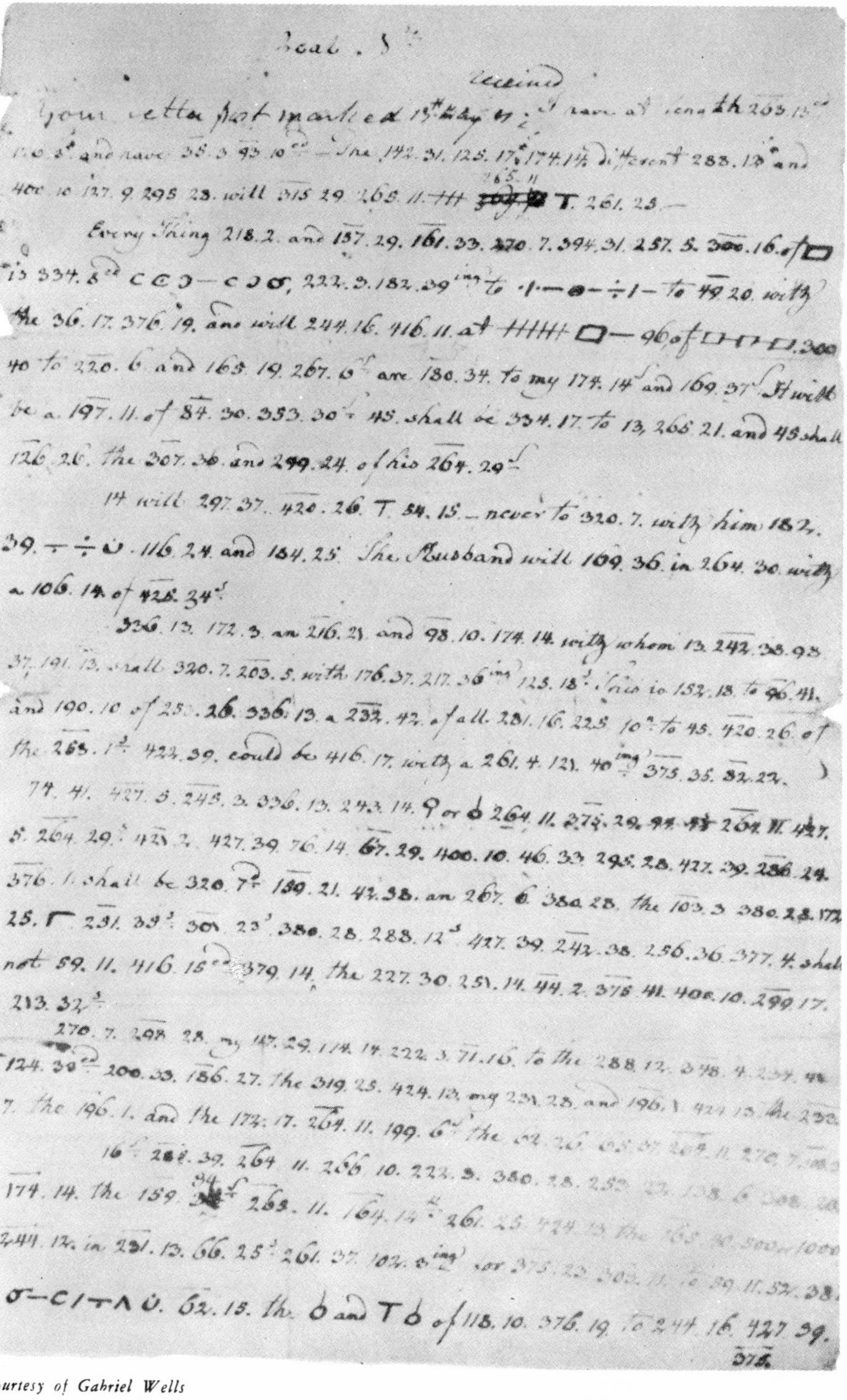

Recd. S^r

received

Your letter post marked 13th May is received. I have at length 263.15 110.5 and have 35.3 93.10 — The 142.31.125.17 174.14 different 288.13 and 400.10 127.9 295.28. will 315.29 265.11. ++++ T. 261.23.

Every Thing 218.2. and 157.29. 161.33. 270.7. 394.31. 257.5. 300.16. of ☐ is 334.8 ... 222.3.182.39 to ... to 49.20. with the 36.17.376.19. and will 244.16.416.11. at ++++ ☐ — 96. of ... 300 40 to 220.6 and 165.19.267.6 are 180.34. to my 174.14 and 169.37. It will be a 197.11. of 84.30.353.30 45. shall be 334.17. to 13, 265.21. and 45 shall 126.26. the 307.36. and 299.24. of his 264.29.

14 will 297.37. 420.26. T 34.15. — never to 320.7. with him 182.39. ... 116.24. and 184.25. The Husband will 109.36. in 264.30. with a 106.14. of 425.34.

336.13. 172.3. an 216.21. and 98.10. 174.14. with whom 13. 242.38.93 37.191.13. shall 320.7. 203.5. with 176.37. 217.36 125.18. This is 152.18 to 96.41. and 190.10 of 25 ... 26. 336.13. a 232.42. of all 231.16. 225.10 to 45. 420.26. of the 265.1. 422.39. could be 416.17. with a 261.4.121.40 375.35. 82.22.

74.41. 427.5. 245.3. 336.13. 243.14. ♀ or ♂ 264.11. 275.29. ... 264.11. 427.5. 264.29. 423.2. 427.39. 76.14. 67.29. 400.10. 46.33. 295.28. 427.39. 286.24. 376.1. shall be 320.7 139.21. 42.38. an 267.6. 380.28. the 103.3. 380.28. 172 25. ┌ 231.33. 301. 23. 380.28. 288.12. 427.39. 242.38. 256.36. 377.4. shall not 59.11. 416.15. 379.14. the 227.30. 251.14. 44.2. 375.41. 400.10. 299.17. 213.32.

270.7. 208.28. my 147.29. 174.14. 222.3. 71.16. to the 288.12. 348.4. 234.48 124.30 200.33. 186.27. the 319.25. 424.13. my 231.28. and 196.1. 424.13. the 232.7. the 196.1. and the 174.17. 264.11. 199.6. the 62.26. 68.37. 264.11. 270.7. ...

16. 281.39. 264.11. 266.10. 222.3. 380.28. 252.23. 138.6. 208.28 174.14. the 159.34. 263.11. 164.14. 261.23. 424.13. the 265.30. 500 or 1000 244.12. in 231.13. 66.25. 261.37. 102.8 or 375.23. 302.11. 12. 89.11. 52.38. ... 62.15. the ♂ and T♂ of 118.10. 376.19. to 244.16. 427.39. 375.

Courtesy of Gabriel Wells

CIPHER LETTER FROM BURR TO WILKINSON, JULY 29, 1806

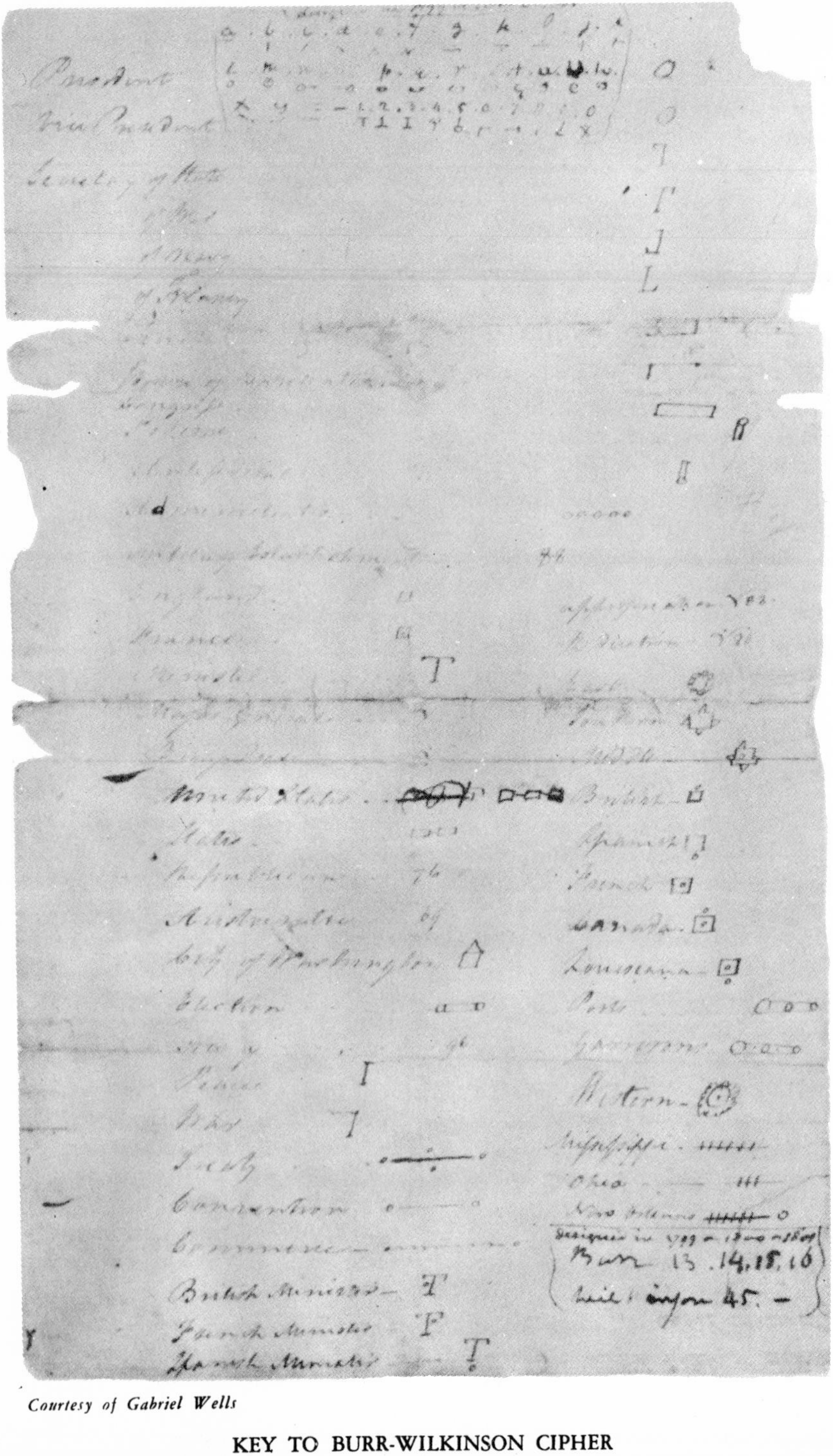

Courtesy of Gabriel Wells

KEY TO BURR-WILKINSON CIPHER

Truxton, of course, had refused to be a party to the filibuster. Burr had some funds — those already received from Alston and those in prospect from Blennerhassett — sufficient for the building of the boats and the launching of a skeleton expedition, though not nearly as much as he wished Wilkinson to believe. The story of England's cooperation was made of whole cloth. The tone of bombast and high optimism was to give the needed fillip to Wilkinson's waning courage.

Ogden and Swartwout started out late in July on their long, overland journey. A second copy of the cipher went by water to New Orleans in the hands of Dr. Justus Erich Bollman, another recruit to Burr's forces. This adventurer's career had been exciting enough. Now thirty-five years old, he had been a graduate of Göttingen, a resident of Paris during the Revolution, a practitioner of medicine in Vienna and London, and famous the world over for his daring rescue of Lafayette from his Austrian prison. Both had been recaptured, however, and Bollman languished in an Austrian dungeon for many months, only to be released on his promise never to return. He came then to the United States, met Burr, was fascinated, and remained to take a prominent part in his activities.

2. The Bastrop Purchase

With the despatch of his code letters, Burr commenced to move on his own account, reasonably satisfied at the turn of events. Wilkinson was a broken reed, but his carefully worded cipher, the sudden warlike disposition of Washington, Spanish aggressions, must stiffen his backbone and carry him along by the very pressure of circumstance. Burr did not know of Wilkinson's secret relations with Spain, could not know that he was about to be betrayed. From his viewpoint, there was no further profit in delay. Enlistments had been carried on with a fair degree of success, some money was at hand, boats were to be ready for him at the Falls of the Ohio. His presence again in the West, he thought, would be the signal for a tumultuous outpouring of volunteers. His reception on the last journey, his private advices since, had left no doubt of that in his mind. By the time his boats were finished, Wilkinson would have already clashed with the Spaniard, and touched off the fuse to a blazing train of events. As for the malignant questions posed in the anonymous *Queries,* the rumors floating through the Western country as to his secret purposes, Burr brushed them aside as beneath contempt. His was essentially a strange compound of mature subtlety and childlike inability to read aright those signs which conflicted with his wishes and illusions. In spite of all that he had already suffered from calumny and a libelous press, to the end of his life he was to labor under the delusion that they were inconsequential and of no effect.

Early in August, 1806, Burr started on his fatal journey westward, that journey from which he had fondly anticipated there would be no return. With him were Theodosia, excited, ardent, blinded with the glamour of her father, a secretary, Charles Willie, and Colonel Julien De Pestre, a refugee from the French Revolution, whom he had formally named his Chief of Staff. The entourage reached Pittsburgh on August 22nd. Here they stopped for a while, and Burr busied himself obtaining recruits for his expedition. Quite a few young men joined, fired with the prospects of wealth and glory. Among them was the young son of Presley Neville, Chief Justice of Pennsylvania. So far so good. But then he made an error. He visited Colonel George Morgan, near Cannonsburg. Morgan, it may be remembered, had known Burr at Princeton when Burr was in college. In fact, it was concerning his niece that the famous legend of the " Forgotten Grave " had flowered into a fine tale of seduction and suicide. Morgan had gone West, as so many others had done, and settled with his sons at a place which he grandiloquently named Morganza. Morgan of Morganza!

Burr had dinner at his house, stayed overnight. They talked, without question, of Burr's plans. Also without question, Burr tried to induce Morgan's two sons to join his venture. Here, however, the parting of the ways is reached, and the rest is darkness and confusion. After Burr's departure — without the sons — Morgan went excitedly to Presley Neville, whose son was already with Burr, and to Samuel Roberts, with a wild tale of conspiracy and treason. The gentlemen listened in some astonishment, and, after some cogitation, decided that the information was sufficiently important to lay before the Administration. Whereupon, on October 7th, they wrote jointly to Madison, the Secretary of State, restating Morgan's charges against Burr, but acknowledging that it was difficult to detail the exact conversation. " Indeed, according to our Informants, much more was to be collected from the *manner* in which certain things were said, and hints given, than from the words used." [8]

But at the Richmond trial, the Morgans were ready with specific conversations; the treason was no longer merely in the *manner*. John Morgan, one of the sons, testified that at the dinner Burr had turned to him and said " that the union of the states could not possibly last; and that a separation of the states must ensue as a natural consequence, in four or five years." An expression of opinion — misguided perhaps, and certainly poor prophecy — but containing nothing of treason; in fact, obviating by its very language, any present seditious intent. But, continued young John, Burr then made the remark " that with two hundred men, he could drive the president and congress into the Potowmac; and with four or five hundred he could take possession of the city of New-York." Vainglorious boasting, of the kind that is made when the wine circulates too long, and of a nature which had never before been associated with Burr's wonted reserve. And even Morgan was driven to admit on cross-examination that the remarks had been tossed off " in a lively or careless manner." [9]

Then the old man, Colonel George Morgan, swore that Burr had tried to feel him out that night, after the others had retired to bed; had asked him if he knew a Mr. Vigo, of Fort Vincent, a Spaniard. Morgan said yes, he knew him as a man who had been deeply involved in the conspiracy of 1788; and went on to say emphatically that it was " a nefarious thing to aim at the division of the states." Whereupon Burr stopped short, bid him a curt goodnight, and rode off early the next morning with De Pestre before breakfast.[10]

A story, which, even if true, left a good deal to be desired in the way of evidencing premeditated treason. But the story is not ended. It seems that the " Morgans of Morganza " had been engaged since 1784 in pressing certain doubtful claims to lands in Indiana before an indifferent Congress.[11] It is a strange coincidence that so many of the witnesses against Burr were involved in pending matters before Congress, and hopeful of governmental favors. (*Vide* " General " William Eaton.) So warm, in fact, were the Morgans on Burr's trail, that the father wrote to Jefferson direct on January 19, 1807, in which communication he repeated the old charges, questioned Neville's patriotism, and bragged how his sons " have imbibed the principles of their father and of Thomas Jefferson from the commencement of our revolutionary war to the present day." [12] Yet even his son was compelled to admit that his " father was old and infirm; and like other old men, told long stories and was apt to forget his repetitions." [13]

From Pittsburgh, Burr went on to his chief rendezvous, Blennerhassett's Island. This time Harman Blennerhassett was at home. The transplanted Irish gentleman farmer met him with eagerness and abounding hospitality. His already slightly addled head was still further addled by the visions of grandeur which Burr painted for his delectation. Every pithy sentence of the great man became a volume; every slight remark a conspiratorial ecstasy. He was eager for anything; he flew beyond his guest on the viewless wings of fantasy. Never was Burr to have such an enthusiastic convert — too enthusiastic, much too imprudent, as time was to disclose. Playful remarks, such as are in abundant evidence in Burr's correspondence with his daughter, were taken at full face value, and builded on *ad infinitum*. Burr was to become Emperor of Mexico and Theodosia the Heir-Apparent? Immediately Blennerhassett grew anxious over his own particular titles. When Burr gravely pronounced him Ambassador to England, he was in the seventh heaven of delight. Burr spoke of the likelihood of the West — in the dim future — breaking off peacefully to become a great nation on its own. Blennerhassett, without Burr's knowledge, promptly sat down and wrote a series of lengthy dissertations preaching Western secession, to be published in the *Ohio Gazette* under the pseudonym of *Querist,* and which silly productions were to plague both Blennerhassett and Burr himself in the not distant future.[14] As for Theodosia, lovely, cultured, charming, woman of the world, she completed the conquest her father had made. Mrs. Blennerhassett fell wholly in love with her. Even when husband and wife were bitter against Burr for the troubles into which they had been led, they continued to worship Theo.

Blennerhassett turned over all his free funds to the enterprise, endorsed bills against Philadelphia with a reckless profusion, mortgaged his Island as security. In October, Theo's husband, Joseph Alston, appeared at the Blennerhassetts'. Alston guaranteed to his host the loans and advancements which were being made, and offered his own vast estates as collateral security. A succession of rice crop failures had left Alston destitute of ready funds.[15]

By the last of August, Burr and Blennerhassett were at Marietta purchasing a hundred barrels of pork, and contracting for fifteen boats to be delivered on December 9th. These were ordered from the firm of Woodbridge and Company, of which Blennerhassett was a former partner. The Island became the center of Burr's organizing activities. Everything was bustle and confusion; a kiln was erected to dry corn, which was then ground into meal, supplies were purchased, the household effects on the Island were packed for removal. For the Blennerhassetts were going along *en masse* — Mrs. Blennerhassett and their two small sons — pulling up stakes to seek their fortune in a new country. Strong evidence that by this time even the military invasion of Mexico was doubtful; that primarily the entire scheme had become a colonization and settlement venture.

Recruiting went on apace. Burr and Blennerhassett both scoured the countryside, trying to induce the footloose and the adventurous to join. Seven young men had come on from Pittsburgh, larger contingents were soon due from the East. The degree of success with which they met was not very encouraging. For strange rumors were flying through the West, causing the bold to pause, the timid to withdraw.

On September 4th, Burr was the guest of John Smith, contractor, storekeeper and United States Senator, in Cincinnati. Then he crossed the Ohio to Lexington and journeyed on to Nashville, once more to meet Andrew Jackson. Here he was among friends. Tennessee was still untouched by suspicion. Jackson wrote to a friend: "Colonel Burr is with me; he arrived last night . . . Would it not be well for us to do something as a mark of attention to the Colonel? He has always and is still a true and trusty friend to Tennessee." [16]

They did a good deal. The leading men of Nashville rode out to the Hermitage to pay their respects to the distinguished visitor. A great ball was organized, and Burr was again the cynosure of all eyes. In private, Jackson and he discussed matters. As a result of their conference, all Tennessee was roused by a proclamation of General Jackson on October 4th, requiring the Militia to be ready for instant duty, as the Spanish forces were " already encamped within the limits of our Government." With his usual impetuosity, Jackson sent off an express to Jefferson offering his services in the pending war, to which the President replied in vague language.

By the first week in October, Burr was back in Lexington, where he met Blennerhassett, Theodosia and her husband. Mrs. Blennerhassett remained behind, in charge of the Island. Lexington was to be the new Headquarters, as nearer to the boats then building, and a better base for collecting supplies. Here he concluded his purchase of the Bastrop claim from Lynch — 400,000 acres on the Washita River, in what is now Louisiana, and not too far away from the Sabine and the Texan border.

" I have bought of Col. Lynch 400 M. acres of the tract called Bastroph's lying on the Washita," he wrote. " The excellence of the soil and climate are established by the report of impartial persons. I shall send on forty or fifty men this autumn to clear and build cabins. These men are to be paid in land, and to be found for one year in provisions. It is my intention to go there with several of my friends next year. If you should incline to partake and to join us, I will *give you 10000 acres.*" [17] To Lynch, to the Kentuckians, to friends in the East like Biddle and Latrobe, to Wilkins, an old friend whom he had been unable to meet in Pittsburgh, all the talk was of the Bastrop Purchase, of cabins and soil and settlement, and peaceful pursuits. [18] In the nebulous, contingent future, possible exploits in Mexico; in the meantime, good, sound pioneering. Nowhere in private, confidential correspondence with trusted friends, is there breathed a word during the autumn of 1806 of secession, disunion, the West or New Orleans.

The purchase price was supplied by the funds raised between Blennerhassett and Alston. Lynch received in cash four or five thousand dollars, some thirty thousand dollars of his paper obligations were assumed, and Burr agreed to make good his contract with Edward Livingston in New Orleans. It has been said that the title was bad. Burr was too good a lawyer to pay out a considerable sum on a title without merit. By international law, the United States must acknowledge as valid all pre-existing contracts and titles in the Louisiana Territory. The Bastrop grant had been released from its conditions by the Spanish Governor, and must therefore stand as an outright grant. And, on the frontier, a doubtful title could be easily made good by solid, tangible possession, as Burr well knew.

There was considerable talk afterwards that Burr, in his endeavors to raise forces for the Washita and Mexico, had hinted, if not said outright, that his plans had the secret and unofficial approval of the Administration. Jefferson went so far as to allege the showing of a forged letter, purporting to be from the Secretary of War. But this was during the heat of the trial, and was based on vague statements concerning a letter left unguarded on a table while Burr pretended to leave the room, with a hasty, running glance by the honorable witness at its contents before Burr should return. [19] Blennerhassett, his tongue wagging on oiled hinges, was without doubt talking recklessly to all and sundry — of gold, of jewels, of empire, of titles, of Emperor Burr, of plunder, of benevolent Washington — doing infinite damage to Burr without Burr being in the slightest degree aware of what was going on.

On October 25, 1806, Burr sent his aide, De Pestre, back to New York and Philadelphia to communicate with his Eastern friends and to see Yrujo. Burr had not yielded up hope of squeezing money out of Spain. Given enough, with the new turn of events on the

Sabine, of which they were just beginning to receive magnified reports, and Mexico might still be in sight. Even if Yrujo would not pay, at least he could be lulled to a state of quiescence concerning Burr's activities.

But before De Pestre arrived, Yrujo was already sending Cevallos a weird account of Burr's army of 500 men, of his purpose to seize Government arms, descend on Natchez and New Orleans and start the Revolution. In fact, wrote Yrujo with conviction, Burr had already composed a Declaration of Independence for New Orleans and the West. Yet, in spite of his gullibility, an uneasy suspicion persisted that all was not well. Though he had been assured that Burr's project against Spain had been abandoned, and that " on the contrary he wishes to live on good terms with Spain, I have written to Governor Folch of West Florida to be on his guard; and although I am persuaded that by means of Governor Folch's connection with General Wilkinson, he must be perfectly informed of the state of things and of Burr's intentions, I shall write to-day or to-morrow another letter to the Governor of Baton Rouge to be on the alert." [20] Wilkinson, who was ostensibly facing the Spaniards at the Sabine in hostile attitude!

On December 4th, Yrujo wrote again, in some perplexity. By this time the fat was in the fire, and all the country was rocking with wild alarms over what Burr was really planning in the West. De Pestre had visited him, and assured him that the Spanish possessions were not to be involved; that any reports to the contrary were dust clouds to hide the real purposes. Yrujo was not convinced. He began to see that he had been made a dupe from the very beginning. " I wrote to the governors of both Floridas and to the Viceroy of Mexico . . ." he told Cevallos, " recommending them to watch the movements of Colonel Burr and of his adventurers. This is an excess of precaution, since by this time they must not only know through the New Orleans and Natchez newspapers of the projects attributed to Colonel Burr, but also through the confidential channel of the No. 13 of the Marquis of Casa Calvo's cipher with the Prince of Peace [Godoy] who is one of the conspirators, and who is to contribute very efficaciously to the execution of the scheme in case it shall be carried into effect." *No. 13,* Spanish spy, was, of course, Wilkinson. But Yrujo had become suspicious even of Wilkinson, hitherto seemingly faithful in disclosing to Spain Burr's plans as they unfolded. With a fine knowledge of that agile gentleman's character, he sent warnings broadcast that " although No. 13 seems to have acted in good faith hitherto, his fidelity could not be depended upon if he had a greater interest in violating it, and that therefore they must be cautious in listening to him and be very vigilant in regard to events that would probably happen in their neighborhood." [21] Yrujo need not have worried. Already Wilkinson had consulted his own interest and decided to betray Burr. Already the damning accusation was on its way to Jefferson.

3. THE CAT JUMPS

Meanwhile, what had been happening on the Sabine? Wilkinson's activities were super-Protean in their character; Janus, the two-faced God of the Romans, Brahma, Vishnu and Shiva, the Indian Triad, with their many faces and a thousand eyes, were but a simple homogeneity compared to him. No wonder that Burr, without word from his fellow conspirator, depending solely on rumor and counter-rumor, was himself compelled to daily inconsistency. One day the news was such as seemed to indicate that Wilkinson was proceeding according to a predetermined schedule — and Mexico and West Florida came to the fore; the next day his apparent supineness reduced Burr to anxious despair — and peaceful settlement on the Washita submerged all thoughts of present conquest. Wilkinson himself was for a long time not quite sure of his own course. Of one thing only was he certain, as Yrujo had justly observed: his own peculiar interests must be served first, last and always.

In October, 1805, almost a year before, Spain had advanced a small force across the Sabine to occupy the posts of Bayou Pierre and Nana, in what Jefferson claimed to be American territory. On February 1, 1806, Major Porter, commanding at Natchitoches, was ordered by the War Department to dislodge the intruders, even at the cost of bloodshed. On February 5th, a detail of sixty men reached the Spanish camp at Bayou Pierre. The Spanish commander, after due protest, bowed to overwhelming force — he had only *twenty* men — and signed an agreement that he would withdraw within six days. But Salcedo, Captain-General of Mexico, ordered six hundred militia to the front. He had no intention of abandoning his positions. The Arroyo Hondo, he claimed, was the western boundary of Louisiana, not the Sabine. There was also Burr's expedition in the offing. To the Spanish officials, the sudden aggression of the Americans was but part and parcel of Burr's plans. Governor Claiborne of Orleans worked himself into a tremendous case of nerves over the proximity of the alien, and bombarded Jefferson with pleas for reinforcements against *Spanish* aggression. The border was in a state of touchiness where anything might happen.

By July, the Spanish troops, with Salcedo's militia, were back again over the Sabine. The news threw the Americans into a fever of alarm. Claiborne and Mead, Acting Governor of Mississippi, called for volunteers to repel the invasion. Major Porter was on the ground, and, according to his instructions, should have proceeded at once into action. But Wilkinson, who should have been on hand, was still in St. Louis. From that distant coign of vantage, he had sent private orders to Porter forbidding any attempt on the Spanish positions. Claiborne heard of this and complained to Mead, " My present impression is that ' all is not right.' I know not whom to censure, but it seems to me that there is wrong somewhere. Either the orders to Major Porter (which have been published) ought not to have been issued or they should have been adhered to and supported." [22] Poor Claiborne was to continue in a sad state of befuddlement for many a day.

Wilkinson, however, knew what he was doing. He had no intention of precipitating a war with Spain — especially when he was not on the ground to direct its movements — until he had definitely made up his mind which way the cat was going to jump. Even though Dearborn's orders to him had been explicit and final: he was to proceed at once — the order was dated May 6, 1806 — to Orleans to take command and " by all means in your power, repel any invasion of the territory of the United States east of the River Sabine, or north or west of the bounds of what has been called West Florida." [23] Yet Wilkinson calmly remained in St. Louis, and countermanded all War Department orders. There were several inducing considerations for this outright insubordination in the face of the enemy. He was still at cross-purposes with himself; playing around with the Burr project, and keeping in communication with Spain as *No. 13.*

On September 7th, however, he finally came to Natchez. Claiborne and Mead were pushing matters, and might create an impossible situation for him if he did not arrive to take command. The day after his arrival he wrote ingenuously to Dearborn that the Territorial militia were proposing to expel the enemy, " but I shall discourage their march until I have penetrated the designs of the Spaniard, and may find him deaf to the solemn appeal which I shall make to his understanding, his interest and his duty." [24] The war was rapidly assuming an *opéra bouffe* aspect.

Nevertheless he called for the Mississippi volunteers to join him, enlarged his posts, and made active preparations for an invasion of the Spanish frontier. On September 19th he demanded from Claiborne the assemblage at Natchitoches, which he had constituted his Headquarters, of all troops and militia in New Orleans. The Territories responded with enthusiasm. The militia poured in. Here at last was the long-delayed war with Spain.

For something had happened — something which seems to have decided Wilkinson to turn on his old employer, Spain, and commit the United States to war. For the moment he was definitely determined to cast his lot with Burr. The first news of a battle, the first attack on Spanish forces, would be the signal for Burr to rally the West, to come out into the open with a forthright declaration of his intentions, and sweep down the Ohio and Mississippi, like a gigantic, accreting snowball, gathering new volunteers on his way. Then — on to Baton Rouge, Pensacola, Vera Cruz and Mexico City — once and forever to sweep the Spaniard off the northern continent!

Such was the idea. Just what it was that had made up Wilkinson's mind for him — for the moment — is not readily discernible from the evidence. Perhaps it was the unbounded enthusiasm for war he had seen displayed in the Territories, perhaps the thought of himself as an all-conquering hero had created a state of auto-intoxication; perhaps some Spanish official had hurt his vanity by an indiscretion. Whatever the inducing cause, for a short period he was resolved. He even committed himself to paper, something he had been hitherto very careful to avoid. On September 28th he wrote to General John Adair, one of the conspirators: " The time long looked for by many & wished for by more has now arrived, for subverting the Spanish government in Mexico — be ready & join me; we will want little more than light armed troops . . . More will be done by marching than by fighting . . . Unless you fear to join a Spanish intriguer [Wilkinson] come immediately — without your aid I can do nothing." [25]

The same day he sent off another letter — this one to Senator John Smith, also one of the initiate. " I shall as surely push them [the Spaniards] over the Sabine — and out of Nacogdoches as that you are alive, although they outnumber me three to one," he declared vaingloriously. " You must speedily send me a force to support our pretensions . . . 5000 mounted infantry . . . may suffice to carry us forward as far as Grand River, there we shall require 5000 more to conduct us to Mount el Rey . . . after which from 20 to 30,000 will be necessary to carry our conquests to California and the Isthmus of Darien. I write in haste, freely and confidentially, being ever your friend." [26] Strangely enough, no letter to Burr, the head and front of the movement, whose followers, then gathering on the Ohio, were obviously the troops to which he referred in such geometric progression.

On September 23rd, Wilkinson was as good as his word — temporarily. He wrote sternly to the Spaniards that if they did not evacuate the west bank of the Sabine immediately, he would march on them in force. To which Cordero, in command at Nacogdoches, replied that he could do nothing in the premises until he heard from Salcedo.[27] The situation bristled with warlike consequences. But suddenly it cleared through the act of Herrera, in command at Bayou Pierre. Without any orders from his superiors, he commanded a retreat on September 27th, before Wilkinson, now hot for war, could proceed to carry his threat into execution. The west bank of the Sabine was clear of the Spaniard, Wilkinson had won a great — and bloodless — victory, and the crisis in the relations of Spain and the United States was over.

McCaleb considers that this unexpected retreat had set at naught Wilkinson's plans to force the issue of war; that without war, Burr's filibuster must prove futile, and it was then and there that Wilkinson determined to jettison his old comrade, and make his peace with Spain. In a limited sense this is true. In the short period from September 8th to the end of the month, he had been ready to carry on according to schedule. In a measure, his shift had been forced on him by circumstance. Now the circumstance had changed back to the old norm. The fever died. He was ready once again to betray all and sundry to his own advantage. But in fact he had determined on such a course — subject to contingencies like the little passage of arms on the Sabine — long before. As long before, in fact, as the receipt of Daniel Clark's warning; as long before, it may be, as the very initiation of the conspiracy, which might have been merely a threat directed at Spain to be more liberal and open-pocketed to such an extremely valuable agent as No. 13 was proving himself to be.

In proof of his new change of purpose, it is only necessary to view his ensuing actions. Where, heretofore, he had been bold — in speech, at least — now that there were no Spaniards between him and the Sabine, he temporized. He wrote Dearborn on October 4th that he would proceed in a few days to the Sabine,[28] but on October 8th, two weeks after the retreat of the Spaniards, he was still in camp. On that fatal day, Samuel Swartwout, who had missed him at St. Louis and followed him down the Mississippi, appeared at Wilkinson's quarters, armed with Burr's cipher letter of July 29th. It was a cruel jest of fate that he arrived at this particular moment. A short two weeks earlier, and he would have caught Wilkinson in the full flush of warlike intent. Burr's letter, breathing false information and spurious ardor, would have kindled the General's vanity to the bursting-point. A quick march, a sudden attack on Bayou Pierre, and not all Jefferson's pacific intentions, not all Wilkinson's own after-hesitations, could have stopped the forward sweep of events. Willy-nilly, he must have thrown in his lot with Burr, and the course of American history would have been considerably changed.

Now, however, the complexion of things had altered. The Spaniards were gone, two weeks had elapsed, and the General's first rush of hot blood had had much time to cool. Perhaps he had received assurances from Folch that he would be well taken care of. In any event, he had resumed his old role — as comfortable to him as a well-worn glove — No. 13 in the pay of Spain. And — he was the heroic Generalissimo of the American forces.

The sudden apparition of Swartwout was like that of an unbidden ghost at the feast. It was the evening of October 8th. When the unexpected messenger entered his quarters, Colonel Cushing was present. Much was to be made later of the *manner* in which Swartwout handed him the incriminating despatch. Wilkinson swore it was slipped to him surreptitiously, after Cushing had retired.[29] Swartwout denied that there was anything secretive about his movements. It really does not matter.

Wilkinson read the slightly bombastic text with increasing perturbation of mind, received Swartwout's help in the decipherment. Then he retired into the silences to consider his course of action. Burr, he noted with an awful clarity, had already commenced operations. They were too far forward to be abandoned now. In fact, as far as Burr was concerned, there was nothing else he could do; he was too deeply committed. But Burr's inevitable coming must necessarily upset Wilkinson's apple cart. The Spaniards, already suspicious of his good faith, would be sure he, Wilkinson, was involved, and a lucrative source of income would be abruptly cut off. Should he urge Burr to give up the entire scheme, Burr, in his resentment, might embroil him with the Administration in Washington. There were certain letters that might be wrongly construed in certain quarters. In which case he stood an excellent chance of losing his command, which, in turn, would mean the abatement of Spain's pension; for his services to Spain must then fall considerably in value. He was damned if he did, and he was damned if he didn't.

In the agony of these wrestlings of spirit, a brilliant resolvement of all his difficulties occurred to him. The letter he had just received from Burr, instead of spelling disaster, actually meant his salvation. By the alteration of a few phrases which too closely incriminated him, he would use it as an instrument to denounce Burr as a traitor to the United States, and as proof to Spain that he had actively warded off a terrible danger from its possessions. Thereby he would kill two birds with one stone, establish himself more solidly than ever in the confidence of Jefferson and Spain alike, and reap the proper rewards of his virtue. The fact that, in the doing, Burr, his old comrade in arms, Dayton, Smith, Adair, Truxton, all friends, and a host of others whom he did not even know, might be ruined beyond redemption, their very lives imperiled, seemingly made no difference to the supple General. He was about to consolidate his own position, and that was all that mattered. In all history, there is no record of a more sinister or vicious betrayal.[30]

4. The Betrayal

Early the following morning, Wilkinson took Colonel Cushing aside and told him in a frightened voice and with much swearing of secrecy that he had just discovered that Burr was plotting to overthrow the United States Government. Young Swartwout was his emissary, but he, Wilkinson, would save the Union, come what may. There was, in fact, only one course to pursue. March at once to the Sabine, make immediate peace with the Spaniards, and then devote all his might to crush the traitors.[31] Thereby — though he forgot to tell Cushing this — he would serve Spain, prove later to Jefferson that he had promptly denounced the conspiracy, and open the way for those measures which would place the unsuspecting Burr in his power immediately upon his arrival.

But to Swartwout he said nothing. He welcomed him with effusive cordiality, kept him as his guest at Natchitoches for a full week — pumping him dry of all the details of the nefarious plot, he was to declare later — actually, because he wished no suspicions of his betrayal to leak out. Then Swartwout went on to New Orleans as had been arranged, there to meet Peter Ogden, who had gone down the river direct with his despatch.

For still another week after Swartwout's departure, Wilkinson dallied in camp, doing nothing, saying nothing, while the nation ostensibly was in the direst peril. Why? Perhaps he was still not quite sure of his course; perhaps he was waiting to hear from his Spanish friends.

Then, one day, he found himself confronted with a situation in which further delay might prove disastrous. Newspapers had filtered down from the West, newspapers filled with denunciations of Burr and an alleged scheme of disunion, and, *mirabile dictu,* daring actually to accuse him, General James Wilkinson, as an " intriguer and pensioner of Spain, now associated with Aaron Burr in reviving the old Spanish Conspiracy." His hand was forced.

On October 20, 1806, he wrote a letter to Jefferson, cautious, feeling his way, mentioning no names. " A numerous and powerful association, extending from New York through the Western States, to the territory bordering on the Mississippi, has been formed, with the design to levy and rendezvous eight or ten thousand men in New Orleans, at a very near period; and from thence, with the co-operation of a naval armament, to carry an expedition against Vera Cruz. Agents from Mexico, who were in Philadelphia in the beginning of August, are engaged in this enterprise; these persons have given assurances, that the landing of the proposed expedition will be seconded by so general an insurrection, as to insure the sub-version of the present government, and silence all opposition in three or four weeks. . . . It is unknown under what authority this enterprise has been projected, from whence the means of its sup-port are derived, or what may be the intentions of its leaders, in relation to the territory of Orleans. But it is believed that the maritime co-operation will depend on a British squadron from the West Indies, under ostensible command of American masters. . . . This information has recently reached the reporter through sev-eral channels so direct and confidential, that he cannot doubt the facts set forth; and, therefore, he considers it his duty to make this representation to the executive by a courier extraordinary, to whom he has furnished five hundred dollars." [32]

In the main, a truthful description of the expedition, except that Wilkinson *knew* who the leaders were. But this was a mere fili-buster, nothing treasonable to the United States, except for the vague reference to possible intentions as to New Orleans. To sup-port this official communication, however, Wilkinson sent an-other, dated October 21st, addressed also to Jefferson, but marked " personal and confidential." Here he unbosomed himself, became truly terrifying, and rose to heights of insinuation, deceit, bom-bast.

" Although my information appears too direct & circumstantial to be fictitious," he wrote, " yet the magnitude of the Enterprise, the desperation of the Plan, and the stupendous consequences with which it seems pregnant, stagger my belief & excite doubts of the reality, against the conviction of my senses; and it is for this reason I shall forbear to commit Names, because it is my desire to avert a great public Calamity, & not to mar a salutary design, or to injure anyone undeservedly. I have never in my whole Life found myself in such circumstances of perplexity and Embarrassment as at present; for I am not only uninformed of the prime mover & ultimate Objects of this daring Enterprize, but am ignorant of the foundations on which it rests, of the means by which it is to be supported, and whether any immediate or Colateral *protection,* internal or external, is expected. . . . Should this association be formed, in opposition to the Laws and in defiance of Government, then I have no doubt the revolt of this Territory, will be made an auxiliary Step to the main design of attacking Mexico, to give it a new Master in the place of promised Liberty. Could the fact be ascertained to me, I believe I should hazard my discretion, make the best compromise with Salcedo in my Power, and throw myself with my little Band into New Orleans to be ready, to defend that Capital against usurpation & violence." After which stupendous exposé, the General hesitated, then added a postscript. " Should Spain be disposed to War seriously with us, might not some plan be adopted to correct the delirium of the associates, & by a suitable appeal to their patriotism to engage them in the service of their Country? I merely offer the suggestion as a possible expedient to prevent the Horrors of a civil contest, and I do believe that, with competent authority I could accomplish the object." [33]

This private letter, with its postscript, is truly an astounding production. In one and the same breath, these mysterious conspirators, of whose names and ultimate objects Wilkinson is wholly ignorant, are traitors and villains of the deepest dye, and men on whose patriotism Wilkinson is certain he can rely. A discrepancy that may be explained by the fact that General Wilkinson is still facing two ways. In the body of the letter, his manifest anxiety is clearly to make peace with Spain. But he has not heard as yet from Folch or Salcedo as to his reward for so doing. Should the Spaniards prove indisposed to make him a proper return, then, with Jefferson's consent, he could still ally himself with Burr, hurl himself upon Spain, and proceed as indicated.

But Wilkinson was not through with his furious letter writing. Still a third letter, also " personal and private," went by the same courier, bearing the same date line. In this address to Jefferson, he discloses the real reason for his sudden outburst of accusations. The *Western World,* Kentucky newspaper, had accused him of being associated with Burr. " I have at times been fearful your confidence might be shaken, by the boldness of the vile Calumnies leveled at me," he whines. He is sending along for Jefferson's inspection " numerous public and private testimonials of Honor & applause "; exercises in laudation, garnered with care from his officers for just such an occasion. Surely Jefferson will read the nice things therein stated about his, Wilkinson's, character, and pay no heed to the libelous *Western World*. In fact, he was even suing that newspaper for defamation, and the truth would come out.[34] Unfortunately there is no record of any such action.

The one sorry thing in this entire business, aside from the obvious Wilkinson, is the picture of Jefferson, who certainly cannot be accused of a lack of intelligence, being taken in by such a fraudulent concoction, in which every line shrieks its glaring inconsistencies. Or was he? Was not Jefferson's willingness to believe every word of Wilkinson as the truth and the gospel a mere pretense? Did he not welcome even the aid of the malodorous Wilkinson, as once he had welcomed that of the ineffable Cheetham, to pursue the victim he had marked for final and definitive destruction? Queries to which the end result may give the answer.

Lieutenant Smith, the courier, left with his assorted despatches and testimonials for Washington on October 22nd. The following day, Wilkinson sent off a despatch to Colonel Freeman, commander in New Orleans, requiring him to rush the completion of all fortifications, and hinting mysteriously at causes " too imperious to be resisted, and too highly confidential to be whispered, or even suspected." [35] Thereby he was certain to start a train of whispered alarm in New Orleans, of which he intended taking later advantage.

Within another few days — perhaps he had heard from Salcedo, and the information had been sufficiently encouraging to decide his course — he commenced his long-postponed march to the Sabine. This was a full month after Herrera had retreated, leaving the disputed area clear of even a solitary enemy. But this knowledge did not prevent Wilkinson from acting the conquering hero. He went in overwhelming force, flags flying, drums beating, scouts spread fanwise before him in the most approved military fashion, stopping at every bush for fear of lurking Spaniards. The rabbits stared, and the squirrels chattered volubly.

On October 29th, he was at the bank of the Sabine. The day before he had sent his conditions to Cordero. The two parties, he requested, should retire to Nacogdoches and Natchitoches respectively, far from the possibility of contact. The Spaniards were to agree not to cross the Sabine again, and the Americans were to retrace all the steps they had taken with such martial display, and agree to hold the Arroyo Hondo as a boundary inviolate. All the territory between the Sabine and the Arroyo Hondo, in effect, was to become neutral ground. Then, proposed Wilkinson, let the home Governments decide the moot question of boundaries. In short, Wilkinson was giving up everything he had gained, his expedition had been wholly unnecessary, and he had disobeyed specific orders. More, he had assumed diplomatic and plenipotentiary powers for which he had absolutely no authorization.

The Spaniards were more than willing — the proposals were entirely in their favor. If they were surprised, they concealed it admirably. It is impossible to avoid the suspicion that they knew in advance what Wilkinson's moves were going to be. On November 5, 1806, the pact known as the " Neutral Ground Treaty " was signed on the terms proposed, and Wilkinson marched back to Natchitoches, carefully concealing from his troops, however, the fact that any such treaty had been made. The whole arrangement was to become a thing of mystery and doubt for a long time after.

Wilkinson's confidence that Jefferson would uphold his course was not misplaced. On November 8th, three days after the signing of the treaty, and of course without any knowledge thereof, Jefferson wrote him that he was extremely desirous of avoiding conflict with Spain, and that he left it to Wilkinson's discretion to arrange such terms and such boundaries as he could.[36] Wilkinson had simply anticipated him.

As for Salcedo, his elation knew no bounds. " This treaty," he wrote Viceroy Iturrigaray on December 3rd, " insures the integrity of the Spanish dominions along the whole of the great extension of frontier." [37] Irregular, unauthorized, unsanctioned by Congress, the arrangement actually held until 1819, when a final and definitive agreement was reached between the contracting powers. Once more Wilkinson had proved that the laborer is worthy of his hire.

The way was now clear to crush Burr. Wilkinson, back in Natchitoches, declaimed to Cushing, now in New Orleans: " The plot thickens, yet all but those concerned, sleep profoundly. My God! what a situation has our country reached. Let us save it if we can . . . I think officers who have families at Fort Adams should be advised to leave them there, for if I mistake not, we shall have an insurrection of blacks as well as whites." This indeed was a novel touch, intended to excite New Orleans to such a pitch of alarm that it would yield without protest to all of Wilkinson's measures. " No consideration, my friend," he continued impressively, " of family, or personal inconvenience, must detain the troops a moment longer than can be avoided, either by land or by water; they must come, and rapidly. On the fifteenth of this month, Burr's declaration is to be made in Tennessee and Kentucky; hurry, hurry after me, and if necessary, let us be buried together in the ruins of the place we shall defend." [38] Wild talk, yes — but serving a purpose. Passions must be inflamed to a degree which would leave Burr speechless, should he attempt to confront Wilkinson. If he should be slain in an access of righteous anger, and his mouth stopped forever, so much the better.

On November 12th, he sent another courier to Jefferson — one Isaac Briggs — with more horrendous news. " Many circumstances have intervened since my last, confirmatory of the information received, and demonstrative of a deep, dark and wicked conspiracy." It embraced the " young and old, the Democrat and the Federalist, the native and the foreigner, the patriot of '76 and the exotic of yesterday, the opulent and the needy, the ins and the outs; and I fear it will receive strong support in New Orleans, from a quarter little suspected." Stopping a moment for breath, he added further masterly touches. He expected a descent of 7000 men, and he had only a handful. " We must be sacrificed unless you should be able to succor me seasonably by sea, with two thousand men and a naval armament, to command the mouth of the Mississippi. To give effect to my military arrangements, it is absolutely indispensable New Orleans and its environs should be placed under martial law." [39] There indeed was the root of the matter. Martial law! Himself dictator of Orleans, able to ride roughshod over protesting citizens and Governor Claiborne alike (was Claiborne the " quarter little suspected "?) . More, martial law would be an effective way of dealing with Burr on his arrival, a justification of a drumhead trial and summary execution even.

The following day he was whistling another tune. But this was to his confidential friend, Walter Burling, whom he wrote privately to proceed to Mexico " to avail yourself of the present alarm produced by Colonel Burr's projects [engineered by himself], to effect a visit to the city of Mexico by the interior and to return by water, in order to examine both routes, relatively to their practicability and the means of defence the Spaniards possess. I have long been in quest of this information." [40] And with Burling went a passport from Wilkinson, announcing to all and sundry that he was being sent to the Viceroy of Mexico for the purpose of handing him a detailed report of Burr's plans and designs, to wit,

" to carry an expedition against the Territories of his Catholic Majesty, a prince at peace with the United States." Wilkinson was attempting the almost incredible feat of riding three plunging and diverging horses at once!

Over two months later Burling rode into Mexico City and delivered his despatches to the Viceroy, who sent copies along to Spain. " In it you will see," he wrote Cevallos, " that he [Wilkinson] lays great stress on the measures which he has taken, at the risk of his life, fame, and fortune in order to save, or at least to protect this kingdom from the attacks of the insurgents." But the Viceroy had had dealings with the American General, *No. 13* in the Spanish cipher, before. " He finally comes to what I had anticipated," he remarked ironically, " the question of payment for his services. He asks for $85,000 in one sum, and $26,000 in another. But, not content with this, he says he considers it just and equitable to be reimbursed for those sums he has been obliged to spend in order to sustain the cause of good government, order, and humanity. Understanding the desires of the General I destroyed his letter, after it had been translated, in the presence of his aide-de-camp." The General becomes positively fascinating in his stupendous audacity as the story unfolds! The Viceroy, amused at these demands, put Burling off with fair words, insinuated that he " wished him happiness in the pursuit of his righteous intentions," and made preparations to return the messenger forthwith to the United States.[41]

Defeated in his modest demands, Wilkinson still was able to make a profit out of the journey. He turned now to Jefferson, whom he had found always most accommodating, sent him a report of conditions in Mexico, purporting to have come from Burling, and requested a modest $1,500 for the expenses of the exploration. Which Jefferson actually caused to be paid to him.[42]

CHAPTER XXII

THE MAN HUNT STARTS

1. ACCUSATIONS IN KENTUCKY

THE "Conspiracy" was now developing on three different stages, flung far over the uttermost stretches of the United States. New Orleans — and Wilkinson; Washington — and Jefferson; Kentucky — and Burr.

Of what was happening in New Orleans and Washington, Burr was blissfully ignorant. Just at the moment, he was having troubles of his own in Kentucky. Blennerhassett's loose talk, his silly series of articles on the philosophy of Western disunion, the rumors started by Stephen Minor, and, above all, the publications of the *Western World,* were beginning to have their cumulative effect.

Joseph Hamilton Daveiss was the United States District Attorney for Kentucky, and one of the few Federalists in that area. He himself had adopted his middle name as a token of his idolatry for the great Federalist leader. Burr had slain his idol. Associated with him was Humphrey Marshall, former Federalist Senator, related to him by marriage. Neither had any use for Republicanism in any form, nor for Burr. These gentlemen, oases in a political desert, were positive from the very first that Aaron Burr, the murderer of Hamilton, meant no good by his projects and journeys. Furthermore, a show of activity on their part might sooner or later be converted into political coin of the realm, and, in any event, it was an excellent opportunity for embarrassing the administration of Mr. Jefferson, for whom they had nothing but the heartiest contempt.

As early as January 10, 1806, following Burr's first tour, Daveiss had written Jefferson to warn him of an intrigue looking to the separation of the West. "This plot," he insisted, "is laid wider than you imagine. Mention the subject to no man from the Western country, however high in office he may be." [1]

Not hearing from the President, Daveiss wrote again, on February 10th, this time accusing Burr directly, and repeating his admonition to "show this letter to nobody. Mr. Burr's connections are more extensive than any man supposes." Enclosed was a list of suspects.[2]

344

On February 15th, Jefferson finally answered by a letter that crossed Daveiss's second in the mails, asking for further information. Daveiss was only too happy to furnish it again, with embellishments. Thereafter he bombarded the President with letter after letter, only to meet with a stone wall of silence. Finally, choking with indignation, he turned to Madison on August 14, 1806, wondering if " it is possible the president might have known that my politics were of the federal kind, on main questions, and have suffered himself to be influenced by it." [3]

This was answered by Madison, enclosing a letter of Jefferson dated September 12th, in which the President blandly acknowledged the receipt of each and every letter, and informed Daveiss that " you may rely on the most inviolable secrecy as to the past and any future communications you may think proper to make." Nothing else! [4]

Daveiss, by this time filled to the bursting-point, determined to make all the capital possible out of the situation. Like a veritable David, he alone would crush the Goliath who was trying to disrupt the Union, and thereby gain the admiring gratitude of the nation.

There was an instrument ready at hand. By one of those remarkable coincidences frowned on in novels and quite common in real life, one John Wood, and one Joseph M. Street, had come to Frankfort, Kentucky, during the winter of 1805–06, journeying from Richmond " on a voyage of adventure, for employment and support." [5] They were printers and writers by trade, and, if the field were right, intended to publish a newspaper in the interests of the uplift in Kentucky.

By July 1, 1806, they had contracted with the *Palladium*, printing plant and newspaper, for their own venture, the *Western World*. In spite of the fact that it was to be a Republican sheet, Daveiss and Marshall were profoundly interested. For, strangely enough, this John Wood was the very same gentleman whose libelous history of John Adams had been so poorly suppressed by Burr, and with such disastrous results. The pair discovered this, and thereupon the editors' fortunes were made. On July 4th the *Western World* initiated a series of articles, in which Wood's old knowledge of Burr, as well as of Miranda, was mingled in a hellish broth with information furnished by Daveiss and Marshall of Wilkinson, Brown, Sebastian, Innes — all of them hitherto opposed to Daveiss. The concoction was spewed out as the " Old Spanish Conspiracy," revived in a new and more terrible form. The *Western World* was an instant success; it became the general topic of conversation wherever people met, its copies were snatched away as fast as they could be printed. " Society was agitated," those whose names were mentioned fumed, " Wood kept his closet" prudently, but Street roamed the streets defiantly. He suffered as a result of his temerity. Those he had maligned set upon him in the streets, assaulted and wounded him, and, to cap the climax, had him hustled off to jail. Whereupon Daveiss and Marshall promptly appeared and went his bail.[6]

On October 15th, " An Observer," probably Marshall himself, published an address in the *Western World* to arouse Kentucky to a sense of its peril. Burr, he declaimed, was working for disunion, and had become the present head and front of the old Spanish Associates. This man, he declared dramatically, is now in your midst, and the Federal Government must act, Congress must act, the people must act.[7] A clear invitation to violence.

Already the people had been aroused by the constant baiting. On October 6th, the citizens of Wood County, across the river in Virginia — in which County Blennerhassett's Island was situated — had held a mass meeting, denouncing the " apparently hostile movements and designs of a certain character [Burr]," and ordering the mustering of the militia.[8] Blennerhassett was then in Kentucky with the Alstons; Burr was absent at Lexington.

Mrs. Blennerhassett, alone on the Island, heard of the excitement, the mutterings of the people, the open threats, and, fearing mob violence, sent Peter Taylor, her gardener, on October 20th with a note to Burr warning him that trouble was brewing. Not knowing where to locate him, however, she sent Taylor first to Senator Smith at Cincinnati to discover his whereabouts. Smith, by this time alarmed for his own personal safety, would have disavowed all knowledge of both Burr and Blennerhassett to the gardener. But Taylor persisted, and Smith, who was serving customers at the time in his store, feared that continued argument would attract unpleasant attention. Whereupon he yielded, took Taylor upstairs, and, with a great show of secrecy, told him Burr was at Lexington. He also gave him a hastily penned note to deliver. This note was a masterpiece of evasion, an attempt by an affectation of ignorance to dissociate himself from Burr in the public eye.

Taylor went on to Lexington, where he found Burr at Jourdan's place. Though he had never seen Burr before, he told him at once — according to his testimony — " If you come up our way, the people will shoot you." On October 27th, the gardener started back for the Island with Blennerhassett, leaving Burr alone to face the gradually rising storm. On the way back — Taylor later testified — Blennerhassett opened himself even more volubly than he had to any one else; spoke of Mexico, of Burr's becoming King, and Mrs. Alston the Queen after him; that all of them would make their fortunes, that the Spaniards were only waiting for their arrival to revolt.[9] Even if the gardener's story were true, there was not even a hint of treasonable design in the tale.

Burr read both letters and frowned. As for Mrs. Blennerhassett's warning, he dismissed that without much thought. Burr had never been the man to fear mob violence. But Smith's note cut him to the quick. Already, at the first hint of trouble, his associates were hastening to quit him. He sat down and wrote back sharply. " I was greatly surprised and really hurt by the unusual tenor of your letter of the 23d, and I hasten to reply to it, as well for your satisfaction as my own. If there exists any design to separate the Western from the Eastern States, I am totally ignorant of it. I never harbored or expressed any such intention to any one, nor did any person ever intimate such design to me." [10]

Burr was alone now. Blennerhassett had gone back to the Island to safeguard his property, the Alstons, all unknowing, had returned to South Carolina, De Pestre had returned to the East to see Yrujo, Smith had cut adrift, and Daveiss was now preparing to act on his own, for the greater glory of the United States and the aggrandizement of the Federalist party. Nevertheless, Burr drove calmly ahead with the work in hand, disdaining all thoughts of personal danger, of making his retreat while there was yet time.

On November 3rd he visited Jackson and placed an order with him for five additional boats and large quantities of provisions. His Eastern contingents of recruits were shortly expected, those from Pittsburgh and elsewhere were on the way, and it was necessary to make haste now, before winter closed in on them and made progress perilous. The title deeds to the Bastrop grant were safely recorded, and, for the present, colonization and home building were all that could be considered. He gave Jackson $3,500 as an advance on the orders, and Jackson turned them over to John Coffee, his partner, for execution. Jackson and his friends had been busy raising recruits — to the number of some seventy-five.[11]

On November 5th, District Attorney Daveiss struck his first blow. He appeared before the United States District Court at Frankfort, and, amid a sudden hush, moved Judge Harry Innes for the issuance of a compulsory process directed to the arrest of Aaron Burr, and for a second process to compel the attendance of witnesses.

Judge Innes denied the motion with some acerbity — pointing out certain irregularities in the application. He and Daveiss were political opponents, and Innes was still smarting under various accusations against himself instigated by the District Attorney. But Burr, then at Lexington, heard of the motion, sent word that he would appear voluntarily, and followed almost on the heels of the messenger. On November 8th he appeared in court and quietly demanded an examination of his acts, in spite of the quashing of Daveiss' motion. Innes thereupon impaneled a Grand Jury, and adjourned court until November 12th for the summoning of witnesses. On the day set, the courtroom was crowded. All the countryside flocked to the trial of the ex-Vice-President of the United States: partisans of Burr and partisans of Daveiss.

Innes arose and prepared to address the usual remarks to the Grand Jury. Daveiss interrupted and moved for the discharge of the Jury, on the ground that a witness, Davis Floyd, of Indiana, one of Burr's adherents, had failed to appear. The crowd shouted its ridicule of the prosecutor. He had boasted of what he would do to Burr, and now he was turning tail. Burr walked out of the courtroom, accompanied by the cheers of the populace. Remarked the *Palladium,* Republican newspaper and friendly to Burr, " Colonel Burr has throughout this business conducted himself with the calmness, moderation, and firmness which have characterized him through life. He evinced an earnest desire for a full and speedy investigation — free from irritation or emotion; he excited the strongest sensation of respect and friendship in the breast of every impartial person present." [12]

By his exemplary conduct Burr had recovered his failing popularity. Daveiss, Marshall, *et al.* had retired in chagrin at the collapse of their untimely move. But the *Western World* continued to hammer home its charges, shouting Burr and secession to all who would listen. And Daveiss hastened to write vindictively to Jefferson that " the genuine Republicans left no efforts unemployed to injure me . . . The people seemed to vie with each other in folly and a zeal to distinguish and caress this persecuted patriot. . . . You remark in history that there are times in which whole nations are blind; this seemed to me to be one." [13]

The clouds seemed to have cleared from Burr's troubled horizon. He was free to go ahead with his preparations. He could not possibly have known that even then Wilkinson had denounced him to the President, that Jefferson, hitherto quiescent under a growing avalanche of accusations, had finally moved against him, and would not rest until he was destroyed. And, in the meantime, another associate, all unknowing to Burr, had fallen temporarily by the wayside. This was Andrew Jackson. It is not a particularly lovely episode in his life.

On November 12th, almost at the very moment that Burr was triumphing in the crowded courtroom at Frankfort, Jackson, alarmed at the growing clamor, wrote a violent epistle to Governor Claiborne of Orleans, weird in thought and weirder in manner. " Put your Town in a State of Defence organize your Militia, and defend your City as well against internal enemies as external. . . . Be upon the alert — keep a watchful eye upon our General [Wilkinson] — and beware of an attack, as well from your own Country as Spain, I fear there is something rotten in the State of Denmark — you have enemies within your own City, that may try to subvert your Government, and try to separate it from the Union . . . beware of the month of December — I love my Country and Government, I hate the Dons — I would delight to see Mexico reduced, but I will die in the last ditch before I would yield a part to the Dons or see the Union disunited." [14]

Jackson's biographer claimed that this hasty communication was the result of the visit of a friend who had filled his ears with horrific tales of a gigantic conspiracy.[15] If so, it is but another evidence of Jackson's trigger-like nature. Later he was to repent of this letter and become again one of Burr's most loyal supporters. But not until after Burr's final acquittal on all charges in Kentucky, and a formal meeting had been held between the two men on December 14th.

On November 25th, while Burr was at Louisville, getting his boats and supplies into shape for the final venture, Daveiss appeared once more before Judge Innes, and moved for a warrant to summon a Grand Jury and for subpoenas to compel the attendance of witnesses on a proposed indictment against Burr. When the news was brought to Burr in Louisville, he wrote immediately to Henry Clay, young Kentucky lawyer, to appear for him in the pending proceedings, and started out at once for Frankfort. Clay, to protect his own rising popularity as an attorney and politician, demanded and received from Burr a formal repudiation of all intent on his part to dissever the Union.[16]

On December 2nd, the Grand Jury was impaneled and sworn in by Innes. Then Clay arose to say that Burr courted an investigation, but that the District Attorney, who once before had shrunk from proceeding, now when he thought Burr was beyond the jurisdiction of the Court, had renewed his application for the sole purpose of alarming the Western country with " rumors of an immediate insurrection." But Burr, Clay announced, had foiled his plan, was there in court, and ready to meet the issue immediately.[17]

Daveiss rose somewhat sheepishly and requested an adjournment. Once again material witnesses were absent. This time they were General John Adair and a Mr. Luckett. In spite of Clay's insistence on an immediate joinder of issue, an adjournment was granted to the following day.

On December 3rd, Daveiss laid an indictment against the absent Adair, as an accomplice of Burr in the preparation of an expedition to invade Mexico. In the courtroom nothing was said of Western secession, though outside, Daveiss and his cohorts were stirring up the populace with tales of treason. Daveiss next demanded permission to go before the Grand Jury to aid in the examination of witnesses. Clay, and his associate counsel, John Allen, were instantly on their feet to declare such a procedure novel and indefensible. Daveiss, in a pet, retorted, " I shall consider it as thoroughly smothering this business; if I am prevented from the examining of witnesses." Whereupon Burr arose to inform him quietly that he, too, had been a State Attorney General, that never once had he entered the Grand Jury room, that there was no precedent anywhere for such a practice. To which the presiding Judge assented, and ruled that the District Attorney might confer with the Jury " in matters of law but not as regards facts." [18]

The following day the redoubtable Daveiss appeared with written interrogatories to submit to the Jury for their guidance in the examination of the witness, Thomas Read, in the presentation against Adair. Read jumped to his feet, hot against what he branded a " malicious fabrication " and an attempted impeachment of his character. The passage of arms in the courtroom grew so heated that Innes remarked, with a malicious side glance at Daveiss, whom he detested, that " they had better retire and settle the cause of difference in some other place." [19]

The Grand Jury filed in after the excitement had subsided, and brought in " not a true bill " on Adair. It was a crushing blow to Daveiss, but he rallied to present them with the proposed indictment against Burr. On December 5th, the Jury sent in a request for the files of the *Western World,* and for the attendance of its editors. Street was examined first. He testified that " he was possessed of no information in respect to Colonel Burr that would amount to evidence, and that the articles of agreement mentioned in the second number of the Western World said to have been entered into between Colonel Burr and John Brown, he had been since informed related to the Ohio Canal Company." [20]

John Wood, Burr's ancient Nemesis, was called next. He testified, " I am possessed of no information that will amount to evidence," and that, though he had hitherto believed in Burr's guilt, he was now convinced " the present designs of Colonel Burr is neither against the government or laws of the United States." [21] In fact, so convinced was he, that for the second time in his devious career he came to Burr's rescue with a pamphlet purporting to clear the name of the man he had besmirched.

The case of Daveiss had collapsed ingloriously, the *Western World* and its denunciations stood exposed to the jeers of the country. The Grand Jury hastened to bring in " not a true bill " on Burr, and accompanied it with a ringing exoneration of Burr and Adair.

" The grand jury is happy to inform the court," it read, " that no violent disturbance of the public tranquillity, or breach of laws has come to their knowledge. We have no hesitation in declaring, that having carefully examined and scrutinized all testimony which has come before us, as well on the charges against Burr, as those contained in the indictment preferred to us against John Adair, that there has been no testimony before us which does in the smallest degree criminate the conduct of either of those persons; nor can we, from all the inquiries and investigation of the subject, discover that anything improper or injurious to the interest of the Government of the United States, or contrary to the laws thereof, is designed or contemplated by either of them." [22]

The courtroom rang with cheers. Burr was now the hero of the hour. Daveiss retired in discomfiture, eventually to be dismissed from office by Jefferson for his clumsy handling of the situation. A great ball was given in Burr's honor — the West gave balls on every possible occasion. Once more Burr was in the full floodtide of popularity. The plan to conquer Mexico, even if proved, would certainly not alienate Western favor from its proponent. Not until Jefferson's Proclamation, even then traveling with inexplicable slowness over the Alleghanies, hit the West was there a revulsion of feeling against Burr. Then, for the first time, the accusation that he was intending forcibly to wrest them from the Union, gained belief. Surely the President of the United States, arch-exponent of Republicanism, of homespun democracy against monarchical tendencies, knew whereof he spoke. What Daveiss and Marshall, Federalists, had failed to accomplish, the Proclamation did with lightning swiftness. It is therefore necessary to shift the scene to Washington and hark back a bit in time to understand the consequential course of events.

2. ACTION IN WASHINGTON

Jefferson's attitude toward Burr and the so-called " Conspiracy " is, in its beginnings, extremely puzzling. For over a year the newspapers had been bristling with accusations; Daveiss had written him innumerable letters; George Morgan had charged specific intention of treason; Eaton had been closeted with him as far back as October, 1805; Judge Rufus Easton had written from St. Louis that Wilkinson was fomenting a conspiracy; [23] on October 13, 1806, one James Taylor, of Kentucky, had told Madison that there was a scheme on foot to separate the States, and that Woodbridge & Company, of Marietta, was even then engaged in the construction of ten strong boats, suspiciously resembling gunboats; [24] he had heard vague rumors of Burr's conferences with Merry and Yrujo; the *Western World* had thundered its filth, to be taken up and repeated in every Eastern paper — yet Jefferson had done nothing.

He certainly could not be accused of kindly feelings toward Burr — from 1800 on, his distrust, his aversion, his determination to put Burr effectually out of the way, had steadily increased. Here was an excellent chance to crush his rival. What held him back for long months? Was Burr's contention correct that Jefferson, as well as members of his Cabinet, was well informed concerning his plans; that, in fact, they had unofficially approved of them? It is difficult to say. During all that period the United States quivered time and again on the verge of war with Spain. Miranda's expedition, in spite of later official disavowals, had at least been openly winked at by the Administration. A descent by Burr and a picked corps of volunteer adventurers on Spanish possessions would keep the Spaniards busily occupied, and immeasurably strengthen the position of the United States. Jefferson hated an open and public war, but was not averse to connivance at irregular excursions. Furthermore, with Burr fighting his way through Mexico — and perhaps meeting with death on the field of battle or before a firing-squad, a constant thorn in his own side would be thus painlessly removed. Or, perhaps, he was only waiting for Burr to embroil himself beyond redemption before pouncing upon him. All arid speculation, it may be, but possessing a certain colorable plausibility in accounting for Jefferson's inaction over a period of a year.

On October 22nd, 1806, the Cabinet met and continued in session until October 25th. Jefferson made notes of its transactions. He had a passion for reducing everything to writing. The matter of Burr came up for discussion. All the information at hand, the various accusations, were spread open. It was unanimously decided to write confidential letters to the Governors of Ohio, Mississippi, Indiana and Orleans, to the District Attorneys of Kentucky, Tennessee, and Louisiana, to keep a sharp eye open for Burr, and " on his committing any overt act, to have him arrested and tried for treason, misdemeanor, or whatever other offence the act may amount to." Gunboats were to be ordered up to Fort Adams to stop the passage of any suspicious force. Inasmuch as Wilkinson had been involved by Eaton in his accusations against Burr, and because he had disobeyed peremptory orders to leave St. Louis and proceed to New Orleans, some member of the Cabinet proposed the question " what is proper to be done as to him? " But Jefferson hastily adjourned the first day's session.[25] He was willing enough now to adopt a strong stand on Burr, but Wilkinson was another matter. At that very moment Wilkinson was facing the Spaniards across the Sabine. An order of arrest, a reprimand even, might be fraught with the gravest consequences.

The Cabinet resumed its sessions the following day. It was agreed to send Captain Preble and Decatur to New Orleans to take command, to order eight warships to the troubled waters, and that John Graham, then on his way to New Orleans to assume the duties of Secretary of the Territory, be sent " through Kentucky on Burr's trail, with discretionary powers to consult confidentially with the Governors to arrest Burr if he has made himself liable." But " the question as to General Wilkinson [was] postponed till Preble's departure, for further information." [26]

Then, on October 25th, came a complete reversal of the Cabinet's stand. A mail, it seemed, had just arrived from the West. " Not one word is heard from that quarter of any movements by Colonel Burr. This total silence of the officers of the government, of the members of Congress, of the newspapers, proves he is committing no overt act against law." Therefore all former orders were countermanded, and Graham alone was to proceed as previously directed.[27] It seems as if the Cabinet were only too willing to drop the entire matter. The possibility of the implication of at least some of its members grows more and more plausible. And the Sabine was still dangerous ground.

John Graham started at once on his mission, and the Cabinet turned to other business. Yet Jefferson, on November 3rd, was writing that " Burr is unquestionably very actively engaged in the westward in preparations to sever that from this part of the Union. We learn that he is actually building 10 or 15 boats able to take a large gun & fit for the navigation of those waters. We give him all the attention our situation admits; as yet we have no legal proof of any overt act which the law can lay hold of." [28] The very next day, however, he changed the story. " In the western quarter great things have been meditated," he wrote Duane, the editor of the *Aurora,* " but they will probably end in an attempt upon the public lands, and the question will be whether we have authority legally to oppose them with force." [29] In other words, the colonization of the Bastrop grant, of which part of Burr's scheme Jefferson was obviously aware.

On November 25th, Lieutenant Smith rode into Washington, bearing Wilkinson's three letters; one for public consumption and two addressed privately to Jefferson. Here at last, thought the President, as he hastily tore open the seals, was the legal proof for which he had been waiting before denouncing Burr and his activities. Of course they were no such thing. They contained no more legal evidence of treason than a host of other communications he had already received. Nevertheless Jefferson now acted, where he had unaccountably held back before; and acted from this day on with a persistence and decisiveness that was tantamount to persecution. Why this sudden change of heart? The answer is obvious, though seemingly it has never been pointed out before. Deep down in his heart Jefferson had believed that Wilkinson was allied with Burr. There had been rumors, too, of Wilkinson's suspicious relations with Spain. As long as Wilkinson was attached to Burr, and in command of the far-distant forces on the Sabine, Jefferson's hands were paralyzed. He dared not make any untoward move which might precipitate Wilkinson either into the arms of Spain, or, joined with Burr, into a war of their own. Such a war might even be directed, as Eaton had whispered, against himself and the Government of the United States.

Now he had proof positive that Wilkinson was on his side. Wilkinson had turned on Burr and intended to make peace with Spain. At once the border was safe, the army was loyal, and Burr was cut off from all competent help. It was time to destroy him, once and for all. He called a Cabinet meeting that very same day, laid the revelatory letters before the assembled Secretaries, called now for prompt and vigorous action. Astounded, they agreed to his moves. It was determined to issue a public proclamation denouncing Burr and his " Conspiracy "; to send orders to the military officer at Pittsburgh, if one could be found, to stop all assemblages of armed men on the Ohio; to the collector at Marietta to seize the " gunboats " building in that neighborhood; to General Jackson demanding the aid of his militia; to Captain Bissell at Fort Massac to stop all armed vessels; similar orders to the officers at Chickasaw Bluffs and Fort Adams; and to General Wilkinson at New Orleans giving him *carte blanche* in the prevention of any unlawful expedition.[30]

Two days later, Jefferson issued his famous Proclamation.[31] "Whereas," declared the preamble, "information has been received that sundry persons, citizens of the United States or residents within the same, are conspiring and confederating together to begin and set on foot, provide, and prepare the means for a military expedition or enterprise against the dominions of Spain; that for this purpose they are fitting out and arming vessels in the western waters of the United States, collecting provisions, arms, military stores, and means; are deceiving and seducing honest and well-meaning citizens, under various pretenses, to engage in their criminal enterprises; are organizing, officering, and arming themselves for the same, contrary to the laws in such cases made and provided"; now therefore, the President issues his warning, bidding all participants to cease their activities, on pain and penalty, etc., etc.

Strangely enough, not a single word of a treasonable conspiracy to alienate the West; nothing but a bald statement of a filibuster against Spain. At the very time that this Proclamation was issued, Burr was being triumphantly acquitted of similar charges in Kentucky. Not a word, either, of the author of the alleged expedition against Spain. But every one knew who was meant — as well as if it had been blazoned in letters of fire. More — the nation knew that it was not merely a filibuster which had released the Presidential Proclamation: it was something far more serious, a treasonable plot against the United States itself. From that moment on, all the forces of the nation, all the thoughts of patriotic men, turned in revulsion against the man indicated by the merest indirection.

Five days later, Jefferson reiterated his charges and amplified his explanations in his Annual Message to Congress. Still there was no mention of names, still no description of the conspiracy as aught but a filibuster against Spain. He ended, however, on a significant hint. Would the powers of prevention granted by the laws of the United States, he queried, " not be as reasonable and useful where the enterprise preparing is against the United States? " [32] Jefferson was a master at the gentle art of leading public opinion.

No one was deceived by his methods. Erskine, who had only recently relieved the plaintive Merry as Minister from Great Britain, wrote home that " it is necessary further to remark upon the Proclamation, though it is apparently leveled against sundry persons engaged in military and unlawful enterprises against Spain, yet that it is also well known to allude to supposed conspiracies to effect a separation of the Western States from the rest of the Union, and which Mr. Burr is suspected to be engaged in forming . . . it is not reasonably to be supposed that Mr. Jefferson who has always pursued a temporizing line of conduct, in domestic politics . . . should have adopted such strong measures without having very strong proof of the existence of such conspiracies and of the importance of suppressing them." [33]

So thought the rest of the world. Overnight, Burr's support evaporated into thin air. Friends and sympathizers alike displayed sincere or meretricious belief in his treason, and left him naked to the shafts of his enemies.

3. ATTACK ON THE ISLAND

John Graham, confidential Government emissary, reached Pittsburgh on November 12th, and found everything calm, with no apprehension of any plots unfriendly to the Union.[34] From there he pushed down the Ohio, but at a rate of speed not much greater than that of a snail. One wonders what specific, secret instructions had been given him by Jefferson. Certainly he seemed not in the least anxious to catch up with Burr, or to invoke the majesty of the law against him.

Meanwhile Blennerhassett, on being apprised of the expected attack on his Island by the militia of Wood County, had ridden furiously back to protect his property and family. But Colonel Phelps, in command of the militia, and already uneasy as to his course, had assured Mrs. Blennerhassett that for the present she had nothing to fear. So jubilant was Blennerhassett at this unexpected surcease to his anxieties, that he even tried to induce the courteous Colonel to join their expedition; which offer Phelps declined, avowing nevertheless that he would recommend the speculation to the young men of Wood County.[35] The first fright was over.

A few days later, Blennerhassett received word of Burr's arrest; then of his subsequent acquittal. The Island became a hive of increased activity. Even Blennerhassett perceived by this time that the temper of the country was getting ugly, and that he must rush his preparations and get away at the earliest possible date. Not every one would be as obliging as Colonel Phelps. Then John Graham reached Marietta and talked to him, without, however, revealing the nature of his mission. Blennerhassett, as expansive as ever, took time off to brag of the Washita, of Mexican emprise, of gold and glory. Whereupon Graham continued on his increasingly leisurely journey. On November 28th, he was in Chillicothe, reporting once more that everything was quiet, and that there were no signs of Burr or his agents at work to arouse disaffection.[36]

Nevertheless, obedient to his instructions, he went on to meet Governor Tiffin of Ohio, and disclosed the orders he had received in Washington. The Governor, albeit somewhat skeptical, mentioned the alleged conspiracy in his message to the Ohio Legislature on December 2nd. Four days later the complaisant members passed "An Act to Prevent certain Acts hostile to the Peace and Tranquillity of the United States within the Jurisdiction of the State of Ohio." Armed with this weapon, Tiffin issued orders to arrest the flotilla being constructed on the Muskigum River, and called out three hundred militiamen to invade and capture Blennerhassett Island. On December 9th, Judge Meigs and General Buell proceeded to the Muskigum, where they seized fifteen boats in various stages of completion, some 200 barrels of provisions, but made no arrests.

The Wood County militia, a rather disorganized mob of volunteers inflamed in equal portions with patriotism and the prospect of plunder, prepared to attack the Island. In the meantime, Comfort Tyler of New York, one of Burr's recruiting agents in the East, had landed with four boats and twenty men. On December 10th, he and Blennerhassett received word that the militia intended to attack on the following day. They held a hasty conference, and determined to leave that very night, shoving off under cover of darkness, and abandoning all supplies that could not be stowed into the boats at their command.

But General Edward W. Tupper, of the Ohio militia, was on the Island while the last-minute preparations for departure were being made to the light of torches and bonfires to warm the chilled adventurers. As to what happened next, there is a wide disparity in the evidence. It was on this incident especially that the Government was to attempt to pin the fatal charge of treason and armed insurrection upon Burr and Blennerhassett alike. At the trial in Richmond, the prosecution produced one Jacob Allbright, a slow-witted laborer who had been hired by Blennerhassett "to help build a kiln for drying corn." He testified that on this night of terror and confusion, just as the boats were on the verge of shoving off, General Tupper stepped suddenly forward into the light of the fires, clapped his hands on Blennerhassett's shoulder, and said loudly, " Your body is in my hands, in the name of the common-wealth." But, continued Allbright, even as Tupper made his motion, " seven or eight muskets leveled at him." Tupper looked about him and said, so swore the witness, " Gentlemen, I hope you will not do the like." One of the nearest men, about two yards off, retorted ominously, " I'd as lieve as not." Whereupon, continued Allbright, Tupper changed his speech incontinently, and said that he had all along wished them to escape safe down the river, and bade them Godspeed on their journey. But before he changed his tune, Tupper had first advised Blennerhassett to stay and stand trial, which the latter refused to do.[37]

Strangely enough, Tupper was in court at the time this evidence was given, under subpoena as a Government witness, yet he was not called upon to testify to this most important scene in which he was allegedly the chief actor. The reason for the prosecution's reluctance to place him on the stand was not discovered until long after, when Tupper's deposition, taken by the Government attorneys and Burr jointly, after the event, was found in the obscure and forgotten archives of an Ohio court.[38] The manner in which his testimony was suppressed speaks unflattering volumes on the ethical standards of the Government in conducting its case against Burr.

Tupper deposed that he knew of Burr's proposed expedition, that Burr had told him it was intended for the settlement of the Washita country, that " indeed a man high in office and in the confidence of the Pres. told me [Burr] that I should render a very great service to the public and afford pleasure to the administration, if I should take ten thousand men to that country." Blennerhassett too had recruited his men openly in his presence, offering acreage on the Red River, a year's provisions, and return expenses if they were dissatisfied at the end of that period.

That on the night of December 10th, he had landed on the Island at Blennerhassett's *own invitation,* and was greeted warmly. That it was Blennerhassett himself who told him of the existence of a warrant against him, and of the seizure of the boats — matters of which Tupper had known nothing. Whereupon Tupper advised him to remain and stand trial, " that if their object was such as had been represented, he could have nothing to fear." It would be difficult, he said, to escape with the State in commotion. He, hoped, he went on to tell Blennerhassett, " that you have no idea of making any resistance in case attempts shall be made to arrest you." To which Blennerhassett replied, " No, certainly not, nothing is further from our intention. We shall surrender ourselves to the civil authority whenever it shall present itself." To which Comfort Tyler chimed in, that even " if we were disposed to defend ourselves, we are not in a situation to do it, having but 3 Or 4 Or 5 Guns some Pistols and Dirks on board. At the same time," he added with determination, " should any unauthorized attempts be made to arrest them, they would defend themselves as well as they could." That was all. As for Allbright's testimony, Tupper denied it *in toto*.

Late that night, the frightened men, fearing instant attack, knowing that all the country was aroused against them, shoved off with half a dozen boats and thirty to forty men, poorly armed, insufficiently provisioned, to brave the unknown dangers of the Ohio.

Early the next morning, Colonel Phelps and his brave militia poured tumultuously upon the Island, only to find it deserted. In the ecstasy of their glorious victory they spread over the lovely, landscaped grounds, tore up the fences and used them for firewood, rioted through the stately mansion, burst open the cellars and drank themselves into a stupor with costly liquors, invaded the smokehouse and helped themselves to all the provisions, and in general, conducted themselves like a conquering army sacking a beleaguered town.

On December 13th, fourteen young men in a flatboat, on their way down from Pittsburgh to join Burr, put in at Marietta, and were warned to push off, that mobs were threatening violence to all and sundry connected with Burr. Somewhat bewildered, they continued down the river to the Island, their rendezvous, where they found Blennerhassett and Tyler decamped, and the riotous militia in full possession. Before they knew exactly what was happening, they were seized, their arms confiscated, and themselves placed under arrest. Mrs. Blennerhassett, who had been away to Marietta to get another boat in which to follow her husband, returned to " a sorrowful scene." Her lovely island home was ruined beyond redemption, and herself subjected to insult.

The militia hastily constituted a court on the Island — wholly illegal, of course — to try the prisoners they had captured. After proceedings that were wholly farcical, cooler heads prevailed, and most of the obviously bewildered boys were released. The rest, with Mrs. Blennerhassett, were held temporary prisoners on a boat, but they were permitted to " live elegantly." [39] Finally all were let go, and they followed the others down the Ohio and Mississippi, to reach Bayou Pierre a month later.

Meanwhile the whole West was in a state of panic. The people saw vast armies behind every bush, the country echoed and re-echoed with tales that lost nothing in the telling.

The newspapers outdid each other in retailing the wildest stories. The *Palladium,* hitherto friendly to Burr, testified on December 11th to " vast military preparations " on his part; the *Western Spy,* on December 23rd, declared Blennerhassett to have four keelboats loaded with "military stores," and that 20,000 men were ready to march at Burr's given signal. Cincinnati had an extreme case of nerves. A report that Burr was about to descend on the city with three armed gunboats sent the people into hiding. When, that same night, an anonymous practical joker exploded a bomb on the waterfront, the militia was called out, preparations for defense feverishly rushed, and frantic calls for assistance broadcast by galloping couriers. The next morning the frightened populace felt a bit sheepish. The armed gunboats proved to be quite peaceful vessels belonging to a Louisville merchant and laden with most unwarlike drygoods.[40]

During all this frenzy Graham was pursuing his most leisurely course. From Ohio he moved on to Frankfort, Kentucky, which he reached barely in time for Christmas. Here, too, he obtained an Act similar to that in Ohio. Orders were issued to stop Burr's boats on the Ohio River, the militia was mobilized. But, thanks to Graham's inexplicable delays, the birds had already flown out of the jurisdiction.

4. ODYSSEY

Burr, after his second triumph against Daveiss in Frankfort, returned to Lexington, still unaware of the slow sweep of accusation and mob violence down the river. In October there had been a brief flurry of excitement in which he had been an unwilling participant. He had been at a house in Wilmington, a town near Cincinnati, when a rabble collected " with drums and fifes, beat the rogue's march, and made much disturbance." Burr's host, in a rage, was going to call upon the authorities to disperse the insulting mob, but Burr " begged him not to trouble himself; for he was extremely fond of martial music; that it would not interrupt him should they play all Night." His coolness and courage shamed the mob into sanity, and the next day the ringleaders " called and begged the Col. pardon." [41] But that was two months before, when the loud cheers of the Frankfort populace were still ringing in his ears.

At Lexington he met Adair, and the two rode on to Nashville, arriving on December 14th. Here they parted. Adair went overland to New Orleans, while Burr remained with Jackson, who accepted his assurances (in the presence of a witness) that he meditated no treason, and made no mention of that damning letter he had posted to Claiborne a month before.

Of the five boats which Jackson and his partner, John Coffee, had contracted to build for him, only two were in a fair state of completion. It took eight days longer for even these to be put into shape. It was increasingly necessary now for Burr to get away, so the unfinished boats were abandoned, and a settlement made, whereby $1725.62 was repaid to Burr on his advances. On December 22nd, Burr cast off with two unarmed boats and a few followers.[42]

All this while Jefferson's Proclamation was coming down the river, at a faster pace, it must be acknowledged, than John Graham's peregrinations, who had preceded it by a month, but unconscionably slow nevertheless. This immensely tardy progress of Government orders, issued for the ostensible purpose of arresting a terrible conspiracy, a conspiracy which endangered the very structure of the nation, must always remain one of the mysteries of Jeffersonian politics. Had there been any earnest desire to catch up with Burr while he was still on the Ohio, the time could easily have been halved, and the culprit captured right then and there. First Graham, now the Proclamation. Even *that* Proclamation did not say quite what it meant, and which it was obvious it wished to be surmised.

There is a dispute as to just when the Proclamation reached Nashville. Parton maintains it came to the city on December 23rd, the day *after* Burr's departure; Beveridge is equally positive that it reached there three days *before* Burr left.[43] Unfortunately, Beveridge cites no authority for his statement. The probabilities are much in favor of Parton's position. For Burr would not have got away as easily as he did. The Proclamation threw Nashville into a delirium of alarm and indignation. Jefferson, by implication, had made Burr into a traitor. All the rumors they had heard, all the wild reports in the air, were thereby confirmed. Burr was burned in effigy in the public square, and threats against the conspirators split the heavens. Jackson, now once more on good terms with Burr, had even permitted his nephew to accompany him, and furnished him with a letter to Claiborne, a course he certainly would not have taken in the face of Presidential prohibition.[44] Doubtless the real truth is that Burr, whose methods of obtaining advance information have already been commented on, had received secret notice and had decided to leave in good time.

The Proclamation arrived on his very heels; on January 1st, Jackson received special orders from Washington to mobilize his militia, to hold them in readiness to march, and to use every means available to frustrate the designs of the traitors. Tongue in cheek, Jackson passed on the news to Captain Bissell at Fort Massac, practically the last armed post at which Burr could be stopped before reaching Natchez. Bissell wrote back satirically that he had not even heard of the Proclamation, and knew nothing of any armed forces such as Jackson had described, but that " on, or about the 31st ult., Colonel Burr, late Vice President of the United States, passed this with about ten boats, of different descriptions, navigated with about six men each, having nothing on board that would even suffer a conjecture more than a man bound to a market; he has descended the rivers toward Orleans." [45] Which, no doubt, was just what Jackson had expected, knowing that Burr had had ample time to escape.

But now the whirlwind of events caught up the excitable Border Captain and puffed him aloft. He accepted the proffered services of aged Revolutionary veterans with a tremendous harangue, he mustered his companies, marched them and reviewed them over and over in full view of the admiring citizenry, he strutted and bragged, and spoke of Bissell's sarcastic reply with explosive allusions to Spaniards and traitors.[46]

This was all for public consumption and edification, however. Privately, he sang another tune. The Secretary of War, he wrote his friend, Patten Anderson, on January 4, 1807, is " not fit for a granny "; his order to Jackson was " the merest old-woman letter . . . you ever saw." As for Wilkinson, he " has denounced Burr as a traitor, after he found that he was implicated. This is deep policy. He has obtained thereby the command of New Orleans, the gun boats armed; and his plan can now be executed without resistance. But we must be there in due time, before fortifications can be erected, and restore to our government New Orleans and the western commerce." [47] Jackson never had any use for the General. And, during those long days at Richmond, when advocacy of Burr was proof positive of seditious sentiments, no one clamored more his belief in Burr's utter innocence.

Meanwhile Burr was floating down the Ohio, floating steadily toward his doom. He had sent an express to Blennerhassett to meet him at the mouth of the Cumberland, where it emptied into the Ohio. He still did not know that the boats building on the Muskigum had been seized, that Blennerhassett even then was fleeing arrest. Blennerhassett and Tyler ran the gauntlet of drunken

Wood County sentries in safety, and met him on the 27th of December. There, for the first time, Burr heard the news. The country was inflamed against him, the full forces of the Government were on his trail. There was only one thing he could do, aside from submitting to arrest and the benevolent mercies of Jefferson. That was to continue down the Mississippi to New Orleans, where he had powerful friends — and, above all, General James Wilkinson — awaiting him.

The combined flotilla consisted of some nine boats — roofed in, of the modern houseboat variety — and some sixty men, mostly mere youths, attracted by the thought of adventure and a new life on the Washita. The leaders were Burr, Blennerhassett, Comfort Tyler and Davis Floyd, of Indiana, who had joined them at the Ohio Falls with three boats and thirty men. This, then, was the mighty flotilla, the armed gunboats belching fire from every port, the tons of munitions, the vast concourse of armed and desperate men, ranging in numbers from a paltry few thousand to as many as twenty thousand, with shuddering tales of which the whole nation was to be regaled, Washington to be thrown into panic fear, the West frightened out of its wits, and New Orleans placed under martial law, to experience a reign of terror never before or since seen on American soil.

On December 29th, the small, rootless band reached Fort Massac. There they anchored, and Burr sent a note of greeting to the commander, Captain Bissell — he of the satiric note. Bissell rowed out to meet them, and invited Burr to the fort to dine with him. Burr refused, but, when he left, he took along with him one Sergeant Jacob Dunbaugh, who had asked, and received, a furlough from Bissell to go down to New Orleans. Of this Jacob Dunbaugh we shall hear much more in the near future. And, it seems, Burr knew already that Wilkinson was not living up to his part of the bargain. For, testified Bissell, Burr remarked that " General Wilkinson had made a compromise with the Spaniards. He said he was sorry for it; and that General Wilkinson ought to have fought them." [48]

But Burr did not know the worst — that he had been betrayed. He did not know of the reception that was waiting for him at the end of the river down which he was floating so leisurely and peaceably.

CHAPTER XXIII

DICTATORSHIP IN NEW ORLEANS

1. GOOSEFLESH AND SWORD RATTLING

ON October 21, 1806, Wilkinson had sent his famous warning to Jefferson; on November 12th he had written that he was about to be overwhelmed by furious bands of descending Burrites, and on the same day he was alarming poor, befuddled Claiborne with a letter well calculated to shake the heart of the stoutest man. *Sacredly Confidential.* " You are surrounded by dangers of which you dream not and the destruction of the American Union is seriously menaced. The Storm will probably burst on New Orleans, when I shall meet it & triumph or perish." There are spies in every nook and cranny; be secret, oh, Claiborne, and act so " that no Emotions may be betrayed." The plot " implicates thousands and among them some of your particular friends as well as my own." Hasten and fortify the town, turn over artillery, troops, everything, to the savior, Wilkinson! [1]

Turgid bombast, of course, but quite effective for its purpose, which was to scare both Claiborne and New Orleans out of their respective wits, to sow the seeds of distrust between friend and friend, to prepare the way for his assumption of all power and unrestricted authority. If this letter were not sufficient to throw Claiborne into a state of panic, the letter soon to follow from Jackson completed the task.

Yet, in spite of denunciation, of hobgoblins thick and threatening, the amazing Savior of his Country took his good and leisurely time in reaching the threatened town. It was not until November 25th that Wilkinson rode with pomp and circumstance into the city of New Orleans. Bursting with importance, yet maintaining an ominous silence, he took up his Headquarters. The way had been well paved. The citizens were uneasy, alarmed with vague rumors; treachery and conspiracy were in the air, the fortifications were being hastily strengthened, the Governor looked grim and a bit frightened. The conditions were ideal for utter panic, for utter relaxation of power to a self-announced Dictator.

Claiborne had been having his own difficulties with the populace over whom he was placed. He was the uneasy master of a rest-

THEODOSIA BURR ALSTON, 1811

From a portrait by John Vanderlyn

THE ARREST OF AARON BURR

From an old engraving

less volcano, which might at any moment erupt and bury him under the ruins. A week before receiving Wilkinson's agitated communication, he himself had written to Jefferson that he had heard Burr was in the Western States, and that he feared his views to be " political and of a kind the most injurious." [2] In fact, soon he was telling Cowles Mead, the Acting Governor of the adjoining Mississippi Territory, that Daniel Clark was plotting his downfall, that " I may fall; but I can never be disgraced." [3] Unconsciously he was adopting Wilkinson's style.

When the doughty General rode into town, the panicky Governor breathed a sigh of relief and hastened to inform Madison in far-off Washington that " General Wilkinson and myself will, to the *best* of our *judgments* and *abilities* support the *honor* and *welfare* of our *Country*." [4] He did not yet realize that Wilkinson had no intention of permitting any one to share that glorious burden with him.

Claiborne met him in secret conference with Captain Shaw, who commanded the naval flotilla in the port, and clamored for an explanation. Wilkinson locked all doors, impressed upon his startled hearers the necessity for the utmost secrecy, intimating that his own life would not be worth a rush if the truth leaked out. Thus, in deep conspiratorial seclusion, did he unfold the dark tale to the astounded men. He read to them the cipher letter from Burr, in his own inimitable translation; then he spoke impressively of Swartwout's alleged disclosures — that the West would secede, New Orleans be revolutionized, and Claiborne slaughtered in his bed; that the money in the banks would be seized — perhaps to be returned at some future date — and that " a Mr. Spence of the Navy, a Mr. Ogden and a Doctor Bollman, who either were or had been in New Orleans, were agents of Colonel Burr." [5]

But outwardly, to the city at large, to Burr's adherents, Wilkinson maintained a bland face and air of impenetrability. Bollman had arrived some time before and had sent his credentials on to Wilkinson. Now, on November 30th, the General called on him in confidential interview, disclosing nothing of his purposes. In fact, he seemed still to the unsuspecting Bollman to be the willing partner in the project. For the brave General was taking no chances. To overcome Bollman, Swartwout *et al.*, he was gathering all the troops at his and Claiborne's command, rushing fortifications behind which he could retire in case of need, calling all units of the navy to his assistance. Once the troops from Natchitoches arrived, there would be some 800 regulars available, volunteers to the number of 180, two bomb ketches and four gun-boats.[6] Until they were all gathered, however, the desperate Boll-man must be temporized with.

On December 5th, with the troops in sight, Wilkinson felt brave enough to inform Bollman that he intended to oppose Burr's schemes, but even then he managed to leave the Doctor a trifle puzzled as to his intentions. On December 6th, Wilkinson dis-closed himself to Claiborne. " The dangers which impend over this City and menace the laws and Government of the United States, from an unorthorized [sic] — and formidable association, must be successfully opposed at this point, or the fair fabric of our independence, purchased by the the best blood of our Country will be prostrated, and the Goddess of Liberty will take her flight from this globe forever." After which exordium, Wilkinson settles down to business. " Under circumstances so imperious, extraor-dinary measures must be resorted to, and the ordinary forms of our Civil institutions must, for a short period, yield to the Strong arm of Military Law." He therefore " most earnestly " en-treats Claiborne " to proclaim martial law over this City its ports and percints [sic]."

As for Claiborne's idea of moving his militia up the river and taking a position against the oncoming hordes, he disposes of it with dark words, for it would have meant the collapse of his pri-vate plans. " You could not for a moment," he warned Claiborne, " withstand the desperation and superiority of numbers opposed to you, and the Brigands provoked by the opposition, might resort to the dreadful expedient of exciting a revolt of the negroes. If we devide our force we shall be beaten in detail, we must there-fore condense it here." [7] If it were not for the tragedy that stalked in his wake, here in truth was the very essence of a comic-opera general. But the matter was too grim for that. Martial law was what he demanded, and martial law was what he was going to get — the Governor, courts and civil authorities notwithstanding.

The following day he returned to the attack. " I believe I have been betrayed," he told Claiborne, " & therefore shall abandon the Idea of temporizing or concealment, the moment after I have secured two persons now in this City." He must have martial law, he insists, as " I apprehend Burr with his Rebelious Bands may soon be at hand." [8]

But Claiborne, frightened though he was by the General's bogies, stuck obstinately to the strange idea that suspension of habeas corpus " properly devolves upon the Legislature," though, he hastened to add, if the danger should augment, he would not hesitate to suspend the saving Constitutional clauses by proclamation. Wilkinson's revelations together with Jackson's wild letter, had convinced him of Burr's plan to dismember the Union.[9]

On December 9th, he called a meeting of the New Orleans Chamber of Commerce to consider the situation. The members met in considerable excitement, not quite knowing what to expect. Rumors there had been aplenty, but Wilkinson had not seen fit as yet to take the city into his confidence. It would be easier, he had thought, to wrest martial law from the single hand of the Governor. But Claiborne, for the moment at least, had proved of more stubborn fiber than he had anticipated. And, as he informed the national Government with considerable naïveté, " I had concealed my intentions from the double view of preserving my person from assassination, and to keep open the channels of communication by which I received information of their secret designs and movements." [10]

Now, however, it was necessary to throw New Orleans into a state of such alarm that the citizens would turn to him as the single savior. Dramatically, the fearful conspiracy was presented to the startled merchants. They were a trifle skeptical perhaps — some of them were members of the Mexican Association and friendly to Burr — and they did not fall down on their knees in terror; but they could do no better than yield on certain points to Wilkinson's insistence. Reluctantly they agreed to furnish sailors and carpenters from their own vessels for the needs of the United States Navy, in the person of Captain Shaw; and even more reluctantly they agreed to a temporary embargo of the port, and to force their idle sailors into the service of the United States.[11] These measures were immediately carried into effect.

Now in truth the town was in a state of panic. Burr was an unspecified distance up the river, traveling fast with thousands of men, desperadoes all, bent on plunder and rapine; he intended raising the blacks in frightful insurrection; he was going to loot the banks and commandeer the shipping. In every corner of their city lurked conspirators, ready at a word to rise and burn and slay. Wilkinson said so, Claiborne chimed in, Shaw was convinced. Unfortunately, Daniel Clark, who might have quieted the storm, was then in Washington as Territorial Delegate.

But there were skeptics, and there were even base wretches who openly mocked at the doughty General who was braving the dangers of assassination to defend them from tremendous perils. Burr, they insisted, had no thoughts of New Orleans or secession. In fact, Mexico was his goal, as it was the goal of all patriotic

Americans. They pointed out that, strangely enough, no word had reached them of the imminent approach of this mighty armada except through the General himself, and they went so far as to laugh loud and long at the frantic preparations, the dread that mantled every official face. The bluster, the braggadocio, the seclusive hiding of the General from his fictitious enemies, were beginning to turn the citizens from their induced fears to smiles, and smiles were on the verge of giving way to ridicule.

Claiborne himself was sadly addled, and knew not which way to turn. " I am sincerely desirous to co-operate with you, in all your measures," he wrote Wilkinson, but " many good disposed Citizens do not appear to think the danger considerable, and there are others who (perhaps from wicked Intentions), endeavour to turn our preparations into ridicule." He had done everything possible, even to authorizing an embargo, though this, he was afraid, " can alone be exercised legally by the General Government," and the Collector of the Port will no longer submit to it, he apprehends.[12]

Wilkinson witnessed these manifestations of turning public sentiment with dismay. If he did not act promptly and decisively, the whole fantastic specter he had evolved would be dissolved in gusts of ridicule, and his own strutting self blown away on the wind of public disapproval. Cursing Claiborne as a fool and weak-kneed idiot, he acted on his own. He had the power, if not the authority. He was the military commander of the troops who swarmed the city, Claiborne had given him the militia also, and Shaw of the Navy was prepared to back him up.

On December 12th, he initiated his own private reign of terror. Burr, the ostensible cause of all the alarm, was just then entering Nashville, quietly and with only a few companions, about a thousand miles away. Swartwout and Ogden, to their own considerable astonishment, were arrested at Fort Adams by Wilkinson's personal orders. On December 14th, a file of the military seized Bollman in New Orleans. All three were hurried incommunicado aboard the bomb ketch *Aetna*, under strict guard. Swartwout's watch was stolen from him by the General himself, his clothing and personal apparel refused him. On board the ship, he, as the most dangerous of the conspirators, was placed in chains, and was so to be held on the voyage to Washington.[13]

On December 15th, Wilkinson wrote the Governor, upon whose legal authority he had just trespassed, that " in the *impending awful moment,* when I am myself absolutely hazarding every thing for the National Safety, by unauthorized dispositions of the Troops and treasure of our Country, you must pardon me should I lament & indeed have felt a little impatient when I could no-where find authority, for the apprehension and safe custody of men, either the Known Agent, Emissaries, or Supporters of the dark and destructive combinations formed or forming in the Heart of the nation." There was only one way out, he cried. Martial law! Compulsory enlistment of seamen to man the navy! While his own life and character had been placed in opposition to the " flagitious enterprize of one of the ablest men of our Country, supported by a crowd of coequals," Claiborne, he charged, had suffered himself to be " unduly biased by the solicitation of the timid, the capricious or the wicked " against himself. Unless, he threatened, sufficient seamen were granted him, he will have to " abandon the City, and suspend further labour on its defences." [14]

To which Claiborne replied on the following day, beginning to yield to the repeated clamors, " believe me, that I am fully sensible of the impending Danger, and am disposed to exert all my constitutional *powers* in support of our Country and even *these* I will exceed, if the means at present pursued, should not (in a short time) produce the desired effects." [15] The Civil Government could no longer stand out against the Military.

But in the city the stupefaction of the people gave way to a mounting indignation and wrath at this ruthless assumption of military rule. On the afternoon of the 15th, an application was made for a writ of habeas corpus before the Superior Court in behalf of Bollman. Similar applications were made before Judge Workman, of the County Court, for Swartwout and Ogden. On the 16th, all writs were granted. But they were too late to save Bollman and Swartwout. For, under secret orders from Wilkinson, they were already on the high seas, sailing for Washington in the custody of Lieutenant Wilson. Young Ogden, however, by some oversight, had been left behind, and after a consultation with Claiborne, he was delivered to the jurisdiction of the Court by Captain Shaw.

On the return day of the writs, Wilkinson sent his aide to court, with a prepared statement, blustering in tone, to the effect that Bollman's arrest and removal had been accomplished on his own responsibility, and avowing openly that he intended to continue his military arrests as long as he saw fit.[16] As for Ogden, there being absolutely no evidence against him, he was freed. But not for long. Within twenty-four hours, he was re-arrested by Wilkinson, together with James Alexander, a young member of the New Orleans Bar, whose sole crime had been to appear in behalf of the imprisoned men. They were hastily transported across the river, then taken to Fort Saint Philip, out of the jurisdiction of the Court, and Alexander was later hustled to Washington, also without extra clothes, to stand trial for an unknown offense.

Edward Livingston had held his peace thus far, though immensely indignant over the treatment meted out to Bollman. Bollman, in fact, had been the bearer of a draft on him from Burr. "Doctor Bollman will receive whatever you may be disposed to pay him on my account, and will give you a discharge on payment of fifteen hundred dollars." [17] Livingston explained this later to be a sum due on a judgment against himself before he had left New York, and which had been assigned to Burr.

Now, however, on Alexander's disappearance, he roused himself to action. No doubt the young lawyer had intervened for Bollman at his request. He applied to Workman for new writs, which were granted. Wilkinson replied contemptuously that his answers in the case of " the traitor Bollman are applicable to the traitors who are the subjects of this writ." [18] Livingston pressed for an order to show cause why an attachment should not issue against the raging Wilkinson himself. Whereupon Workman, who had no love for the General, and who had been included by him in broad denunciation as a member of the Conspiracy, adjourned court to inquire of Claiborne if he would assist the civil authorities against Wilkinson. He received no satisfaction, however. Claiborne had at last yielded unconditionally to the formidable General. On December 26th, Livingston appeared again, and moved for the attachment, which was granted. Defiantly, Wilkinson informed the Court that Ogden was not " in his power, possession or custody." [19]

Again Workman turned to Claiborne to uphold the arm of the Court in its controversy with the Military. Claiborne, in sore distress, had already justified the arrests to Wilkinson, but thought, rather weakly, that when any prisoner " was claimed by the Civil authority, I did think, that (if within your power) it would have been right and proper to have surrendered him." [20] Weasel words, to be arrogantly ignored; indeed, they were in effect a complete abdication of the civil to the military power.

Despairing of further efforts, Workman wrote formally to the Governor. " Not having received any answer to my letter to your excellency . . . and considering your silence on the subject of it as a proof, in addition to those that previously existed, that your excellency not only declines the performance of your duties as chief magistrate of this territory, but actually supports the lawless measures of its oppressor, I have adjourned the court of the County of Orleans *sine die*." [21] Following that, he resigned forthwith and sent a strong protest to the Territorial Legislature.

Meanwhile New Orleans was held fast in the iron grip of Wilkinson's soldiers. No one dared dispute his progress, no man's liberty was safe. Secret visitations were the order of the day; the press — at least those newspapers who dared raise their voices in protest — was suppressed; indiscriminate arrests were made daily, and the prisoners hurried no one knew where. Workman himself was to fall into the toils, Livingston was in hourly peril of seizure, Lewis Kerr was rushed off to jail. So, too, was Bradford, editor of the *Orleans Gazette*. And, on January 14, 1807, John Adair rode into New Orleans, all unsuspecting. A detachment of regular troops, 150 strong, burst suddenly and violently into his hotel, dragged him away from his meal, and hurried him off to the barracks. A writ of habeas corpus was sued out and ignored as a mere scrap of paper. He, too, went the way of all others — the sea route to Washington, trophy of Wilkinson's valor.[22] On February 25th, Lieutenant Spence, the bearer of messages to Burr in Kentucky, followed in the well-trodden path of arrest and imprisonment.

Claiborne fluttered helplessly back and forth, tossed by storms not of his own contriving, not knowing exactly what to do. Events were moving too swiftly for his addled senses. On December 16th he had issued a Proclamation against unlawful combinations, in the manner of Jefferson, but the next day he was writing Madison " that the Danger is not as great, as the General apprehends; but in no event will I take upon myself to suspend the privilege of the *Writ of habeas Corpus,* & to proclaim *martial Law.*" [23]

Bold words, but without meaning. Wilkinson had gaged him only too well, and knew he could proceed without fear of opposition. " Cet bête," he wrote contemptuously of the Governor, " is at present up to the chin in folly and vanity. He cannot be supported much longer; for Burr or no Burr, we shall have a revolt, if he is not removed speedily." [24]

Wilkinson now had the city at his mercy. Claiborne had proved a muddle-headed nonentity, the civil government was prostrate, the courts were closed. He purloined letters from the post-office, set an army of secret agents to work ferreting out evidence of the Conspiracy, and they found — exactly nothing. And all the while he was bombarding Jefferson with bragging details of his exploits — it was not until Swartwout and Bollman were *en route* to the North that he condescended to send the President a much garbled version of the notorious cipher letter which had precipitated the entire unwarranted proceedings. Nor did he, even then, see fit to inform the President that he had actually answered Burr's letter with a cipher of his own, which he had posted, only to suffer a change of heart immediately after. He had raced after it all the way from Natchitoches to Natchez, caught up with it in time, and destroyed it. Had the letter eluded his retrieving grasp, and gone through, he would never have dared send warning to Jefferson and act as he did, for Swartwout, who had helped him encode the response, testified later that it had contained the words, " I am ready." Which impelled Wilkinson to admit that the expression actually was, " I fancy Miranda has taken the bread out of your mouth — and I shall be ready for the grand expedition before you are." [25] On such little threads does the course of history depend. Nor did Wilkinson breathe a word of his constant correspondence, during all this troublous period, with the Spaniards. Was it possible that he was also considering, while Dictator, a sudden shift to Spain — if the price were right?

But the end of the reign of terror was soon in sight. In fact, Cowles Mead, Acting Governor of Mississippi, was already planting disturbing seeds in Claiborne's mind as to Wilkinson's purpose and integrity. On December 14th, he wrote his fellow Governor that " Burr may come — and he is no doubt desperate," but, " should he pass us your fate will depend on the Genl. not on the Col: If I stop Burr — this may hold the Genl. in his allegiance to the U. States — but if Burr passes this Territory with two thousand men, I have no doubt but the Genl. will be your worst enemy. Be on your guard against the wily General — he is not much better than Cataline — consider him a traitor and act as if certain thereof — you may save yourself by it." [26] Mead knew Wilkinson, even if he did not know Aaron Burr.

And then the bubble burst, when Burr's much rumored expedition actually hove into sight, and the frightened Orleaners crept out of their holes. They started asking each other the questions Mead had long before propounded to Claiborne. " Is New Orleans invaded? is it threatened? or is it believed that any enemy is nearer, than the General Himself? " [27]

But by the time they bestirred themselves, still a bit fearful of the shadow of the military, Wilkinson had departed from their midst, to strut anew on a different stage. At a time when New Orleans had accurately gaged the remarkable talents of the General, and the Territorial Legislature, after an investigation, had laid all the facts in a scathing memorial before Congress, he was aiding the Government in its prosecution of Burr, and hence became a

" sacred cow," against whom not the slightest suspicion might be murmured.[28] In fact, the *Orleans Gazette* was to charge that the whole uproar was but a method of extracting financial profit by the interested parties, who had " some snug contracts for supplying the government with materials of defense." [29]

2. SURRENDER IN MISSISSIPPI

Farther up the river, in the Territory of Mississippi, under the jurisdiction of Secretary Cowles Mead, Acting Governor in place of Robert Williams, then absent in the East, the excitement was almost as intense, if not as provocative of harsh repression and dictatorial methods. On December 15th, a day before Claiborne issued his similar Proclamation, Mead sent a message to the Territorial Legislature announcing the existence of a plot to dissever the Union; on the 23rd, he proclaimed it to the inhabitants.[30] Yet to him Wilkinson was even more of a menace than the faintly mythical Burr. He was taking no chances, however. Wherefore he mustered the Territorial regiments for service, and ordered them to take stations to repel invasion.

" It is apprehended that Colo. Burr may land at or near the walnut Hills," he instructed Colonel Woolridge. " You are therefore ordered to appoint such number of persons as you may think sufficient to act as a guard along the river." [31] Orders of mobilization flew thick and fast. Rumors multiplied. The oncoming Burr swelled to monstrous proportions. On January 12th, Mead prorogued the Legislature so that, he told them, " you who blend the civil & the military characters must relinquish for the moment the functions of the first, while you assume the prerogatives of the latter." [32]

Then, on January 13th, came the dreadful news. Aaron Burr had arrived at Bayou Pierre, not a great distance up the river.[33] At once the feverish preparations for defense multiplied. Wilkinson, down in New Orleans, proposed to ascend the stream with 1000 men to cooperate with Shaw's flotilla of gunboats. There were, he warned, numerous adherents of Burr in the city, ready at a signal to rise and pillage the town, seize the shipping, and carry on an expedition against Spain. It pained him to declare that he had " the strongest grounds for believing that Judge Workman, has been deeply and actively engaged in these nefarious projects." [34]

Burr had floated down the river with his little fleet of unarmed houseboats, wholly ignorant of the tremendous alarm to the

southward, of the marchings and countermarchings, proclama-
tions, reign of terror and all. On the placid drift of the Mississippi everything was singularly peaceful and bucolic. Fort Massac
had been left behind, and New Year's Day was spent at New Madrid, opposite the mouth of the Ohio. Three days later they
were at Chickasaw Bluffs, where Lieutenant Jacob Jackson was
in command of a small garrison. It was an oasis of quiet. Jackson
was even ready to join the expedition in any move against Mexico, and took money from Burr to raise recruits against the day.[35]

On January 10th, they reached the boundaries of the Mississippi Territory, after some misadventures due to squalls and
treacherous eddies. Burr pushed on ahead with a single bateau
and twelve men to Bayou Pierre, where the other boats caught up
with him on the 11th. Here, for the first time, they learned of
the rousing of the country against them. Already Captain Ryan
was marching with a detachment of troops, and a civil warrant
in his pocket, to arrest the traitor, Burr.[36]

The bewildered adventurers, seeing a party of militia take their
station in the woods, some distance from the boats, pushed off
hurriedly in the night, and landed four miles below on the opposite shore, within the jurisdiction of Louisiana. There, for the
moment, they were safe.

Colonel Woolridge, in obedience to Mead's instructions, had
hastened to Bayou Pierre with 35 men to intercept Burr, but
found that the quarry had escaped. He followed the flotilla down
the river, and gazed impotently at the broad river that interposed itself between them. Burr had anchored his boats on the
Louisiana side, opposite the mouth of Cole's Creek.

But Burr politely sent a skiff across, so that Woolridge and two
of his officers might visit him in camp. Woolridge reported later
that Burr seemed glad to see him, and declared the complete innocence of his intentions. He returned to his own encampment
baffled and fuming, because he had no boats to bring his men
across to capture Burr. His detachment was surprisingly still " in
good Order but Darn hungry." He confessed, however, that there
were only some 55 men in Burr's expedition, a few women and
children, and some negro servants; and that he had seen no stand
of arms or other evidences of warlike intent. Meanwhile his
own " malish " were discontented and resigning from service in
groups.[37]

Burr, exceedingly surprised at the tumult his coming had raised,
had issued from Bayou Pierre a public letter, and another personally addressed to Mead, in which he had strongly avowed the

innocence of his views and protested vigorously his patriotic motives. His sole objects, he averred, were agriculture and the settlement of the lands he had purchased, and his boats were merely the vehicle of emigration.[38]

Mead forwarded the letter to Colonel Fitzpatrick with the comment that he " should be proud to find him as innocent as he there professes himself." In fact, " should Colo. Burr be disposed to pay due regard to the authority of our Government, you are requested to assure him from me that every security shall be given to private property and every respect paid him and his associates, which can be done after being assured that his plans are not directed against the United States or its Territories — You may further assure him of the particular solicitude I feel for the verification of his professions to me — and further if he has been vilified or injured by rumour or the *Pensioned* he shall receive all the benefits of my individual civility and the full and complete protection of the laws of the Territory." [39] The disgusted Acting Governor was already smelling a rat. The armed invasion had petered out to a mere handful of boys, women and children, unarmed, in peaceful emigrant boats. Very rightly he placed the blame for the alarm upon Wilkinson, the *Pensioned,* and began to hold serious doubts of Burr's alleged guilt. The skies were clearing.

Accordingly, Mead sent Colonel Shields, his confidential Aide-de-Camp, with an explanatory letter to Burr.[40] But before he arrived, Colonel Fitzpatrick had already rowed across the river, where Burr met him courteously, disclaimed indignantly any treasonable purposes, and expressed his willingness to surrender and stand trial on the charges against him, provided such trial would take place in the Mississippi Territory and nowhere else. By this time he was fully apprised of Wilkinson's inexplicable betrayal, and feared that, to protect himself, his erstwhile friend would not stop at any measures to close his mouth forever. Fitzpatrick agreed to submit his offer to Mead, and started back to Natchez. But on the way he heard that Colonel Claiborne (of the Mississippi militia, not to be confused with Governor Claiborne of Orleans) was on his way up the river with a considerable force to arrest Burr. Whereupon he returned to Burr's encampment and told him he must " under these circumstances summit [*sic*] to the civil authority, or trust to events." [41]

Claiborne arrived on January 16th with 275 men and took his position on the Mississippi side of the river, where he captured four unsuspecting members of the encampment who had just landed from a boat. But Natchez was becoming restless at all these manifestations of force. Burr's friends were numerous and powerful. Mead, in some alarm at their expressed hostility to himself, ordered Claiborne to seize all malcontents and send them under guard to Judge Rodney of the Federal Court. "The number of Burrs friends require much vigilance," he wrote. "Their licentiousness must be curbed." [42]

On the 16th, Shields and Poindexter, U. S. District Attorney, clothed with plenipotentiary powers, conferred with Burr and an agreement was reached, after a further meeting with Mead himself. Burr offered to surrender to the Mississippi civil authorities and to permit his boats to be searched for the rumored munitions of war. The next day he crossed the river with Mead's aides, and rode with them to the little village of Washington, the capital of the Territory, and there was committed for trial. "Thus Sir," reported Mead to the national Administration, "this mighty alarm (with all its exagerations) has eventuated in nine boats and one hundred men and the major part are boys or young men just from school — many of their depositions have been taken before Judge Rodney, but they bespeak ignorance of the views or designs of the Col. — I believe them really ignorant and deluded, I believe that they are the dupes of stratagems, if the asservations of Gen'l Eaton and Wilkinson are to be accredited." [43] Manifestly, Cowles Mead held many mental reservations concerning the latter.

As for Burr, he had adopted the wisest course. He had thrust his head unwittingly into the lion's mouth. He could not remain long on the Louisiana side. Shaw and Wilkinson would soon be appearing, in such overwhelming force that resistance would be futile. And the thought of falling into his former partner's clutches was not to be viewed with equanimity. Across the river, on the Mississippi side, lay Colonel Claiborne with a formidable force to block passage that way. He, too, was of the military, and liable to instructions from far-off Washington. To abandon the boats and attempt to force a desperate passage through trackless woods and tangled swamps into Spanish territory was equally unthinkable. His expedition was small and unused, most of them, to frontier hardships. There were women and children along, and the Spaniards would welcome him only too warmly. Already Governor Folch was marching at the head of 400 men from Pensacola to protect Baton Rouge against the dreaded American. By surrendering to the civil authorities, Burr assured himself of a civil trial, surrounded by all the Constitutional safeguards which he knew so well how to invoke. Besides, as Mead had complained, his friends were numerous and powerful in the Territory. Burr anticipated nothing more than a quick trial, acquittal, and permission to continue peacefully on his journey to the Washita. New Orleans, of course, was now definitely out of the picture.

3. VINDICATION

On January 18, 1807, Burr appeared before Judge Thomas Rodney and was bound over in $5,000 bail for the Grand Jury. Substantial citizens of the Territory immediately came forward and produced the necessary bail, with the result that he was once more a free man. It was extremely unfortunate, however, that Rodney was the Federal Judge in the Territory; for he was father to Caesar A. Rodney, Jefferson's Attorney General, and therefore closely attuned to the desires of the Administration. Burr could expect no even-handed justice from him.

But he had plenty of other friends; old comrades from Revolutionary times, men in sympathy with his views and resentful of what seemed vindictive persecution. They were tired of the uproar Wilkinson had managed to create with such obviously insubstantial materials. In Natchez, the induced hysteria of a few days before was subsiding. On January 7th, Silas Dinsmore had written satirically of the local situation. " We are all in a flurry here hourly expecting Colonel Burr & all Kentucky & half of Tennessee at his [back] to punish General Wilkinson, set the negroes free, Rob the banks & take Mexico. Come & help me laugh at the fun." [44]

Back in their camp, the little band, under the leadership of Blennerhassett, huddled in their boats, cooked their meals to the accompaniment of constant searches, and awaited the return of their Chief. Fitzpatrick, with a squad of men, searched in vain for the warlike equipment they had been led to expect. They found nothing but a few hunting rifles, blunderbusses, some small arms and pistols, such as are the essential equipment of all pioneers, frontiersmen and emigrants. Burr's men watched and jeered the discomfited snoopers, and hot-headed Davis Floyd became involved in an argument with the newly arrived Major Flaharty, at the head of 30 Territorials, and swelling with his own importance. Flaharty would not permit the boats to shift their positions and was firing on all traffic as it tried to pass down the river. Floyd sent him a letter of defiance, tantamount to an offer to discuss the matter on the field of honor. Blennerhassett, cowed by the excitement of the past few days, dissociated himself completely from the altercation, which ended inconclusively. On January 22nd, Comfort Tyler was removed from the camp by a squad of militia for appearance in the Territorial capital to answer charges alongside of Burr. Others of the camp, mere enlisted men, were taken for examination and deposition, and attempts were made to get them to swear to the treasonable purposes of the expedition, and to the secretion of warlike armaments by Burr before the militia had arrived. One and all, however, swore with the utmost sincerity to lack of knowledge of the one and the complete absence of the other.

Burr rejoined his men on the 24th. He was not required to appear in Washington (the Territorial capital) until the Grand Jury convened in February. Rodney, he said, had expressed his indignation at the exercise of military law against Burr, and threatened " if Wilkinson, or any other military force, should attempt to remove his person out of the Mississippi Territory, prior to his trial, he, the Judge, would again . . . put on old ' '76 ', and march out in support of Col. Burr and the Constitution." [45]

This was no vain fear. Immediately upon the receipt of news in New Orleans that Burr had come to the Mississippi Territory, Wilkinson and Claiborne sent off a joint express to Mead, in which they urged " the expediency of placing him without delay on board one of our armed vessels in the river with an order to the officers to descend with him to this city. Otherwise, if his followers are numerous, as they are represented to be, it is probable it may not be in your power to bring him to trial." [46]

Wilkinson was determined to lay his hands on Burr, at whatever cost. As early as December 4th, before Burr had appeared on the scene, he had laid his plans " to cut off the two principal leaders." As soon as they reached Natchez, he wrote a resident of that place, " it is my wish to have them arrested and carried off from that place, to be delivered to the Executive authority of the Union . . . If you fail, your expences shall be paid. If you succeed I pledge the Government to you for Five Thousand Dollars." [47] An exceedingly sinister note. Once in Wilkinson's power, the chances for Burr to reach the " Executive authority " would be rather remote. This kidnaping scheme failed, but Wilkinson was to try again.

Trouble piled up. Mrs. Blennerhassett and her two children, after much perilous journeying, had finally joined her distracted husband at Cole's Creek. Ominous reports drifted up the river from Natchez that Shaw was coming full speed with nine or ten gunboats, armed with express orders from the Secretary of the Navy to " capture or destroy all of Burr's boats." [48] There was other disturbing news. Burr's drafts on New York had been protested, and he now found himself without any funds to pay his men or supply them with additional provisions. They were beginning to turn on him, and to accuse him as the author of all their misfortunes. They became drunk and mutinous, and refused to perform the most necessary tasks about the boats. There were threats that they would decamp and take with them the remaining supplies on board. It required all of Burr's tact and presence of mind to quiet the grumblers.

A new element was now injected into the situation. Governor Williams had returned to the Territory to take up his duties, and Burr rode immediately to Washington Town to pay his respects and sound out his attitude. Seemingly it was friendly. On the first Monday in February the Grand Jury convened, with Judges Rodney, he of " '76," and Bruin, friendly to Burr, presiding. On Tuesday, at the opening of Court, United States District Attorney Poindexter suddenly arose and moved for a dismissal of the proposed bill of indictment on the ground that there was no evidence of any criminal acts within the jurisdiction of the Court, and on the further ground that the Supreme Court, being an appellate tribunal, had no jurisdiction over original causes.

Judge Rodney was manifestly upset and annoyed at this unexpected motion, which sounded as if it had been prepared for the prosecutor by Burr himself, and differed angrily. In spite of his fine speech to Burr at the time of bail, he owed it to his son and to his political connections in the national capital to press Burr with all the rigors of the law. Judge Bruin, however, inclined to the position of the District Attorney, and argued, even, that should the motion be granted, the bail must likewise be discharged. There being a tie vote in the Court, the motion was considered overruled, and the evidence, consisting wholly of depositions, was placed before the Grand Jury for consideration.[49]

The Jury soon returned without an indictment, and, following the example of an earlier Kentucky jury, went out of its true province to excoriate the Government, Wilkinson and Claiborne, and to denounce all and sundry who had participated in the persecution of Burr. An astonishing document indeed. " The grand jury of the Mississippi Territory," they declared, " on a due investigation of the evidence brought before them, are of the opinion that Aaron Burr has not been guilty of any crime or misdemeanor against the laws of the United States, or of this Territory; or given any just cause of alarm or inquietude to the good people of the same." Then they paid their respects to Wilkinson and Claiborne, and to Mead himself, in scathing phrases. " The grand jurors present, as a grievance, the late military expedition, unnecessarily, as they conceive, fitted out against the person and property of the said Aaron Burr, when no resistance had been made to the civil authorities. The grand jurors also present, as a grievance, destructive of personal liberty the late military arrest [at New Orleans], made without warrant, and, as they conceive, without other lawful authority; and they do sincerely regret that so much cause has been given to the enemies of our glorious Constitution, to rejoice at such measures being adopted, in a neighboring Territory, as, if sanctioned by the Executive of our country, must sap the vitals of our political existence, and crumble this glorious fabric in the dust." [50] They did not hesitate even to lash out at Jefferson himself.

For the third time Burr had appeared in a Federal Court and been acquitted of any criminal intent.

Burr's friends carried him off in triumph. They were wealthy planters, Federalists chiefly, and openly scornful of Jefferson and his satellites. On February 4th, Burr demanded his release from bail. Rodney, furious at the prospect of this easy escape of the man on whose destruction the Government was determined, denied the motion, and bound him over to appear from day to day before him. This was wholly illegal, an unheard-of proceeding, and in violation of Burr's constitutional rights. The bail had been set to compel his appearance before the Grand Jury. That body had considered the evidence and had refused to indict. Instead, it had brought in a ringing vindication of the accused. The bail, therefore, should necessarily have been annulled. There was no charge, no accusation, upon which it could be predicated.

It was obvious now that constitutional guaranties and orderly legal processes alike would not avail Burr any more. His enemies were determined to destroy him, and would use every weapon at hand to do the trick. More ominous even than the procedure of Judge Rodney were the activities of Wilkinson, whose long arm was reaching up from New Orleans to pluck his prey. His earlier attempt at kidnaping had failed; he tried again and with more effective weapons. He sent Dr. Carmichael, a civilian, and Lieutenants Peter and Jones, as well as men in disguise, " armed with Dirks & Pistolls," to seize and convey Burr to him, or to assassinate him if possible. In the case of Dr. Carmichael, the remonstrances of Governor Williams were sufficient to dissuade him from his task, but Peter announced that he " felt himself bound to obey the orders of his General like a good soldier." The assassins were bound by no moral scruples whatever.[51]

Burr went into conference with his friends to determine on his course of action. They pointed out to him that the laws of the Territory no longer sufficed for his protection, that each moment he remained, increased the danger of illegal incarceration or private assassination. On their advice he decided to go into hiding.

From his place of concealment Burr wrote the Governor that because of the " vindictive temper and unprincipled conduct of Judge Rodney he withdrew for the present from the public," but offered to appear before the court again whenever his rights as a citizen could be assured.[52] The Governor's answer was to declare his bond forfeited, and to offer a reward of $2,000 for his arrest. To which Burr, still in hiding, protested that his bond had been merely for appearance before the Grand Jury, that he had obeyed that provision, and therefore it could not legally be forfeited.[53] Williams retorted sharply that he could only regard him as a fugitive from justice, and that all questions as to legality or illegality of proceedings were the province of the courts, and not his to consider.[54]

Burr was in despair. He had stood three legal proceedings and been acquitted of all wrongdoing; yet the acquittals were of no avail. Hourly his situation was becoming more dangerous. Mississippi had turned against him as well as Orleans and Louisiana. He consulted his friends again and they strongly advised his immediate flight. Reluctantly he bowed to the inevitable.

But before he went, he visited secretly his disheartened and somewhat mutinous followers in the unguarded boats. It was a sorrowful farewell. *They* were certain of eventual freedom; *he* could expect only unrelenting public and private vengeance. He made them a little speech that moved them to tears. He told them that they might sell all his property in the flotilla, and divide the proceeds among themselves; that if they wished, they might go on to the Washita lands and take up such shares as they desired. With a heavy heart he told them " that he stood his trial and was acquitted; but that they were going to take him again, and that he was going to flee from oppression." [55] Then he disappeared from their midst as suddenly as he had come, leaving them with renewed faith and belief in their tormented leader. Later, they took the boats and provisions to Natchez, sold what they could, stored the balance, and divided the money. Of all the members of the expedition, in spite of arrest, in spite of Wilkinson's threats and promises of reward to any one who turned informer, only one man was later to testify to damaging circumstances against Burr. That man was Dunbaugh, the soldier on furlough, and peculiarly amenable to Wilkinson's threats.

The saga of their journey's end is soon told. Williams, furious at Burr's escape, ordered their wholesale arrest. The pretext was ready at hand. A negro boy, so it was said, had been discovered near the mouth of Cole's Creek, riding on Burr's horse and wearing Burr's coat. It was alleged that within the folds of his cape there was a note, dated February 1st, and addressed to Tyler and Floyd. It read, " If you are yet together, keep together, and I will join you to-morrow night. In the meantime, put all your arms in perfect order. Ask the bearer no questions, but tell him all you may think I wish to know. He does not know that this is from me, nor where I am." The note was unsigned, but it was claimed to be in Burr's handwriting.[56]

This seems to be the clumsiest of forgeries. The original was never produced for inspection, and it was never disclosed when it had been seized. Furthermore, why had such a note been written at all? On its purported date, Burr was openly in Washington Town, awaiting the Grand Jury proceedings. He was confident of gaining a dismissal; there was no need for the utter secrecy. The note was an obvious attempt to pin a new crime upon Burr — the reference to arms could mean only resistance to authority. But it had been intended to date it as of Burr's escape, and in the hurry of the forgery, the forger had miscalculated.

Nevertheless, on the strength of this, some sixty were arrested at Natchez, most of them to be freed in a few days. But Blennerhassett, Floyd, Ralston and Tyler continued to be held. After many vicissitudes, Ralston was freed; so was Blennerhassett, only to be re-arrested in Kentucky and sent to Richmond to stand trial with Burr; Floyd and Tyler were also indicted by the Richmond Grand Jury.

As for the rank and file of the expedition, they soon made friends with the people of Natchez, and finding conditions to their liking, " dispersed themselves through the territory and supplied it with school masters, singing masters, dancing masters, clerks, tavern keepers, and doctors." [57]

4. Escape and Arrest

Mounted on a fleet horse given him by Colonel Osmun, one of his most loyal friends in the Territory, accompanied by Chester Ashley as a guide, and disguised, according to Wilkinson's account, in " an old blanket coat begirt with a leathern strap, to which a tin cup was suspended on the left and a scalping knife on the right," Aaron Burr galloped into the tangled wilderness. Despair was in his heart and a settled melancholy in his voice — this man who had always been gay and sanguine. Behind him lay oppression and death; before him — what? Everywhere he turned, a hostile nature and more hostile men awaited him. It is asserted that he meant to seek refuge within Spanish territory, but there he would have been subjected to rather brief shrift. The United States by and large was hostile country — the government, the courts, the minds of the people themselves, were poisoned by the constant propaganda. Wilkinson told Jefferson that " Burr's destination was France beyond all doubt." [58] Which was plausible; but the probabilities lay more in favor of England — and Charles Williamson.

The problem was how to get there. The ports would be guarded, and the way to Canada was long and difficult. The elements were also against him. Heavy rains had rendered the streams swollen and unfordable, necessitating a change in route over the one first mapped.

On the 18th of February, 1807, Nicholas Perkins, a young lawyer, and Thomas Malone, Clerk of the Court, were seated in their cabin, in the village of Wakefield, Washington County, deeply immersed in an exciting game of backgammon. It was late at night and the scattered citizens were mostly in bed and fast asleep. A knock sounded on the outer door. Perkins arose, thrust open the door. Two mounted travelers loomed dark in the road. One came forward with an inquiry for the village tavern. Perkins pointed it out in the distance. Then the traveler, muffled to the chin in a blanket coat, asked also the way to Colonel Hinson, a local celebrity. That, too, was pointed out, and the travelers rode away.

But Perkins had been studying the broadcast descriptions. By the dim light of the fire as it eddied out through the open door into the night, he observed that the inquirer wore exquisitely shaped boots under the coarse pantaloons of a farmer, and that his eyes, even in the semi-darkness, sparkled and glowed. There could be only one man in all the Territory with eyes like that. He turned at once to Malone and exclaimed, " *That* is Aaron Burr! "

The thought of the reward — two thousand dollars — was a huge temptation to a penniless young lawyer. He seized his cloak and hastened over to the cabin of Theodore Brightwell, the sheriff, awoke him from his sleep, and breathlessly told him that he had found the fugitive. The sheriff dressed, and together they went to Hinson's. Perkins hid outside in the woods so as not to awaken suspicion, while the sheriff went in alone. Mrs. Hinson, the mistress of the house, was his relative. She welcomed him, all unsuspecting; her husband, the Colonel, was not at home. The sheriff went casually into the kitchen and there discovered the two travelers who had inquired the way of Perkins. One of them was obviously muffled and avoiding observation. They stayed overnight; so did the sheriff. It seems that he had regretted his hasty action, and was not disposed to bear the onus of Burr's arrest. The next morning the two gentlemen left, politely taking their leave of Mrs. Hinson and expressing disappointment at her husband's absence.

In the meantime, Perkins had become impatient at the sheriff's non-appearance. He mounted and rode away to Fort Stoddard, the nearest military post. There he explained the situation to Lieutenant Edmund P. Gaines, in command. Gaines, with Perkins and four soldiers, heavily armed, hastened back on the road to Hinson's. About two miles out of Wakefield they came upon Burr and Ashley, and Sheriff Brightwell, who, far from arresting Burr, had volunteered to guide him on his way. No resistance was possible, as the soldiers presented their arms. Burr at first refused to answer questions, but finally admitted his identity.[59]

He was taken to the Fort, and imprisoned. But Gaines was uneasy over his unexpected prisoner. He was afraid that the country might rouse at the news and rescue him by force. Ashley, who had been allowed to go free, was popular in the neighborhood, and Burr himself had many friends. Burr was also making friends daily within the Fort by reason of his attractive personality and considerateness. It was necessary to get rid of him at once. Nicholas Perkins, hot after the reward, volunteered to escort him all the arduous miles to distant Washington, and to deliver his prisoner direct to the President. Gaines, glad of this solution to his difficulties, gave Perkins a file of eight soldiers to guard the prisoner, and wished them Godspeed. He declared to Wilkinson in justification of his course that the inhabitants were ready to follow Ashley to the rescue, that " the plans of Burr are now spoken of in terms of approbation, and Burr in terms of sympathy and regard. I am convinced if Burr had remained here a week longer the consequences would have been of the most serious nature." [60]

But the countryside seethed with adverse criticism. Gaines, in self-defense, denied he had arrested Burr " militarily," and shifted all the blame to Perkins.[61] But Perkins did not mind. By that time he was in Washington, and had already collected $3,331 as his share of various rewards for Burr's capture.

John Graham, the Government agent, whose dilatory following in the footsteps of Burr still excites incredulous wonder, reported also to the Administration a change of heart in the Southwestern

Territories. He had come up with Burr in Washington Town on January 30th, to find Burr already awaiting trial. He interviewed Burr, who spoke to him frankly, disclaiming, as always, any treasonable intentions. On February 8th, he was writing mournfully to Madison, " I am sorry to say that since my arrival in this Territory I have met with many people who either openly or indirectly attack the government for not countenancing Colonel Burr in the invasion of Mexico, for it is generally considered here that that was his object. I am well persuaded that most of his followers were of this opinion." [62]

When he proceeded to New Orleans, he discovered a similar state of public feeling. The city was rent by factions, and only just recovering from Wilkinson's tyrannical yoke. It was, he admitted, most " unpleasant." [63] Workman and Kerr had been tried on Wilkinson's trumped-up charges and speedily acquitted. Burr's friends once more raised their voices in protest, and Claiborne was vainly trying to have a reluctant Legislature suspend the writ of habeas corpus so that he could deal properly with them.

5. VIA DOLOROSA

About March 6, 1807, Perkins, with eight soldiers and Aaron Burr, started out from Fort Stoddard on the long Via Dolorosa to Washington, the capital of the United States. Burr was still attired in the homespun pantaloons, the flapping, wide-brimmed beaver hat in which he had been arrested. It was a perilous and a fatiguing journey for escort and prisoner as well. They traveled in secrecy, avoiding towns and settled communities for fear of rescue of their distinguished prisoner; through swamps and trackless forests, swimming their horses over unbridged rivers, in daily danger from hostile Indians. They rode hard and fast, making forty miles a day; but never once was Aaron Burr " heard to complain that he was sick, or even fatigued."

Then they reached comparatively settled country, and their precautions redoubled against the chance of rescue. Burr had been biding his time. In South Carolina, the State of his son-in-law, Joseph Alston, the cavalcade was galloping fast near the courthouse of the Chester District. As they passed a tavern before which a group of people were assembled, Burr suddenly flung himself from his horse, and exclaimed in a loud voice, " I am Aaron Burr, under military arrest, and claim the protection of the civil authorities! " Perkins and his men immediately dismounted, presented their pistols, and ordered him back on his horse again. Burr refused; whereupon Perkins, who was a large man, seized him around the waist and heaved him bodily into the saddle. Thomas Malone, the Court Clerk who had played backgammon with Perkins that fateful night, and now a member of the escort, caught the reins and urged the horse along, while the soldiers whipped it from behind. Thus, still struggling, Burr was whisked out of sight in a cloud of dust before the astonished citizens could recover their wits. For the first time in his life Burr, fatigued, oppressed with emotion, gave way to tears, and Malone sobbed with him.[64]

Perkins took no more chances with his prisoner. He placed him in a closed and shaded gig, and conveyed him by stealth to Fredericksburg, there to find orders awaiting him from Jefferson to carry Burr to Richmond, where the President had determined to set the stage for his trial on the charge of high treason.

John Randolph of Roanoke, in the town of Bizarre, looked out of his window and beheld a strange sight the afternoon of March 23rd. "Col. Burr (quantum mutatus ab illo!) passed by my door the day before yesterday under a strong guard."[65]

On March 26th, in the evening, the sorry cavalcade cantered into Richmond — and journey's end.

CHAPTER XXIV

THE STAGE IS SET

1. CONVICTED IN ADVANCE

IN Washington, the President of the United States was jubilant. Burr was at last in his power, and he was determined that he should not escape this time. He proclaimed exultantly that " Burr has indeed made a most inglorious exhibition of his much overrated talents. He is now on his way to Richmond for trial." [1] But the following day, with a fine inconsistency, he was informing an anonymous correspondent, " No man's history proves better the value of honesty. With that, what might he [Burr] not have been! " [2]

Since Wilkinson's vague alarms had come to trouble his ears the preceding November, he had steadily increased his already overabundant spleen toward the man who had made him President. He became judge, prosecutor and jury, all in one. He had tried the question of Burr's guilt in the public eye before his capture; he had given the impression that he had in his possession the most irrefutable proofs of his treason and convicted him accordingly. He had utilized every resource of the Government to achieve his purpose — to blacken the name of Aaron Burr forever — whether the means were legal or illegal; and now, during the course of the ensuing trial, he injected himself into what was a judicial proceeding in a way that bespoke the most vindictive persecution and interference with the orderly processes of the law of the land. It is indeed a strange episode in the life of an otherwise great figure in American history. A philosopher displaying spleen, passion and enmity; a democrat acting the tyrant; a scientist rearing a structure of hate on the flimsiest premises; the ardent prophet of the Bill of Rights tearing every constitutional guaranty of personal liberty to shreds; the disciple of the Enlightenment adopting the Jesuitical doctrine that the end justifies the means!

Had Jefferson been sincerely convinced of Burr's guilt, and that the nation was in danger of subversion, his course might at least be understandable, if not wholly to be approved. But the record casts serious doubts on Jefferson's own convictions, no matter what he pretended to the public. His first Proclamation made no mention of internal treason, though obviously he intended the people to read between the lines. A filibustering expedition against Spain did not justify the pursuit of the proponent with such unrelenting vigor. In the eyes of the nation, it was considerably less than an offense. But he was feeling his way, slowly and carefully, building up public opinion to the boiling-point.

The Proclamation was followed a few days later by detailed references in the annual message to Congress. Burr's crime was still merely the technical misdemeanor of an expedition against Mexico. But the people waited breathlessly for revelations they knew must soon be forthcoming. They were not disappointed. Rumors of Wilkinson's charges, of Eaton's fantastic story, were skilfully placed in circulation. Dark looks and muttered words hinted at other and more definitive proof in the possession of the Government, so damning in its implications that, for reasons of State, it could not be released for public consumption.

To the general populace, these were sufficient. The hints and rumors were magnified and distorted, until Aaron Burr, the traitor, became an execration and a byword. But winks, and portentous shakings of heads, and the carefully released stories of Wilkinson and Eaton, met with incredulity on the part of those who knew Burr well and intimately. Wrote Senator Plumer to a friend, " I am too well acquainted with the man to believe him guilty of all the absurdity that is ascribed to him. He is a man of first rate talents. He may be capable of much wickedness, but not of folly." [3]

This was indeed to be the constant cry of well-informed men, and one which Jefferson could only overcome by constant reiteration, assiduous propaganda, and a horde of witnesses. They had known Aaron Burr for years; it was incredible that such fantastic, insane schemes could be the product of that brilliant mind. It was the " folly," not the " wickedness," that led to total disbelief. A little later, Plumer was to repeat, " I must have plenary evidence before I believe him capable of committing the hundredth part of the absurd & foolish things that are ascribed to him." In fact, " the president of the United States, a day or two since, informed me that he knew of no evidence sufficient to convict him of either high crimes or misdemeanors . . ." [4] And, in that very conversation, Jefferson had remarked that " he believed Yrujo was duped by Burr " into advancing him money.[5] In other words, at the turn of the year, Jefferson had no evidence of guilt, and, by his reference to the *duping* of Yrujo, was not at all himself convinced of a design for disunion.

Yet when John Randolph, bitter critic of Jefferson, rose in the House on January 16, 1807, and demanded that the President of the United States lay before them any information he possessed touching the conspiracies mentioned in his Message, the President showed no such public qualms as he had exhibited in private. His response on January 22nd to the Resolution was positive, unequivocal, detailed. No longer was it merely an expedition against Spain; it was now as well a plot to disrupt the Union; Aaron Burr, he stated emphatically, is " the principal actor, whose guilt is placed beyond question." On information received from Wilkinson and Eaton, as well as on a mass of " letters, often containing such a mixture of rumors, conjectures, and suspicions as renders it difficult to sift out the real facts and unadvisable to hazard more than general outlines," he was enabled to inform Congress of every move, of every thought, of Burr. He had intended to sever the Union beyond the Alleghanies, Jefferson declared; he had intended also to attack Mexico; his scheme for the colonization of the Bastrop grant was a mere blind for his treasonable purposes. Then, finding the West impervious to his designs, he had formed the desperate scheme of descending on New Orleans, of robbing the banks, and plundering the city. But Wilkinson, "with the honor of a soldier and fidelity of a good citizen," had punctured the plot and arrested the conspirators within his reach, and had hastened to notify the President of the United States of the base treason which had unwittingly been opened to him. In fact, on January 18th, only a few days before, Jefferson had received from that singular patriot a translation of the damning cipher from Burr, which, to Jefferson, was convincing evidence of Burr's infamy. Furthermore, Swartwout, Bollman and the others were even then on the high seas, bound for Atlantic ports as prisoners of state. To this extraordinary document he attached Wilkinson's letters — but not the private despatch of October 21st — and Wilkinson's affidavit justifying the arrests, as well as the famous translation.[6]

The Message created a profound sensation. Here was convincing evidence, statements made without any hesitation. The Chief Executive of the United States had declared positively that Burr was guilty beyond question. The story was complete in every detail. Even the men who had known Burr began to waver. Though Plumer thought the cipher letter sounded more like Wilkinson's style than Burr's, and doubted the accuracy of the translation, the overwhelming mass of detail led him, by January 26th, reluctantly to the conclusion that Burr must in truth be guilty as charged.[7]

Only crusty, obstinate old John Adams held out against the tremendous clamor. " I have never believed him [Burr] to be a Fool," he declared. " But he must be an Idiot or a Lunatick if he has really planned and attempted to execute such a Project as imputed to him." But, he remarked dryly, politicians have " no more regard to Truth than the Devil . . . I suspect that this Lying Spirit has been at work concerning Burr." However, regardless of everything else — and here old Adams rose to incontrovertible heights, " if his guilt is as clear as the Noon day Sun, the first Magistrate ought not to have pronounced it so before a Jury had tryed him." [8]

Jefferson was not troubled with such trifling scruples. He proceeded on his subtle, tortuous way to enmesh and bedevil Burr in advance of arrest, in advance of trial, in advance of conviction — and with utter disregard of Constitutional provisions.

On January 23, 1807, the day following the receipt of the Message, William B. Giles, the Administration whip, brought before the Senate in secret session a resolution for the suspension of the Constitutional right of habeas corpus. This was introduced for one purpose — to hold Bollman and Swartwout, who were already in Baltimore, in the clutch of the military, without affidavit or formal accusation of specified crimes. It went through almost *viva voce,* with only Bayard of Delaware vehemently opposed to this determination to impose what was tantamount to a military dictatorship upon the country. The Bill then went immediately before the House, where an attempt was made to rush it through behind closed doors. But the House revolted in disgust and astonishment. By a vote of 123 to 3 the doors were flung open to public audience, and, after an angry debate, led, astonishingly enough, by John W. Eppes, Jefferson's son-in-law, who shouted that " never, under this Government, has personal liberty been held at the will of a single individual," the House rejected the Senate measure by a vote of 113 to 19.[9] The Bill had proved a boomerang.

But the Message had already done its deadly work. All over the country, as the news of it penetrated to the most distant parts, the people blazed into indignation and fury at the unspeakable Burr. No further evidence was needed to deepen the conviction of guilt: the President had spoken, and the trial was an unnecessary formality. Even Joseph Alston, Burr's own son-in-law and partner, hastened to humble himself in abject dissociation from the treason. On February 6th, he wrote to Governor Pinckney of South Carolina in imploring accents. " I have received and read the President's Message with deep mortification and concern; but the letter annexed to it, stated to be a *communication in cyphers* from Col. Burr to Gen. Wilkinson, excites my unfeigned astonishment. I solemnly avow that, when that letter was written, I had never heard, directly or indirectly, from Col. Burr, or any other person, of the meditated attack on New Orleans . . . On the other hand, I had long had strong grounds for believing that Col. Burr was engaged by other objects, of a very different nature from those attributed to him, and which I confess the best sentiments of my heart approved. I need not add that those objects involved not the interests of my country . . . I confess," he submitted hesitantly, " there are times even now, when, in spite of the strong facts which have been exhibited, I am almost inclined to believe my suspicions [of Burr] injurious. Whatever may be thought of the *heart* of Mr. Burr, his *talents* are great beyond question, and to reconcile with such talents, the chimerical project of dismembering the Union, or wresting from it any part of its Territory, is difficult indeed." Let not the fact, he begged, that he was Burr's son-in-law involve him; " let me," he said, " always be judged by *my own acts,* and I shall be satisfied." [10] A disgusting, cowardly performance, indeed, and one which, when discovered by his wife, must have filled her with scornful fury for her impotent husband. Even Blennerhassett spoke of him always with words of contempt.

Yet Jefferson himself was under no particular illusions as to the magnitude of Burr's enterprise, or the danger to the country. On January 3rd, he told Wilkinson that " I do not believe that the number of persons engaged for Burr has ever amounted to five hundred," and " that the enterprise may be considered as crushed." As for the fear of an attack on New Orleans from the West Indies, " be assured there is not any foundation for such an expectation. . . . The very man whom they represented to you as gone to Jamaica, [Truxton] and to bring the fleet, has never been from home, and has regularly communicated to me everything which had passed between Burr and him. No such proposition was ever hazarded to him." [11]

On February 3rd, in answer to the flow of frightened bombast from Wilkinson, he was assuring him that Burr " began his descent of the Mississippi January 1st, with ten boats, from eighty to one hundred men of his party, navigated by sixty oarsmen not at all of his party." While he approved in the main of Wilkinson's arrests and deportations, he cautioned him not to " extend this deportation to persons against whom there is only suspicion, or shades of offence not strongly marked. In that case, I fear the public sentiment would desert you; because, seeing no danger here, violations of law are felt with strength." In other words, illegalities and outrage of personal liberty are quite all right as long as the public will stand for it. But, continued Jefferson, Wilkinson could rest assured of his support in whatever measures he takes. " You have doubtless seen a good deal of malicious insinuation in the papers against you. This, of course, begot suspicion and distrust in those unacquainted with the line of your conduct. We, who knew it, have not failed to strengthen the public confidence in you; and I can assure you that your conduct, as now known, has placed you on ground extremely favorable with the public. Burr and his emissaries found it convenient to sow a distrust in your mind of our dispositions towards you; but be assured that you will be cordially supported in the line of your duties." [12]

And, on the same day, he amplified this amazing doctrine that the violation of private rights by military force was justified as long as it was limited to specified individuals. " On great occasions," he wrote Claiborne, " every good officer must be ready to risk himself in going beyond the strict line of law, when the public preservation requires it . . . The Feds, and the little band of Quids, in opposition, will try to make something of the infringement of liberty by the military arrest and deportation of citizens, but if it does not go beyond such offenders as Swartwout, Bollman, Burr, Blennerhassett, Tyler, etc. they will be supported by the public approbation." [13] What had happened to the man who had listed in the Declaration of Independence as a cardinal grievance against the King of England that " he has affected to render the Military independent of and superior to the Civil power "; who had insisted on a Bill of Rights before he would approve of the new Constitution; who had written the Kentucky Resolutions — that ringing declaration against the Federal Government for usurpation of power in enacting the Sedition Laws?

But no better evidence can be adduced of the President's knowledge of the chief purposes of the man he was hounding than his confidential letter to the American Minister in Madrid, to whom he unbosomed himself so that Spain might be apprised of the gracious efforts of the United States in its behalf — à la Wilkinson! " No better proof of the good faith of the United States [toward Spain] could have been given than the vigor with which we acted . . . in suppressing the enterprise meditated lately by Burr against Mexico. Although at first, he proposed a separation of the western country, and on that ground received encouragement and aid from Yrujo, according to the usual spirit of his government towards us, yet he very early saw that the fidelity of the western country was not to be shaken, *and turned himself wholly towards Mexico*. And so popular is an enterprise on that country in this, *that we had only to lie still, and he would have had followers enough to have been in the city of Mexico in six weeks.*" [14] Yet, at the very time that this was written, Burr was on trial for his life, with Jefferson himself as Prosecutor-in-Chief!

2. PRELIMINARY TRIALS

Bollman and Swartwout were the first of Wilkinson's prisoners to arrive. From Baltimore, the point of debarkation, they were hustled to Washington, and, on January 22, 1807, thrown into a military prison, to be " guarded, night and day, by an officer & 15 soldiers of the Marine Corps." [15] Rumbles of habeas corpus proceedings reaching the Presidential ear; it was attempted, as already stated, to suspend altogether that invaluable weapon against oppression. The attempt not only failed, but a resolution to strengthen the privilege barely missed passing in the House by the narrowest of margins — the Federalists and Randolph's band of Quids working harmoniously together in its favor.

On January 23rd, a squad of soldiers escorted Bollman to the Secretary of State's office, where he found Jefferson and Madison awaiting him. He was entirely willing, he professed, to disclose all that he knew of Burr's conspiracy, provided he were assured that nothing which he might divulge or admit to them, would be thereafter used for any purpose. With imperfectly restrained eagerness, they assured him that such would be their course. Now they would hear the truth — that truth which would place Aaron Burr's neck in the noose.

Bollman told them, and they wrote busily, that the plan was to revolutionize Mexico and make a monarchy of it, that it was intended to seize the French artillery still in New Orleans (to which the United States had no title) , but to avoid violence and invasion of private rights; then to seize the harbor shipping, by force if necessary, and convey their forces to Vera Cruz. That, as soon as Burr was embarked, Bollman was to hasten back to Washington to acquaint the Government of the enterprise, and urge it on to war with Spain. He frankly avowed that Yrujo had been duped into a belief that Burr's object was to revolutionize Louisiana and separate the Western States, but that this had been done to lull the suspicions of Spain. Then he went on to spin elaborate embroidery. Yrujo had been most eager, had offered arms and money, but Burr had " despised the dirty character of Yrujo, and never would accept either money or any thing else from that quarter."

To Merry, however, the real truth had been told — that the sole object was Mexico. More embroidery! The English government had been warm in favor, but Pitt's death had changed the complexion of things. As for Merry, Bollman was at pains to assure his listeners that he " had no wish to injure the interests or infringe the authority of the United States, but solely to advance those of Great Britain." [16] A dexterous concoction, in which fact and fancy were inextricably mingled, and which left Jefferson and Madison sorely puzzled.

A writ of habeas corpus was in the meantime sued out in behalf of Swartwout and Bollman, but before it could be properly tested, a superseding bench warrant charging high treason had placed them in the custody of the Civil Courts. Whereupon a motion was made for their discharge on the ground that the supporting evidence failed to make out a *prima facie* case against them. Jefferson hastened then to procure Eaton's affidavit, with its tale of horrors and proposed assassinations, in order to bolster that of Wilkinson. Charles Lee, Robert G. Harper and Francis S. Key represented the prisoners. After long argument before a vast concourse of curious people, the Court sustained the warrant and committed them to jail for trial by a vote of two to one — two Republican judges to one Federalist.

An appeal was taken from the District Court to the Supreme Court, with the redoubtable Luther Martin now associated with the defense. On February 21, 1807, Chief Justice John Marshall delivered the majority opinion of the Court. After an elaborate analysis of the famous cipher letter (in Wilkinson's translation), after a consideration of the various affidavits produced in support of the charge of treason, it was their opinion that there was no evidence whatsoever of acts constituting treason under the Constitution. Whereupon the two men were discharged from custody.

The next prisoner to arrive was Alexander, the New Orleans attorney whose sole offense it had been to act as counsel for the victims of Wilkinson's despotic seizures. He, too, was promptly released on a writ of habeas corpus. On February 17th, the endless procession of deportations brought John Adair and Peter V. Ogden to Baltimore's shore. More writs — and they likewise found themselves freed of custody and restraint.

" Very much to my surprise and mortification," wrote the Justice who had signed the writs, to Jefferson, " there was no proof of any nature whatsoever with them, although I administered an oath to Lieutenant Luckett with a view to acquire the necessary information from him. He could give none except the common conversation of the day. And I was under the necessity of discharging the prisoners." [17] Impartial justice indeed! But Jefferson consoled the disgruntled Nicholson, Republican friend whom he had placed upon the Bench, with the remark that "their crimes are defeated, and whether they should be punished or not belongs to another department, and is not the subject of even a wish on my part." [18] It is a pity that the President of the United States did not pursue this wise and tolerant course in the case of Aaron Burr, soon to be tried before another court.

Chapter XXV

TRIED FOR TREASON

1. The Titans Gather

THE stage was now set for the final act in the tremendous drama of conspiracy and treason with which the nation had been regaled. For months the country had been tossing in a confused welter of rumors, alarms, tales of phantom armies and desperate rebellion; now the mists had cleared to disclose the slight, elegantly dressed figure of Aaron Burr, pale but composed of face, eyes as brilliantly inscrutable as ever, as the focal-point of all the tumult. The beating spotlight which had hitherto dissipated its energies on diverse and remote sections of the land, now concentrated its blinding gleam on the town of Richmond, in the State of Virginia, and upon the spare, erect little man with hair carefully brushed back from his high, intellectual forehead. Aaron Burr, against whom all the resources of Government, all the ingenuity of President and Cabinet, all the power of public propaganda and an envenomed press, were to be directed in a mighty effort to convict him of high treason and sedition, and thereupon hang him high upon a gallows, his head snapping in the encircling noose, his trim feet dancing for the last time on the insubstantial breeze. No wonder the nation quivered and thrilled with an emotional orgy, and all eyes — and numerous feet — were directed to the gracious, aristocratic precincts of Richmond. The drama was approaching its climax.

Richmond had been chosen as the seat of the trial because of an unfortunate dictum tossed off by Marshall in the course of his opinion discharging Swartwout and Bollman from custody. To support the charge of treason, he had said, " war must be actually levied . . . To conspire to levy war, and actually to levy war, are distinct offenses. The first must be brought into open action by an assemblage of men for a purpose treasonable in itself, or the fact of levying war cannot have been committed." This was sound constitutional law. For the Constitution of the United States had clearly defined treason against the United States to consist " only in levying war against them, or in adhering to their enemies, giving them aid and comfort." Obviously the two prisoners had neither assembled nor levied war. But Marshall, as too many judges are prone to do, added more than was essential to a decision of the instant case. It was not necessary, however, he continued, that one should in fact " appear in arms against his country . . . If a body of men be actually assembled for the purpose of effecting by force a treasonable purpose; all those who perform any part, however minute, or however remote from the scene of the action, and who are actually leagued in the general conspiracy, are to be considered as traitors." [1] This *obiter dicta* was to cause the Chief Justice many uncomfortable moments during the trial of Aaron Burr.

For the Government attorneys, studying the decision, seized upon this section of the opinion as the thin wedge whereby their more important prisoner could be convicted. In most of those territories where Burr had actually appeared in an assemblage of armed men, he had already been held guiltless of any crime by qualified Grand Juries. These were Kentucky and Mississippi. Which left Ohio and Indiana as possibilities — questionable because of the fleeting nature of his sojourn, and the prospect that in those remote places, far from the vigilant eye of the Government, trial would again mean speedy acquittal.

But if it were not necessary for Burr to have been present at the place of assemblage — and Marshall had so stated — then the matter was simplified. The real place of gathering of men armed for desperate emprise had been Blennerhassett's Island — where the militia had attacked and wreaked vengeance on wine barrels and defenseless fences. And Blennerhassett's Island was providentially situated in Wood County, in the State of Virginia. Wherefore Richmond became the *situs* of trial, not far from Washington, and the unfaltering regard of Jefferson himself.

There was, however, one ironical fly in the ointment. The Justice of the Supreme Court in whose Circuit Richmond lay was none other than that redoubtable upholder of Federalist principles and the inviolability of judicial supremacy, Chief Justice John Marshall himself. The battle thereby became triangular, with Burr, Marshall, and Jefferson occupying the apexes. The three most impressive and titanic personalities of the day were thus joined in mutual conflict, on the result of which one man's life depended, and the reputations of the other two. But to Jefferson's jaundiced eye, it seemed more like a coalition of judge and prisoner against the Administration, and he prepared his course cannily to lime the one and snare the other. Let him but catch Marshall showing favor and bias towards Burr, and he would have him, as well as the entire judiciary, discredited before the country.

There were many angles to this last great battle of the gods. Marshall stood like an impassive stone colossus in Jefferson's way. So did Burr, who should have trembled at the bar of justice, yet did not. The Federalists had plucked up courage, after years of supine acquiescence, and were hammering once more at Jeffersonian policies. The present *cause célèbre* was their opportunity. Worse still, the irrepressible John Randolph and his little band of recalcitrant Republicans, known to all and sundry as the *Quids,* were hovering on his flanks like stinging hornets. Let him make but one false step and the opposition would grow to an irresistible clamor. The lone figure of Aaron Burr, therefore, had become more than that of a mere traitor, of a man against whom Jefferson had held peculiar personal animosity; he was the focal-point for all the latent and open opposition against the Administration, the symbol and rallying-cry for all discontent. It was therefore necessary to convict and hang him at all costs — for Jefferson's own political sake. The question of meticulous, abstract justice, of due process of law, could not be permitted to be entertained. Aaron Burr *must* be destroyed! And if John Marshall attempted to block the path of political expediency, he, too, must be destroyed — discredited, impeached, removed from office, and the power of a hated judiciary forever obliterated.

The opposition planned its attacks skilfully. It did not cry out the innocence of Aaron Burr, though informed men like Senator Plumer, after much shifting, had come finally to the conclusion that "Burr's object was the Mexican provinces — not a seperation [*sic*] of the Union." [2] The people of the country had been propagandized into an ineradicable belief in the guilt of the former Vice-President. Instead, those opposed to the President began to snipe persistently at his Achilles' heel — to wit, one General James Wilkinson. The latter's reign of terror at New Orleans — of which reports were coming thick and fast — his devious courses, the deep cloud of suspicion which surrounded his every move, were meat and drink to the snipers. They fulminated against the General in the halls of Congress; they howled against him at every possible opportunity — and the public was listening. Wilkinson himself wrote in fear and trembling to his protector, Jefferson, "You must long before this perusal have heard . . . of the persecution and abuse I have suffered and am suffering in consequence of it . . . But sir, when the tempest has passed away and dangers have disappeared I must hope I shall not be left alone to buffet a combination of bar and bench." [3]

Jefferson was compelled to give him aid and comfort. Willy-nilly, he had to assume the ungrateful role of protector to the malodorous General, to approve of his acts — no matter how indefensible, and to safeguard him from all attacks. For the General was the chief and almost only real witness against Burr. Let his reputation be destroyed, and the case of the Government *versus* Burr failed of its own weight. Thus it came about in March, 1807, when Major Bruff told Secretary of War Dearborn that he could prove Wilkinson's treasonable complicity in the conspiracy, Dearborn blandly replied " there might be an enquiry after the present bustle was over, but at present, he [Wilkinson] must and would be supported." And further, that Wilkinson " had stood low in the estimation of government before his energetic measures at New Orleans, but now he stood very high." When Bruff, astounded at this exhibition of Administration ethics, went to the Attorney General with his story, it was to meet with a cynical shrug of shoulders and an inquiry — " what would be the result if all this should be proven? — why just what the federalists and the enemies of the present administration wish — it would turn the indignation of the people from Burr on Wilkinson; Burr would escape, and Wilkinson take his place." [4] All of which was to come to light at the trial, and must take its place in history as an example of the unbiased, open-minded and judicial spirit with which the Government of the United States, under the guidance of that philosopher and believer in " the rights of man," Thomas Jefferson, proceeded to try the question of the guilt or innocence of Aaron Burr.

2. MARSHALL DEFINES TREASON

John Marshall hastened down from Washington to Richmond, and issued a warrant whereby the prisoner, Aaron Burr, was taken out of the custody of the military, in whose grasp he had been ever since his initial arrest, and delivered over to the civil authorities for examination.

On March 30, 1807, Burr, under close guard at the Eagle Tavern, was taken before the Chief Justice, in a retired room in the same building, for the preliminary hearing and commitment. A celebrated array of counsel crowded into the small chamber behind the prisoner — the greatest assemblage of legal talent ever witnessed at one time in America, to participate in the most famous criminal trial in American history. To the disappointment of the curious citizenry the door swung shut behind them, and they were compelled to cool their heels in the tap-room of the Tavern, there to wait expectantly for the news as it filtered out from the sanctum, meanwhile consoling themselves with small beer and headier potations, to the great delight of mine host, the innkeeper.

For the defense, there was first and foremost Aaron Burr himself, one of the finest lawyers the nation had yet produced, resourceful, technical, familiar with every loophole and cranny of the law, logically formidable and coolly intellectual, even when his own life was the stake. Around him he had gathered the flower of the country's bar — great lawyers who had volunteered their services in behalf of their accused compeer. All of them were Virginians — Edmund Randolph, who had held the offices of Attorney General and Secretary of State under Washington; Benjamin Botts, learned and thorough; John Baker, acquainted with the ways of juries; and, later, Charles Lee, former Attorney General of Maryland. But the weight of the defense rested on two men — John Wickham, a truly great lawyer whose talents have not been adequately appreciated, whose close marshaling of facts rivaled the talent of Burr himself, and who was more philosophical and comprehensive in his grasp of the material. He was to make the greatest speech and finest forensic effort of the entire trial. With him was Luther Martin, who had thundered and roared at the impeachment trial of Justice Chase, and who detested and was reciprocally hated by Jefferson with wholesome cordiality. It was upon this nicknamed "bulldog of Federalism" that the defense was to rely for epithet and denunciation, the flowery periods so impressive to the lay mind, and the political scarification of the President. For the defense had no illusions as to the master mind in back of the prosecution: every move, every detail of strategy, was dictated by Thomas Jefferson himself, of the Executive branch of Government.

For the prosecution the array of attorneys was considerably lighter in number and in legal weight. Caesar A. Rodney, the Attorney General, whose province it should have been to direct the case, hastily dissociated himself from the prosecution under one lame pretense or another. He saw no profit for himself in the proceedings, and wisely foresaw only a considerable lessening of prestige. The chief burden rested upon George Hay, United States District Attorney for Virginia, a capable enough attorney, but blundering confusedly throughout the trial — possibly because his heart was not in it, possibly because of the constant interference by the President of the United States. Associated with him were William Wirt, young and aggressive, of the flowery school of oratory to counterbalance Luther Martin, yet possessed of considerable wit and talent; and Alexander McRae, Lieutenant-

Governor of Virginia, a definitely inferior lawyer, brought into the case for political reasons.

In the judicial chair of this tavern court sat Chief Justice John Marshall, under whose powerful sway the Supreme Court had steadily forged ahead to assume a commanding position in the structure of government possibly not contemplated by the authors of the Constitution. Beveridge describes him as " towering, ramshackle, bony, loose-jointed, negligently dressed, simple and unconventional of manner," physically a perfect contrast to the scrupulously elegant, short, erect Burr. Burr was fifty years of age, Marshall six months older. Both were logical, clear, purposeful thinkers; both were subtle and astute, both were lucid in statement, though Marshall was prone to tiresome repetition, while Burr was concise and irrefutable. There they stood facing each other, as once before they had done, when Marshall had administered and Burr had repeated the oath of the Vice-President of the United States.[5]

George Hay opened the hearing by introducing into evidence a copy of the record in the case of Bollman and Swartwout, which included the depositions of Wilkinson and Eaton; then Nicholas Perkins took the stand to testify to the capture of the prisoner. When he had finished, Hay moved to commit Burr for the Grand Jury on two grounds: first, high misdemeanor " in setting on foot, within the United States, a military expedition against the dominions of the King of Spain "; second, and more important, " for treason in assembling an armed force, with a design to seize the city of New-Orleans, to revolutionize the territory attached to it, and to separate the western from the Atlantic states." [6]

Whereupon Marshall adjourned court for argument on this crucial motion until the following day, and directed that further hearings be held in the State Capitol building. Meanwhile he admitted Burr to bail of $5,000 *pendente lite.* Hay had insisted on a larger arena for the trial of the cause, and even for the preliminary motions. This was Jefferson's idea, to dramatize and hold the proceedings in the full glare of publicity, both to arouse the popular emotion and to keep every move of Marshall under open scrutiny.

When court opened again in its new quarters, the great room was immediately jammed to capacity, and hundreds clamored vainly outside for admission. Hay, still under orders, demanded that they adjourn to the Hall of Delegates, to give all and sundry a chance to hear and see the show. Marshall, curiously enough, complied, and that too was promptly filled in every nook and cranny. Mob spirit was in the air; though Burr was not without friends, and daily he was making more by his composure, his conduct before his accusers, and the more and more obvious malice of the prosecution. Daily the Federalists rallied to his standard, and the more fearless and disinterested Republicans.

For two days the argument swung back and forth on the motion, with Hay the proponent and Wickham in opposition. Hay declared that Burr's cipher letter to Wilkinson was proof positive of treasonable intent, while Wickham was equally certain that it was evidence of an innocent design. Where is there a single phrase that could possibly be construed as traitorous? Here is specified only an expedition against Spanish possessions, *if and when* the United States declared war. Perfectly innocent, perfectly laudable; in fact, the project of a true patriot.

Burr himself rose to speak, but only " to repel some observations [by Hay] of a personal nature." He was being persecuted, he said, on a series of mere conjectures, with which the infamous Wilkinson had only too easily frightened the President and the country. He spoke feelingly of his military incarceration, the illegality of his arrest, his denial of all civil privileges; and called attention to his three former trials for the same offenses, in which he had been uniformly found guiltless, his conduct praised and that of his persecutors severely scored. Then he sat down, having made his points for the benefit of the spectators as well as for the Court.[7]

On April 1st, Marshall delivered his opinion. It was lengthy and carefully prepared. On the question of the misdemeanor, he said, the cipher letter and Wilkinson's deposition sufficiently constituted a *prima facie* case to warrant committing Burr for Grand Jury action. But as for the graver charge of treason — and here the spectators leaned forward breathlessly in their seats — the Constitution of the United States had defined it plainly and with precise detail. " Treason against the United States," declared that sacred document, " shall consist only in levying war against them, or in adhering to their enemies, giving them aid and comfort." Further to safeguard the individual against governmental tyranny, the Constitution stated emphatically that " no person shall be convicted of treason unless on the testimony of two witnesses to the same overt act, or on confession in open court."

Marshall then amplified the Constitutional provisions in the light of Blackstone and other eminent English commentators. He analyzed the affidavits of Wilkinson and Eaton, sole evidence before the Court to the charge, and found nothing but mere rumor and conjecture, mere intention as against commission. " An intention to commit treason," he argued, " is an offence entirely distinct from the actual commission of that crime. War can only be levied by the employment of actual force. Troops must be embodied, men must be assembled in order to levy war . . . these are facts which cannot remain invisible. Treason may be machinated in secret, but it can be perpetrated only in open day and in the eye of the world. Testimony of a fact which in its own nature is so notorious ought to be unequivocal."

He proceeded now from the general to the particular. " The fact to be proved in this case is an act of public notoriety. It must exist in the view of the world, or it cannot exist at all. The assembling of forces to levy war is a visible transaction, and numbers must witness it. It is therefore capable of proof; and when time to collect this proof has been given, it ought to be adduced, or suspicion becomes ground too weak to stand upon.

" Several months have elapsed," he continued reading, " since this fact did occur, if it ever occurred. More than five weeks have elapsed, since the opinion of the supreme court [in re Swartwout and Bollman] has declared the necessity of proving the fact, if it exists. Why is it not proved? " He paused, and an audible sigh came from the crowded courtroom. This was obviously a direct thrust at Jefferson. Then he resumed. " If, in November or December last, a body of troops had been assembled on the Ohio, it is impossible to suppose that affidavits establishing the fact could not have been obtained by the last of March . . . I cannot doubt that means to obtain information have been taken on the part of the prosecution; if it existed, I cannot doubt the practicability of obtaining it; and its nonproduction, at this late hour, does not, in my opinion, leave me at liberty to give to those suspicions which grow out of other circumstances, that weight to which at an earlier day they might have been entitled. I shall not therefore," he closed, " insert in the commitment the charge of high treason." Bail was fixed on the misdemeanor count at $10,000, which was furnished that same day by five sureties, and Burr walked out, temporarily at least, a free man.[8] For seven weeks he was to remain free, until the next term of the United States Circuit Court, on May 22nd.

The prosecution was stunned, and Jefferson, to whom the news was sent by fast courier, was furious. The prey, of which he had been so certain, was escaping. The misdemeanor charge — levying war against Spain — was trivial in the eyes of the nation. Surely it was not enough to justify the extraordinary measures both he and Wilkinson had taken. He was discomfited; more, he was discredited. And John Marshall, the Federalist, the third formidable antagonist of his career — after Hamilton and Burr — had administered the blow.

The very next day he was writing James Bowdoin in a rage that " hitherto we have believed our law to be, that suspicion on probable grounds was sufficient ground to commit a person for trial, allowing time to collect witnesses till the trial. But the judges here have decided, that conclusive evidence of guilt must be ready in the moment of arrest, or they will discharge the malefactor. If this is still insisted on, Burr will be discharged; because his crimes having been sown from Maine, through the whole line of the western waters, to New Orleans, we cannot bring witnesses here under four months. The fact is, that the federalists make Burr's cause their own, and exert their whole influence to shield him from punishment, as they did the adherents of Miranda. And it is unfortunate that federalism is still predominant in our judiciary department, which is consequently in opposition to the legislative and executive branches, and is able to baffle their measures often." [9]

Jefferson was permitting his spleen to disturb his reasoning powers. At no time had mere suspicion of a crime been sufficient to hold a prisoner for trial, after a preliminary hearing. This was the instrument of autocracy and unbridled tyranny, not of the English common law. There must always be adduced sufficient testimony to make out a *prima facie* case, such a case as would be sufficient to convict on a trial, if uncontradicted or not explained away. The rest of his dissertation is mere rhetoric. It was not necessary to obtain witnesses from Maine to New Orleans; it was sufficient to have two competent witnesses to a single act of treason anywhere along the line — in this particular instance, Wood County, Virginia, not very far away.

The fact is, as Marshall pertinently pointed out, that the whole might of the Administration had been concentrated from an earlier period in an eager search for testimony. As far back as February 27th, the Cabinet had decided to " institute an inquiry into the proceedings of Burr and his adherents from New York to New Orleans," and to appoint men in all the places along that route to take affidavits as to his alleged crimes.[10] Attorney General Rodney acted immediately on these instructions. He printed lists of questions, and broadcast them throughout the land, with appeals to all good citizens having knowledge of the facts to come forward and make affidavit thereto; while Government agents scoured the

THOMAS JEFFERSON

From a bust by Jean-Antoine Houdon

JOHN MARSHALL

From a portrait by John Wesley Jarvis

country, ferreting out every scrap of evidence. No pains were spared, and no expense, to make the search as extensive and thorough as possible.

But now, in the face of Marshall's decision, Jefferson ordered renewed activity, on a scale before and since unexampled in the history of American justice. Government agents swarmed everywhere, prying and snooping; a deputy marshal and special messenger went forthwith to Wood County to collect depositions and summon witnesses. Jackson was solicited by Madison as well as by Rodney to disclose what he knew. Wilkinson sent agents into the Mississippi Territory to collect all available testimony, and to manufacture it, if necessary. He blustered and threatened and bribed members of Burr's expedition, in a desperate attempt to obtain proof against Burr. Jefferson was not content with the misdemeanor charge; he hoped and expected to be able to hang Burr for high treason.

On April 20th, he was still complaining bitterly of the perfidy of the Federalist Chief Justice. " That there should be anxiety and doubt in the public mind, in the present defective state of the proof, is not wonderful; and this has been sedulously encouraged by the tricks of the judges to force trials before it is possible to collect the evidence." Five weeks? Five months was barely time enough. He had instructed Rodney to inform Marshall of this condition unofficially, but the Chief Justice had refused to listen. " All this, however, will work well," Jefferson exclaimed. " The nation will judge both the offender and judges for themselves. If a member of the executive or legislature does wrong, the day is never far distant when the people will remove him. They will see then and amend the error in our Constitution, which makes any branch independent of the nation. They will see that one of the great coordinate branches of the government, setting itself in opposition to the other two, and to the common sense of the nation, proclaims impunity to that class of offenders which endeavors to overturn the Constitution, and are themselves protected in it by the Constitution itself; for impeachment is a farce which will not be tried again. If their protection of Burr produces this amendment, it will do more good than his condemnation would have done." The trial was rapidly broadening out into a wholesale battle of political principles and parties, and involving the fundamental structure of the government itself.

Jefferson ended his letter in a manner highly reminiscent of similar remarks by Hamilton, and, like them, outraging every sense of truth or probability. " Against Burr, personally," he said,

" I never had one hostile sentiment. I never indeed thought him
an honest, frank-dealing man, but considered him as a crooked
gun, or other perverted machine, whose aim or shot you could
never be sure of. Still, while he possessed the confidence of the
nation, I thought it my duty to respect in him their confidence,
and to treat him as if he deserved it; and if his punishment can
be commuted now for an useful amendment of the Constitution,
I shall rejoice in it." [11] Words entirely belied by his actions.
Every effort was concentrated to crush and destroy Burr, and, in
the process, Marshall and the judiciary. Jefferson's own prestige
depended on it. He had gone too far to retract now; had he not
said that Burr was guilty beyond all question?

Surrounded thus by the baying hounds of the Administration,
Aaron Burr was not dismayed. He realized to the full that his
initial victory in having the charges against him reduced to a
mere misdemeanor was but a temporary one; that his enemies
would not rest or cease to harry him with all the resources at their
command. Nevertheless he retained, as always, that perfect outward composure and inner calm which had marked him throughout his career. He had never been known to complain at the
keenest arrows of misfortune, nor would he permit others to lament for him.

Poor Theo was taking her father's imprisonment and pending
trial with that anguish of spirit which comes only to a keenly sensitive and imaginative mind. Burr would have none of that, and
reproved her sharply. " Your letters of the 10th and those preceding seemed to indicate a sort of stupor; but now you rise into
phrenzy. Another ten days will, it is hoped, have brought you
back to reason." He was beginning to be very skeptical of democracy now — at least the particular brand devised by Jefferson.
" You have read to very little purpose," he admonished his daughter, " if you have not remarked that such things happen in all
democratic governments. Was there in Greece or Rome a man of
virtue and independence, and supposed to possess great talents,
who was not the object of vindictive and unrelenting persecution." [12]

Hay, the prosecuting attorney, wondered at the defendant's
calmness and seeming lack of interest. He wrote his superior in
office that " Burr lies here entirely dormant. I do not understand
that he pays visits, and I believe he receives very few. The disposition manifested by the enemies of the administration to pat-
ronise him, and raise a clamor, seems to have gone off." [13]

But Hay was not very observant. Burr was extremely busy, and never less dormant than now. He was engaged closely with his counsel in mapping his defense against all contingencies, in planning, searching and briefing the law of treason with a diligence and perspicuity hardly to be equaled in the annals of law. He was also carefully and slowly gathering around him, by the infinite charm of his manner, the leading families of Richmond, socially if not politically powerful, and whose influence was therefore all the more subtle and penetrating. John Wickham, of counsel, gave notable dinners at which the flower of Virginia society was gathered — there to meet the man whom Jefferson had called a traitor. At one of these dinners the Chief Justice, John Marshall, was present. So, too, was Aaron Burr. It is certain they did not discuss the case, or exchange any remarks except the normal courtesies, yet the Jeffersonian partisans seized upon the episode with loud clamors as an effective means of destroying public confidence in the integrity of the Court. Judge and prisoner hobnobbing over wine, and toasting " treason " arm in arm!

Nor did the Administration permit the intervening time to pass in idleness. The Republican papers teemed with abuse, depositions were gathered by the ream, witnesses were dragooned and subpoenaed to Richmond from the ends of the earth. A Grand Jury was drawn for the ensuing term, and it had been selected with care for the purpose in hand. " The grand jury," Burr advised his daughter, " is composed of twenty democrats and four federalists. Among the former is W. C. Nicholas, my vindictive and avowed personal enemy — the most so that could be found in this state [Virginia]. The most indefatigable industry is used by the agents of government, and they have money at command without stint. If I were possessed of the same means, I could not only foil the prosecutors, but render them ridiculous and infamous. The democratic papers teem with abuse against me and my counsel, and even against the chief justice. Nothing is left undone or unsaid which can tend to prejudice the public mind, and produce a conviction without evidence." [14]

3. COURT CONVENES

On May 22, 1807, the hitherto placid town of Richmond was a seething, swarming hive of humanity. Overnight, the population of five thousand had been almost doubled. Rough men from the mountains, clad in coarse woolens and deerskin jackets, jostled with scant ceremony elegant gentlemen in silk knee-breeches, and long queues carefully powdered and beribboned. Dainty ladies with parasols against the Southern sun tripped along the narrow sidewalks to the round-eyed envy of frontier women in red flannel petticoats and to the rude snickers of the frontier louts. Politicians rubbed shoulders with small farmers, mere visitors from far-off New York and Boston disputed the streets with a horde of witnesses, willing and reluctant alike, come from Maine and New Orleans, flanked day and night by watchful agents, vigilant against unholy contact with the defense, prodding their memories, conning their well-taught lessons for them.

Such a swarm had never descended upon the town within the memory of man. The taverns were full to bursting, every private house in town in reduced circumstances, and many with bolder fronts, took in guests who paid in coin of the realm for the courtesy; and still the clamor for beds and accommodations was unabated. The country folk perforce slept in tents or wagons on bedded straw, or on the river banks under the open starlight. The taverns emptied all day to the courtroom and rang all night with oaths and loud talk and calls for liquor and more liquor. Bets were freely made on the outcome — wagers of substantial size — while tobacco-juice spattered sand-box and floor and walls with indiscriminate liberality. It was a show they had come to see, and they would not be denied. The greatest show America had ever offered for the entertainment of its populace — the proud spectacle of a solitary man, bankrupt in fortune, pitting his strength against the mighty government of the United States in a dramatic battle for his life. Gentlemen of the press watched the crowd, the Court, the shifting pageantry of tavern and counsel bench, and sharpened their quills to the task in approved modern fashion.

It was chiefly a Republican audience, come to see their idol, Jefferson, overthrow the son of Belial, the traitor Burr. For months it had been beaten into their ears with trumpets and drums — Burr was a traitor, a scoundrel who had sought to break up the glorious Union. It would take more than mere logic, more than esoteric legalisms, to make them change the stubborn mold of their minds. Only here and there, among the Federalists, or the more thoughtful Republicans — aside from Burr's own personal friends and immediate circle — was there a doubt as to the ultimate guilt of this prisoner whose bearing and dignity made all forget his stature, and whose eye could not be met without an inward quailing. That doubt grew more and more formidable as the weary, yet infinitely dramatic trials wore on from day to day; others joined the band of those who had come to curse and remained to wonder; but even at the end they were but a small, and for the most part discreetly voiceless, minority. Jefferson and Wilkinson had done their task but too well.

The hall of the House of Delegates was crowded to the rafters when Chief Justice Marshall banged his gavel a little past noon to demand some modicum of order from the motley throng of spectators. It was an impressive sight, for all its mingling of urban polish and frontier crudeness. Two men dominated the proceedings from beginning to end. John Marshall, in the seat of the mighty, and Aaron Burr, prisoner before the bar. They were foemen — in a sense — worthy of each other's steel. " There he stood," exclaimed young Winfield Scott, later to become Lieutenant-General and hero of the Mexican War, " in the hands of power, on the brink of danger, as composed, as immovable, as one of Canova's living marbles." [15] Clad in black silk, elegant, distinguished, slim, eyes blackly brilliant, hair brushed neatly back and tied in the fashionable powdered queue; speaking in quiet, even tones, yet whose least syllable penetrated the stir and bustle of the courtroom, Aaron Burr was a figure to impress the rudest. On the bench next to the tall, loose-jointed Chief Justice sat an Associate Justice for that Circuit, one Cyrus Griffin, conceived in anonymity and dedicated throughout the long proceedings to silences more utter than those of frozen Antarctica. No arguments were addressed to him by opposing counsel, no sign of his presence exists in the three-volume record except for a faint few words, modest in tone and thought, followed by quick relapse into the caverns of discreet darkness. One wonders at his thoughts as he sat, day after day, a lay figure, while his towering colleague delivered pathfinding opinions and the oratorical thunder burst in salvos about him.

Surrounding Burr were his counsel — Edmund Randolph, John Wickham, Benjamin Botts, and John Baker. Luther Martin and Charles Lee were to enter the proceedings later. Across the way sat the prosecution — George Hay, William Wirt, and Alexander McRae, fumbling their papers, nervous, reading the latest instructions from the master-mind, Jefferson, cocking ears toward the door for sound of a new messenger, direct from Washington, with more instructions. Advice, strategy, documents, in an endless stream from the President of the United States.

The Court opened with the impaneling of the Grand Jury — that Jury which had been handpicked for the task. To it was to be entrusted the task of considering *in camera* the evidence against Aaron Burr, and deciding on indictment or dismissal of the charges of filibustering and treason. As the clerk droned the names of the assembled jurymen, Burr arose and made his objections. After a preliminary skirmish addressed to the method of summoning the jurors, he challenged specifically Senator William B. Giles, who had, he said, made public and private statements evidencing a formal prejudgment of the case; and also Wilson C. Nicholas, former Congressman, who had always evinced for Burr the bitterest personal animosity. With much reluctance these two gentlemen withdrew. John Randolph of Roanoke appeared, and Marshall promptly appointed him foreman of the Grand Jury. A clever stroke, but not creditable to Marshall's judicial conduct. For Randolph hated Jefferson and loathed Wilkinson. Yet he was convinced of Burr's guilt as well, and asked to be excused from duty on that ground. Burr looked at him quietly, and observed, " I am afraid we shall not be able to find any man without this prepossession," and permitted him to remain. In fact, as juror after juror was examined for his opinions, it was discovered that practically every one had already formed an opinion prejudicial to Burr. George Hay, the prosecutor, remarked with thinly veiled triumph, " There was not a man in the United States, who probably had not formed an opinion on the subject; and if such objections as these were to prevail, Mr. Burr might as well be acquitted at once." [16] Whereupon the defense objected no more, and permitted the impaneling of a Grand Jury notable for the political and personal prominence of its members, and notable also for the antagonism it displayed to the defendant in advance of submitted evidence. Fourteen of them were Republican and two were Federalist.

After Marshall had charged the Grand Jury, the battle opened; to be conducted, at least on the side of the defense, with infinite resource, learning and a maze of legal technicalities that obviously bewildered the prosecution and astounded even Marshall himself. When Hay objected to Burr's request for certain instructions to the jury on the admissibility of evidence, and declared with heat that Burr " stood on the same footing with every other man charged with crime," Burr raised his voice for almost the only time in the long contest. " Would to God," he exclaimed, " that I did stand on the same ground with every other man. This is the first time that I have been permitted to enjoy the rights of a citizen." [17] Whereupon court was adjourned for further argument and the presentation of evidence to the Jury.

But Wilkinson, the star witness for the prosecution, was still on his way to Richmond from New Orleans, and the Jury was compelled to adjourn from day to day, marking time, pending the

General's arrival. In spite of this, Hay moved on May 25th to commit Burr for treason on the ground of newly adduced evidence. At once Burr and his battery of lawyers were on their feet protesting that no notice of this new motion had been given them, as previously agreed, and that Hay was now attempting to compel the Court to usurp the functions of the Grand Jury, then in session. Hay retorted that the reason he had given no notice was because Wilkinson was soon to come, and, he added sneeringly, " I do not pretend to say what effect it might produce upon Colonel Burr's mind; but certainly Colonel Burr would be able to effect his escape, merely upon paying the recognisance of his present bail." [18] Whereupon the floodgates on both sides burst loose. Botts poured the vials of his scorn upon government and Wilkinson alike, inquired sarcastically of Hay whether he was trying his case in a court of law or in the public press and the poisoned minds of the populace, and demanded why this star witness was not already there. Wirt and Hay answered in kind. Burr summed up coldly to the effect that the Government, with six months of accumulating evidence, was admitting by its constant adjournments that it had not enough to go before the Grand Jury to obtain indictments, yet now wished the court to usurp those functions and commit him to jail on the flimsiest of rumors and suspicions. Wirt had charged them with declamation against the Government. It was no mere declamation, Burr declared, when a democratic government aped the despotism of European autocracy, shanghaied his friends, robbed post-offices, utilized military authority while civil courts were functioning. The President had shouted war, yet for six months they had hunted for this mythical war and found no traces of it.

Again and again, during every argument, on every motion, Burr and his counsel were to hammer at Jefferson, at the malignancy of his persecution, at the illegality of his acts, until the Government attorneys writhed and frothed at the mouth. It was grand strategy, plotted in advance. Before they were through, a bewildered court and spectators alike were not quite sure who actually was on trial: Burr — or Jefferson and Wilkinson. The court was a sounding-board for political speeches and accusations on both sides, addressed to the spectators' benches as well as to the gangling figure of Marshall; addressed still more to the wide country outside, in attempt to sway public opinion. What a trial it would have been for the modern broadcaster and his magic tubes and wires!

On May 26th, Marshall rendered his decision on the question of jurisdiction. He overruled Burr's objections, and declared that such a motion to commit was proper in form, and could be used instead of presenting bills for indictment to the Grand Jury then sitting.[19]

On the same day, Jefferson, from his watchtower in Washington, was telling Hay that "it becomes our duty to provide that full testimony [of the proceedings] shall be laid before the Legislature, and through them the public. For this purpose, it is necessary that we be furnished with the testimony of every person who shall be with you as a witness. If the Grand jury find a bill, the evidence given in court, taken as verbatim as possible, will be what we desire. If there be no bill, and consequently no examination before court, then I must beseech you to have every man privately examined by way of affidavit, and to furnish me with the whole testimony . . . Go into any expense necessary for this purpose, and meet it from the funds provided by the Attorney General for the other expenses." [20]

Hay demanded that Burr post heavy additional bail. Burr refused. Whereupon he produced his witnesses in support of the motion to commit for treason, and announced that he would place them on the stand and read the depositions of the absent in "chronological order." But Wickham rose to insist that a "strict legal order" be followed: i.e., that first the overt act itself be proved, and then Burr's complicity therein. Hay was taken aback, spoke vaguely of one great plot, involving both treason to the United States and an attack on Spain, and demanded a free hand. But Burr was in no mood to grant any favors. He intended to take advantage of every legal technicality arising out of the situation, as indeed he ought and must. He was on trial for his life, and it was no time for so-called "courtesies."

Hay, badgered beyond endurance by the proddings of the defense, their constant flow of technical objections to his every move, cried out angrily, "If, sir, exceptions are thus to be continually taken to the most common measures; if in this way every inch of ground is to be disputed, contrary to every practice that has prevailed in our country; instead of ten hours, or ten days, this trial will take up ten years." [21]

Marshall ultimately ruled that the Government be permitted a certain latitude in the introduction of its testimony. Whereupon Hay triumphantly offered Wilkinson's famous affidavit. Botts objected with tireless vigor. The *overt act!* he clamored. First submit evidence as to that, as to the *war* in Virginia, the *situs* of the alleged treason. He flung Marshall's own opinion *in re* Bollman and Swartwout back at him. This affidavit represents mere talk, he said, mere asseverations supposed to have been made by Swartwout to Wilkinson far from the scene of the war. Show us first that there had been a war; for without a war the charge of treason fails. " In this country," he finished impressively, " as there cannot be a constructive treasonable war, plans, and acts of associates, can only come in when the former have been executed, and the latter have been visibly and publicly assisted." 22 This was to be the crux of the defense, and the cry was ever to be raised, at every move of the prosecution, of *overt act* and *no constructive treason* until a bedeviled Hay and his associates heartily wished that such words and phrases had never been invented.

Marshall gently inquired of Hay why he produced Wilkinson's affidavit, inasmuch as the Supreme Court in the former case had already decided it contained no proof of the *overt act,* and was therefore inadmissible.

Hay then called his witnesses to prove the act: i.e., that war had been waged by the conspirators on Blennerhassett's Island. Peter Taylor, the gardener, told the story of his journey to warn Burr of impending mobs, of Blennerhassett's confused, rambling talk, of the assemblage of armed men on the Island that fateful night of December 10th when Blennerhassett and Tyler fled; and Jacob Allbright, the day laborer, unfolded his fantastic story of leveled muskets and Tupper's breast. But both admitted that Burr had not been on the Island during these alleged acts of war against the Government of the United States.

Then Hay attempted to read into evidence the affidavit of Jacob Dunbaugh. This was that sergeant from Fort Massac whom Bissell had given a furlough to accompany Burr. Inasmuch as he was a soldier, and subject to military discipline, Wilkinson had been more successful with him than with any others of Burr's entourage. Dunbaugh, it seemed, had exceeded the term of his furlough and had accordingly been posted as a deserter. To avoid certain obvious penalties, Wilkinson had *induced* him to sign an affidavit alleging the hasty destruction by Burr of large stands of arms and warlike material just before the flotilla was searched in Mississippi. But of this testimony, more later.

At the hearing, however, the defense objected to the introduction of this affidavit, and succeeded in keeping it out on technical grounds. Hay had no further evidence to produce until Wilkinson's arrival. Nevertheless he had the audacity to demand a heavy increase in the defendant's bail pending that event. Marshall, in some embarrassment, preferred not to render an opinion on this point, whereupon Burr came to the prosecutor's rescue by offering voluntarily an additional ten thousand, though Luther Martin, now joined in the defense, remarked sarcastically, " The motion of the gentleman [Hay] amounts to this: ' We have no evidence of treason, and are not ready to go to trial for the purpose of proving it; we therefore move the court to increase the bail.' " [23]

And now court, jurors, lawyers, defendant, spectators, the nation itself, settled back to await with varying degrees of patience the advent of the long-heralded, but never-appearing General Wilkinson. Without him the prosecution admitted it could not present its case. All depended on him. The country was raised skilfully to a fever-pitch of expectation. The redoubtable General became enlarged through propaganda to mythical proportions. Bets were freely offered in the Richmond taverns that Burr, rather than face the righteous accuser, would abscond before his arrival, bail or no bail. The witnesses loitered in town, at Government expense, waiting for the chief of them all. Eaton, in red sash and tremendous hat, swaggered with boon companions from pothouse to pothouse, drinking himself to the color of his sash, bragging and blustering against Burr. The ten thousand awarded him by a grateful Government for his affidavit itched in his pockets, demanding to be spent. General Jackson, summoned as witness by the prosecution, was now convinced of Burr's innocence. Whereupon he acted with his accustomed fiery courage. In an atmosphere of menace and threats, he harangued the crowds in Capitol Square, almost in front of the court, defending his friend, Burr, and denouncing the mighty Jefferson as a man afflicted with the demon of persecution.[24] More, he accused Wilkinson outright as a pensioner of Spain, and prophesied that he would not dare show his face in Richmond.[25]

And so it began to seem as June came, with its sweltering heat, and the overcrowded town waited and waited, while the long, lazy days slipped by. Young Washington Irving, in Richmond as a newspaper correspondent of sorts, and friendly to Burr — his brother, Dr. Peter Irving, was the editor of the *Morning Chronicle,* which Burr had godfathered — wrote home on June 4th that " we are now enjoying a kind of suspension of hostilities; the grand jury having been dismissed the day before yesterday for five or six days, that they might go home, see their wives, get their clothes washed, and flog their negroes." As for Burr, he " retains his serenity and self-possession unshaken, and wears the same aspect in all times and situations." [26]

While Wilkinson dawdled somewhere on the way, and hundreds wasted precious days in idleness, Burr was preparing himself, sawing wood with quiet assiduity. "Busy, busy, busy from morning till night — " he wrote Theo, still in Charleston, confused with a thousand alarms, " from night till morning, yet there are daily amusing incidents; things at which you will laugh, also things at which you will pout and scold." [27] The results of these midnight activities were soon to become visible. Burr was preparing *sub rosa* a bombshell to explode under the noses of the prosecution, whose repercussions were to extend even to the Executive Mansion itself.

4. THE PRESIDENT IS SUBPOENAED

On June 9, 1807, when court had opened for what seemed another day of futile wonderment at Wilkinson's whereabouts, Burr quietly arose from his seat, a sheaf of papers in his hand. He had a motion to direct to the presiding Justices. Marshall cocked his head wearily to listen to another of the interminable petty technicalities; Cyrus Griffin, his alleged colleague, was frankly half asleep; the prosecution table barely stirred. The few spectators in court sprawled with the sultry June torpor. It was time, thought most, to pack up and go home. There never would be a trial.

Speaking in his clear, even voice, Burr called the Court's attention to Jefferson's message to Congress in which he had spoken of a certain letter and other documents, all dated October 21, 1806, which he had received from General Wilkinson. The President had also mentioned various orders of the army and navy. Burr paused, patted his carefully knotted stock. He had applied for copies of the latter to Robert Smith, Secretary of the Navy, and had been refused. It was necessary, he continued, for the preparation of a proper defense that these several documents be made available to him, and therefore he requested the honorable Court to issue a subpoena *duces tecum* to the President of the United States to produce these papers in open court, unless, and he turned courteously to the now thoroughly aroused lawyers of the prosecution, they would consent to submit them to the inspection of the defense.

Here at last was sensation! The news spread through the town, and the spectators' benches rapidly filled. Hay was hot and fuming, and stammering as well. He would try and obtain those papers which the Court thought material. How could he decide on their materiality, inquired Marshall gently, when they were not before him? Hay's voice rose in anger. The Court had no power to compel the Executive's attendance by means of a subpoena. Marshall himself was doubtful. It was a ticklish point, and in the existing exacerbated state of emotions, a dangerous one — the judiciary attempting to haul the President of the United States before its judgment seat by compulsory process. He would call for argument on the moot question by counsel, he declared. Whereupon court adjourned for the day.

Hay hastened to his rooms and sent off an agonized letter to Jefferson, appealing to him to forward the papers without delay, because the " detention of them will afford [Burr] pretext for clamor." [28]

On June 10th, the historic argument opened. The heat was forgotten, except as it inflamed further already inflamed tempers. Hay invoked a technicality. This was a proceeding to commit, he argued, not a trial after indictment. Burr had no standing in court as yet, and was therefore not entitled to any legal process.

Luther Martin lumbered to his feet: he of the thundering voice and beet-red face, colored by years of assiduous potations. He was the spearhead of Burr's forensic army, the vituperative bludgeoner, the tickler of groundlings, even as John Wickham was the wielder of briefs and documented logic, while Burr himself remained the canny general and marshaler of his forces. " We did apply for copies; and were refused under presidential influence," he rumbled. " In New-York, on the farcical trials of Ogden and Smith the officers of the government screened themselves from attending, under the sanction of the president's name. Perhaps the same farce may be repeated here." He turned and looked squarely at his friend, John Marshall. " This is a peculiar case, sir. The president has undertaken to prejudge my client by declaring, that ' Of his guilt there can be no doubt.' He has assumed to himself the knowledge of the Supreme Being himself . . . He has proclaimed him a traitor in the face of that country, which has rewarded him. He has let slip the dogs of war, the hell-hounds of persecution, to hunt down my friend. And would this president of the United States, who has raised all this absurd clamour, pretend to keep back the papers which are wanted for this trial, where life itself is at stake? . . . Can it be presumed that the president would be sorry to have colonel Burr's innocence proved? " [29]

Sensation upon sensation. A direct, vitriolic attack on the sacrosanct person of the President himself. The courtroom reverberated with his thunder, while the spectators gasped and the

government lawyers grew pale with anger. Magnificent vituperation, well calculated to speed on the wings of rumor up and down
the land.

McRae tried vainly to establish a definitive position for the
prosecution, and failed. He admitted that Jefferson *as a private
individual* could be subpoenaed, but tried to show there was
something inherently different in a subpoena *duces tecum,* which
required the President to produce papers. These were, he said,
" confidential communications." Whereupon all of the lawyers
leaped joyously into the fray, and the discussion went on, day in
and day out, until June 13th, when Hay came into court with
Jefferson's reply to his letter of June 9th.

" Reserving the necessary right of the President of the United
States to decide, independently of all other authority," he wrote
cautiously, " what papers, coming to him as President, the public
interests permit to be communicated, and to whom, I assure you
of my readiness under that restriction, voluntarily to furnish on
all occasions, whatever the purposes of justice may require." Thus
hedged in against judicial compulsion, he authorized the production by Hay of Wilkinson's letter of October 21st, *but,* he was to
withhold those parts which were not material. As for the Army
and Navy orders, these should be specified by proper description.[30]

On June 13th, Marshall delivered his opinion. The point at
issue, he said, was " whether a subpoena *duces tecum* can be directed to the president of the United States, and whether it ought
to be directed in this case? " His decision was sweeping. He could
find nowhere in the Constitution, or the Statute, any exception
whatever to the right of the accused to compulsory process. " The
single reservation," he added significantly, " is the case of the
king." There were many points of difference, he went on ironically, between a president and a king. Of these he need mention
only two. " The king can do no wrong, that no blame can be imputed to him, that he cannot be named in debate." The tables
were being reversed with a vengeance when a Federalist could
insinuate, even by indirection, an attempt by Thomas Jefferson,
Democrat, to assume the perquisites of kingship. Wherefore, he
directed that a subpoena *duces tecum* issue against the President.[31]

Hay was thunderstruck, and wrote his usual daily letter to the
strategist in Washington. " There never was such a trial from
the beginning of the world to this day," he cried plaintively. And,
in the course of his opinion, Marshall had dared also to say that
the Government *expected* Burr's conviction, but he had later

hastened to apologize privately to Hay for the unfortunate expression.[32]

When the messenger brought the news to Jefferson, his wrath knew no bounds. Yet deep within his heart he realized that the decision had been rendered on good republican principles; that the President was not superior to or different from any other citizen before the law. By a process of rationalization, he turned on Luther Martin.

Something must be done about this " unprincipled & impudent federal bull-dog," he fumed. He had just heard that Martin had known all along about Burr's treasonable enterprise. " Shall we move to commit L M as *particeps criminis* with Burr? " he asked Hay, or just summon him as a witness?[33] To such tortuous measures was Jefferson descending in the vindictiveness of his wrath.

In the meantime, an even more unlovely situation had arisen. Not on account of the subpoena, for Jefferson had acquiesced in that, albeit reluctantly and with reservations; but because of one Erich Justus Bollman. Hay had finally proceeded to call additional witnesses on the long-delayed motion to commit. Bollman was his first. Now, that European emigré and confidant of Burr had made certain statements to Jefferson and Madison which Jefferson himself had promised would remain inviolate, and that the paper would never go out of his hand. Yet Jefferson, with a fine disregard for his promises, had forwarded the written statement to Hay, so that, if Bollman " should prevaricate, ask him whether he did not say so and so to Mr. Madison and myself." He also enclosed a sheaf of blank pardons, which Hay was to fill in at his own discretion, and distribute them among the petty offenders, and even to " the gross offenders," if it should ever " be visible that the principal will otherwise escape." [34] One of these especially was to be offered to Bollman. In other words, if only Burr could be convicted of treason, Jefferson did not care if all the others went scot free.

But Bollman, when placed on the stand, where he had the right to refuse to answer incriminating questions, unaccountably and with a fine scorn turned down the proffered pardon. He was not guilty of any crime, he insisted, and hence the pardon was at once an insult and an admission of guilt on his part. Hay insisted that the pardon was nevertheless effective, willy-nilly, and Marshall reserved decision on that point; never, somehow, to decide it. Hay hastened to ask Jefferson's advice as to his course if Marshall should uphold Bollman, and Jefferson ordered angrily that Hay

" move to commit him [Bollman] immediately for treason or misdemeanor, as you think the evidence will support." [35]

5. THE MAMMOTH OF INIQUITY

The Grand Jury had also commenced its inquiry into the indictments before it. News had come that the elusive Wilkinson was definitely on his way, and would be in Richmond shortly. So that there were now two separate and distinct moves on the part of the prosecution against Burr. A Grand Jury inquiry on bills of indictment, and a simultaneous motion to commit him to jail before the Court as committing Magistrates. Thomas Truxton, Benjamin Stoddert, Stephen Decatur, and others, were sworn by Marshall as witnesses, and sent before the Grand Jury to testify. But Bollman was another matter. He had refused a pardon, dramatically; hence, he could refuse to testify on the ground that he would incriminate himself. After a heated argument, he went into the deliberative chamber, with reservations as to the legal purport of his testimony and the proffered and rejected pardon.[36]

And now, General James Wilkinson himself appeared, gross of body, eyes deep-sunk in folds of fat, resplendent in full uniform, strutting, striding the streets of the town like long-expected Deity. Large sums passed hands on his appearance. For, wrote Irving, " the bets were against Burr that he would abscond, should W. come to Richmond; but he still maintains his ground, and still enters the Court every morning with the same serene and placid air that he would show were he brought there to plead another man's cause, and not his own." [37]

The prosecution heaved a sigh of relief. With their star witness safely in town, the battle was as good as won. But the defense was not impressed. When, on June 15th, it was the General's turn to appear before the Grand Jury, they promptly objected to his taking any papers along with him, even if only to refresh his recollection, unless the Court had first passed on their evidential pertinence. After lengthy argument, and much citation of law, Marshall permitted the Jury to inspect only such papers as represented an integral part of Wilkinson's narrative, and which had been written by the accused himself.

Wilkinson was a bit flustered and bewildered. He had expected to find Burr a cowering, trembling wretch, overwhelmed with the terror of expected conviction. Instead . . . but let him tell his own story. " I dreampt not of the importance attached to my presence," he wrote Jefferson in plaintive accents. " For I had anticipated that a deluge of testimony would have been poured forth from all quarters to overwhelm him [Burr] with guilt and dishonor. Sadly, indeed, was I mistaken, and to my astonishment I found the traitor vindicated, and myself condemned by a mass of wealth, character, influence, and talents. — Merciful God, what a spectacle did I behold — integrity and truth perverted and trampled under foot by turpitude and guilt, patriotism appalled and usurpation triumphant. Did I ever expect it would depend on my humble self to stop the current of such a polluted stream? Never, never."

He was beginning to feel inward qualms at the spectacle. But he did not disclose these to Jefferson. Instead, he narrated for the President's delectation how, on first meeting the man in court whom he had basely betrayed, " in spite of myself my eyes darted a flash of indignation at the little traitor, on whom they continued fixed until I was called to the Book; — here, sir, I found my expectations verified — this lion-hearted, eagle-eyed Hero, jerking under the weight of conscious guilt, with haggard eyes in an effort to meet the indignant salutation of outraged honor; but it was in vain, his audacity failed him. He averted his face, grew pale, and affected passion to conceal his perturbation." [38]

But Washington Irving, observing both antagonists from a spectator's bench, had a different story to narrate of the celebrated meeting. " Wilkinson strutted into court . . ." he reported, " swelling like a turkey-cock." But Burr " did not take notice of him until the judge directed the clerk to swear General Wilkinson; at the mention of the name Burr turned his head, looked him full in the face with one of his piercing regards, swept his eye over his whole person from head to foot, as if to scan its dimensions, and then coolly resumed his former position, and went on conversing with his counsel as tranquilly as ever. The whole look was over in an instant; but it was an admirable one. There was no appearance of study or constraint in it; no affectation of disdain or defiance; a slight expression of contempt played over his countenance." [39]

For four days Wilkinson held the center of proceedings in the Grand Jury room. His trump card, the cipher letter Burr had sent him, was examined, re-examined, re-deciphered and skeptically questioned by the implacable foreman, John Randolph. Outside, the world waited breathlessly. " Wilkinson is now before the grand jury," Irving reported, " and has such a mighty mass of *words* to deliver himself of, that he claims at least two days more to discharge the wondrous cargo." [40] There were others as well —

Swartwout, Dunbaugh, Taylor, Allbright, the Morgans — a continuous stream of witnesses who disappeared into the sinister maw of the jury room, later to be disgorged with admonitions of secrecy.

On June 17th, within the surcharged atmosphere of the courtroom, Burr exploded another bomb. This was a motion to attach Wilkinson, Judge Toulmin of the Mississippi Territory, and Congressman John G. Jackson for improper practices in the examination and intimidation of witnesses, and for the illegal transport of such witnesses from New Orleans by military force. Wilkinson blustered and quaked. His own sacred person was in danger of judicial process. It was then that he cried upon the remote Jefferson for aid and comfort.[41]

Hay tried desperately to save his favored witness from such malignant persecution. Such a motion, if ever to be heard, he cried, should be postponed until after the completion of the trial. But Marshall summarily brushed aside the objection and ordered a hearing.[42] Burr submitted affidavits by James Knox and Chandler Lindsley in support of his latest move. Knox deposed that Wilkinson had carried him before Judge Hall in New Orleans, who refused him counsel, and threatened him with deportation to Richmond if he did not sign a deposition. Under persistent pressure, Knox answered some questions, and refused to answer others; whereupon he was placed in jail and sent, a prisoner, to Richmond without other clothes than those on his back. But he weakened the effect of his tale of coercion by admitting that Wilkinson had used no terroristic tactics against him, that he had told Wilkinson he had no objection to going to Richmond if he were properly treated, and that Wilkinson had given him money to purchase clothes.[43] Whereupon Marshall decided that the illegal acts, if any, were those of Judge Hall, and denied the attachment against the General — much to that worthy's manifest relief.

And, while the Grand Jury heard evidence and deliberated, the tilts in Court grew ever sharper. Every slightest move by either side was made the basis of impassioned oratory and exhaustive, and exhausting, citations of authority. Wearily, delicately, Marshall trod his judicial way between the embattled forces. Jefferson had not obeyed the subpoena, though he had offered certain copies, and Burr contemplated a body attachment against him to compel attendance.

Behind closed doors, an exciting drama was also taking place. From accuser, Randolph was endeavoring to place his especial aversion, James Wilkinson, in the position of the accused. He had the cipher letter brought before the Jury, forced the perspiring

General to an admission that he had made certain erasures and alterations of phrases tending to implicate him with Burr, and pressed vigorously for an indictment of the Administration hero. He failed by the narrowest of margins, and then only on a technicality adduced by some lawyer member of the Jury, who, incidentally, was a Republican.

While Jefferson was writing approvingly to the favorite that " your enemies have filled the public ear with slanders, and your mind with trouble on that account," and that " no one is more sensible than myself of the injustice which has been aimed at you," [44] the Grand Jury, by a vote of 9 to 7, decided against an indictment of his quaking protégé. The disgusted Randolph wrote Nicholson that " the mammoth of iniquity escaped; not that any man pretended to think him *innocent,* but upon certain wire-drawn distinctions that I will not pester you with. W——n is the only man that I ever saw who was from the bark to the very core a villain." [45] And, a few days later, he repeated to Nicholson, " W. is the most finished scoundrel that ever lived; a ream of paper would not contain all the proofs; but what of that? He is ' the man whom the king delights to honor! ' " Randolph had no use for Jefferson either. As to Wilkinson's demeanor before the Jury, " all was confusion of language and looks. Such a countenance never did I behold. There was scarcely a variance of opinion amongst us as to his guilt." [46]

6. THE GRAND JURY INDICTS

Meanwhile, the suspense grew to unbearable proportions. The witnesses filed in and out, but still the Grand Jury had not come to a decision. Burr's attitude was admirable, as even the much-harried Hay was obliged to confess.[47] Public opinion in Richmond was veering in his favor; the heralded Wilkinson had left a bad taste in many mouths. Burr's partisans became bolder. The society and elite of the town, at least, were favorable to Burr. The accused's progress to and from court each day resembled a triumphal procession. Two hundred gentlemen accompanied him as a bodyguard, breathing defiance to Government.[48] Parties were given in his honor, and everywhere the houses of fashion and planter aristocracy were open to him. His friends were loyal and devoted. Young Swartwout met the somewhat bedraggled General in the street, and deliberately and painstakingly shoved him flying from the narrow sidewalk into the muddy gutter. Wilkinson hastened away to the jeers of the bystanders. Andrew Jackson, still haranguing all who would listen on the persecutions of the Government, the craven villainy of Wilkinson, and the exalted innocence of his friend Burr, went "wild with delight." [49]

Wilkinson pocketed the gross insult, and did not challenge. Whereupon Swartwout challenged *him*. Wilkinson turned poltroon, and refused to fight. Swartwout then published him in the public press as a traitor, a forger, a perjurer and a coward.[50] Thereafter, Wilkinson slunk along the streets where once he had preened himself and strutted, while the Virginians looked on him with contempt and loathing. From a hero he had turned to something less than a worm.

But, on June 24th, the thunderbolt descended with crushing force. John Randolph marched into the suddenly hushed courtroom, where only a moment before counsel had been wrangling over the motion to attach Wilkinson. The Grand Jury, he announced, had brought in indictments against Aaron Burr and Harman Blennerhassett, charging them with treason against the United States, and misdemeanor in preparing an expedition against Spain.

For a moment there was silence. Burr was the first to recover his wits. He immediately asked that he be admitted to bail, instead of being sent to jail like a common felon. But neither he nor Luther Martin could produce any precedents for such a course, and Marshall accordingly committed him to the Richmond Municipal Jail.

From his cell Burr exhorted Theo, waiting anxiously for news in far-off South Carolina, " I beg and expect it of you that you will conduct yourself as becomes my daughter, and that you manifest no signs of weakness or alarm." [51] The Spartan daughter of a Spartan father!

It was later to be discovered that the indictment had been based on a misapprehension of Marshall's charge as to what constituted the *overt act* in treason, as delivered in the Swartwout and Bollman case — that famous *obiter dicta* which was to be a continuing source of embarrassment to the Chief Justice during the instant trial.[52]

CHAPTER XXVI

ON TRIAL

1. ORANGES AND JAIL

WITH morning came new expedients. A writ of *habeas corpus* was sued out, whereby Burr was brought back into court to continue the everlasting discussions. John Randolph left the jury room again, this time to demand from Burr the letter addressed by Wilkinson to him, dated May 13th, the reference to which Wilkinson had eliminated from the cipher letter. Burr refused to deliver any communication which had been made to him confidentially, even from such a scoundrel as Wilkinson, and Randolph retired discomfited.[1] Later, when Wilkinson himself challenged its disclosure, Burr was to say that he had placed it out of his power to deliver. It must be admitted that it was probably more than motives of honor which animated Burr in his persistent refusal. Doubtless, the missing letter contained material which would have definitely proved his filibustering intentions against Mexico, and thus rendered him liable to conviction on the misdemeanor charge.

The same day the Jury brought in additional indictments against Jonathan Dayton, John Smith, Comfort Tyler and Davis Floyd. They were making a clean sweep.

The next day, Burr's counsel appeared with an eloquent request for the removal of their client from the sultry, unsanitary jail to more comfortable and commodious quarters. Marshall looked inquiringly at Hay, who remained silent. Thereupon he ordered Burr's removal to his former lodgings near the Capitol, provided that they were first made sufficiently strong for safekeeping. Pursuant to this order Burr was shifted to the front room of Luther Martin's house, the windows were barred, the door padlocked, and a guard of seven men placed in the adjoining house to keep constant watch on the distinguished prisoner.[2] But he remained in these quarters only two days, for the Government could not brook such unusual favors to the man whose life it was seeking. The Executive Council of Virginia came to the rescue with an offer of three large rooms on the third floor of its penitentiary for Federal prisoners, and promised uninterrupted access to his counsel. The proposition was accepted, and Burr was to make this his home, his reception chamber, his library and study, until August 2nd, when the trial commenced, and he was once more returned to Luther Martin's house.

Though the penitentiary was a mile and a half out of Richmond, and inhabited with the usual quota of thieves, cutthroats, and incendiaries, Burr found his life there not unpleasant. The jailer was friendly and permitted him many liberties. Well-wishers sent him " messages, notes and inquiries, bringing oranges, lemons, pineapples, raspberries, apricots, cream, butter, ice, and some ordinary articles " along with them as they streamed out to the distant penitentiary.[3] He wrote regularly to Theo, and all his letters are calm and reasoned, discussing the pending trial dispassionately and as an acute exercise in law, interspersed with flashes of wit and the comic incidents of jail existence. It was August, however, before his daughter could come to Richmond, and when she did, she took, as always, the hearts of susceptible males by storm. Especially did she make a conquest of the elderly and bibulous, but redoubtable, Luther Martin. Thereafter he was more firmly than ever devoted to the interests of his client.

While Theo was fluttering male hearts in Richmond, her father, even when in jail, was making similar inroads upon feminine dispositions. While " it has almost been considered as culpable to evince towards him [Burr] the least sympathy or support; and many a hollow-hearted caitiff have I seen, who basked in the sunshine of his bounty, when in power, who now skulked from his side, and even mingled among the most clamorous of his enemies," there was " not a lady, I believe, in Richmond, whatever may be her husband's sentiments on the subject, who would not rejoice on seeing Col. Burr at liberty." [4] The remarkable fascination of the man was timeless.

For five weeks Burr remained in the penitentiary, awaiting the opening of the new term for his trial. Five weeks, during which period the American frigate *Chesapeake* was fired on by the British warship *Leopard* in American territorial waters, an outrage to be swallowed supinely by Jefferson while he strained every nerve to force a conviction of Aaron Burr.

Meanwhile, Blennerhassett had left the Mississippi Territory in June to return to his Island and ascertain the condition of his property. After a long and arduous journey, beset with anxieties and knowing that his future was dark and uncertain, he came to Nashville on June 29th, there to hear of the proceedings against Burr. " I think," he wrote his wife bitterly, " if I should be prosecuted with the virulence that has marked the proceedings against Burr, my acquittal, by the trouble and expense that would be incurred to obtain it, would be worth little more than a condemnation. One thing is certain, I shall take nothing from you to fee lawyers." [5]

At Lexington, he found trouble waiting for him in the guise of a sheriff's attachment for some unpaid bills of Burr which he had indorsed. There was some ten thousand dollars' worth of these, though Burr, as far back as May, had been negotiating for their settlement. Alston had paid some of the many notes outstanding, but, with the collapse of the venture, they were coming due at a rate which his depleted resources were unable to meet.

While Henry Clay was attempting to extricate Blennerhassett from his financial difficulties by arranging an assignment of Alston's guaranties to his creditors, news came of his indictment for treason, and hard on its heels, one David Meade to arrest and convey him to Richmond for trial.[6] Downcast, bitter, seeing the entire world through jaundiced eyes, all his dreams shattered, the poor Irish gentleman was taken away to battle for his life. His beloved Island had been sold to satisfy a modicum of his debts, Alston was pleading poverty on *his* obligations, and he was beginning to blame Burr as the author of all his misfortunes. Yet, when Blennerhassett arrived in Richmond, and refused point-blank to hire any lawyers in his behalf, Burr arranged with his own counsel — Wickham, Botts and Randolph — to represent him, and engaged himself and Alston to pay for their services at such later date as would be possible.[7]

2. ARREST OF TESTIMONY

On August 3rd, to the accompaniment of tremendous national excitement and a courtroom crowded to the very bursting, John Marshall, Chief Justice of the United States, opened the trial of the People of the United States against Aaron Burr, on a charge of treason. Once more Cyrus Griffin sat at his side, voiceless, mute. Joseph Alston of South Carolina, Burr's son-in-law, made public display of his reconciliation — after that unfortunate letter of hasty disavowal — by entering the court arm in arm with the accused. For the duration of the trial, Burr had been brought back to Martin's house for safekeeping, as nearer to the Hall of Burgesses in which the proceedings were being held.

But it took exactly a week, after the fanfare of opening, for the trial actually to get under way. A hundred Government witnesses wandered around town, eating and sleeping well at Government expense, while the prosecution lawyers scurried madly about, interviewing, consulting, keeping in constant touch with Jefferson, getting their case prepared. Burr had no such difficulties. His witnesses were few; they had come to Richmond at their own expense, and the event showed that they might just as well have stayed at home. But the law of the matter was dug into with exceeding thoroughness; law books were studied and precedents searched. And Blennerhassett — in jail, and seemingly the forgotten man — was being told by a kind friend " that Col. Burr and myself could not be too much on our guard, for he was persuaded that every Democrat, to a man, now in this town, was thirsting for our blood." [8]

But Blennerhassett was more occupied with his troubled finances and bitter rage against Alston for not living up to his endorsements than with worrying about life and limb and the looming gallows. He displays a trenchant pen in the Journal which he kept while cooling his heels in jail. " The once redoubted Eaton," he writes, " has dwindled down in the eyes of this sarcastic town, into a ridiculous mountebank, strutting about the streets, under a tremendous hat, with a Turkish sash over colored clothes, when he is not tippling in the taverns, where he offers up with his libations the bitter effusions of his sorrows, in audibly bewailing to the sympathies of the bystanders." [9] Eaton, Wilkinson, Dunbaugh, Allbright — the more Richmond saw of these witnesses who had been brought by a paternal Government from the ends of its domains to testify against Burr — the more it wondered whether it might not be possible, after all, that Burr's constant cry of persecution and hounding had considerable truth in it.

George Hay was at last ready to proceed on August 10th and the examination of prospective jurors commenced. But as man after man was called, and examined, it was found with monotonous regularity that one and all were strongly convinced of Burr's guilt. They had formed their rooted opinions, they said, from the newspapers, from the President's Proclamation, from the depositions of Wilkinson and Eaton which had been printed and reprinted and strewn broadcast until not a child but knew them *verbatim*. It was impossible to obtain a jury of twelve without fixed prepossessions. The tremendous outpouring of prejudicial propaganda had seen to that. Of the jurors finally chosen, only *two* had not at some time or other expressed an opinion unfavorable to Burr.

Nevertheless, four were chosen the first day — as men who might change their beliefs after hearing the testimony — and nine were suspended for further consideration. When these came up for examination the following day, an extended argument took place concerning the general principles involved in rejecting prospective jurors because of avowed opinions. Marshall, in a masterful decision, enunciated the doctrine that any *deliberate* opinion was sufficient to disqualify from jury duty; that only such light impressions which might fairly be supposed to yield to the evidence would not be sufficient ground for rejection. With these criteria to guide the inquisition, all of the suspended jurors were rejected for cause.

Hay was in a rage. He moved sarcastically for a new panel — of 150, of 500 talesmen even — and talked of the expense. Burr was immediately on his feet to object to the insinuation that a jury could not be drawn under the Chief Justice's ruling, *provided* — and now it was he who was doing the insinuating — the marshal was really disposed to seek proper jurymen. Wickham chimed in with the remark that the first panel of 48 had contained " too many members of assembly and candidates for public favour and office." [10] The Court disregarded Hay's fantastic figures, and called for a new venire of 48 talesmen.

It was August 15th before this additional panel appeared for examination. In the meantime, Hay had written complainingly to Jefferson that " the bias of Judge Marshall is as obvious as if it was stamped on his forehead. I may do him injustice, but I do not believe that I am, when I say that he is endeavoring to work himself up to a state of firmness which will enable [him] to aid Burr throughout the trial without appearing to be conscious of doing wrong." [11]

Burr now did a brave thing. He could have forced the prosecution to the calling of panel after panel, and dragged out the proceedings to interminable lengths. Instead, he cut the Gordian knot by suggesting that if he were permitted to pick eight men out of the existing panel, he would permit them to be sworn in, regardless of their opinions as to himself. Hay was suspicious of this unusual proposition at first, but ultimately could see no ground for disapproval. Burr took his men practically at random, and expressed his satisfaction even with those who had already proclaimed opinions adverse to himself. He even permitted one Miles Bott to remain in the jury box, though he had boasted that his mind was completely made up, and it had been proved that he had publicly said that " colonel Burr ought to be hanged." [12] By this time, Burr was convinced that if the case were permitted to go to the jury, *any* jury would convict him. He must win, if at all, on matters of law.

Two days later, the completed jury filed into the jury box, the lawyers clustered like a swarm of bees at the counsel tables, every available inch of space was taken, and George Hay rose to make his opening address. He intended to prove, he told the straining audience, that Aaron Burr, on December 10th, 1806, at Blennerhassett's Island, had congregated with persons, to the number of 30 and upward, with arms in their hands, for the purpose of levying war against the United States. He would further prove, he continued impressively, that with the persons aforesaid, Burr did, on December 11, 1806, descend the Ohio and the Mississippi with force and arms to take possession of New Orleans.[13]

General William Eaton — of the colored clothes and flaming sash — was called as the first witness. He had hardly taken his seat in the witness chair before Burr began his objections. The Court had, he argued, already determined the proper course of procedure. *First* the *overt act* must be proved; *then and then only,* could corroborative evidence, such as Eaton's, be introduced into court. At once the big guns on both sides were unlimbered. William Wirt claimed that it was the prosecutor's privilege to introduce his evidence in any way he saw fit; that in this instance it was his intention to trace the chronological continuity of the treason from its birth to completion. Martin took up the cudgels for the defense, and the remainder of the day was spent in resounding oratory, a wealth of citations, both English and American, and considerable ingenuity of argument.

Marshall retired to his chamber that night to write his opinion, which he delivered on the 18th. The crime of treason, he read, consisted of both the fact and the intention; both must be proved. The Court would not interfere with the prosecution if it saw fit to introduce first its evidence of the intention, but, he added significantly, *it must be relevant to the crime charged,* and not merely corroborative of a general course outside the actual crime.[14] On the face of it, the decision was a victory for the Government; actually, it was to play its part in saving Burr's life.

Whereupon the impatient Eaton was returned to the stand, to admit at once that "concerning any overt act, which goes to prove Aaron Burr guilty of treason I know nothing," but that of Burr's treasonable intentions he knew much. His testimony, thereafter rendered with many protestations, followed the familiar pattern of his deposition, with all the fantasy and embroidery intact, and has already been considered in detail. Because of Marshall's ruling, however, the juicy bits about assassination were omitted.

There was little cross-examination, though the important point was elucidated that on or about March 1st the Government had paid him the sum of $10,000 on his long-unheeded claim.[15] When he left the stand, he had strutted and pirouetted, but had only succeeded in amusing the spectators. His concoction no longer excited belief as in former days.[16]

Thomas Truxton was the next witness for the prosecution. Hay could extract but cold comfort from *his* testimony. This, too, has already been described. It was a plain, unadorned account of conversations with Burr and propositions which held nothing of treason and much of Mexican conquest, if and when the United States decided to declare war. On cross-examination he testified that " we [Burr and he] were very intimate. There seemed no reserve on your [Burr's] part. I never heard you speak of a division of the Union."

McRae: " Did he wish to fill your mind with resentment against the government? "

Truxton: " I was pretty full of it myself, and he joined me in opinion." [17]

Before the day's session ended, Peter Taylor, the gardener, had once more recited his story of the warning message to Burr, of Blennerhassett's wild talk, of the men on the Island; that some of them had guns, whether rifles or muskets he did not know, and that they had powder and lead. But Burr, he admitted, was not present on the Island during the assemblage of the men and the ensuing flight.

The defense had reason to be satisfied with the first day's proceedings. Aside from Eaton's pretty well discredited testimony, nothing had been harmful, and much had been favorable.

Nor was Burr uncomfortable in his new quarters. In fact, Blennerhassett, not as well situated, was bursting with envy. He noted in his Journal, " Jourdan tells me, Burr lives in great style, and sees much company within his gratings, where it is as difficult to get an audience as if he really were an Emperor." Solitary, broken in fortunes and in health, the Irishman added bitterly of his erstwhile confederate that " the vivacity of his wit, and the exercise of his proper talents, now constantly solicited here in private and public exhibition, while they display his powers and address at the levee and the bar, must engross more of his time than he can spare for the demands of other gratifications." [18] Blennerhasset could never understand this buoyancy and childlike optimism which animated Burr in the darkest hours, when he should have been submissively crushed under the weight of his misfortunes, and attributed it wrongly to an insensitivity of spirit and an indifference to his, Blennerhassett's, personal difficulties.

In accordance with Jefferson's scheme of blank pardons and other more devious methods of obtaining essential evidence against Burr, Colonel De Pestre, Burr's Chief of Staff, was approached with an offer to provide for him handsomely in the American Army, " if his principles or engagements were not adverse to the administration. The Col. replied, that he understood the hint, but it neither suited his honor nor character to serve in such employment." [19] Baffled, the secret agents turned their attention to Blennerhassett. Editor Duane, of the *Aurora,* visited him in his cell, and under the guise of a pretended friendship, warned him that Burr was intending to make him the scapegoat, but that he could save himself, if only he would confess in writing to the entire plot.[20] Evidently Blennerhassett could not or would not deliver the requisite information, for the matter was quietly dropped.

On the following day, August 19th, the trial was resumed with the appearance of the Morgans on the stand, who repeated their tale of innuendoes and *manner* of speech rather than of actual words. They were followed by Jacob Allbright, the Dutch hired hand, who stumblingly went through his story of seven — or was it eight? — muskets that were leveled at General Tupper. And all the while, the protagonist of his story sat listening attentively, yet not once did Hay dream of calling *him* to the witness chair to confirm this remarkably pat evidence that a war had been declared and levied against the United States on that night of December 10th.

Then the witnesses came in quick succession, most of them contributing but little of value to the proceedings. William Love, Blennerhassett's personal servant; Dudley Woodbridge, the contractor for the expedition, and Blennerhassett's former partner. From what that worthy had told him, he testified, he had inferred " that his object was Mexico." He also enlivened the day by declaring that " it was mentioned among the people in the country, that he [Blennerhassett] had every kind of sense but common sense." [21] A statement for which he was later to apologize to the indignant Irishman, as well as for other derogatory references.

On the 20th, Simeon Poole testified that he had been sent by the Governor of Ohio to arrest Blennerhassett, and, hiding himself on the opposite shore that night of December 10th, had seen men moving about a fire, that there were men stationed on the island shore who " appeared to have guns, and looked like sentinels."

After several other witnesses had described the doings on the

Island, Burr arose to object to further *collateral* testimony of this kind. All the witnesses had testified, and the prosecution had admitted, that on the night of December 10th, he, Burr, had been far away from the place where, it was maintained, acts of war were occurring. In fact, he had then been in Kentucky, a good many miles away. Marshall turned to Hay and inquired if he had any other witnesses to the *overt act*. Hay admitted he had not; that as to this phase of the counts against Burr all the evidence was in.

Whereupon the defense formally moved for an arrest of all further testimony. This was the supreme effort, the move toward which all their strategy had been directed. John Wickham had been chosen to make the opening address in support of the motion.

For two whole days he hammered home his argument, while judges and lawyers and laymen listened agape. Such a wealth of closely reasoned logic, of brilliant phraseology, of learned citations and happy wit, of marshaled facts and masterful weaving into an ordered fabric, had never been heard in an American court before, and perhaps not since. Tazewell, a member of the Grand Jury which had indicted Burr, and himself a lawyer of note, declared that it was " the greatest forensic effort of the American bar." [22]

Wickham took the position that no person could be convicted of treason in levying war who was not personally present at the commission of the act charged. There was, he admitted, an ancient English doctrine of *constructive* treason, whereby the overt act of associates could be imputed to another, no matter how far distant from the scene; but in a magnificent argument he shredded that doctrine into little pieces, citing and subjecting to a merciless analysis every case that had ever been reported on the subject, pointing out with irrefutable logic the obvious errors piled on errors in the reasoning of the judges, the misconceptions of legal elementals, the barbarous prejudices and the injustices committed in its name. That doctrine, he declared, had been based on artificial constructions and to bolster an artificial tyranny. The Constitution of the United States, being a new and original compact, should be judged *per se,* and for the plain intent of the words employed. There was no common law of the United States, derived from England, he argued forcibly; only the common law of the several states that made up the Union. The Constitution *created* the offense of treason, and by the exact wording of the appropriate sections must they be bound. Nothing was contained in those plain and emphatic words about the overt acts of *others;* only of the overt acts of the *accused.*

And, Wickham continued, even if he were wrong on his first

point, the indictment had been drawn in defective fashion. It had charged Burr with the overt act itself, instead of naming an act committed by others, with Burr aiding and abetting, as the testimony had been intended to prove, and that therefore the indictment must be dismissed. For a third point: as an accessory, Burr could not be convicted of treason until the principals had been found guilty, and that therefore the entire proceeding was premature. For a fourth point: that the *facts* disclosed no such criminal assemblage on the Island as charged. It was lawful for guns to be carried in the Western country; they were part of the indispensable equipment of every man. There was no evidence anywhere of a military plot of any kind.

Marshall, following him closely, interrupted to inquire whether there were any reported cases in which it was shown that the presiding judge had the right to decide whether or not the evidence submitted to the jury was or was not proof of an overt act. Wickham contended that such a right was inherent, that the jury might find the *truth* of the facts, but the judge must decide as a matter of law whether such facts so found, constituted in law an overt act. Which was sound doctrine, and universally followed today.

He proceeded with his argument. Force was necessary to accompany any levying of war. Only Allbright had in anywise testified to forcible resistance to General Tupper. Even if his evidence were true, it was not enough. The Constitution called for *two* witnesses to the overt act. And why, he demanded pertinently, had Tupper himself not been called? Furthermore, there was no evidence that Tupper had acted on a warrant or authority; that none could be presumed from his office, as he was from Ohio, and the Island was in Virginia; and that, in any event, resistance to process is a crime, but not the crime of treason.

When he finally sat down, he had covered every possible point, exhausted every possible precedent, and had established himself as one of the great lawyers of the age. His argument had taken two days, and filled some 65 pages of the printed Reports.

The prosecution was in a panic. Evidently they had expected nothing like this motion in arrest of further testimony, or such a magnificent effort as that of Wickham. Hay asked for leave to submit further evidence to prove the act, thereby admitting that his case was weak and required bolstering. But his additional witnesses proved of little help. Israel Miller, a member of Tyler's party, testified to the presence of 32 men, of the existence of about 5 rifles, 3 or 4 pair of pistols; and that on the Island itself there had been 1 blunderbuss, 2 pairs of pistols, and 1 fusee. Nothing else.

Purley Howe swore that he had called to deliver 40 boat poles, that a boat with two men carrying rifles had ferried over to the Ohio shore for them, and that they had refused to permit his companion to accompany them back to the Island in their boat.[23] This was all that the desperate Hay could supply to make up deficiencies in evidence.

When once more the prosecution rested, Edmund Randolph arose for the defense to continue the thread of Wickham's argument. But his efforts added little to the rich, lustrous weave of his predecessor. On August 21st he had closed. The prosecution lawyers huddled in indecision; then Hay asked for a lengthy adjournment to " enable them to answer the elaborate arguments of the counsel for the accused; which having occupied two whole days in the delivery must have been prepared with infinite labour and industry." The defense objected to a lengthy postponement, arguing rightly " that the counsel for the United States ought to have come prepared to prosecute and to understand and repel every argument and every defense of which the cause was susceptible." [24] Hay and his associates, with months of preparation, with the resources of the Government in back of them, were still not adequately armed at all points. Yet Marshall, with an eye to public opinion and the open whispers about his probity, granted an adjournment until August 24th.

When Court opened again, it was discovered that McRae had been chosen to lead the forces of rebuttal. He argued that the Constitutional provisions concerning treason were not new or novel, but were identical in every word with the English Statute governing the same offense; hence English decisions and English precedents must control in the interpretation of the law. And, cried he, in England those words have been held sufficient to convict traitors even though they personally were far away from the scene of the overt act. Burr, he thundered, was a *principal,* not an accessory; hence Burr was *legally* present at Blennerhassett Island the night of December 10th, though perhaps not in corporeal body.

William Wirt took up the argument on August 25th. He was a brilliant orator, of the florid, imaginative school. Yet he started prosaically enough with the evocation of Marshall's own words in the prior case of Bollman and Swartwout, words which had been tossed off redundantly without adequate consideration, and which, like Banquo's ghost, rose ever to plague him anew. Relentlessly he hammered them home — " If a body of men be assembled, for the purpose of effecting by force a treasonable purpose, all those who perform any part, however minute, *or however remote from the scene of action* . . . are to be considered as traitors " — while Marshall twisted uncomfortably in his seat.

Turning to look squarely at the composed prisoner, Wirt insisted that Burr was the principal in the atrocious crime, not a mere underling, and that in any event the distinction between principal and accessory was not recognized by the Constitution and the Statutes of the United States; *that* distinction, he said scornfully, is recognized only by the English common law, which the defense had attempted with much labor to prove inapplicable. But dry law and cogent reasoning were too much for Wirt's particular talents. He swung gratefully into that passionate apostrophe to Harman Blennerhassett, the dupe, the innocent victim of Burr's machinations, that " man of letters, who fled from the storms of his own country to find quiet in ours," that man who had " carried with him taste and science and wealth; and lo, the desert smiled! " that man who " on a beautiful island in the Ohio " reared " a palace and decorates it with every romantic embellishment of fancy," the wife of whose bosom was " lovely even beyond her sex "; and then, he shouted dramatically, as he rose on the viewless wings of fancy, " in the midst of all this peace, this innocent simplicity, and this tranquillity, this feast of the mind, this pure banquet of the heart, the destroyer comes; he comes to change this paradise into a hell." Is this poor gentleman the principal and is Burr then the accessory? [25] Exhausted with this lovely word-painting he had evoked — a painting that was to fix the picture of the serpentine Burr in the minds of generations to come — Wirt ended prosaically enough with an etymological dissection of the word *levy*, and sat down — having taken the better part of two days and 67 pages in the Reports for his effort. It represented the best speech on the part of the prosecution, though on a considerably lower level than the cool, logical reasoning of Wickham for the defense.

Benjamin Botts next arose, to take up cudgels once more for Burr. Wirt's flowery designs had made a deep impression upon the spectators and jury, if not on the judges themselves. Whereupon Botts opened with mock apologetics. " I cannot promise you, sir, a speech manufactured out of tropes and figures," and proceeded then with sharp satire to ridicule and bring to naught the florid rhetoric of his opponent. While Wirt, he smiled, sports with sleeping Venuses with voluptuous limbs and wanton nakedness, " *I* am compelled to plod heavily and meekly through the dull doctrines of Hale and Foster." Every one rocked with laughter, and the spell was broken. That much accomplished, he turned to the discussion of a point heretofore overlooked. The prosecution itself had admitted that all those on the Island, with the possible exceptions of Blennerhassett and Tyler, had been ignorant of Burr's purposes, not knowing them to be treasonable. How then, he demanded, was it a treasonable assemblage, where those involved meditated no war on the United States, would have shrunk in horror from the very thought of it? Taylor's testimony was next taken up and demolished with nimble satire until nothing was left of that worthy's bellicose descriptions. Then he turned his attention to the President himself, and paid his respects in no uncertain language. The whole prosecution, he charged, was but an attempt to bolster the waning prestige of an Administration beyond contempt; he traced in damning detail the devices, the fraud, the chicanery employed to place Burr high on the gallows, the clever manipulation of public sentiment to that end. The courtroom was a sounding-board to reach the ears and minds of the nation.

Hay rose in rebuttal, and took nearly two days for his speech. He had been ill, and perhaps that accounts for the listlessness of his argument. But he was not above making thinly veiled threats against Marshall. He adverted to the case of Fries before Justice Chase, "for his conduct in which," he was speaking directly now to Marshall, "with other causes, he was afterwards impeached." Yes, he continued — and there was no doubt in the minds of the crowded courtroom as to his meaning — "the censure which the judge drew on himself was not on account of his opinions, however incorrect they might be, but for his arbitrary and irregular conduct at the trial; which was one of the principal causes for which he was afterwards impeached. He attempted to wrest the decision from the jury, and prejudge the case before hearing all the evidence in it; the identical thing," he exclaimed, "which this court is now called upon by these gentlemen themselves to do." [26]

Marshall overlooked the open threat, but not so Charles Lee, next counsel to be heard. He pounced upon it with glee, shook it like a rag, held it up for the inspection of all and sundry, thereby forcing Hay to a faint denial that such had been his meaning, and a mild acceptance of his disclaimer by Marshall himself.

On August 28th, Luther Martin, the heavy artillery of the defense, went into action to end the interminable argument on the motion. It was the longest, as well as the most impassioned thundering of the entire proceedings. It also took two days and 118 pages of reported text. The fires of constant potations burned in his veins and exalted his rhetoric and tremendous invective. He attacked the reasoning of Marshall himself in the Bollman and Swartwout case, he attacked the Government and Jefferson with bitter words, he called on Marshall to tread the path of righteousness and undeviating justice amid the bloodthirsty clamor of prosecution and populace alike, and he spoke in idolatrous accents of Theodosia, the lovely daughter of his client. After him, as an anti-climax, Edmund Randolph said a few words. It was the afternoon of August 29th when the historic debate, one of the longest and most brilliant in history, came to a close. The issue rested now in the hands of the judges.

After two days of consideration, Chief Justice Marshall read his decision on the motion of the defense to arrest further testimony. It took three hours to read, and represents his longest reported opinion. First he paid his respects to the assemblage of counsel. Said he, " A degree of eloquence seldom displayed on any occasion has embellished a solidity of argument and a depth of research by which the court has been greatly aided in forming the opinion it is about to deliver." [27] In fact, to a large extent he followed almost verbatim the citations, the logic and the reasoning of the defense, especially that of John Wickham in his notable address.

It would not profit to attempt a thorough analysis of his decision, which is a landmark in American jurisprudence, and settled definitively for all time that the pernicious doctrine of constructive treason held no place in American law and *mores*. But the pertinent parts of his decision are as follows. " The present indictment charges the prisoner with levying war against the United States," he declared, " and alleges an overt act of levying war. That overt act must be proved, according to the mandates of the constitution and of the act of congress, by two witnesses. It is not proved by a single witness." At one swift stroke he had struck the prosecution down in its tracks. " The presence of the accused," he resumed, " has been stated to be an essential component part of the overt act in this indictment, unless the common law principle respecting accessories should render it unnecessary; and there is not only no witness who has proved his actual or legal presence, but the fact of his absence is not controverted. The counsel for the prosecution offer to give in evidence subsequent transactions at a different place and in a different state, in order to prove — what? the overt act laid in the indictment? that the prisoner was one of those who assembled at Blannerhassett's [*sic*] island? No: that is not alleged. It is well known that such testimony is not competent to establish such a fact. The constitution and law require that the fact should be established by two witnesses; not by the establishment of other facts from which the jury might reason to this fact. The testimony then is not relevant." Hence, he ended impressively, the jury, having heard the opinion of the Court on the *law*, " will apply that law to the facts, and will find a verdict of guilty or not guilty as their own consciences may direct." [28]

The defense was jubilant, the prosecution downcast and sullen. Hay asked for an adjournment to September 1st to consider his course under the Court's opinion. It was granted. On the adjourned day, he shrugged his shoulders. He had nothing further to offer. Whereupon the jury retired to consider its verdict, and returned shortly. " We of the jury say that Aaron Burr is not proved to be guilty under this indictment by any evidence submitted to us. We therefore find him not guilty." [29]

Instantly the entire battery of defense lawyers were on their feet, protesting against the form of the verdict as unusual, informal and irregular. Burr demanded that the Court either send the jury back with instructions to alter it to the proper form, or make the correction itself. Colonel Carrington, foreman of the jury, interposed that it was intended as a verdict of acquittal, but that if it were informal, the jury had agreed to alter it. He was immediately contradicted by Mr. Parker, another juryman, who vehemently declared he would not consent to any alteration of the verdict. Marshall ruled the verdict in effect to be a verdict of acquittal, and directed an entry on the record of " not guilty." [30]

The trial of treason was over, and Burr had once more repelled the malignancy of fate and the Administration. The one flaw in the ointment was the illegal verdict — an attempt by Parker, a Jeffersonian partisan, to leave the poison of doubt still in the minds of the people. Though the defense was right, and the verdict should have been corrected, Marshall preferred to arouse no further violent debates and cries of favoritism. It was let stand.

3. THE MISDEMEANOR IS TRIED

With the principal discharged, the underlings were swiftly disposed of. A *nolle prosequi* was entered on the treason charge against Dayton. But Hay had not exhausted the arsenal of his weapons. Immediately following the verdict he had written to Jefferson that " Wirt, who has hitherto advocated the *integrity* of the chief-justice, now abandons him. This last opinion has opened his eyes, and he speaks in the strongest terms of reprobation." [31]

" The event has been (what was evidently intended from the beginning of the trial) . . .'' raged Jefferson in return, '' not only to clear Burr, but to prevent the evidence from ever going before the world. But this latter case must not take place. It is now, therefore, more than ever indispensable, that not a single witness be paid or permitted to depart until his testimony has been committed to writing, either as delivered in court, or as taken by yourself in the presence of any of Burr's counsel, who may choose to attend to cross-examine. These whole proceedings will be laid before Congress, that they may decide whether the defect has been in the evidence of guilt, or in the law, or in the application of the law, and that they may provide the proper remedy for the past and the future.'' Burr and Marshall alike were to feel the full impact of his wrath. '' The criminal is preserved,'' he exclaimed, '' to become the rallying point of all the disaffected and the worthless of the United States, and to be the pivot on which all the intrigues and the conspiracies which foreign governments may wish to disturb us with, are to turn. If he is convicted of the misdemeanor, the Judge must in decency give us a respite by some short confinement of him; but we must expect it to be very short.'' [32]

Obediently Hay moved, on September 2nd, to commit Burr on a new treason charge, this time predicated on a continuing overt act, starting at the mouth of the Cumberland and extending all the way down the rivers to Bayou Pierre, and that he be forwarded to the appropriate district for trial. In another jurisdiction, he thought, the Federal judges might be more pliant to the avowed will of the Administration. But the defense smelled the rat, and so did Marshall. It was necessary, they argued, and he ruled, that the misdemeanor indictment be first disposed of at Richmond. On September 3rd, after a heated discussion, Burr was admitted to bail in the sum of $5,000, which Dayton and William Langbourne promptly furnished, and the prisoner once more walked the streets of Richmond, a free man.

Burr, turning on his enemies, counterattacked with a demand for the production of a subpoenaed letter from Wilkinson to Jefferson, dated November 12, 1806. Hay declared he was willing to place it in the hands of the court for inspection, but that it must not be made a matter of public record. Burr insisted, whereupon Hay declared dramatically he would rather rot in jail than be recreant to his trust. Marshall ruled gravely that Burr might see the letter, but he would later decide whether it should be entered into the record, either in whole or in part. The battle was in progress all over again.

But it was in the nature of an anti-climax. The misdemeanor

charge was comparatively unimportant, and it was recognized on all sides that it was merely Jefferson's peculiar method of making a record for the benefit of Congress. Burr was legally still the defendant; actually Chief Justice Marshall was now, from the point of view of the Administration, the prisoner at the bar; and all efforts were to be directed to prove his bias so conclusively that Congress must necessarily impeach and remove him from the path of Republican principles.

Blennerhassett, freed on a *nolle prosequi* on the treason count, and admitted to bail on the lesser charge, visited Burr. He was bitter against him and Alston, though he was compelled to admit that Alston had taken over some of his notes, had paid others, and had never failed to acknowledge his indebtedness. All his comments during this period are colored by his spleen and resentment, which was only human. His Island, his personal property, had all been sold to cover his notes; his family was far away to the south struggling in the grip of poverty; he was a ruined man. He could not understand how Burr, against whom civil suits had already been commenced on his financial obligations, and equally a ruined man, could be " as gay as usual, and as busy in speculations on re-organizing his projects for action as if he had never suffered the least interruption. He [Burr] observed to Major Smith and me, that in six months our schemes could be all remounted; that we could now new-model them in a better mould than formerly, having a clearer view of the ground, and a more perfect knowledge of our men."

Misfortune could not defeat Burr as it had Blennerhassett. The latter was amazed, and somewhat contemptuous of his former idol. Instead of formulating vain, impossible schemes, Burr, he insisted, should devote all his energies to the " destruction of those enemies who have so long and so cruelly wreaked their malicious vengeance upon him." [33] But Burr was incapable of striking back at his persecutors with the weapons they had employed against him. In all his long life there is no instance of a vengeful disposition on his part.

The second trial opened on September 9, 1807. The count was the preparation of a military expedition against Spain on United States soil. It was as short and speedy as the first had been long-drawn-out. Almost identic evidence was offered as to acts and declarations in Wood County; then, following a familiar path, Hay proffered evidence as to acts committed outside the jurisdiction of Virginia. On swift objection, Marshall rejected such testimony, and gave further opinion that the declarations of a third party, or acts of accomplices, not in the presence of the accused, were inadmissible.

On September 15th, Hay, finding once more that most of his testimony was under legal prohibition, moved to discharge the jury, but Burr insisted on a verdict. Accordingly, the jury went through the necessary motions and brought in a straight verdict of "not guilty."

4. FURTHER COMMITMENT

Hay was not through. He now opened his strategy — as directed by Jefferson — to compel the judicial recording of *all* the evidence in the case. He moved to commit Burr on the new charge of treason, which would bring with it trial in Ohio, Kentucky or Mississippi, or all of them. Once again Marshall sat as a committing magistrate, without benefit of jury, while Hay placed all the witnesses hitherto debarred upon the stand to give their testimony, as well for Congress and the listening public as for the benefit of the Court. To the great disgust of the defense, Marshall permitted the widest latitude before himself in the introduction of this testimony. Evidently he had an eye open for the political effect, and was doubly cautious to avoid even the appearance of shutting off the Government case. He had no stomach for impeachment possibilities; during the trial of Judge Chase he had shown himself rather a badly frightened man than a fearless exponent of what he conceived to be judicial sanctity.

The witnesses were numerous, and the testimony interminable. Only the most important of these will be considered here. Jacob Dunbaugh, for example, the sergeant from Fort Massac, who had been posted as a deserter by Captain Bissell when he had failed to return to the fort at the expiration of his furlough. Wilkinson had found him apt material for his purposes, inasmuch as he could have imposed a rigorous sentence upon him for his offense. He was accordingly prodded into a long, complicated story. Burr had asked him to persuade ten or twelve of the garrison at Fort Massac to desert and accompany him; he had tried to get him to steal arms and munitions from the fort. Dunbaugh even implicated his superior officer, Bissell, as an accessory to Burr's plot. But most important of all, from the point of view of the prosecution, was his testimony of what took place at Cole's Creek. When the militia, he averred, were about to seize the expedition, Burr and Willie, his secretary, secretly chopped with axes in Burr's private room on the boat, while Dunbaugh, in hiding, watched the weird proceedings. He saw, he swore, two bundles of arms lowered through the holes they had made in the gunwales, and deposited with a great splash into the muddy waters of the Mississippi. He had also seen, he testified veraciously, over forty stands of arms, pistols, blunderbusses, swords, tomahawks, bayonets and fusees in great profusion.[34]

But on cross-examination his evidence was completely and thoroughly discredited. The facts as to his desertion and subsequent pardon by Wilkinson were elucidated, and he was forced to admit that he had written Bissell that " as both of us might be injured by this transaction, if he would say that he had sent me as a spy, it would clear both him and myself." [35] The most damning evidence against Dunbaugh's integrity, however, was discovered later in the form of a letter to Bissell. " With sorrow I take Pen in hand to inform you," he wrote lachrimosely, " that I had to tell the officers that you sent me as a Spy against Colonel Burr and had to make outt what I new againg him. I wrote that you sent me on that Purpes. The[y] thought My Captain [Bissell] was interested. I told them that he did not know what Burr's mening was to take some men down the River with him. . . . I should be thankful if my Captain would send some money if their is any for me and my Boots if my detes air paid." [36]

But the grand event was the second performance of General James Wilkinson, who rehashed all his old testimony, made certain notable contradictions in details, and finally produced the much-advertised cipher letter. It was Botts who noted the erasures, and compelled Wilkinson to admit, after much hemming and hawing and shifting of ground, that such erasures and alterations had been made to protect himself. All through his days on the stand, he was self-contradictory, evasive, asking permission continually to change testimony formerly given, standing on his privilege as to State secrets, declining to answer questions on the ground of self-incrimination. A sorry performance, indeed, and one that Jefferson could not possibly have relished. Instead of clinching his case against Burr and Marshall, it only excited ridicule and contempt among informed people.

Eaton, too, came in for a barrage from the defense. It was asserted, and evidence was introduced as tending to prove, that the " hero of Derne " had been court-martialed and convicted on a charge of selling soldiers' rations and public supplies for his own profit. Major Bruff followed, to pour his hot-shot into the aching sides of Wilkinson. Burr then called Thomas Power, Spanish spy and former agent of Wilkinson, to prove that Wilkinson was in the pay of Spain. But Power took refuge in a question of privilege — he was Spanish born and still an officer in the service of Spain — and refused to testify. Thus ended at last the examination of over fifty witnesses, with Burr unwell, lawyers exhausted, and Marshall so patient, and yet so wavering that Burr declared angrily that he " did not for two days together understand either the questions or himself . . . and should in future be put right by strong language." [37]

On October 19th, Marshall ruled there was not sufficient evidence to commit on another charge of treason, but there was on the misdemeanor, and accordingly he committed both Burr and Blennerhassett to Ohio for trial in bail of $3,000 each, which was furnished. Thus one sorry farce had come to an end, and another seemingly was opening. Burr had been tried on various charges in various courts to the number of seven, and each time had been acquitted or released. Was the malice of the Administration to pursue him forever and ever? Burr wrote bitterly to Theo, now returned to her home, " This opinion [of Marshall] was a matter of regret and surprise to the friends of the chief justice, and of ridicule to his enemies — all believing that it was a sacrifice of principle to conciliate *Jack Cade*. Mr. Hay immediately said that he should advise the government to *desist from further prosecution*. That he has actually so advised there is no doubt." [38]

This was true. Hay had no stomach for any further proceedings. He was infinitely weary of the whole tangled mess. He was disgusted, too, with the king's favorite, General Wilkinson. " My confidence in him is shaken, if not destroyed," he wrote Jefferson. " I am sorry for it, on his own account, on the public account, and because you have expressed opinions in his favor; but you did not know then what you soon will know." [39]

But Jefferson was never to repudiate the General, even after the facts were known. To do so would have entailed a loss of his own prestige. He had entangled himself too thoroughly to break loose now. And Jefferson was not honest enough or courageous enough to admit publicly and frankly that he had made a mistake, that he had been deceived. Wilkinson was to be protected, not only through the remainder of his own Administration, but in succeeding ones. A Congressional investigation of the double-jointed General resulted in a hasty whitewashing which convinced no one; at the outbreak of the War of 1812 he was actually given high command, with inglorious results. He ended rather sorrily in Mexico, unhonored, unwept, a stench in the nostrils of Spaniards and Americans alike.

5. MOB SPIRIT

Burr was free temporarily, though the new indictment still hung over him, never to be dismissed, a sword of Damocles, to be released at any whim of the Government. That, contrary to the general belief, Jefferson still persisted in his determination to try Burr again and again until somewhere, somehow, a conviction could be attained, is evidenced by a letter addressed by him to Albert Gallatin, dated March 10, 1808. A rumor had reached him that Burr had sailed to New Orleans, and he wished Gallatin to warn Claiborne and the colonel of militia in that territory. " I presume," he added, " that a writ may be obtained from Ohio grounded on the indictment, by which Burr may be arrested any where and brought back to trial." [40]

Even as late as 1809, when Burr was actually in Europe, the officers of Government were still nosing like bloodhounds on their victim's trail. Rodney thought Burr was in Philadelphia, and was trying to get a warrant issued against him on the hoary charge of *treason,* and have him returned again to Richmond for trial.[41]

It is no wonder, then, that Burr decided at length that the time had come for him to seek fresh fields and pastures new. In the eyes of the general public he was guilty, in spite of acquittals and *nolle prosses*. Popular indignation still ran high. And his creditors were descending upon him like a horde of devouring locusts. They harried him with writs and held him under civil arrest in his own house, pending bail for security. Luther Martin did yeoman service for his friend, putting up his personal security in the sum of $15,000. He was willing, declared Blennerhassett, even to sacrifice his money, if need be, because of his idolatrous admiration for Mrs. Alston.[42]

Jefferson forthwith laid the records of the case before Congress, seeking Marshall's impeachment, while that Judge very prudently retired to the hills until the storm blew over. Burr traveled to Baltimore in the company of Luther Martin, Blennerhassett and others. The Republican press raged and ranted, and incited to violence. They went to a hotel and engaged a suite of rooms. Immediately, all the political Democrats threatened to leave the tainted quarters. That evening, November 2nd, excitement ran high in town. A printer named Frely led a mob under the windows of their suite, drew them up in straggling order, had a fife and drum play the " Rogues' March," gave three derisive cheers, interspersed with hoots and catcalls, and marched off. Luther Martin almost suffered a stroke in his wrath, but Burr had not been present to witness the shameful scene.[43]

The following day the excitement grew more intense. Incendiary speeches were made, and even more incendiary handbills distributed, inciting to mob violence.

AWFUL! ! !

The public are hereby notified that four " choice spirits " are this afternoon, at 3 o'clock, to be marshaled for execution by the hangman, on Gallows Hill, in consequence of the sentence pronounced against them by the unanimous voice of every honest man in the community. The respective crimes for which they suffer are thus stated on the record: first, Chief Justice M. for a repetition of his X.Y.Z. tricks, which are said to be much aggravated by his *felonious* capers in open Court, on the plea of irrelevancy; secondly, His Quid Majesty, charged with the trifling fault of wishing to divide the Union, and farm *Baron* Bastrop's grant; thirdly B——, the chemist, convicted of conspiring to destroy the tone of the public Fiddle; fourthly, and lastly, but not least, *Lawyer* Brandy-Bottle, for a false, scandalous, malicious Prophecy, that, before six months, " Aaron Burr would divide the Union." N.B. The execution of accomplices is postponed to a future day.[44]

Marshall, Burr, Blennerhassett and Martin — all involved in the indiscriminate fury of the mob.

Tyler fled precipitately from the city, Blennerhassett, in alarm, hastened to Burr's quarters to seek aid, Luther Martin demanded protection from the Mayor and received consoling assurances. But the latter would not guarantee Burr's safety. Instead, he sent a police guard to escort him and Swartwout hurriedly to the stage-coach then leaving for Philadelphia, which was boarded, the horses whipped up, and they clattered away " under the good wishes of many spectators." Two troops of horse and police drew up in front of the house in which Martin and the others had barricaded themselves, heavily armed and swearing to defend themselves to the death. A mob of about 1500 maddened people swarmed through the streets, shouting and yelling, prepared with viscous tar and sticky feathers, and dragging after them carts with the effigies of the " four choice spirits " attired for execution. The police wisely refrained from interfering, and, after a few windows had been broken, and the effigies hanged, the wild emotion spent itself, and the rioters scattered to their holes.[45]

Hounded, proscribed, threatened with tar and feathers by mobs, soon to be indicted in Ohio, harried by creditors with civil actions — where could the hunted man turn now?

In Philadelphia he found temporary refuge at the house of George Pollock, where he remained in hiding for a while. His old friend, Charles Biddle, found him " concealed in a French boarding-house . . . pale and dejected . . . generally alone," and talking of suicide. He was shocked at the change which a few short months had made. " How different from what he had been a short time before," he exclaimed, " when few persons in the city were not gratified at seeing him at their tables, where he was always one of the most lively and entertaining of the company." [46]

Fallen and proscribed!

Blennerhassett followed Burr to Philadelphia with the fixed monomania of his own misfortunes. He demanded from the bankrupt man payment of the $7,000 due him on their open account, and made a scene. He even started suit in Philadelphia, only to find himself forestalled by Luckett, another creditor. Burr was to be permitted no peace, no breathing-space. Barely had he managed to raise bail to release himself from Luckett's suit, than Wilkins of Pittsburgh filed action for money lent. Late one night the sheriff descended again upon the luckless man. In despair, Burr turned to his sole source of help — Charles Biddle. But Biddle was not at home. Finally a Mr. Hollowell, a lawyer, was reached and consented to go bail for the former Vice-President of the United States.[47] Nicholas Biddle, brother to Charles, found him completely " broken in fortune & character, & . . . pursued by his creditors." Though himself without partiality for Burr, he tendered his legal services free in the many pending suits for the sake of old family friendship, and felt called upon to explain the matter in apologetic tones to others.[48] The touch of the disgraced is a leprosy to be avoided.

Yet Jefferson was writing " He cannot see what shape Burr's machinations will take next. If we have war with Spain, he will become a Spanish General. If with England, he will go to Canada and be employed there. Internal convulsion may be attempted if no game more hopeful offers. But it will be a difficult one, and the more so as having once failed." [49] Had it not been for the gravity of the foreign situation, to which Jefferson was at last compelled to turn his attention, the President would not have let his victim slip so easily.

The other members of the Conspiracy suffered varying fortunes. Blennerhassett finally quit Philadelphia to join his wife and children at Natchez, to make his home in the Mississippi Territory and farm a thousand acres of cotton. All his fortune had disappeared in the deluge; creditors hounded him as well as Burr, his Island was gone, his mansion in ruins, his beloved library, chemical apparatus, furniture, everything, was attached and sold to satisfy insatiable claims.

But real dirt farming was not for him, and he busied himself in brooding over his wrongs, making constant demands on Alston for all the damage he had suffered; until finally, desperate, he yielded to the ways of blackmail. He would, he threatened Alston, show " other motives of action besides those already offered. These are certainly of a character and complexion I regret it should be my lot to exhibit to the public. To you, however, it belongs to say whether they shall remain shrouded within the sanctuary of your own breast, or stalk forth the heralds of the private treason and public *perjury* they will proclaim infallibly to the honest Democratic electors of South Carolina, who would thence remove you from the chair of their assembly with a different kind of zeal from that through which they placed you in it." He has written an account of all the proceedings, he went on darkly, and intended to publish it, together with all correspondence, if Alston did not pay him forthwith.[50] Alston was Governor then, and hence politically vulnerable. The baseness of the attempt may be extenuated only by the despairing condition of the man. It failed him, yet the book still remained unpublished, to be used again as a threat against Burr in 1813.

He removed to New York in 1812, and later to Montreal, where he practiced law obscurely. In 1822 he sailed to Ireland to seek a reversionary claim, there to die nine years later, aged 63, on the Island of Guernsey.

Senator John Smith, the Kentucky storekeeper, avoided expulsion from the Senate by a single vote; Jonathan Dayton went West and rebuilded his fortunes; General John Adair served with distinction in the War of 1812 and was finally chosen Governor of Kentucky; Bollman tried to establish himself as a physician in the United States, failed, and returned to Europe after many vicissitudes; Samuel Swartwout, thirty years later, became Collector of the New York Port and embezzled the public funds; Jackson won enduring fame in the forthcoming war and rose to the Presidency of the United States. Varying fortunes, and a wide scattering of the men who had followed Burr in his glamorous schemes.

But for Aaron Burr himself there was no peace. All the forces of an outraged society were unleashed against him, he was an outlaw, an outcast, still in danger of life and liberty. Europe beckoned him as at once a mode of escape and a means to a new life. For, in spite of misfortunes that would have crushed another man, he had not given up his plans. Mexico still lured with irresistible force, a guiding beacon to all the remaining years of his life. And only in the Chancellories of Europe was there hope now for success and rehabilitation. He would go to England first and try his luck. From his hiding-place in Philadelphia he sent Samuel Swartwout, still unswervingly loyal, to London with a letter to his fellow-conspirator, Charles Williamson, announcing that he was on his way. But Williamson, before Burr could meet him, had been sent by the British ministry on a mission to the West Indies, to die of yellow fever in Havana, thus shattering, unknown to him, Burr's last hopes of success.[51]

Chapter XXVII

MAN WITHOUT A COUNTRY

1. Flight

A T the age of 51, Aaron Burr stood on the threshold, his past life in ruins, with eyes turned to Europe, eternally optimistic. Yet his flight from the shores of the country that had spurned him required stealth and finesse. Too many were eager to know his whereabouts, and chain him, if they could, to the very soil he wished to leave. He made his way by devious means to New York, and engaged passage on the British packet, *Clarissa Ann,* under the pseudonym of H. E. Edwards. For a month preceding the date of departure he lay concealed in the houses of his friends, not daring to show his face. To cast off suspicion, he wrote Theo, " Make — publish, about the time you get these, that Gamp. passed through that place on the — day of June, on his way to Canada, accompanied by one Frenchman and two Americans or Englishmen." [1] Which announcement duly appeared in the public prints. *Gamp, Gampy, Gampillo, Gampasso,* were pet names current in the family, and were used indiscriminately for Aaron Burr himself and his little grandson, Aaron Burr Alston.

On June 7, 1808, muffled against inquiring looks, H. E. Edwards boarded the packet, anchor was weighed, sails bellied to catch the vagrant breeze, and Burr had set sail for the unknown. But first there had been a tragic leave-taking from one Mary Ann Edwards, likewise muffled, and otherwise known to fame as Theodosia Burr Alston, with tears and desperate affection on the one side, and smiling, albeit Spartan fortitude on the other.

Halifax was the packet's first port of call, and Burr held to the seclusion of his cabin most of the way, shunning the usual seagoing intimacy with the other twenty-six passengers on board. At that Nova Scotian port he was welcomed by Sir George Prevost, a relative on his deceased wife's side, who furnished him with letters of introduction to family and friends in England, as well as a passport certifying that " G. H. Edwards was bearer of dispatches to the Right Honorable Lord Castlereagh, at whose office he was immediately to present himself on his arrival at London." [2]

The passage was comparatively swift; by July 13th, he had

reached Falmouth, and three days later he was in London. He had a definite mission to perform. Williamson and Merry had failed him at an earlier date, but he was still hopeful that if he appeared in person before the members of the English Cabinet he could gain their support, or at least approval and a certain authorization, for his plans to render Mexico independent of Spain. They were, he insisted, and continued so to insist all his life, perfectly good and feasible plans, and events were to justify him. But the events were not of his making, for he was under a cloud; the malignancy of the American Government was to pursue him even to the uttermost reaches of Europe, and the Continental situation, hitherto seemingly favorable to his hopes, was changing with rapidity and secrecy.

He kept a Private Journal of his Odyssean wanderings, as a shorthand aid to his memories for the benefit of Theo, anxiously awaiting news in South Carolina. It is an astounding document: there is nothing like it in American letters, and hardly anything to which it could be compared on the franker Continent. Pepys's Diary is a model of reticence by comparison; its matter-of-fact references to things ordinarily concealed strip the human animal to the few bare wants of nature; its wit, gayety and high courage in the face of despair, misfortune, starvation even, are electric. Here is the man himself — for all to see.

His coming created a sensation in certain circles. The American Minister, William Pinkney, was not fooled by the disguise. Already he had learned of the arrival of Samuel Swartwout, who, he informed Madison, "may be bearer of dispatches from Burr to Englishmen. Had him followed, but learnt nothing." [3] Now the arch-conspirator himself was in London, and the perturbed Minister wrote home again, "Burr arrived in England by the last Packet . . . It has been suggested that his object was to engage in some Enterprize against Spanish America under British auspices. This plan is of course defeated (at least for the present) by the late Change in the Relations of G. B. & Spain." Troops then gathering under Sir Arthur Wellesley, later to be better known as the Duke of Wellington, were rumored to be for South America, and perhaps, thought Pinkney, Burr had expected to participate. It was also hinted that Burr was planning a rupture between Great Britain and the United States, and the Minister felt certain that Burr's interviews with the Government had been responsible for the change for the worse in the attitude of Canning toward himself.[4] Nothing, of course, could have been further from the truth. There was sufficient explosive material in the Orders in Council and the Embargo to justify an attitude toward America, without Burr's intervention. But such insinuations, traveling to Jefferson and Madison, but confirmed them in their previous exceeding hostility to the exile.

Had Pinkney but known it, Burr ran into insuperable difficulties almost at once in his attempts to gain the ear of the British Government. Joseph Bonaparte, mediocre brother to the Dictator of Europe, was even then entering Madrid to be proclaimed the King of Spain by the ambitious Napoleon. It was part of his grandiose scheme to intrench his dynasty on the thrones of the mighty. With Spain in his grip, Napoleon would certainly not be interested in any scheme to dissipate its possessions. But England, hitherto hostile to Spain, now took the long, and opposite view. She immediately espoused the cause of the dethroned King and threw her forces into the Peninsula to oppose the Marshals of France. Allied now with the regnant dynasty, she, too, could hardly be a party to revolution in Mexico. *Both* doors were closed with irrevocable suddenness to Burr.

2. ENGLAND IS NOT INTERESTED

But these considerations were for the future. Immediately upon his arrival in London, Burr called on John Reeves, official of the British Alien Office, who was to befriend him later under dramatic circumstances. He was cordially received. Then, with his despatches from Prevost, he went to see Lord Castlereagh, who, however, was out, and continued to remain out for a considerable period. Castlereagh, the War Secretary, had no intention of helping Burr.

Dismayed at finding Williamson already gone from England, with only a note from him at hand to acknowledge receipt of his New York letter, and realizing with painful perspicuity that the European situation had wholly changed since he had set sail for England with such high hopes, he wrote his absent friend, " Your absence is extremely distressing and embarrassing, as it is a contingency against which I had made no provision. Though the new state of things defeats, for the present, the speculations we had proposed, yet it opens new views, not less important." [5] What these " new views " were, it is difficult to determine. Perhaps they were the suggestions of Williamson himself, left behind in his note, that Burr had the " power to advise [the English Cabinet] what means would most certainly prevent the French in the present crisis from having command of the Floridas and Mexico. No man can give so valuable information as yourself." [6] Doubtless Burr also figured on the long view. Mexico and the Floridas in Napoleon's iron grip meant the end of all his dreams; but, freed from French domination by English aid, the next shift in the kaleidoscope of European politics might place England and Spain once more in age-old opposition, and he could then descend with considerable prospect of success on the weak-held colonies of that dying Power.

On August 10th, he made out his alien declaration, as was required under the law, and gave as the reason for his presence in England that " I am known personally to Lord Mulgrave and Mr. Canning, to whom the motives to my visit have been declared. These reasons have long been known to Lord Melville." [7] For Burr had finally achieved that much measure of success. Canning, Cooke, Castlereagh and Mulgrave, all of the Cabinet, had at length opened their doors to him and his schemes. At least they had listened and questioned.

But if Burr met with scant success in thus knocking at the doors of the hard-headed statesmen of the Empire, all social doors swung wide at his coming. The Prevost family was well connected in England, and Charles Williamson had a host of friends and relations among the nobility. Baron Balgray was his brother, and he took to Burr immediately. So did the second Lord Melville. Military circles treated his soldierly qualities with respect, ladies of high and low degree discovered that same irresistible attraction toward the middle-aged widower which had been a prevalent disease in America, his courtly bearing and polished manner charmed aristocratic gatherings and country week-ends; while those circles in which intellect, wit and culture reigned supreme, hailed him as an equal and a brother.

Amid all his weary waiting at political doors, amid sightseeing of ruins and picture galleries, amid a bewildering succession of routs, entertainments, dances, cards, visits, parties _à deux,_ nothing delighted him more than the simple invitation of Jeremy Bentham to " pass some days, _chez lui._" [8] Burr had been among the very first in the United States to recognize the genius of that economist and moral philosopher, and now, his " amiable simplicity," his unaffected goodness and kindliness of spirit, earned an equally warm admiration for the man. And it was reciprocated. Burr spent a week-end at Barrow Green, Bentham's country residence, and, on returning to town, was forthwith lodged at the philosopher's town house in Queen's Square Place.

He met also, and became intimate with, William Godwin, whose advanced ideas had struck sympathetic chords; Charles Lamb, the

Courtesy of Estate of Dr. John E. Stillwell

AARON BURR, IN OLD AGE

From a portrait by Henry Inman

LETTER FROM BURR TO G. W. LATHROP, 1814-1815 (?)

gentle essayist; William Cobbett, the fierce "Peter Porcupine," whose quills were tipped with pamphleteering poison. Cobbett even tried to persuade Burr to stand for Parliament and rise to those heights in British political life for which his talents eminently fitted him. Faseli, the fashionable painter, took his commissions, lords and ladies vied with each other in extending the utmost hospitality. But it was Jeremy Bentham who commanded his complete idolatry — for the first time in his life Burr was humble in the presence of his fellow-man. " I hasten to make you acquainted with Jeremy Bentham," he wrote enthusiastically to Theo, " author of a work entitled Principles of Morals and Legislation . . . and of many other works of less labour and research. You will recollect to have heard me place this man second to no one, ancient or modern, in profound thinking, in logical and analytic reasoning." [9] To Bentham he had been equally enthusiastic in his descriptions of Theo and little *Gampy* (his grandson) ; so much so that Bentham insisted on receiving a portrait of the beloved daughter, and requested Burr to send " my dear little Theodosia " a package of all his works.

Meanwhile, at regular intervals, Burr continued to cool his heels in the anterooms of Cabinet members, and to meet with frigid evasions when he actually penetrated to the inner sanctums. England was strangely cold to *X,* as Burr had designated his Mexican scheme in cipher to Theo. As the autumn waned, he grew more and more discouraged. " I have no longer the slightest hope of the countenance of the ministry for anything which might be proposed," he told Bentham sadly. " I am an object of suspicion and alarm." [10] For this there were several good and sufficient reasons. One was that Spain was now an ally, and must have looked askance at the presence of Aaron Burr, her arch-enemy. The second was the attitude of the American Ministry, to whom Burr was a traitor and a fugitive from justice. The final reason was England's own uneasiness over this restless, talented individual within its borders, whose activities no one had ever fathomed fully, and whose course was as unpredictable as the vagaries of chance.

To add to his discouragement, about this time he received a letter from Bollman, his fellow-conspirator. Bollman had attempted to settle in New Orleans to the prosaic practice of medicine, but found that " the Americans shun me; and Clark himself, on his return, anxious to make his peace with his enemies . . . rather avoided me; wished me not to call on him, and came to see me by stealth." Only Judge Workman, " now practicing as a lawyer . . . is constantly excited in the old cause. His looks are steadfastly turned to the South." Disgusted, Bollman had tried his luck in New York; failing there, he intended to return to France.[11] This was a considerable blow to Burr. He had still hugged to his bosom the delusion that New Orleans was only awaiting the magic of his presence and the clarion-call to arms to rise *en masse* and pour its men and treasure into the long-anticipated advance on Mexico. Even with the members of the Mexican Association, Jefferson had triumphed.

Nor were matters much better with his adored Theo. She was sick, suffering constantly, worn out with anxiety for her father, and a pariah in her native surroundings. With tragic pathos she wrote Burr, " The world begins to cool terribly around me. You would be surprised how many I supposed attached to me have abandoned the sorry, losing game of disinterested friendship. Frederic alone [her half-brother] however, is worth a host." [12] She was in New York now, feeling to the full the weight of loneliness and execration that enveloped everything pertaining to Burr. Her husband, back in South Carolina, meant very little to her now. He had failed her worshiped father in his hour of need; he was but a poor stick to lean upon. More, he was parsimonious and kept a tight hold on the purse-strings. Very few words of endearment were hereafter to pass between them.[13] In all the world she had but three passions — her father, her child, and X.

And now X was gone from the trinity! " You are well and happy," she wrote her father on hearing the mournful news, " but X is abandoned! This certainly was inevitable, but I cannot part with what had so long lain near my heart, and not feel some regret, some sorrow. No doubt there are many other roads to happiness, but this appeared so perfectly suitable to you, so complete a remuneration for all the past . . . that I cherished it as my comfort." *Eheu fugaces!* Then bravely, smiling through her tears, " My knowledge of your character, however, consoles me greatly. You will not remain idle. The situation in which you are placed would excite apathy itself, and your mind needs no external impetus." Then, turning to more cheerful topics, she exclaims, " When shall I receive the journal? Good Heaven, how it will delight me! " [14] Alas, she was never to see it, never to read that naked, stripped account of indomitable gesturing against the pursuing gods. She alone would have understood the childlike disclosures of his soul, the casual obscenities with which the original text is studded. He held no secrets from *her*. But an ironic, cruelly sportive fate decreed otherwise.

She was ill now, desperately so. Burr was terribly alarmed. He haunted the offices of the English practitioners, describing her symptoms as they came to him through slow and unsatisfactory mails, seeking advice, the possibility of cures. In final desperation he determined to bring her to England to obtain the best medical advice. He wrote strongly about it to Alston, " As to money, I have transferred over to Theodosia the small sum which had been destined for my own expenses (say four or five hundred guineas) ; this will pay her passage and expenses to this place, and maintain her in the way I propose she shall live for four or five months . . . It is probable that her fate will be determined within six or eight months. If she survive, I shall return with her to the United States." [15]

But Alston refused to permit her to go. Instead, he insisted that she return to the hot, miasmic lowlands of their South Carolinian home, and fulfil her wifely duties. When Burr heard of it, he was furious. He scolded Theo for her meek subservience, and berated Alston. " He gave me his word before marriage," he exclaimed to his daughter, " and I claim now the renewal of that promise. You may be made to do anything; to say anything; to write anything. After four experiments, all nearly fatal, I would not have made *a fifth with a dog*." [16]

Meanwhile, the ever-bubbling Anthony Merry had promised his assistance. Burr waited and possessed his soul in patience for his arrival, " and till I shall see whether no other engines can be brought into use for the occasion. If it fail, heighho for the Mediterranean," he told Bentham. " Nevertheless, if there should remain even a remote hope of obtaining the countenance of this government, I will not quit the field. My American friends have very sagaciously concluded that the present state of things in Spain is calculated to promote my views! Hence some ferment." [17] An l he was in constant communication with revolutionists in Spain itself, through the medium of Don Castella, who likewise was interested in Mexican independence. [18]

But Merry was mournfully to report that " although I could not see Mr. Canning . . . I conversed with another person of nearly equal authority, who told me he was sure that what you proposed to me yesterday could never be consented to, pointing it out in every way to be impracticable." [19] The last small door had been firmly and decisively shut in Burr's face.

There was nothing left for Burr to do but seek his fortunes elsewhere. In the Mediterranean were troubled waters, in which possibly he could fish to some profit. X — the conquest of Mexico — had become the ruling passion of his life, a fixed monomania.

Psychologically it was a defense mechanism — a justification for the shattered ruins in which his whole life lay. Taken away, nothing remained but dust and ashes.

There had been intimations too — rather pointed, in fact — that his presence in England was not exactly welcome. He was an alien, and his license to remain was revocable at will. Without such license, he could be deported summarily, and no passport granted him to the places he wished to visit. Faced with this situation, Burr determined on a desperate course. On November 23, 1808, he went boldly to the Alien Office, where his friend, Reeve, was in charge, and flung the license on the table. " I am a Briton," he exclaimed, " and claim the privilege of a British subject as a birthright, which I have a right to resume. I hereby give you notice that I shall go wherever I please." This little comedy, however, Burr confessed, had been Reeve's own suggestion as one way in which to avoid forcible deportation to America. Reeve gravely made a report of the incident, and submitted it to Lord Hawkesbury, who, he said, would probably refer it to the Attorney General for an opinion.[20]

For this course he was to suffer much criticism in the United States — that country which had spewed him forth as a traitor. In later years, Burr himself was ashamed of this sudden action, and tried to deny it. But at the moment it seemed the only way in which he could remain in England, or travel where he willed under the protecting egis of a British passport. It was a novel and rather amazing point — this claim of his to British citizenship. His argument was a strange compound of subtlety, naïveté and sophistry. At his birth, he maintained, he had been a British subject. The Colonies had rebelled and cast off their citizenship. But, *in English law*, he insisted, once an Englishman, always an Englishman. His very attempt to cast off his obligations was a futility, and now he was returning to the fold. A doctrine which would have had the strange consequence of making the millions of independent Americans, *in English law*, still subjects of His Majesty.

Yet this farrago received the careful and somewhat bewildered attention of the legists of the kingdom. There was even a violent dispute over the merits of the argument. Dampier, it seemed, " has given opinion that I may resume at pleasure," Burr noted in his Journal; " the Lord Chancellor, Eldon, that I cannot, and am forever an alien. The Attorney-General is doubting. Lord Hawkesbury thinks the claim monstrous." And cooler thought had come to Burr. " I begin to think," he confessed, " the policy of this brusque movement very doubtful." [21] But it had served its immediate purpose. While the lawyers were arguing and puzzling, there was no further talk of deportation.

He had moved into Bentham's lodgings, and the nights were replete with high talk of morals, of the legal basis of the State, of such various subjects as " tattooing, and how to be made useful; of infanticide; of crimes against Nature, etc., etc." [22] He sat for a portrait to the famous Turnevelli, for transport to Theo, but it turned out villainously. X was still in his thoughts, but infinitely remote of accomplishment. Whereupon he decided on making the *Grand Tour* of all the British Isles as a mode of occupying his restless mind and inquiring senses. While he was making preparations for his travels, Jefferson, in America, was getting somewhat garbled reports of his activities. " Burr is in London," he wrote, " and is giving out to his friends that that government offers him two millions of dollars the moment he can raise an ensign of rebellion as big as a handkerchief . . . For myself," he went on vaingloriously, " even in his most flattering periods of conspiracy, I never entertained one moment's fear." [23]

3. THE GRAND TOUR

On December 21st, Burr started on his tour, armed with numerous letters of introduction. His first stop was Oxford, and on the stagecoach he met " a very pretty, graceful, arch-looking girl, about 18." But alas, " M'lle. was reserved and distant," and even when he finally progressed to breakfast " *tete-a-tete* ", he could go no further. Somewhat ruefully he made a memorandum, some day " to write an essay, historical and critical, on the education and treatment of women in England. Its influence on morals and happiness." [24] Burr could never resist a pretty face, a trim figure, the speaking eye.

The next day he was equally at home dining gravely with the Oxford Provost, who " though he speaks of Bentham with reverence, and, probably prays for him, I presume he thinks that he will be eternally damned [Bentham's views on revealed religion were rather unorthodox], and I have no doubt he expects to be lolling in Abraham's bosom with great complacency, hearing Bentham sing out for a drop of water. Such," exclaimed Burr in amused indignation, " is the mild genius of our holy religion." [25] He was Bentham's most enthusiastic disciple, and wherever he went, in whatever gathering, Bentham's name, Bentham's genius, Bentham's doctrines were his constant theme.

Christmas Eve found him in Birmingham, and here begins the

record of his amorous adventures, described so casually and with no moral undertones. He mingled with the gay throngs until " at length I got so well suited with a couple that we agreed to walk and see the town. I have always had a passion for certain branches of natural history." [26] An overpowering passion, it seems. To almost the very end of his long life his sexual prowess remained unimpaired and of an abounding vitality. The flesh to him was a natural need, and the appeasement of desire an equally natural function. Ordinary moral criteria cannot be applied to such men — the case books of medical history are full of similar instances; and medical men understand — and are tolerant.

But this particular adventure had a tawdry ending. In the course of it he found himself robbed of his passage ticket to Liverpool, he had lost, spent or had stolen from him 28 shillings, and a pair of gloves disappeared. Accordingly, he was compelled to take an outside passage on the coach to Liverpool at half price, unregenerate, unrepentant.

On New Year's Day he was in Edinburgh, where he was immediately taken into the bosom of aristocracy, literati, bench and bar alike. For over a month he remained in that hospitable Scottish town, tasting to the full all manner of things. He met and became intimate boon companions with Lord Justice Clerk, Alexander McKenzie, the author, Francis Jeffrey, founder and for 26 years the editor of the famous *Edinburgh Review,* whose savage criticism was later falsely assumed to have been the inducing cause of John Keats' death; the Lord Mayor welcomed him, and Sir Walter Scott, at the height of his powers, treated his literary criticism with respect. Not to speak of a horde of lesser lights — lords and ladies, dukes and marquises, men of wealth and men of fashion, admirals, generals, authors, editors, judges and lawyers. In fact, the cream of Scotch society. Life became a round of invitations, suppers, dances, music and amorous adventures. " I lead a life of the utmost dissipation," he confessed to Bentham. " Driving out every day and at some party almost every night. Wasting time and doing many silly things." But wisely taking cream of tartar punch — his favorite remedy for indigestion — the following mornings.[27]

But in the maze of flattering attentions, he had not forgotten the *raison d'être* of his European wanderings. He found a warm ally in Lord Justice Clerk, who corresponded about X with Lord Melville in London, but, thought Burr, he " does not go to work right." [28] Clerk considered it advisable for Burr to return at once to London, abandoning the rest of his tour. Burr's claim to British citizenship was still pending " and has made a very considerable sensation in the Cabinet," he was told. " Cobbett very deeply impregnated with the magnitude of your talents as a statesman and a soldier. They [Cobbett and some one in power active in Burr's behalf] had been consulting together how it was possible that you should be brought into Parliament, supposing the above question to form no obstacle." [29]

For the first time the prospects were encouraging. It was with considerable reluctance, however, that Burr tore himself away from his friendly hosts, and reached London on February 7th. Bentham sent for him immediately, and he was rushed to a conference with General Hope, who had considerable influence, and in whom Charles Williamson had confided the old plans, even to the extent of divulging Burr's secret cipher. But the excitement died out as quickly as it had arisen. Once more Burr found himself adrift.

New matters rose to plague him. His slender resources — funds borrowed chiefly from American friends before he sailed — were evaporating rapidly in the careless profusion of his daily expense; and suddenly a London bookseller threatened him with arrest for debt on a four-year-old claim for books he had ordered while in the United States, but which had been seized by the United States Government at the port of entry. The amount was 117 pounds, a " trifling " sum, Burr advised Alston, but " by no means convenient to pay it out of my slender resources." So he determined to shift his residence from Bentham's house, where he had made his home ever since his arrival in England. " The benevolent heart of J. B. shall never be saddened by the spectacle of Gamp's arrest," he declared.[30] It is a significant disclosure of his character that never once, in the darkest hours of destitution and starvation, did he make known his plight to Jeremy Bentham, who, though of modest means himself, would have been only too happy to have shared with him.

To avoid arrest, he took obscure quarters on February 12th, at 35 St. James Street, under an assumed name. His new landlady, whose name, strangely enough, turned out to be Madame Prevost was young and personable, and became " extremely attentive — *Un air d'elegance et d'abbatement. Peutetre 28.*" (An air of elegance and dejection. Perhaps 28.) Indeed, " Sent by the Devil to sed. [seduce] Gamp," he protested to his Diary.[31] Burr usually descended to a particularly barbarous French, interlarded with obscure abbreviations and obscurer phrases when jotting down these daily mementoes of his amorous adventurings.

Within two days, " foreseeing that we might go the round of

sentiment, though I think we shall go rapidly through it, thought it necessary to coo dow [kowtow?]." He went through it rapidly enough. " An hour with Madame P. *La 2 lecon car. et souprs.*" (The second lesson consists of caresses and sighs.) The next jotting was optimistic. *" Des progres; ça je finira en deux jours."* (Progress. I'll finish that in two days.) He surprised himself. For, that very night, is the significant entry, " *Couche at 1/2 p 10 . . . Des. progr. rapides."* [32]

The course of true love did not run quite smooth. There were blushes, tears, protests; all in all, " *Jo. melange* " (pretty mess!). But soon the too-charming landlady became more moderate in her transports, and life in hiding ran smoothly along for several weeks. On March 4th, however, someone had inquired about him in the neighborhood, and he shifted his quarters hastily to the house of some friends. There was a civil warrant of arrest out for him on the bookseller's claim. Two weeks later, he decided it was safe again to move back to Mme. Prevost. To such illicit subterfuges was the man who had been exalted to the seats of the mighty now compelled to descend.

But he had been watched. On April 4, 1809, " having a confused presentiment that something was wrong, packed up my papers and clothes with intent to go out and seek other lodgings." It was too late. " At 1 o'clock came in, without knocking, four coarse-looking men, who said they had a state warrant for seizing me and my papers; but refused to show the warrant. I was peremptory, and the warrant was produced, signed Liverpool." [33] This was far worse than the mere civil arrest from which he had been hiding. " They took possession of my trunks," the Journal narrates, " searched every part of the room for papers, threw all the loose articles into a sack, called a coach, and away we went to the Alien Office." Reeve came out to the prisoning coach with serious mien, told him hastily " he could not then explain, but . . . I must have patience." Immediately he was whisked away to the house of one of his captors, and held there *incommunicado,* although treated with proper respect, and the mistress of the house, he soon discovered, was pretty and quite bearable. [34] Burr by this time was well accustomed to arrests and imprisonments, and took them with a careless gayety.

But powerful friends were at work. On the third day, he was taken back to the Alien Office, his papers and effects restored unopened, and there was a letter of apology for his arrest from Lord Liverpool, who had signed the warrant. It was but temporary surcease, however. Crude methods had been employed, and had failed because of active opposition by men like Reeve, Cobbett, Lord Melville, General Hope, Baron Balgray, all partisans of Burr. Politer methods were to succeed, however.

The British Government was determined to rid itself of this constant thorn in its side. It mistrusted him, was a little afraid of his bold and enterprising spirit; while the American and Spanish embassies alike agitated incessantly for stern measures against him. The most powerful nations of the world presented a united hostile front to this solitary little man. One against the world — yet the world feared, while it scourged him!

On April 14, 1809, still at Madame Prevost's, he received a message, " Lord Liverpool expects that you will leave town this day and the kingdom tomorrow." [35] To enforce the peremptory demand, Burr's young secretary, Hosack, was arrested, and freed only with the greatest difficulty. Burr defied the order, though agreeing to leave in due time and to the place of his own choice. He won.

Eleven days later, on April 25th, he received passports for himself and his secretary for Sweden, which, he thought, was " the most proper asylum," for almost every other port in Europe was under the control of France and its allies, and hence barred to his entrance or dangerous to his person. Spanish ports were even worse. To a friend in New York, he wrote bitterly, " Mr. Jefferson, or the Spanish Juntas, or probably both, have had influence enough to drive me out of this country." [36] Homeless, a wanderer on the face of the earth, there was only Sweden to which he could turn for a certain neutrality. Yet not a word of complaint to Theo, not a moment of hopeless repining in the privacy of the Journal, no clamoring against inimical Fate.

" I witness your extraordinary fortitude with new wonder at every new misfortune," wrote Theo in almost breathless adoration. " You appear to me so superior, so elevated above all other men, I contemplate you with such a strange mixture of humility, admiration, reverence, love, and pride, that very little superstition would be necessary to make me worship you as a superior being: such enthusiasm does your character excite in me. . . . I had rather not live than not be the daughter of such a man." [37]

The very day the passports came, he boarded His Britannic Majesty's packet, the *Diana*, a 60-ton sloop, and set sail for Sweden. England had spewed him forth; what adventures lay ahead on the Continent?

4. Swedish Journey

Burr landed in Gothenburg, neat and very trim Swedish port, on May 2nd. Hosack, left behind to settle his affairs, came by a later boat, and joined him on the 6th. Burr's first impression was unappetizing. He lost his trunk with all his clothes — an irremediable loss in the precarious state of his finances — but fortunately it was recovered intact in a few days. Whereupon the pair journeyed on to Stockholm, the nation's capital.

At Stockholm Burr was once more in his element. He had a sheaf of letters of introduction, and the kindly Swedish folk took him into their collective bosoms. With the very highest and the very lowest, he was equally at home, and equally attractive. At the top of the social ladder he met and was cordially entertained by Colonel and Professor Gahn, the historian and geographer Catteau-Calleville and Baron Munck, and was given the freedom of the very exclusive Society of Nobles. He was even presented to the Swedish Regent, and " you would have laughed to see Gamp with his sword and immense three-cornered hat." [38]

At the other end of the scale, he was equally irresistible to a maid at his lodgings, who came to his room and whom " *Ne saur. renvoir.*" (I couldn't send back.) [39] His Journal now contains almost daily references to certain peculiar lessons in natural history, expressed invariably in a vile shorthand French, with the price of each lesson unblushingly affixed. Casual encounters with prostitutes — pale and pretty ones, stout and otherwise, blondes, brunettes, country girls and servants — as well as countesses and court ladies, with no price tags; all were grist for the mill.

And, interspersed with these, constant visiting, dances, concerts, drives, walks — with the inevitable amorous encounter at the end — art galleries, levees, to bed long after midnight and up at six every morning, and, withal, long conversations with legists on the Swedish law. " You will be charmed to hear the results of my inquiries on this head," he wrote for the later edification of Theo. " Only to think of a people, the most honest and peaceable in the world, and not a lawyer! No such animal, (according to English ideas of a lawyer) , in Sweden! But again and again I remind you that this Journal is only a memorandum to talk from. The most interesting and amusing incidents are not noted at all, because I am sure to remember them." [40]

His acute intellect required constant satisfaction as well as his body and senses. He read extensively in Swedish jurisprudence and on the civil administration, making copious notes and inquiring of judges and famous lawyers. The Swedish law and system of government fascinated him, and he had every intention of some day publishing on the subject. Nor were his interests confined to the law. He read considerably in the drama, history, military science, travels, moral and social studies, and, always, Bentham. Breda, the famous painter, was his intimate, and found him a connoisseur. In short, Burr, at the age of 53, an exile, an outcast, was displaying an intellectual and physical vitality that would have sadly taxed the resources of men of half his years and under happier conditions. Misfortune could not touch him; age could not wither or stale his infinite variety. He lived in the present and the future; the past was ever a resolutely closed book. He was indifferent to criticism and malignity. There is a significant item in the Journal that explains much that might otherwise have sounded incredible in his previous career. " Aug. 20, 1809 — It was not till yesterday that I learnt that I have been a subject of newspaper discussion for several weeks. What is said about me I have neither heard nor inquired." [41]

After four months of Sweden he took stock of himself. The life had been so full, so interesting, so physically involved, that even his insatiable appetites were glutted. He had paid out innumerable rix-dollars for the flesh, and had satisfied the spirit with scenery, museums, private collections, art galleries, and with long, judicious talks with scientists, literary men, philosophers and savants in the law. He had visited mines and shown puzzled Swedish engineers how to drain a lake; he still was preoccupied with his favorite topic — the emancipation of women and the discovery that they have souls and brains as well as men. He read essays on the subject and found that the moralists were on the wrong track, " and of course [had] not found the remedy; this will remain for Gamp." [42] His notes on law and government were slowly taking form.

But he had not forgotten Theo, or his friends in America, or X. On September 2, 1809, the stocktaking had its effect. " It is no easy matter, *ma Min.* [my Minerva]," he told his Journal, " to determine how to dispose of myself. Why stay here? To be sure I am unmolested and live at no great expense, but *tem. fug.* [*tempus fugit*] and nothing done. When I came here it was with intent to stay till answers should be received to my letters written to the United States." But there had been no mail for four months. Evidently the British Government, mistress of the high seas, was not permitting his letters to pass through the cordon. " The summary is," he concluded, " that I am resolved to go without knowing exactly why or where . . . The facility of getting to a particular place may of itself determine my course. To be sure the *embarras* of traveling on the Continent is very great, but I am in utter despair of receiving letters through England." [43]

This hasty jotting throws a flood of light on Burr's motives in this Continental tour. It was not as aimless, as dilatory, as feckless as most commentators have thought. When the European situation closed all doors to an outlet for his Mexican plans, he had determined to return to the United States. But various indictments still hung over his head — the one for murder in New Jersey, which was a dead letter; the one for sending a challenge in New York, which might require political manipulation. This, however, had already been taken care of by Tammany and the Swartwouts.

De Witt Clinton, engaged in a political squabble with Governor Morgan Lewis, approached the Burrites with an offer of peace if they would aid him in the party warfare. In December, 1805, his agent had promised Tammany and those loyal to Burr the discount facilities of the Manhattan Bank, recognition as party members in good standing, appointments to office, a cessation of Cheetham's attacks, and even, under pressure, that Burr, their leader and idol, would be unmolested in New York. A secret meeting was held with John Swartwout, Peter Irving and Matthew L. Davis, at which the terms were arranged. On February 29, 1806, Clintonians and Burrites joined in a love feast at Dyde's Hotel in celebration of the union. The banquet was a secret, but the newspapers got wind of it, and a howl went up from unreconstructed Clintonians and Burrites alike. The uninvited Burrites, fearing they would be left out in the cold, joined the followers of Morgan Lewis in a meeting at Martling's Long Room, the home of Tammany, and organized a protestant faction, known as the Martling Men, whose enmity followed De Witt Clinton to his ultimate downfall.[44] In any event, this indictment, too, was a dead letter.

But the Ohio indictment on the filibuster charge was in Jefferson's unrelenting hands, and Burr's numerous creditors with their threats of civil arrest were just as adamant in their determination to collect. It was these matters which required clearing up. Burr had been forced from England before he could hear from his correspondents. The Swedish mails went through English ports, and England was holding up all letters to and from Burr. When, finally on October 12th, a letter was smuggled through to him by private hand from Theo, he was so overjoyed that he " could have kissed the fellow! " [45] It was necessary, therefore, to find some other place where the mails would not be subject to the censorship of England. This intense interest of the political police of many European countries in the correspondence of Aaron Burr explains the shorthand of the Journal, the villainous French, the total lack of all political comment. His effects had been seized once; there was no telling when it might happen again.

" Be very careful what you write," he warned an unnamed correspondent. " Every letter is liable to inspection. One indiscreet expression might expose your letters to be burned, and perhaps me with them. Avoid everything having reference to politics, and there is no danger." [46] One wonders whether the preoccupation of the Journal with *muse* (a slang French expression constantly employed by Burr, meaning " the rutting period in animals "), and the vulgar details set out at length, were not part and parcel of a clever scheme. Should Burr be subject to another visitation, this Journal would be evidence to a cynical police that the owner, so occupied with low pursuits, could not possibly be involved in dangerous conspiracies, and therefore they might be impelled to dismiss him as a harmless voluptuary.

5. HAMLET AND GOETHE

Burr's first thought was of Russia. It was comparatively easy of access from Sweden, and its alliances with the countries hostile to Burr were not particularly entangling. With Russia as a base, he might be in a better position to survey the scene and plan his return. There was also the memory of John Paul Jones, who had carved an adventurous niche for himself in that semi-Oriental country.

But John Quincy Adams was in Russia on an official mission from the United States. Ever since he had turned Republican, and sunned himself in the favors of Republican Administrations, he had joined the baying circle of Burr's enemies. On November 15, 1809, Count Romanzoff, the Russian Minister, informed him " that Colonel Burr, now at Gottenburg, had applied for a passport to come to Petersburg, which had been refused him, unless it should be regularly applied for under the sanction of the representative of his country at this Court." [47] Some three months later, Romanzoff told Adams again that if Burr " wanted to come here he must make his application through me [J. Q. A.], and, if I had desired it, no difficulty would have been made." [48] Evidently, John Quincy Adams did *not* desire it.

Thus rebuffed, Burr turned elsewhere, and succeeded finally

in obtaining passports for himself and his secretary to Denmark. He had started on his travels again.

He landed at Elsinore, famous for its castle and more famous for Hamlet's ghost. He did not stop to walk the hoary battlements at midnight but continued on to Copenhagen, where, the very evening of his arrival, " after strolling an hour, during which *mus. mauv.;* 1 d. [bad *muse,* 1 dollar] came home," where " the chambermaid, fat, not bad; *muse* again." [49]

Owing to the heavy depreciation of the paper currency, Burr found living cheap in Denmark, but, even so, his funds were beginning to be a constant source of anxiety to him. A most welcome, though embarrassing addition came in the form of a draft for 1,000 marks from Lüning, a friend he had made in Sweden. It was a wholly unexpected, unsolicited loan. With it was a note. " I cannot tell you how much I am thankful to Providence for having given me the pleasure to get acquainted with a man whom I admired long ago. I esteemed you before; now I love you." [50] Aaron Burr excited either idolatry or unremitting hate in the bosoms of men; as for women, they uniformly adored him.

In Denmark he met Friedrich Schlegel, the great critic, whose " Treatise on Neutral Rights " he had read and much admired. He went by slow stages through that tiny kingdom, mostly by wagon, and taking along with him, throughout his travels, the painted lineaments of Theo, which he never left out of his sight, even holding the large portrait in his lap, as " I could not bear to see you," he wrote, " bouncing about at the bottom of the wagon." [51]

On November 8, 1809, he was over its borders and into what is now modern Germany, finally coming to rest in the little town of Altona, close to Hamburg, on the Elbe River. His funds, even with Lüning's windfall, were very low. He remained here for over a month, making frequent trips into neighboring Hamburg. There were a good many Americans in the town, and, for the first time since leaving London, Burr felt a decided coolness in the air. He was not given ordinarily to complaining, so that his allusions to the situation must have been the result of a full heart. " I find that, among the great number of Americans here and *there,*" he wrote in his Journal, " all are hostile to A. B. — all. What a lot of rascals they must be to make war on one whom they do not know; on one who never did harm or wished harm to a human being. Yet they, perhaps, ought not to be blamed, for they are influenced by what they hear. I learn further that A. B. is announced in the Paris papers in a manner no way auspicious."⁵² The former was discouraging, the latter disastrous.

His last chance on the Continent lay in France. In the kaleidoscopic whirl of politics and arms, at this particular moment Napoleon might be willing to listen to his schemes. Victory seemed perched on British arms in Spain, and Spanish possessions in America were at the mercy of the British fleet. Burr had no further love for England, after his unceremonious deportation from that tight little isle, and France had always been the object of his admiration. But the French Minister at Hamburg, De Bourrienne, was exceedingly evasive on the subject of a passport to Paris. Burr's money was now exhausted, and there was no prospect of any more. He persisted with De Bourrienne until the Minister finally granted him a passport to a frontier town in France, and advised him that he would have to write direct to Paris if he wished to go further. Later, De Bourrienne was to remember this episode: " At the height of his glory and power, Bonaparte was so suspicious that the veriest trifle sufficed to alarm him. . . . I recollect . . . Colonel Burr, formerly Vice-President of the United States, who had recently arrived at Altona, was pointed out to me as a dangerous man, and I received orders to watch him very closely, and to arrest him on the slightest ground of suspicion if he should come to Hamburg. Colonel Burr was one of those in favor of whom I ventured to disobey the orders I received from the restless police of Paris. As soon as the Minister of Police heard of his arrival in Altona, he directed me to adopt towards him those violent measures which are equivalent to persecution. In answer to these instructions, I stated that Colonel Burr conducted himself at Altona with much prudence and propriety; that he kept but little company, and he was scarcely spoken of. Far from regarding him as a man who required watching, having learned that he wished to go to Paris, I caused a passport to be procured for him, which he was to receive at Frankfort, and I never heard that this dangerous citizen had compromised the safety of the state in any way."⁵³

Burr was suffering physically as well as mentally at the time. An ulcerated tooth drove him nearly frantic, and into the competent arms of a lady dentist. Also, " a lip which was bitten by a venomous animal on Friday last has swollen, and is very painful." The " venomous animal " seems to have been suspiciously two-legged and female in sex, for, narrates the Journal, " the origin of the thing is so ridiculous that I wished to hush it up; for the bite was given in a paroxysm of great good humor." [54] Yet it took days for that bite to heal.

In spite of bite, in spite of toothache, Burr started for France on December 11, 1809. His journey took him first to Göttingen, where he met Karl Friedrich Gauss, the famous mathematician and Director of the Astronomical Observatory. He was taken through the observatory and the library, and was properly impressed. Then on to Cassel, Westphalia, where, as in every land and clime, the children trooped to him and adored him. He had a remarkable gift for capturing their fancy, for interesting himself in their little affairs. Little *Gampy*, his grandson, was constantly in his thoughts. He was forever sending him trinkets, toys, medals, old coins; whatever might interest the sturdy little boy – even when the purchase price meant the lack of a supper that night. At Cassel we find this charming entry in the Journal, expressive of much in Burr's character and the loyalty he inspired: " Dec. 28 – Yesterday I must have been possessed by the devil. A pretty little girl about 15 years old came into my room [at the post house] with a little *guittare* in her hand and muttering a few words in German began to sing and play. Could you imagine anything more calculated to fascinate me? I drove her rudely out. To be sure, I did give her a *gooden-groshen*, which was probably much more than she expected; but I was unkind. One minute after, I was sorry and sent for her, but she was not to be found; and I have been all day looking out for her in vain." [55]

But it was at Göttingen that he received most important news from Professor Heeren, with whom he had corresponded from the United States. It was nothing more or less than " the Emperor's assent to the independence of Mexico and the other Spanish colonies! " In great anguish of spirit Burr exclaimed, " Now, why the devil didn't he tell me of this two years ago? " [56] Two years before, when Burr was seeking aid through all the world for his imminent expedition against Mexico, and Napoleon as well as England had turned him coldly down. He had been two years too early. What thoughts must have coursed through his mind at the twists and ironic turns of Fate! With Napoleon's help he might now have been monarch of Mexico, ruler of Central and South America, one of the world's great, the arbiter of the destiny of millions. Instead, he was a threadbare little man, eating potatoes for lunch and supper, hardly knowing where his next meal would come from, a wanderer on the face of the earth, harried from pillar to post, subject to the vigilant attentions of the police in many lands, an object of scorn, suspicion and wrath.

But it was not in his nature to repine. More than ever was he determined to get to Paris. Napoleon favored the independence of the Spanish colonies? Very well; he had plans to submit, memorials to offer which might interest the Dictator of half of Europe.

On January 2, 1810, Burr was in Weimar. That little capital was then at the height of its glory, the intellectual center of Europe. In spite of his slightly shabby, though painfully elegant, clothes, in spite of his obvious poverty, he was welcomed at once into the innermost circles by the aristocracy of birth as well as that of the intellect. He met Frau von Stein, lady of the court, beloved of Goethe, and the Princess Caroline; he dined in state with Charles Augustus, the Duke of Saxe-Weimar and the genial patron of the glorious figures with whom he had surrounded himself; he was greeted by the royal family and the whole of that brilliant circle of wits, lovely ladies, and courtiers. Then he was introduced to Wieland, the poet; the wife of Knebel; Wilhelm, the brother of the great naturalist, Alexander von Humboldt; the mother of Schopenhauer, the philosopher of pessimism; and finally — the great, the overwhelming Goethe himself. Name after glittering name, until the reader is left breathless. And everywhere, in whatever company, Burr was an equal, a comrade, a man of taste, of breeding, of intellectual comprehension. What a pity that Burr chose this particular period to hurry his Diary, to avoid extended comments, to jot down, " but I must stop with details and only make short notes to talk from," that on the day he met Goethe, his whole comment should be, " this day would make about 200 pages if written out." [57] To cap the climax, he was never to talk from his notes to Theo, to any one; and his observations must forever remain buried in the grave at Princeton.

A complication arose at Weimar — an amatory one. A certain lady of the court — Mademoiselle de Reizenstein — had aroused in him a depth of passion of which he had no longer believed himself capable, and the passion had been reciprocated. On January 8, 1810, he packed his belongings in great haste and in utter secrecy, and fled incontinently from Weimar, never stopping for breath until he had reached Erfurt. Dates were left unfilled, friends, the Duke himself, were deserted without a word of farewell. That night he scribbled by candlelight, still shaken with the danger he had just escaped: she is " a sorceress," and " if I were President of the secret tribunal she should be burnt alive tomorrow. Another interview and I might have been lost, my hopes and projects blasted and abandoned." [58]

There could now be but one ruling passion in his life — Mexico.

Professor Heeren had opened up new vistas; he must get to Napoleon and strike while the iron was hot. The dazzling De Reizenstein would have married him, settled him down to a secure, graceful, elegant position in a German court. His ambitions were on a grander scale; they *must* be fulfilled.

From Erfurt he continued his breakneck flight to Gotha, as though he feared the siren might follow and he might weaken. There he was royally entertained by Ernst I, Duke of Saxe-Coburg, and met Bernard de Lindenau, Director of the Observatory, famous mathematician and astronomer, as well as Galletti, the historian. And, on January 18th, he was in Frankfort, where he settled down to await word from Paris on his application for a passport. Five days later, he was still waiting, " but there were advices from Paris concerning me extremely unfavorable, and requesting I might be advised by no means to hazard my person within the territories of France." [59] Nevertheless, he made the hazard, and on the 25th was in Mayence, in the sphere of French influence. No passport was forthcoming, and he was placed under a modified arrest pending disposition of his case from Paris. He found distant cousins here in Mayence, representing a branch of the Burr family which had settled in Holland more than a century before, and they did what they could to ease his condition. And, at the beginning of February, came good news. Paris had decided to grant him his passport, and he was free to proceed.

Chapter XXVIII

FAILURE IN FRANCE

1. Proposals to Napoleon

ARON BURR reached Paris on February 16, 1810. He wrote at once for an audience with the Duc de Cadore, the Minister of Foreign Relations, which was granted, and he submitted his plans. Then he retired to his shabby lodgings and waited for a reply. The wait was to be long and tiring. In the interval he renewed his acquaintance with Comte de Volney, scholar and author, and M. Adet, former French Minister to the United States, both of whom he had entertained in the days of affluence at Richmond Hill. There was also a joyful reunion with John Vanderlyn, the painter, to further whose genius Burr had given unstintedly of his time and money. Vanderlyn was famous now, and in a position to turn the tables in the matter of financial help. But Burr was singularly delicate in this respect. He had had no hesitation in borrowing vast sums from usurers and those to whom lending was a business procedure, but he resisted as long as possible borrowing — with little prospect of return — from those who were personal friends. Bentham, Lüning, whose draft he had cashed with the greatest reluctance only when he had not another *sou* in his pocket, and now Vanderlyn.

His first flush of optimism was slowly dying. He heard nothing from Cadore, French officialdom was cool, if not openly hostile, and his scanty funds were steadily growing less. So much so that on February 24th, he was reduced to " rice soup for dinner, 8 sous. Go out at 6. Bought bread and cheese." *But,* the same evening, he records " two rencounters, one good; another, the third, 13 francs! That's economy for you! " [1] Burr knew his own failings, but could not resist them. He had no money for food, but the cries of the flesh were irresistible.

A few days later Cadore informed him that he had appointed Deputy Louis Roux to treat with him concerning the proposals he had submitted to His Majesty, the Emperor. Burr dined with Roux several times, and recorded mournfully, " have no reason to believe that my business advances, or that I shall do anything here." [2] Officialdom grew more and more rude and overbearing, doors remained closed in spite of repeated attempts to get past guards, food was held at a minimum, and life was kept bearable only by repeated *muse* and the solace derived from a certain yielding Madame Paschaud, whose husband was quite fortunately away in Geneva. Because of her, Burr had no time to make any entries in his Journal from March 12th to March 28th.

What were these projects which he had submitted to Napoleon, and to which the French Ministry opposed a discreet silence? On March 21st, he had written in desperation to the Duc d'Otrante — better known to fame as Fouché, dreaded Chief of Police to Napoleon — " Mr. Burr, from the United States of North America, having some months ago seen published in the Moniteur the expression of his majesty's assent to the independence of the Spanish American colonies, came to Paris to offer his services to accomplish that object and others connected therewith. He asked neither men nor money. He asked only the authorization of his majesty." Failing answers to his previous communications, he now asks an audience from the Duke relating to his schemes.[3]

Seemingly this letter is plain enough in its language. The independence of Spanish America was the single object of his heart, the only plan to be discussed. Nothing else. Nothing of treasonable designs upon the territory of the United States. Yet, up to a few years ago, there was no period in Burr's long career more shrouded in impenetrable obscurity, more murmurous in the whispering-galleries of history with treason, turncoatism and renegade proposals. The older view was based chiefly on rumors, fugitive letters and inquiries addressed by the State Department to correspondents in France and their replies — or rather, the bruited rumors of their replies. These documents, as they come to light among the Madison papers in various repositories, require close examination.

The first and most important is a lengthy communication, addressed to James Madison from Paris, dated Dec. 11, 1811. Herein is stated positively that " to the Duke [of Otranto], he [Burr] delivered a memorial of 63 folio pages . . . The object of this memorial was: to procure peace between France and England. France was to offer to secure to England, with all her forces, even by the loan of 100,000 men, or more; the conquest of the Northern parts of the United States. With such a secret treaty or an understanding between the two nations, it was proposed that English fleets should carry, from time to time, to Canada and Nova Scotia as many troops, as would be judged necessary, and there wait under some pretence till the moment was favorable for the operation. That time was provisionally stated by B[urr] to be the next election of

P. & V. P. He added: that he strongly relied on his consummate local knowledge of the various dispositions & inclinations of the inhabitants of the Eastern and Southern states, and of the local prejudices which he could, between this and that time, encite by means of his numerous friends, who were dispersed over every part of the Country." These were to act in " concert with the Chief of an insurrection that was to be raised in New Mexico, the Province of Texas, W. Florida. This chief was to be himself with the appointment from his F. M. [French Majesty] of Generalissimo over the armies in the South, 1,500,000 francs was required for this part of the expedition." [4]

Proposals that are obviously treasonable, even if somewhat contradictory and fantastic in their total disregard of political, military and nationalistic considerations. Yet they are set forth in this letter with such a wealth of precise detail as almost to compel belief. Who, then, had sent this warning to the Department of State? One who merely signed himself " Citizen of the United States," who received the information second-hand from another personage equally unknown. Such anonymity must naturally render the warning highly suspicious — Burr had many American enemies in Paris at the time — unless it contains internal evidence of authenticity, or there is external corroboration. But only a crank or a madman could propose seriously that France and England, battling for the supremacy of the world, with antagonisms that were deep-seatedly political, economic and philosophical, could unite on a scatterbrained plot involving remote and unessential issues. Such a memorial, if offered, would have found its way immediately into the nearest fire, and the promulgator himself clapped into a lunatic asylum.

But Burr's letter to the Duke of Otranto, or Fouché, quoted above, not only makes no mention of such phantasms, but speaks specifically and sharply of Spanish-American independence alone, and " *asked neither men nor money.*" Joel Barlow, ex-Hartford wit and poet, and charged with a commercial mission to France, was asked by Madison to verify these accusations against Burr. He wrote back in cipher that such seemed to be the case, that both France and England did not dislike Burr's project of dividing the United States between them, that the scheme was rather applauded by Napoleon, and that " it is with great inquietude that I contemplate these possibilities." [5] But this seeming confirmation was dated Sept. 26, 1812, long after Burr's memorials had retired to gather dust in forgotten archives, and the proponent himself was safely back in the very country he was supposed to have divided.

Furthermore, Barlow, a polemic writer chiefly, and the author of such poems as " The Vision of Columbus," had not reached France until late in 1811, after Burr had left, discomfited. And, though it was Barlow's mission to see Napoleon, he never achieved even that. Obviously his information, such as it was, had come from the whispering-gallery of rumors that represented the American colony, who one and all hated Burr, or even from that " Citizen of the United States " whose anonymous letter he was supposed to investigate.

Thus the situation stood until a few years ago, when research workers, under the direction of Dr. Waldo G. Leland, of the Carnegie Institution, unearthed in the *Archives Nationales* of France certain memoranda and *précis* relating directly to the memorials and proposals of Aaron Burr. Now indeed should the matter of Burr's alleged treasonable designs have been cleared up definitively, once and for all. But, surprisingly, the darkness became worse confounded. Unfortunately, the transcriptions and summaries of these documents have remained hidden in the working notebooks of the researchers, penciled in great haste, and seen only by a very few in the safekeeping of the Carnegie Institution. Perhaps because of the crabbed handwriting, the vagueness of Burr's phrasing — an old failing of his — the notoriously poor French, and certain misinterpretations by an openly puzzled and much harried clerk in the French Ministry, these documents have lent themselves to assertions that Burr, at least in his later years, was openly advocating treason against the United States. One of the commentators even goes so far as to explain the lapse upon the theory that Burr, always mentally somewhat unbalanced, was now definitely insane.[6]

But let the documents speak for themselves. The first is a summary by a French departmental clerk of all the others. The second is a " Note on the United States," submitted by Burr through Deputy Roux. The Americans, he said, are not content with the present form of government, but a great many of them would not consent to a change. Concerning the political parties in the United States, he maintained that, aside from the Republicans, whom he admitted to be in the majority, the Federalists were without zeal and energy, and without a leader. However, " there is a third party quite superior — in talent and energy . . . they wish for something grand and stable, something which, requiring the employment of active spirits, will assure the tranquillity of reasonable men . . . This party has a recognized chief [Burr]; they ask only to follow and obey him." Three-quarters of the Americans, he as-

sured the French, hate England. It is a favorable moment for per-
suading the United States to make war on that country. Forty
thousand sailors, idle because of the embargo, are ready to undertake anything.

To which Note the puzzled clerk added his own admittedly
doubtful interpretation. His *addendum* has been the responsible
cause of most of the misconceptions concerning Burr's thesis.
" This note," he wrote for the information of the Ministry, " is not
at all clear: the author seems hardly willing to explain himself
openly — it seems that he is the chief of the third party which in-
clines to monarchy; and that this plan would employ the 40 thousand sailors for the overthrow of the republican government — the
declaration of War against the English would follow this change —
it ought to be remarked, for the rest, that since the writing of this
note, the embargo has been lifted." [7]

Which is indeed an outrageous interpretation of a rather plain
document by an underpaid, much harried clerk. To his French
mind, obsequiously eager to flatter His Majesty, the Emperor,
a grand and stable government could only mean a monarchy;
though not a syllable is breathed by Burr relating to such a form
of government. Nor, even by a twisting of meanings, can any intention be ascribed to him for the employment of the inactive sailors
to overthrow the American forms. Burr, in fact, stated quite
plainly that a great many of the people would not consent to any
change, though discontented. He had been asked for an analysis
of the political situation, and he had given it. That was all. Of
course there was a third party, naturally it was superior in talents
and energy to the others, and he was its chief — what else could he
have told the French if he wished to be considered as a person of
weight and influence? But obviously, the whole tenor of the proposal was for a war with England. Three-quarters of the Americans
hated England; the forty thousand sailors, idle in American ports
because of the embargo induced by England's high-handed Orders
in Council and seizures on the seas, would leap at the opportunity
to avenge themselves on the country responsible for their ills. The
third party — of superior talents — would follow Burr blindly to
the attack. The " grand and stable " occupation of " active spirits "
would be war — war on England, on Spain as well, with strong governments in the conquered provinces of Canada, Mexico, Cuba,
Florida — and the strong ruler would be Burr. Nowhere in this
note is there a hint of treason, except in the overheated imagination of a French clerk. Burr had simply enlarged his old scheme
against Spain to include a now hated England, chiefly because he

had suffered indignities, and Napoleon's interest could be more readily caught in a plan against his formidable rival. The United States could also be drawn into the grand scheme because of the pending situation. While the big powers squabbled and fought, he would quietly seize those provinces which he had always passionately desired, and thus set up for all time the dynasty of Burr.

The next Note in the series is a Memoir on Louisiana. He described its government, its population, and remarked that in spite of union, the inhabitants did not enjoy the privileges of American citizens. "The government of the United States," he continued, "has become quite odious to the Inhabitants. When I was in the district of Orleans, about three years ago, I saw a memorial already signed by several respectable citizens, addressed to the Emperor. I advised them to suppress this memorial and promised them to come to their assistance in another manner. They are still waiting for me to keep my promise." [8]

It is on this Note that Wandell and Minnigerode base their contention that Burr was plotting the seizure of Louisiana, and its annexation to France. But the Memoir bears no such far-fetched interpretation. Quite the contrary. When the disgruntled inhabitants had wished to address Napoleon, obviously for assistance, Burr had advised them against such a course, and promised to help them " in another manner." This " manner " fits in as well with his old schemes as with his new. They were still the same. He had, as we have seen, promised the Orleaners the conquest of Mexico and the adjoining Spanish provinces of Texas and West Florida. With himself as the ruler of these territories, prosperity must necessarily come to Louisiana and New Orleans by free and untrammeled trade with these dominions; and with prosperity, the population must soon increase to the figures set by Congressional Statute as requisite for full citizenship. Here, however, as has also been noted in the initial conspiracy, lingers the vague doubt whether or not, at some unspecified future time, Burr was not considering the possibility that Orleans would find it advantageous to associate itself with his dream empire of Mexico. In this, and this only, may be found the adumbrations of possible treason, if such it could be considered, when the plan depended on the will of the people involved, and not on forcible seizure.

The next Note is a straightforward proposal concerning the " Spanish Colonies." Cuba, Florida and Mexico, he declared, desire independence but have no means of achieving it. England's attitude was now one of hostility to such attempts, because Spain was her ally. The moment, therefore, has come for the Emperor to be the means of liberating the colonies. Such a course would naturally involve the United States in a war with England, and would necessarily bring about the loss of the English colonies to the United States.[9]

The next document is a " Memorial on the means of wresting the Spanish Colonies from the Influence of England." Burr proposed to make the Spanish colonies independent, and array them under his control against England. He would begin with Mexico and New Granada. With 1200 men he could take Pensacola. St. Augustine, Mobile and Baton Rouge would fall without any resistance. In West Florida alone he could enroll under his standard a corps of 4000 men in six weeks; and as many in New Orleans and along the left bank of the Mississippi. With this force he could overthrow the Spanish power east of the Rio del Norte in short order. There would be plenty of volunteers for this enterprise from the Mississippi boatmen and the Western States, whose inhabitants, he said, believed in him.[10]

On March 13, 1810, an employee of the Ministry of Foreign Relations was assigned to confer with Burr. This was the Deputy Roux, who wrote out an account of a conversation, in which, according to him, Burr discussed his plans for expeditions against the Lucca Islands, Florida, Louisiana, New Mexico, Jamaica, Canada, and Nova Scotia, or any of them.[11] Aside from the vast reaches of territory involved in these grandiose schemes, the chief interest lies in the mention of Louisiana. The other colonies were either English or Spanish. But already the *written* proposals of Burr had been misinterpreted completely; how much more chance for Roux to become wholly befogged in the mist of Burr's cryptic talk. Senator Plumer had long before remarked that Burr's speech was all things to all men, and that it required careful after-analysis to discover that he had not actually said the things his auditors thought he had.

This clerical memorandum was submitted by the Duc de Cadore to the Emperor on March 14th with a notation that Burr could not initiate anything except in Florida and Louisiana, " and he could not be employed without giving grave offense to the United States." [12]

On March 19th, Roux conferred again with Burr, this time to receive a detailed plan for an expedition against Canada, which was duly reported to the Ministry.[13] Almost four months later, on July 27th, Roux submitted a final report in which he referred to his previous notes, and gave an account of a new interview with

Burr on July 14th, in which Burr had urged that the attention of the Emperor be called to the plans he had presented for his consideration. These were, Roux now stated distinctly, for the independence of Florida and Mexico.[14]

The Minister of Foreign Relations, the Duc de Cadore, sent these *précis* along to Napoleon on July 29th, with the illuminating comment that " he [Burr] spoke only of the Floridas and of Canada. It would seem then that he proposed to hush the rumor which had redounded from the reports directed against his own country (*qui s'etait répondu des communications dirigées contre son propre pays*) and which he was accused of having made to the Duc d'Otrante [Fouché]." [15]

This communication of Cadore is most important for a final view of what Burr's somewhat involved, and always grandiose, schemes actually portended. Had they been, in truth, treasonable to the United States, and so known to the French to whom they were submitted, certainly he could not now be protesting to them that they entailed no such purpose, that the rumor prevalent in Paris concerning his conversations with Fouché, *not with Roux or Cadore,* was false.

It was *that* rumor to which Joel Barlow referred, and which the anonymous " Citizen " had obligingly sent along to Madison. A careful examination of the actual notes, memoirs and reports, as elicited from the French Archives, discloses at once the absurdity of those rumors. Instead of a proposition by Burr for an amicable agreement between England and France at the expense of the United States, all energies were to be directed to a war by France and the United States, in association, against England and Spain. The charge of treason on the last, and what has appeared hitherto to be the most damning count against Burr, seems to have very little substantiation in the facts.

Burr's appeals to Napoleon for aid failed, not because his proposals were impracticable, when limited in extent of operations, but because, as the Ministerial clerk had justly noted, Madison had lifted the Jeffersonian embargo, and relations between the United States and England had eased for the moment. Napoleon was also engaged, about this period, in diplomatic negotiations with England over Holland, and did not wish to endanger these by an open advocacy of Burr. Then, too, Napoleon must have recognized in the slight figure of Aaron Burr something of his own boundless ambition and thirst for power, and had no intention of aiding such a dangerously able and talented man to set himself up as the ruler of a huge and glamorous territory in the Americas. He had no assurance, that, once in power, Burr would crook the pregnant knee to him and follow French leadership in vassal obedience.

2. Desperate Straits

On July 27, 1810, the very day that Roux submitted his final report to his superior, Burr confided to his Journal that, "despairing of any success in my project, a few days ago asked passport to go to the United States, which was refused. . . . Was told that I could not have a passport to go out of the empire. *Me voila prisonier d'etat et presque sans sous.*" (Here I am a prisoner of state and almost without a cent.) [16]

Burr had given up all hope of French participation, and wished to return to the United States, there to take his chances with a vindictive Government and creditors alike. His friends had meanwhile been active in his behalf, and Theo had exerted herself to the utmost — so far, without success, though Burr did not know of it at the time.

She had made a desperate appeal to Dolly Madison, wife of the President of the United States. "Why . . . is my Father banished from a country for which he has encountered wounds & dangers & fatigue for years?" she demanded passionately. "Why is he driven from his friends, from an only child, to pass an unlimited time in exile, and that too at an age when others are reaping the harvest of past toils?" Then, as if ashamed of her outburst, she concluded with dignified words, "To whatever fate Mr. Madison may doom this application, I trust it will be treated with delicacy; of this I am more desirous as Mr. Alston is ignorant of the step I have taken in writing to you." Dolly Madison must indeed attribute it to the zeal of a daughter for a "Father almost adored." [17]

Aaron Burr had peculiar claims on Dolly Madison. As Dolly P. Todd, left a widow with an infant son, she had helped her mother run an exclusive boarding-house in Philadelphia. Burr had been of the greatest assistance to both. He had advised the mother on points of law — without a fee; and he had been responsible for the introduction of Madison and Dolly to each other, and their consequent marriage. So close had been their friendship that the young widow, in a will dated May 13, 1794, had appointed Burr as the sole guardian of her son.[18] Madison, too, had much to remember gratefully of the friendship of Aaron Burr, but these things are soon forgotten in the heat of politics and the exigencies of personal ambition. The record is barren of any reply to Theo's impassioned plea, and evidently the application was discreetly forgotten.

Napoleon's course in refusing either to approve of Burr's designs or to permit him out of his realm is puzzling from the point of view of any other explanation than the one offered. If Burr would be dangerous as the conqueror of Mexico, he was also sufficiently dangerous out of the Emperor's grasp. Desperate, ambitious, talented, he might evolve some other scheme in that fertile brain of his which would disturb the delicate balances set up by Napoleon, and impede, if not bring to grief, some of his own grandiose plans. It would be better to keep him in France, under the eye of his secret police — and harmless. And there was also the American Embassy, of which more will be said later.

This was flattering enough to any vanity Burr might have possessed, but decidedly disagreeable otherwise. He had no more money, Theo was trying hard in the United States to collect funds for him, and not succeeding; winter was approaching, and the prospect of Paris in a penniless state was frightening. He wrote a note to a friend, Edward Griswold, requesting the loan of 150 guineas, and told him that he attributed the refusal of a passport to " the machinations of our worthy minister, General Armstrong, who has been, and still is, indefatigable in his exertions to my prejudice." [19] Armstrong was related to the Livingston clan, and had been a party to the shuffling of Senatorial seats with De Witt Clinton.

But Griswold was no longer a friend, and refused the loan. Burr records mournfully, " winter approaches, no prospect of leave to quit the empire, and still less of any means of living in it. So must economize most rigidly my few remaining louis." To add to his troubles, Madame Paschaud, his mistress, had left for Geneva to join her husband, and " truly, her absence makes me sad." [20]

There were tragic days ahead. Life became a constant effort to keep from starving and freezing, and a weary routine of repeated applications for the coveted passport. Item after item in the Journal discloses a most painstaking economy in food and coal; meals of bread and cheese and potatoes, and sometimes just potatoes. Burr cut himself off from the luxuries of tea and coffee, and shivered in his cold, bare little attic room without a warming fire in the grate. But, in the midst of heroic privations, suddenly an entry appears, in startling contrast. He had given a girl 6 francs for *muse*, and, the same day, another, " pretty, good, voluptuous, stayed with her two hours; 7 francs." Hustling then to bed, penitent, apprehensive of physical consequences, and — walking twenty miles the next day to save coach fare.[21]

The story goes on and on — of dire poverty interspersed with reckless extravagances in the things of the flesh; and of presents for Theo and *Gampillo,* the grandson. Though it had become " so cold I should be glad of a fire," he bought books to send to Theo, and medals, ancient coins and toys to thrill *Gampillo.* " I never spend a livre that I do not calculate what pretty thing it might have bought for you and Gampillo; hence my economy," he wrote pathetically.[22] In fact, so determined was he on this, that on September 11th may be seen this proud entry: " Not a cent for *muse* since last Saturday week," but, alas, the sentence was thereafter crossed out, as if he had remembered.[23]

Meanwhile, he was cooling his heels almost daily at the forbidding door of the Duc de Rovigo, the new Minister of Police, seeking a passport to get out of this most inhospitable country and return to one more inhospitable, perhaps. After days of weary waiting, and wrenching agony of heart, September 13th brought most joyful news. The Duc de Rovigo notified him that his passport had been granted; and Griswold, repenting of his former churlishness, came through with a loan of 2000 francs, sufficient to pay his passage to the United States.

The silver pieces glittered in welcome profusion, but the equally glittering words of the Minister of Police were a cruel mockery. Day by day, the assurances were repeated, with no passport forthcoming; until, on September 25th, Burr was stunned to hear that the Emperor had in fact neither granted the passport nor returned any answer to his repeated demands.

Black despair enveloped him; he was doomed to a lingering starvation — yet, " alas! on my way a pair of demoiselles, and so 8 francs." He knew his weaknesses, fought against them, but they were too strong for will, for self-respect, for self-preservation even. " How many curses have I heaped on poor Gam.," he upbraided himself, " and yet he is rather to be pitied; only see how for the last fifteen days he has been so good and considering his habits, and considering, etc., etc." [24]

Yet, in the midst of darkness, his keen mind remained undimmed; his intellectual curiosity was as alert as ever. Every new discovery, every new inventive process, of which he heard, attracted his instant attention — from the practical as well as the purely scientific point of view. " A very important discovery has been made here, viz., to make vinegar, of excellent quality, from the sap of any trees," he wrote. " The process gives you all the moisture in vinegar, and all the wood in carbon. I shall get the details if I can find money to pay for it." And, also, he went " to see Mons. Cagniard, and his new invention of raising water and

performing any mechanical operation. His apparatus is a screw of
Archimedes turned the reverse, air, water, and quicksilver . . . If
the thing performs what is said, I will apply it to give water to
Charleston." [25] He was quick to see the financial possibilities in all
things. He lived before his time; had he been born a century later,
he might possibly have become a formidable captain of industry —
or, and this is equally likely, a glorified Colonel Sellers, flitting
from scheme to scheme with the agility, and the futility, of a
butterfly sportive in the sun.

Back he went to the weary, interminable task of renewed peti-
tions for leave to quit French shores, studying Spanish withal, just
in case . . . and spending Griswold's money on food, shelter, prostitutes and presents — that money which should have transported
him to his native land. And now a new speculation dawned on his
vision, dazzling him with its possibilities of millions. The old Holland Land Company venture, on its native heath, *redivivus*. By
1810, the Holland Company shares had fallen to their lowest ebb
— war, the collapse of land values, Dutch fear of reprisals by the
United States for the Napoleonic seizures of American property —
all contributed to the result. But canny speculators in Paris commenced buying up these depreciated shares which were glutting
the market, expecting an upswing, and consequent enormous
profits. Burr, more than most, was well acquainted with the actual
value of the Company's holdings in Western lands, and saw his opportunity in the existing slump. He had no money himself, but he
tried to interest others in the speculation. Among them were Griswold, Valkenaer, Nicholas Hubbard, and Theophile Cazenove —
that same gentleman who had been his associate in New York, and
who was now in Paris. Griswold was interested — so much so that
Burr recorded that a liberal proposition had been made to him,
" so very liberal that if I had now a passport to go to Amsterdam,
I would clear for myself 10,000 dollars in a fortnight." [26]

Once more he haunted the anteroom of the Minister of Police,
only to be informed that he must first apply to the American consul in Paris. This consul turned out to be a gentleman named Alexander McRae, one of the government attorneys in the Richmond
trial. " What a prospect! " Burr noted bitterly in his Journal.[27]

Nevertheless, undaunted, he tried his luck. McRae turned him
down with malicious satisfaction. He turned then to Jonathan
Russell, American *chargé d'affaires,* with a demand for a certificate
of citizenship. Russell replied that was the consul's duty, not his.
Reluctantly, Burr was forced back to McRae, noting grimly, " if
the latter answers insolently, the only revenge I will take, for re-

venge, you know, is not in my nature, will be to publish his letter." [28] The answer was prompt and insolent enough. Said McRae, on October 29, 1810, " that his knowledge of the circumstances under which Mr. Burr left the United States renders it his duty to decline giving Mr. Burr either a passport or a *permis de séjour.*" And, if Burr felt aggrieved, there was always Russell.[29]

Feeling rather like a shuttlecock, Burr applied again to Russell, this time with firm language. He was ignorant, he wrote, " of any statute or instruction which authorizes a foreign minister or agent to inquire into any circumstances other than those which tend to establish the fact of citizen or not." [30] This gave Russell, who once had been glad enough to fawn on Burr, the chance to extract a miserable triumph from the reversal of their fortunes. He replied on November 4th, that " the man who evades the offended laws of his country, abandons, for the time, the right to their protection. This fugitive from justice, during his voluntary exile, has a claim to no other passport than one which shall enable him to surrender himself for trial for the offences with which he stands charged. Such a passport Mr. Russell will furnish to Mr. Burr, but no other." [31]

The malice of the Virginians was pursuing him with vengeful relentlessness to the farthermost shores. It affected even the American sojourners in Paris. For, reported Burr, " the Americans here have entered into a combination against A. B.; that every man who speaks to him shall be shunned as unworthy of society; that no master of vessel, or any other person, shall take any letter or parcel for him, and other like benevolent things; all of which amused me." [32] Amusing, yes, but with a bitter tinge to it. No matter how armored with pride, with stoic philosophy, Burr must have felt the keen sting. Scorned, hated, shunned, proscribed, a pariah in a foreign land, forbidden to leave, almost forbidden to remain, the last few dollars of a loan dribbling through his hands, the future black, the present insupportable, the past but vain regrets, one wonders that in truth, as has been claimed, the doors of sanity did not swing slightly ajar.

Griswold was still willing to back him in the Holland Company venture, if he could only get to Holland to buy and sell the necessary shares. But Americans and French alike blocked the way to seeming fortune. In desperation, he composed a long memorial to Napoleon, in which he recited his grievances, the lack of response to his proposals, the refusal to grant him his passport, the blank walls he encountered on every side. He is hurt and surprised, he told the Emperor; he merited better at French hands; his home had always been open to distinguished French visitors, and, he pointed out, " at a period when the administration of the government of the United States was hostile to France and Frenchmen, they received from me efficient protection." [33] Which was true enough; but past benefits, if remembered, are but added causes for present resentment. Napoleon never took the trouble to answer Burr's lengthy effort.

Yet, on November 1st, he was buying a watch for Theo, only to pawn it the following day, together with his ring, for $200; which sum, together with the $300 left from Griswold's loan, was deposited with Valkenaer to cover his share in the Holland Company speculation. This left him with but $21 in his pocket. By November 8th, his funds were so low that he was compelled to sell some of the curious coins he had intended for his grandson's collection; his boots, left at the shoemaker's for resoling, could not be redeemed; and, on November 17th, he had changed his last two guineas into francs. There were 52 of the latter at the existing rate of exchange. " Then began to calculate how I should dispose of so much money," he wrote. " Having on Monday evening engaged with two dancing girls of good demeanor to take coffee with them this evening, thought I would devote a crown to that. Took in my pocket 7 francs 10 sous, lest the devil might induce me to spend more. It all went, and ran into debt 6 francs more, having been deb'd by one — that one which liked least. Got home very penitent and humble." [34] Only to repeat such sorry incidents, however, again and again.

Two days later, in fact, he borrowed 50 francs from the complaisant Griswold, paid off some small debts, and " with the most deliberate malice and forethought, have resolved to dine with Fleury to-morrow or next day, which will be an affair of 6 or 8 francs." [35] As a result of this adventure, he lived for three days on 10 sous — a pittance one gives a beggar — yet rode home in a fiacre, borrowing from his housekeeper and the family in whose shabby quarters he resided the three francs necessary to pay off the indignant cabman. Recording, the very same day, " Nothing from Amsterdam, and verily I shall starve." [36]

In the midst of all this a kind friend furnished him with the recently arrived American newspapers, " from which I learn that I have a pension of 2,000 sterling from his Majesty the Emperor. An extract from an English paper, also, that I am on a project for dismembering the United States." [37] Cause for loud and bitter laughter, sometimes not far from tears.

He was living now on soup and potatoes, or bread and cheese, or bread, baked pears and milk, trying hard not to show his famishment when he was infrequently invited out to dine; playing whist without a sou in his pocket, and fortunately winning 60 before he arose from the table; resorting to all sorts of shabby expedients to keep body and soul together — yet discovering in himself an ineradicable need for women. He described his own condition with unsparing pen. "For some days past, and more particularly to-day, I have been in a state of irritability very unusual. Answer brusque and rapid. Say things almost rude; even to the good Valkenaer I was unkind. . . . Can you imagine from what this arises? The want of *muse*." For ten days the lack of a sou had deprived him of such consolations, and "really I suffer and am scarcely fit for society." [38]

By December 10th, he could stand his parlous state no more. Again there was but one way, to rob "poor little Gampy" of his cherished coins, which were duly sold, and the proceeds invested in sugar, coffee, tea, "segars." The balance was intended for the payment of his debt to his washerwoman, but, meeting a girl of the streets instead, the washerwoman, all unknowing, was perforce compelled to wait. [39]

These were the darkest days of his life. Then, on December 23rd, came a faint ray of sunshine. "I am about to undertake the translation from English to French of two octavo volumes for 100 louis. It will take me three months hard work. Better than to starve. But the most curious part of the story is that the book in question contains a quantity of abuse and libels on A. B." [40]

The Holland speculation seemed in dire straits. Griswold decided to withdraw, and warned him against Valkenaer, with whom all of Burr's scanty speculative capital had been placed. But Burr, in order to display his complete trust in his partner, made the grand gesture of returning to him the receipt evidencing the deposit. With Griswold out, it was necessary to find another backer. Crede, a friend, agreed to advance the necessary moneys for equal participation in the profits, and, in the meantime, took 10 shares for future delivery from Burr at a price which, at the existing market, gave Burr a supposed profit of some $300. In high spirits now, the eternally optimistic Burr noted for Theo's later edification, "Now, if I can get a passport to Bremen and Amsterdam, I will send you a million of francs within six months; but one-half of it must be laid out in pretty things. Oh, what beautiful things I will send you. Gampillus, too, shall have a beautiful little watch, and at least fifty trumpets of different sorts and sizes. Home at 10, and have been casting up my millions and spending it. Lord, how

many people I have made happy! " [41] Colonel Sellers was rapidly
coming to the fore!

In fact, his own enthusiasm was infecting his friends. The canny
Griswold caught the contagion again, and also took ten of Burr's
mythical shares, giving Burr an additional profit of $400. The fol-
lowing day, the fever waxing, he raised his purchases to fifteen
shares, thereby increasing Burr's capital to $1000. All these were
paper transactions, however, contingent on his getting to Amsterdam to take up the shares for which he had contracted. The market value had increased in the interim, but evidently the regulations forbade the export of the certificates. On January 21, 1811,
his application for a passport to Amsterdam was definitely turned
down, and all was gloom again. " Thus end all my fine projects,"
he wrote mournfully, " and hopes, and with them the fortune, and
it is quite doubtful whether I get a penny of the 800 dollars which
I thought I had made." [42] The bubble had burst.

Once more he was reduced to petty borrowings; Valkenaer, now
that the mythical fortunes had vanished, turned cool, and Crede,
the friend, had worked secretly behind Burr's back to reap the
profits of the speculation which Burr had disclosed to him in strict
confidence. An unusual cry of anguish welled from Burr's heart
at the collapse of fortune, friendship, everything. " My dear
T[heo], I am sick at heart, having made the most afflicting of all
discoveries, the perfidy of a friend." [43] All was lost.

From February 18th to May 14th, 1811, there is a significant gap
in the Journal, as if misfortune had so completely overwhelmed
him that he had no heart to put pen to paper. During this period,
too, came bitter news from Theo. All their friends, she wrote, had
deserted them. John P. Van Ness " is like the rest of the world.
When I was in New-York, W. P. [William P. Van Ness] was doubtful whether it would be quite safe to visit me. John Swartwout is
true, invariably and nobly conspicuous as the sun. He retrieves the
character of man." [44] Poor Theo, she was aging rapidly in experience!

Yet her indomitable will carried her on. She had not heard from
Dolly Madison, nor from her husband, the President of the United
States. Now she tried Albert Gallatin, another old friend of her
father.[45] But this inquiry also was destined to remain unanswered.
Whereupon she marshaled a certain desperate courage, and wrote
to Burr, " I say *come;* . . . Go to New-York. Make your stand
there. If you are attacked, you will be in the midst of the tenth
legion." She was forgetting how the " tenth legion," with the shining exception of John Swartwout, had deserted them. " Civil debts

may be procrastinated, for a time, by confinement to the limits. There you can take breath; openly see your friends; make your arrangements; and soon, I think, you will be able to throw off those momentary shackles, and resume your station." [46] Yet over a year was to pass before the advice could be followed.

3. ENGLAND AGAIN

When the Journal resumes, on May 14, 1811, Burr is discovered in Arras, headed for the French border. He had received his passport, that precious document which had been dangled before him so tantalizingly for long, weary months. Powerful French friends had been working quietly and secretly to this end. Among these were M. Denon, Director of Fine Arts, who had been captivated by Burr's knowledge and appreciation of art, and the Duc de Bassano, who advanced him sufficient money to pay entangling debts and leave the country. The vindictive Russell, even, under pressure from Bassano, yielded to the extent of furnishing him with the coveted certificate of citizenship. [47]

Burr hastened by diligence to Amsterdam, seeking information on the affairs of the Holland Company. But the directors were noticeably cool to their stockholder, and refused to open their books or issue any statements. Nevertheless, Burr subscribed to more of the Company's stock, to the value of 7000 francs — so positive was he of its eventual enhancement. From Amsterdam he went to Bremen, where he took ill with his usual stomach complaint, and was forced to come back to Amsterdam for adequate treatment. There had also been a hitch in the matter of the elusive passport; the final application and attached papers had been lost in one of the many French bureaus, and red tape must spin interminable coils, while Burr perforce possessed his soul in patience.

On June 14th, he fell in with an American captain of a 400-ton ship, who was most " anxious to serve me. Sais [sic] he has often kept awake whole nights about me, though he had never seen me. Will fit up a cabin to my own caprice, and appears to think he can never do enough." [48] Passage to the United States seemed at last in sight. The captain was so amiable, so eager to please! How should Burr know he was a smooth, cozening rascal, who was to cause him more trouble and sickening exasperation than any one in all the rest of his exile? This was but another example of Burr's total inability to penetrate the superficial surfaces of men to the mainsprings of their characters.

Burr, ill, suffering from headaches and piles, went on to Paris for better treatment, and arrived there on June 22nd. But in his Journal one comes across the gay nonsense that he had gone for " a thousand nothings, of which, probably, the most important are to buy Gampy some beautiful marbles, and you some silk stockings, and father a pail to water his horses on the road. A pail that you may put in your pocket." [49]

But the passport continued elusive. Again he took up the weary round of calls, to meet with the usual shrugs and futile promises. Russell had repented of his former pliability, and now that all papers were lost, refused point-blank to issue another certificate. On July 17th a letter arrived from Captain Combes that he was sailing on July 23rd. Six days, barely time to make Amsterdam by hard riding, and the precious passport was still not in sight. Combes' ship, it seemed, was the only one sailing under a flag of truce, and therefore immune from capture. Practically every other American vessel that stuck its nose out of port was promptly seized by the patrolling warships of the warring powers. Denon heard of Burr's plight, and took it up with Bassano. The Duke intimated it would be wiser to have Russell, the American *chargé d'affaires,* issue the passport. Burr shook his head despondingly. That meant his last hope was gone. But Bassano only smiled with Gallic subtlety, and, on July 18th, the next day, lo and behold! the courtly Frenchman had received the necessary assurances that the priceless document was on its way.

The method employed by Bassano to achieve the seemingly impossible reflects the utmost discredit on the moralistic Jonathan Russell, so touchy about his country's honor, so ethically virtuous in his judgments on Burr. Bassano explained it all in a letter to Denon, " The person through whom I could have communicated to Mr. Russell that he should not have refused a new passport to Mr. Burr," he said discreetly, " was in the country. I wrote to *her* [italics mine] yesterday to return. She arrived at the moment that your note was received. I shall have the passport in the course of the day, and shall forward it immediately to the Duke [Rovigo], and I am convinced that you will receive it to-morrow, to transmit to Mr. Burr." [50] The result was to justify his calm omniscience. He *knew* that strait-laced Puritan, Mr. Jonathan Russell.

Posthaste, Burr raced for Amsterdam to catch the poised Captain Combes. But news evidently reached him *en route* of delay, for he remained unaccountably at Anvers from July 22nd to August 3rd, while Combes' ship was detained at Trexel, an island in the North Sea. Something had gone wrong. So wrong, that on August 15th, Combes was begging Burr to use *his* influence to get him a passport to go to the United States with Burr. The explanation of this topsy-turvy business proved to be that the honest Captain had run heavily into debt, in reliance on the forthcoming passage money of some fifty passengers, only a few of whom had paid anything on account — and even these were suing him for the return of their money.

On September 8th, they were still in port, and new trouble in sight. Combes, writes Burr, " demands of me 450 guilders immediately, or that he should break up the voyage and sell the ship; by which I understand that, if I do not pay the 450, he will go off without me . . . I have not ⅓ of the sum he demands, nor have I any hope of getting it." [51] The Captain was coming forth in his true colors — the amount demanded was far in excess of the original contract price. But Burr could not help himself. Four days later he had raised 480 guilders, by the sale of most of his personal effects — only to find that the rascally Captain had summarily raised the price to 500. Accordingly, Theo's watch followed the rest. His baggage was on board the *Vigilant,* Combes' ship, on September 14th. All worries were over. " I feel as if I were already on the way to you," he told Theo *via* the Journal, " and my heart beats with joy. Yet alas! that country which I am so anxious to revisit will perhaps reject me with horror . . . My windows look over the ocean; that ocean which separates me from all that is dear. With what pleasure I did greet it after three year's absence . . . There seems to be no obstacle between us, and I almost fancy I see you and Gampy, with the sheep about the door, and he ' driving the great ram with a little stick.' " [52]

Alas, Burr was still far away from native land and dear ones. More delays, more gougings by the Captain, and dilatory negotiations with the authorities to permit passengers of Dutch extraction — and most of them were in that category — to sail. Finally, in the latter part of September — the Journal entry of October 9th is an obvious error — to Burr's inexpressible joy, the *Vigilant* actually sailed. Two ducats represented Burr's entire fortune. Combes had bled him clean. But all was forgotten now as the homecoming exile sniffed the salt sea air, saw the sails belly in the favoring wind, and strained his eyes westward toward the distant shore his fancy almost persuaded him that he could see. What did it matter that he was " on board a small ship, very badly accomodated, fifty-four passengers, of whom a majority women and children; thirty-one sailors, thirty-three hogs, and about one hundred other quadrupeds and bipeds." And pockets bare.[53] He was going home!

But the sportive gods were not through with their victim. On

September 29th, the British frigate, *Le Desirée,* lying off Holland waters, seized the *Vigilant,* in spite of flag of truce, and sent it on to Yarmouth roads as a prize. There they huddled in discomfort, human passengers and porcine, waiting the august decision of the Admiralty Court as to their ultimate fate. Combes, seeing his profits slip out of his hands, brutally refused to feed his passengers, and Burr was forced ashore, if he would not starve. Once more he was on inhospitable English soil, that soil from which he had been deported three years before.

October 16th found him in London with exactly two shillings in his pocket. The *Vigilant* was being detained for trial, but there was another vessel due to sail shortly for Charleston. " But how," Burr asked in despair, " to pay and how to get my baggage in time are grave questions." [54]

Once more he met Jeremy Bentham, but withheld from him all knowledge of his desperate financial plight. He was reduced to selling his cambrics, rare bits that he had carefully hoarded, the last of the things he had thought to bring Theo. On October 30th, he encountered Combes and demanded the return of his passage money. Combes laughed in his face. His troubles multiplied. His French passport, secured after so much incredible hardship, was no longer of any value. He required an English document now to leave the country.

Again he was starving — a condition that had become monotonously, and tragically, usual. Bit by bit the last of his precious little gifts for Theo and little Aaron Burr Alston found their way into strange hands, while the paltry pence into which they had been converted went for the barest necessities of life. And, on December 14th, he counted his money and found exactly 18 sous on hand. The *Vigilant's* case was again postponed for a month; there seemed no chance ever to realize on his passage money in that vessel. In despair he made his way somehow back to Yarmouth to remove his baggage, and try for another boat. But principally, he wished to get his French pamphlet on the new method of making vinegar. Brunel, the distinguished engineer, to whom he had explained the process, had thought it of great value. But the pamphlet had been lost or stolen from his effects. His brain teemed with a thousand inventive and ingenious projects for making money — perhaps the sparse diet was responsible for the brilliant schemes. There was the matter of making vinegar, which, unfortunately, required cash for acid and barrels; he was keenly interested in steam engines, and visited all the factories, attentive, questioning, alert; a shoe-making machine caught his fancy; he

became enamored of a wholly new idea in steamboats — and, finally, there was a new kind of false teeth, made by Fonzi for himself, so excellent that he wished to promote their manufacture on
a large scale for all of suffering humanity. Visions, schemes, processes, inventions — which in another day and age, backed by his
restless energy, might actually have brought him the millions that
forever tossed about in his fancy.

But, with millions in the clouds, on solid earth " held a consultation with myself about dining. Instead of having bread for
the day, had not a mouthful, and was sick for want of Tobacco. To
dine and drink a pint of ale would just ruin me. So sent my little
maid for 4 pence worth of bread and an ounce of tobacco, 3 pence
half penny; for which had to borrow a penny and a half of her;
and having only coffee for the morning, and very scant." [55]

On January 4, 1812, good news came. The *Vigilant* had been
acquitted, and was ready to sail. But Combes was not through —
he had an infinite talent for causing Burr trouble. He had char-
tered his boat for a voyage to New Orleans without consulting his
passengers. New Orleans was the last place to which Burr wished
to go. There he would be directly within the jurisdiction of the
Federal Government, and of all his old enemies — Wilkinson,
Claiborne, *et al.* But Combes told him he could take it or leave
it. Finally Burr decided to go — it was the only way he could save
his passage money — when more blows fell on his devoted head.
The American Government had intervened in the persons of the
consuls at Yarmouth and London. Both warned Combes that if he
transported Burr to the United States he personally must abide
the consequences. Jonathan Russell had tracked Burr like an
avenging Fury, and was now *chargé d'affaires* in London. His fine
Italian hand was detectable in these proceedings. Burr tried other
American boats, and actually engaged passage on two occasions,
only to have the captains come to him with troubled countenances
and break the contract. The only way to get out of England now
was by British packet.[56]

The month of March found Burr still in London — almost six
months of weary sojourning. Finally there was a rift in the clouds.
He heard of a ship clearing for Boston, commanded by a Captain
Potter. The bluff sea-dog asked no questions, though he looked
queerly enough at *Monsieur Arnot,* Burr's latest *alias.* The price
for passage on the *Aurora,* he said, was 30 guineas, and she sailed
on the 25th.

At last he could get away — *if* he could raise the necessary funds.
Again he sold some of that lovely cambric — one begins to won-

der what magic store of gifts he had on hand — and received ten pounds. Within a few days this sum had dwindled to six pounds. He tried to sell his precious volumes of *Bayle,* which he had carted with him all over Europe, to Reeve, his good friend in the Alien Office. But he received a loan of ten pounds from him instead. Reeve had been of infinite assistance. It was he who issued a passport to *M. Arnot,* and, he told him obligingly, " if you are tired of the name Arnot, and wish any other, you may have it."

On March 21st, through the good offices of Robert Morris, then in London, Burr realized another ten pounds from the sale of the balance of his cambric, ribands, medals and handkerchiefs — the magic store was at length thoroughly exhausted. Five pounds more came from seltzer water he had somehow accumulated.

The day before sailing time found his baggage on board the *Aurora,* but the passenger himself was still twenty pounds shy of the passage money. The morning of the 25th dawned cold and clear, and the balance seemed as far away of attainment as the moon. At the turn of the tide, Captain Potter intended to weigh anchor, Burr or no Burr. In desperation, not knowing where else to turn, Burr went once more to Reeve. That official listened to him in silence, and, without a word, " drew a check on his banker for 20 pounds; and how I did gallop across the park," confided M. Arnot to his Journal that night, " to get my 20 pounds." [57] Luckily, there was a delay in sailing, and he had time to bid his friends good-bye, especially Bentham and the Godwins, before galloping once more to the ship.

The next day, March 26, 1812, the *Aurora* weighed anchor, spread its wings, and westward ho, for America! Only Captain Potter knew the true identity of *A. Arnot,* the modest, retiring, gray-templed passenger with eyes of undimmed brilliance. He was cargo more dangerous than stored gunpowder. Potter feared impending war between England and the United States, but not Burr. For the first time in his travels, he dared commit political thoughts to his Journal. " If the British should hang or roast every American they can catch, and seize all their property," he wrote acidly, " no war would be declared by the United States under present rulers . . . Now at some future day we will read this over, and see whether I know those folks. I did not dare write such things while on shore, for I never felt perfectly secure against another seizure." [58] Burr was a true prophet, even though war was actually to be declared within the year. He had rightly gaged Madison's temper, and the temper of the Virginia Dynasty. In fact, the war was forced upon Madison by the expansionists who stemmed from Burr himself, and who, wittingly or unwittingly, were but following in the paths he had indicated. It was the hunger of the Western and Southern frontiersmen for Canada and Florida, *not* the outrages on American shipping, that pushed the new Administration into the War of 1812.

4. EXILE'S RETURN

On May 5, 1812, M. Adolphus Arnot, " a grave, silent, strange sort of animal," who had let his whiskers grow to disguise him, landed in Boston port. The exile had returned to his native land, after four years of wandering which read like some fantastic adventure out of the Arabian Nights — a tale of unbelievable hardships and impossible splendors; one day hobnobbing with kings and princes and ladies fair, and the intellectual giants of the earth — the next lying hidden in a filthy garret, gnawing dry bread, and making assignations with servants and prostitutes of the gutter; feted and honored — and pursued with hate and misunderstanding; exalted to the skies — and ground by a malignant destiny into the mud; a tale of indomitable courage, gallantry and defiance — and saturated with the lowest physical instincts of man. A tapestry of rich and varied threads, a story which has quite no counterpart in the history of man, and told, day by day, in unvarnished, matter-of-fact style, always with humor, always without complaints or bitterness or vain regrets. Here, if anywhere, may the curious reader discover the man, Aaron Burr.

Aaron Burr was back, but not a soul was there to greet him, not a person knew of his homecoming. For he had sent no word ahead; he dared not. What welcome could possibly await the returned traitor, the man whom all the nation cursed? Jail awaited him possibly; jail, or worse. He must feel his way, remain unknown, unseen, until he could be sure of his course.

He took obscure lodgings in a boarding-house in Cornhill Square, and wrote at once to Samuel Swartwout in New York, and to Theo, notifying them of his arrival. In every corner, at every crossing, he expected some one to start, peer in his face, and exclaim, " But you are Colonel Burr! " No one did; his whiskers and wig kept his secret. But his baggage was in the Customs, and the Collector was the son of General Dearborn, knew him well, and was " extremely vindictive." The gauntlet was run, however, without the busy Collector realizing that the whiskers and wig of the unassuming M. Arnot hid the presence of the family enemy; and the baggage was freed.

The next thing to do was to get in touch with friends in Boston whom he could trust. He hunted in the directory for familiar names. There he found a Benjamin Fessenden, who had served under him as ensign in the Westchester campaign. Fessenden seemed not delighted to see his old commander, but this was evidently due to the touchiness of Burr himself; for later the Journal notes that he became most obliging, and helped Burr in sundry ways. He found as well another name — that of Jonathan Mason, a friend of college days. He sent him a letter, " I pray you not to conjecture *aloud* who may be the writer of this note; he wishes to remain *incog.* a few days . . . If you will take the trouble of calling at Mrs. Goodrich's, Cornhill Square . . . you will find an old acquaintance who wishes half an hour's conversation with you." [59]

But Mason had grown cautious with the years. He wrote back apologetically that he dared not come, and " that the motive to it is a respect to the prejudices of others." Neither would he buy the books which Burr offered in order to get cash, nor advance his old friend a loan in any amount.

Better and more heartening, however, was the enthusiastic response of Samuel Swartwout. A letter came on May 19th, " with assurance that I have very many and warm friends and no enemies. The letter," Burr noted dryly, " is stamped with that enthusiasm which marks his character. As regards business, however, things are not propitious. The two creditors who have judgments against me are inexorable. Nothing will satisfy them but money or approved security, neither of which are in my power. The alternative is to be taken on execution and go the [jail] limits." [60]

There were serious objections in Burr's mind to the latter course. There was the blow to Theo's pride; it would interfere with the prospect of marriage to an old and wealthy woman (as a means of extrication from his financial difficulties) , and it would confine him to the tedious practice of law within New York City and prevent those larger speculations outside by which his fortune might be speedily recouped. He was already an aging man, and impatient. But Theo's letter of a year before, which, through unaccountable vicissitudes, had just caught up with him, was strong in urging that very method — she would feel no blow to her pride if her father were confined to the jail limits. Her heartening tone encouraged and decided him to follow her advice. But, alas, another degrading circumstance intervened. His luggage was being held in the boarding-house as security for the unpaid room rent. Fessenden came to his rescue by introducing him to President Kirkland of Harvard, who purchased his stock of books and thereby released him from durance vile.

Still in disguise, still hiding from prying eyes, Mr. De Gamelli — his latest *alias* — sailed on May 30th out of Boston harbor in the sloop *Rose,* bound for New York. The captain of the boat and his wife, strangely enough, were Burr's distant cousins, and Mrs. Hall, a passenger, had known him well in those fabulous days at Fairfield, but they did not recognize him. On June 7th, he set foot after years in the streets of New York, so familiar, yet so haunted with the pathos of distance.

The Swartwouts, Samuel and Robert, took their old leader into their house, and kept him there *incognito* while the future was charted and the horizon anxiously scanned. Here the Journal, having fulfilled its purpose, comes abruptly to an end. Aaron Burr had come home!

1. Double Tragedy

FOR several weeks Burr lay concealed in the home of his faithful friends, while they bestirred themselves to sound out government officials, politicians, old friends and creditors alike as to the steps that might be taken against him should he reveal his presence in the United States. The results were fairly encouraging. Madison had other fish to fry now — the Anglo-American situation was daily becoming more alarming, and perhaps Dolly Madison had spoken privately to her husband of Theo's letter. John Wickham replied from Richmond to Swartwout's discreet inquiries about the forfeited bail in Ohio and pending civil suits, to the effect that some $4000 had been paid to the unfortunate bailor " or is about to be by Col. Burr's Friend in Phila (Mr. Pollock I think) & that the other suits have been dismissed "; while Luther Martin, who had also been on the bail bond, " has never mentioned any proceeding against him on his recognizance to appear in Ohio, & I think that nothing has been done on it." And, in closing, Wickham was " glad to hear that after so many sufferings Col. Burr has the prospect of being restored to his country & of being permitted again to employ his talents with advantage." [1]

At length it was deemed safe to disclose his presence. An item was inserted in a Boston newspaper, to be quoted by the New York *Columbian,* that " Colonel Burr, . . . once so celebrated for his talents and latterly so much talked of for his sufferings, arrived at Newburyport from France and England, and passed through this town on his way to New York." [2] The paragraph seemed to produce no untoward reactions and Burr was sufficiently heartened to come into the open.

A few days later another item appeared in the *Columbian* — a very modest and discreet line of type. " Aaron Burr," it read, " had returned to the city and had resumed the practice of law at [9] Nassau Street." [3] This had the desired effect. The city rubbed its collective eyes, and rocked with excitement. For the moment everything was forgotten — the political enmities, the riot of accusations — there was a feeling that he had been dealt with too severely, no matter what his crimes; and there was that irresistible curiosity which always animates the human race. The tiny tin sign, proclaiming the lawyer, was that same day a magnet calculated to attract all New York. The small cubbyhole of an office was crowded with friends, well-wishers, prospective clients and the merely curious. By nightfall some five hundred gentlemen had come to pay their respects and shake the hand of the man who once had held the destiny of the nation in his grasp.

Burr had started law practice anew with a borrowed $10 and that badge of his profession, the tin sign. Robert Troup, the close friend of youthful days, and bitter political enemy of later days, forgot all rancors, the harsh judgments he had pronounced, and offered him the use of his law library until his son should require it. Troup had retired from the practice of law. So eminent had Burr been in the profession, so tremendous his former prestige as an infallible winner of cases, that in the first twelve days of his practice he had taken in $2,000 in fees. Aaron Burr, aged now 56, had picked up the threads of existence, and seemed once more on the highroad to at least a moderate success. He wrote joyfully of his good fortune to Theo in South Carolina and settled down to work.

But Fortune proved but a sorry jade. She took an infinite delight in aping the malignity of the human race, permitting her victim to raise his head only that he might be smashed to earth again. This time she delivered her most telling blows in rapid succession — blows that accomplished what all the varied, heartsick years before had failed to do — they crushed and caused to die his indomitable spirit.

First came two letters in a single mail from the South. Wrote a tragic Theo, " A few miserable days past, my dear father, and your late letters would have gladdened my soul; and even now I rejoice at their contents as much as it is possible for me to rejoice at anything; but there is no more joy for me; the world is a blank. I have lost my boy. My child is gone for ever. He expired on the 30th of June. My head is not now sufficiently collected to say any thing further. May Heaven, by other blessings, make you some amends for the noble grandson you have lost." [4] Blindly, with suddenly shaking hand, Burr ripped open the seal of the other letter. It was from Alston; longer, but of the same terrible tenor. " That boy, on whom all rested; " he wrote in anguish, " our companion, our friend . . . he who was to have redeemed all your glory, and shed new lustre upon our families — that boy, at once our happiness and our pride, is taken from us — is dead." Poor

Theodosia! She has "endured all that a human being could endure; but her admirable mind will triumph. She supports herself in a manner worthy of your daughter. We have not yet been able to form any definite plan of life. My present wish is that Theodosia should join you, with or without me, as soon as possible." Gone are the old rancors, the old jealousies. "I not only recognize your claim to her after such a separation," he declared magnanimously, "but change of scene and your society will aid her, I am conscious, in recovering at least that tone of mind which we are destined to carry through life with us." [5]

One half of Burr's life was thereafter a closed chamber. Little *Gampy, Gampillo,* wearer of an hundred endearing names, the sturdy little boy of eleven, for whom he had collected toys, trophies, medals, coins — while he had starved in Europe; the boy who had been destined to recreate his name and glory, and push on to those higher reaches which unaccountably had been denied himself — was dead!

But there was still Theo — a Theo who needed him now more desperately than ever. Disease had taken its full toll of her — it was doubtless cancer — and her powers of resistance were terribly weakened. It was determined that she come north to join her father. He sent a messenger to South Carolina to escort her back in safety — one Timothy Green, a retired lawyer. He found her very low, emaciated, feeble, and suffering from an incessant nervous fever. The long, overland trip, it was decided, would be too arduous. But luckily, there was a fast pilot boat, erstwhile privateer — the *Patriot,* Captain Overstocks commanding — which was due to leave Charleston for New York. Under her hatches were the spoils of months of successful privateering on the high seas, to be sold at satisfactory prices in New York. If the British should catch her . . . But Alston, now Governor of his State, furnished the captain with a letter requesting the courtesies of the chivalrous British for the sick lady, his wife, on board — a letter which actually succeeded in passing the disguised privateer through the British blockading fleet.

The *Patriot* sailed on December 30, 1812, from Charleston, carrying a most wretched passenger, and all of Burr's papers and documents which he had left with Theo for safekeeping while he was in exile. A British warship hove the *Patriot* to off Cape Hatteras, read Alston's plea, and chivalrously waved her on her way. That was the last ever to be heard of the *Patriot.* That same night a terrific gale blew up, raking those stormy waters with unheard-of violence. Then all was silence!

The days passed; weary, interminable days for anxious father in New York and worried husband in South Carolina. The *Patriot,* fast, seaworthy, should long since have glided into New York Harbor. On January 15th, 1813, Alston wrote a supposedly safely arrived Theo in New York that he had heard no news of her. But there had been rumors of a gale off Cape Hatteras at the beginning of the month. Would she please write and relieve his mind.[6] Four days later he was writing again, frantically: " Forebodings! wretched, heartrending forebodings distract my mind. I may no longer have a wife; and yet my impatient restlessness addresses her a letter. To-morrow will be three weeks since our separation, and not yet one line. Gracious God! for what am I reserved? " [7] Under separate cover, a letter to Burr, lamenting, " I do not know why I write, but I feel I am miserable." [8]

Burr read, and his heart died completely within him. Daily he walked the Battery, looking out over the harbor, peering in vain for the topsails of the *Patriot.* Hope flared, and died, and flared again. He wrote to Alston, seeking comfort. Alston answered tragically. " You ask of me to relieve your suspense. Alas! it was to you I looked for similar relief." [9]

By the end of February, Alston had yielded to the ultimate despair. Advices from Bermuda, from Nassau, had brought their tale of that terrific gale which had twisted upward from the Caribbean, to leave only death and destruction in its wake. They had " forced upon me the dreadful conviction that we had no more to hope." Heartbrokenly he cries, " My boy — my wife — gone, both! " But there are compensations. " The man who has been deemed worthy of the heart of Theodosia Burr, and who has felt what it was to be blessed with such a woman's, will never forget his elevation." [10]

Hope died more slowly in Burr's breast. Perhaps she had been captured, and taken to some far port by a vagrant privateer. But as the weeks became months, even that poor consolation was gone. The second half of Burr's life was now dust and ashes. In all history there is no record of a greater or more passionate communion and understanding between father and daughter. She was not merely the child of his loins; she was the paragon he had slowly and laboriously created with his brain. She was the living justification of his very existence. And now she, too, had been taken away from him, to leave life itself a meaningless, echoing shell. Fate had done its worst — had triumphed over the bright armor of his soul — had found with unerring instinct the vulnerable slits through which to enter and deal its fatal thrusts. He was to live on another twenty-three years, to an age beyond the usual mortal span — but Aaron Burr actually died early in 1813.

Legend took up the vanishment of Theodosia, and embroidered the bare, paltry bones with glamour and romance and shuddering thrills. She had not gone down in a storm, it cried; she had been captured by pirates, and forced to walk a plank with her babe in her arms — Dame Legend forgot that her boy was already dead and she had no other child — and so calm and majestic was her presence as she plunged into the salt, salt sea that the hardened pirates sniffled and sobbed aloud. Or the tale changed, and it was the crew itself that had mutinied and compelled her to walk the plank. So, at least, confessed a member of that very crew as he died, forty years later, in an agony of remorse for the foul deed.

More malignant was the odious story promulgated by the Carolina *Spartan,* to the effect that Burr had compassed the ruin of the wife of a coasting sea-captain. To remove this latter obstacle from the path of his lust, Burr had corrupted the sailors to mutiny and sink the vessel with all on board. Unfortunately, it was the very ship on which Theodosia had taken passage, and thus, ended the account in an orgy of moral gratulation, " her fate was an awful retribution upon her abandoned father." No tale was too gross, too fantastic, to merit credence. One of these even enlisted the support of the late Dr. John Stillwell, a lifelong laborer in Burriana and a collector of portraits relating to him. This was the story that the *Patriot* had been driven on the rocks at Kitty Hawk, that the wreckers who infested that treacherous shore boarded the vessel, killed all the crew and passengers, and bore off the rich spoil in triumph to their huts and cabins. Among the spoil was a portrait — that of Theodosia herself — later to be discovered in a cottage on Nag's Head, and to become famous as the Nag's Head portrait. Dr. Stillwell was firmly convinced of the authenticity of this picture, but the excellent reproduction contained in his privately printed " The History of the Burr Portraits " leaves at least one observer wholly unconvinced that it is in truth a portrait of Theodosia Burr.[11] The most sensible solution of what has been elevated to the dignity of a mystery is the prosaic conclusion that the *Patriot* sank in the storm, as boats occasionally do, and that the poor, sick lady went down with the others.

2. THE EDEN CASE

Life somehow went on after the death of child and grandchild. Burr encased himself in a new armor of seeming outward indiffer-

AARON BURR, AGED 78

From a portrait by James Vandyck

MADAME JUMEL

From a portrait by Henry Inman

ence — he was too essentially reserved, too proud of himself to show to the world his grief. He was a lawyer once more, practising in the various courts of the State as he had in those obliterated days when he had been young and eager, with the future a shining upward path before him. Now it was stale and unprofitable to this lonely old man; on his death the line of Burr — direct, that is, and sequential — would cease to be.

But he had not lost his old cunning, or the keen razor-edge of his intellect. Clients continued to flock to him — he was still the great advocate who practically never had lost a case. Socially he might have been an outcast, the man to be pointed out in the streets with scorning finger as the murderer of Hamilton, the schemer who plotted to disrupt his country — but business was business, and those with doubtful cases, those who wished assurance of success, those whose claims had been turned down by other counsel as hopeless, came to him for succor. Nor did he fail them, once he had examined the matter and assumed responsibility.

There was, for example, the famous Mecdef Eden case. Mecdef Eden had been a New York brewer who had died in 1798, leaving behind him two sons and a considerable fortune in Manhattan real estate. The sons, however, were the idle sons of a self-made man, and managed to run through their fortune, with the happy aid of dishonest creditors and usurers, in a very short time. Bankruptcy followed, the parcels were foreclosed, and they lived on in dire poverty. The case was then submitted to Hamilton and Burr, both then at the height of their powers. Hamilton was of the firm opinion that absolutely nothing could be done to salvage the wreck of the estate; Burr advised that much could be done. Hamilton's advice was followed, and no proceedings were taken.

On Burr's return, however, he heard of the death of one of the brothers, and, remembering the old claim, hunted up the survivor, who was poor, bedraggled, and heavily in debt. He undertook to recover the estate for him — the real property had increased enormously in value over the years — and brought Eden, his wife and two daughters into his own home, fed and clothed them all, and provided for the education of the young girls through the long years that the case dragged in chancery.

Meanwhile he went skilfully to work. The most valuable of the parcels were within the city limits, and in the possession of powerful banks and corporations who could be counted on to fight desperately and with ample resources for the protection of their titles. He left them severely alone, and concentrated his efforts on a small farm, of no great monetary value, in the upper part of Manhattan Island. He started suit to recover this parcel for the Eden Estate, claiming fraud, coercion and usury in the original assignments and foreclosures. Privately it was intimated to the existing owner that if he did not contest the case very vigorously, he would be permitted to buy it back at a nominal price. Burr won in the lower court, urged that it be appealed to establish a record, and won again on the appeal.

With this single case as an established precedent, he then moved swiftly and with despatch upon the holders of all the other alienated parcels. Writs of ejectment were served by the score. The city buzzed with excitement; there was a vast scurrying for legal advice and a checking up of titles long thought to be secure. Martin Van Buren, who had deserted Burr in time of need, now came back to assist him. For years the courts echoed with the litigation. The owners fought bitterly, desperately; yet in suit after suit Burr won and won again. But his resources were small, and those of his opponents huge. Appeals and constant litigation, even with eventual victory at the end of the trail, were costly, and Burr was compelled to go to the usurers to finance the legal costs as well as to maintain himself and the Edens over the years. By the time it was over, the usurers had won heavily, with only a sufficient modicum to maintain the Edens in some decency. When the father died, he nominated Burr as the guardian of his two daughters.[12]

The story of that guardianship makes pleasant reading. The pedagogue in Burr was always close to the surface, to burst forth at the slightest provocation. He trained his wards rigorously in the arts and sciences, and supervised their reading, their sports, their every activity. They, and Charles Burdett, an adopted — and, it was whispered, a natural — son, were placed under a private tutor, subject to Burr's strict control. His "ideas of education," Burdett was to remember gratefully long after, "differed from those of every other person with whom I ever came in contact . . . He believed and acted upon the principle that a woman should be educated so as to be fitted for any position, any sphere, or to be equal to any circumstances." Accordingly, their studies ranged over such diverse subjects as the classics, modern languages, astronomy and navigation, the violin and flageolet. "Nothing was neglected. Their studies were regulated by system; their health was cared for by incessant injunctions to take air and exercise." They were all three domiciled in Albany, where a room was devoted to Burr's sole use on his frequent trips on legal business to that capital, and "it was his wont to review the studies that they had pursued during his absence." The girls acted as his secretaries, and, said Burdett, " exercised a greater influence over Burr's later years than any who had ever been connected with him, except by ties of consanguinity." It is a wholly pleasant picture. " He was perfectly wrapped up in them and . . . they were the only human beings who ever filled the void caused by the death of Theodosia Alston. They reciprocated his affection as strongly as it was bestowed. They loved and honored him . . . His word was their law." [13]

All the remaining years of his life, there was to exist increasingly this reciprocal attraction between Burr and the young. He gravitated to them naturally, reared and educated them — his purse was always being drained by numerous protégés — and his system of education justified itself in the remarkable results achieved. Burdett himself, born in 1814, worked in his office, lived with the Misses Eden, and was sent first to the school of Dr. Hazelins at Cooperstown, later to Captain Partridge's military academy at Middletown, and finally entered the Navy.

There were others, many others; a constant succession of wards. In 1829 he was inquiring of the Principal of the Bethlehem Seminary as to the tuition charges at his school for " a young lady of rare talents and extraordinary industry, who has been placed under my guardianship [and] is desirous of learning the German and Latin languages and also of perfecting herself in music and drawing, in both of which branches she has made considerable proficiency . . . Her character and temperament are entirely amiable and her habits the most simple." [14]

And, in 1828, in answer to a query as to the wifely possibilities of one of his wards, he replied with characteristic humor. " The young woman about whom you have made inquiries," he told Alden Partridge, the founder of Norwich University, " is 21 years of age. She possesses no single one of those talents which are commonly called useful in a female — i.e., she can neither ' darn a stocking ' nor make a pudding, — though in common justice I ought to add that she is eminently useful to me as a private secretary and reader, and that she is well qualified to assist in the education of her children, should she ever become a mother." He had a definite philosophy of education for women, as is apparent in his concluding paragraph. " She has been educated wholly under my superintendence, the principal aim of which has been to form her manners, to teach her knowledge of the world, the duties, disabilities and the privileges of her sex; to appear to advantage in any society, to do the honors of her own house with grace and dignity and, in short, to be the friend and companion of a man of sense, of education and of taste." [15]

Parton reports a conversation with one of these female protégées in after years. " I never ask and never answer an impertinent question," she told him proudly. " I was brought up in the *Burr* school." And a man who had been helped by Burr stated emphatically: " He made me iron! " [16] His educational ideas were far in advance of his age; they dispensed wholly with corporal punishment, and invariably drew from the recipients of his bounty a lifelong admiration and love. The widening circle of his influence among the younger generation was an incalculable, but obviously important factor.

3. Of Many Matters

But this is peering into the future. For the first few years after his return, though his law business prospered, life was a constant effort to avoid creditors and keep out of the dreaded " jail limits." His debts were enormous, accumulated over a period of many years. The fundamental base rested upon his extravagances prior to 1800. On this was reared the heavy structure of his borrowings to finance the ill-fated Mexican expedition and Bastrop purchase; and, superimposed, sat the debts he had incurred in Europe for the mere purposes of continued existence and return to the United States.

In 1815, Burr was writing Alston, " my business affords me a decent support." That is, if he were left alone. But, " my old creditors (principally the holders of the Mexican debts) came upon me last winter with vindictive fury. I was held to bail in large sums, and saw no probability of keeping out of prison for six months. This danger is still menacing, but not quite so imminent. I shall neither borrow nor receive from any one, not even from you. I have determined not to begin to pay unless I see a prospect of paying all." [17]

They were indeed far beyond the possibilities of payment from any law practice, no matter how lucrative. His debts aggregated in the total several hundred thousand dollars, and a goodly part of this sum was due to usurers who had already exacted their pound of flesh. The remainder of Burr's life was a struggle to keep out of their clutches, to stave them off with small payments as long as possible. He carried the burden of most of his debts to his grave. The Le Guen litigation bobbed up again, with claim and counter-claim, and indignant allegations by Burr that he had made payments on account, of which Le Guen had, or pretended to have, no knowledge. Judgments piled up.

There is the record of a judgment obtained by Luther Martin against Burr for some $20,000, ostensibly for legal services rendered, but it was obviously a friendly suit, interposed to protect Burr against importunate creditors. Lathrop, Burr's friend and law assistant, was Martin's attorney, and the judgment was eventually satisfied of record in 1833.[18]

Martin, one of the greatest lawyers of his day, had come to a bibulous, poverty-stricken old age. His talents and his money alike had been dissipated in riotous excesses and the taverns. Burr, grateful to the memory of those hectic days in Richmond, took the defeated, palsied old war horse into his own house, shared with him his meager resources, and cared for him tenderly and uncomplainingly until his death in 1826, aged 81.

It was a difficult old age for Burr, yet he never repined, and met reverses, arrests, ostracism, creditors and friends alike with a smiling fortitude and outward cheer. Biddle saw him in 1814, soon after the double tragedy, and wrote in some surprise that "he . . . did not appear to me or my family much altered. He called several times at my lodgings to see me, and was at times cheerful as usual, but the loss of his amiable daughter, Mrs. Alston, and his grandson had weaned him from the world, and it was a matter of perfect indifference to him when he left it. I was sorry to find that some of his old friends did not visit him." [19]

In fact, after the first stir and acclaim of his spectacular return, the old clouds of suspicion, of ingrained propaganda, had cast their muddy veils over the bright-eyed, still erect little man. It was considered political suicide to be intimate with him, and socially disreputable to invite him to one's house. Studied slights and discourtesies were placed upon him, in court and out. He affected not to notice them, but if they became too obvious, he turned upon the offender, whether judge or opposing lawyer, with crushing and unanswerable rebuke. Henry Clay, his own advocate in Kentucky, while on a visit to New York, pretended not to recognize him at first. But Henry Clay was in the full flight of his political career, and he wished no unnecessary burdens upon that delicate structure.

Yet some of his friends remained faithful, and all the more loyal because of the possible consequences to themselves. The Van Nesses had fallen away, but the Swartwout clan remained, a tower of strength. Davis still clung to him, though to become most disloyal after his death; Charles Biddle never deserted him; Robert Troup, after years of political invective, returned; and to his old Alma Mater, Princeton, and the society of Cliosophia, he was ever one of their most distinguished graduates. Bollman continued to correspond with him, Vanderlyn to the end of his days remembered with the warmest gratitude the solicitude of his patron, and European dignitaries, such as the Duke of Saxe-Weimar, did not disdain to visit the old man in his not very exclusive quarters.

And, while he maintained at the last a considerable degree of indifference to his debts, no appeal to his charity was ever disregarded. His self-appointed wards, those who had at any time shown him kindness, his old Revolutionary soldiers, never went away empty-handed. In fact, the claims upon his charity grew to unscrupulous proportions, as the news was bruited around. While he himself lived in Spartan simplicity, satisfied with meager surroundings and the least amount of food, a constant stream of applicants for his bounty left him utterly penniless. In desperation, his law partners took charge of the firm funds, permitting him only his current expense. Yet he managed, somehow, to secrete sufficient for the benefit of utter strangers. He forgot indignities, insults, but never a favor. He was the most loyal of friends. Besides Martin, he took care of a poor relation of Dr. Hosack, who had befriended him; and he gave to a son of Benjamin Botts, another of his Richmond lawyers, when he had but few remaining years, a very valuable farm near Jamaica in return for an annuity of $500. The exchange was considerably to Burr's disadvantage.

He was vigorous, hale and hearty to almost the end of his long life. He attributed his good health to the fact that he never took any medicine. Fasting was his sole remedy for all disorders. He was extremely impatient with whiners and complainers; he advocated and cultivated for himself the Stoic attitude toward life's ills. While on a sea voyage he remarked, " For a sick woman he could feel pity and sympathy, but for a sick man he had no feeling but contempt." [20] There was another story current, which, if not true ought to have been true — it expresses the man so thoroughly. He was asked by a lady how to get through an emergency. " Live through it," he replied. But when she insisted that she could not possibly survive her predicament, he exclaimed angrily, " Well, die then, Madam; we must all die, but bless me, die game! "

His income consisted of his law practice, an annuity of 50 pounds which he had purchased in England long before, a Revolutionary pension of $500 annually, and, toward the end of his life, the annuity of $500 from young Botts. He petitioned the Federal Government for reimbursement of the very large sums of money which he had expended out of his own pocket during the dark days of the Revolution, when Continental money was worthless and the soldiers' pay rarely met. The preparation of affidavits as to his services occupied a good deal of his time. But all his efforts were fruitless. He had enlisted the services of Congressman G. C. Verplanck in his fight, but they were evidently of little value. For, almost at the close of his life, he was writing to him, " Sir, I have to acknowledge the receipt of your letter of the 25th Ult., in which you are pleased to inform me that you had put the papers, which I had transmitted to you, in the hands of the Chairman of the Standing Committee. I regret very much this disposition of the papers and have now only to request that you would have the goodness to get the papers from the Chairman of that Committee and hand them to my friend Col. A. Ogden." [21]

He was never to receive a single penny for his efforts. The story goes that it was Andrew Jackson, then President, who effectively put the brakes upon his claim, but the tale is not authenticated. The New York State Legislature, on the motion òf some of Burr's friends, considered granting him a pension in return for former services. For the moment hopes were high. " With respect to my personal concern," he wrote G. W. Lathrop, his office manager, from Albany, " my hopes are not diminished. [The bill] will be taken up on Wednesday, having been already referred to the Com [mittee] of the whole. I think something decent will pass the Senate — of the other house no Judgment can be formed . . . Pray observe that I present no petition or memorial — make no claim, but the Legislature of their own mere motion, offer me remuneration, because it has been merited & because *it is wanted.*" [22]

But a little later, hope gave way to despair. Burr was still in Albany, without funds to leave. " a. b.' — bill not introduced," he told Lathrop, " owing to the illness of the gentleman who gave the notice — he has promised to be well tomorrow. It is possible, & barely probable, that the bill will be referred to a select committee who may make a handsome report; and there it will repose." [23] Nothing, in fact, ever came of it.

In his law practice Burr proved himself as keen and successful as ever. Published and unpublished letters alike testify to the number of his cases, the meticulous attention he gave to each, the remarkable grasp of their subject matter, the technical and involved procedure he loved to follow, to the vast confusion of his opponents, and the sharp eye he kept on his office staff, even when away on business for weeks. W. D. Craft, G. W. Lathrop, M. H. Flandrau, and Pelletreau were at various times his partners, associates and managing attorneys. In financial matters, they ruled him, but in the domain of law, he was the guiding genius, the great lawyer to whom they submitted all points for final consideration. His letters are replete with exact and careful instructions for procedures to be followed while he was away, and he was insistent on strict attention to his remarks.

While Craft was training in his office, he advised him in kindly fashion, " Your letters are very satisfactory — they shew me the actual state of things and I pray you to continue in the same Way . . . I hope you are improving & perfecting yourself in the practical part of the attorney's business; though I see nothing of it in your Journal. I shall hope to find you, at my return, qualified to take charge of the whole of the attorney's business of the office." [24]

With Lathrop, an older man, he unbuttoned himself more. " your drunken letter and your sober one have both been [received]," he wrote lightly. " It is with pleasure I remark that your frolic did not render you inattentive to business — at this rate one may now and then Venture on a debauch." [25] And, at another time, in even more bawdy vein, " You have adopted the only genuine antidote to Hypocondria — " he jested, " *Testisical dissipation,* which always imports the presence of Women. Thank my fair dreamer. We will dream together, if she so please, on my return." [26]

The years and the onslaughts of age had not diminished, it seems, his powers of venery. His interest in women — almost *any* woman — continued through years when other men are content to hug the fireside and dream philosophically, with perhaps a tinge of vain regrets, of past exploits. In 1828, aged 72, there was a lovely " syren " of some 20 years, with whom he was infatuated. Charles Burdett, on furlough from school, " was daily dispatched . . . with notes and presents. The notes invariably contained money; the presents consisted of fruits or flowers," as well as crusted bottles of wine from his cellar. The " syren " was obviously no innocent. " She harassed him daily with clamorous demands for money. Bills against her came in to him with terrible rapidity and frightful in amount." Finally Burr could pay no more; she had used his name to defraud others, and had been driven from the school in which he had obtained for her a dancing teacher's position. New York became entirely too warm a place for her wiles and arts. So, with her mother and sister, kindred leeches, she was shipped South at Burr's expense, and he wryly washed his hands of her; only soon to be ensnared by another " syren." [27] Burr still possessed his remarkable fascination, and his childlike inability to differentiate between adventurers and honest men.

Politically, of course, he was *persona non grata*. Yet he maintained an active, if personally discreet interest in the political situation of the day. He was possibly the first to realize the military qualities and Presidential timber of General Andrew Jackson. At the outbreak of the War of 1812 he had told Dr. John Sage, Congressman from New York, " I know . . . my word is not worth much with Madison; but you may tell him from me that there is an unknown man in the West, named Andrew Jackson, who will do credit to a commission in the army if conferred on him." [28]

And, after the War, and Jackson's signal services therein, he started a one-man boom for Jackson for President. He tried to enlist his son-in-law, Governor Alston, in the campaign. He was impatient and a bit disgusted with Alston's lackadaisical nature. He wished him to precipitate himself into the campaign of 1815. Monroe was to be nominated by the usual Congressional caucus on the Republican ticket, and Burr thought him " one of the most improper and incompetent that could be selected. Naturally dull and stupid; extremely illiterate; indecisive to a degree . . . . , pusillanimous, and, of course, hypocritical; has no opinion on any subject, and will be always under the government of the worst men." Not only was Monroe excoriated, but the Virginia junto, whose candidate he was, and who had held the government of the United States in its control since Jefferson's time. " If there be a man in the United States of firmness and decision, and having standing enough to afford even a hope of success," he exhorted Alston, " it is your duty to hold him up to public view. That man is Andrew Jackson." As for Alston himself, " Exhibit yourself," he cried impatiently, " and emerge from this state of nullity. You owe it to yourself, you owe it to me, you owe it to your country, you owe it to the memory of the dead." [29]

But not even these fiery words could stir the sluggish Alston. The Governor claimed he had received the letter too late to do anything about it, and even if it had been received in time, he was ill, and, said he, while " I fully coincide with you in sentiment . . . the spirit, the energy, the health necessary to give practical effect to sentiment are all gone. I feel too much alone,

too entirely unconnected with the world, to take much interest in
any thing." [30] He died that summer; a poor, broken reed, a hollow
shell, entirely unpossessed of that indomitable spirit which animated his father-in-law. Perhaps Burr had thought to re-enter
politics in the guise of Alston; if so, he was bitterly disappointed,
and from that day on, devoted himself exclusively to his personal
affairs.

When Jackson finally fulfilled his prophecies and became President, fortune smiled once more — at least upon the old associates
of Burr. Samuel Swartwout became Collector of the New York
Port and betrayed his trust. Others received minor appointments,
but there was nothing for Burr himself. Perhaps Jackson dared do
nothing, for fear of reviving old wounds. His own complicity in
the " Conspiracy " had been used with considerable effect against
him in the campaign. And certain it is that Burr was too proud to
ask for anything outright.

The revolutionists in Mexico and South America, however, did
not forget the man who had dramatized their cause. In 1816, José
Alvarez de Toledo, in command of the Mexican revolutionary
forces, came to the United States to seek the sinews of warfare, and
to offer Burr " the management of our political and military
affairs in the dangerous crisis in which we find ourselves." [31] Burr
must have smiled ironically at this offer; it was years too late.

Venezuela was the next revolutionary province to ask for his
distinguished aid. Burr was authorized in 1819 " to raise troops
for sea and land service, to aid this government or any other now
struggling in the same cause against the despotism of Spain." [32]
Which Burr pigeonholed with the Mexican letter, especially as
the Venezuelans would have graciously permitted him to finance
the expedition out of his own pocket. He was through with all such
endeavors. The Burr Dynasty would become extinct with him; to
what profit then an Empire?

But he had pointed out the path, and others — not to be called
traitors, but patriots — were following the trail. After his ill-fated
attempt, a horde of filibusterers descended on the Spanish possessions, and the Spanish consul in New Orleans wrote in some alarm
to Salcedo, " From what I can hear and penetrate it seems that
the project of Burr is coming to life." [33]

Animated in part by the winds of ferment generated on
the Ohio and Mississippi, revolution soon swept all of Spanish
America, eventually to cleanse the Continent of Spain. And when
Texas, under the leadership of American settlers, fought and won
its independence, Burr, then an old man, flashed out with the

old fires. " There! " he exclaimed. " You see? I was right! I was only thirty years too soon! What was treason in me thirty years ago, is patriotism now! " [34]

4. OLD AND WEALTHY WOMAN

On Wednesday, July 3, 1833, Philip Hone, New York merchant, noted in his Diary with ironic emphasis, " The celebrated Colonel Burr was married on Monday evening to the equally celebrated Mrs. Jumel, widow of Stephen Jumel. It is benevolent in her to keep the old man in his later days. One good turn deserves another." [35]

It was the astounding climax of an astounding career. The town buzzed with excitement, and snickered a little. The groom was 77, and the bride was 58. It is always difficult to gage the processes of a man's mind inducing to marriage, especially those of a septuagenarian, but it is quite likely that Burr was tired of the futile struggle — he was still practicing law at that advanced age — and Mrs. Jumel was an exceptionally wealthy widow. Once before, on his return from Europe, he had cast a quizzical eye at the available market of wealthy old women, without, it seems, having discovered anything notable. And Mrs. Eliza Jumel *was* notable; there was no doubt as to that.

Born " Betsy," or Eliza Bowen, of a roving sailor and a woman of the streets, in illegitimate union, her childhood knew only the most sordid scenes and surroundings. At the age of 7, she and her mother were compelled to flee hastily from a most virtuous mob, who thereupon proceeded to tear down the house in which they lived as a house of ill fame. This was in Providence, the place of her birth. Later, her mother was sent to jail on the charge of keeping a house of prostitution, and young Betsy, at the age of 12, was bound out as a servant.[36]

When she grew older, however, she abandoned the drudgery and dullness of domestic service for the excitement of her mother's ancient profession. She soon achieved a certain reputation as the handsomest girl in Providence, and in 1794, she bore a son, father unknown, whom she as promptly abandoned.

At the age of 19, New York beckoned, and in the metropolis she drifted from man to man, until, aged 25, she blossomed out as the mistress of Stephen Jumel, naturalized Frenchman and one of the richest merchants in New York. Jumel persisted in flaunting his handsome mistress in the face of an outraged society, and attempted to force her acceptance by the wildest extravagances, the most elaborate balls New York had yet seen. But society would have none of her, and after four years of vain endeavor, Jumel suddenly married Eliza. To console her for her isolation he purchased the stately Roger Morris House, near the tip of the Island, to be renamed and known thereafter as the Jumel Mansion. It was lavishly redecorated and furnished, and Mrs. Eliza Jumel was thus installed in the most elegant home in New York. But still society remained away from its colonial portals in droves.

After five years of splendid isolation, the couple went to France, where Madame Jumel achieved the success to which her beauty, her adventuress's talent, her wealth, entitled her. But within a year she had suddenly returned to the United States, leaving her husband abroad. Perhaps there was a quarrel — perhaps there had been a lover. For five years more she lived alone in the great house, solitary, neither visiting nor visited, until in 1821, she returned to Paris for a reconciliation with Stephen Jumel. But her extravagances and financial reverses had brought him to the verge of bankruptcy, and, in 1825, to protect himself from creditors, he deeded to her the Mansion and other valuable parcels of real estate in New York, and gave her a power of attorney to sell all the rest. She returned hastily to the United States, while he remained in Paris. When the smoke of her operations had lifted, she was in possession of every bit of her husband's property — and he was penniless. He came over in 1828 to retrieve his stolen assets, but she had been clever enough to keep within the law. One wonders whether Aaron Burr had been her advisory counsel, though there is no evidence on the point, and it was always insisted, on her side, that she had never known Burr until after the death of her husband. Poor Jumel died in 1832, poverty-stricken and raging against the woman he had lifted from the gutter.

She was now the wealthiest widow in New York, with a certain ravaged beauty, and a reputation for eccentricity and violence of temper. But she was still outside the social barriers of New York, and Aaron Burr, though somewhat of an outcast, was possessed of a most distinguished heritage and fame. With her money and his background, the stubborn doors might possibly yield to her avid touch.

The details of the courtship are veiled in considerable mystery. On her side it was to be asserted that he had forced his attentions upon her, even to the extent of bringing a minister to the Mansion that night of July 1, 1833, after repeated refusals on her part, and placing her thus in such a compromising situation that marriage was the only way out. A story based on gossip and the vanity of a very eccentric and somewhat insane old woman at a much later date. It is impossible to think of Betsy Bowen as compromised. On Burr's side, his law partner, Craft, insisted that it was she who pestered and harried the old man into marriage. It makes very little difference either way. It was folly on both sides, and the relationship terminated very rapidly and under deplorable circumstances.

They started out in grand style on their honeymoon, traveling in a huge yellow carriage — the bride's, of course — to Connecticut, where they visited Governor Edwards, Burr's nephew. There was business to be transacted in Hartford. The new Mrs. Burr owned a number of shares of stock in a Connecticut Toll Bridge Company, which, on her husband's advice, she now sold for $6,000 and turned over the proceeds to him. He promptly re-invested it, without her knowledge, in an emigration scheme to settle Germans on Texan lands. But the scheme was foredoomed to failure, and the money vanished in the ruins of the speculation. As the story goes, when she questioned him about the money, he turned on her grandly to exclaim, " Madam, I would have you know that you now have a master, and I will care for your money hereafter."

Pursuant to this assertion, Burr proceeded to spend his wife's money with reckless abandon, multiplying many-fold his charities, his gifts, his extravagances. His old creditors heard of his new state, and descended upon him with a storm of executions. Even his bewildered wife's carriage and horses were seized. Such domestic bliss could naturally last but a little time, and after four months of wrangling, and a concomitant attack of paralysis on his part, Burr left the Mansion to live with Aaron Columbus Burr in the City, and later to remove to Jersey City — no doubt once more to escape the importunities of his creditors. Aaron Columbus Burr was the product of a Paris adventure. He had come over to New York at an early age, and his education had been directed by his father. On reaching maturity, he had become a silversmith, and was prospering. There were two other illegitimate children, issue of an aged father. Frances Ann, aged 6 when Burr died, and Elizabeth, aged 2.

The first act in the nuptial drama was ended. The second act was described by William Dunlap in his Diary:

" June 19, 1834. Today in the street a woman accosted me by name, who I immediately recognized as the Madam Jumel Aaron Burr married about a year back. She had been a supernumerary at the Theatre before Jumel married her.

" ' You dont know me Mr. Dunlap? '

" ' Oh yes Mrs. Burr. How does Col. Burr do? '

" ' Oh I don't see him any more. He got $13000 dollars of my property & spent it all or gave it away & had no money to buy him a dinner. I had a new carriage & a pair of horses cost me 1000 dollars — he took them and sold them for 500.' " [37]

Shortly after this encounter, the tawdry show entered its final phase. On July 12, 1834, Madame Eliza Burr brought suit for divorce against her husband, then in Jersey City, alleging the usual infidelities as the cause of action. Attached to the petition was a prayer for an injunction to prevent Burr from interfering with her property. Burr at first showed fight, and interposed denials and counterclaims alleging misconduct on her part. But he thought better of it later, the answer was withdrawn, and the suit was permitted to be tried before a Master in Chancery undefended. The final decree was eventually entered on September 14, 1836, which was, tragically enough, the very day that Burr lay on his deathbed on Staten Island. But the farce was over; a most discreditable episode, and well ended.

5. FINALE

Life itself was fast approaching the end. For two years Burr lingered. At the age of 78, after the excitation of marriage and divorce, his marvelous vitality ebbed away. The Reverend William Hague, as a schoolboy, remembered Burr in the years between 1821 and 1824, when Burr was nearing 70. " His *physique*," he then thought, " style of movement, realize a boy's highest ideal of the soldier and gentleman; while his keen glance and sunny smile, expressive of a personal interest as real as if I had been a Senator, awaken a feeling quickly responsive to the tone of cheer in his greeting." [38] To the idolatrous schoolboy, Burr was " actually the ancient Stoic and the primitive Epicurean fused into a live unity. Never could I conceive of an ancient Stoic . . . more fully ' possessing himself,' and persistently imperturbable, than was Aaron Burr . . . His perfect poise, his equanimity, his power of endurance, his apparent superiority to all changes of condition, even from affluence to a poverty that he could dignify like Diogenes . . . were exceptionally wonderful, seeming almost superhuman." [39]

It was to Hague that Burr made his famous remark anent his duel with Hamilton. He had been reading Sterne's tolerant and mellowly wise " Tristram Shandy." He closed the book, stared at the worshiping youngster, and mused half to himself: " Had I read

Voltaire less, and Sterne more, I might have thought the world wide enough for Hamilton and me! " [40] It was the only time he had ever been known to evince a regret for what was past.

In 1830, he had already suffered a stroke of paralysis on his right side. His cousin, Mrs. Hawes (née Catherine Bartow), hastened to his office, then at the corner of Gold and Fulton Streets, and had him removed to her home in Brooklyn for nursing and treatment. There he exercised his limbs with rigid discipline until he had recovered their use, to return again to active life and practice.

But now, in 1834, he suffered another stroke, this time never to recover. He was carried from Jersey City to the old Jay Mansion, now a boarding-house, where he was tenderly nursed by Mrs. Newton, the housekeeper. He persisted in receiving clients while propped up in bed or on a sofa, applying his still acute mind to the solution of their difficulties; but soon that exertion was too much for him. For two years he lingered, calm, peaceful, alert to the end, spinning yarns of the brave old days to his frequent callers, no doubt tinctured with the golden glow that hazes the past in the minds of the aged, and awaiting without repining the inevitable end.

In the summer of 1836, however, the Jay Mansion was to be torn down, in accordance with the restless spirit of New York, and his friends and relatives gathered to decide what should be done. Judge Ogden Edwards, who resided on Staten Island, thought the country air and ocean breezes of that hilly adjunct of New York would be pleasant for his few remaining days, and so it was agreed. On a warm, sunny day, he was carried to a boat in the Bay, and removed to a hotel, later called the Continental, at Port Richmond, Staten Island, not far from Judge Edwards' own house. There he was installed in style, his room overlooking the harbor and Newark Bay. There the sands of life ebbed slowly away, his last few wants supplied by relatives and friends. On September 14, 1836, the day on which the decree of divorce became final, he died.

6. L'Envoi

Even in death, the malignity of the newspapers pursued him, and the evil legends clustered. He was buried in stealth at night, it was alleged, and the stone placed on his grave, also at night, by unknown hands.

In fact, Princeton, his old Alma Mater, paid his poor dead body the highest honors; and the funeral was a public and solemn occasion. On September 16, 1836, the body reached Princeton in state and was deposited in the chapel of the college, " within the walls where his own novitiate was passed, and where his sire and grand-sire were wont to offer prayer to God." In the afternoon, the exercises were held in the chapel, attended by the entire student body, citizens of the town, and friends and relatives of the deceased, come to do him honor. Dr. Carnahan preached a moving sermon, other ministers officiated as well. Then the funeral procession was formed in order, " the Military, the Hearse, the Pall Bearers, the Clergy, Mourners, Professors, Students of the Colleges, and Citizens." They proceeded to the college cemetery, where the " Mercer Guards " fired a military volley over the grave. The pallbearers were General Robert Swartwout, Colonel Romeyn, Colonel Joseph W. Scott, Colonel Samuel Swartwout, Major Popham, General Bogardus, H. M. Western and Samuel Corp. Faithful old friends, who had witnessed the dazzling career, meteoric flight, and hissing oblivion of one of the most fascinating figures in all history.[41]

Cliosophic Society, always proud of its most distinguished member, paid tribute to his memory in a series of resolutions, and decreed that they be published in the newspapers, and that the members wear mourning for their departed brother for a space of thirty days.[42] But the restless spirit was at rest, oblivious of honors, of slander and execration alike.

For twenty years the grave remained unmarked; then Alfred Edwards, a relative, erected a simple stone, giving dates of birth and death, with the added notations that he had been a " Colonel in the Army of the Revolution " and " Vice-President of the United States from 1801 to 1805." Nothing else. Yet even this brief and unadorned reminder suffered mutilation from some patriotic vandal. In death as well as in life Aaron Burr was hated as no man had been hated in American history. Only now are the mists of obloquy gradually rising and the true picture taking shape and form — of a man of extraordinary talents, approaching genius, of a man of human mold and human failings, of one who remained to the end erect against the gods. It was his inherent limitations that prevented him from assaulting the highest places; it was his energy and talents that earned him the hatred and opposition of his fellows.

Yet his place in history is secure. In an era of giants, he, too, was of the elect. He helped make possible the rise of Jeffersonian democracy, he discovered and perfected the smoothly geared party machine with its reliance upon the masses, which was to culminate in that last sweep of democracy under Andrew Jackson; while his ideas on education and feminism were remarkably in advance of his age. He may be considered the catalyst *par excellence* in hastening certain social, political and legal reactions. His contest with Jefferson led to the adoption of the Twelfth Amendment, his duel with Hamilton not only martyred the latter, but caused a revulsion of popular feeling against that venerable institution. His trial for treason developed the judicial theory of the overt act and demolished the English doctrine of constructive treason. It also laid the basis, by its very concentration on the issue, for a true nationalism in this country. He initiated the movement of expansion which led to the War of 1812, the Texan Revolution, and the acquisition of a vast Continent.

The tumult is over, the hatreds are dying. Burr is slowly regaining his rightful place and niche in time. He was not all greatness, not all fault. His greatest limitation was the lack of a rounded, well-organized philosophy applicable to the issues of the day. It is to Hamilton, to Jefferson, to Jackson, to John and Samuel Adams, that one looks for comprehensive plans, whether good or bad, to bolster the infant government and adapt its course to the social, political and economic problems that confronted it at its inception. One looks in vain to Burr for such matters and theories; he was essentially a practical man, not an idealist; one who viewed government in terms of men rather than in terms of ideals and philosophic concepts. Modern machine politics may look to him as its founder, yet in his time it was the only organization possible to the masses as against the aristocracy of wealth and birth. Treason has been placed at his door, and treachery to Jefferson; yet both charges do not survive the cold light of the documents. He, the practical politician, was indeed singularly faithful to his code and to his friends. In all his life there were but two incidents that merit complete censure — his negotiations with Merry and Yrujo, and the doubtful ethics of his Holland Land Company connections while in the Legislature. Yet these were small enough, compared to the vast texture of his career, the numerous temptations and openings that, caught in the full tide, would have swung him aloft to the heights. Who in history has not similar smirches on his character; who in history would not be content with such a paucity of spots on an effulgent sun? Who in history has survived a more venomous brood of decriers?

THE END

NOTES

CHAPTER I

1. John Adams to James Lloyd, Feb. 17, 1815; John Adams, *Works*, C. F. Adams, *ed.*, X, 123.

2. I am indebted chiefly for genealogical data on the Burrs to *A General History of the Burr Family*, by Charles Burr Todd, 1902.

3. Parton's *Burr*, 31.

4. *Ibid*, 31-2.

5. Davis' *Burr*, I, 17-18.

6. *Ibid*, 18.

7. MSS. Sermons, Yale Univ.; MSS. Letter, Burr to Mr. Hogg, Dec. 3, 1775 [an obvious error for 1755], Princeton Univ.

8. *A General Account of . . . the College lately established in the Province of New-Jersey . . . by the Trustees of the College*, 4.

9. Both Davis and Parton yield Burr the honor of being its first President. But see Princeton Univ. Archives.

10. *A General Account*, etc., *supra*, 5.

11. New York *Gazette*, July 20, 1752; Davis' *Burr*, I, 20.

12. Joseph Shippen, Jr., to his father, July 6, 1752; N. J. Hist. Soc. Proc., First Series, V, 169.

13. Joseph Shippen, Jr., to his stepmother, August 1, 1752; *ibid*, 169-70.

14. MSS. Letter, Princeton Univ.

15. MSS. Letter, Esther Burr to Lucy Edwards, Nov. 4, 1754; Princeton Univ.

16. MSS. Diary, Esther Burr; Yale Univ.

17. *Ibid*.

18. MSS. Letter, Burr to Mr. Hogg, Dec. 3, 1755; Princeton Univ.

19. MSS. Letter, Burr to the Gov. & General Court of Conn., May 8, 1754; Conn. State Lib.

20. Esther Burr *Diary; supra*.

21. *Ibid*.

22. *Ibid*.

CHAPTER II

1. Esther Burr *Diary; supra*.

2. *Ibid*.

3. Burr to Mr. Hogg, Dec. 3, 1755; *supra*.

4. Esther Burr *Diary; supra*.

5. *Ibid*.

6. MSS. Letter, Burr to George Whitefield, Feb. 16, 1757; Princeton Univ.

7. Esther Burr *Diary; supra*.

8. MSS. Letter, Burr to Naphalis Daggett, Prof. of Divinity, Yale College, May 10, 1757; Yale Univ.

9. Esther Burr *Diary; supra*.

10. *Diary*, Ezra Stiles, II, 337.

11. A MSS. inventory of the joint estates of Aaron and Esther Burr in 1765 discloses seemingly that the totals received amounted to some 3679 pounds,

with disbursements over the course of years of 1106 pounds, including debts and current expenses; Princeton Univ.

12. Parton's *Burr*, 47.
13. Davis' *Burr*, I, 23–4.
14. *Ibid*, 26.
15. Parton's *Burr*, 53.

CHAPTER III

1. Beam, *American Whig Society*, 60.
2. Williams, *The Cliosophic Society*.
3. Beam, *American Whig Society*, 30.
4. Davis' *Burr*, I, 44.
5. Burr, *Journal*, Bixby, ed., II, 73. See also *ibid*, I, 8.
6. MSS. Letter, McLean to Editors *Presbyterian Journal*, Jan. 27, 1875; Princeton Univ. Archives; Researches of V. Lansing Collins and Jacob Beam, of Princeton.
7. Davis' *Burr*, I, 28; the *Essay on Dancing* is in the Pa. Hist. Soc.
8. Wandell and Minnigerode, *Burr*, I, 27.
9. Davis' *Burr*, I, 27–8.
10. Patterson to Burr, Oct. 26, 1772; Davis' *Burr*, I, 39–40.
11. MSS. Letter, Burr to Jonathan Sergeant, June 12, 1772; Princeton Univ.
12. Same to same, Aug. 15, 1772, *ibid*.
13. Princeton Univ. Archives.
14. Patterson to Spring, Oct. 5, 1772; Davis' *Burr*, I, 40.
15. Patterson to Burr, Jan. 17, 1772; *ibid*, 37.
16. Same to same, Oct. 26, 1772; *ibid*, 37.
17. Spring to Burr, May 15, 1772; *ibid*, 43.
18. Ogden to Burr, Aug. 9, 1774; *ibid*, 47.
19. Davis' *Burr*, I, 45.
20. MSS. Letter, Richard Platt to Burr, undated; N. Y. Pub. Lib.
21. Timothy Edwards to Burr, Feb. 11, 1774; Davis' *Burr*, I, 46.
22. Correspondence between Ogden and Burr; *ibid*, 47–56.
23. Burr to Ogden, Aug. 17, 1774; *ibid*, 48–9.

CHAPTER IV

1. Wandell and Minnigerode, *Burr*, I, 42.
2. Sally Reeve to Burr, Sept. 2, 1775; W. C. Ford, *Some Papers of Aaron Burr*, 22.
3. Davis' *Burr*, I, 65–6.
4. The source material, including the *Journals* of Arnold, Senter, Henry, Ware, Dearborn, Wild, Ogden, etc., as well as secondary works, notably John Codman's *Arnold's Expedition* and the two books of Justin H. Smith, to wit, *Arnold's March* and the *Struggle for the Fourteenth Colony*, has been freely used for this account.
5. Ogden's *Journal*, MSS., Washington Assn. of N. J.; published in N. J. Hist. Soc. Proc., Jan., 1928.
6. *Ibid*. According to Davis, I, 66, this incident occurred to Burr himself.
7. Arnold to his officers, Oct. 27, 1775.
8. Davis (*Burr*, I, 77) avers the doubtful honor was first offered by Arnold to Burr, who refused it as a silly, futile move. He places the incident, however, *after* the assault, which seemingly disposes of it as apocryphal.

9. Ogden's *Journal, supra.*

10. Codman, *Arnold's Expedition.*

11. Maine Hist. Soc. Coll., I, 386.

12. Davis' *Burr*, I, 67–9.

13. The story of Burr's "forlorn hope" is narrated in detail in Davis' *Burr*, I, 70–1, a source always to be viewed with suspicion. But it was obviously based on Burr's own statements in after life, and involves no such self-contradictions as some of the other tales. Codman accepts it whole, while Smith's skeptical attitude is based on nothing more definite than a belief that Montgomery's notable caution precluded any discussion of plans with his men. He forgets that a regular Council of War had been held, and that Burr was Montgomery's aide-de-camp at the time.

14. Testimony of Capt. Richard Platt, cited Davis' *Burr*, I, 177.

15. Statement of Spring to Senator William Plumer; Plumer's *Memorandum of Proceedings*, 612. Here again a merry controversy has raged. Parton embellished the story with lofty language and romantic details. (75–7) Justin H. Smith disbelieves the entire episode (*Struggle for the Fourteenth Colony*, II, note LXV), basing his disbelief on the fact that Spring's account was not given until 45 years later, and not published until 1838, 19 years after Spring's death, and on the more important fact that, according to J. J. Henry's *Journal*, p. 109, Spring had helped the wounded Arnold to the hospital, and therefore could not have been present with Montgomery's column. But Henry did not compose his *Journal* until considerably later, to wit, between 1805 and 1811, when he was in feeble health, and the blurring effect of time may be charged equally to him as to Spring. His testimony is as follows: "Now we saw Colonel Arnold returning, wounded in the leg, and supported by two gentlemen, a Parson Spring was one, and in my belief, a Mr. Ogden the other." But Dr. Isaac Senter, who was in charge of the hospital that night, notes in his *Journal* (MSS., N. Y. Hist. Soc.) that "Col. Arnold was brought in, supported by two Soldiers, wounded in the leg . . . Before the Col. was done with, Major Ogden came in Wounded through the left Shoulder, which proved only a flesh wound." So that Ogden definitely was not one of the good Samaritans, as Henry averred, and it is not likely that Senter, who knew Spring to be a Chaplain, would refer to him anonymously as a "Soldier."

16. Arnold to Gen. Wooster, Dec. 31, 1775; *Correspondence of the Revolution*, Sparks, ed., I, 500.

17. Wm. Bradford, Jr., to Burr, Jan. 24, 1776; Davis' *Burr*, I, 75.

18. Reeve to Burr, Jan. 27, 1776; *ibid*, 75–6.

19. Ogden to Burr, Mar. 20, 1776; *ibid*, 77–8.

20. Burr to Sally Reeve; Wandell and Minnigerode, *Burr*, I, 56. (Italics mine.)

21. Ogden to Burr, June 5, 1776; Davis' *Burr*, I, 80.

22. Burr to Ogden, June 18, 1776; *ibid*, 81.

23. Mrs. Coghlan's *Memoirs.*

24. *Ibid.*

25. Davis' *Burr*, I, 90–2.

26. Mrs. Coghlan's *Memoirs.*

27. G. W. Greene, *Life of Greene*, I, 212; Wm. Jay, *Life of Jay*, II, 7.

28. Eyewitness account, Van Tyne, *The War of Independence, American Phase*, 250.

29. Depositions of Hezekiah Ripley, Nathaniel Judson, Isaac Jennings and Andrew Wakeman, all of Silliman's Brigade; Davis' *Burr*, I, 102–6.

30. MSS. Letter, Burr to Sally Reeve, Oct. 27, 1776; Yale Univ.

31. Burr to Ogden, Mar. 7, 1777; Davis' *Burr*, I, 109.
32. Horatio Gates Papers, N. Y. Hist. Soc.
33. Putnam to Burr, July 14, 1777; Davis' *Burr*, I, 110.

CHAPTER V

1. Burr to Washington July 21, 1777; Davis' *Burr*, I, 111.
2. Davis' *Burr*, 112.
3. Statement, Lt. Robert Hunter; *ibid*, 116.
4. Statement, Judge George Gardner; *ibid*, 113–4; Statement, Lt. Hunter, *supra;* Putnam to Burr, Sept. 27, 1777, Force Transcripts, Lib. of Congress.
5. Col. Burr's *Orderly Books*, Whitemarsh, 1777; N. Y. Hist. Soc.
6. Col. Burr's *Orderly Books*, Valley Forge, 1778; N. Y. Hist. Soc.
7. MSS. Letter, Burr to Lord Stirling, Apr. 10, 1778; Princeton Univ.
8. Stirling to Burr, July 4, 1778; Davis' *Burr*, I, 129.
9. Benson to Burr, Aug. 2, 1778; *ibid*, 131–2.
10. Stirling to Burr, July 4, 1778, *supra*.
11. W. C. Ford, *Some Papers of Aaron Burr*, 39.
12. MSS. Letter, Commissioners for conspiracies to Col. John Fisher, Sept. 7, 1778; Emmett Coll., N. Y. Pub. Lib.
13. Lee to Burr, Oct. 1778; MSS. Letter, Pa. Hist. Soc.
14. Burr to Washington, Oct. 24, 1778; Davis' *Burr*, I, 136–7.
15. Washington to Burr, Oct. 26, 1778; *ibid*, 137.
16. MSS. Letter, McDougall to Parsons, Jan. 9, 1779; McDougall Papers, N. Y. Hist. Soc.
17. Burr to McDougall, Jan. 13, 1779; Davis' *Burr*, I, 142–3.
18. McDougall to Burr, Jan. 15, 1779; *ibid*, 145.
19. Burr to McDougall, Jan. 12, 1779; *ibid*, 140.
20. Same to same, McDougall Papers, N. Y. Hist. Soc.
21. Burr's *Orderly Books;* N. Y. Hist. Soc.
22. Statement of Samuel Young; Davis' *Burr*, I, 158–66.
23. Washington to Burr; *ibid*, 168.
24. Patterson to Burr, Mar. 18, 1779; *ibid*, 170.
25. Hull to Burr, May 29, 1779; W. C. Ford, *Some Papers of Aaron Burr*, 48–9.
26. Davis' *Burr*, I, 172.
27. Ezra Stiles, *Diary*, II, 351.
28. *Ibid*.

CHAPTER VI

1. Monroe to Mrs. Prevost, Nov. 8, 1778; Davis' *Burr*, I, 185–6.
2. Washington to Mrs. Prevost, May 19, 1779; *ibid*, 186.
3. See p. 60.
4. Patterson to Burr, Sept. 29, 1779; Davis' *Burr*, I, 187–8.
5. Troup to Burr, Jan. 16, 1780; *ibid*, 188–91.
6. Burr to Patterson; *ibid*, 193–4.
7. Troup to Burr, Feb. 29, 1780; *ibid*, 194–7.
8. Troup to Burr, June 27, 1780; *ibid*, 204–5.
9. Burr to Alden, Feb. 15, 1781; *ibid*, 221–2.
10. Peter Colt to Burr, July 7, 1780; *ibid*, 206.
11. Smith to Burr, Mar. 1, 1781; *ibid*, 223.
12. Theodosia Prevost to Burr, May, 1781; *ibid*, 226–7.
13. Same to same, Feb. 12, 1781; *ibid*, 224–5.

14. Same to Tapping Reeve, May 29, 1781; Tapping Reeve Papers, Yale Univ.

15. Theodosia Prevost to Burr, Sept. 11, 1781; Davis' *Burr*, I, 228.

16. Burr to Morris, Oct. 21, 1781; *ibid*, 231-2.

17. Burr to Mrs. Prevost, Dec. 6, 1781; *ibid*, 234.

18. *Ibid*, 234-5.

19. Burr to Mrs. Prevost, Dec. 23, 1781; *ibid*, 241-3.

20. Marriage Certificate; *Some Papers of Aaron Burr*, W. C. Ford, ed., 52.

21. MSS. Letter, undated, copy in Princeton Univ. Archives.

22. Burr to an uncle, Nov. 1783; Wandell and Minnigerode, *Burr*, I, 102.

23. Aug. 19, 1783, Tapping Reeve Papers; Yale Univ.

24. MSS. Letter, Burr to Barnard Gratz, June 21, 1785; Pa. Hist. Soc. "Yesterday Mrs. Burr presented me another Daughter, and is as well as can be expected." This unpublished letter has been overlooked by previous biographers, and settles definitively the long controversy over Burr's second child.

25. Mar. 22, 1784; Davis' *Burr*, I, 247-8.

26. Oct. 29, 1784; *ibid*, 248.

27. MSS. Letter, undated; Tapping Reeve Papers, Yale Univ.

28. MSS. Letter, May 1, 1786; *ibid*.

29. Hobart to Burr, June 17. 1783; Pa. Hist. Soc.

CHAPTER VII

1. N. Y. State Assembly Journal, Session Oct. 12, 1784.

2. *Ibid*, Session Jan. 27, 1785; 77-9.

3. *Ibid*, Session Jan. 1785; 53, 64, 76, 77.

4. *Life of Hamilton*, H. J. Ford, 331.

5. MSS. Docket of Cases; N. Y. Hist. Soc.

6. MSS. Letter, Jan. 12, 1790; N. J. Hist. Soc.

7. *Greene* Folio Vol., Case I; N. Y. Hist. Soc.

8. *De Peyster Papers*, Vol. I, III; *ibid*.

9. *Ibid*, Vol. VIII.

10. Parton's *Burr*, 154.

11. Davis' *Burr*, II, 14.

12. *Ibid*.

13. MSS. Brief of Law Suit re Title of Wayawanda Patent; N. Y. Pub. Lib.

14. Parton's *Burr*, 152.

15. *Ibid*.

16. *Travels . . . in the U. S. A.*, J. Davis, 24-5. Nevertheless this *was* the language of panegyric. Davis had come to America in 1798 to seek his fortune with a translation of Bonaparte's *Campaign in Italy*. Burr sought him out, opened his house, table, purse and library to the young poetaster. His accounts of his Travels are full of airy flights of fancy and the poetic touch, and are famous for his misleading eye-witness account of Jefferson's inauguration.

17. Apr. 1785; Davis' *Burr*, I, 253.

18. Apr. 1785; *ibid*.

19. May 1785; *ibid*, 256-7.

20. Aug. 28, 1785; *ibid*, 269.

21. Aug. 29, 1785; *ibid*, 270.

22. Nov. 1787; *ibid*, 279.

23. Maunsell to Mrs. Watkins, Dec. 14, 1783; *My Forefathers*, A. M. Bradhurst, 40.

24. *Ibid*, 116. *Cf.* Wandell and Minnigerode, *Burr*, I, 141.

25. Maunsell to Miss Watkins, *ca.* spring, 1791; *My Forefathers*, A. M. Bradhurst, 117.

26. Burr to Mrs. Burr, June 1791; Wandell and Minnigerode, *Burr*, I, 112.

CHAPTER VIII

1. *A Political Hist. of N. Y.*, D. S. Alexander, I, 15.

2. Parton's *Burr*, 169.

3. Davis' *Burr*, I, 286.

4. *Hist of Polit. Parties in N. Y.*, J. D. Hammond, I, 39.

5. Davis' *Burr*, I, 329.

6. *Hist. of Polit. Parties in N. Y.*, J. D. Hammond, I, 56–61.

7. See Wandel and Minnigerode, *Burr*, I, 110; Davis' *Burr*, I, 291 *et seq.*

8. *Travels . . . in the U. S. A.*, J. Davis, 25.

9. Schuyler to Hamilton, Jan. 29, 1792; Hamilton, *Works* (J. C. Hamilton, ed.) , V, 494.

CHAPTER IX

1. July 23, 1791; Davis' *Burr*, I, 298.

2. Burr to Mrs. Burr, Oct. 30, 1791; *ibid*, 304.

3. Same to same, Dec. 15, 1791; *ibid*, 312.

4. *Travels . . . in the U. S. A.*, J. Davis, 25. His account, however, cannot be considered as impartial. Burr was his patron.

5. Annals of Congress (Gales & Seaton) , III, 15.

6. *Ibid*, 15, 26, 30, 50, 90, 104, 110.

7. *Ibid*, 638.

8. Feb. 19, 1792; Davis' *Burr*, I, 315.

9. Jefferson to Burr; *ibid*, 331.

10. Schuyler to Hamilton, Jan. 29, 1792; Hamilton, *Works* (J. C. Hamilton, ed.) , V, 492–4.

11. Isaac Ledyard to Hamilton, Feb. 1, 1792; *ibid*, 494–5.

12. *Hist. of Polit. Parties in N. Y.*, J. D. Hammond, I, 56.

13. Davis' *Burr*, I, 354–5.

14. Burr's opinion; *ibid*, 339–41.

15. Statement of Canvassers; *ibid*, 335–6.

16. *Ibid*, 338, 341.

17. Hunt *vs.* Burrill, 5 John R. 137.

18. Burr to Tapping Reeve, undated; Tapping Reeve Papers, Yale Univ.

19. Burr to James Monroe, Sept. 10, 1792; Monroe Papers, Lib. of Congress.

20. Burr to Jacob De Lamater, June 15, 1792; Davis' *Burr*, I, 357.

CHAPTER X

1. Dr. Benjamin Rush to Burr, Sept. 24, 1792; Davis' *Burr*, I, 316–7.

2. MSS. Letter in cipher, Theodore Sedgwick to Burr, Sept. 9, 1791; Pa. Hist. Soc.

3. King to Hamilton, Sept. 17, 1792; Hamilton, *Works*, V, 526.

4. MSS. Letter, Hamilton to Washington, Sept. 23, 1792; Pa. Hist. Soc.

5. Hamilton to ——, Sept. 21, 1792; Hamilton, *Works*, V, 527.

6. Hamilton to ——, Sept. 26, 1792; *ibid*, 529.

7. Hamilton to Steele, Oct. 15, 1792; *ibid*, 535.

8. Same to King, Sept. 23, 1792; *ibid*, 528.

9. MSS. Letter, John Beckley to Madison, Oct. 17, 1792; James Madison Papers, N. Y. Pub. Lib.

10. Abigail Adams to Mrs. Shaw, Sept. 27, 1789; *Letters of A. Adams* (C. F. Adams, ed.) , 399–400.

11. Same to Brand-Hollis, Sept. 6, 1790; *ibid*, 402–3.

12. Same to Mrs. Smith, Nov. 21, 1790; *ibid*, 405.

13. *Travels . . . in the U. S. A.*, J. Davis, 26.

14. MSS. Letter, Burr to Peter Van Gaasbeck, June 21, 1795; possession of Edward Coykendall.

15. *Ibid*, same date.

16. For the essential data on Vanderlyn, I am indebted to a manuscript *Biographical Sketch of John Vanderlyn*, by Robert Gossman, deposited with the N. Y. Hist. Soc.

17. Burr to Marinus Willett, Dec. 9, ——; Burr MSS., N. Y. Hist. Soc.

18. Burr to ——, Feb. 27, 1796; *ibid*.

19. Troup to King, Jan. 20, 1797; Rufus King Papers, *ibid*.

20. Memo. of Acct., undated, Lamb Papers, *ibid*.

21. Lamb Papers, *ibid*.

22. Deed of Sale, Burr to Sir John Temple; Burr MSS., *ibid*.

23. *The Golden Earth*, Arthur Pound, 271–3.

24. June 7, 1797; Burr MSS., N. Y. Pub. Lib.

25. Jan. 12, 1798; Lamb Papers, N. Y. Hist. Soc.

26. Burr to Lamb, May 6, 1799; Harison to Burr, May 6, 1799; *ibid*.

27. Burr to Mrs. Burr, Feb. 15, 1793; Davis' *Burr*, I, 362.

28. Same to same, Feb. 16, 1793; *ibid*, 363.

29. Same to same, July 17, 1791; *ibid*, 297.

30. Mrs. Burr to Burr, July 2, 1791; *ibid*, 292–4.

31. Same to same, July 23, 1791; *ibid*, 298.

32. Burr to Mrs. Burr, Dec. 4, 1791; *ibid*, 308–10.

33. Same to same, Feb. 8, 1793; *ibid*, 361–2.

34. MSS. Letter, Burr to Theo Burr, Jan. 2, 1792; Pa. Hist. Soc.

35. Burr to Theo, Feb. 24, 1793; Davis' *Burr*, I, 365.

36. Same to same, Dec. 16, 1793; *ibid*, 366–7.

37. Same to same, Jan. 23, 1797; *ibid*, 395.

38. *Travels . . . in the U. S. A.*, J. Davis, 26

39. Burr to Theo, Jan. 4, 1799; Davis' *Burr*, I, 396.

CHAPTER XI

1. MSS. Letter, Burr to Nicholson, July 16, 1793; Pa. Hist. Soc.

2. Annals of Congress, IV, 32, 33.

3. *Ibid*, 46–7.

4. *Ibid*, 58.

5. *Ibid*, 78, 79.

6. *Ibid*, 90.

7. *John Jay*, Frank Monaghan, 367; Davis' *Burr*, I, 408.

8. Annals of Congress, IV, 116, 120.

9. *Life . . . of Manasseh Cutler*, W. P. Cutler, I, 522.

10. *Memoirs of the Administrations of Washington and Adams* (G. Gibbs, ed.) , I, 379–80.

11. Davis' *Burr*, I, 408–9.

12. *Administrations of Washington and Adams* (G. Gibbs, ed.) , II, 24.

13. Annals of Congress, IV, 794.

14. *Ibid*, 840, 843.

15. Annals of Congress, *Senate Executive Journal*, IV, 860–1.

16. June 29, 1795, Adams' *Gallatin*, 151.

17. Annals of Congress, *Senate Executive Journal*, IV, 862–3.

18. MSS. Letter, Burr to Monroe, July 5, 1795; Monroe Papers, Lib. of Congress.

19. Parton's *Jackson*, I, 173.

20. Annals of Congress, V, 99.

21. MSS. Letter, Madison Papers, N. Y. Pub. Lib.

22. Burr to Monroe, Sept. 6, 1796; Monroe Papers, Lib. of Congress.

23. Williamson to McHenry, Oct. 20, 1796; *Life of McHenry*, Steiner, 200.

24. Burr Misc. MSS., N. Y. Pub. Lib.

25. Parton's *Burr*, 198.

CHAPTER XII

1. Parton's *Burr*, 232.

2. Correspondence between Hamilton and Monroe, Monroe and Burr; quoted in American Book Prices Current, 1926–7; also Hamilton, *Works* (Lodge, ed.) , VII, 125.

3. Jefferson to Burr, June 17, 1797; Jefferson MSS., Lib. of Congress.

4. Burr to Jefferson, June 21, 1797; *ibid*.

5. Adams to James Lloyd, Feb. 17, 1815; John Adams, *Works*, X, 123–4.

6. Boston *Patriot*, 1809; *ibid*, IX, 294.

7. Troup to King, June 10, 1798; Rufus King Papers, N. Y. Hist. Soc.

8. Burr to Ebenezer Stevens, August 17, 1798; Stevens MSS., N. Y. Hist. Soc.

9. Same to same, August 8, 1798; *ibid*.

10. N. Y. State Assembly Journal, Session, Aug. 9, 1798; 8, 9, 23–30.

11. Troup to King, Oct. 2, 1798; Rufus King Papers, *supra*.

12. *Ibid; cf.* Albany *Centinel*, July 13, 1798.

13. N. Y. State Assembly Journal, Session, Jan. 2, 1799; 41 *et seq*.

14. *Ibid*, 241; *cf. Hist. of Polit. Parties in N. Y.*, Hammond, I, 122–4.

15. N. Y. State Assembly Journal, *supra*, 114–123.

16. For the data of the ensuing narrative I am chiefly indebted to a doctoral thesis by Paul D. Evans, entitled *The Holland Land Company*, appearing in 1924 in the Buffalo Historical Society Publications, XXIV. Mr. Evans had access to the original records of the Company in Holland. All references to such records are taken from his monograph.

17. MSS. Letter, Burr to John Nicholson, July 16, 1793; Pa. Hist. Soc.

18. MSS. Letter, same to same, Mar. 26, 1795; *ibid*.

19. Burr to ——, Oct. 6, 1799; Davis' *Burr*, I, 419.

20. *Laws of N. Y.*, Chap. 58, 19th Sess., April 11, 1796.

21. *Ibid*, Chap. 36, 20th Sess., Mar. 17, 1797.

22. Cazenove to P. & C. Van Eeghen, Feb. 22, 1798; Holland Co. Papers, possession of Van Eeghen & Co., Amsterdam.

23. Holland Co. Papers, possession of Van Eeghen & Co., Amsterdam.

24. *Ibid*.

25. Benson to Cazenove, Apr. 4, 1798; *ibid*.

26. Cazenove to P. & C. Van Eeghen, May 21, 1798; *ibid*.

27. Troup to King, Sept. 2, 1799; Rufus King Papers, *supra*.

28. Burr to ——, Oct. 6, 1799; Davis' *Burr*, I, 418–23.

29. *Memorial Hist. of N. Y. C.* (J. G. Wilson, ed.), II, 46.

30. *An Act of Incorporation of the Manhattan Company,* 1830; N. Y. Pub. Lib.

31. *Ibid.*

32. N. Y. State Assembly Journal, Session, 1799; 263.

33. Davis' *Burr,* I, 414.

34. Troup to King, Apr. 19, 1799; Rufus King Papers, *supra.*

35. See Parton's *Burr,* 238–9; Wandell and Minnigerode, *Burr,* I, 177–8.

36. Report of the Manhattan Committee, 1799; N. Y. Pub. Lib.

37. Burr's *Journal* (Bixby, ed.) I, 211.

38. *An Act of Incorporation of the Manhattan Company; supra.*

39. Troup to King, May 6, 1799; Rufus King Papers, *supra.*

40. Same to same, June 5, 1799; *ibid.* (Italics mine.)

CHAPTER XIII

1. See p. 165.

2. Jefferson, *Works* (Ford, ed.), X, 134–6, 154–9.

3. *Gallatin,* H. Adams, 232–4.

4. John Adams, *Works,* X, 125.

5. See Horatio Gates Papers, N. Y. Hist. Soc.

6. Davis' *Burr,* II, 58–9. See also *An Examination of the Charges against Aaron Burr,* by Aristides (Wm. P. Van Ness). Clinton, however, was to deny these allegations, which emerged as a result of a campaign of mutual recriminations, charges and countercharges.

7. *Commercial Advertiser,* Apr. 26, 1800. See also *Jefferson and Hamilton,* by Bowers.

8. *The History of Tammany Hall,* by Gustavus Myers.

9. *American Citizen,* July 18, 1809.

10. *The History of Tammany Hall,* Gustavus Myers, 15–16.

11. Davis' *Burr,* II, 16–17.

12. May 1, 1800; *Gallatin,* H. Adams, 237–8.

13. N. Y. *Spectator,* May 7, 10, 1800.

14. May 7, 1800; Hamilton, *Works,* VI, 438–40.

15. See p. 152.

16. The Correspondence and Public Papers of John Jay, IV, 271–3.

17. May 5, 1800; *Gallatin,* H. Adams, 239–40.

18. May 6, 1800; *ibid,* 240–1.

19. Nicholson to Gallatin, May 7, 1800; *Gallatin,* H. Adams, 242.

20. De Witt Clinton Papers, Columbia Univ.

21. Statement of James Nicholson, Dec. 26, 1803; De Witt Clinton Papers, Columbia Univ.

22. Gallatin to his wife, May 12, 1800; *Gallatin,* H. Adams, 243.

23. Hamilton, *Works,* VI, 440.

24. *Ibid,* 441.

25. Aug. 9, 1800; Rufus King Papers, *supra.*

26. Sept. 14, 1800; *ibid.*

27. Aug. 6, 1800; Hamilton, *Works,* VI, 453.

28. Aug. 10, 1800; *ibid,* 454.

29. Nov. 26, 1800; Burr Misc. MSS., N. Y. Pub. Lib.

30. Nov. 29, 1800; *ibid.*

31. Burr to P. Edwards (?), Nov. 20, 1800; *ibid.*

32. Date unknown, 1800; Madison, *Writings* (Congress Ed.), II, 160.

33. Oct. 21, 1800; *ibid,* 162.

CHAPTER XIV

1. Madison to Monroe, Nov. 10, 1800; Madison, *Writings* (Congress Ed.), II, 163.

2. Am. Hist. Rev., IV, 120.

3. Mass. Hist. Coll., *Seventh Series*, I, 80.

4. *Some Papers of Aaron Burr*, W. C. Ford, ed., 60–1.

5. Davis' *Burr*, II, 75.

6. Burr to Jefferson, Dec. 23, 1800; Jefferson MSS., Lib. of Cong. McMaster, in his *Hist. of the U. S.*, Vol. II, cites this letter by date, without, however, giving any inkling as to its contents.

7. Gouverneur Morris, *Diary* (A. C. Morris, ed.), II, 396–7.

8. Harper to Burr, Dec. 24, 1800; *Life of Matthew Lyon*, McLaughlin, 386.

9. Hamilton to Wolcott, Dec. 16, 1800; Hamilton, *Works*, VI, 486.

10. Gouverneur Morris, *Diary*, II, 397.

11. Sedgwick to Hamilton, Jan. 10, 1801; Hamilton, *Works*, VI, 511–14.

12. Troup to King, Dec. 31, 1800; Rufus King, *Works* (C. R. King, ed.), III, 358–9.

13. Parsons to Otis, Jan. 23, 1801; *Harrison Gray Otis*, S. E. Morison, I, 213–4.

14. Hamilton to Wolcott, Dec. 17, 1800; Hamilton, *Works*, VI, 487.

15. Hamilton to G. Morris, Dec. 26, 1800; *ibid*, 498–9.

16. Same to Bayard, Dec. 27, 1800; *ibid*, 499–500.

17. Same to same, Jan. 16, 1801; *ibid*, 419–24.

18. Jefferson to Madison, Dec. 19, 1800; Davis' *Burr*, II, 69–70.

19. Sewell to Otis, Dec. 29, 1800; *Otis*, S. E. Morison, I, 212.

20. McHenry to King, Jan. 2, 1801; Rufus King, *Works* (C. R. King, ed.), III, 362–3.

21. *Ibid.*

22. Jefferson, *Works* (Ford, ed.), IX, 166.

23. George Clinton to De Witt Clinton, Jan. 13, 1801; De Witt Clinton Papers, Columbia Univ.

24. Rodney to Nicholson, Jan. 3, 1801; Nicholson MSS., Lib. of Congress.

25. Madison to Jefferson, Jan. 10, 1801; Madison, *Writings* (Congress Ed.), II, 166–7.

26. MSS. Letter, Nicholson to a Constituent, Jan. 15, 1801; Pa. Hist. Soc.

27. Jefferson to Tench Coxe, Dec. 31, 1800; Jefferson, *Writings* (Monticello Ed.), X, 188.

28. Burr to Theodosia Alston, Feb. 17, 1801; Davis' *Burr*, II, 145.

29. Burr to Gallatin, Jan. 16, 1801; *Gallatin*, H. Adams, 245.

30. Livingston to Davis, Feb. 5, 1801; *Some Papers of Aaron Burr*, W. C. Ford, 64.

31. Gallatin to his wife, Jan. 15, 1801; *Gallatin*, H. Adams, 254.

32. Jefferson, *Writings* (*Anas*, Feb. 14 and Dec. 31, 1801– Monticello Ed.), I, 440, 442. There were many other rumors and charges which Jefferson was careful to set down in his *Anas*, for future publication. Such as reports from Edward Livingston anent attempts by Bayard of Delaware to tempt him to change his vote; of an offer to General Samuel Smith, Jefferson's political henchman, of the Secretaryship of the Navy, if he voted for Burr; of a proposal to Dr. Linn of New Jersey to make him Governor. (*Ibid*, I, 439–40). Even in 1804 Jefferson was still recording matters prejudicial to Burr. These *Anas*, however, are singularly unreliable. Jefferson, great man though he was, was not averse to certain small distortions of the truth in this private *Diary*, which he knew would some day reach the public eye. Livingston was to deny,

years later, when Jefferson's *Anas* were published, any recollection of having made such a report to Jefferson. General Samuel Smith, of Maryland, then a United States Senator, on Jan. 28, 1830, emphatically denied that any such proposition was ever made to him.

33. Jefferson to Burr, Feb. 1, 1801; Jefferson, *Writings* (Monticello Ed.), X, 193-4.

34. Burr to Jefferson, Feb. 12, 1801; Jefferson MSS., Lib. of Congress. Claude G. Bowers, in his *Jefferson and Hamilton*, p. 500, comments on the alleged fact that Burr had never responded to Jefferson's denouncement of the forgery, and deduces therefrom implications that are decidedly unfavorable to Burr. To same effect, see Chinard's *Jefferson* (1929), p. 371.

35. Boston *Centinel*, Jan. 28, 1801.

36. *Ibid*, Feb. 18, 1801.

37. N. Y. *Commercial Advertiser*, Jan. 17, 1801.

38. Conn. *Courant*, Feb. 11, 1801.

39. As given in a *Circular Letter* by Robert G. Harper to his Constituents, Feb. 24, 1801; *Papers of James A. Bayard* (Donnan, ed.), in Annual Report of the Amer. Hist. Assn., II, 132-7. McMaster, in his *Hist. of the U. S.*, II, 524, cites a different set of figures without quoting any authority. In his table, Jefferson had a majority of the individual votes.

40. John Randolph to St. George Tucker, Feb. 11, 1801; *Randolph*, W. C. Bruce, I, 168.

41. H. G. Otis to his wife, Feb. 11, 1801; *Otis*, Morison, I, 207-8.

42. Gallatin to his wife, Feb. 12, 1801; *Gallatin*, H. Adams, 260-1.

43. MSS. Letter, Uriah Tracy to Mr. Gould, Feb. 16, 1801; Pa. Hist. Soc.

44. Burr to Gallatin, Feb. 12, 1801; *Gallatin*, H. Adams, 246.

45. Jefferson, *Writings* (Monticello Ed.), X, 201-2.

46. David A. Ogden to Peter Irving, Nov. 24, 1802; N. Y. *Morning Chronicle*, Nov. 25, 1802.

47. Bayard to Hamilton, Mar. 8, 1801; Hamilton, *Works*, VI, 522-4.

48. Cooper to Morris, Feb. 13, 1801; Davis' *Burr*, II, 113.

49. MSS. Memorandum, Feb. 8, 1858; Van Buren Papers, Lib. of Congress. In connection with this controversy, the New York *Times*, Sept. 22, 1886, quoted an alleged letter from Burr to Peter Van Gaasbeck, Congressman from Orange County. The letter is undated, and was copied from the Rondout *Freeman*, Sept. 21, 1886. The *Freeman* alleged that the autograph letter had just been found in a bundle of old papers, and that this letter was positive evidence that Burr in fact had been intriguing to displace Jefferson. I have made every attempt to trace the original of this published letter, but without success. It seems to have disappeared from sight. On the face of it, if in truth Burr's autograph, the letter seems wholly incriminating. " From the returns in Pennsylvania," it reads, " it is certain that Adams cannot be elected. The President and Vice-President must therefore be taken from Jefferson, Pinckney and Burr. Six or seven votes for Burr in this State will make him President or Vice-President. You know, I suppose, that no distinction can be made by the Electors. They vote for two men without declaring the offices for which they intend them. You see how important and critical this is, and must therefore spare no pains. It will be surprising, indeed, if you, Addison Bivier, and others cannot influence Miller and Cantine so far as to induce them to do what is right. Burr must be spoken of, however, only as Vice-President for the present. This caution must not be neglected for cogent reasons, which will in due time be communicated. Somebody must confer with Miller and Cantine personally and without delay."

A little consideration, however, discloses innumerable inconsistencies in this alleged find. For one thing it is absurd to believe that Burr had to tutor Van Gaasbeck, a Congressman, in the method of electing a President. It is an all too obvious effort by the writer of the incriminating document to enlighten the *modern* reader. For another, Burr still did not know the returns from Pennsylvania on November 22nd or even on November 26, 1800. (See p. 185, *supra*.) On November 6th, however, New York had already chosen its Presidential Electors. Neither Miller nor Cantine was on the list of Electors. Hence it would have been futile to urge certain measures upon men who had nothing to do with the election one way or another. On this alone the letter must be pronounced a forgery. There are other minor inconsistencies as well. Such as the statement that Pinckney would overshadow Adams. At the time of the Pennsylvania vote Burr knew Adams to be in the lead. The statement that " six or seven votes for Burr in this State will make him President or Vice-President " does not make sense. New York had *twelve* Electors, and all twelve were already pledged to vote for Burr. The forger was very clumsy indeed.

50. Interrogatories of James A. Bayard, *in re* James Gillespie *vs* Abraham Smith, Apr. 3, 1806; Davis' *Burr*, II, 129–33.

51. Jefferson to Monroe, Feb. 15, 1801; *supra*.

52. Jefferson, *Writings* (Anas, Monticello Ed.), Apr. 15, 1806: I, 448–53.

53. Interrogatories of Gen. Samuel Smith, *in re* Gillespie *vs* Smith, Apr. 15, 1806; Davis' *Burr*, II, 133–7.

54. Papers of James A. Bayard (Donnan, ed.), *supra*, 126.

55. *Hist. of the U. S.*, H. Adams, I, 294–5.

56. Troup to King, May 27, 1801; Rufus King, *Works* (C. R. King, ed.), III, 459–60.

CHAPTER XV

1. *Hist. of the U. S.*, H. Adams, I, 207.

2. May 17, 1801; Jefferson, *Works* (Ford, ed.), VIII, 67–70.

3. *Constitutional History of New York*, Chas. Z. Lincoln, I, 600 *et seq.*

4. See Letter from Burr to Wm. Edgar, Nov. 7, 1801; William Edgar Photostats, N. Y. Pub. Lib.

5. Amer. Hist. Rev., III, 290.

6. Jefferson, *Works* (Ford, ed.), IX, 254–5.

7. Burr to Gallatin, June 28, 1801; *Gallatin*, H. Adams, 283.

8. Gallatin to Jefferson, Sept. 12, 1801; Gallatin, *Writings* (Adams, ed.), I, 47–8.

9. Same to same, Sept. 14, 1801; *ibid*, 51–3.

10. Jefferson to Gallatin, Sept. 18, 1801; *ibid*, 54.

11. Burr to Gallatin; *Gallatin*, H. Adams, 289.

12. Jefferson to Burr, Nov. 18, 1801; Jefferson MSS., Lib. of Congress.

13. MSS. Letter, Osgood to Madison, Apr. 24, 1801; Madison Papers, *ibid*.

14. William Edgar Photostats, N. Y. Pub. Lib.

15. *Hist. of the U. S.*, H. Adams, I, 332.

16. Truxton to Burr, Feb. 14, 1802; *Some Papers of Aaron Burr*, W. C. Ford, 73–4.

17. T. Sedgwick to King, Feb. 20, 1802; Rufus King, *Works* (C. R. King, ed.), IV, 74.

18. MSS. Letter, Emmett Collection, N. Y. Pub. Lib.

19. Burr to Edgar, Nov. 18, 1801; William Edgar Photostats, *ibid*.

20. Same to same, Nov. 7, 1801; *ibid*.

21. Richmond *Examiner*, Feb. 6, 1801.

22. Bayard to Bassett, Jan. 25, 1802; Papers of James A. Bayard (Donnan, ed.), 147.

23. *Annals of Congress*, XI, 147.

24. Morris to R. Livingston, Aug. 21, 1802; Morris, *Diary and Letters*, II, 426.

25. *Annals of Congress*, XI, 148–9.

26. *Ibid*, 150. Burr devoted a good deal of thought to this bill. He had sought the advice of his Republican friends who were also Constitutional lawyers. To Joseph Alston he wrote, Feb. 2, 1802, " Of the constitutionality of repealing the law I have no doubt, but the equity and expediency of depriving the twenty-six judges of office and pay is not quite so obvious. Read the Constitution, and . . . write me how you view the thing." Davis' *Burr*, II, 171. To the same effect, see communication addressed to Barnabas Biddle, *ibid*, 169, as well as congratulatory letters from A. J. Dallas and Nathaniel Miles, *ibid*, 81, 83–4. Pierpont Edwards sent him, in response to an inquiry, a detailed series of amendments which he conceived necessary to the old system. See unpublished letter, Burr to Edwards, Mar. 12, 1802, Pa. Hist. Soc.

27. *Annals of Congress*, XI, 154, 160, 183.

28. *Life of Marshall*, Beveridge, III, 68, *footnote*.

29. Cited in newspaper clipping, name missing, Feb. 1802; N. Y. Pub. Lib.

30. Bayard to Hamilton, Apr. 12, 1802; Hamilton, *Works* (Hamilton, ed.) , VI, 539.

31. Hamilton to G. Morris, Mar. 4, 1802; Hamilton, *Works* (Lodge, ed.) , X, 427–8. But Burr's version of the incident, according to John P. Van Ness, made the whole affair a mere impromptu accident. In an unpublished letter to his brother, Van Ness informed him that " Mr. Townsend was to explain the transaction of the federal Dinner. Burr did not dine with the federalists, but was politely invited to dine with a party of their Gentlemen on that day which he declined. After dinner, however, he went into their Room, and to his astonishment found the whole corps there celebrating Washington's birthday; he immediately discovered the object of the business, not knowing it before, and after having sat a moment or two retired: — In the mean time, however, they called on him for a Toast — and he gave the one you mention." (John P. to William P. Van Ness, Apr. 2, 1802; Van Ness Papers, N. Y. Pub. Lib.) The attempted explanation makes Burr more naive in his conduct than can readily be believed.

32. *A Correct Statement*, etc., John Wood, 15.

33. Davis' *Burr*, II, 87–9.

34. *A Correct Statement*, etc., John Wood (1802) .

35. N. Y. *Evening Post*, May 26, 1802.

36. Burr to Alston, July 3, 1802; Davis' *Burr*, II, 205.

37. N. Y. *Evening Post*, Aug. 9, 1802.

38. *American Citizen*, Aug. 4, 1802.

39. N. Y. *Evening Post*, Aug. 10, 1802.

40. N. Y. *Chronicle-Express*, Nov. 25, 1802, May 2, 1803, Feb. 9, 1804.

41. Mass. Hist. Soc. Proc., 1907–8, *Third Series*, I, 46–51.

42. *Ibid*, 58.

43. *Nine Letters*, etc., Cheetham (1803) , 41.

44. *Ibid*, 90.

45. *An Examination*, etc., Aristides.

46. Dec. 11, 1803; De Witt Clinton Papers, Columbia Univ.

47. MSS. Letters between Clinton and Ward & Gould; *ibid*.

48. Jefferson to De Witt Clinton, Oct. 6, 1804; De Witt Clinton Papers, *supra*.

49. W. C. Nicholas to De Witt Clinton, Aug. 13, 1802; *ibid*.

50. Gallatin to Jefferson, Sept. 21, 1802; Gallatin, *Writings*, I, 101.

51. MSS. Letter, Van Ness to Van Buren, Feb. 22, 1804; Van Buren Papers, Lib. of Congress.

52. Van Buren to Van Ness, Mar. 13, 1804; *ibid.*

CHAPTER XVI

1. Theodosia Alston to Burr, June 9, 1803; Davis' *Burr*, II, 227.

2. Same to same, June 14, 1803; *ibid*, 232.

3. Plumer to Judge Smith, Feb. 21, 1803; *Life of Wm. Plumer*, Wm. Plumer, Jr., 256–7.

4. Bloomfield to Burr, Apr. 16, 1803; Princeton Univ.

5. Pres. Samuel S. Smith to same, Jan. 2, 1804; *ibid.*

6. Jefferson, *Writings* (*Anas*, Monticello Ed.) , Jan. 26, 1804; I, 443–8.

7. Nov. 26, 1803; Jefferson MSS., Lib. of Congress.

8. Jefferson, *Writings* (Ford, ed.) , VIII, 282.

9. *Anas*. See note 6, *supra.*

10. Jefferson to Gideon Granger, Mar. 9, 1814; Jefferson, *Writings* (Monticello Ed.) , XIV, 113.

11. *Pol. Hist. of N. Y.*, J. D. Hammond, I, 202–4.

12. Albany *Morning Chronicle*, Feb. 17, 1804; also Hamilton, *Works* (Lodge, ed.) , VII, 851.

13. *Pol. Hist. of N. Y.*, J. D. Hammond, I, 208.

14. Plumer to Jeremiah Smith, Feb. 10, 1804, and Feb. 28, 1804; Plumer MSS., Lib. of Congress.

15. Jan. 29, 1804; *New England Federalism*, H. Adams, 341.

16. Plumer, *Memorandum of Proceedings* (E. S. Brown, ed.), 517–8.

17. Mar. 4, 1804; *New England Federalism*, H. Adams, 351–2.

18. Mar. 11, 1804; *ibid*, 354–6.

19. *Hist. of the Republic of the U. S.*, J. C. Hamilton, VII, 781 *et seq.* See also Rufus King, *Works*, IV, 356.

20. Campaign Poster, 1804, signed *Sylphid*, N. Y. Pub. Lib. See also, for a more moderate tone, a Broadside, signed *A Republican and no Burrite*, in the Emmett Coll., *ibid.* The worst of all is merely entitled *Burr*, a copy of which is in the N. Y. Hist. Soc.

CHAPTER XVII

1. Charles Biddle, *Autobiography*, 305.

2. Albany *Register*, Apr. 24, 1804.

3. *Ibid.*

4. The famous correspondence leading up to the duel may be found in various sources. Davis' *Burr*, II, 294 *et seq.* gives it complete, together with Van Ness's notes of his conversations with Hamilton. It has also been published separately, culled from the columns of the *Evening Post*, by William Coleman, under the title, *The Death of Hamilton.*

5. Charles Biddle, *Autobiography*, 303.

6. Burr to Theo, June 24, 1804; Davis' *Burr*, II, 290.

7. Same to same, July 10, 1804; *ibid*, 322–3.

8. Burr to Alston, July 10, 1804; *ibid*, 324–6.

9. Hamilton's Statement; *ibid*, 318–21.

10. Van Ness to Biddle; Biddle, *Autobiography*, 304–5; see also, Davis' *Burr*, II, 309–10.

11. Gouverneur Morris, *Diary and Letters*, II, 456–7.

12. A. M. Bradhurst, in *My Forefathers*, p. 65, tells of a family tradition to the effect that, prior to the Hamilton duel, Burr had fought a secret duel

with Samuel Bradhurst, in which Bradhurst had received a sword cut. There exists no corroborating evidence, and the story must accordingly be treated with marked reservations.

13. Randolph to Nicholson; Nicholson MSS., Lib. of Congress.

14. Davis' *Burr*, II, 327-8.

15. Burr to Theo, July 20, 1804; *ibid*, 328.

16. Burr to Alston, July 29, 1804; *ibid*, 328-9.

17. Davis' *Burr*, II, 329-30.

18. Aug. 11, 1804; *ibid*, 332.

19. Davis' *Burr*, II, 171.

20. *Ibid*, 348.

21. *Ibid*, 349.

22. *Ibid*, 351-2.

23. Burr to Alston, Dec. 15, 1804; *ibid*, 353; John Quincy Adams, *Memoirs* (C. F. Adams, ed.) , I, 317-8.

24. Charles Biddle, *Autobiography*, 308.

25. Jan. 28, 1805; Davis' *Burr*, II, 355.

26. MSS. Letter, Jan. 31, 1805; Pa. Hist. Soc.

CHAPTER XVIII

1. Plumer to Daniel Treadwell, Nov. 6, 1804; Plumer MSS., Lib. of Congress.

2. Plumer to Jeremiah Smith, Dec. 6, 1804; *ibid*.

3. Cutler to Dr. Torrey, Mar. 13, 1804; *Life . . . of Manasseh Cutler*, by W. P. and J. P. Cutler, I, 166.

4. Plumer to Thompson; Plumer MSS., Lib. of Congress.

5. Plumer, *Memorandum of Proceedings* (E. S. Brown, ed.) , Nov. 26, 1804; 203-4.

6. Gideon Granger wrote Judge Rufus Easton on Mar. 16, 1805 that " Doctor Browne of New York is appointed Secretary upon the special and single recommendation of Aaron Burr." Cited in *The Bench and Bar of Missouri*, by W. V. N. Bay, 598.

7. Plumer, *Memorandum of Proceedings*, 220-1.

8. Plumer to Sheafe, Jan. 9, 1805; Plumer MSS., Lib. of Congress.

9. Annals of Congress, *Trial of Samuel Chase*, reported by Smith and Lloyd, XIV, 100.

10. Mar. 1, 1805; *Life . . . of Cutler*, W. P. and J. P. Cutler, I, 193.

11. Plumer, *Memorandum of Proceedings*, 239, 278, 282-3, 285.

12. *Ibid*, 310.

13. Washington *Federalist*, Mar. 13, 1805.

14. Annals of Congress, XIV, 71. See also Washington *Federalist, supra;* John Quincy Adams, *Memoirs* (C. F. Adams, ed.) , I, 365-7; Plumer to his wife, Mar. 2, 1805, Plumer MSS., Lib. of Congress.

15. John Quincy Adams, *Memoirs, supra*, I, 367.

16. Annals of Congress, XIV, 68, 1211.

17. Mar. 10, 1805; Plumer MSS., Lib. of Congress.

CHAPTER XIX

1. *Life of Henry Clay*, Prentice, 77.

2. Jefferson to Claiborne, July 13, 1801; Jefferson MSS., Lib. of Congress.

3. See p. 258.

4. Dec. 22, 1802; cited in *Hist. of the U. S.*, Henry Adams, I, 429.

5. *Hist. of the U. S.*, Adams, II, 58.

6. *Ibid*, 61.

7. Nov. 15, 1803; Amer. State Papers, II, 573.

8. Merry to Hawkesbury, Mar. 1, 1804; Adams Transcripts, Lib. of Congress.

9. Miranda to Hamilton, Oct. 19, 1798; Davis' *Burr*, II, 377.

10. Aug. 22, 1798; Hamilton, *Works*, VI, 347–8.

11. June 27, 1799; *ibid*, V, 283–4.

12. Jan. 22, 1806; Madison MSS., State Dept. Archives.

13. Biddle, *Autobiography*, 314.

14. Burr to Jeremy Bentham, Oct. 16, 1811; Burr, *Journal* (Davis, ed.), II, 254–5.

15. *Some Papers of Aaron Burr*, W. C. Ford, 82–3.

16. See unpublished letter, Burr to Williamson, Oct. 19, 1798; N. Y. Hist. Soc.

17. Charles Williamson was of noble English birth, brother to Baron Balgray, protégé of Lord Melville, First Lord of the Admiralty, and intimate friend of General Hope.

18. *Life of Marshall*, III, 287.

19. Merry to Lord Harrowby, Aug. 6, 1804; Adams Transcripts, Library of Congress. These transcripts were made by Henry Adams from the original documents in the archives of the British, French and Spanish Foreign offices. Many of them are quoted in Adams' *History of the United States*.

20. See the article by I. J. Cox, entitled *Hispanic-American Phases of the "Burr Conspiracy,"* in the *Hispanic American Historical Review*, XII, No. 2, 1932, pp. 145–75.

21. Williamson to Melville, Oct. 6, 1804; *Hisp. Amer. Hist. Rev., supra*, 151.

22. *Ibid*, 151.

23. *Ibid*, 150.

24. Williamson to Melville, Feb. 19, 1805; *ibid*, 152.

25. *Hisp. Amer. Hist. Rev.*, Cox, *supra*, 166.

26. Merry to Harrowby, Mar. 29, 1805 (No. 14) ; Adams Transcripts, Lib. of Congress.

27. Same to same, Mar. 29, 1805 (No. 15) ; *ibid*.

28. May 23, 1805; *Hisp. Amer. Hist. Rev.*, Cox, *supra*, 157.

29. Turreau to Talleyrand, Mar. 9, 1805; Adams Transcripts.

30. Navarro to King of Spain, Apr. 30, 1789. See *Wilkinson and the Beginnings of the Spanish Conspiracy*, by W. L. Shepherd, in *American Historical Review*, IX, (1904), 494. This monograph is based on source material in the various Spanish archives.

31. *Ibid*, 496–503. For the text of the memorial, or " Reflections," see *Louisiana Under the Rule of Spain*, J. M. Robertson, II, 325–47, where, however, it is wrongly attributed to Folch. Folch had merely translated the " Reflections " into Spanish for home consumption, and had certified to its accurate rendition.

32. Cited by W. L. Shepherd, in *Amer. Hist. Rev.*, IX, (1904), 765.

33. McHenry to Hamilton, June 27, 1799; Hamilton, *Works*, V, 282–3.

34. Hamilton to Washington, June 15, 1799; *ibid*, 270–1.

35. *Proofs of the Corruption of Gen. James Wilkinson*, etc., Daniel Clark, App., 33.

36. *Ibid*, App., 25; also *General Wilkinson and His Later Intrigues with the Spaniards*, by I. J. Cox, in *Amer. Hist. Rev.* XIX (1914), 794–812, based on Spanish documents in *Papeles de Cuba*.

37. *Report of the Committee Appointed to Inquire into the Conduct of Brig. Gen. J. Wilkinson*, May 1, 1810.

38. Folch was correct in his prophecy. The Cuban archives remained in the control of Spain until the end of the century. It was the second decade of the twentieth century before Professor I. J. Cox discovered the pertinent documents which proved conclusively Wilkinson's infamy. See *Amer. Hist. Rev.*, XIX (1914), 807–8.

CHAPTER XX

1. Davis' *Burr*, II, 366–7.

2. Mar. 22, 1805; *ibid*, 365.

3. Burr to Theo, Apr. 30, 1805; *ibid*, 368.

4. Feb. 25, 1811; Wilkinson, *Memoirs*, II, App., LXVIII.

5. See the Blennerhassett Papers (Wm. H. Safford, ed.) for the life and career of Harman Blennerhassett.

6. Laws of the Indiana Territory, 1801–1806, pp. 94–108.

7. For complete details of this interesting episode see *The Burr Conspiracy in Indiana*, by I. J. Cox, in the *Indiana Mag. of Hist.*, XXV (1929), No. 4.

8. May 28, 1805; Clark's *Proofs of the Corruption*, etc., App., 158.

9. Mar., 1807; Davis' *Burr*, II, 380.

10. Davis' *Burr*, II, 370.

11. *Ibid*.

12. Wilkinson, *Memoirs*, II, App., No. LXXI.

13. Mar. 18, 1805; June 9, 1805; *Audienca de Santo Domingo*, cited in *Amer. Hist. Rev.*, XIX, *supra*, 801.

14. Davis' *Burr*, II, 371.

15. McCaleb argues that Burr met only Americans in New Orleans, that he could not possibly have had any dealings with the Creoles, who hated the American interlopers and wished for independence. But the Ursuline nuns were Creoles; so, too, were the Catholic authorities with whom he consorted, and who entered into his schemes. Mexican freedom was as dear to the Creole heart as to the American, and they cared little for Spanish rule. Nor were the Deputies with whom Burr had become so intimate in Washington of American lineage.

16. Burr to Theo; Davis' *Burr*, II, 373.

17. Davis' *Burr*, II, 372.

18. Testimony, Major Bruff; *Trial of Aaron Burr*, Carpenter, III, 340, 346. It should be noted that it was *Burr* who called him as a witness. Furthermore, he was obviously animated by a hatred of Wilkinson, who had court-martialed him for insubordination, though the conviction had been reversed.

19. *West Florida Controversy*, Cox, 189; *Aaron Burr Conspiracy*, McCaleb, 32–3.

20. Wilkinson, *Memoirs*, II, App., XXXIII.

21. *Ibid*, LXXXVI.

22. Clark's *Proofs of the Corruption*, etc., App., 141–2.

23. Wilkinson, *Memoirs*, II, 303.

24. Copied by the Lexington *Gazette*, and quoted in turn by the *Kentucky Palladium*, Sept. 7, 1805, which used them as the base for a structure of charges and insinuations all its own.

25. Merry to Mulgrave, Aug. 4, 1805; Adams Transcripts, *supra*.

26. Same to same, Nov. 25, 1805; *ibid*.

27. Yrujo to Cevallos, Aug. 5, 1805; Spanish Archives.

28. MSS. Cuban Papers, Lib. of Congress; quoted in *Amer. Hist. Rev.*, X, 837-40.

29. Blennerhassett Papers (W. H. Safford, ed.), 115-6.

30. *Ibid*, 116-9.

31. Yrujo to Cevallos, Dec. 5, 1805; Adams Transcripts, *supra*.

32. Dec. 12, 1806; Wilkinson, *Memoirs*, II, App. LXXXIV.

33. Yrujo to Cevallos, Jan. 1, 1806; Adams Transcripts, *supra*.

34. Same to same, Feb. 13, 1806; Spanish Archives, cited by McCaleb.

35. Cevallos to Yrujo, Feb. 3, 1806; *ibid*.

36. Plumer, *Memorandum of Proceedings*, 436.

37. Jefferson, *Writings*, Apr. 15, 1806 (*Anas*, Monticello Ed.), I, 448 *et seq*.

38. Apr. 15, 1806; Blennerhassett Papers, 119-21. It has been claimed that Burr had never met Blennerhassett before August, 1806. This letter shows a definite personal acquaintance of long standing.

39. *Trials of Aaron Burr*, reported by David Robertson, I, 473 *et seq*.

40. Eaton's deposition, Jan. 26, 1807; *Life of Eaton*, Prentiss, 396-403. See also *Trial of Aaron Burr*, Carpenter, III, 233-4.

41. *Trials of Aaron Burr*, Robertson, I, 474-8.

42. *Ibid*, 479, 483-4.

43. Plumer, *Memorandum of Proceedings*, 583.

44. *Trials of Aaron Burr*, Robertson, I, 486-90.

45. Biddle, *Autobiography*, 313-4.

46. Wilkinson, *Memoirs*, II, App., LXXXIII.

47. Yrujo to Cevallos, May 14, 1806; Adams Transcripts, *supra*.

48. Same to same, June 9, 1806; *ibid*.

49. Cevallos to Yrujo, Mar. 28, 1806, July 12, 1806; *ibid*.

50. Merry to Fox, Nov. 2, 1806; *ibid*.

CHAPTER XXI

1. Parton's *Jackson*, I, 313-4.

2. Viana to Cordero, June 3, 1806; Bexar Archives, cited in *Aaron Burr Conspiracy*, McCaleb, 64.

3. *Trials of Aaron Burr*, Robertson, I, 328-9.

4. *Trial of Aaron Burr*, Carpenter, III, App. L.

5. *Ibid*, 243-4, 249, 252.

6. *Ibid*, App. L.

7. *Hist. of the U. S.*, Adams, III, 253-4. The original cipher manuscript and the key to it are now in the possession of Gabriel Wells, of New York.

8. *Letters in Relation to Burr's Conspiracy;* Lib. of Congress.

9. *Trials of Aaron Burr*, Robertson, I, 497-9.

10. *Ibid*, 502.

11. Journal of Congress, IV, 341.

12. *Letters in Relation*, etc., Lib. of Congress.

13. *Trials of Aaron Burr*, Robertson, I, 504.

14. Blennerhassett Papers, 132-40.

15. *Ibid*, 142-3.

16. Sept. —, 1806; Parton's *Jackson*, I, 315-6.

17. Burr to B. H. Latrobe, Oct. 26, 1806; Burr Misc. MSS., N. Y. Pub. Lib.

18. Same to Wm. Wilkins, Oct. 21, 1806; *ibid*.

19. Jefferson to Hay, June 5, 1807; Jefferson, *Writings* (Monticello Ed.), XI, 218-9.

20. Yrujo to Cevallos, Nov. 10, 1806; Adams Transcripts.

21. Same to same, Dec. 4, 1806; *ibid.*

22. Sept. 9, 1806, *Official Letter Books*, Claiborne (D. Rowland, ed.), IV.

23. *Aaron Burr Conspiracy*, McCaleb, 121.

24. Sept. 8, 1806, Annals of Congress, 1807–08, App., 568.

25. Quoted partly in letter by Adair to Orleans *Gazette*, May 16, 1807, partly in Plumer MSS., Feb. 20, 1807, Lib. of Congress.

26. *Letters in Relation*, etc., Lib. of Congress. Wilkinson's plethora of italics has been omitted as confusing.

27. Wilkinson to Cordero, Sept. 23, 1806; Cordero to Wilkinson, Sept. 29, 1806; Bexar Archives, cited in *Aaron Burr Conspiracy*, McCaleb, 134.

28. Annals of Congress, 1807–08, App., 570.

29. *Trial of Aaron Burr*, Carpenter, III, 237.

30. Yrujo, hearing of Burr's betrayal by Wilkinson, analyzed his conduct with a just and accurate perception of motives. He had no illusions about No. 13! Nevertheless, he was convinced that Wilkinson had saved Mexico and West Florida for Spain, no matter what his underlying reason might have been for the act of salvation. (Yrujo to Cevallos, Jan. 28, 1807; Adams Transcripts.)

31. Wilkinson, *Memoirs*, II, App. XCII.

32. *Letters in Relation*, etc., Lib. of Congress.

33. *Ibid.*

34. Oct. 21, 1806; *ibid.*

35. Wilkinson, *Memoirs*, II, App. CI.

36. Cabinet Memo; Jefferson MSS., Lib. of Congress.

37. Bexar Archives, cited in *Aaron Burr Conspiracy*, McCaleb.

38. Wilkinson, *Memoirs*, II, App. XCIX.

39. *Ibid*, App. C.

40. Nov. 13, 1806; *Letters in Relation*, etc., Lib. of Congress.

41. Iturrigaray to Cevallos, Mar. 12, 1807; Mexican Archives, cited in McCaleb, *Aaron Burr Conspiracy*, 169.

42. Mar. 12, 1807; *Letters in Relation*, etc., Lib. of Congress.

CHAPTER XXII

1. *A View of the President's Conduct*, Daveiss, 10–11.

2. *Ibid*, 12, 13.

3. *Ibid*, 25.

4. *Ibid*, 25–6.

5. *Hist. of Kentucky*, Marshall, II, 375. A highly colored and biased account of the proceedings by a man who was one of the chief actors.

6. *Hist. of Kentucky*, Marshall, II, 377–8.

7. *Ibid*, 386–92.

8. *Moniteur de la Louisiane*, Dec. 31, 1806.

9. *Trials of Aaron Burr*, Robertson, I, 493–4.

10. Oct. 26, 1806, Senate Report, 33.

11. Parton's *Jackson*, I, 316–7.

12. *Palladium*, Nov. 13, 1806.

13. *A View of the President's Conduct*, Daveiss, 30.

14. *Letter Books*, Claiborne, IV, 53–4.

15. Parton's *Jackson*, I, 318–9.

16. Burr to Clay, Dec. 1, 1806; *Private Corresp. of Henry Clay* (C. Colton, ed.), 13–14.

17. *A Full Statement of the Trial . . . of Aaron Burr*, John Wood, 9.

18. *Ibid*, 18–32.

19. *Ibid,* 33.

20. *Ibid,* 34.

21. *Ibid,* 34–5.

22. *Palladium,* Dec. 11, 1806.

23. Easton to Granger, Feb. 17, 1807; *Bench and Bar of Missouri,* W. V. N. Bay, 598.

24. Madison MSS., Lib. of Congress.

25. Cabinet Memoranda; Jefferson, *Writings* (Monticello Ed.), I, 459–60.

26. *Ibid,* 460 *et seq.*

27. *Ibid.*

28. Jefferson to T. M. Randolph; Mass. Hist. Coll., *Seventh Series,* I, (1900), 118.

29. Nov. 4, 1806; Jefferson MSS., Lib. of Congress.

30. Cabinet Memoranda, Jefferson, *Writings* (Monticello Ed.), I, 462–5.

31. Nov. 27, 1806; *Messages of the Presidents,* J. D. Richardson, I, 404.

32. Dec. 2, 1806; *ibid,* 405.

33. Erskine to Fox, Dec. 4, 1806; Adams Transcripts.

34. Graham to Madison, Nov. 12, 1806; *Letters in Relation,* etc., Lib. of Congress.

35. Blennerhassett Papers, 148–52.

36. Graham to Madison; *Letters in Relation,* etc., Lib. of Congress.

37. *Trials of Aaron Burr,* Robertson, I, 507–12.

38. Tupper's deposition, Sept. 8, 1807; Quarterly Publ. of the Historical and Philosophical Soc. of Ohio. IX, (1914), No. 1.

39. Letter dated Dec. 21, 1806, by a participant, to the Pittsburgh *Gazette,* issue of Jan. 13, 1806; copy in *Letters in Relation,* etc., Lib. of Congress.

40. McCaleb, *Aaron Burr Conspiracy,* 248–9.

41. Belknap to Danielson, Oct. 11, 1806; *Letters in Relation,* etc., Lib. of Congress.

42. Affidavit of John Coffee; 1815; Parton's *Jackson,* I, 322.

43. Parton's *Jackson,* I, 322; Beveridge's *Marshall,* III, 326.

44. Parton's *Jackson,* I, 321.

45. Bissell to Jackson, Jan. 5, 1807; Annals, 9th Cong. 2nd Sess., 1017–8.

46. Parton's *Jackson,* I, 326–7.

47. *Ibid,* 328–9.

48. *Trial of Aaron Burr,* Carpenter, III, 300.

CHAPTER XXIII

1. Nov. 12, 1806; Claiborne, *Letter Books,* IV, 55.

2. Claiborne to Jefferson, Nov. 5, 1806; *ibid,* 33.

3. Same to Mead, Nov. 18, 1806; *ibid,* 36.

4. Same to Madison, Nov. 25, 1806; *ibid,* 37–8.

5. Claiborne and Shaw to Madison, Dec. 4, 1806; *ibid,* 39–40.

6. Claiborne to Madison, Dec. 4, 1806; *ibid,* 41.

7. Wilkinson to Claiborne, Dec. 6, 1806; *ibid,* 46–7.

8. Same to same, Dec. 7, 1806; *ibid,* 49.

9. Claiborne to Madison, Dec. 9, 1806; *ibid,* 50–2.

10. Wilkinson, *Statement,* Dec. 6, 1806; *Letters in Relation,* etc., Lib. of Congress.

11. Claiborne to Madison, Dec. 9, 1806; (two letters), Claiborne, *Letter Books,* IV, 51–2; 52–3.

12. Dec. 12, 1806; *ibid,* 57.

13. Plumer, Feb. 21, 1807; Plumer MSS., Lib. of Congress.

14. Claiborne, *Letter Books*, IV, 58–61.

15. *Ibid*, 61.

16. Orleans *Gazette*, Dec. 18, 1806.

17. Burr to Livingston, July 26, 1806; *Life of Edward Livingston*, C. H. Hunt, 130.

18. *A Letter*, etc., James Workman, 14.

19. *Ibid*.

20. Claiborne to Wilkinson, Dec. 25, 1806; Claiborne, *Letter Books*, IV, 69.

21. McCaleb, *Aaron Burr Conspiracy*, 220–1.

22. This time, however, Wilkinson stumbled. No doubt his outrageous seizure and abduction of Adair were intended to head off any disclosures by the latter. He had written Adair certain letters which might have made uncomfortable reading. A year later, Adair brought suit against him for false arrest and imprisonment. The action dragged for ten years, to result finally in a verdict for Adair of $2500, the jury declaring that they would have awarded far more substantial damages if it were not well known that Wilkinson was then wholly penniless. But a complaisant Congress proceeded to indemnify the defendant.

23. Dec. 17, 1806; Claiborne, *Letter Books*, IV, 68.

24. Wilkinson to Clark, Jan., 1807; Clark's *Proofs*, Note 71.

25. *Trial of Aaron Burr*, Carpenter, III, 268, 291–2.

26. Claiborne, *Letter Books*, IV, 65–6.

27. Nov. 23, 1806; *ibid*, 82–3.

28. Gayarré, *Hist. of Louisiana*, IV, 178; Orleans *Gazette*, Extra, Mar. 20, 1807.

29. May 8, 1807.

30. Third Annual Report of the Dept. of Archives and History of Mississippi (1903–4), App. II, 40, 42–3.

31. Mead to Woolridge, Jan. 12, 1807; *ibid*, 49.

32. Mead to the Legislature, Jan. 12, 1807; *ibid*, 49–51.

33. Shields to Baker, Jan. 13, 1807; *ibid*, 51.

34. Wilkinson to Claiborne, Jan. 14, 1807; Claiborne, *Letter Books*, IV, 94–5.

35. Annals of Congress, 1807–8, 683.

36. Fitzpatrick to Mead, Jan. 12, 1807; Report of the Miss. Dept. of Archives, *supra*, App. II, 51.

37. Wool[d]ridge to Mead, Jan. 14, 1807; *ibid*, 54–5.

38. Burr to Mead, Jan. 12, 1807; *Trial of Aaron Burr*, Carpenter, III, App. C.

39. Jan. 13, 1807; Report of the Miss. Dept. of Archives, App. II, 52–3.

40. Mead to Burr, Jan. 15, 1807; *ibid*, 57–58.

41. Fitzpatrick to Mead, Jan. 15, 1807; *ibid*, 60–1.

42. Mead to Claiborne, Jan. 16, 1807; *ibid*, 62–3.

43. Mead to Dearborn, Jan. 19, 1807; *ibid*, 64–6. The manuscript of the formal agreement for an interview between Burr and Mead is now in the possession of Gabriel Wells, of New York. It is dated Jan. 16, 1807.

44. Dinsmore to Col. McKee; Transactions of the Alabama Hist. Soc., III, (1898–9), 168.

45. Blennerhassett Papers, 184–92.

46. *Hist. of Louisiana*, Gayarré, IV, 177.

47. Wilkinson to Silas Dinsmore, Dec. 4, 1806; *Letters in Relation*, etc., Lib. of Congress.

48. Robert Smith to Capt. Shaw, Dec. 20, 1806; *ibid.*

49. Harry Toulmin to Capt. P. P. Schuyler, Feb. 7, 1807; *ibid.*

50. Miss. Dept. of Archives, *supra*, App. III, 101.

51. *Trial of Aaron Burr*, Carpenter, III, 217–8; Amer. State Papers, Misc., I, 566; Quarterly Publ., Hist. and Philos. Soc. of Ohio, IX, Nos. 1 and 2, 35–8.

52. Undated; *Trial of Aaron Burr*, Carpenter, III, App. F.

53. Burr to Williams, Feb. 12, 1807; *Letters in Relation*, etc., Lib. of Congress.

54. Williams to Burr, Feb. 13, 1807; Miss. Dept. of Archives, *supra*, App. II, 75.

55. Testimony of David Fisk; *Trial of Aaron Burr*, Carpenter, III, 188.

56. Annals of Congress, 1807–8, 589. McCaleb asserts that the name of the discoverer of the note was never disclosed. but the *Mississippi Messenger*, Feb. 17, 1807, (cited in Miss. Dept. of Archives, *supra*, App. III), gives his name as William Fairbanks.

57. *Hist. of Mississippi*, Claiborne, 282.

58. Mar. 20, 1807; *Letters in Relation*, etc., Lib. of Congress.

59. The narrative of Burr's arrest follows in the main Chapter XXIX of A. J. Pickett's *History of Alabama*. Pickett had personally interviewed the chief actors in the drama.

60. Gaines to Wilkinson, Mar. 4, 1807; Jefferson MSS., Lib. of Congress.

61. Same to Jefferson, July 23, 1807; *ibid.*

62. *Letters in Relation*, etc., Lib. of Congress.

63. Graham to Madison, Mar. 5, 1807; *ibid.*

64. *Hist. of Alabama*, Pickett, II, 227.

65. Randolph to Nicholson, Mar. 25, 1807; Nicholson MSS., Lib. of Congress.

CHAPTER XXIV

1. Jefferson to Robert R. Livingston, Mar. 24, 1807; Jefferson, *Writings* (Monticello Ed.), XI, 171–2.

2. Same to ——, Mar. 25, 1807; *ibid*, 55.

3. Plumer to B. Cilley, Dec. 9, 1806; Plumer MSS., Lib. of Congress.

4. Plumer to Jeremiah Mason, Jan. 4, 1807; *ibid.*

5. Plumer, *Memorandum of Proceedings*, 543.

6. Jan. 22, 1807; *Messages of the Presidents*, Richardson, I, 412 *et seq.*

7. Plumer, *Memorandum of Proceedings*, 591.

8. John Adams to Rush, Feb. 2, 1807; *Old Family Letters, Series A* (1892), 128–9.

9. Annals of Congress, XVI; 44, 403.

10. Blennerhassett Papers, 227–30.

11. Jefferson, *Writings* (Monticello Ed.), XI, 127–30.

12. *Ibid*, 147–50.

13. Jefferson to Claiborne, Feb. 3, 1807; *ibid*, 150–1.

14. Jefferson to James Bowdoin, Apr. 2, 1807; *ibid*, 185–6. (Italics mine.)

15. Plumer, Jan. 30, 1807; Plumer MSS., Lib. of Congress.

16. Madison, *Writings* (Congress Ed.), II, 393–400.

17. Nicholson to Jefferson, Feb. 18, 1807; Jefferson MSS., Lib. of Congress.

18. Jefferson to Nicholson, Feb. 20, 1807; *ibid.*

CHAPTER XXV

1. 4 *Cranch Reports,* U. S., 125–6.

2. Plumer's *Memorandum of Proceedings,* Feb. 21, 1807, p. 619.

3. Feb. 13, 1807; *Letters in Relation,* etc., Lib. of Congress.

4. *Trial of Aaron Burr,* Carpenter, III, 346, 348.

5. Beveridge's *Marshall,* III, 371–2.

6. *Trials,* Robertson, I, 3–4.

7. *Ibid,* 6–8.

8. *Ibid,* 14–18.

9. Jefferson to Bowdoin, Apr. 2, 1807; Jefferson, *Writings* (Monticello Ed.), XI, 185–6.

10. Cabinet Memoranda, Feb. 27, 1807; Jefferson MSS., Lib. of Congress.

11. Jefferson to Giles, Apr. 20, 1807; Jefferson, *Writings* (Monticello Ed.), XI, 187–91.

12. Apr. 26, 1807; Davis' *Burr,* II, 405.

13. MSS. Letter, Hay to Caesar A. Rodney, Apr. 15, 1807; Pa. Hist. Soc.

14. May 15, 1807; Davis' *Burr,* II, 405–6.

15. Lt. Gen. Scott, *Memoirs,* I, 13.

16. *Trials,* Robertson, I, 45.

17. *Ibid,* 46.

18. *Ibid,* 55.

19. *Ibid,* 79–81.

20. May 26, 1807; Jefferson, *Writings* (Monticello Ed.), XI, 209–10.

21. *Trials,* Robertson, I, 83.

22. *Ibid,* 88–9.

23. *Ibid,* 102.

24. Parton's *Jackson,* I, 333.

25. Randolph to Monroe, May 30, 1807; Monroe MSS., Lib. of Congress.

26. Irving to Mrs. Hoffman, June 4, 1807; *Life of Irving,* P. M. Irving, I, 191–2.

27. June 3, 1807; Davis' *Burr,* II, 406.

28. Hay to Jefferson, June 9, 1807; Jefferson MSS., Lib. of Congress.

29. *Trials,* Robertson, I, 128.

30. Jefferson to Hay, June 12, 1807; Jefferson, *Writings* (Monticello Ed.), XI, 228–30.

31. *Trials,* Robertson, I, 180–8.

32. Hay to Jefferson, June 14, 1807; Jefferson MSS., Lib. of Congress.

33. Jefferson to Hay, June 19, 1807; Jefferson, *Writings* (Monticello Ed.), XI, 233–6.

34. Same to same, May 20, 1807; Jefferson, *Writings* (Ford, ed.), X, 394–401.

35. Same to same, June 19, 1807; *supra.*

36. *Trials,* Robertson, I, 191 *et seq.*

37. Irving to Paulding, June 22, 1807; *Life of Irving,* P. M. Irving, I, 194.

38. Wilkinson to Jefferson, June 17, 1807; *Letters in Relation,* etc., Lib. of Congress.

39. Irving to Paulding, June 22, 1807; *supra.*

40. *Ibid.*

41. See Wilkinson to Jefferson, June 17, 1807; *supra.*

42. *Trials,* Robertson, I, 238, 242.

43. *Ibid,* 268–72.

44. June 21, 1807; Jefferson, *Writings* (Monticello Ed.), XI, 248–50.

45. June 25, 1807; Nicholson MSS., Lib. of Congress.

46. June 28, 1807; *ibid.*
47. Hay to Jefferson, June 25, 1807; Jefferson MSS., Lib. of Congress.
48. Blennerhassett Papers, 298.
49. Parton's *Jackson*, I, 335.
50. Blennerhassett Papers, 459–60.
51. June 24, 1807; Davis' *Burr*, II, 408.
52. Blennerhassett Papers, 314. For the opinion itself, see pp. 396–7.

CHAPTER XXVI

1. *Trials*, Robertson, I, 328–9.
2. *Ibid*, 351.
3. Burr to Theo, July 3, 1807; Davis' *Burr*, II, 409.
4. *Life of Irving*, P. M. Irving, I, 201–2.
5. June 29, 1807; Blennerhassett Papers, 244–5. He had left his wife and two young sons behind to find a new home at Bayou Sara.
6. Blennerhassett to his wife, July 14, 1807; Blennerhassett Papers, 259–62.
7. Blennerhassett Papers, 279 *et seq.*
8. *Ibid*, 313.
9. *Ibid*, 315–6.
10. *Trials*, Robertson, I, 420.
11. Aug. 11, 1807; Jefferson MSS., Lib. of Congress.
12. *Trials*, Robertson, I, 426.
13. *Ibid*, 446.
14. *Ibid*, 469–72.
15. *Ibid*, 483.
16. Blennerhassett Papers, 343.
17. *Trials*, Robertson, I, 489–90.
18. Blennerhassett Papers, Aug. 13, 14, 1807; 324, 327.
19. *Ibid*, Aug. 14, 1807; 328–9.
20. *Ibid*, Aug. 23, 1807; 356–8.
21. *Trials*, Robertson, I, 520 *et seq.*
22. *Life of Tazewell*, Grigsby, 73.
23. *Trials*, Robertson, II, 1–2.
24. *Ibid*, 25–6.
25. *Ibid*, 96–7.
26. *Ibid*, 193.
27. *Ibid*, 401.
28. *Ibid*, 443–5.
29. *Ibid*, 446.
30. *Ibid*, 446–7.
31. Sept. 1, 1807; Jefferson MSS., Lib. of Congress.
32. Jefferson to Hay, Sept. 4, 1807; Jefferson, *Writings* (Monticello Ed.), XI, 360–1.
33. Blennerhassett Papers, Sept. 13, 1807, p. 402.
34. *Trial of Aaron Burr*, Carpenter, III, 160 *et seq.*
35. *Ibid*, 180.
36. Undated, *Letters in Relation*, etc., Lib. of Congress.
37. Blennerhassett Papers, 412–3.
38. Oct. 23, 1807; Davis' *Burr*, II, 411–2.
39. Oct. 15, 1807; Jefferson MSS., Lib. of Congress.
40. Gallatin, *Writings*, I, 375–6.

41. Rodney to Madison, May 11, 1809; *Letters in Relation,* etc., Lib. of Congress.

42. Blennerhassett Papers, Oct. 21 and 28, 1807; 461, 467–8.

43. *Ibid,* Nov. 2, 1807; 475–6.

44. *Ibid,* 477.

45. *Ibid,* 477–82.

46. *Autobiography,* Chas. Biddle, 323.

47. *Ibid.*

48. Nicholas Biddle to Monroe, Jan. 2, 1808; Monroe MSS., Lib. of Congress.

49. Jefferson to Edward Tiffin, Jan. 30, 1808; Jefferson, *Writings* (Monticello Ed.), XI, 435.

50. Blennerhassett Papers, Mar. 2, 1811, 533–8.

51. I. J. Cox, in *Hisp. Amer. Hist. Rev., supra,* 170–1; citing Melville Papers.

CHAPTER XXVII

1. Burr's *Journal* (Davis, ed.), I, 20–1.

2. *Ibid,* 21. The Davis edition is considerably bowdlerized, and often inaccurately transcribed. " G. H. Edwards," instead of " H. E. Edwards," is an example. The edition of Wm. K. Bixby (1903) is complete and unexpurgated, and will be used as the preferred reference for the text of the *Journal.* The Davis edition, however, contains copies of letters not found elsewhere.

3. Pinkney to Madison, Apr. 2, 1808; Madison MSS., Lib. of Congress.

4. Same to same, August 2, 1808; *ibid.*

5. Burr to Williamson, July 19, 1808; Burr's *Journal* (Davis, ed.), I, 23.

6. Williamson to Burr, June 19, 1808; *ibid,* 24.

7. Burr's *Journal* (Bixby, ed.), I, 3.

8. *Ibid,* 3.

9. Sept. 9, 1808; Burr's *Journal* (Davis, ed.), I, 47.

10. Oct. 14, 1808; Burr's *Journal* (Bixby, ed.), I, 10, note 1.

11. Bollman to Burr, Aug. 11, 1808; Burr's *Journal* (Davis, ed.), I, 29–30.

12. Theo to Burr, Sept. 30, 1808; *ibid,* 58.

13. See MSS. Letter, Theo Burr Alston to Joseph Alston, Dec. 3, 1809; Pa. Hist. Soc.

14. Theo to Burr, Oct. 31, 1808; Burr's *Journal* (Davis, ed.), I, 72.

15. Burr to Alston, Nov. 10, 1808; *ibid,* 83–4.

16. Same to Theo, Apr. 22, 1809; *ibid,* 210–11.

17. Same to Bentham, Oct. 1, 1808; *ibid,* 61.

18. Burr's *Journal* (Bixby, ed.), I, 11.

19. Merry to Burr, Nov. 6, 1808; Davis' *Burr,* II, 413.

20. Burr's *Journal* (Bixby, ed.), I, 15–6.

21. *Ibid,* 19–20.

22. *Ibid,* 11–12.

23. Jefferson to Dr. Brown, Oct. 27, 1808; Jefferson, *Writings* (Monticello Ed.), XII, 182–4.

24. Burr's *Journal* (Bixby, ed.), I, 41–2.

25. *Ibid,* 44.

26. *Ibid,* 45–6. See Voltaire's *Candide* for the origin of this expression.

27. Burr to Bentham, Jan. 13, 1809; *ibid,* 54.

28. Jan. 29, 1809; *ibid,* 69.

29. J. H. Koe to Burr, Jan. 17, 1809; Burr's *Journal* (Davis, ed.), I, 137.

30. Burr's *Journal* (Bixby, ed.), I, 77.

31. *Ibid*, 80–1.

32. *Ibid*, 82.

33. *Ibid*, 93.

34. *Ibid*.

35. *Ibid*, 99.

36. Burr to Mrs. ——, Apr. 25, 1809; Burr's *Journal* (Davis, ed.) , I, 212.

37. Theo to Burr, Aug. 1, 1809; *ibid*, 285.

38. Burr's *Journal* (Bixby, ed.) , I, 128.

39. *Ibid*, 116.

40. *Ibid*, 165.

41. *Ibid*, 198.

42. *Ibid*, 221.

43. *Ibid*, 226–7.

44. *A Narrative of the Celebrated Dyde Supper*, Wm. Rose; also *Polit. Hist. of New York*, Alexander, I, 152.

45. Burr's *Journal* (Bixby, ed.) , I, 243.

46. Burr to Mme. ——, Sept. 26, 1809; Burr's *Journal* (Davis, ed.) , I, 310–1.

47. John Quincy Adams, *Memoirs* (C. F. Adams, ed.) , II, 67.

48. *Ibid*, 103.

49. Burr's *Journal* (Bixby, ed.) , I, 250.

50. Lüning to Burr, Oct. 21, 1809; *ibid*, 255.

51. Burr's *Journal* (Bixby, ed.) , I, 263.

52. *Ibid*, 274.

53. *Memoirs of Napoleon*, De Bourrienne, IV, 108.

54. Burr's *Journal* (Bixby, ed.) , I, 291.

55. *Ibid*, 337.

56. *Ibid*, 338.

57. *Ibid*, 352–3.

58. *Ibid*, 358.

59. *Ibid*, 386–7.

CHAPTER XXVIII

1. Burr's *Journal* (Bixby, ed.) , I, 419.

2. *Ibid*, 430.

3. Burr's *Journal* (Davis, ed.) , I, 441–2.

4. Anonymous Letter to Madison; Madison MSS., N. Y. Pub. Library.

5. Joel Barlow to Madison, Sept. 26, 1812; Madison MSS., Lib. of Congress.

6. See Wandell and Minnigerode, *Burr*, II, 262–9. See also article on *Aaron Burr*, by Prof. I. J. Cox, in the Dictionary of American Biography.

7. *Archives Nationales*, AF IV, 1681A, No. 37; MSS. Notes, possession of Dr. Waldo G. Leland, deposited with the Carnegie Institution of Washington.

8. *Ibid*, No. 38.

9. *Ibid*, No. 39.

10. *Ibid*, No. 40.

11. *Ibid*, No. 107.

12. *Ibid*, No. 106.

13. *Ibid*, No. 110.

14. *Ibid*, No. 115.

15. *Ibid*, No. 114.

16. Burr's *Journal* (Bixby, ed.) , I, 454.

17. June 24, 1809; copy in Princeton Univ. Records.

18. Copy in Sales Catalogue, Stan V. Henkels, Jr., no. 1478.

19. Burr to Griswold, Aug. 3, 1810; Burr's *Journal* (Davis, ed.) , II, 29.

20. Burr's *Journal* (Bixby, ed.), I, 463, 460.
21. *Ibid*, 468.
22. *Ibid*, 482.
23. *Ibid*, 483.
24. *Ibid*, 489.
25. *Ibid*, 494.
26. *Ibid*, II, 15.
27. *Ibid*, 16.
28. *Ibid*, 25.
29. Davis' *Burr*, II, 422.
30. Nov. 1, 1810; *ibid*, 422–3.
31. *Ibid*, 423.
32. Burr's *Journal* (Bixby, ed.), II, 28.
33. Davis' *Burr*, II, 419–21.
34. Burr's *Journal* (Bixby, ed.), II, 47–8.
35. *Ibid*, 51.
36. *Ibid*, 55.
37. *Ibid*, 60.
38. *Ibid*, 73–4.
39. *Ibid*, 76–7.
40. *Ibid*, 87.
41. *Ibid*, 114.
42. *Ibid*, 118.
43. *Ibid*, 131.
44. Theo to Burr, Feb. 14, 1811; Burr's *Journal* (Davis, ed.), II, 139.
45. Theo to Gallatin, Mar. 9, 1811; *ibid*, 139.
46. Same to Burr, May 10, 1811; *ibid*, 159–60.
47. Burr to Russell, Mar. 9, 1811; Burr's *Journal* (Bixby, ed.), II, 141.
48. *Ibid*, 175.
49. *Ibid*, 175.
50. July 18, 1811; *ibid*, 229.
51. *Ibid*, 242–3.
52. *Ibid*, 244–5.
53. Burr to J. Reeves, Oct. 5, 1811; Burr's *Journal* (Davis, ed.), II, 240–1.
54. Burr's *Journal* (Bixby, ed.), II, 250.
55. *Ibid*, 313.
56. Burr to Edward Livingston, Feb. 28, 1812; Burr's *Journal* (Davis, ed.), II, 326–7.
57. Burr's *Journal* (Bixby, ed.), II, 395.
58. *Ibid*, 402.
59. Burr to Mason, May 14, 1812; Burr's *Journal* (Davis, ed.), II, 397.
60. Burr's *Journal* (Bixby, ed.), II, 448.

CHAPTER XXIX

1. MSS. Letter, Wickham to Samuel Swartwout, July 4, 1812; Pa. Hist. Soc.
2. Parton's *Burr*, 595–6.
3. *Ibid*, 596.
4. *Ibid*, 597.
5. July 26, 1812; Davis' *Burr*, II, 426.
6. *Ibid*, 428.
7. *Ibid*, 429.
8. *Ibid*, 429.

9. *Ibid*, 430.

10. Alston to Burr, Feb. 25, 1813; *ibid*, 430–2.

11. For the curious reader, there are collections of newspaper clippings anent the several legends in the New York Public Library and in Dr. Stillwell's Scrapbook, deposited with the New York Historical Society.

12. Parton's *Burr*, 608–10.

13. *Reminiscences of Aaron Burr, by One Who Knew and Loved Him* (Chas. Burdett); Newspaper Clipping, N. Y. Pub. Library.

14. Burr to Rev. Charles Seidel, July 6, 1829; quoted in T. F. Madigan Catalogue, #104, Jan., 1933.

15. Burr to Partridge, Feb. 22, 1828; Partridge Papers, cited in the Burlington *Free Press*, Nov. 8, 1929.

16. Parton's *Burr*, 623.

17. Burr to Alston, Oct. 16, 1815; Davis' *Burr*, II, 433.

18. Judgment Docket, N. Y. County Clerk's Office, Oct. 24, 1817.

19. Chas. Biddle, *Autobiography*, 348.

20. *Reminiscences of Aaron Burr*, Burdett, *supra*, N. Y. Pub. Library.

21. Feb., 1833; Lamb Papers, N. Y. Hist. Soc.

22. Mar. 28, ——, Burr MSS., Princeton Univ.

23. MSS. Letter, undated; Pa. Hist. Soc.

24. Burr to Craft, Mar. 17, 1823; Burr MSS., Princeton Univ.

25. Burr to Lathrop, undated; Burr MSS., N. Y. Hist. Soc.

26. Burr to Lathrop, Mar. 28, ——; Burr MSS., Princeton Univ.

27. *Reminiscences*, etc., Burdett, *supra*; N. Y. Pub. Library.

28. Parton's *Jackson*, I, 361, citing *General Jackson's Fine*, by C. J. Ingersoll, 28.

29. Burr to Alston, Nov. 20, 1815; Davis' *Burr*, II, 433–6.

30. Alston to Burr, Feb. 16, 1816; *ibid*, 437–8.

31. Toledo to Burr, Sept. 20, 1816; *ibid*, 442–3.

32. *Ibid*, 443–5.

33. De Clovet to Salcedo, June 22, 1808; Mexican Archives, cited in McCaleb, *Aaron Burr Conspiracy*.

34. Parton's *Burr*, 670.

35. *Diary*, Philip Hone, I, 78.

36. I am indebted in the main for the story of Mrs. Jumel to the account in *The Jumel Mansion*, by Wm. Henry Shelton.

37. MSS. *Diary*, William Dunlap; N. Y. Hist. Soc.

38. *Life Notes*, William Hague, 70.

39. *Ibid*, 72–3.

40. *Ibid*, 78.

41. Princeton *Whig*, Sept. 16, 1836; see also letter of John McLean, President of Princeton, to Editors, *Presbyterian Journal*, Jan. 27, 1875; Princeton Univ. Archives.

42. Davis' *Burr*, II, 448–9.

BIBLIOGRAPHY

Manuscript Sources

American Antiquarian Society
  Burr MSS.
Carnegie Institution of Washington
  Leland Transcripts of Archives Nationales, AF IV, 1681A, Nos. 36–40, 106,
    107, 110, 114, 115
Chicago Historical Society
  Wilkinson Papers
Columbia University
  De Witt Clinton Papers
Library of Congress
  Adams Transcripts from British, French and Spanish Archives
  Burr Misc. Folder
  Cuban Papers
  East Florida Papers
  Force Transcripts of Revolutionary Correspondence
  Innes, Harry, Papers of, v. XVIII
  Jefferson MSS.
  Letters in Relation to Burr's Conspiracy, 1806–8
  Madison MSS.
  Monroe MSS.
  Nicholson MSS.
  Plumer MSS.
  Van Buren Papers
Massachusetts Historical Society
  Pickering Papers
Newberry Library, Chicago
  Melville Papers
New Jersey Historical Society
  Burr MSS.
New York Historical Society
  Burr Misc. MSS.
  Burr Orderly Books
  De Peyster Papers
  Dunlap, Wm., MSS. Journal
  Gates, Horatio, Papers
  Gosman, Robert, MSS. Life of John Vanderlyn
  Green Folio Volumes
  King, Rufus, Papers
  Lamb, John, Papers
  McDougall Papers
  Senter, Isaac, Journal
  Stevens, Ebenezer, MSS.
  Stillwell, Dr. John E., A Compilation Scrap Book

New York Public Library
  Burr Misc. MSS.
  Clay, Joseph, Papers
  Edgar, William, Papers
  Emmett Collection
  Madison Papers
  Van Ness Papers
Pennsylvania Historical Society
  Burr MSS.
Princeton University
  Burr MSS.
  Burr Folders (Secretary's Office)
  Burr, Rev. Aaron, MSS.
Spanish Archives
  Havana, Madrid, Mexico City, Seville
University of Chicago
  Durrett Papers
University of Texas
  Bexar Archives
Washington Association of New Jersey
  Ogden, Matthias, MSS. Journal
Yale University
  Burr MSS.
  Burr, Esther, MSS. Diary
  Burr, Rev. Aaron, MSS.
  Burr, Rev. Aaron, MSS. Sermons
  Reeve, Tapping, Papers

Printed Sources

Adams, Abigail, Letters of, Chas. F. Adams, ed., 1840
Adams, Henry, ed., New England Federalism, 1877
Adams, John, The Works of, Chas. F. Adams, ed., 10 v., 1851–6
Adams, John Quincy, Memoirs of, Chas. F. Adams, ed., 12 v., 1874–7
A General Account of the Rise and State of the College lately established in the Province of New-Jersey in America, published by the Trustees of the College, 1752, reprinted 1754
Alabama Historical Society, Transactions of, v. 3, 1898–9
Alston, Joseph (Agrestis), A Short Review of the Late Proceedings at New Orleans, 1807
American Book Prices Current, 1926–7
American Historical Review, III, VIII, XIX
American State Papers
An Act of Incorporation of the Manhattan Company, 1830
Annals of the Congress of the United States, Gales and Seaton, eds., 1849

Bayard, James A., Papers of, Elizabeth Donnan, ed. (Annual Report of the American Hist. Assoc., II, 1913)
Biddle, Charles, Autobiography, 1883
Biggs, James, History of Don Francisco de Miranda's Attempt to Effect a Revolution in South America, 1810
Blennerhassett Papers, The, Wm. H. Safford, ed., 1864

Burr, Aaron, Memoirs of, by Matthew L. Davis, 2 v., 1852
Burr, Aaron, The Private Journal of, reprinted in full from the Original Manuscript in the Library of Mr. William K. Bixby, 2 v., 1903
Burr, Aaron, The Private Journal of, Matthew L. Davis, ed., 2 v., 1838
Burr, Aaron, The Trial of Col., by T. Carpenter, 3 v., 1807
Burr, Aaron, Reports of the Trials of Colonel, by David Robertson, 2 v., 1808
Burr, Aaron, Some Papers of, W. C. Ford, ed. (Proceedings of the American Antiquarian Society, 1919)

Cheetham, James, A Narrative of the Suppression by Col. Burr of the History of the Administration of John Adams, 1802
Cheetham, James, An Antidote to John Wood's Poison, 1802
Cheetham, James, A view of the Political Conduct of Aaron Burr, 1802
Cheetham, James, Nine Letters on the Subject of Aaron Burr's Political Defection, 1803
Cheetham, James, A Reply to Aristides, 1804
Claiborne, W. C. C., Official Letter Books of, 1801–1816, Dunbar Rowland, ed., 6 v., 1917
Clark, Daniel, Proofs of the Corruption of Gen. James Wilkinson and of his Connexion with Aaron Burr, 1809
Clay, Henry, Private Correspondence of, Calvin Colton, ed., 1855
Coghlan, Mrs., Memoirs of, reprinted 1864
Cutler, Rev. Manasseh, Life, Journals and Correspondence of, by W. P. & J. P. Cutler, 2 v., 1888

Daveiss, J. H., A View of the President's Conduct Concerning the Conspiracy of 1806, printed in 1807
Davis, John, Travels of Four Years and a Half in the United States of America, reprinted 1909

Filson Club, The, History Quarterly, v. 10 (1936), pp. 31–40

Gallatin, Albert, The Writings of, Henry Adams, ed., 3 v., 1879

Hague, William, Life Notes, 1888
Hamilton, Alexander, The Works of, John C. Hamilton, ed., 7 v., 1851 (citations in text otherwise unlisted are from this edition)
Hamilton, Alexander, The Works of, Henry Cabot Lodge, ed., 12 v., 1904
Henry, John Joseph, Account of Arnold's Campaign against Quebec, 1877
Hispanic American Historical Review, XII, No. 2, 1932
Hone, Philip, Diary of, v. 1, 1889

Irving, Washington, The Life and Letters of, by Pierre M. Irving, 3 v., 1868

Jay, John, The Correspondence and Public Papers of, H. P. Johnston, ed., 4 v., 1890–3
Jefferson, Thomas, Works of, Paul L. Ford, ed., 12 v., 1904–5
Jefferson, Thomas, The Writings of, Monticello Edition, A. A. Lipscomb, ed., 20 v., 1904
Jefferson, Thomas, The Writings of, H. A. Washington, ed., 9 v., 1861

King, Rufus, The Life and Correspondence of, Chas. R. King, ed., 6 v., 1894

Lloyd, Thomas, reporter, Trials for Misdemeanor of W. S. Smith and S. G. Ogden, 1807

Madison, James, Letters and other Writings of, Congress Edition, 4 v., 1865
Madison, James, The Writings of, Gaillard Hunt, ed., 9 v., 1908
Maine Historical Society Collections, v. I
Massachusetts Historical Collections, Seventh Series, I, 1900
Massachusetts Historical Society Proceedings, 1907–8, Third Series, v. I
Mississippi, Third Annual Report of the Director of the Department of Archives and History of the State of, Dunbar Rowland, ed., 1903–4
Morris, Gouverneur, The Diary and Letters of, Anne C. Morris, ed., 2 v., 1888

New Jersey Historical Society Proceedings, First Series, v. 5; also January, 1928
New York State Assembly Journal, 1784, 1785, 1788, 1789, 1801

Ohio, Quarterly Publication of the Historical and Philosophical Society of, v. IX, 1914, Nos. 1–9, 13–20
Old Family Letters, Series A, 1892

Patterson, William, Glimpses of Colonial Society and the Life at Princeton College, 1766–1773, as described in the Letters of, W. Jay Mills, ed., 1903
Plumer, William, Memorandum of Proceedings in the United States Senate, 1803–1807, E. S. Brown, ed., 1923

Report of the Commissioners relative to Supplying the City of New-York with Pure and Wholesome Water, 1835
Report of the Committee appointed to Inquire into the Conduct of Brigadier Gen. J. Wilkinson, May 1, 1810
Report of the Manhattan Committee, 1799
Richardson, J. D., ed., A Compilation of the Messages and Papers of the Presidents, v. I, 1898
Robertson, James A., ed., Louisiana under the Rule of Spain, France and the United States, 2 v., 1911
Rose, William, A Narrative of the Celebrated Dyde Supper, 1811

Scott, Lt. Gen. Winfield, Memoirs of, 2 v., 1864
Sparks, Jared, ed., Correspondence of the Revolution, v. I, 1853
Stiles, Ezra, The Literary Diary of, F. B. Dexter, ed., 3 v., 1901

Van Ness, William Peter (Aristides), An Examination of the various charges exhibited against Aaron Burr, 1803

Ware, Joseph, Journal of the Expedition against Quebec (Magazine of History, extra no. 133, v. 34, No. I)
Wilkinson, General James, Memoirs of My Own Times, 3 v., 1816
Wolcott, Oliver, Memoirs of the Administrations of Washington and John Adams, edited from the Papers of, by George Gibbs, 2 v., 1846
Wood, John, A Correct Statement of the Various Sources from which the History of the Administration of John Adams was Compiled, and the Motives for its Suppression by Col. Burr, 1802
Wood, John, A Full Statement of the Trial and Acquittal of Aaron Burr, etc., 1807
Workman, James, Essays and Letters on Various Political Subjects, 1809

Newspapers

Albany Centinel, 1798, 1804
Albany Register, 1804
Baltimore American, 1801
Boston Centinel, 1801
Burlington Free Press, 1929
Connecticut Courant, 1801
Frankfort, Ky. Palladium, 1805–6
Moniteur de la Louisiane, 1806
Nashville Impartial Review, 1806–7
N. Y. American Citizen, 1802–4, 1809

N. Y. Chronicle Express, 1802–4
N. Y. Commercial Advertiser, 1800–1
N. Y. Corrector, 1804
N. Y. Evening Post, 1802–4
N. Y. Spectator, 1800
Orleans Gazette, 1807
Philadelphia Aurora, 1801
Princeton Whig, 1836
Richmond Examiner, 1801
Washington Federalist, 1805

Public Records and Laws

Cranch, Wm., (U. S.) Reports, 6 v., 1812
Indiana Territory, Laws, 1801–1806
New York Court of Chancery, Divorce Records, 1834–6
New York County Clerk, Judgment Dockets
New York County Surrogate's Court, Wills
New York State Laws
Ohio Statutes
Tammany Society, Records

Secondary Works

Adams, Henry, History of the United States of America during the Administrations of Thomas Jefferson and James Madison (A. & C. Boni), 4 v., 1930
Adams, Henry, The Life of Albert Gallatin, 1879
Alexander, De Alva S., A Political History of the State of New York, v. I, 1906
American Historical Review, IX

Bassett, John Spencer, The Federalist System, 1906
Bassett, John Spencer, The Life of Andrew Jackson, 2 v., 1911
Bay, W. V. N., The Bench and Bar of Missouri, 1878
Beam, Jacob M., The American Whig Society, 1933
Beard, Charles A., Economic Origins of Jeffersonian Democracy, 1915
Beveridge, Albert, The Life of John Marshall, 4 v., 1919
Bobbé, Dorothie, De Witt Clinton, 1933
Bowers, Claude G., Jefferson and Hamilton, 1925
Bowers, Claude G., Jefferson in Power, 1936
Bradhurst, A. Maunsell, My Forefathers, 1910
Bruce, Wm. Cabell, John Randolph of Roanoke, 2 v., 1922
Buell, Rowena, The Memoirs of Rufus Putnam, 1903
Butler, Mann, A History of the Commonwealth of Kentucky, 1834
Brady, J. P., Trial of Aaron Burr, 1913

Channing, Edward, A History of the United States, 4 v., 1905–17
Channing, Edward, The Jeffersonian System, 1906
Chinard, Gilbert, Thomas Jefferson, 1929
Claiborne, J. F. H., Mississippi as a Province, Territory and State, v. I, 1880
Clark, Allen C., Life and Letters of Dolly Madison, 1914

Codman, John, Arnold's Expedition to Quebec, 1901
Cox, Isaac Joslin, Article on Aaron Burr in Dictionary of American Biography
Cox, Isaac Joslin, The West Florida Controversy, 1918

Evans, Paul D., The Holland Land Company, 1924 (Buffalo Historical Society Publications, v. 24)

Ford, Henry Jones, Alexander Hamilton, 1929

Gayarré, Charles, History of Louisiana, v. 4, 1903
Giger, G. M., The History of the Cliosophic Society from 1765 to 1865, 1865
Green, T. M., The Spanish Conspiracy, 1891
Groves, Joseph A., The Alstons and Allstons of North and South Carolina, 1901

Hamilton, J. C., History of the Republic of the United States, 7 v., 1864
Hammond, Jabez D., The History of Political Parties in the State of New-York, v. I, 1852
Hildreth, Richard, History of the United States of America, 6 v., 1854-5
Hopkins, Samuel, The Life and Character of Jonathan Edwards, 1815
Hunt, Charles H., Life of Edward Livingston, 1864

Illinois State Historical Society Publications, v. 35, 1928
Indiana Magazine of History, v. 25, No. 4, 1929

Jenkinson, Isaac, Aaron Burr, 1902
Journal of Southern History, The, v. II (1936), pp. 175-210

Kennedy, John P., Memoirs of the Life of William Wirt, 2 v., 1854
Knapp, Samuel L., Life of Aaron Burr, 1835

Lincoln, Chas. Z., Constitutional History of New York, v. I, 1906
Lodge, Henry Cabot, Alexander Hamilton, 1882
Lossing, B. J., The Life and Times of Philip Schuyler, 2 v., 1873

McCaleb, Walter F., The Aaron Burr Conspiracy, 1903
McLaughlin, J. F., Matthew Lyon, 1900
McMaster, James B., A History of the People of the United States, 8 v., 1883-1914
Marshall, Humphrey, The History of Kentucky, 2 v., 1824
Martin, F. X., The History of Louisiana, v. 2, 1827
Minnigerode, Meade, Lives and Times, 1925
Monaghan, Frank, John Jay, 1935
Morison, S. E., The Life and Letters of Harrison Gray Otis, 2 v., 1913
Morris, Ira K., Memorial History of Staten Island, 2 v., 1898
Myers, Gustavus, The History of Tammany Hall, 1917

Parkes, Bamford, Jonathan Edwards, 1930
Parton, James, The Life and Times of Aaron Burr, 1858
Parton, James, Life of Andrew Jackson, 3 v., 1860
Parton, James, Life of Thomas Jefferson, 1874
Pickett, Albert J., History of Alabama, 2 v., 1851
Pidgin, Chas. F., Theodosia, 1907

Plumer, Wm., Jr., Life of William Plumer, 1856
Pound, Arthur, The Golden Earth, 1935
Prentice, George D., Life of Henry Clay, 1831
Prentiss, Chas., The Life of Gen. William Eaton, 1813

Randall, H. S., Life of Thomas Jefferson, 3 v., 1858

Schuyler, John, The Society of the Cincinnati, 1886
Shelton, Wm. H., The Jumel Mansion, 1916
Shreve, Royal O., The Finished Scoundrel, 1933
Smith, Justin H., Arnold's March from Cambridge to Quebec, 1903
Smith, Justin H., Our Struggle for the Fourteenth Colony, 2 v., 1907
Steiner, Bernard C., The Life and Correspondence of James McHenry, 1907
Stillwell, John E., The History of the Burr Portraits, 1928

Tennessee History Magazine, Series 2, v. I, 1930–1
Todd, Chas. Burr, A General History of the Burr Family, 1902

Van Tyne, Claude H., The War of Independence, American Phase, 1929

Wandell, Samuel H., and Minnigerode, Meade, Aaron Burr, 2 v., 1925
Wharton, A. H., Salons Colonial and Republican, 1900
Wharton, A. H., Social Life in the Early Republic, 1902
Williams, Chas. R., The Cliosophic Society, 1916
Wilson, James G., ed., The Memorial History of the City of New York, v. 2, 1893

INDEX